REFERENCE

W9-AYE-708

FISCAL YEAR 2019

EFFICIENT, EFFECTIVE, ACCOUNTABLE

AN
AMERICAN
BUDGET

WITHDRAWN

ANALYTICAL
PERSPECTIVES

DES PLAINES PUBLIC LIBRARY
1501 ELLINWOOD STREET
DES PLAINES, IL 60016

BUDGET OF THE U.S. GOVERNMENT

OFFICE OF MANAGEMENT AND BUDGET | OMB.GOV

Budget of the United States Government, Fiscal Year 2019 contains the Budget Message of the President, information on the President's priorities, and summary tables.

Analytical Perspectives, Budget of the United States Government, Fiscal Year 2019 contains analyses that are designed to highlight specified subject areas or provide other significant presentations of budget data that place the budget in perspective. This volume includes economic and accounting analyses; information on Federal receipts and collections; analyses of Federal spending; information on Federal borrowing and debt; baseline or current services estimates; and other technical presentations.

The **Analytical Perspectives** volume also has supplemental materials that are available on the internet at *www.whitehouse.gov/omb/analytical-perspectives/* and on the Budget CD-ROM. These supplemental materials include tables showing the budget by agency and account and by function, subfunction, and program.

Appendix, Budget of the United States Government, Fiscal Year 2019 contains detailed information on the various appropriations and funds that constitute the budget and is designed primarily for the use of the Appropriations Committees. The **Appendix** contains more detailed financial information on individual programs and appropriation accounts than any of the other budget documents. It includes for each agency: the proposed text of appropriations language; budget schedules for each account; legislative proposals; narrative explanations of each budget account; and proposed general provisions applicable to the appropriations of entire agencies or group of agencies.

Information is also provided on certain activities whose transactions are not part of the budget totals.

ELECTRONIC SOURCES OF BUDGET INFORMATION

The information contained in these documents is available in electronic format from the following sources:

Internet. All budget documents, including documents that are released at a future date, spreadsheets of many of the budget tables, and a public use budget database are available for downloading in several formats from the internet at *www.whitehouse.gov/omb/budget/.* Links to documents and materials from budgets of prior years are also provided.

Budget CD-ROM. The CD-ROM contains all of the printed budget documents in fully indexed PDF format along with the software required for viewing the documents.

The Internet and CD-ROM also include many of the budget tables in spreadsheet format, and supplemental materials that are part of the *Analytical Perspectives* volume. It also includes *Historical Tables* that provide data on budget receipts, outlays, surpluses or deficits, Federal debt, and Federal employment over an extended time period, generally from 1940 or earlier to 2019 or 2023.

For more information on access to electronic versions of the budget documents (except CD-ROMs), call (202) 512-1530 in the D.C. area or toll-free (888) 293-6498. To purchase the Budget CD-ROM or printed documents call (202) 512-1800.

GENERAL NOTES

1. All years referenced for budget data are fiscal years unless otherwise noted. All years referenced for economic data are calendar years unless otherwise noted.

2. At the time of this writing, none of the full-year appropriations bills for 2018 have been enacted, therefore, the programs and activities normally provided for in the full-year appropriations bills were operating under a continuing resolution (Public Law 115-56, division D, as amended). In addition, the Additional Supplemental Appropriations for Disaster Relief Requirements Act, 2017 (Public Law 115-72, division A) provided additional appropriations for 2018 for certain accounts within the Departments of Agriculture, Homeland Security, and the Interior. The Department of Defense Missile Defeat and Defense Enhancements Appropriations Act, 2018 (Public Law 115-96, division B) also provided additional appropriations for 2018 for certain accounts within the Department of Defense. Accordingly, references to 2018 spending in the text and tables reflect the levels provided by the continuing resolution and, if applicable, Public Laws 115-72 (division A) and 115-96 (division B).

3. The Budget does not incorporate the effects of Public Law 115-120, including the reauthorization of the Children's Health Insurance Program and amendments to the tax code in that law.

4. Detail in this document may not add to the totals due to rounding.

The Office of Management and Budget (OMB) has prepared an addendum to the Fiscal year 2019 President's Budget to account for changes to discretionary spending limits pursuant to the recently enacted Bipartisan budget Act of 208. To view this addendum, please visit: http://www.whithouse.gov/omb/budget.

ISBN: 978-164143-294-8

Bernan does not claim copyright in U.S. government information.

TABLE OF CONTENTS

LIST OF TABLES

*Available on the Internet at *http://www.whitehouse.gov/omb/analytical-perspectives/* and on the *Budget* CD-ROM

Technical Budget Analyses

*Available on the Internet at *http://www.whitehouse.gov/omb/analytical-perspectives/* and on the *Budget* CD-ROM

*Available on the Internet at *http://www.whitehouse.gov/omb/analytical-perspectives/* and on the *Budget* CD-R

**Available on the Internet at *http://www.whitehouse.gov/omb/analytical-perspectives/* only

INTRODUCTION

1. INTRODUCTION

The *Analytical Perspectives* volume presents analyses that highlight specific subject areas or provide other significant data that place the President's 2019 Budget in context and assist the public, policymakers, the media, and researchers in better understanding the budget. This volume complements the main Budget volume, which presents the President's budget policies and priorities, and the Budget Appendix volume, which provides appropriations language, schedules for budget expenditure accounts, and schedules for selected receipt accounts.

Presidential budgets have included separate analytical presentations of this kind for many years. The 1947 Budget and subsequent budgets included a separate section entitled "Special Analyses and Tables" that covered four, and later more, topics. For the 1952 Budget, the section was expanded to 10 analyses, including many subjects still covered today, such as receipts, investment, credit programs, and aid to State and local governments. With the 1967 Budget this material became a separate volume entitled "Special Analyses," and included 13 chapters. The material has remained a separate volume since then, with the exception of the Budgets for 1991–1994, when all of the budget material was included in one volume. Beginning with the 1995 Budget, the volume has been named *Analytical Perspectives*.

Several supplemental tables as well as several longer tables that were previously published within the volume are available at *http://www.whitehouse.gov/omb/analytical-perspectives* and on the Budget CD-ROM. These tables are shown in the List of Tables in the front of this volume with an asterisk instead of a page number.

Overview of the Chapters

Economic and Budget Analyses

Economic Assumptions and Interactions with the Budget. This chapter reviews recent economic developments; presents the Administration's assessment of the economic situation and outlook; compares the economic assumptions on which the 2019 Budget is based with the assumptions for last year's Budget and those of other forecasters; provides sensitivity estimates for the effects on the Budget of changes in specified economic assumptions; and reviews past errors in economic projections.

Long-Term Budget Outlook. This chapter assesses the long-term budget outlook under current policies and under the Budget's proposals. It focuses on 25-year projections of Federal deficits and debt to illustrate the long-term impact of the Administration's proposed policies, and shows how alternative long-term budget assumptions affect the results. It also discusses the uncertainties of the long-term budget projections and discusses the actuarial status of the Social Security and Medicare programs.

Federal Borrowing and Debt. This chapter analyzes Federal borrowing and debt and explains the budget estimates. It includes sections on special topics such as trends in debt, debt held by the public net of financial assets and liabilities, investment by Government accounts, and the statutory debt limit.

Management

Social Indicators. This chapter presents a selection of statistics that offers a numerical picture of the United States and illustrates how this picture has changed over time. Included are economic, demographic and civic, socioeconomic, health, security and safety, and environmental and energy statistics.

Building and Using Evidence to Improve Government Effectiveness. This chapter discusses evidence and its role in improving government programs and policies. It articulates important principles and practices including building and using a portfolio of evidence, developing a learning agenda, building an evidence infrastructure, and making better use of administrative data.

Strengthening the Federal Workforce. This chapter presents summary data on Federal employment and compensation, and discusses the approach the Administration is taking with Federal human capital management.

Budget Concepts and Budget Process

Budget Concepts. This chapter includes a basic description of the budget process, concepts, laws, and terminology, and includes a glossary of budget terms.

Coverage of the Budget. This chapter describes activities that are included in budget receipts and outlays (and are therefore classified as "budgetary") as well as those activities that are not included in the Budget (and are therefore classified as "non-budgetary"). The chapter also defines the terms "on-budget" and "off-budget" and includes illustrative examples.

Budget Process. This chapter discusses proposals to improve budgeting and fiscal sustainability within individual programs as well as across Government.

Federal Receipts

Governmental Receipts. This chapter presents information on estimates of governmental receipts, which consist of taxes and other compulsory collections. It includes descriptions of tax-related legislation enacted in the last year and describes proposals affecting receipts in the 2019 Budget.

Offsetting Collections and Offsetting Receipts. This chapter presents information on collections that offset outlays, including collections from transactions with the public and intragovernmental transactions. In addition, this chapter presents information on "user fees," charges associated with market-oriented activities and regulatory fees. The user fee information includes a description of each of the user fee proposals in the 2019 Budget. A detailed table, "Table 12–5, Offsetting Receipts by Type" is available at the Internet address cited above and on the Budget CD-ROM.

Tax Expenditures. This chapter describes and presents estimates of tax expenditures, which are defined as revenue losses from special exemptions, credits, or other preferences in the tax code.

Special Topics

Aid to State and Local Governments. This chapter presents crosscutting information on Federal grants to State and local governments. The chapter also includes a table showing historical grant spending, and a table with budget authority and outlays for grants in this Budget. Tables showing State-by-State spending for major grant programs are available at the Internet address cited above and on the Budget CD-ROM.

Strengthening Federal Statistics. This chapter discusses the vital role of the Federal Government's statistical agencies and programs in generating data that citizens, businesses, and governments need to make informed decisions. This chapter also provides examples of innovative developments and applications throughout the Federal statistical community and highlights 2019 Budget proposals for the Government's principal statistical programs.

Information Technology. This chapter addresses Federal information technology (IT), highlighting initiatives to improve IT management through modern solutions to enhance service delivery. The Administration will invest in modern, secure technologies and services to drive enhanced efficiency and effectiveness. This will include undertaking complex Government-wide modernization efforts, driving improved delivery of citizen-facing services, and improving the overall management of the Federal IT portfolio. The Administration will also continue its efforts to further build the Federal IT workforce and strategically reduce the Federal Government's cybersecurity risk.

Federal Investment. This chapter discusses Federally-financed spending that yields long-term benefits. It presents information on annual spending on physical capital, research and development, and education and training.

Research and Development. This chapter presents a crosscutting review of research and development funding in the Budget.

Credit and Insurance. This chapter provides crosscutting analyses of the roles, risks, and performance of Federal credit and insurance programs and Government-sponsored enterprises (GSEs). The chapter covers the major categories of Federal credit (housing, education, small business and farming, energy and infrastructure, and international) and insurance programs (deposit insurance, pension guarantees, disaster insurance, and

insurance against terrorism-related risks). Five additional tables address transactions including direct loans, guaranteed loans, and Government-sponsored enterprises. These tables are available at the Internet address cited above and on the Budget CD-ROM.

Budgetary Effects of the Troubled Asset Relief Program. The chapter provides special analyses of the Troubled Asset Relief Program (TARP) as described in Sections 202 and 203 of the Emergency Economic Stabilization Act of 2008, including information on the costs of TARP activity and its effects on the deficit and debt.

Cybersecurity Funding. This chapter displays enacted and proposed cybersecurity funding for Federal departments and agencies, and includes analysis of broad cybersecurity trends across government.

Federal Drug Control Funding. This chapter displays enacted and proposed drug control funding for Federal departments and agencies.

Technical Budget Analyses

Current Services Estimates. This chapter discusses the conceptual basis of the Budget's current services, or "baseline," estimates, which are generally consistent with the baseline rules in the Balanced Budget and Emergency Deficit Control Act of 1985 (BBEDCA). The chapter presents estimates of receipts, outlays, and the deficit under this baseline. Two detailed tables addressing factors that affect the baseline and providing details of baseline budget authority and outlays are available at the Internet address cited above and on the Budget CD-ROM.

Trust Funds and Federal Funds. This chapter provides summary information about the two fund groups in the budget—Federal funds and trust funds. In addition, for the major trust funds and certain Federal fund programs, the chapter provides detailed information about income, outgo, and balances.

Comparison of Actual to Estimated Totals. This chapter compares the actual receipts, outlays, and deficit for 2017 with the estimates for that year published in the 2017 Budget, published in February 2016.

The following materials are available at the Internet address cited above and on the Budget CD-ROM:

Detailed Functional Table

Detailed Functional Table. Table 26–1, "Budget Authority and Outlays by Function, Category, and Program," displays budget authority and outlays for major Federal program categories, organized by budget function (such as health care, transportation, or national defense), category, and program.

Federal Budget by Agency and Account

The Federal Budget by Agency and Account. Table 27–1, "Federal Budget by Agency and Account," displays budget authority and outlays for each account, organized by agency, bureau, fund type, and account.

The following report is available at the Internet address cited above:

California Bay-Delta Federal Budget Crosscut

California Bay-Delta Federal Budget Crosscut. The California Bay-Delta interagency budget crosscut report includes an estimate of Federal funding by each of the participating Federal agencies to carry out its responsibilities under the California Bay-Delta Program, fulfilling the reporting requirements of section 106 of Public Law 108-361.

ECONOMIC ASSUMPTIONS AND INTERACTIONS WITH THE BUDGET

2. ECONOMIC ASSUMPTIONS AND INTERACTIONS WITH THE BUDGET

This chapter presents the economic assumptions that underlie the Administration's Fiscal Year 2019 Budget.[1] It describes the recent performance of the U.S. economy, explains the Administration's projections for key macroeconomic variables, compares them with forecasts prepared by other prominent institutions and discusses the uncertainty inherent in producing an eleven-year forecast.

After contracting by more than 4 percent over 2007Q4 to 2009Q2, the United States economy has experienced stable but relatively modest growth, especially when compared with past recoveries. From the trough in the second quarter of 2009, it took about two years for the economy to recover to its previous output peak, much longer than in the other post-World War II recoveries. Over the first three years of recoveries from previous postwar recessions, average output growth averaged 4.5 percent annually. In the first three years following the most recent recession, average annual growth was only about 2.3 percent.

The disappointing recovery has motivated this Administration's aggressive economic strategy, two key elements of which are cutting taxes and reforming the tax code along with reducing the burden of Federal regulations. The Administration's efforts succeeded on both of these fronts in its first year, with the passage of the Tax Cut and Jobs Act in December 2017 and the elimination of scores of unnecessary regulations under Executive Orders 13771 and 13777. In addition, the Administration is pursuing policies to encourage domestic energy development and investments in infrastructure, reform welfare programs to encourage work, establish paid family leave for new parents, negotiate more attractive trade agreements, and reduce Federal budget deficits. Taken together, these actions should encourage investment by American firms, stimulate productivity growth, and slow the expected decline in the labor force participation rate, leading to stronger growth in output and putting more Americans to work.

This chapter proceeds as follows:

- The first section reviews the recent performance of the U.S. economy, examining a broad array of economic outcomes.

- The second section provides a detailed exposition of the Administration's economic forecast for the FY 2019 Budget, discussing how a number of macroeconomic variables are expected to evolve over the years 2018 to 2028.

- The third section compares the forecast of the Administration with those prepared by the Congressio-

nal Budget Office, the Federal Open Market Committee of the Federal Reserve, and the Blue Chip panel of private sector forecasters.

- The fourth section discusses the sensitivity of the Administration's projections of Federal receipts and outlays to fluctuations in the main macroeconomic variables discussed in the forecast.

- The fifth section considers the errors and possible biases[2] in past Administration forecasts, comparing them with the errors in forecasts produced by the Congressional Budget Office, and the Blue Chip panel of private professional forecasters. The sixth section uses information on past accuracy of Administration forecasts to provide a sense of the uncertainty associated with the Administration's current forecast of the budget balance.

Recent Economic Performance[3]

The U.S. economy continued to exhibit robust growth in the fourth quarter of 2017, growing at 2.6 percent after having grown 3.1 and 3.2 percent in the second and third quarter, respectively. The first quarter had lackluster growth at 1.2 percent. For the four quarters ending December 2017, real Gross Domestic Product (GDP) growth averaged 2.5 percent. In contrast, during the four quarters of 2016, real GDP grew by 1.8 percent. This came on the heels of real GDP growing at 2.0 percent during 2015, and an average growth rate of 2.1 percent (fourth quarter-on-fourth quarter) since 2010. Among the demand components of GDP, real consumer spending has accounted for 76 percent of the demand growth in 2017, with consumption of nondurables and services contributing 54 percent and consumption of durable goods contributing the remaining 22 percent. Gross private domestic investment contributed 22 percent to real GDP growth, government consumption and gross investment have been slightly positive and net exports have made a negative contribution of 3 percent to real GDP growth. On the supply side, weak labor productivity growth limited overall growth during 2017, as it has over the past several years. Over the four quarters through 2017Q4, nonfarm productivity increased at 1.1 percent compared to 0.8 percent a year ago. Productivity growth has been relatively sluggish since the end of 2007, increasing by 1.2 percent at an annual rate; over the past two years, through 2017Q4, labor productivity (output per hour) in

---

[1] Economic performance, unless otherwise specified, is generally discussed in terms of calendar years. Budget figures are discussed in terms of fiscal years.

[2] As discussed later in this chapter, "bias" here is defined in the statistical sense and refers to whether previous Administrations' forecasts have tended to make positive or negative forecast errors on average.

[3] The statistics in this section are based on information available in late January 2018.

the nonfarm business sector has increased just 1.0 percent at an annual rate. These rates are notably slower than the rate of 2.6 percent annual rate observed over the period from 1994Q4 through 2007Q4 and the long run average of 2.1 percent during the post-World War II period from 1947 to 2016.

Labor Markets.—Labor markets continued to improve in 2017 across a broad array of metrics. The unemployment rate continued to decline, falling from 5.0 percent at the end of 2015 to 4.7 percent at the end of 2016, and further to 4.1 percent in January of 2018, the lowest level since December 2000, and well below the long-term average of 5.8 percent. During the 12 months of 2017, the labor force participation rate averaged 62.8 percent, up from 62.7 percent in 2015 but about the same as in 2016. Although the participation rate has stabilized somewhat following a steep decline since 2000, demographic forces are expected to exert continued downward pressure as the baby boom generation continues retiring in large numbers. The proportion of the labor force employed part-time for economic reasons has fallen to 3.1 percent in December 2017, well below its peak of over 6.0 percent during the Great Recession. Furthermore, the proportion of the labor force unemployed for longer than 27 weeks has fallen to 0.9 percent from a peak of nearly 4.4 percent.

In spite of these improvements, several metrics suggest that the labor market has not regained the ground it had lost. Compared with the last business cycle peak at the end of 2007, the proportion of the labor force working part-time for economic reasons and the proportion unemployed for more than 27 weeks are still elevated, as are the shares of the working-age population only marginally attached to the labor force or too discouraged to look for work. The aging of the baby boom cohorts into retirement does not explain the drop in the labor force participation rates for prime-age men and women (age 25-54). From 2007 to 2017, the participation rate for prime-age men (aged 20-54) fell 2.2 percentage points from 2007 to 2017, while the rate for prime-age women fell 0.4 percentage point. Real average hourly wages for production and non-supervisory workers have grown only 0.7 percent at an annual rate during the 10 years since 2007. In December 2017, the employment-to-population ratio for Americans aged between 25 and 54 years old was still 0.6 percentage point below where it was at the start of the "Great Recession."

Housing.—The effect of the housing market on the broader economy was mixed in 2017. House prices, as measured by the Federal Housing Finance Agency's (FHFA) purchase-only index, were 6.5 percent higher in November 2017 than in November 2016. Higher house prices help fortify household balance sheets and support personal consumption expenditures. They also encourage further activity in the housing sector, with sales volumes rising for both new and existing homes. Despite the rising house prices, measures of new construction edged up only slightly or were roughly flat. The number of housing starts decreased from an annual rate of about 1.33 million in October 2016 to 1.29 million in October 2017. Building permits increased 2.4 percent over the same period. And

residential fixed investment increased 2.3 percent over the four quarters ending in December 2017.

Some weaknesses still remain in the housing market, however. As of November 2017, while the FHFA house-price index was about 13.1 percent higher than its pre-crisis peak, the S&P-Case Shiller index was only about 6 percent above its previous apex. Homeownership rates steadily declined since the recession began and after matching the lowest rate on record in the middle of 2016, started edging up in 2017.

Consumption.—Consumer spending was a primary driver of demand growth in 2017, growing by 2.8 percent over the four quarters ending December 2017. At close to 70 percent of the economy, consumption is essential to overall growth. Consumption growth was spread over a number of different categories, including motor vehicles and parts (4.5 percent), furnishings and household equipment (9.5 percent), recreational goods and vehicles (9.3 percent), food and beverages (3.0 percent), medical care (2.6 percent), and financial services and insurance (3.4 percent).

Investment.—For the four quarters ending in December 2017, growth in nonresidential fixed investment was strong, coming in at 6.3 percent relative to 0.7 percent during the year-earlier period. Equipment spending was up 8.8 percent, spending on structures was up 3.7 percent, and spending on intellectual property products increased 4.8 percent. Growth in overall private fixed investment (residential and nonresidential) was 5.4 percent compared with virtually zero growth over the four quarters ending December 2016, and 2.4 percent the year prior.

Government.—Overall demand growth by the government sector has been 0.7 percent over the four quarters ending in December 2017. State and local spending grew 0.5 percent, while Federal purchases were up 1.1 percent. The Federal deficit as a percentage of GDP increased to 3.5 percent in fiscal year 2017 from 3.2 percent in fiscal year 2016. While increasing deficits might be expected to lead to higher interest rates and subsequent crowding out of private investment, the low interest rate environment in recent years has mitigated this potentially negative force.

Monetary Policy.—After holding the nominal Federal funds rate near zero for seven years, the Federal Open Market Committee of the Federal Reserve raised the target range for the Federal funds rate by 25 basis points at the end of 2015. After a moderate pause, the Federal Reserve continued the normalization of monetary policy, with a 25 basis point increase in each meeting held in December 2016, March 2017, June 2017, and December 2017. In its December policy statement, the FOMC characterized as "solid" the job gains and the rising rate of economic activity with expectations for continued strengthening of labor markets, as well as rates of inflation around the 2.0 percent target in the medium term. The yield on the 10-year Treasury note has also increased recently, from an average of 1.6 percent in the third quarter of 2016 to an average of 2.4 percent during the fourth quarter of 2017.

Oil and Natural Gas Supply.—After reaching a post-financial crisis peak above $100 per barrel, crude oil prices began to tumble in mid-2014. They continued to fall in 2015 and bottomed out around $30 in early 2016. Prices have since rebounded, rising above the $50 mark in late 2016 where they have stayed in the latter half of 2017. Higher oil prices act as a kind of tax on consumers' purchasing power, so their net decline from $100 per barrel in early 2014 to above $50 per barrel raised disposable incomes, which has supported consumer spending. With new technology such as hydraulic fracturing, U.S. oil producers have emerged as important swing producers in global oil markets, helping to lower prices and moderate price fluctuations. Domestic production of crude oil for the year ending September 2017 averaged about 9.0 million barrels per day (mbd), up from 8.9 mbd in calendar year 2016 and 7.5 mbd in calendar year 2013, although down from 9.4 million barrels per day in 2015 (calendar year). The decline from 2015 likely reflects the decline in oil prices. Production of natural gas has averaged about 89.2 billion cubic feet per day in the year ending September 2017, down 0.6 percent from year-earlier production levels, but 13.4 percent higher than in the year ending September 2013.

Table 2–1. ECONOMIC ASSUMPTIONS [1]

(Calendar Years, Dollar Amounts in Billions)

	Actual 2016	2017	2018	2019	2020	2021	2022	2023	2024	2025	2026	2027	2028
							Projections						
Gross Domestic Product (GDP):													
Levels, Dollar Amounts in Billions:													
Current Dollars	18,624	19,372	20,262	21,263	22,345	23,482	24,672	25,923	27,234	28,598	30,001	31,461	32,991
Real, Chained (2009) Dollars	16,716	17,090	17,601	18,157	18,727	19,296	19,875	20,471	21,085	21,705	22,320	22,945	23,588
Chained Price Index (2009=100), Annual Average	111.4	113.4	115.1	117.1	119.3	121.7	124.1	126.6	129.2	131.8	134.4	137.1	139.9
Percent Change, Fourth Quarter over Fourth Quarter:													
Current Dollars	3.4	4.1	4.7	5.1	5.1	5.1	5.1	5.1	5.1	5.0	4.9	4.9	4.9
Real, Chained (2009) Dollars	1.8	2.5	3.1	3.2	3.1	3.0	3.0	3.0	3.0	2.9	2.8	2.8	2.8
Chained Price Index (2009=100)	1.5	1.6	1.6	1.8	1.9	2.0	2.0	2.0	2.0	2.0	2.0	2.0	2.0
Percent Change, Year over Year:													
Current Dollars	2.8	4.0	4.6	4.9	5.1	5.1	5.1	5.1	5.1	5.0	4.9	4.9	4.9
Real, Chained (2009) Dollars	1.5	2.2	3.0	3.2	3.1	3.0	3.0	3.0	3.0	2.9	2.8	2.8	2.8
Chained Price Index (2009=100)	1.3	1.7	1.6	1.7	1.9	2.0	2.0	2.0	2.0	2.0	2.0	2.0	2.0
Incomes, Billions of Current Dollars:													
Domestic Corporate Profits	1,679	1,753	1,893	1,985	2,050	2,060	2,047	2,035	2,043	2,048	2,041	2,049	2,046
Employee Compensation	9,979	10,320	10,750	11,225	11,774	12,408	13,104	13,843	14,622	15,438	16,291	17,160	18,092
Wages and Salaries	8,085	8,365	8,713	9,094	9,550	10,058	10,620	11,217	11,844	12,506	13,195	13,902	14,642
Other Taxable Income [2]	4,427	4,576	4,793	5,068	5,386	5,704	6,053	6,398	6,738	7,072	7,360	7,683	7,943
Consumer Price Index (All Urban): [3]													
Level (1982–1984 = 100), Annual Average	240.0	245.1	250.2	255.1	260.7	266.7	272.7	278.9	285.2	291.7	298.3	305.1	312.0
Percent Change, Fourth Quarter over Fourth Quarter	1.8	2.1	1.9	2.0	2.3	2.3	2.3	2.3	2.3	2.3	2.3	2.3	2.3
Percent Change, Year over Year	1.3	2.1	2.1	2.0	2.2	2.3	2.3	2.3	2.3	2.3	2.3	2.3	2.3
Unemployment Rate, Civilian, Percent:													
Fourth Quarter Level	4.7	4.1	3.8	3.7	3.8	3.9	4.1	4.2	4.4	4.5	4.8	4.8	4.8
Annual Average	4.9	4.4	3.9	3.7	3.8	3.9	4.0	4.2	4.3	4.5	4.7	4.8	4.8
Federal Pay Raises, January, Percent:													
Military [4]	1.3	2.1	2.4	2.6	N/A	N/A	N/A	N/A	N/A	N/A	N/A	N/A	N/A
Civilian [5]	1.3	2.1	1.9	0.0	N/A	N/A	N/A	N/A	N/A	N/A	N/A	N/A	N/A
Interest Rates, Percent:													
91-Day Treasury Bills [6]	0.3	0.9	1.5	2.3	2.9	3.0	3.0	2.9	2.9	2.9	2.9	2.9	2.9
10-Year Treasury Notes	1.8	2.3	2.6	3.1	3.4	3.6	3.7	3.7	3.6	3.6	3.6	3.6	3.6

N/A=Not Available

[1] Based on information available as of mid-November 2017.

[2] Rent, interest, dividend, and proprietors' income components of personal income.

[3] Seasonally adjusted CPI for all urban consumers.

[4] Percentages apply to basic pay only; percentages to be proposed for years after 2019 have not yet been determined.

[5] Overall average increase, including locality pay adjustments. Percentages to be proposed for years after 2019 have not yet been determined.

[6] Average rate, secondary market (bank discount basis).

* 0.05 percent or less.

External Sector.—Real exports grew 4.9 percent over the last four quarters ending in December 2017, while real imports grew 4.6 percent. Net exports made less of a negative contribution to real GDP growth in 2017 than in 2016. Worldwide, 2017 is projected to have been a better year for economic growth than 2016. According to the International Monetary Fund's World Economic Outlook, October 2017, the advanced economies were poised to grow by 2.2 percent (year over year) in 2017 versus 1.7 percent in 2016. The emerging and developing economies were expected to collectively grow by 4.6 percent in 2017 versus 4.3 percent in 2016.[4] Many large emerging market countries (with the exception of India) have experienced lower growth rates, relative to the past, in recent years, while Brazil and Russia went through recessions in 2015-16. These developments, as well as a strengthening dollar, have contributed to the soft performance of U.S. exports. Looking ahead, the faster global growth expected by the IMF and other forecasters, and better trade agreements will support U.S. export performance.

Economic Projections

The Administration's economic forecast is based on information available as of mid-November 2017. The forecast informs the Fiscal Year 2019 Budget and rests on the central assumption that all of the President's policy proposals will be enacted. The Administration's projections are reported in Table 2-1 and summarized below.

Real GDP.—In mid-November, when the forecast was finalized, the Administration projected that real GDP growth would average 2.5 percent during the four quarters of 2017. It appears that 2017 growth was in line with expectations. The pace of growth is projected to increase to 3.1 percent over the four quarters of 2018. The enactment of tax reform and the Administration's additional policies for cutting regulation, building infrastructure, reforming health care, and boosting domestic energy production are expected to improve the supply side of the U.S. economy to allow these growth rates. As for demand, lower taxes and an expected pick up in global growth in 2017 and 2018 should bolster demand for American goods and services.[5]

Medium and Long-Run Growth.—In the medium term the rate of real GDP growth is expected to remain strong at 3.0 percent as the effects of growth-enhancing

policies play out in terms of an increasing capital stock per employed worker and consequently higher labor productivity growth. As the economy settles into a new steady state with higher capital stock per worker, the annual rate of real GDP growth is expected to edge down to a pace of 2.8 percent by 2026. While expected GDP growth of 2.8 percent per year at the end of the forecast is below the average growth rate seen in the post-World War II period, it is consistent with present-day and expected demographic trends for the U.S.

Unemployment.—As of January 2018, the unemployment rate stood at 4.1 percent. The Administration expects the unemployment rate to decrease as a result of increasing business investment and higher real GDP growth, reaching a low of 3.7 percent in 2019. After that, the forecast assumes that it will rise back toward 4.8 percent, a rate roughly consistent with stable inflation. Theory suggests that when the unemployment rate is at this rate, pressures on inflation are broadly in balance, so that inflation neither creeps up nor down.

Interest Rates.—As growth increases, the Administration expects that interest rates will begin to rise to values more consistent with historical experience. The rate on the 91-day Treasury bill is expected to increase from 0.9 percent in 2017 to 3.0 percent in 2021 and then taper down to 2.9 percent in the last 6 years of the forecast window. The interest rate on the 10-year Treasury note is expected to rise in a similar fashion, from 2.3 percent in 2017 to 3.6 percent in the long run. Economic theory suggests that real GDP growth rates and interest rates are positively correlated, so interest rates are expected to be propelled higher by the stronger growth that the Administration anticipates.

Inflation.—Since the onset of the financial crisis, inflation, whether measured by the GDP price index, the Consumer Price Index (CPI), or the price index for Personal Consumption Expenditures (PCE), has been subdued compared with the post-World War II average. This observation holds even when looking at the "core" indexes that exclude volatile food and energy prices. The Administration expects CPI inflation to rise 1.9 percent in 2018 (on a fourth quarter-over-fourth quarter basis), before rising to 2.3 percent in the long run. The GDP price index is forecast to rise by 1.6 percent in 2018 (on a fourth-quarter-over-fourth-quarter basis) and, with stronger aggregate demand for goods and labor, rise by 2021 to 2.0 percent where it is expected to stay through the longer term.

Changes in Economic Assumptions from Last Year's Budget.—Table 2-2 compares the Administration's forecast for the FY 2019 Budget with that from the FY 2018 Budget. Compared with the previous forecast, the Administration expects output growth to rise earlier before edging down to growth of 2.8 percent annually whereas the previous forecast expected growth to rise more gradually and stabilize at a slightly higher growth path of 3.0 percent annually. In 2027, both forecasts predict similar levels of nominal and real GDP. Both forecasts are predicated on the implementation of the Administration's policies designed to boost productivity

---

[4] Besides the U.S.A. the other advanced economies are: Australia, Austria, Belgium, Canada, Cyprus, Czech Republic, Denmark, Estonia, Finland, France, Germany, Greece, Hong Kong SAR, Iceland, Ireland, Israel, Italy, Japan, Korea, Latvia, Lithuania, Luxembourg, Macao SAR, Malta, Netherlands, New Zealand, Norway, Portugal, Puerto Rico, San Marino, Singapore, Slovak Republic, Slovenia, Spain, Sweden, Switzerland, Taiwan, Province of China, and the United Kingdom.

[5] For estimates on productivity enhancing and economic growth effects of tax and regulation policies, see: The Growth Effects of Corporate Tax Reform and Implications for Wages, The Council of Economic Advisers October 2017, *https://www.whitehouse.gov/sites/whitehouse.gov/files/images/Corporate%20Tax%20Reform%20and%20Growth%20Final.pdf*; The Growth Potential of Deregulation, The Council of Economic Advisers October 2, 2017, *https://www.whitehouse.gov/sites/whitehouse.gov/files/documents/The%20Growth%20Potential%20of%20Deregulation_1.pdf*

Table 2–2. COMPARISON OF ECONOMIC ASSUMPTIONS IN THE 2018 AND 2019 BUDGETS

(Calendar Years, Dollar Amounts in Billions)

	2017	2018	2019	2020	2021	2022	2023	2024	2025	2026	2027
Nominal GDP:											
2018 Budget Assumptions[1]	19,419	20,291	21,253	22,313	23,442	24,628	25,874	27,183	28,558	30,003	31,522
2019 Budget Assumptions	19,372	20,262	21,263	22,345	23,482	24,672	25,923	27,234	28,598	30,001	31,461
Real GDP (2009 Dollars):											
2018 Budget Assumptions[1]	17,093	17,508	17,978	18,504	19,059	19,631	20,220	20,826	21,451	22,095	22,758
2019 Budget Assumptions	17,090	17,601	18,157	18,727	19,296	19,875	20,471	21,085	21,705	22,320	22,945
Real GDP (Percent Change):[2]											
2018 Budget Assumptions[1]	2.3	2.4	2.7	2.9	3.0	3.0	3.0	3.0	3.0	3.0	3.0
2019 Budget Assumptions	2.2	3.0	3.2	3.1	3.0	3.0	3.0	3.0	2.9	2.8	2.8
GDP Price Index (Percent Change):[2]											
2018 Budget Assumptions[1]	1.9	2.0	2.0	2.0	2.0	2.0	2.0	2.0	2.0	2.0	2.0
2019 Budget Assumptions	1.7	1.6	1.7	1.9	2.0	2.0	2.0	2.0	2.0	2.0	2.0
Consumer Price Index (All-Urban; Percent Change):[2]											
2018 Budget Assumptions	2.6	2.3	2.3	2.3	2.3	2.3	2.3	2.3	2.3	2.3	2.3
2019 Budget Assumptions	2.1	2.1	2.0	2.2	2.3	2.3	2.3	2.3	2.3	2.3	2.3
Civilian Unemployment Rate (Percent):[3]											
2018 Budget Assumptions	4.6	4.4	4.6	4.7	4.8	4.8	4.8	4.8	4.8	4.8	4.8
2019 Budget Assumptions	4.4	3.9	3.7	3.8	3.9	4.0	4.2	4.3	4.5	4.7	4.8
91-Day Treasury Bill Rate (Percent):[3]											
2018 Budget Assumptions	0.8	1.5	2.1	2.6	2.9	3.0	3.0	3.1	3.1	3.1	3.1
2019 Budget Assumptions	0.9	1.5	2.3	2.9	3.0	3.0	2.9	2.9	2.9	2.9	2.9
10-Year Treasury Note Rate (Percent):[3]											
2018 Budget Assumptions	2.7	3.3	3.4	3.8	3.8	3.8	3.8	3.8	3.8	3.8	3.8
2019 Budget Assumptions	2.3	2.6	3.1	3.4	3.6	3.7	3.7	3.6	3.6	3.6	3.6

[1] Adjusted for July 2017 NIPA Revisions
[2] Calendar Year over Calendar Year
[3] Calendar Year Average

and labor force participation. These include deregulation, tax reform, an improved fiscal outlook, and inducements for infrastructure investment, which should boost investment and bolster the incentives to work and save. The Administration's expectations for inflation differ little from the previous forecast, except for lower CPI inflation in the near term in light of the fact that price pressures in the economy have been remarkably contained despite falling unemployment and higher economic growth. The forecast for the unemployment rate is also broadly similar, although the 2019 Budget projections have the unemployment rate dropping to a trough of 3.7 percent, lower than was previously expected, but the unemployment rate in both projections gradually edges up to 4.8 percent, the rate at which inflation pressures are broadly balanced in the long term. On the 91-day Treasury bill rate, the 2019 Budget expects it to rise more rapidly in the near term before settling at a steady state rate. The steady-state Treasury bill rate in the latter half of the forecast window is expected to be below that of the 2018 Budget. The yield on the 10-year Treasury note is lower at all points of the forecast horizon relative to the 2018 Budget. This lowering of the yield, relative to the 2018 Budget projection in the near term, is largely driven by lower long-term interest rates observed in the recent data. Over the medium term, the yield rises rap-

idly to levels consistent with the steady state annual GDP growth projection of 2.8 percent in contrast to the 3.0 percent growth forecast in the 2018 Budget.

Comparison with Other Forecasts

For some additional perspective on the Administration's forecast, this section compares it with forecasts prepared by the Congressional Budget Office (CBO), the Federal Open Market Committee of the Federal Reserve (FOMC), and the Blue Chip panel of private-sector forecasters. There are some important differences to bear in mind when making such a comparison.

The most important difference between these forecasts is that they make different assumptions about the implementation of the Administration's policies. As already noted, the Administration's forecast assumes full implementation of these proposals. At the opposite end of the spectrum, CBO produces a forecast that assumes no changes to current law. It is not clear to what extent the FOMC participants and the Blue Chip panel incorporate policy implementation in their respective outlooks. The Blue Chip panel, in particular, compiles a large number of private-sector forecasts, which are marked by considerable heterogeneity across individual forecasters and their policy expectations.

Table 2–3. COMPARISON OF ECONOMIC ASSUMPTIONS
(Calendar Years)

	2017	2018	2019	2020	2021	2022	2023	2024	2025	2026	2027	2028
Nominal GDP:												
2019 Budget	19,372	20,262	21,263	22,345	23,482	24,672	25,923	27,234	28,598	30,001	31,461	32,991
CBO	19,310	20,118	20,847	21,566	22,378	23,262	24,186	25,150	26,150	27,191	28,273	N/A
Blue Chip	19,351	20,105	20,950	21,830	22,725	23,657	24,626	25,661	26,739	27,862	29,032	30,251
Real GDP (Year-over-Year):												
2019 Budget	2.2	3.0	3.2	3.1	3.0	3.0	3.0	3.0	2.9	2.8	2.8	2.8
CBO	2.1	2.2	1.7	1.4	1.7	1.9	1.9	1.9	1.9	1.9	1.9	N/A
Blue Chip	2.2	2.4	2.1	2.1	2.0	2.0	2.1	2.1	2.1	2.1	2.1	2.1
Real GDP (Fourth Quarter-over-Fourth Quarter):												
2019 Budget	2.5	3.1	3.2	3.1	3.0	3.0	3.0	3.0	2.9	2.8	2.8	2.8
CBO	2.2	2.0	1.5	1.5	1.8	1.9	1.9	1.9	1.9	1.9	1.9	N/A
Blue Chip	2.3	2.3	2.1	2.1	2.0	2.0	2.1	2.1	2.1	2.1	2.1	2.1
Federal Reserve Median Projection	2.5	2.5	2.1	2	-------------				1.8 longer run			-------------
GDP Price Index: [1]												
2019 Budget	1.7	1.6	1.7	1.9	2.0	2.0	2.0	2.0	2.0	2.0	2.0	2.0
CBO	1.8	2.0	1.9	2.0	2.0	2.0	2.0	2.0	2.1	2.1	2.1	N/A
Blue Chip	1.7	1.9	2.1	2.1	2.1	2.1	2.1	2.1	2.1	2.1	2.1	2.1
Consumer Price Index (CPI-U): [1]												
2019 Budget	2.1	2.1	2.0	2.2	2.3	2.3	2.3	2.3	2.3	2.3	2.3	2.3
CBO	2.3	2.2	2.3	2.4	2.4	2.4	2.4	2.4	2.4	2.4	2.4	N/A
Blue Chip	2.1	1.9	2.3	2.3	2.3	2.3	2.3	2.3	2.3	2.3	2.3	2.3
Unemployment Rate: [2]												
2019 Budget	4.4	3.9	3.7	3.8	3.9	4.0	4.2	4.3	4.5	4.7	4.8	4.8
CBO	4.4	4.2	4.4	4.7	4.9	5.0	4.9	4.9	4.9	4.9	4.9	N/A
Blue Chip	4.4	4.1	4.2	4.3	4.4	4.5	4.5	4.9	4.9	4.9	4.9	4.6
Federal Reserve Median Projection [3]	4.1	3.9	3.9	4	-------------				4.6 longer run			-------------
Interest Rates: [2]												
91-Day Treasury Bills (discount basis):												
2019 Budget	0.9	1.5	2.3	2.9	3.0	3.0	2.9	2.9	2.9	2.9	2.9	2.9
CBO	0.9	1.5	2.2	2.6	2.8	2.8	2.8	2.8	2.8	2.8	2.8	N/A
Blue Chip	0.9	1.7	2.4	2.7	2.8	2.8	2.8	2.8	2.9	2.9	2.9	2.9
10-Year Treasury Notes:												
2019 Budget	2.3	2.6	3.1	3.4	3.6	3.7	3.7	3.6	3.6	3.6	3.6	3.6
CBO	2.4	2.8	3.2	3.5	3.6	3.7	3.7	3.7	3.7	3.7	3.7	N/A
Blue Chip	2.3	2.8	3.4	3.5	3.5	3.6	3.6	3.7	3.7	3.7	3.7	3.7

Sources: Administration; CBO, An Update to the Budget and Economic Outlook: 2017 to 2027, June 2017; October 2017 Blue Chip Economic Indicators, Aspen Publishers, Inc.; Federal Reserve Open Market Committee, December 13, 2017

N/A=Number is not available.

[1] Year-over-Year Percent Change

[2] Annual Averages, Percent

[3] Median of Fourth Quarter Values

A second difference is the publication dates of the various forecasts. While the forecast put out by the Administration is based on actual data available in mid-November, the Blue Chip long-term forecast is based on their October Survey, the FOMC projections were released on December 13, and the CBO forecast was published much earlier, in June of 2017.

In spite of these differences, the forecasts share several attributes. All of them project a further short-run decline in unemployment, followed by a rise back toward a rate consistent with stable inflation. They all forecast a rise in inflation, followed by a stable path at its long-run rate.

Finally, they all foresee a gradual rise in interest rates over the course of the forecast horizon. What separates the Administration's forecast from those of the other bodies is their respective views on real output growth.

Real GDP.—The Administration forecasts a higher path for real GDP growth compared with the CBO, FOMC, and Blue Chip forecasts throughout the forecast period after 2017. After 2017, the Administration's forecast diverges from the other forecasts, with a growth rate 0.6 percentage point faster than the next fastest in 2018 and 0.7 percentage point faster than the others at the end of the forecast window. This reflects the Administration's expectation

Table 2–4. SENSITIVITY OF THE BUDGET TO ECONOMIC ASSUMPTIONS
(Fiscal Years; In Billions Of Dollars)

Budget Effect	2018	2019	2020	2021	2022	2023	2024	2025	2026	2027	2028	Total of Budget Effects: 2018-2028
Real Growth and Employment:												
Budgetary effects of 1 percent lower real GDP growth:												
(1) For calendar year 2018 only, with real GDP recovery in 2018–2019:[1]												
Receipts	–16.1	–25.5	–13.1	–2.1	0.2	0.2	0.2	0.2	0.2	0.2	0.2	–55.7
Outlays	8.4	18.9	9.2	3.0	2.8	2.8	2.7	2.8	2.8	2.9	2.9	59.1
Increase in deficit (+)	24.5	44.4	22.3	5.1	2.6	2.6	2.6	2.6	2.6	2.7	2.8	114.7
(2) For calendar year 2018 only, with no subsequent recovery:[1]												
Receipts	–16.1	–33.7	–39.4	–41.7	–43.7	–46.0	–48.3	–50.8	–53.6	–56.3	–58.9	–488.3
Outlays	8.4	23.0	23.8	25.3	27.2	29.0	31.0	33.2	35.3	37.4	40.5	314.1
Increase in deficit (+)	24.5	56.6	63.2	67.0	70.9	75.0	79.3	83.9	88.9	93.7	99.4	802.4
(3) Sustained during 2018–2028, with no change in unemployment:												
Receipts	–16.1	–50.0	–91.3	–137.5	–187.1	–241.6	–300.8	–364.7	–436.3	–511.3	–590.3	–2,927.2
Outlays	0.0	0.5	2.4	5.5	9.4	14.2	20.0	27.2	35.6	45.2	56.6	216.6
Increase in deficit (+)	16.1	50.6	93.7	143.0	196.4	255.8	320.9	391.9	471.9	556.6	646.9	3,143.7
Inflation and Interest Rates:												
Budgetary effects of 1 percentage point higher rate of:												
(4) Inflation and interest rates during calendar year 2018 only:												
Receipts	17.2	33.9	36.4	37.1	39.0	41.0	43.1	45.2	47.7	50.1	52.4	443.0
Outlays	25.6	50.0	45.7	45.2	45.0	44.8	43.0	44.1	43.3	45.1	47.0	478.8
Increase in deficit (+)	8.4	16.1	9.4	8.1	6.0	3.8	–0.1	–1.1	–4.4	–5.0	–5.4	35.8
(5) Inflation and interest rates, sustained during 2018–2028:												
Receipts	17.2	51.7	91.0	134.2	181.8	234.3	292.1	355.2	426.6	502.3	583.3	2,869.7
Outlays	23.7	73.3	120.9	170.6	225.9	279.9	332.7	395.3	456.5	522.8	601.8	3,203.4
Increase in deficit (+)	6.5	21.6	29.9	36.4	44.1	45.6	40.6	40.1	29.9	20.5	18.5	333.7
(6) Interest rates only, sustained during 2018–2028:												
Receipts	1.1	2.5	3.1	3.5	3.8	4.0	4.3	4.6	4.9	5.2	5.4	42.4
Outlays	11.5	38.1	62.0	83.9	105.2	126.1	143.9	160.4	175.0	189.7	204.1	1,299.8
Increase in deficit (+)	10.4	35.6	58.9	80.4	101.5	122.1	139.6	155.8	170.1	184.6	198.7	1,257.5
(7) Inflation only, sustained during 2018–2028:												
Receipts	16.0	49.1	87.8	130.7	177.9	230.0	287.5	350.3	421.3	496.7	577.4	2,824.6
Outlays	12.2	35.1	58.8	86.7	120.8	154.0	189.2	235.5	282.2	334.1	398.9	1,907.5
Decrease in deficit (–)	–3.9	–13.9	–29.0	–44.0	–57.1	–76.0	–98.3	–114.8	–139.1	–162.6	–178.5	–917.1
Interest Cost of Higher Federal Borrowing:												
(8) Outlay effect of 100 billion increase in borrowing in 2018	0.7	2.1	3.0	3.4	3.5	3.5	3.6	3.7	3.8	3.9	4.1	35.3

[1] The unemployment rate is assumed to be 0.5 percentage point higher per 1 percent shortfall in the level of real GDP.

of full implementation of its policy proposals, while other forecasters are unlikely to be operating under the same assumption. The CBO in particular is constrained to assume a continuation of current law in its forecast, which in the case of its June 2017 forecast was prepared prior to the enactment of the Tax Cuts and Jobs Act.

Unemployment.—On the unemployment rate, the Administration's expectations are largely aligned with those of the other forecasters. Along with the Administration, all forecasters expect further declines in unemployment in 2018. After 2018 other forecasters expect the unemployment rate to rise gradually while the Administration believes that because of its policies there is more room for the economy to grow and for the unemployment rate to decrease. After 2019, all forecasters project a gradual uptick in the unemployment rate to their respective estimates of the long-term rate (4.8 percent for the Administration, 4.9 percent for the CBO, and 4.6 percent for the FOMC and the Blue Chip panel).

Interest Rates.—There are not significant differences in the outlooks for interest rates. For both short- and long-term rates, all forecasters agree that they will tend to gradually rise, the Treasury bill rate is expected to rise to a steady-state level of around 2.9 percent and the 10-

Table 2–5. FORECAST ERRORS, JANUARY 1982–PRESENT

REAL GDP ERRORS

2-Year Average Annual Real GDP Growth	Administration	CBO	Blue Chip
Mean Error	0.2	−0.1	−0.1
Mean Absolute Error	1.2	1.0	1.1
Root Mean Square Error	1.5	1.3	1.4

6-Year Average Annual Real GDP Growth			
Mean Error	0.4	0.1	0.1
Mean Absolute Error	1.1	1.0	0.9
Root Mean Square Error	1.3	1.2	1.1

INFLATION ERRORS

2-Year Average Annual Change in the GDP Price Index	Administration	CBO	Blue Chip
Mean Error	0.3	0.3	0.4
Mean Absolute Error	0.7	0.7	0.7
Root Mean Square Error	0.9	0.9	0.8

6-Year Average Annual Change in the GDP Index			
Mean Error	0.4	0.5	0.7
Mean Absolute Error	0.6	0.8	0.9
Root Mean Square Error	0.8	1.0	1.0

INTEREST RATE ERRORS

2-Year Average 91-Day Treasury Bill Rate	Administration	CBO	Blue Chip
Mean Error	0.3	0.5	0.6
Mean Absolute Error	1.0	0.9	1.0
Root Mean Square Error	1.2	1.3	1.2

6-Year Average 91-Day Treasury Bill Rate			
Mean Error	0.9	1.4	1.5
Mean Absolute Error	1.4	1.5	1.6
Root Mean Square Error	1.7	1.8	1.9

year Treasury note yield is expected to lie between 3.6 percent and 3.7 percent.

Inflation.—Expectations for inflation are similar across the Administration, the CBO, and the Blue Chip. The CBO expects a CPI inflation rate of 2.4 percent in the long run, while the Administration and the Blue Chip expect a 2.3 percent long run rate. For the GDP price index, the three forecasts also exhibit little disagreement, other than a marginally higher long-run rate from the Blue Chip panel and CBO.

Sensitivity of the Budget to Economic Assumptions

Federal spending and tax collections are heavily influenced by developments in the economy. Tax receipts are a function of growth in incomes for households and firms. Spending on social assistance programs may rise when the economy enters a downturn, while increases in spending on Social Security and other programs are dependent on consumer price inflation. A robust set of projections for macroeconomic variables assists in budget planning, but unexpected developments in the economy have ripple effects for Federal spending and revenues. This section seeks to provide an understanding of the magnitude of

the effects that unforeseen changes in the economy can have on the budget.

To make these assessments, the Administration relies on a set of rules of thumb that can predict how certain spending and revenue categories will react to a change in a given subset of macroeconomic variables, holding almost everything else constant. These rules of thumb provide a sense of the broad changes one would expect after a given development, but they cannot anticipate how policy makers would react and potentially change course in such an event. For example, if the economy were to suffer an unexpected recession, the rules of thumb suggest that tax revenues would decline and that spending on programs such as unemployment insurance would go up. In such a situation, however, policy makers might cut tax rates to stimulate the economy, and such behavior would not be accounted for by the historical relationships captured by these rules of thumb.

Another caveat is that it is often unrealistic to suppose that one macroeconomic variable might change while others would remain constant. Most macroeconomic variables interact with each other in complex and subtle ways. These are important considerations to bear in mind when examining Table 2-4.

Table 2–6. DIFFERENCES BETWEEN ESTIMATED AND ACTUAL SURPLUSES OR DEFICITS FOR FIVE-YEAR BUDGET ESTIMATES SINCE 1986 (AS A PERCENT OF GDP)

	Current Year Estimate	Budget Year Estimate	Estimate for Budget Year Plus:			
			One Year (BY + 1)	Two Years (BY + 2)	Three Years (BY + 3)	Four Years (BY + 4)
Average Difference [1]	−0.8	0.2	1.1	1.7	2.1	2.5
Average Absolute Difference [2]	1.1	1.4	2.2	2.8	3.4	3.7
Standard Deviation	1.0	2.0	2.8	3.3	3.5	3.5
Root Mean Squared Error	1.3	2.0	3.0	3.7	4.0	4.2

[1] A positive number represents an overestimate of the surplus or an underestimate of the deficit. A negative number represents an overestimate of the deficit or an underestimate of the surplus.

[2] Average absolute difference is the difference without regard to sign

For real growth and employment:

- The first panel in the table illustrates the effect on the deficit resulting from a one percentage point reduction in real GDP growth, relative to the Administration's forecast, in 2018 that is followed by a subsequent recovery in 2019 and 2020. The unemployment rate is assumed to be half a percentage point higher in 2018 before returning to the baseline level in 2019 and 2020. The table shows that receipts would temporarily be somewhat lower and outlays would temporarily be higher. The long run effect on the budget deficit would be an increase of $114.7 billion over the eleven-year forecast horizon due to lower receipts and higher interest payments resulting from higher short-run deficits.

- The next panel in the table reports the effect of a reduction of one percentage point in real GDP growth in 2018 that is not subsequently made up by faster growth in 2019 and 2020. Consistent with this output path, the rate of unemployment is assumed to rise by half a percentage point relative to that assumed in the Administration's forecasts. Here, the effect on the budget deficit is more substantial, as receipts are lowered in every year of the forecast, while outlays rise gradually over the forecast window. This is because unemployment will be higher, leading to lower tax revenues and higher outlays on unemployment insurance, as well as higher interest payments that follow from increased short-run deficits.

- The third panel in the table shows the impact of a GDP growth rate that is permanently reduced by one percentage point, while the unemployment rate is not affected. This is the sort of situation that would arise if, for example, the economy were hit by a permanent decline in productivity growth. In this case, the effect on the budget deficit is large, with receipts being reduced substantially throughout the forecast window and outlays rising due to higher interest payments. The accumulated effect over the eleven-year horizon is an additional $3.1 trillion of deficits.

For inflation and interest rates:

- The fourth panel in Table 2-4 shows the effect on the Budget in the case of a one percentage point higher rate of inflation and a 1 percentage point higher nominal interest rate in 2018. Both inflation and interest rates return to their assumed levels in 2019. This would result in a permanently higher price level and nominal GDP over the course of the forecast horizon. The effect on the Budget deficit would be fairly modest, as receipts would increase slightly less than outlays over the eleven years. This is because revenues, interest payments, and nondiscretionary outlays rise with inflation while discretionary outlays are assumed fixed. Over the years from 2018-2028, the budget deficit would increase by about $36 billion.

- The fifth panel in the table illustrates the effects on the budget deficit of an inflation rate and an interest rate one percentage point higher than projected in every year of the forecast. The overall effect on the deficit over the forecast is $334 billion accumulated as both receipts, interest payments, and mandatory outlays (on Social Security and Federal pensions rise with inflation while discretionary outlays are presumed to be fixed. It is still important to note, however, that faster inflation implies that the real value of Federal discretionary spending would be eroded.

- The next panel reports the effect on the deficit resulting from an increase in interest rates in every year of the forecast, with no accompanying increase in inflation. The result is a much higher accumulated deficit, as the Federal Government would have to make much higher interest payments on its debt. Receipts would be slightly higher as households would pay higher taxes on interest income.

- The seventh panel in the table reports the effect on the budget deficit of an inflation rate one percentage point higher than projected in every year of the forecast window, while the interest rate remains as forecast. In this case, the result is a much smaller deficit over the eleven years of the forecast relative to the baseline. Permanently higher inflation results in much higher revenues over the next eleven years, which helps to reduce interest payments on debt.

Outlays rise due to higher cost-of-living increases on items such as Social Security, though not so much as to offset the revenue increases.

- Finally, the table shows the effect on the budget deficit if the Federal government were to borrow an additional $100 billion in 2018, while all of the other projections remain constant. Outlays rise over the forecast window by an accumulated $35 billion, due to higher interest payments.

These simple approximations that inform the sensitivity analysis are symmetric. This means that the effect of, for example, a one percentage point higher rate of growth over the forecast horizon would be of the same magnitude as a one percentage point reduction in growth, though with the opposite sign.

Forecast Errors for Growth, Inflation, and Interest Rates

As with any forecast, the Administration's projections will not be fully accurate. It is impossible to foresee every eventuality over a one–year horizon, much less ten or more years. This section evaluates the historical accuracy of the forecasts of past Administrations for real GDP, inflation, and short-term interest rates, especially as compared with the accuracy of forecasts produced by the CBO or Blue Chip panel. For this exercise, forecasts produced by all three entities going as far back as the Fiscal Year 1983 Budget are compared with realized values of these important variables.

The results of this exercise are reported in Table 2-5 and contain three different measures of accuracy. The first is the average forecast error. When a forecaster has an average forecast error of zero, it may be said that the forecast has historically been unbiased, in the sense that realized values of the variables have not been systematically above or below the forecasted value. The second is the average absolute value of the forecast error, which offers a sense of the magnitude of errors. Even if the past forecast errors average to zero, the errors may have been of a very large magnitude, with both positive and negative values. Finally, the table reports the square root of the mean of squared forecast error (RMSE). This metric applies an especially harsh penalty to forecasting systems prone to large errors. The table reports these measures of accuracy at both the 2-year and the 6-year horizons, thus evaluating the relative success of different forecasts in the short run and in the medium term.

For real GDP growth rates, at both the 2-year and 6-year horizons, the mean forecast error suggests that all of the forecasts (Administration, the CBO, and the Blue Chip panel) have been broadly unbiased, with small average errors close to zero. The mean absolute error and the RMSE both suggest that the Administration's past forecasts have tended to make slightly larger errors than the others. This could be due to partial adoption of the various Administrations' proposed policies in the past.

When it comes to inflation, there is more evidence of some systematic bias in all three forecasts. The mean er-

rors at the 2- and 6-year horizons are all positive and larger than the errors in projecting real GDP growth. This implies that the Administration, the CBO, and the Blue Chip have expected faster inflation than ultimately materialized. A closer look at the data reveals that the errors were largest in the 1980s, as the U.S. economy shifted from a period of high inflation in the 1970s to a period of more moderate price rises. The mean absolute error and the RMSE metrics imply that the errors in the Administration's inflation forecast have tended to be of equal or smaller magnitude than those of the CBO or Blue Chip panel.

Finally, on interest rates, the story is similar to that for inflation. All of the forecasts have historically projected interest rates that were higher than what later occurred, probably because they expected higher inflation as shown above. Across the three forecasters, the Administration has generally made errors of lesser magnitude than the other two.

Uncertainty and the Deficit Projections

This section assesses the accuracy of past Budget forecasts for the deficit or surplus, measured at different time horizons. The results of this exercise are reported in Table 2-6, where the average error, the average absolute error, and the RMSE (as well as the standard deviation of the forecast error) are reported.

In the table, a negative number means that the Federal Government ran a greater surplus than was expected, while a positive number in the table indicates a smaller surplus or a larger deficit. In the current year in which the Budget is published, the Administration has tended to understate the surplus (or, equivalently, overstate the deficit). For every year beyond the current year, however, the historical pattern has been for the budget deficit to be larger than the Administration expected. One possible reason for this is that past Administrations' policy proposals have not all been implemented. The forecast errors tend to grow with the time horizon, which is not surprising given that there is much greater uncertainty in the medium run about both the macroeconomic situation and the specific details of policy enactments.

It is possible to construct a probabilistic range of outcomes for the deficit. This is accomplished by taking the RMSE of previous forecast errors and assuming that these errors are drawn from a normal distribution. This exercise is undertaken at every forecast horizon from the current year to five years down the road. Chart 2-1 displays the projected range of possible deficits. In the chart, the middle line represents the Administration's expected budget balance and can be interpreted as the 50th percentile outcome. The rest of the lines in the chart may be read in the following fashion. The top line reports the 95th percentile of the distribution of outcomes over 2018 to 2023, meaning that there is a 95 percent probability that the actual balance in those years will be more negative than expressed by the line. Similarly, there is a 95 percent probability that the balance will be more positive than suggested by the bottom line in the chart. In 2018, there is a 95 percent chance of a budget deficit greater than 2.0 percent of GDP. By 2023, there is only a 5 percent chance of a budget deficit greater than 9.9 percent of GDP. In addition, the chart reports that there is a significant probability of a budget surplus by 2023.

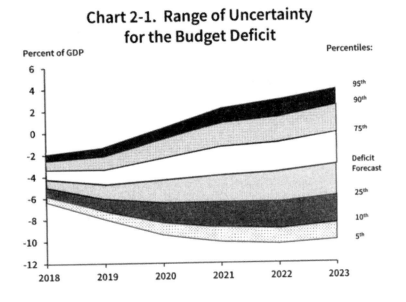

Chart 2-1. Range of Uncertainty for the Budget Deficit

3. LONG-TERM BUDGET OUTLOOK

The 2019 President's Budget improves the Federal Government's long-term fiscal picture by promoting rapid economic growth, responsibly controlling spending, and increasing efficiencies Government-wide. This chapter demonstrates the positive impact of the Administration's policies by comparing long-term budget forecasts under current policy (baseline projections) with forecasts based on the 2019 Budget proposals (policy projections). Baseline projections indicate that the deficit will continue at elevated levels beyond the 10-year window and that publicly held debt will continue to rise as a share of the economy. Conversely, policy projections indicate that enacting the Budget's proposed reforms could dramatically reduce deficits and publicly held debt as a percentage of GDP.

Chart 3-1 shows the path of debt as a percent of GDP under continuation of current policy, *without* the proposed changes in the President's Budget, as well as the debt trajectory under the President's policies. Under current policy, the ratio of debt to GDP will rise from 78.8 percent in 2018 to 88.3 percent in 2028, an increase of about 9.5 percentage points over that period. In contrast, the debt ratio is projected to be 72.6 percent in 2028 under the proposed policy changes. By the end of the 25-year horizon, the difference in the debt burden—93.7 percent of GDP under current policy compared to 39.2 percent of GDP under Budget policy—is even starker. The savings proposed by the Administration from 2019-2028 are a significant down payment towards reducing debt and reaching a balanced budget by 2039.

While the detailed estimates of receipts and outlays in the President's Budget extend only 10 years, this chapter presents the longer-term budget outlook, both under a continuation of current policies and under the policies proposed in the Budget. The projections in this chapter are highly uncertain. Small changes in economic or other assumptions can cause large differences to the results especially for projections over longer horizons.

The chapter is organized as follows:

- The first section details the assumptions used to create the baseline projection and analyzes the long-term implications of leaving current policies in place. This forecast serves as a point of comparison against the proposals in the 2019 Budget in the second section.

- The second section demonstrates how the Administration's policies will significantly alter the current trajectory of the Federal budget by reducing deficits and debt, and by balancing the budget by 2039 under a long-term term extension of the Budget's policies.

- The third section discusses alternative assumptions about the evolution of key variables and uncertainties in the resulting projections.

- The fourth section discusses the actuarial projections for Social Security and Medicare.

- The appendix provides further detail on data sources, assumptions, and other methods for estimation.

Chart 3-1. Comparison of Publicly Held Debt

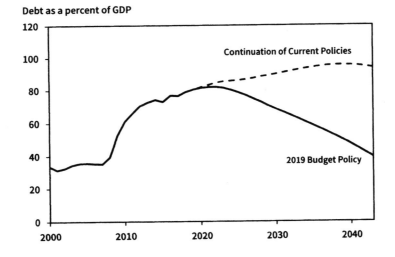

Long-Run Projections under Continuation of Current Policies

For the 10-year budget window, the Administration produces both baseline projections, which show how deficits and debt would evolve under current policies, and projections showing the impact of proposed policy changes. Like the budget baseline more generally, long-term projections should provide policymakers with information about the Nation's expected fiscal trajectory in the absence of spending and tax changes. For this reason, a set of economic assumptions based in current law, including the projected effects of the 2017 tax reform and excluding the growth-increasing effects of the Administration's proposed fiscal policies, underlie the baseline projections in this chapter. Using the same set of economic assumptions for baseline and policy projections would understate the severity of the current-law fiscal problem and fail to illustrate the full impact of the 2019 Budget policies.

The baseline long-term projections assume that current policy continues for Social Security, Medicare, Medicaid, other mandatory programs, and revenues.[1] For discretionary spending, it is less clear how to project a continuation of current policy. After the expiration of the statutory caps in 2021, both the Administration's and CBO's 10-year baselines assume that discretionary funding levels generally grow slightly above the rate of inflation (about 2.5 percent per year) per statutory baseline rules. Thereafter, the baseline long-run projections assume that per-person discretionary funding remains constant, which implies an annual nominal growth rate of about 2.9 percent.

Over the next 10 years, debt in the baseline projection rises from 78.8 percent of GDP in 2018 to 88.3 percent of GDP in 2028. Beyond the 10-year horizon, debt continues to increase, reaching 93.7 percent of GDP by 2043, the end of the 25-year projection window. The key drivers of that increase are an aging population and rapid health care cost growth, which are only partly offset by growth in Federal revenues and a decline in discretionary spending relative to GDP. Without policy changes, the public debt will continue to grow, increasing the burden on future generations.

Aging Population.—Over the next 10 years, an aging population will put significant pressure on the budget. In 2008, when the oldest members of the baby boom generation became eligible for early retirement under Social Security, the ratio of workers to Social Security beneficiaries was 3.2. By the end of the 10-year budget window, that ratio will fall to 2.3, and it will reach about 2.1 in the mid-2030s, at which point most of the baby boomers will have retired.

With fewer active workers paying taxes and more retired workers eligible for Social Security, Medicare, and Medicaid (including long-term care), budgetary pressures will increase. Social Security program costs will grow from 4.9 percent of GDP today to 5.6 percent of GDP by 2043, with most of that growth occurring within the 10-year budget window. Likewise, even if per-beneficiary health care costs grew at the same rate as GDP per capita, Medicare and Medicaid costs would still increase substantially, as a percent of GDP, due solely to the aging population.

Health Costs.—Health care costs per capita have risen much faster than per-capita GDP growth for decades, thus requiring both public and private spending on health care to increase as a share of the economy. While in recent years spending per enrollee has grown roughly in line with, or more slowly than, per-capita GDP in both the public and private sectors, this slower per-enrollee growth is not projected to continue. Trends in per-enrollee costs, together with the demographic trends discussed above, are the primary drivers of long-term fiscal projections.

Based on projections of Medicare enrollment and expenditures included in the 2017 Medicare Trustees Report, the projections here assume that Medicare per-beneficiary spending growth will increase, with the growth rate averaging about 1.0 percentage points above the growth rate of per-capita GDP over the next 25 years. (This average growth rate is still below the historical average for the last 25 years.) Under these assumptions, Medicare and Medicaid costs increase by a total of 2.5 percentage points as a percent of GDP by 2043.

Revenues and Discretionary Spending.—Under the 2017 tax reform law, receipts will grow slightly faster than GDP over the long run. The increase in revenues as a percent of GDP occurs primarily because individuals' real, inflation-adjusted incomes grow over time, and so a portion of their income falls into higher tax brackets. (Bracket thresholds are indexed for inflation but do not grow in real terms.) In addition, under baseline assumptions discretionary spending grows slower than GDP. Both of these factors act to restrain deficits relative to GDP, partially offsetting the pressure from increases in spending for Social Security and health programs.

The Impact of 2019 Budget Policies on the Long-Term Fiscal Outlook

To show the long-term effects of implementing new policies, expenditures and revenues are extended through the 25-year timeframe. The President's 2019 Budget proposals reduce deficits while continuing to invest in national security and other critical priorities that promote economic growth by decreasing non-defense discretionary and mandatory spending over the next 10 years. Beyond the 10-year window, most categories of mandatory spending grow at the same rates as under the baseline projection, discretionary spending keeps up with inflation and population, and revenues continue as a fixed percentage of GDP based on their level in 2028. Details about the assumptions are available in the appendix.

---

[1] The long-run baseline projections are consistent with the Budget's baseline concept, which is explained in more detail in Chapter 22, "Current Services Estimates," in this volume. The projections assume extension of the individual income tax and estate tax provisions of the Tax Cuts and Jobs Act beyond their expiration in 2025, and also assume full payment of scheduled Social Security and Medicare benefits without regard to the projected depletion of the trust funds for these programs. Additional baseline assumptions beyond the 10-year window are detailed in the appendix to this chapter.

Chart 3-2. Comparison of Annual Surplus/Deficit

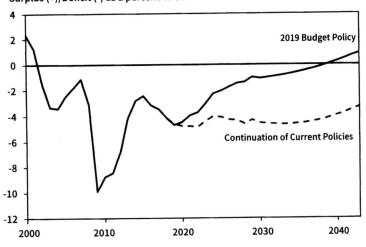

Surplus (+)/Deficit (-) as a percent of GDP

As shown in Chart 3-2, 2019 Budget policies reduce the deficit to 1.4 percent of GDP by 2028 and ultimately lead to a balanced budget by 2039. Over the decade and a half after 2028, the debt-to-GDP ratio continues to decline. At the end of the 25-year horizon, the debt ratio would be the lowest since before 2008, representing significant progress in reducing the Federal debt burden.

One way to quantify the size of the Nation's long-term fiscal challenges is to determine the size of the increase in taxes or reduction in non-interest spending needed to reach a target debt-to-GDP ratio over a given period. There is no one optimal debt ratio, but two illustrative targets are keeping the debt ratio stable, and reaching the average postwar debt ratio of 45 percent. Policy adjustments of about 0.7 percent of GDP to baseline projections would be needed each year to keep the debt ratio stable at 79 percent. Alternatively, policy adjustments of about 2.2 percent of GDP would steer the debt ratio to the postwar average by the end of the 25-year horizon. In comparison, the President's Budget policies are projected to decrease the debt ratio within the 10-year window and reduce it by nearly 40 percentage points by 2043, more than satisfying the definition of fiscal sustainability.

The Budget achieves these fiscal goals through prioritizing expenditures that promote economic growth and security while improving the efficiency of the Federal government. For example, the President's Budget includes a $200 billion initiative to improve the Nation's crumbling infrastructure and an increase of $65 billion to defense spending for 2019 above the current discretionary caps. Continuing reductions of regulatory burden will promote job creation, and extending tax reform will allow families to keep more of their earnings. In addition, the Budget proposes streamlining Medicare to make it a better deal for seniors and the Government. Eliminating fraud, waste, and abuse from Medicare contributes to a lower debt and deficit in the long run.

Table 3–1. 25-YEAR DEBT PROJECTIONS UNDER ALTERNATIVE BUDGET SCENARIOS
(Percent of GDP)

2019 Budget Policy	39.2
Health:	
Excess cost growth averages 1.5%	51.3
Zero excess cost growth	32.1
Discretionary Outlays:	
Grow with inflation	37.1
Grow with GDP	45.6
Revenues:	
Revenues rise as as a share of GDP, with bracket creep	32.7
Productivity and Interest:[1]	
Productivity grows by 0.25 percentage point per year faster than the base case	24.2
Productivity grows by 0.25 percentage point per year slower than the base case	56.1

[1] Interest rates adjust commensurately with increases or decreases in productivity.

Uncertainty and Alternative Assumptions

Future budget outcomes depend on a host of unknowns: changing economic conditions, unforeseen international developments, unexpected demographic shifts, and unpredictable technological advances. The longer budget projections are extended, the more the uncertainties increase. These uncertainties make even accurate short-run budget forecasting quite difficult. For example, the Budget's projection of the deficit in five years is 3.0 percent of GDP, but a distribution of probable outcomes ranges from a deficit of 8.4 percent of GDP to a surplus

Chart 3-3. Alternative Productivity and Interest Assumptions

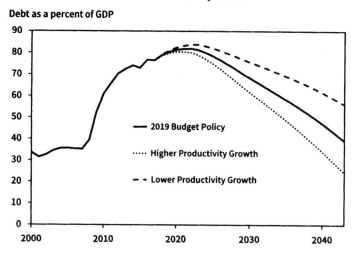

of 2.4 percent of GDP, at the 10th and 90th percentiles, respectively.

Productivity and Interest Rates.—The rate of future productivity growth has a major effect on the long-run budget outlook (see Chart 3-3). Higher productivity growth improves the budget outlook, because it adds directly to the growth of the major tax bases while having a smaller effect on outlay growth. Productivity growth is also highly uncertain. For much of the last century, output per hour in nonfarm business grew at an average rate of around 2.1 percent per year, but there were long periods of sustained productivity growth at notably higher and lower rates than the long-term average. The base case long-run projections assume that real GDP per hour worked will grow at an average annual rate of 2.0 percent per year and assume interest rates on 10-year Treasury securities of 3.6 percent. The alternative scenarios il-

lustrate the effect of raising and lowering the projected productivity growth rate by 0.25 percentage point and changing interest rates commensurately. At the end of the 25-year horizon, the public debt ranges from 24.2 percent of GDP in the high productivity scenario to 56.1 percent of GDP in the low productivity scenario. This variation highlights the importance of investment and smarter tax policy, which can contribute to higher productivity.

Health Spending.—Health care cost growth represents another major source of uncertainty in the long-term budget projections. As noted above, the baseline projections follow the Medicare Trustees in assuming that Medicare per-beneficiary costs grow an average of about 1.0 percentage points faster than per-capita GDP growth over the next 25 years. However, in the past, especially prior to 1990, health care costs grew even more rapidly. Over the last few years, per-enrollee health care costs

Chart 3-4. Alternative Health Care Costs

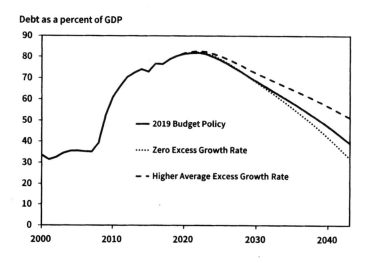

Chart 3-5. Alternative Discretionary Assumptions

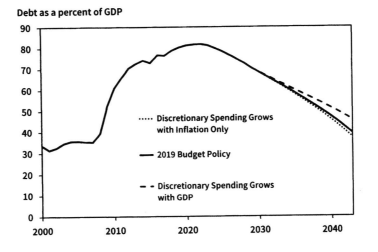

Debt as a percent of GDP

..... Discretionary Spending Grows with Inflation Only

—— 2019 Budget Policy

- - Discretionary Spending Grows with GDP

have grown roughly in line with or more slowly than GDP per capita, with particularly slow growth in Medicare and Medicaid.

Chart 3-4 shows the large impacts that either slower or faster health care cost growth would have on the budget. If health care cost growth averaged 1.5 percentage points faster than per-capita GDP growth, the debt ratio in 25 years would increase from 39.2 percent of GDP under the base case Budget policy to 51.3 percent of GDP. If health care costs grew with GDP per-capita, the debt ratio in 25 years would be 32.1 percent of GDP.

Policy Assumptions.—As evident from the discussion of the 2019 Budget proposals, policy choices will also have a large impact on long-term budget deficits and debt. The base case policy projection for discretionary spending assumes that after 2028, discretionary spending grows with inflation and population (see Chart 3-5). Alternative assumptions are to grow discretionary spending with GDP or inflation only. At the end of the 25-year horizon, the debt ratio ranges from 37.1 percent of GDP if discretion-

ary spending grows with inflation only to 39.2 percent of GDP in the base case and 45.6 percent of GDP if discretionary spending grows with GDP.

In the base case policy projection, tax receipts remain a constant percent of GDP after the budget window. Chart 3-6 shows an alternative receipts assumption. Without changes in law, revenues would gradually increase with rising real incomes adding to budget surpluses that can further improve the debt outlook. At the end of the 25-year horizon, the debt ratio falls from 39.2 percent of GDP in the base case to 32.7 percent of GDP in the alternative case where tax brackets are not regularly increased after 2028.

Finally, Chart 3-7 shows how uncertainties compound over the forecast horizon. As the chart shows, under the base case Budget policy projections, debt declines to 39.2 percent of GDP. Alternatively, assuming a combination of slower productivity growth and higher health care cost growth results in less debt reduction, with the debt ratio reaching 69.0 percent by the end of the window.

Chart 3-6. Alternative Revenue Assumptions

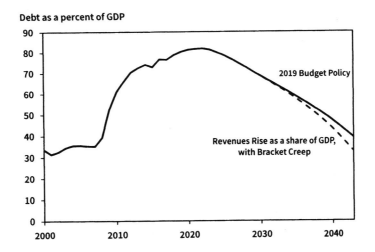

Debt as a percent of GDP

2019 Budget Policy

Revenues Rise as a share of GDP, with Bracket Creep

Chart 3-7. Long-Term Uncertainties

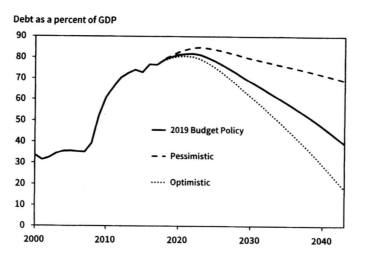

Debt as a percent of GDP

Meanwhile, assuming a combination of higher productivity growth and slower health care cost growth results in the debt ratio reaching 17.5 percent in 2043.

Despite considerable uncertainties, long-term projections are helpful in highlighting some of the budget challenges on the horizon, especially the impact of an aging population. In addition, the wide range of the projections highlight the need for policy awareness of key drivers of future budgetary costs and potential action to address them.

Actuarial Projections for Social Security and Medicare

While the Administration's long-run projections focus on the unified budget outlook, Social Security and Medicare Hospital Insurance benefits are paid out of trust funds financed by dedicated payroll tax revenues. Projected trust fund revenues fall short of the levels necessary to finance projected benefits over the next 75 years.

The Social Security and Medicare Trustees' reports feature the actuarial balance of the trust funds as a summary measure of their financial status. For each trust fund, the balance is calculated as the change in receipts or program benefits (expressed as a percentage of taxable payroll) that would be needed to preserve a small positive balance in the trust fund at the end of a specified time period. The estimates cover periods ranging in length from 25 to 75 years.

Under the Medicare Modernization Act (MMA) of 2003, the Medicare Trustees must issue a "warning" when two consecutive Trustees' reports project that the share of Medicare funded by general revenues will exceed 45 percent in the current year or any of the subsequent six years. The 2017 Trustees' Report made a determination of excess revenues, but did not issue a warning since no such determination was made in the 2016 Trustees' Report. The MMA requires that, if there is a Medicare funding warning, the President submit proposed legislation responding to that warning, within 15 days of submitting

the Budget. In accordance with the Recommendations Clause of the Constitution and as the Executive Branch has noted in prior years, the Executive Branch considers a requirement to propose specific legislation to be advisory.

Table 3-2 shows the projected income rate, cost rate, and annual balance for the Medicare HI and combined OASDI trust funds at selected dates under the Trustees' intermediate assumptions in the 2017 reports. There is a continued imbalance in the long-run projections of the HI program due to demographic trends and continued high per-person costs. The HI trust fund is projected to become insolvent in 2029.

As a result of reforms legislated in 1983, Social Security had been running a cash surplus with taxes exceeding costs up until 2009. This surplus in the Social Security trust fund helped to hold down the unified budget deficit. The cash surplus ended in 2009, when the trust fund began using a portion of its interest earnings to cover benefit payments. The 2017 Social Security Trustees' report projects that the trust fund will not return to cash surplus, but the program will continue to experience an overall surplus for a few more years because of the interest earnings. After that, however, Social Security will begin to draw on its trust fund balances to cover current expenditures. Over time, as the ratio of workers to retirees falls, costs are projected to rise further while revenues excluding interest are projected to rise slightly. In the process, the Social Security trust fund, which was built up since 1983, would be drawn down and eventually be exhausted in 2034. These projections assume that benefits would continue to be paid in full despite the projected exhaustion of the trust fund to show the long-run implications of current benefit formulas. Under current law, not all scheduled benefits could be paid after the trust funds are exhausted. However, benefits could still be partially funded from current revenues. According to the 2017 Trustees' report, beginning in 2034, 77 percent of projected Social Security scheduled benefits would be funded. This percentage would eventually decline to 73 percent by 2091.

Table 3-2. INTERMEDIATE ACTUARIAL PROJECTIONS FOR OASDI AND HI, 2017 TRUSTEES' REPORTS

	2015	2020	2030	2040	2080
	Percent of Payroll				
Medicare Hospital Insurance (HI):					
Income Rate	3.4	3.4	3.6	3.8	4.3
Cost Rate	3.4	3.4	4.2	4.7	5.0
Annual Balance	−0.1	*	−0.5	−0.9	−0.7
Projection Interval			25 years	50 years	75 years
Actuarial Balance			−0.5	−0.6	−0.6
	Percent of Payroll				
Old Age Survivors and Disability Insurance (OASDI):					
Income Rate	12.8	13.0	13.2	13.3	13.3
Cost Rate	13.9	13.9	16.3	17.0	17.5
Annual Balance	−1.1	−0.9	−3.1	−3.7	−4.2
Projection Interval			25 years	50 years	75 years
Actuarial Balance			−1.7	−2.4	−2.8

* 0.05 percent or less.

TECHNICAL NOTE: SOURCES OF DATA AND METHODS OF ESTIMATING

The long-run budget projections are based on actuarial projections for Social Security and Medicare as well as demographic and economic assumptions. A simplified model of the Federal budget, developed at OMB, is used to compute the budgetary implications of these assumptions.

Demographic and Economic Assumptions.—For the years 2018-2028, the assumptions are drawn from the Administration's economic projections used for the 2019 Budget. The economic assumptions are extended beyond this interval by holding the inflation rate, interest rates, and the unemployment rate constant at the levels assumed in the final year (2028) of the budget forecast. Population growth and labor force growth are extended using the intermediate assumptions from the 2017 Social Security Trustees' report. The projected rate of growth for real GDP is built up from the labor force assumptions and an assumed rate of productivity growth. Productivity growth, measured as real GDP per hour, is assumed to equal its average annual rate of growth in the Budget's economic assumptions—2.3 percent per year. For the baseline projections, GDP growth is adjusted to remove the growth-increasing effects of the Administration's fiscal policies.

Under Budget policies, the CPI inflation rate is held constant at 2.3 percent per year, the unemployment rate is held constant at 4.8 percent, the yield to maturity on 10-year Treasury notes is constant at 3.6 percent, and the 91-day Treasury bill rate is kept at 2.9 percent. Consistent with the demographic assumptions in the Trustees' reports, U.S. population growth slows from an average of 0.8 percent per year during the budget window to about three-quarters of that rate by 2035, and slower rates of growth beyond that point. By the end of the 25-year projection period total population growth is slightly above 0.5 percent per year. Real GDP growth is projected to be less than its historical average of around 3.3 percent per year because the slowdown in population growth and the increase in the population over age 65 reduce labor supply growth. In these projections, real GDP growth averages between 2.7 percent and 2.8 percent per year for the period following the end of the 10-year budget window.

The economic and demographic projections described above are set exogenously and do not change in response to changes in the budget outlook. This makes it easier to interpret the comparisons of alternative policies.

Budget Projections.—For the period through 2028, receipts and outlays in the baseline and policy projections follow the 2019 Budget's baseline and policy estimates respectively. Under Budget policies, total tax receipts are constant relative to GDP after 2028. Discretionary spending grows at the rate of growth in inflation and population outside the budget window. Long-run Social Security spending is projected by the Social Security actuaries using this chapter's long-run economic and demographic assumptions. Medicare benefits are projected based on a projection of beneficiary growth and excess health care cost growth from the 2017 Medicare Trustees' report current law baseline. For the policy projections, these assumptions are adjusted based on the Budget proposal to streamline Medicare. Medicaid outlays are based on the economic and demographic projections[2] in the model, which assume average excess cost growth of approximately 1.0 percentage point above growth in GDP per capita after 2028. For the policy projections, these assumptions are adjusted based on the Budget proposals to reform Medicaid funding. Other entitlement programs are projected based on rules of thumb linking program spending to elements of the economic and demographic projections such as the poverty rate.

---

[2] The Medicaid per capita projections assumed in this chapter contain a higher degree of uncertainty than they have in past years. This is due to ongoing system changes that have resulted in complete Medicaid claims and enrollment data being unavailable for the most recent several years.

4. FEDERAL BORROWING AND DEBT

Debt is the largest legally and contractually binding obligation of the Federal Government. At the end of 2017, the Government owed $14,665 billion of principal to the individuals and institutions who had loaned it the money to fund past deficits. During that year, the Government paid the public approximately $310 billion of interest on this debt. At the same time, the Government also held financial assets, net of financial liabilities other than debt, of $1,515 billion. Therefore, debt held by the public net of financial assets was $13,151 billion.

In addition, at the end of 2017 the Treasury had issued $5,540 billion of debt to Government accounts. As a result, gross Federal debt, which is the sum of debt held by the public and debt held by Government accounts, was $20,206 billion. Interest on the gross Federal debt was $457 billion in 2017. Gross Federal debt is discussed in more detail later in the chapter.

The $14,665 billion debt held by the public at the end of 2017 represents an increase of $498 billion over the level at the end of 2016. This increase is the result of the $665 billion deficit in 2017 and other financing transactions that reduced the need to borrow by $168 billion. Debt held by the public fell from 76.7 percent of Gross Domestic Product (GDP) at the end of 2016 to 76.5 percent of GDP at the end of 2017. The deficit is estimated to increase to $833 billion, or 4.2 percent of GDP, in 2018, and to $984 billion, or 4.7 percent of GDP, in 2019. After 2019, the deficit is projected to begin to decrease as a percent of GDP, falling to 1.4 percent of GDP by 2027. Debt held by the public is projected to grow to 78.8 percent of GDP at the end of 2018 and 80.3 percent of GDP at the end of 2019. Debt held by the public as a percent of GDP is projected to begin to decline in 2023, falling to 72.6 percent of GDP in 2028. Debt held by the public net of financial assets is expected to similarly grow to 69.8 percent of GDP at the end of 2018 and to 71.3 at the end of 2019, then to begin to decline in 2023, falling to 64.9 percent of GDP at the end of 2028.

Trends in Debt Since World War II

Table 4–1 depicts trends in Federal debt held by the public from World War II to the present and estimates from the present through 2028. (It is supplemented for earlier years by Tables 7.1–7.3 in the Budget's historical tables, available as supplemental budget material.[1]) Federal debt peaked at 106.1 percent of GDP in 1946, just after the end of the war. From that point until the 1970s, Federal debt as a percentage of GDP decreased almost every year because of relatively small deficits, an expanding economy, and unanticipated inflation. With households borrowing large amounts to buy homes and consumer durables, and with businesses borrowing large amounts to buy plant and equipment, Federal debt also decreased almost every year as a percentage of total credit market debt outstanding. The cumulative effect was impressive. From 1950 to 1975, debt held by the public declined from 78.5 percent of GDP to 24.5 percent, and from 53.3 percent of credit market debt to 17.9 percent. Despite rising interest rates, interest outlays became a smaller share of the budget and were roughly stable as a percentage of GDP.

Federal debt relative to GDP is a function of the Nation's fiscal policy as well as overall economic conditions. During the 1970s, large budget deficits emerged as spending grew faster than receipts and as the economy was disrupted by oil shocks and rising inflation. The nominal amount of Federal debt more than doubled, and Federal debt relative to GDP and credit market debt stopped declining for several years in the middle of the decade. Federal debt started growing again at the beginning of the 1980s, and increased to almost 48 percent of GDP by 1993. The ratio of Federal debt to credit market debt also rose during this period, though to a lesser extent. Interest outlays on debt held by the public, calculated as a percentage of either total Federal outlays or GDP, increased as well.

The growth of Federal debt held by the public was slowing by the mid-1990s. In addition to a growing economy, three major budget agreements were enacted in the 1990s, implementing spending cuts and revenue increases and significantly reducing deficits. The debt declined markedly relative to both GDP and total credit market debt, with the decline accelerating as budget surpluses emerged from 1997 to 2001. Debt fell from 47.8 percent of GDP in 1993 to 31.4 percent of GDP in 2001. Over that same period, debt fell from 26.3 percent of total credit market debt to 17.4 percent. Interest as a share of outlays peaked at 16.5 percent in 1989 and then fell to 8.9 percent by 2002; interest as a percentage of GDP fell by a similar proportion.

The progress in reducing the debt burden stopped and then reversed course beginning in 2002. A decline in the stock market, a recession, the attacks of September 11, 2001, and two major wars, and other policy changes all contributed to increasing deficits, causing debt to rise, both in nominal terms and as a percentage of GDP. Following the most recent recession, which began in December 2007, the deficit began increasing rapidly in 2008 and 2009, as the Government acted to rescue several major corporations and financial institutions as well as enact a major stimulus bill. Since 2008, debt as a percent of GDP has grown rapidly, increasing from 35.2 percent at the end of 2007 to 76.7 percent at the end of 2016. In 2017, debt as a percent of GDP fell to 76.5 percent.

---

[1] The historical tables are available at *https://www.whitehouse.gov/omb/historical-tables/* and on the Budget CD-ROM.

Under the proposals in the Budget, the deficit is projected to grow to $833 billion in 2018. The deficit is projected to stabilize in nominal terms in 2020 and then begin to decrease in subsequent years, falling to $445 billion, or 1.4 percent of GDP, in 2028. Gross Federal debt is projected to grow to 107.2 percent of GDP in 2018 and then begin to fall after 2020, to 91.8 percent of GDP in 2028. Debt held by the public as a percent of GDP is es-timated to be 78.8 percent at the end of 2018, to continue to grow gradually through 2022, and then to begin to de-cline, falling to 72.6 percent of GDP by 2028. Debt held by the public net of financial assets as a percent of GDP is estimated to similarly grow to 69.8 percent of GDP at the end of 2018, grow gradually through 2022, and then begin to fall, reaching 64.9 percent of GDP by the end of 2028.

Table 4–1. TRENDS IN FEDERAL DEBT HELD BY THE PUBLIC AND INTEREST ON THE DEBT HELD BY THE PUBLIC

(Dollar amounts in billions)

Fiscal Year	Debt held by the public		Debt held by the public as a percent of		Interest on the debt held by the public [3]		Interest on the debt held by the public as a percent of [3]	
	Current dollars	FY 2017 dollars [1]	GDP	Credit market debt [2]	Current dollars	FY 2017 dollars [1]	Total outlays	GDP
1946	241.9	2,492.6	106.1	N/A	4.2	43.1	7.6	1.8
1950	219.0	1,826.1	78.5	53.3	4.8	40.4	11.4	1.7
1955	226.6	1,660.5	55.7	42.1	5.2	38.0	7.6	1.3
1960	236.8	1,537.6	44.3	33.1	7.8	50.8	8.5	1.5
1965	260.8	1,585.7	36.7	26.4	9.6	58.2	8.1	1.3
1970	283.2	1,434.8	27.0	20.3	15.4	77.9	7.9	1.5
1975	394.7	1,473.8	24.5	17.9	25.0	93.4	7.5	1.6
1980	711.9	1,850.0	25.5	18.5	62.8	163.1	10.6	2.2
1985	1,507.3	2,989.5	35.3	22.2	152.9	303.3	16.2	3.6
1990	2,411.6	4,112.4	40.8	22.5	202.4	345.1	16.2	3.4
1995	3,604.4	5,424.2	47.5	26.8	239.2	360.0	15.8	3.2
2000	3,409.8	4,730.3	33.6	18.8	232.8	323.0	13.0	2.3
2005	4,592.2	5,683.6	35.6	17.1	191.4	236.8	7.7	1.5
2010	9,018.9	10,103.9	60.9	25.2	228.2	255.6	6.6	1.5
2011	10,128.2	11,120.9	65.9	27.5	266.0	292.0	7.4	1.7
2012	11,281.1	12,163.7	70.4	29.4	232.1	250.2	6.6	1.4
2013	11,982.7	12,705.5	72.6	30.1	259.0	274.6	7.5	1.6
2014	12,779.9	13,309.0	74.1	30.8	271.4	282.7	7.7	1.6
2015	13,116.7	13,497.0	72.9	30.6	260.6	268.2	7.1	1.4
2016	14,167.6	14,411.2	76.7	31.4	283.8	288.7	7.4	1.5
2017	14,665.5	14,665.5	76.5	31.3	309.9	309.9	7.8	1.6
2018 estimate	15,789.7	15,546.5	78.8	N/A	360.4	354.9	8.6	1.8
2019 estimate	16,871.7	16,338.7	80.3	N/A	415.2	402.1	9.4	2.0
2020 estimate	17,946.8	17,063.7	81.3	N/A	498.6	474.0	10.8	2.3
2021 estimate	18,950.5	17,669.3	81.7	N/A	566.8	528.5	11.9	2.4
2022 estimate	19,946.3	18,232.1	81.9	N/A	627.5	573.6	12.6	2.6
2023 estimate	20,808.6	18,644.9	81.3	N/A	681.5	610.6	13.2	2.7
2024 estimate	21,495.3	18,882.7	79.9	N/A	724.4	636.4	13.7	2.7
2025 estimate	22,137.0	19,063.5	78.4	N/A	757.2	652.1	13.7	2.7
2026 estimate	22,703.3	19,165.6	76.6	N/A	784.9	662.6	13.7	2.6
2027 estimate	23,194.0	19,194.0	74.6	N/A	813.1	672.9	13.7	2.6
2028 estimate	23,683.6	19,213.3	72.6	N/A	835.8	678.1	13.3	2.6

N/A = Not available.

[1] Amounts in current dollars deflated by the GDP chain-type price index with fiscal year 2017 equal to 100.

[2] Total credit market debt owed by domestic nonfinancial sectors. Financial sectors are omitted to avoid double counting, since financial intermediaries borrow in the credit market primarily in order to finance lending in the credit market. Source: Federal Reserve Board flow of funds accounts. Projections are not available.

[3] Interest on debt held by the public is estimated as the interest on Treasury debt securities less the "interest received by trust funds" (subfunction 901 less subfunctions 902 and 903). The estimate of interest on debt held by the public does not include the comparatively small amount of interest paid on agency debt or the offsets for interest on Treasury debt received by other Government accounts (revolving funds and special funds).

Debt Held by the Public and Gross Federal Debt

The Federal Government issues debt securities for two main purposes. First, it borrows from the public to provide for the Federal Government's financing needs, including both the deficit and the other transactions requiring financing, most notably disbursements for direct student loans and other Federal credit programs.[2] Second, it issues debt to Federal Government accounts, primarily trust funds, that accumulate surpluses. By law, trust fund surpluses must generally be invested in Federal securities. The gross Federal debt is defined to consist of both the debt held by the public and the debt held by Government accounts. Nearly all the Federal debt has been issued by the Treasury and is sometimes called "public debt," but a small portion has been issued by other Government agencies and is called "agency debt."[3]

Borrowing from the public, whether by the Treasury or by some other Federal agency, is important because it represents the Federal demand on credit markets. Regardless of whether the proceeds are used for tangible or intangible investments or to finance current consumption, the Federal demand on credit markets has to be financed out of the saving of households and businesses, the State and local sector, or the rest of the world. Federal borrowing thereby competes with the borrowing of other sectors of the domestic or international economy for financial resources in the credit market. Borrowing from the public thus affects the size and composition of assets held by the private sector and the amount of saving imported from abroad. It also increases the amount of future resources required to pay interest to the public on Federal debt. Borrowing from the public is therefore an important concern of Federal fiscal policy. Borrowing from the public, however, is an incomplete measure of the Federal impact on credit markets. Different types of Federal activities can affect the credit markets in different ways. For example, under its direct loan programs, the Government uses borrowed funds to acquire financial assets that might otherwise require financing in the credit markets directly. (For more information on other ways in which Federal activities impact the credit market, see the discussion at the end of this chapter.) By incorporating the change in direct loan and other financial assets, debt held by the public net of financial assets adds useful insight into the Government's financial condition.

Issuing debt securities to Government accounts performs an essential function in accounting for the operation of these funds. The balances of debt represent the cumulative surpluses of these funds due to the excess of their tax receipts, interest receipts, and other collections over their spending. The interest on the debt that is credited to these funds accounts for the fact that some earmarked taxes and user fees will be spent at a later time than when the funds receive the monies. The debt securities are assets of those funds but are a liability of the general fund to the funds that hold the securities, and are a mechanism for crediting interest to those funds on their recorded balances. These balances generally provide the fund with authority to draw upon the U.S. Treasury in later years to make future payments on its behalf to the public. Public policy may result in the Government's running surpluses and accumulating debt in trust funds and other Government accounts in anticipation of future spending.

However, issuing debt to Government accounts does not have any of the credit market effects of borrowing from the public. It is an internal transaction of the Government, made between two accounts that are both within the Government itself. Issuing debt to a Government account is not a current transaction of the Government with the public; it is not financed by private saving and does not compete with the private sector for available funds in the credit market. While such issuance provides the account with assets—a binding claim against the Treasury—those assets are fully offset by the increased liability of the Treasury to pay the claims, which will ultimately be covered by the collection of revenues or by borrowing. Similarly, the current interest earned by the Government account on its Treasury securities does not need to be financed by other resources.

Furthermore, the debt held by Government accounts does not represent the estimated amount of the account's obligations or responsibilities to make future payments to the public. For example, if the account records the transactions of a social insurance program, the debt that it holds does not necessarily represent the actuarial present value of estimated future benefits (or future benefits less taxes) for the current participants in the program; nor does it necessarily represent the actuarial present value of estimated future benefits (or future benefits less taxes) for the current participants plus the estimated future participants over some stated time period. The future transactions of Federal social insurance and employee retirement programs, which own 90 percent of the debt held by Government accounts, are important in their own right and need to be analyzed separately. This can be done through information published in the actuarial and financial reports for these programs.[4]

This Budget uses a variety of information sources to analyze the condition of Social Security and Medicare, the Government's two largest social insurance programs. The excess of future Social Security and Medicare benefits rel-

---

[2] For the purposes of the Budget, "debt held by the public" is defined as debt held by investors outside of the Federal Government, both domestic and foreign, including U.S. State and local governments and foreign governments. It also includes debt held by the Federal Reserve.

[3] The term "agency debt" is defined more narrowly in the budget than customarily in the securities market, where it includes not only the debt of the Federal agencies listed in Table 4–4, but also certain Government-guaranteed securities and the debt of the Government-sponsored enterprises listed in Table 19–7 in the supplemental materials to the "Credit and Insurance" chapter. (Table 19–7 is available on the Internet at: *https://www.whitehouse.gov/omb/analytical-perspectives* and on the Budget CD-ROM.)

[4] Extensive actuarial analyses of the Social Security and Medicare programs are published in the annual reports of the boards of trustees of these funds. The actuarial estimates for Social Security, Medicare, and the major Federal employee retirement programs are summarized in the *Financial Report of the United States Government*, prepared annually by the Department of the Treasury in coordination with the Office of Management and Budget, and presented in more detail in the financial statements of the agencies administering those programs.

Table 4–2.   FEDERAL GOVERNMENT FINANCING AND DEBT
(In billions of dollars)

	Actual 2017	Estimate										
		2018	2019	2020	2021	2022	2023	2024	2025	2026	2027	2028
Financing:												
Unified budget deficit	665.4	832.6	984.4	986.9	915.9	907.8	778.5	612.1	579.2	517.4	449.7	445.0
Other transactions affecting borrowing from the public:												
Changes in financial assets and liabilities: [1]												
Change in Treasury operating cash balance	−194.0	190.7	....	....	....	....	....	....	....	....	....	....
Net disbursements of credit financing accounts:												
Direct loan accounts	54.7	101.0	93.9	86.9	87.0	89.6	87.0	79.6	69.0	59.0	49.9	45.7
Guaranteed loan accounts	−13.7	0.9	5.1	2.7	2.1	−0.1	−2.0	−3.8	−5.4	−9.1	−8.1	−0.5
Troubled Asset Relief Program equity purchase accounts	−0.3	−0.1	−*	−*	−*	−*	−*	....	....	....	....	....
Subtotal, net disbursements	40.7	101.8	99.0	89.6	89.2	89.5	85.0	75.8	63.6	49.9	41.8	45.2
Net purchases of non-Federal securities by the National Railroad Retirement Investment Trust	1.2	−0.5	−1.0	−1.1	−1.0	−1.1	−0.7	−0.8	−0.7	−0.6	−0.3	−0.1
Net change in other financial assets and liabilities [2]	−15.2	....	....	....	....	....	....	....	....	....	....	....
Subtotal, changes in financial assets and liabilities ...	−167.3	292.0	97.9	88.5	88.2	88.4	84.3	75.0	62.9	49.3	41.5	45.1
Seigniorage on coins	−0.2	−0.4	−0.4	−0.4	−0.4	−0.4	−0.4	−0.4	−0.4	−0.4	−0.4	−0.4
Total, other transactions affecting borrowing from the public	−167.5	291.6	97.6	88.1	87.8	88.0	83.9	74.6	62.5	48.9	41.0	44.6
Total, requirement to borrow from the public (equals change in debt held by the public)	497.8	1,124.3	1,082.0	1,075.1	1,003.7	995.8	862.4	686.7	641.7	566.3	490.7	489.6
Changes in Debt Subject to Statutory Limitation:												
Change in debt held by the public	497.8	1,124.3	1,082.0	1,075.1	1,003.7	995.8	862.4	686.7	641.7	566.3	490.7	489.6
Change in debt held by Government accounts	168.4	148.3	142.6	123.0	115.6	65.0	88.8	119.4	56.0	52.6	−54.8	−138.4
Less: change in debt not subject to limit and other adjustments	3.9	1.5	2.2	2.8	2.0	2.0	2.1	2.2	1.4	1.5	1.9	1.8
Total, change in debt subject to statutory limitation	670.2	1,274.0	1,226.8	1,200.9	1,121.3	1,062.8	953.2	808.3	699.1	620.3	437.9	353.0
Debt Subject to Statutory Limitation, End of Year:												
Debt issued by Treasury	20,179.5	21,452.4	22,677.7	23,877.0	24,997.1	26,058.6	27,010.6	27,818.0	28,517.1	29,137.1	29,574.2	29,926.4
Less: Treasury debt not subject to limitation (−) [3]	−11.9	−10.8	−9.3	−7.7	−6.5	−5.3	−4.1	−3.2	−3.2	−2.8	−2.0	−1.1
Agency debt subject to limitation	*	*	*	*	*	*	*	*	*	*	*	*
Adjustment for discount and premium [4]	41.1	41.1	41.1	41.1	41.1	41.1	41.1	41.1	41.1	41.1	41.1	41.1
Total, debt subject to statutory limitation [5]	20,208.6	21,482.6	22,709.4	23,910.3	25,031.6	26,094.4	27,047.6	27,855.9	28,555.0	29,175.3	29,613.2	29,966.3
Debt Outstanding, End of Year:												
Gross Federal debt: [6]												
Debt issued by Treasury	20,179.5	21,452.4	22,677.7	23,877.0	24,997.1	26,058.6	27,010.6	27,818.0	28,517.1	29,137.1	29,574.2	29,926.4
Debt issued by other agencies	26.2	25.8	25.1	23.9	23.1	22.3	21.5	20.2	18.8	17.7	16.6	15.6
Total, gross Federal debt	20,205.7	21,478.2	22,702.8	23,900.9	25,020.2	26,081.0	27,032.1	27,838.2	28,535.9	29,154.8	29,590.7	29,942.0
As a percent of GDP	105.4%	107.2%	108.1%	108.3%	107.9%	107.0%	105.6%	103.5%	101.0%	98.3%	95.2%	91.8%
Held by:												
Debt held by Government accounts	5,540.3	5,688.5	5,831.1	5,954.2	6,069.7	6,134.7	6,223.5	6,342.9	6,398.9	6,451.5	6,396.8	6,258.4
Debt held by the public [7]	14,665.5	15,789.7	16,871.7	17,946.8	18,950.5	19,946.3	20,808.6	21,495.3	22,137.0	22,703.3	23,194.0	23,683.6
As a percent of GDP	76.5%	78.8%	80.3%	81.3%	81.7%	81.9%	81.3%	79.9%	78.4%	76.6%	74.6%	72.6%

*$50 million or less.

[1] A decrease in the Treasury operating cash balance (which is an asset) is a means of financing a deficit and therefore has a negative sign. An increase in checks outstanding (which is a liability) is also a means of financing a deficit and therefore also has a negative sign.

[2] Includes checks outstanding, accrued interest payable on Treasury debt, uninvested deposit fund balances, allocations of special drawing rights, and other liability accounts; and, as an offset, cash and monetary assets (other than the Treasury operating cash balance), other asset accounts, and profit on sale of gold.

[3] Consists primarily of debt issued by the Federal Financing Bank.

[4] Consists mainly of unamortized discount (less premium) on public issues of Treasury notes and bonds (other than zero-coupon bonds) and unrealized discount on Government account series securities.

[5] The statutory debt limit is approximately $20,456 billion, as increased after December 8, 2017.

[6] Treasury securities held by the public and zero-coupon bonds held by Government accounts are almost all measured at sales price plus amortized discount or less amortized premium. Agency debt securities are almost all measured at face value. Treasury securities in the Government account series are otherwise measured at face value less unrealized discount (if any).

[7] At the end of 2017, the Federal Reserve Banks held $2,465.4 billion of Federal securities and the rest of the public held $12,200.0 billion. Debt held by the Federal Reserve Banks is not estimated for future years.

ative to their dedicated income is very different in concept and much larger in size than the amount of Treasury securities that these programs hold.

For all these reasons, debt held by the public and debt held by the public net of financial assets are both better gauges of the effect of the budget on the credit markets than gross Federal debt.

Government Deficits or Surpluses and the Change in Debt

Table 4–2 summarizes Federal borrowing and debt from 2017 through 2028.[5] In 2017 the Government borrowed $498 billion, increasing the debt held by the public from $14,168 billion at the end of 2016 to $14,665 billion at the end of 2017. The debt held by Government accounts grew by $168 billion, and gross Federal debt increased by $666 billion to $20,206 billion.

Debt held by the public.—The Federal Government primarily finances deficits by borrowing from the public, and it primarily uses surpluses to repay debt held by the public.[6] Table 4–2 shows the relationship between the Federal deficit or surplus and the change in debt held by the public. The borrowing or debt repayment depends on the Government's expenditure programs and tax laws, on the economic conditions that influence tax receipts and outlays, and on debt management policy. The sensitivity of the budget to economic conditions is analyzed in Chapter 2, "Economic Assumptions and Interactions with the Budget," in this volume.

The total or unified budget consists of two parts: the on-budget portion; and the off-budget Federal entities, which have been excluded from the budget by law. Under present law, the off-budget Federal entities are the two Social Security trust funds (Old-Age and Survivors Insurance and Disability Insurance) and the Postal Service Fund.[7] The on-budget and off-budget surpluses or deficits are added together to determine the Government's financing needs.

Over the long run, it is a good approximation to say that "the deficit is financed by borrowing from the public" or "the surplus is used to repay debt held by the public." However, the Government's need to borrow in any given year has always depended on several other factors besides the unified budget surplus or deficit, such as the change in the Treasury operating cash balance. These other factors—"other transactions affecting borrowing from the public"—can either increase or decrease the Government's need to borrow and can vary considerably

in size from year to year. The other transactions affecting borrowing from the public are presented in Table 4–2 (where an increase in the need to borrow is represented by a positive sign, like the deficit).

In 2017 the deficit was $665 billion while these other factors reduced the need to borrow by $168 billion, or 34 percent of total borrowing from the public. As a result, the Government borrowed $498 billion from the public. The other factors are estimated to increase borrowing by $292 billion (26 percent of total borrowing from the public) in 2018, and $98 billion (9 percent) in 2019. In 2020–2028, these other factors are expected to increase borrowing by annual amounts ranging from $41 billion to $88 billion.

Three specific factors presented in Table 4–2 have historically been especially important.

Change in Treasury operating cash balance.—The cash balance increased by $155 billion in 2016, to $353 billion, and decreased by $194 billion in 2017, to $159 billion. The large 2017 decrease in the cash balance is primarily due to Treasury drawing down the cash balance as it took measures to continue to finance Federal Government operations while at the debt ceiling. For risk management purposes, Treasury seeks to maintain a cash balance roughly equal to one week of Government outflows, with a minimum balance of about $150 billion. The operating cash balance is projected to increase by $191 billion, to $350 billion at the end of 2018. Changes in the operating cash balance, while occasionally large, are inherently limited over time. Decreases in cash—a means of financing the Government—are limited by the amount of past accumulations, which themselves required financing when they were built up. Increases are limited because it is generally more efficient to repay debt.

Net financing disbursements of the direct loan and guaranteed loan financing accounts.—Under the Federal Credit Reform Act of 1990 (FCRA), the budgetary program account for each credit program records the estimated subsidy costs—the present value of estimated net losses—at the time when the direct or guaranteed loans are disbursed. The individual cash flows to and from the public associated with the loans or guarantees, such as the disbursement and repayment of loans, the default payments on loan guarantees, the collection of interest and fees, and so forth, are recorded in the credit program's non-budgetary financing account. Although the non-budgetary financing account's cash flows to and from the public are not included in the deficit (except for their impact on subsidy costs), they affect Treasury's net borrowing requirements.[8]

In addition to the transactions with the public, the financing accounts include several types of intragovernmental transactions. They receive payment from the credit program accounts for the subsidy costs of new direct loans and loan guarantees and for any upward reestimate of the costs of outstanding direct and guaranteed loans. They also receive interest from Treasury on balances of uninvested funds. The financing accounts pay

---

[5] For projections of the debt beyond 2028, see Chapter 3, "Long-Term Budget Outlook."

[6] Treasury debt held by the public is measured as the sales price plus the amortized discount (or less the amortized premium). At the time of sale, the book value equals the sales price. Subsequently, it equals the sales price plus the amount of the discount that has been amortized up to that time. In equivalent terms, the book value of the debt equals the principal amount due at maturity (par or face value) less the unamortized discount. (For a security sold at a premium, the definition is symmetrical.) For inflation-indexed notes and bonds, the book value includes a periodic adjustment for inflation. Agency debt is generally recorded at par.

[7] For further explanation of the off-budget Federal entities, see Chapter 9, "Coverage of the Budget."

[8] The FCRA (sec. 505(b)) requires that the financing accounts be non-budgetary. They are non-budgetary in concept because they do not measure cost. For additional discussion of credit programs, see Chapter 19, "Credit and Insurance," and Chapter 8, "Budget Concepts."

any negative subsidy collections or downward reestimate of costs to budgetary receipt accounts and pay interest on borrowings from Treasury. The total net collections and gross disbursements of the financing accounts, consisting of transactions with both the public and the budgetary accounts, are called "net financing disbursements." They occur in the same way as the "outlays" of a budgetary account, even though they do not represent budgetary costs, and therefore affect the requirement for borrowing from the public in the same way as the deficit.

The intragovernmental transactions of the credit program, financing, and downward reestimate receipt accounts do not affect Federal borrowing from the public. Although the deficit changes because of the budgetary account's outlay to, or receipt from, a financing account, the net financing disbursement changes in an equal amount with the opposite sign, so the effects are cancelled out. On the other hand, financing account disbursements to the public increase the requirement for borrowing from the public in the same way as an increase in budget outlays that are disbursed to the public in cash. Likewise, receipts from the public collected by the financing account can be used to finance the payment of the Government's obligations, and therefore they reduce the requirement for Federal borrowing from the public in the same way as an increase in budgetary receipts.

Borrowing due to credit financing accounts was $41 billion in 2017. In 2018 credit financing accounts are projected to increase borrowing by $102 billion. After 2018, the credit financing accounts are expected to increase borrowing by amounts ranging from $42 billion to $99 billion over the next 10 years.

In some years, large net upward or downward reestimates in the cost of outstanding direct and guaranteed loans may cause large swings in the net financing disbursements. In 2017, net upward reestimates received by the financing accounts reduced financing disbursements by $49.3 billion, due largely to upward reestimates for student loan programs and Federal Housing Administration (FHA) Mutual Mortgage Insurance guarantees. In 2018, upward reestimates for FHA guarantees are more than offset by downward reestimates for student loans, resulting in a net downward reestimate of $0.9 billion.

Net purchases of non-Federal securities by the National Railroad Retirement Investment Trust (NRRIT).— This trust fund, which was established by the Railroad Retirement and Survivors' Improvement Act of 2001, invests its assets primarily in private stocks and bonds. The Act required special treatment of the purchase or sale of non-Federal assets by the NRRIT trust fund, treating such purchases as a means of financing rather than as outlays. Therefore, the increased need to borrow from the public to finance NRRIT's purchases of non-Federal assets is part of the "other transactions affecting borrowing from the public" rather than included as an increase in the deficit. While net purchases and redemptions affect borrowing from the public, unrealized gains and losses on NRRIT's portfolio are included in both the "other transactions" and, with the opposite sign, in NRRIT's net outlays

in the deficit, for no net impact on borrowing from the public. In 2017, net increases, including purchases and gains, were $1.2 billion. A $0.5 billion net decrease is projected for 2018 and net annual decreases ranging from $0.1 billion to $1.1 billion are projected for 2019 and subsequent years.[9]

*Debt held by Government accounts.—*The amount of Federal debt issued to Government accounts depends largely on the surpluses of the trust funds, both on-budget and off-budget, which owned 90 percent of the total Federal debt held by Government accounts at the end of 2017. Net investment may differ from the surplus due to changes in the amount of cash assets not currently invested. In 2017, the total trust fund surplus was $154 billion, while trust fund investment in Federal securities increased by $146 billion. The remainder of debt issued to Government accounts is owned by a number of special funds and revolving funds. The debt held in major accounts and the annual investments are shown in Table 4–5.

Debt Held by the Public Net of Financial Assets and Liabilities

While debt held by the public is a key measure for examining the role and impact of the Federal Government in the U.S. and international credit markets and for other purposes, it provides incomplete information on the Government's financial condition. The U.S. Government holds significant financial assets, which can be offset against debt held by the public and other financial liabilities to achieve a more complete understanding of the Government's financial condition. The acquisition of those financial assets represents a transaction with the credit markets, broadening those markets in a way that is analogous to the demand on credit markets that borrowing entails. For this reason, debt held by the public is also an incomplete measure of the impact of the Federal Government in the United States and international credit markets.

One transaction that can increase both borrowing and assets is an increase to the Treasury operating cash balance. When the Government borrows to increase the Treasury operating cash balance, that cash balance also represents an asset that is available to the Federal Government. Looking at both sides of this transaction—the borrowing to obtain the cash and the asset of the cash holdings—provides much more complete information about the Government's financial condition than looking at only the borrowing from the public. Another example of a transaction that simultaneously increases borrowing from the public and Federal assets is Government borrowing to issue direct loans to the public. When the direct loan is made, the Government is also acquiring an asset in the form of future payments of principal and interest, net of the Government's expected losses on the loan. Similarly, when NRRIT increases its holdings of non-Federal securities, the borrowing to purchase those securities is offset by the value of the asset holdings.

[9] The budget treatment of this fund is further discussed in Chapter 8, "Budget Concepts."

The acquisition or disposition of Federal financial assets very largely explains the difference between the deficit for a particular year and that year's increase in debt held by the public. Debt held by the public net of financial assets is a measure that is conceptually closer to the measurement of Federal deficits or surpluses; cumulative deficits and surpluses over time more closely equal the debt held by the public net of financial assets than they do the debt held by the public.

Table 4–3 presents debt held by the public net of the Government's financial assets and liabilities. Treasury debt is presented in the Budget at book value, with no adjustments for the change in economic value that results from fluctuations in interest rates. The balances of credit financing accounts are based on projections of future cash flows. For direct loan financing accounts, the balance generally represents the net present value of anticipated future inflows such as principal and interest payments from borrowers. For guaranteed loan financing accounts, the balance generally represents the net present value of anticipated future outflows, such as default claim payments net of recoveries, and other collections, such as program fees. NRRIT's holdings of non-Federal securities are marked to market on a monthly basis. Government-sponsored enterprise (GSE) preferred stock is measured at market value.

Due largely to the $194 billion decrease in the Treasury operating cash balance, net financial assets fell by $183 billion, to $1,515 billion, in 2017. This $1,515 billion in net financial assets included a cash balance of $159 billion, net credit financing account balances of $1,295 billion, and other assets and liabilities that aggregated to a net asset of $60 billion. At the end of 2017, debt held by the public was $14,665 billion, or 76.5 percent of GDP.

Therefore, debt held by the public net of financial assets was $13,151 billion, or 68.6 percent of GDP. As shown in Table 4–3, the value of the Government's net financial assets is projected to increase to $1,809 billion in 2018, principally due to projected increases in the Treasury cash balance and the value of the direct loan financing accounts. While debt held by the public is expected to increase from 76.5 percent to 78.8 percent of GDP during 2018, debt held by the public net of financial assets is expected to increase by a smaller amount, from 68.6 percent to 69.8 percent of GDP.

Debt securities and other financial assets and liabilities do not encompass all the assets and liabilities of the Federal Government. For example, accounts payable occur in the normal course of buying goods and services; Social Security benefits are due and payable as of the end of the month but, according to statute, are paid during the next month; and Federal employee salaries are paid after they have been earned. Like debt securities sold in the credit market, these liabilities have their own distinctive effects on the economy. The Federal Government also has significant holdings of non-financial assets, such as land, mineral deposits, buildings, and equipment. The different types of assets and liabilities are reported annually in the financial statements of Federal agencies and in the *Financial Report of the United States Government*, prepared by the Treasury Department in coordination with the Office of Management and Budget (OMB).

Treasury Debt

Nearly all Federal debt is issued by the Department of the Treasury. Treasury meets most of the Federal Government's financing needs by issuing marketable securities to the public. These financing needs include both

Table 4–3. DEBT HELD BY THE PUBLIC NET OF FINANCIAL ASSETS AND LIABILITIES

(Dollar amounts in billions)

	Actual 2017	Estimate										
		2018	2019	2020	2021	2022	2023	2024	2025	2026	2027	2028
Debt Held by the Public:												
Debt held by the public	14,665.5	15,789.7	16,871.7	17,946.8	18,950.5	19,946.3	20,808.6	21,495.3	22,137.0	22,703.3	23,194.0	23,683.6
As a percent of GDP	76.5%	78.8%	80.3%	81.3%	81.7%	81.9%	81.3%	79.9%	78.4%	76.6%	74.6%	72.6%
Financial Assets Net of Liabilities:												
Treasury operating cash balance	159.3	350.0	350.0	350.0	350.0	350.0	350.0	350.0	350.0	350.0	350.0	350.0
Credit financing account balances:												
Direct loan accounts	1,281.3	1,382.3	1,476.2	1,563.1	1,650.1	1,739.7	1,826.7	1,906.3	1,975.2	2,034.3	2,084.2	2,129.9
Guaranteed loan accounts	13.9	14.8	19.9	22.6	24.7	24.7	22.7	18.9	13.5	4.4	–3.7	–4.2
Troubled Asset Relief Program equity purchase accounts	0.1	*	*	*	*	*	–*	–*	–*	–*	–*	–*
Subtotal, credit financing account balances	1,295.3	1,397.1	1,496.1	1,585.7	1,674.8	1,764.4	1,849.4	1,925.1	1,988.7	2,038.7	2,080.4	2,125.7
Government-sponsored enterprise preferred stock	92.6	94.6	94.6	94.6	94.6	94.6	94.6	94.6	94.6	94.6	94.6	94.6
Non-Federal securities held by NRRIT	25.3	24.8	23.7	22.7	21.7	20.6	19.9	19.1	18.4	17.8	17.5	17.4
Other assets net of liabilities	–58.0	–58.0	–58.0	–58.0	–58.0	–58.0	–58.0	–58.0	–58.0	–58.0	–58.0	–58.0
Total, financial assets net of liabilities	1,514.6	1,808.6	1,906.5	1,995.0	2,083.2	2,171.6	2,255.9	2,330.9	2,393.8	2,443.1	2,484.6	2,529.7
Debt Held by the Public Net of Financial Assets and Liabilities:												
Debt held by the public net of financial assets	13,150.9	13,981.2	14,965.2	15,951.8	16,867.3	17,774.7	18,552.8	19,164.4	19,743.2	20,260.1	20,709.4	21,153.9
As a percent of GDP	68.6%	69.8%	71.3%	72.3%	72.7%	72.9%	72.5%	71.2%	69.9%	68.3%	66.6%	64.9%

*$50 million or less.

the change in debt held by the public and the refinancing—or rollover—of any outstanding debt that matures during the year. Treasury marketable debt is sold at public auctions on a regular schedule and, because it is very liquid, can be bought and sold on the secondary market at narrow bid-offer spreads. Treasury also sells to the public a relatively small amount of nonmarketable securities, such as savings bonds and State and Local Government Series securities (SLGS).[10] Treasury nonmarketable debt cannot be bought or sold on the secondary market.

Treasury issues marketable securities in a wide range of maturities, and issues both nominal (non-inflation-indexed) and inflation-indexed securities. Treasury's marketable securities include:

Treasury Bills—Treasury bills have maturities of one year or less from their issue date. In addition to the regular auction calendar of bill issuance, Treasury issues cash management bills on an as-needed basis for various reasons such as to offset the seasonal patterns of the Government's receipts and outlays.

Treasury Notes—Treasury notes have maturities of more than one year and up to 10 years.

Treasury Bonds—Treasury bonds have maturities of more than 10 years. The longest-maturity securities issued by Treasury are 30-year bonds.

Treasury Inflation-Protected Securities (TIPS)—Treasury inflation-protected—or inflation-indexed—securities are coupon issues for which the par value of the security rises with inflation. The principal value is adjusted daily to reflect inflation as measured by changes in the Consumer Price Index (CPI-U-NSA, with a two-month lag). Although the principal value may be adjusted downward if inflation is negative, at maturity, the securities will be redeemed at the greater of their inflation-adjusted principal or par amount at original issue.

Floating Rate Securities—Floating rate securities have a fixed par value but bear interest rates that fluctuate based on movements in a specified benchmark market interest rate. Treasury's floating rate notes are benchmarked to the Treasury 13-week bill. Currently, Treasury is issuing floating rate securities with a maturity of two years.

Historically, the average maturity of outstanding debt issued by Treasury has been about five years. The average maturity of outstanding debt was 71 months at the end of 2017. Over the last several years there have been many changes in financial markets that have ultimately resulted in significant structural demand for high-quality, shorter-dated securities such as Treasury bills. At the same time, Treasury bills as a percent of outstanding issuance had fallen to historically low levels of around 10 percent. In recognition of these structural changes, in November 2015, the Treasury announced that it would increase issuance of shorter-dated Treasury securities.

In addition to quarterly announcements about the overall auction calendar, Treasury publicly announces in advance the auction of each security. Individuals can participate directly in Treasury auctions or can purchase securities through brokers, dealers, and other financial institutions. Treasury accepts two types of auction bids: competitive and noncompetitive. In a competitive bid, the bidder specifies the yield. A significant portion of competitive bids are submitted by primary dealers, which are banks and securities brokerages that have been designated to trade in Treasury securities with the Federal Reserve System. In a noncompetitive bid, the bidder agrees to accept the yield determined by the auction.[11] At the close of the auction, Treasury accepts all eligible noncompetitive bids and then accepts competitive bids in ascending order beginning with the lowest yield bid until the offering amount is reached. All winning bidders receive the highest accepted yield bid.

Treasury marketable securities are highly liquid and actively traded on the secondary market, which enhances the demand for Treasuries at initial auction. The demand for Treasury securities is reflected in the ratio of bids received to bids accepted in Treasury auctions; the demand for the securities is substantially greater than the level of issuance. Because they are backed by the full faith and credit of the United States Government, Treasury marketable securities are considered to be credit "risk-free." Therefore, the Treasury yield curve is commonly used as a benchmark for a wide variety of purposes in the financial markets.

Whereas Treasury issuance of marketable debt is based on the Government's financing needs, Treasury's issuance of nonmarketable debt is based on the public's demand for the specific types of investments. Decreases in outstanding balances of nonmarketable debt, such as occurred in 2017, increase the need for marketable borrowing.[12]

Agency Debt

A few Federal agencies other than Treasury, shown in Table 4–4, sell or have sold debt securities to the public and, at times, to other Government accounts. Currently, new debt is issued only by the Tennessee Valley Authority (TVA) and the Federal Housing Administration; the remaining agencies are repaying past borrowing. Agency debt was $26.2 billion at the end of 2017. Agency debt is less than one-quarter of one percent of Federal debt held by the public. Primarily as a result of TVA activity, agency debt is estimated to fall to $25.8 billion at the end of 2018 and to $25.1 billion at the end of 2019.

The predominant agency borrower is TVA, which had borrowings of $26.0 billion from the public as of the end of 2017, or 99 percent of the total debt of all agencies other than Treasury. TVA issues debt primarily to finance capital projects.

TVA has traditionally financed its capital construction by selling bonds and notes to the public. Since 2000, it has also employed two types of alternative financing methods, lease financing obligations and prepayment obligations. Under the lease financing obligations method,

---

[10] Under the SLGS program, the Treasury offers special low-yield securities to State and local governments and other entities for temporary investment of proceeds of tax-exempt bonds.

[11] Noncompetitive bids cannot exceed $5 million per bidder.

[12] Detail on the marketable and nonmarketable securities issued by Treasury is found in the *Monthly Statement of the Public Debt*, published on a monthly basis by the Department of the Treasury.

TVA signs long-term contracts to lease some facilities and equipment. The lease payments under these contracts ultimately secure the repayment of third party capital used to finance construction of the facility. TVA retains substantially all of the economic benefits and risks related to ownership of the assets.[13] Under the prepayment obligations method, TVA's power distributors may prepay a portion of the price of the power they plan to purchase in the future. In return, they obtain a discount on a specific quantity of the future power they buy from TVA. The quantity varies, depending on TVA's estimated cost of borrowing.

OMB determined that each of these alternative financing methods is a means of financing the acquisition of assets owned and used by the Government, or of refinancing debt previously incurred to finance such assets. They are equivalent in concept to other forms of borrowing from the public, although under different terms and conditions. The budget therefore records the upfront cash proceeds from these methods as borrowing from the public, not offsetting collections.[14] The budget presentation

---

[13] This arrangement is at least as governmental as a "lease-purchase without substantial private risk." For further detail on the current budgetary treatment of lease-purchase without substantial private risk, see OMB Circular No. A–11, Appendix B.

[14] This budgetary treatment differs from the treatment in the *Monthly Treasury Statement of Receipts and Outlays of the United States Government (Monthly Treasury Statement)* Table 6 Schedule C, and the *Combined Statement of Receipts, Outlays, and Balances of the United States Government* Schedule 3, both published by the Department of the Treasury. These two schedules, which present debt issued by agencies other than Treasury, exclude the TVA alternative financing arrangements. This difference in treatment is one factor causing minor differences between debt figures reported in the Budget and debt figures reported by Treasury. The other factors are adjustments for the timing of the reporting of Federal debt held by NRRIT and treatment of the Federal debt held by the Securities Investor Protection Corporation and the Public Company Accounting Oversight Board.

is consistent with the reporting of these obligations as liabilities on TVA's balance sheet under generally accepted accounting principles. Table 4–4 presents these alternative financing methods separately from TVA bonds and notes to distinguish between the types of borrowing. At the end of 2017, lease financing obligations were $1.7 billion and obligations for prepayments were $0.1 billion.

Although the FHA generally makes direct disbursements to the public for default claims on FHA-insured mortgages, it may also pay claims by issuing debentures. Issuing debentures to pay the Government's bills is equivalent to selling securities to the public and then paying the bills by disbursing the cash borrowed, so the transaction is recorded as being simultaneously an outlay and borrowing. The debentures are therefore classified as agency debt.

A number of years ago, the Federal Government guaranteed the debt used to finance the construction of buildings for the National Archives and the Architect of the Capitol, and subsequently exercised full control over the design, construction, and operation of the buildings. These arrangements are equivalent to direct Federal construction financed by Federal borrowing. The construction expenditures and interest were therefore classified as Federal outlays, and the borrowing was classified as Federal agency borrowing from the public.

Several Federal agencies borrow from the Bureau of the Fiscal Service (Fiscal Service) or the Federal Financing Bank (FFB), both within the Department of the Treasury. Agency borrowing from the FFB or the Fiscal Service is not included in gross Federal debt. It would be double counting to add together (a) the agency borrowing from the Fiscal Service or FFB and (b) the Treasury borrowing from the public that is needed to provide the Fiscal Service or FFB with the funds to lend to the agencies.

Table 4–4. AGENCY DEBT

(In millions of dollars)

	2017 Actual		2018 Estimate		2019 Estimate	
	Borrowing/ Repayment(-)	Debt, End-of-Year	Borrowing/ Repayment(-)	Debt, End-of-Year	Borrowing/ Repayment(-)	Debt, End-of-Year
Borrowing from the public:						
Housing and Urban Development:						
Federal Housing Administration	....	18.5	....	18.5	....	18.5
Architect of the Capitol	–9.0	89.5	–9.5	80.0	–11.0	69.0
National Archives	–23.0	52.3	–25.0	27.2	–27.2	....
Tennessee Valley Authority:						
Bonds and notes	36.7	24,207.3	–97.0	24,110.3	–514.7	23,595.6
Lease financing obligations	–118.6	1,704.3	–131.1	1,573.1	–122.6	1,450.5
Prepayment obligations	–100.0	109.6	–100.0	9.6	–9.6	....
Total, borrowing from the public	–213.9	26,181.5	–362.7	25,818.9	–685.2	25,133.7
Borrowing from other funds:						
Tennessee Valley Authority [1]	–3.0	1.2	....	1.2	....	1.2
Total, borrowing from other funds	–3.0	1.2	....	1.2	....	1.2
Total, agency borrowing	–211.8	26,182.8	–362.7	25,820.1	–685.2	25,134.9
Memorandum:						
Tennessee Valley Authority bonds and notes, total	33.7	24,208.6	–97.0	24,111.5	–514.7	23,596.8

[1] Represents open market purchases by the National Railroad Retirement Investment Trust.

Debt Held by Government Accounts

Trust funds, and some special funds and public enterprise revolving funds, accumulate cash in excess of current needs in order to meet future obligations. These cash surpluses are generally invested in Treasury debt.

The total investment holdings of trust funds and other Government accounts increased by $168 billion in 2017. Net investment by Government accounts is estimated to be $148 billion in 2018 and $143 billion in 2019, as shown in Table 4–5. The holdings of Federal securities by Government accounts are estimated to increase to $5,831 billion by the end of 2019, or 26 percent of the gross Federal debt. The percentage is estimated to decrease gradually over the next 10 years.

The Government account holdings of Federal securities are concentrated among a few funds: the Social Security Old-Age and Survivors Insurance (OASI) and Disability Insurance (DI) trust funds; the Medicare Hospital Insurance (HI) and Supplementary Medical Insurance (SMI) trust funds; and four Federal employee retirement funds. These Federal employee retirement funds include two trust funds, the Military Retirement Fund and the Civil Service Retirement and Disability Fund (CSRDF), and two special funds, the uniformed services Medicare-Eligible Retiree Health Care Fund (MERHCF) and the Postal Service Retiree Health Benefits Fund (PSRHBF). At the end of 2019, these Social Security, Medicare, and Federal employee retirement funds are estimated to own 86 percent of the total debt held by Government accounts. During 2017–2019, the Military Retirement Fund has a large surplus and is estimated to invest a total of $218 billion, 48 percent of total net investment by Government accounts. Some Government accounts are projected to have net disinvestment in Federal securities during 2017–2019.

Technical note on measurement.—The Treasury securities held by Government accounts consist almost entirely of the Government account series. Most were issued at par value (face value), and the securities issued at a discount or premium are traditionally recorded at par in the OMB and Treasury reports on Federal debt. However, there are two kinds of exceptions.

First, Treasury issues zero-coupon bonds to a very few Government accounts. Because the purchase price is a small fraction of par value and the amounts are large, the holdings are recorded in Table 4–5 at par value less unamortized discount. The only two Government accounts that have held zero-coupon bonds during the period of this table are the Nuclear Waste Disposal Fund in the Department of Energy and the Pension Benefit Guaranty Corporation (PBGC). PBGC disinvested its holdings of zero-coupon bonds during 2017. The unamortized discount on zero-coupon bonds held by the Nuclear Waste Disposal Fund was $15.7 billion at the end of 2017.

Second, Treasury subtracts the unrealized discount on other Government account series securities in calculating "net Federal securities held as investments of Government accounts." Unlike the discount recorded for zero-coupon bonds and debt held by the public, the unrealized discount is the discount at the time of issue and is not amortized over the term of the security. In Table 4–5 it is shown as a separate item at the end of the table and not distributed by account. The amount was $10.3 billion at the end of 2017.

Debt Held by the Federal Reserve

The Federal Reserve acquires marketable Treasury securities as part of its exercise of monetary policy. For purposes of the Budget and reporting by the Department of the Treasury, the transactions of the Federal Reserve are considered to be non-budgetary, and accordingly the Federal Reserve's holdings of Treasury securities are included as part of debt held by the public.[15] Federal Reserve holdings were $2,465 billion (17 percent of debt held by the public) at the end of 2017. Over the last 10 years, the Federal Reserve holdings have averaged 15 percent of debt held by the public. The historical holdings of the Federal Reserve are presented in Table 7.1 in the Budget's historical tables. The Budget does not project Federal Reserve holdings for future years.

Limitations on Federal Debt

Definition of debt subject to limit.—Statutory limitations have usually been placed on Federal debt. Until World War I, the Congress ordinarily authorized a specific amount of debt for each separate issue. Beginning with the Second Liberty Bond Act of 1917, however, the nature of the limitation was modified in several steps until it developed into a ceiling on the total amount of most Federal debt outstanding. This last type of limitation has been in effect since 1941. The limit currently applies to most debt issued by the Treasury since September 1917, whether held by the public or by Government accounts; and other debt issued by Federal agencies that, according to explicit statute, is guaranteed as to principal and interest by the U.S. Government.

The third part of Table 4–2 compares total Treasury debt with the amount of Federal debt that is subject to the limit. Nearly all Treasury debt is subject to the debt limit.

A large portion of the Treasury debt not subject to the general statutory limit was issued by the Federal Financing Bank. The FFB is authorized to have outstanding up to $15 billion of publicly issued debt. The FFB has on occasion issued this debt to CSRDF in exchange for equal amounts of regular Treasury securities. The FFB securities have the same interest rates and maturities as the Treasury securities for which they were exchanged. The FFB issued: $14 billion of securities to the CSRDF on November 15, 2004, with maturity dates ranging from June 30, 2009, through June 30, 2019; $9 billion to the CSRDF on October 1, 2013, with maturity dates from June 30, 2015, through June 30, 2024; and $3 billion of securities to the CSRDF on October 15, 2015, with maturity dates from June 30, 2026, through June 30, 2029. The outstanding balance of FFB debt held by CSRDF was $11

---

[15] For further detail on the monetary policy activities of the Federal Reserve and the treatment of the Federal Reserve in the Budget, see Chapter 9, "Coverage of the Budget."

Table 4–5. DEBT HELD BY GOVERNMENT ACCOUNTS[1]

(In millions of dollars)

Description	Investment or Disinvestment (–)			Holdings, End of 2019 Estimate
	2017 Actual	2018 Estimate	2019 Estimate	
Investment in Treasury debt:				
Commerce:				
Public safety trust fund	....	5,000	3,650	8,983
Defense—Military:				
Host nation support fund for relocation	420	–145	158	1,272
Energy:				
Nuclear waste disposal fund [1]	1,712	415	421	38,193
Uranium enrichment decontamination fund	–156	–176	1,791	3,955
Health and Human Services:				
Federal hospital insurance trust fund	5,626	2,614	9,102	209,551
Federal supplementary medical insurance trust fund	7,253	25,200	6,701	102,490
Vaccine injury compensation fund	–10	94	109	3,798
Child enrollment contingency fund	574	2,327	–2,305	1,167
Homeland Security:				
Aquatic resources trust fund	12	20	–18	1,924
Oil spill liability trust fund	722	355	447	6,474
National flood insurance reserve fund	–1,039	860	40	900
Housing and Urban Development:				
Federal Housing Administration mutual mortgage insurance capital reserve	–5,562	–4,960	7,346	33,265
Guarantees of mortgage-backed securities	1,322	1,058	983	19,317
Interior:				
Abandoned mine reclamation fund	–16	–23	–18	2,719
Federal aid in wildlife restoration fund	139	65	51	2,256
Environmental improvement and restoration fund	37	20	32	1,518
Natural resource damage assessment fund	508	200	100	1,600
Justice: Assets forfeiture fund	–922	–2,773	–1,291	1,187
Labor:				
Unemployment trust fund	6,934	14,389	14,950	90,050
Pension Benefit Guaranty Corporation [1]	4,878	4,868	4,949	38,259
State: Foreign service retirement and disability trust fund	447	317	338	19,447
Transportation:				
Airport and airway trust fund	4	–285	1,521	14,640
Highway trust fund	–12,297	–11,297	–11,297	29,738
Aviation insurance revolving fund	338	37	56	2,303
Treasury:				
Exchange stabilization fund	–590	161	282	22,533
Treasury forfeiture fund	–373	–383	–591	1,343
Gulf Coast Restoration trust fund	262	47	194	1,431
Comptroller of the Currency assessment fund	134	–108	....	1,683
Veterans Affairs:				
National service life insurance trust fund	–641	–703	–560	2,341
Veterans special life insurance fund	–97	–138	–137	1,328
Corps of Engineers: Harbor maintenance trust fund	345	373	519	9,923
Other Defense-Civil:				
Military retirement fund	69,924	69,037	79,417	809,424
Medicare-eligible retiree health care fund	12,365	12,973	11,384	250,204
Education benefits fund	–156	–20	–67	971
Environmental Protection Agency: Hazardous substance superfund	2	2	2	4,804
International Assistance Programs:				
Overseas Private Investment Corporation	72	61	–5,799	....
Development Finance Institution	....	....	5,823	5,823

Table 4–5. DEBT HELD BY GOVERNMENT ACCOUNTS [1]—Continued
(In millions of dollars)

Description	Investment or Disinvestment (–)			Holdings, End of 2019 Estimate
	2017 Actual	2018 Estimate	2019 Estimate	
Office of Personnel Management:				
Civil service retirement and disability trust fund	17,942	17,273	13,876	936,252
Postal Service retiree health benefits fund	–2,004	1,376	–2,536	48,331
Employees life insurance fund	512	444	763	46,887
Employees and retired employees health benefits fund	2,292	68	41	26,130
Social Security Administration:				
Federal old-age and survivors insurance trust fund [2]	23,488	–24,520	–7,048	2,788,632
Federal disability insurance trust fund [2]	23,789	22,367	–1,960	90,076
District of Columbia: Federal pension fund	1	1	–24	3,730
Farm Credit System Insurance Corporation: Farm Credit System Insurance fund	428	476	290	5,219
Federal Communications Commission: Universal service fund	–923	–706	–695	5,695
Federal Deposit Insurance Corporation: Deposit insurance fund	8,638	12,267	10,550	102,978
National Credit Union Administration: Share insurance fund	785	2,358	778	16,225
Postal Service fund [2]	2,438	–2,256	2,067	10,776
Railroad Retirement Board trust funds	155	–486	–181	1,707
Securities Investor Protection Corporation [3]	245	99	115	3,164
United States Enrichment Corporation fund	–16	34	–1,640	....
Other Federal funds	–335	–59	249	5,170
Other trust funds	–716	32	–312	3,587
Unrealized discount [1]	–459	....	....	–10,252
Total, investment in Treasury debt [1]	168,432	148,251	142,616	5,831,120
Investment in agency debt:				
Railroad Retirement Board:				
National Railroad Retirement Investment Trust	–3	....	....	1
Total, investment in agency debt [1]	–3	....	....	1
Total, investment in Federal debt [1]	168,429	148,251	142,616	5,831,122
Memorandum:				
Investment by Federal funds (on-budget)	20,106	30,576	30,341	617,054
Investment by Federal funds (off-budget)	2,438	–2,256	2,067	10,776
Investment by trust funds (on-budget)	99,066	122,085	119,216	2,334,836
Investment by trust funds (off-budget)	47,277	–2,153	–9,008	2,878,708
Unrealized discount [1]	–459	....	....	–10,252

[1] Debt held by Government accounts is measured at face value except for the Treasury zero-coupon bonds held by the Nuclear Waste Disposal Fund and the Pension Benefit Guaranty Corporation (PBGC), which are recorded at market or redemption price; and the unrealized discount on Government account series, which is not distributed by account. Changes are not estimated in the unrealized discount. If recorded at face value, at the end of 2017 the debt figures would be $15.7 billion higher for the Nuclear Waste Disposal Fund than recorded in this table. PBGC disinvested its holdings of zero-coupon bonds during 2017.

[2] Off-budget Federal entity.

[3] Amounts on calendar-year basis.

billion at the end of 2017 and is projected to be $10 billion at the end of 2018.

The other Treasury debt not subject to the general limit consists almost entirely of silver certificates and other currencies no longer being issued. It was $481 million at the end of 2017 and is projected to gradually decline over time.

The sole agency debt currently subject to the general limit, $209 thousand at the end of 2017, is certain debentures issued by the Federal Housing Administration.[16]

Some of the other agency debt, however, is subject to its own statutory limit. For example, the Tennessee Valley

Authority is limited to $30 billion of bonds and notes outstanding.

The comparison between Treasury debt and debt subject to limit also includes an adjustment for measurement differences in the treatment of discounts and premiums. As explained earlier in this chapter, debt securities may be sold at a discount or premium, and the measurement of debt may take this into account rather than recording the face value of the securities. However, the measurement differs between gross Federal debt (and its components) and the statutory definition of debt subject to limit. An adjustment is needed to derive debt subject to limit (as defined by law) from Treasury debt. The amount of the adjustment was $41 billion at the end of 2017 compared

---

[16] At the end of 2017, there were also $18 million of FHA debentures not subject to limit.

with the total unamortized discount (less premium) of $65 billion on all Treasury securities.

Changes in the debt limit.—The statutory debt limit has been changed many times. Since 1960, the Congress has passed 83 separate acts to raise the limit, revise the definition, extend the duration of a temporary increase, or temporarily suspend the limit.[17]

The five most recent laws addressing the debt limit have each provided for a temporary suspension followed by an increase in an amount equivalent to the debt that was issued during that suspension period in order to fund commitments requiring payment through the specified end date. Most recently, the Continuing Appropriations Act, 2018 and Supplemental Appropriations for Disaster Relief Requirements Act, 2017, suspended the $19,809 billion debt ceiling from September 8, 2017, through December 8, 2017, and then raised the debt limit on December 9, 2017, by $647 billion to $20,456 billion.

At many times in the past several decades, including 2014, 2015, and 2017, the Government has reached the statutory debt limit before an increase has been enacted. When this has occurred, it has been necessary for the Department of the Treasury to take "extraordinary measures" to meet the Government's obligation to pay its bills and invest its trust funds while remaining below the statutory limit. On December 6, 2017, near the end of the most recent debt limit suspension period, the Secretary of the Treasury sent a letter to Congress announcing that Treasury would begin to take extraordinary measures on December 9.

One such extraordinary measure is the partial or full suspension of the daily reinvestment of the Thrift Savings Plan (TSP) Government Securities Investment Fund (G-Fund).[18] The Treasury Secretary has statutory authority to suspend investment of the G-Fund in Treasury securities as needed to prevent the debt from exceeding the debt limit. Treasury determines each day the amount of investments that would allow the fund to be invested as fully as possible without exceeding the debt limit. The TSP G-Fund had an outstanding balance of $223 billion at the end of November and $69 billion at the end of December. The Secretary is also authorized to suspend investments in the CSRDF and to declare a debt issuance suspension period, which allows him or her to redeem a limited amount of securities held by the CSRDF. The Postal Accountability and Enhancement Act of 2006 provides that investments in the Postal Service Retiree Health Benefits Fund shall be made in the same manner as investments in the CSRDF.[19] Therefore, Treasury is able to take similar administrative actions with the PSRHBF. The law requires that when any such actions are taken with the G-Fund, the CSRDF, or the PSRHBF, the Secretary is required to make the fund whole after the debt limit has been raised by restoring the forgone

interest and investing the fund fully. Another measure for staying below the debt limit is disinvestment of the Exchange Stabilization Fund. The outstanding balance in the Exchange Stabilization Fund was $22 billion at the end of December 2017.

As the debt has neared the limit, including in 2017, Treasury has also suspended the issuance of SLGS to reduce unanticipated fluctuations in the level of the debt. At times, Treasury has also adjusted the schedule for auctions of marketable securities.

In addition to these steps, Treasury has previously exchanged Treasury securities held by the CSRDF with borrowing by the FFB, which, as explained above, is not subject to the debt limit. This measure was most recently taken in October 2015.

The debt limit has always been increased prior to the exhaustion of Treasury's limited available administrative actions to continue to finance Government operations when the statutory ceiling has been reached. Failure to enact a debt limit increase before these actions were exhausted would have significant and long-term negative consequences. The Federal Government would be forced to delay or discontinue payments on its broad range of obligations, including Social Security and other payments to individuals, Medicaid and other grant payments to States, individual and corporate tax refunds, Federal employee salaries, payments to vendors and contractors, principal and interest payments on Treasury securities, and other obligations. If Treasury were unable to make timely interest payments or redeem securities, investors would cease to view U.S. Treasury securities as free of credit risk and Treasury's interest costs would increase. Because interest rates throughout the economy are benchmarked to the Treasury rates, interest rates for State and local governments, businesses, and individuals would also rise. Foreign investors would likely shift out of dollar-denominated assets, driving down the value of the dollar and further increasing interest rates on non-Federal, as well as Treasury, debt.

The debt subject to limit is estimated to increase to $21,483 billion by the end of 2018 and to $22,709 billion by the end of 2019. The Budget anticipates timely Congressional action to address the statutory limit as necessary before exhaustion of Treasury's extraordinary measures.

Federal funds financing and the change in debt subject to limit.—The change in debt held by the public, as shown in Table 4–2, and the change in debt held by the public net of financial assets are determined primarily by the total Government deficit or surplus. The debt subject to limit, however, includes not only debt held by the public but also debt held by Government accounts. The change in debt subject to limit is therefore determined both by the factors that determine the total Government deficit or surplus and by the factors that determine the change in debt held by Government accounts. The effect of debt held by Government accounts on the total debt subject to limit can be seen in the second part of Table 4–2. The change in debt held by Government accounts results in 7

---

[17] The Acts and the statutory limits since 1940 are listed in Table 7.3 of the Budget's historical tables, available at *https://www.whitehouse.gov/omb/historical-tables/*.

[18] The TSP is a defined contribution pension plan for Federal employees. The G-Fund is one of several components of the TSP.

[19] Both the CSRDF and the PSRHBF are administered by the Office of Personnel Management.

percent of the estimated total increase in debt subject to limit from 2018 through 2028.

The budget is composed of two groups of funds, Federal funds and trust funds. The Federal funds, in the main, are derived from tax receipts and borrowing and are used for the general purposes of the Government. The trust funds, on the other hand, are financed by taxes or other receipts dedicated by law for specified purposes, such as for paying Social Security benefits or making grants to State governments for highway construction.[20]

A Federal funds deficit must generally be financed by borrowing, which can be done either by selling securities to the public or by issuing securities to Government accounts that are not within the Federal funds group. Federal funds borrowing consists almost entirely of Treasury securities that are subject to the statutory debt limit. Very little debt subject to statutory limit has been issued for reasons except to finance the Federal funds deficit. The change in debt subject to limit is therefore determined primarily by the Federal funds deficit, which is equal to the difference between the total Government deficit or surplus and the trust fund surplus. Trust fund surpluses are almost entirely invested in securities subject to the debt limit, and trust funds hold most of the debt held by Government accounts. The trust fund surplus reduces the total budget deficit or increases the total budget surplus, decreasing the need to borrow from the public or increasing the ability to repay borrowing from the public. When the trust fund surplus is invested in Federal securities, the debt held by Government accounts increases, offsetting the decrease in debt held by the pub-

lic by an equal amount. Thus, there is no net effect on gross Federal debt.

Table 4–6 derives the change in debt subject to limit. In 2017 the Federal funds deficit was $819 billion, and other factors reduced financing requirements by $169 billion. The change in the Treasury operating cash balance reduced financing requirements by $194 billion, the net financing disbursements of credit financing accounts increased financing requirements by $41 billion, and other Federal fund factors reduced financing requirements by $15 billion. In addition, special funds and revolving funds, which are part of the Federal funds group, invested a net of $23 billion in Treasury securities. A $6 billion adjustment is also made for the difference between the trust fund surplus or deficit and the trust funds' investment or disinvestment in Federal securities (including the changes in NRRIT's investments in non-Federal securities). As a net result of all these factors, $666 billion in financing was required, increasing gross Federal debt by that amount. Since Federal debt not subject to limit fell by $2 billion and the adjustment for discount and premium changed by $2 billion, the debt subject to limit increased by $670 billion, while debt held by the public increased by $498 billion.

Debt subject to limit is estimated to increase by $1,274 billion in 2018 and by $1,227 billion in 2019. The projected increases in the debt subject to limit are caused by the continued Federal funds deficit, supplemented by the other factors shown in Table 4–6. While debt held by the public increases by $9,018 billion from the end of 2017 through 2028, debt subject to limit increases by $9,758 billion.

---

[20] For further discussion of the trust funds and Federal funds groups, see Chapter 24, "Trust Funds and Federal Funds."

Table 4–6. FEDERAL FUNDS FINANCING AND CHANGE IN DEBT SUBJECT TO STATUTORY LIMIT

(In billions of dollars)

Description	Actual 2017	Estimate										
		2018	2019	2020	2021	2022	2023	2024	2025	2026	2027	2028
Change in Gross Federal Debt:												
Federal funds deficit	819.0	976.3	1,087.7	1,067.2	991.6	933.5	827.7	692.5	597.3	534.8	357.2	268.7
Other transactions affecting borrowing from the public -- Federal funds[1]	−168.7	292.2	98.6	89.2	88.8	89.1	84.6	75.4	63.2	49.5	41.3	44.8
Increase (+) or decrease (−) in Federal debt held by Federal funds	22.5	28.3	32.4	42.8	39.9	39.3	39.5	39.0	38.0	35.1	37.7	37.9
Adjustments for trust fund surplus/deficit not invested/disinvested in Federal securities[2]	−6.1	−24.3	5.8	−1.1	−1.0	−1.1	−0.7	−0.8	−0.7	−0.6	−0.3	−0.1
Change in unrealized discount on Federal debt held by Government accounts	−0.5	....	....	....	....	....	....	....	....	....	....	....
Total financing requirements	666.3	1,272.5	1,224.6	1,198.1	1,119.3	1,060.8	951.1	806.1	697.7	618.9	436.0	351.2
Change in Debt Subject to Limit:												
Change in gross Federal debt	666.3	1,272.5	1,224.6	1,198.1	1,119.3	1,060.8	951.1	806.1	697.7	618.9	436.0	351.2
Less: increase (+) or decrease (−) in Federal debt not subject to limit	−1.8	−1.5	−2.2	−2.8	−2.0	−2.0	−2.1	−2.2	−1.4	−1.5	−1.9	−1.8
Less: change in adjustment for discount and premium[3]	−2.1	....	....	....	....	....	....	....	....	....	....	....
Total, change in debt subject to limit	670.2	1,274.0	1,226.8	1,200.9	1,121.3	1,062.8	953.2	808.3	699.1	620.3	437.9	353.0
Memorandum:												
Debt subject to statutory limit[4]		20,208.6	21,482.6	22,709.4	23,910.3	25,031.6	26,094.4	27,047.6	27,855.9	28,555.0	29,175.3	29,613.2	29,966.3

[1] Includes Federal fund transactions that correspond to those presented in Table 4–2, but that are for Federal funds alone with respect to the public and trust funds.
[2] Includes trust fund holdings in other cash assets and changes in the investments of the National Railroad Retirement Investment Trust in non-Federal securities.
[3] Consists of unamortized discount (less premium) on public issues of Treasury notes and bonds (other than zero-coupon bonds).
[4] The statutory debt limit is approximately $20,456 billion, as increased after December 8, 2017.

Foreign Holdings of Federal Debt

During most of American history, the Federal debt was held almost entirely by individuals and institutions within the United States. In the late 1960s, foreign holdings were just over $10 billion, less than 5 percent of the total Federal debt held by the public. Foreign holdings began to grow significantly starting in the 1970s and since 2004 have represented over 40 percent of outstanding debt. This increase has been almost entirely due to decisions by foreign central banks, corporations, and individuals, rather than the direct marketing of these securities to foreign investors.

Foreign holdings of Federal debt are presented in Table 4–7. At the end of 2017, foreign holdings of Treasury debt were $6,323 billion, which was 43 percent of the total debt held by the public.[21] Foreign central banks and other foreign official institutions owned 64 percent of the foreign holdings of Federal debt; private investors owned nearly all the rest. At the end of 2017, the nations holding the largest shares of U.S. Federal debt were China, which held 19 percent of all foreign holdings, and Japan, which held 17 percent. All of the foreign holdings of Federal debt are denominated in dollars.

Although the amount of foreign holdings of Federal debt has grown greatly over this period, the proportion that foreign entities and individuals own, after increasing abruptly in the very early 1970s, remained about 15–20 percent until the mid-1990s. During 1995–97, however, growth in foreign holdings accelerated, reaching 33 percent by the end of 1997. Foreign holdings of Federal debt resumed growth in the following decade, increasing to 48 percent by the end of 2008. After 2008, foreign holdings as a percent of total Federal debt remained relatively stable through 2015 and then fell from 47 percent at the end of 2015 to 43 percent at the end of 2016. Foreign holdings remained at 43 percent at the end of 2017. The dollar increase in foreign holdings was about 34 percent of total Federal borrowing from the public in 2017 and 25 percent over the last five years.

Foreign holdings of Federal debt are around 20-25 percent of the foreign-owned assets in the United States, depending on the method of measuring total assets. The foreign purchases of Federal debt securities do not measure the full impact of the capital inflow from abroad on the market for Federal debt securities. The capital inflow supplies additional funds to the credit market generally, and thus affects the market for Federal debt. For example, the capital inflow includes deposits in U.S. financial intermediaries that themselves buy Federal debt.

---

[21] The debt calculated by the Bureau of Economic Analysis is different, though similar in size, because of a different method of valuing securities.

Table 4–7. FOREIGN HOLDINGS OF FEDERAL DEBT
(Dollar amounts in billions)

Fiscal Year	Debt held by the public			Change in debt held by the public[2]	
	Total	Foreign[1]	Percentage foreign	Total	Foreign
1965	260.8	12.2	4.7	3.9	0.3
1970	283.2	14.0	4.9	5.1	3.7
1975	394.7	66.0	16.7	51.0	9.1
1980	711.9	126.4	17.8	71.6	1.3
1985	1,507.3	222.9	14.8	200.3	47.3
1990	2,411.6	463.8	19.2	220.8	72.0
1995	3,604.4	820.4	22.8	171.3	138.4
2000	3,409.8	1,038.8	30.5	−222.6	−242.6
2005	4,592.2	1,929.6	42.0	296.7	135.1
2010	9,018.9	4,324.2	47.9	1,474.2	753.6
2011	10,128.2	4,912.1	48.5	1,109.3	587.9
2012	11,281.1	5,476.1	48.5	1,152.9	564.0
2013	11,982.7	5,652.8	47.2	701.6	176.7
2014	12,779.9	6,069.2	47.5	797.2	416.4
2015	13,116.7	6,105.9	46.6	336.8	36.7
2016	14,167.6	6,155.9	43.5	1,050.9	50.0
2017	14,665.5	6,323.0	43.1	497.8	167.1

[1] Estimated by Treasury Department. These estimates exclude agency debt, the holdings of which are believed to be small. The data on foreign holdings are recorded by methods that are not fully comparable with the data on debt held by the public. Projections of foreign holdings are not available.

[2] Change in debt held by the public is defined as equal to the change in debt held by the public from the beginning of the year to the end of the year.

Federal, Federally Guaranteed, and Other Federally Assisted Borrowing

The Government's effects on the credit markets arise not only from its own borrowing but also from the direct loans that it makes to the public and the provision of assistance to certain borrowing by the public. The Government guarantees various types of borrowing by individuals, businesses, and other non-Federal entities, thereby providing assistance to private credit markets. The Government is also assisting borrowing by States through the Build America Bonds program, which subsidizes the interest that States pay on such borrowing. In addition, the Government has established private corporations—Government-sponsored enterprises—to provide financial intermediation for specified public purposes; it exempts the interest on most State and local government debt from income tax; it permits mortgage interest to be deducted in calculating taxable income; and it insures the deposits of banks and thrift institutions, which themselves make loans.

Federal credit programs and other forms of assistance are discussed in Chapter 19, "Credit and Insurance," in this volume. Detailed data are presented in tables accompanying that chapter.

PERFORMANCE AND MANAGEMENT

5. SOCIAL INDICATORS

The social indicators presented in this chapter illustrate in broad terms how the Nation is faring in selected areas. Indicators are drawn from six domains: economic, demographic and civic, socioeconomic, health, security and safety, and environment and energy. The indicators shown in the tables in this chapter were chosen in consultation with statistical and data experts from across the Federal Government. These indicators are only a subset of the vast array of available data on conditions in the United States. In choosing indicators for these tables, priority was given to measures that are broadly relevant to Americans and consistently available over an extended period. Such indicators provide a current snapshot while also making it easier to draw comparisons and establish trends.

The measures in these tables are influenced to varying degrees by many Government policies and programs, as well as by external factors beyond the Government's control. They do not measure the impacts of Government policies. Instead, they provide a quantitative picture of the baseline on which future policies are set and useful context for prioritizing budgetary resources.

Economic.—The 2008-2009 economic downturn produced the worst labor market since the Great Depression. The employment-population ratio dropped sharply from its pre-recession level, and real GDP per person also declined. The unemployment rate has since recovered, standing at 4.1 percent in December 2017, down from a high of 10 percent in October 2009. Despite the recovery in the unemployment rate, the employment-population ratio remains low relative to its pre-recession levels. From 1985 to 2007, the employment-population ratio ranged from 60.1 to 63.1 percent, and in 2007 it stood at 63.0 percent. After the 2008-2009 recession, it fell to 58.4 percent in 2011 and has recovered only partly to 60.1 percent in 2017.

Over the entire period since 1960, the primary pattern has been one of economic growth and rising living standards. Real GDP per person has tripled as technological advancements and accumulation of human and physical capital increased the Nation's productive capacity. The stock of physical capital including consumer durable goods, like cars and appliances, amounted to $55 trillion in 2016, approximately five times the size of the capital stock in 1960 after accounting for inflation.

However, national saving, a key determinant of future prosperity because it supports capital accumulation, remains low relative to historical standards, standing at 2.3 percent of GDP in 2016, down from 10.9 percent in 1960. Meanwhile, the labor force participation rate, also critical for growth, has generally been on the decline since 2000 and fell abruptly during the 2008-2009 recession. Though it increased slightly in the past two years, the labor force participation rate remains far below pre-recession levels.

In addition to the size of the economy, the structure of the economy has also changed considerably. From 2000 to 2016, goods-producing industries declined from 24.9 to 21.0 percent of total private goods and services, measured in value added as a percent of GDP, while services-producing industries increased from 75.1 to 79.0 percent. This period coincided with a steep decline in manufacturing employment, potentially due to import competition from China and changes in technology.[1] The United States has experienced persistent trade deficits since the early 1980s, reaching $714 billion in 2005 and standing at $505 billion in 2016.

Demographic and Civic.—The U.S. population steadily increased from 1970 to 2017, growing from 204 million to 326 million. Since 1970, the foreign born population has rapidly increased, more than quadrupling from about 10 million in 1970 to 44 million in 2016. The U.S. population is getting older, due in part to the aging of the baby boomers, improvements in medical technology, and declining birth rates. From 1970 to 2016, the percent of the population aged 65 and over increased from 9.8 to 15.2, and the percent aged 85 and over increased from 0.7 to 2.0. In contrast, the percent of the population aged 17 and younger declined from 28.0 in 1980 to 22.6 in 2017.

The composition of American households and families has evolved considerably over time. The percent of Americans who have ever married has declined from 78.0 to 68.0 percent of Americans aged 15 and over. Average family sizes have also fallen over this period, a pattern that is typical among developed countries, from 3.7 to 3.1 members per family household. Births to unmarried women aged 15-17 and the fraction of single parent households both reached turning points in 1995 after increasing for over three decades. From 1995 to 2016, the number of births per 1,000 unmarried women aged 15-17 fell from 30 to 9, the lowest level on record. The fraction of single parent households comprised 9.1 percent of all households in 1995, up from only 4.4 percent in 1960, but since 1995 it has stabilized and in recent years has decreased to 8.4 percent in 2017.

Charitable giving among Americans, measured by the average charitable contribution per itemized tax return, has generally increased over the past 50 years.[2] The effects of the 2008-2009 recession are evident in the sharp drop in charitable giving from 2005 to 2010, but that

---

[1] Autor, David H., David Dorn, and Gordon H. Hanson (2013). The China Syndrome: Local Labor Market Effects of Import Competition in the United States, American Economic Review, 103(6).

[2] This measure includes charitable giving only among those who claim itemized deductions. It is therefore influenced by changes in tax laws and in the characteristics of those who itemize.

decline was reversed by 2014 and charitable giving continues to increase.

Socioeconomic.—Education is a critical component of the Nation's economic growth and competitiveness, while also benefiting society in areas such as health, crime, and civic engagement. Between 1960 and 1980, the percentage of 25- to 34-year olds who have graduated from high school increased from 58 percent to 84 percent, a gain of 13 percentage points per decade. The rate of increase has slowed since then with a six percentage point gain over the past 36 years. The percentage of 25- to 34-year olds who have graduated from college continues to rise, from only 11 percent in 1960 to 35 percent in 2016. While the percentage of the population with a graduate degree has risen over time, the percentage of graduate degrees in science and engineering fell by half in the period between 1960 and 1980, from 22 percent to 11 percent. However, since 2010 this decline has partially reversed, with science and engineering degrees rising from 12 to 16 percent of all graduate degrees in 2016.

Although national prosperity has grown considerably over the past 50 years, these gains have not been shared equally. Real disposable income per capita more than tripled since 1960, but for the median household, real income increased by only 23 percent since 1970, and nearly all of those gains took place prior to 2000. The median wealth of households aged 55-64 declined dramatically from $321 thousand in 2005 to only $171 thousand in 2014, before increasing to $187 thousand in 2016. From 2000 to 2010, the poverty rate, the percentage of food-insecure households, and the percentage of Americans receiving benefits from the Supplemental Nutrition Assistance Program (SNAP), increased, with most of this increase taking place during and after the 2008-2009 economic downturn. The poverty rate has recovered to approximately its pre-recession level, while food insecurity and the percentage of the population on SNAP have declined over the past several years but still remain elevated.

After increasing from 1990 to 2005, homeownership rates have fallen continuously since the 2008 housing crisis. The share of families with children and severe housing cost burdens more than doubled from 8 percent in 1980 to 18 percent in 2010, before falling to 15 percent in 2015. The share of families with children and inadequate housing steadily decreased from a high of 9 percent in 1980 to a low of 5 percent in 2013, but has since increased to over 6 percent in 2015.

Health.—America has by far the most expensive health care system in the world. National health expenditures as a share of GDP have increased from 5 percent in 1960 to nearly 18 percent in 2016. This increase in health care spending coincides with improvements in medical technologies that have improved health. However, the level of per capita health care spending in the United States is far greater than in other Organization for Economic Cooperation and Development (OECD) countries that have experienced comparable health improvements.[3]

Average private health insurance premiums paid by individuals with private health insurance increased by 19 percent from 2010 to 2016, after adjusting for inflation.

Some key indicators of national health have improved since 1960. Infant mortality fell from 26 to under 6 per 1,000 live births, with a rapid decline occurring in the 1970s. Life expectancy at birth increased by 8.9 years, from 69.7 in 1960 to 78.6 in 2016. However, between 2014 and 2016, life expectancy declined from its high of 78.9.

Improvements in health-related behaviors among Americans have been mixed. Although the percent of adults who smoke cigarettes in 2016 was less than half of what it was in 1970, rates of obesity have soared. In 1980, 15 percent of adults and 6 percent of children were obese; in 2016, 40 percent of adults and 19 percent of children were obese. Adult obesity continued to rise even as the share of adults engaging in regular physical activity increased from 15 percent in 2000 to 23 percent in 2016.

Security and Safety.—The last three decades have witnessed a remarkable decline in crime. From 1980 to 2016, the property crime rate dropped by 76 percent while the murder rate fell by 48 percent. However, the downward decline in the murder rate ended in 2014, with the rate rising between 2014 and 2016, and the property crime rate rose from 2015 to 2016. The prison incarceration rate increased more than five-fold from 1970 through 2005, before declining by 8 percent from 2005 through 2015. Road transportation has become safer. Safety belt use increased by 19 percentage points from 2000 to 2017, and the annual number of highway fatalities fell by 29 percent from 1970 to 2016 despite the increase in the population.

In recent years, the number of military personnel on active duty has fallen to its lowest levels since at least 1960. The highest count of active duty military personnel was 3.1 million in 1970, reached during the Vietnam War. It now stands at 1.3 million. The number of veterans has declined from 29 million in 1980 to 20 million in 2017.

Environment and Energy.—Substantial progress has been made on air quality in the United States, with the concentration of particulate matter falling 42 percent from 2000 to 2016 and ground level ozone falling by 31 percent from 1980 to 2016. Gross greenhouse gas emissions per capita and per real dollar of GDP have fallen since at least 1990. As of 2016, 91 percent of the population served by community water systems received drinking water in compliance with applicable Federal water quality standards, which has remained relatively constant since 2000.

Technological advances and a shift in production patterns mean that Americans use less than half as much energy per real dollar of GDP as they did 50 years ago, and per capita energy consumption is at its lowest since the 1960s despite rising income levels. From 2005 to 2016, coal production fell by 36 percent, with most of that decrease occurring from 2014 to 2016. The decrease in coal production since 2005 coincided with increases in the production of natural gas, petroleum, and renewable energy as well as new regulatory proposals and requirements.

---

[3] Squires, D. and C. Anderson (2015). U.S. Health Care from a Global Perspective: Spending, Use of Services, Prices and Health in 13 Countries, The Commonwealth Fund.

Table 5-1. SOCIAL INDICATORS

Calendar Years	1960	1970	1980	1990	1995	2000	2005	2010	2014	2015	2016	2017
Economic												
General Economic Conditions												
1 Real GDP per person (chained 2009 dollars)	17,198	23,024	28,325	35,794	38,167	44,475	48,090	47,720	50,216	51,286	51,690	N/A
2 Real GDP per person change, 5-year annual average	0.8	2.4	2.6	2.4	1.3	3.1	1.6	–0.1	1.4	1.5	1.4	N/A
3 Consumer Price Index [1]	12.5	16.4	34.8	55.2	64.4	72.7	82.5	92.1	100.0	100.1	101.4	103.5
4 Private goods producing (%)	N/A	N/A	N/A	N/A	N/A	24.9	23.9	22.3	22.9	21.8	21.0	N/A
5 Private services producing (%)	N/A	N/A	N/A	N/A	N/A	75.1	76.1	77.7	77.1	78.2	79.0	N/A
6 New business starts (thousands) [2]	N/A	N/A	452	477	513	482	544	385	404	414	N/A	N/A
7 Business failures (thousands) [3]	N/A	N/A	371	371	386	406	416	417	392	396	N/A	N/A
8 International trade balance (billions of dollars; + surplus / - deficit) [4]	3.5	2.3	–19.4	–80.9	–96.4	–372.5	–714.2	–494.7	–490.3	–500.4	–504.8	N/A
Jobs and Unemployment												
9 Labor force participation rate (%)	59.4	60.4	63.8	66.5	66.6	67.1	66.0	64.7	62.9	62.7	62.8	62.9
10 Employment (millions)	65.8	78.7	99.3	118.8	124.9	136.9	141.7	139.1	146.3	148.8	151.4	153.3
11 Employment-population ratio (%)	56.1	57.4	59.2	62.8	62.9	64.4	62.7	58.5	59.0	59.3	59.7	60.1
12 Payroll employment change - December to December, SA (millions)	–0.4	–0.5	0.3	0.0	2.2	2.0	2.5	1.1	3.0	2.7	2.2	2.1
13 Payroll employment change - 5-year annual average, NSA (millions)	0.7	2.0	2.7	2.8	1.6	2.9	0.4	–0.7	1.5	2.3	2.5	2.5
14 Civilian unemployment rate (%)	5.5	4.9	7.1	5.6	5.6	4.0	5.1	9.6	6.2	5.3	4.9	4.4
15 Unemployment plus marginally attached and underemployed (%)	N/A	N/A	N/A	N/A	10.1	7.0	8.9	16.7	12.0	10.4	9.6	8.5
16 Receiving Social Security disabled-worker benefits (% of population) [5]	0.9	2.0	2.8	2.5	3.3	3.7	4.5	5.5	6.0	5.8	5.7	N/A
Infrastructure, Innovation, and Capital Investment												
17 Nonfarm business output per hour (average 5 year % change) [6]	1.8	2.1	1.2	1.6	1.6	2.8	3.2	1.9	1.1	0.6	0.6	N/A
18 Corn for grain production (million bushels)	3,907	4,152	6,639	7,934	7,400	9,915	11,112	12,425	14,216	13,601	15,148	14,578
19 Real net stock of fixed assets and consumer durable goods (billions of chained 2009 dollars)	11,383	16,921	23,265	30,870	34,246	40,217	46,305	50,332	52,943	53,814	54,659	N/A
20 Population served by secondary wastewater treatment or better (%) [7]	N/A	41.6	56.4	63.7	61.1	71.4	74.3	72.0	74.5	N/A	N/A	N/A
21 Electricity net generation (kWh per capita)	4,202	7,486	10,076	12,170	12,594	13,475	13,723	13,335	12,850	12,707	12,624	N/A
22 Patents for invention, U.S. origin (per million population) [8]	N/A	231	164	190	209	301	253	348	453	439	N/A	N/A
23 Net national saving rate (% of GDP)	10.9	8.5	7.1	3.9	4.0	5.9	2.7	–0.8	3.5	3.7	2.3	N/A
24 R&D spending (% of GDP) [9]	2.52	2.44	2.21	2.54	2.40	2.61	2.48	2.72	2.73	2.73	2.74	N/A
Demographic and Civic												
Population												
25 Total population (millions) [10]	N/A	204.0	227.2	249.6	266.3	282.2	295.5	309.3	318.6	320.9	323.1	325.7
26 Foreign born population (millions) [11]	9.7	9.6	14.1	19.8	N/A	31.1	37.5	40.0	42.4	43.3	43.7	N/A
27 17 years and younger (%) [10]	N/A	N/A	28.0	25.7	26.1	25.7	24.9	24.0	23.1	22.9	22.8	22.6
28 65 years and older (%) [10]	N/A	9.8	11.3	12.5	12.7	12.4	12.4	13.1	14.5	14.9	15.2	N/A
29 85 years and older (%) [10]	N/A	0.7	1.0	1.2	1.4	1.5	1.6	1.8	1.9	2.0	2.0	N/A
Household Composition												
30 Ever married (% of age 15 and older) [12]	78.0	75.1	74.1	73.8	72.9	71.9	70.9	69.3	68.3	68.2	67.8	68.0
31 Average family size [13]	3.7	3.6	3.3	3.2	3.2	3.2	3.1	3.2	3.1	3.1	3.1	3.1
32 Births to unmarried women age 15–17 (per 1,000 unmarried women age 15–17)	N/A	17.1	20.6	29.6	30.1	23.9	19.4	16.8	10.6	9.6	8.6	N/A
33 Single parent households (%)	4.4	5.2	7.5	8.3	9.1	8.9	8.9	9.1	8.9	8.8	8.7	8.4
Civic and Cultural Engagement												
34 Average charitable contribution per itemized tax return (2015 dollars) [14]	2,242	2,224	2,566	3,226	3,430	4,552	4,569	3,966	4,795	4,978	N/A	N/A
35 Voting for President (% of voting age population) [15]	63.4	57.0	55.1	56.4	49.8	52.1	56.7	58.3	54.9	N/A	55.7	N/A
36 Persons volunteering (% age 16 and older) [16]	N/A	N/A	N/A	20.4	N/A	N/A	28.9	26.3	25.3	24.9	N/A	N/A
37 Attendance at visual or performing arts activity, including movie-going (% age 18 and older) [17]	N/A	N/A	71.7	72.1	N/A	70.1	N/A	63.9	N/A	66.5	N/A	N/A
38 Reading: Novels or short stories, poetry, or plays (not required for work or school; % age 18 and older) [17]	N/A	N/A	56.4	54.2	N/A	46.6	N/A	50.2	N/A	43.1	N/A	N/A

Table 5–1. SOCIAL INDICATORS—Continued

	Calendar Years	1960	1970	1980	1990	1995	2000	2005	2010	2014	2015	2016	2017
	Socioeconomic												
	Education												
39	High school graduates (% of age 25–34) [18]	58.1	71.5	84.2	84.1	N/A	83.9	86.4	87.2	89.1	89.7	90.1	N/A
40	College graduates (% of age 25–34) [19]	11.0	15.5	23.3	22.7	N/A	27.5	29.9	31.1	33.5	34.1	34.9	N/A
41	Reading achievement score (age 17) [20]	N/A	285	285	290	288	288	283	286	N/A	N/A	N/A	N/A
42	Math achievement score (age 17) [21]	N/A	304	298	305	306	308	305	306	N/A	N/A	N/A	N/A
43	Science and engineering graduate degrees (% of total graduate degrees)	22.0	17.2	11.2	14.7	14.2	12.6	12.7	12.1	13.7	15.0	16.3	N/A
44	Receiving special education services (% of age 3–21 public school students)	N/A	N/A	10.1	11.4	12.4	13.3	13.7	13.0	13.0	13.2	N/A	N/A
	Income, Savings, and Inequality												
45	Real median income: all households (2016 dollars) [22]	N/A	48,194	49,131	53,350	53,330	58,544	56,935	54,245	54,398	57,230	59,039	N/A
46	Real disposable income per capita (chained 2009 dollars)	11,877	16,643	20,158	25,555	27,180	31,524	34,424	35,685	37,441	38,720	38,988	N/A
47	Adjusted gross income share of top 1% of all taxpayers	N/A	N/A	8.5	14.0	14.6	20.8	21.2	18.9	20.6	20.7	N/A	N/A
48	Adjusted gross income share of lower 50% of all taxpayers	N/A	N/A	17.7	15.0	14.5	13.0	12.9	11.7	11.3	11.3	N/A	N/A
49	Personal saving rate (% of disposable personal income)	10.0	12.6	10.6	7.8	6.4	4.2	2.6	5.6	5.7	6.1	4.9	N/A
50	Foreign remittances (billions of 2016 dollars) [23]	N/A	N/A	N/A	N/A	N/A	32.6	38.5	40.5	42.4	44.8	46.5	N/A
51	Poverty rate (%) [24]	22.2	12.6	13.0	13.5	13.8	11.3	12.6	15.1	14.8	13.5	12.7	N/A
52	Food-insecure households (% of all households) [25]	N/A	N/A	N/A	N/A	11.9	10.5	11.0	14.5	14.0	12.7	12.3	N/A
53	Supplemental Nutrition Assistance Program (% of population on SNAP)	N/A	3.3	9.5	8.2	9.9	6.1	8.9	13.1	14.7	14.3	13.7	13.0
54	Median wealth of households, age 55–64 (in thousands of 2016 dollars) [26]	80	N/A	158	183	180	251	321	198	171	N/A	187	N/A
	Housing												
55	Homeownership among households with children (%) [27]	N/A	N/A	N/A	63.6	65.1	67.5	68.4	65.5	61.0	59.5	N/A	N/A
56	Families with children and severe housing cost burden (%) [28]	N/A	N/A	8	10	12	11	14.5	17.9	15.4	15.1	N/A	N/A
57	Families with children and inadequate housing (%) [29]	N/A	N/A	9	9	7	7	5.4	5.3	5.6	6.3	N/A	N/A
	Health												
	Health Status												
58	Life expectancy at birth (years)	69.7	70.8	73.7	75.4	75.8	76.8	77.6	78.7	78.9	78.7	78.6	N/A
59	Infant mortality (per 1,000 live births)	26.0	20.0	12.6	9.2	7.6	6.9	6.9	6.1	5.8	5.9	5.9	N/A
60	Low birthweight [<2,500 gms] (% of babies)	7.7	7.9	6.8	7.0	7.3	7.6	8.2	8.2	8.0	8.1	8.2	N/A
61	Disability (% of age 18 and over) [30]	N/A	N/A	N/A	N/A	N/A	N/A	N/A	8.9	9.9	9.5	8.6	N/A
62	Disability (% of age 65 and over) [30]	N/A	N/A	N/A	N/A	N/A	N/A	N/A	22.6	21.6	21.6	18.2	N/A
	Health Behavior												
63	Engaged in regular physical activity (% of age 18 and older) [31]	N/A	N/A	N/A	N/A	N/A	15.0	16.6	20.7	21.5	21.6	22.7	N/A
64	Obesity (% of age 20–74 with BMI 30 or greater) [32]	13.4	N/A	15.0	23.2	N/A	30.9	35.1	36.1	38.2	N/A	40.0	N/A
65	Obesity (% of age 2–19) [33]	N/A	N/A	5.5	10.0	N/A	13.9	15.4	16.9	17.2	N/A	18.5	N/A
66	Cigarette smokers (% of age 18 and older)	N/A	37.1	33.1	25.3	24.6	23.1	20.8	19.3	17.0	15.3	15.9	N/A
67	Heavier drinker (% of age 18 and older) [34]	N/A	N/A	N/A	N/A	N/A	4.3	4.8	5.2	5.2	5.0	5.3	N/A
	Access to Health Care												
68	Total national health expenditures (% of GDP)	5.0	6.9	8.9	12.1	13.3	13.3	15.5	17.4	17.4	17.7	17.9	N/A
69	Average total single premium per enrolled employee at private-sector establishments (2016 dollars) [35]	N/A	N/A	N/A	N/A	N/A	3,700	4,905	5,437	5,913	6,038	6,101	N/A
70	Average health insurance premium paid by an individual or family (2016 dollars) [36]	N/A	N/A	N/A	N/A	N/A	N/A	N/A	3,062	3,438	3,547	3,657	N/A
71	Persons without health insurance (% of age 18–64) [37]	N/A	N/A	N/A	N/A	16.9	18.9	19.3	22.3	16.3	13.0	12.2	N/A
72	Persons without health insurance (% of age 17 and younger) [37]	N/A	N/A	N/A	N/A	13.0	12.6	9.3	7.8	5.5	4.5	5.2	N/A
73	Children age 19–35 months with recommended vaccinations (%) [38]	N/A	N/A	N/A	N/A	N/A	N/A	N/A	56.6	71.6	72.2	70.7	N/A
	Security and Safety												
	Crime												
74	Property crimes (per 100,000 households) [39]	N/A	N/A	49,610	34,890	31,547	19,043	15,947	12,541	11,806	11,072	11,944	N/A
75	Violent crime victimizations (per 100,000 population age 12 or older) [40]	N/A	N/A	4,940	4,410	7,068	3,749	2,842	1,928	2,010	1,858	2,112	N/A
76	Murder rate (per 100,000 persons)	5.1	7.9	10.2	9.4	8.2	5.5	5.6	4.8	4.4	4.9	5.3	N/A
77	Prison incarceration rate (state and federal institutions, rate per 100,000 persons) [41]	118.8	95.8	145.6	311.9	430.4	508.8	518.2	523.3	491.7	476.7	N/A	N/A

Table 5-1. SOCIAL INDICATORS—Continued

Calendar Years	1960	1970	1980	1990	1995	2000	2005	2010	2014	2015	2016	2017
National Security												
78 Military personnel on active duty (thousands) [42]	2,475	3,065	2,051	2,044	1,518	1,384	1,389	1,431	1,338	1,314	1,301	1,307
79 Veterans (thousands)	22,534	26,976	28,640	27,320	26,198	26,206	24,542	22,668	21,250	20,784	20,392	19,999
Transportation Safety												
80 Safety belt use (%)	N/A	N/A	N/A	N/A	N/A	70.7	81.7	85.1	86.7	88.5	90.1	89.7
81 Highway fatalities	36,399	52,627	51,091	44,599	41,817	41,945	43,510	32,999	32,744	35,485	37,461	N/A
Environment and Energy												
Air Quality and Greenhouse Gases												
82 Ground level ozone (ppm) [43]	N/A	N/A	0.10	0.09	0.09	0.08	0.08	0.07	0.07	0.07	0.07	N/A
83 Particulate matter 2.5 (ug/m3) [44]	N/A	N/A	N/A	N/A	N/A	13.4	12.8	9.9	8.8	8.5	7.8	N/A
84 Annual mean atmospheric CO_2 concentration (Mauna Loa, Hawaii; ppm)	316.9	325.7	338.7	354.4	360.8	369.5	379.8	389.9	398.6	400.8	404.2	406.5
85 Gross greenhouse gas emissions (teragrams CO_2 equivalent) [45]	N/A	N/A	N/A	6,363	6,709	7,214	7,313	6,926	6,740	6,587	N/A	N/A
86 Net greenhouse gas emissions, including sinks (teragrams CO_2 equivalent)	N/A	N/A	N/A	5,544	5,923	6,462	6,582	6,208	5,978	5,828	N/A	N/A
87 Gross greenhouse gas emissions per capita (metric tons CO_2 equivalent)	N/A	N/A	N/A	25.1	24.8	25.2	24.4	22.1	20.9	20.2	N/A	N/A
88 Gross greenhouse gas emissions per 2009$ of GDP (kilograms CO_2 equivalent)	N/A	N/A	N/A	0.71	0.66	0.57	0.51	0.47	0.42	0.40	N/A	N/A
89 Population that receives drinking water in compliance with standards (%) [46]	N/A	N/A	N/A	N/A	83.8	90.8	88.5	92.2	92.5	91.1	91.2	N/A
Energy												
90 Energy consumption per capita (million Btu)	250	331	344	338	342	350	339	315	309	303	302	N/A
91 Energy consumption per 2009$ GDP (thousand Btu per 2009$)	14.5	14.4	12.1	9.4	9.0	7.9	7.0	6.6	6.2	5.9	5.9	N/A
92 Electricity net generation from renewable sources, all sectors (% of total) [47]	19.7	16.4	12.4	11.8	11.5	9.4	8.8	10.4	13.2	13.3	14.9	N/A
93 Coal production (million short tons)	434	613	830	1,029	1,033	1,074	1,131	1,084	1,000	897	728	N/A
94 Natural gas production (dry) (trillion cubic feet) [48]	12.2	21.0	19.4	17.8	18.6	19.2	18.1	21.3	25.9	27.1	26.7	N/A
95 Petroleum production (million barrels per day)	8.0	11.3	10.2	8.9	8.3	7.7	6.9	7.5	11.8	12.8	12.4	N/A
96 Renewable energy production (quadrillion Btu)	2.9	4.1	5.4	6.0	6.6	6.1	6.2	8.1	9.6	9.5	10.2	N/A

N/A=Number is not available.

[1] Adjusted CPI-U. 2014=100.

[2] New business starts are defined as firms with positive employment in the current year and no paid employment in any prior year of the LBD. Employment is measured as of the payroll period including March 12th.

[3] Business failures are defined as firms with employment in the prior year that have no paid employees in the current year.

[4] Calculated as the value of U.S. exports of goods and services less the value of U.S. imports of goods and services, on a balance of payments basis. This balance is a component of the U.S. International Transactions Balance of Payments) Accounts.

[5] Gross prevalence rate for persons receiving Social Security disabled-worker benefits among the estimated population insured in the event of disability at end of year. Gross rates do not account for changes in the age and sex composition of the insured population over time.

[6] Values for prior years have been revised from the prior version of this publication.

[7] Data correspond to years 1972, 1982, 1992, 1996, 2000, 2004, 2008, and 2012.

[8] Patent data adjusted by OMB to incorporate total population estimates from U.S. Census Bureau.

[9] The data point for 2016 is estimated and may be revised in the next report of this time series. The R&D to GDP ratio data reflect the new methodology introduced in the 2013 comprehensive revision of the GDP and other National Income and Product Accounts by the U.S. Bureau of Economic Analysis BEA). In late July 2013, BEA reported GDP and related statistics that were revised back to 1929. The new GDP methodology treats R&D as investment in all sectors of the economy, among other methodological changes. For further details see NSF's InfoBrief "R&D Recognized as Investment in U.S. Gross Domestic Product Statistics: GDP Increase Slightly Lowers R&D-to-GDP Ratio" at http://www.nsf.gov/statistics/2015/nsf15315/nsf15315.pdf.

[10] Data source and values for 2010 to 2016 have been updated relative to the prior version of this publication.

[11] Data source for 1960 to 2000 is the decennial census; data source for 2006, 2010, 2011, 2012, 2013, 2014, 2015, and 2016 is the American Community Survey.

[12] For 1960, age 14 and older.

[13] Average size of family households. Family households are those in which there is someone present who is related to the householder by birth, marriage, or adoption.

[14] Charitable giving reported as itemized deductions on Schedule A.

[15] Data correspond to years 1964, 1972, 1980, 1992, 1996, 2000, 2004, 2008, 2012 and 2016. The voting statistics in this table are presented as ratios of official voting tallies, as reported by the U.S. Clerk of the House, to population estimates from the Current Population Survey.

[16] Refers to those who volunteered at least once during a one-year period, from September of the previous year to September of the year specified. For 1990, refers to 1989 estimate from the CPS Supplement on volunteers.

[17] The 1980, 1990, 2000, and 2010 data come from the 1982, 1992, 2002, and 2008 waves of the Survey of Public Participation in the Arts, respectively.

[18] For 1960, includes those who have completed 4 years of high school or beyond. For 1970 and 1980, includes those who have completed 12 years of school or beyond. For 1990 onward, includes those who have completed a high school diploma or the equivalent.

[19] For 1960 to 1980, includes those who have completed 4 or more years of college. From 1990 onward, includes those who have a bachelor's degree or higher.

[20] Data correspond to years 1971, 1980, 1990, 1994, 1999, 2004, 2008, and 2012.

Table 5–1. SOCIAL INDICATORS—Continued

[21] Data correspond to years 1973, 1982, 1990, 1994, 1999, 2004, 2008, and 2012.

[22] Beginning with 2013, data are based on redesigned income questions. The source of the 2013 data is a portion of the CPS ASEC sample which received the redesigned income questions, approximately 30,000 addresses. For more information, please see the report Income and Poverty in the United States: 2014, U.S. Census Bureau, Current Population Reports, P60-252.

[23] Foreign remittances, referred to as 'personal transfers' in the U.S. International Transactions Balance of Payments) Accounts, consist of all transfers in cash or in kind sent by the foreign-born population resident in the United States to households resident abroad. Adjusted by OMB to 2016 dollars using the CPI-U.

[24] The poverty rate does not reflect noncash government transfers. Beginning with 2013, data are based on redesigned income questions. The source of the 2013 data is a portion of the CPS ASEC sample which received the redesigned income questions, approximately 30,000 addresses. For more information, please see the report Income and Poverty in the United States: 2014, U.S. Census Bureau, Current Population Reports, P60-252.

[25] Food-insecure classification is based on reports of three or more conditions that characterize households when they are having difficulty obtaining adequate food, out of a total of 10 such conditions.

[26] Data values shown are 1962, 1983, 1989, 1995, 2001, 2004, 2010, 2013, and 2016. For 1962, the data source is the SFCC; for subsequent years, the data source is the SCF

[27] Some data interpolated.

[28] Expenditures for housing and utilities exceed 50 percent of reported income. Some data interpolated.

[29] Inadequate housing has moderate to severe problems, usually poor plumbing, or heating or upkeep problems. Some data interpolated.

[30] Disability is defined by level of difficulty in six domains of functioning: vision, hearing, mobility, communication, cognition, and self-care. Persons indicating "a lot of difficulty," or "cannot do at all/unable to do" in at least one domain are considered to have a "Disability."

[31] Participation in leisure-time aerobic and muscle-strengthening activities that meet 2008 Federal physical activity guidelines.

[32] BMI refers to body mass index. The 1960, 1980, 1990, 2000, 2005, 2010, 2014, 2016 data correspond to survey years 1960-1962, 1976-1980, 1988-1994, 1999-2000, 2005-2006, 2009-2010, 2013-2014, and 2015-2016, respectively.

[33] Percentage at or above the sex-and age-specific 95th percentile BMI cutoff points from the 2000 CDC growth charts. The 1980, 1990, 2000, 2005, 2010, 2014, 2016 data correspond to survey years 1976-1980, 1988-1994, 1999-2000, 2005-2006, 2009-2010, 2013-2014, and 2015-2016, respectively.

[34] Heavier drinking is based on self-reported responses to questions about average alcohol consumption and is defined as, on average, more than 14 drinks per week for men and more than 7 drinks per week for women.

[35] Includes only employees of private-sector establishments that offer health insurance. Adjusted to 2016 dollars by OMB.

[36] Unpublished data. This is the mean total private health insurance premium paid by an individual or family for the private coverage that person is on. If a person is covered by more than one plan, the premiums for the plans are added together. Those who pay no premiums towards their plans are included in the estimates. Adjusted to 2016 dollars by OMB.

[37] A person was defined as uninsured if he or she did not have any private health insurance, Medicare, Medicaid, CHIP (1999-2016), state-sponsored, other government-sponsored health plan (1997-2016), or military plan. Beginning in 2014, a person with health insurance coverage through the Health Insurance Marketplace or state-based exchanges was considered to have private coverage. A person was also defined as uninsured if he or she had only Indian Health Service coverage or had only a private plan that paid for one type of service such as accidents or dental care. In 1993-1996 Medicaid coverage is estimated through a survey question about having Medicaid in the past month and through participation in Aid to Families with Dependent Children (AFDC) or Supplemental Security Income (SSI) programs. In 1997 to 2016, Medicaid coverage is estimated through a question about current Medicaid coverage. Beginning in the third quarter of 2004, a Medicaid probe question was added to reduce potential errors in reporting Medicaid status. Persons under age 65 with no reported coverage were asked explicitly about Medicaid coverage.

[38] Recommended vaccine series consists of 4 or more doses of either the diphtheria, tetanus toxoids, and pertussis vaccine (DTP), the diphtheria and tetanus toxoids vaccine (DT), or the diphtheria, tetanus toxoids, and acellular pertussis vaccine (DTaP); 3 or more doses of any poliovirus vaccine; 1 or more doses of a measles-containing vaccine (MCV); 3 or more doses or 4 or more doses of Haemophilus influenzae type b vaccine (Hib) depending on Hib vaccine product type (full series Hib); 3 or more doses of hepatitis B vaccine; 1 or more doses of varicella vaccine; and 4 or more doses of pneumococcal conjugate vaccine (PCV).

[39] Property crimes, including burglary, motor vehicle theft, and property theft, reported by a sample of households. Includes property crimes both reported and not reported to law enforcement. Due to methodological changes in the 2016 NCVS, use caution when comparing 2016 criminal victimization estimates to other years. See Criminal Victimization, 2016 (BJS Web, NCJ 251150, December, 2017) for more information.

[40] Violent crimes include rape, robbery, aggravated assault, and simple assault. Includes crimes both reported and not reported to law enforcement. Due to methodological changes in the enumeration method for NCVS estimates from 1993 to present, use caution when comparing 1980 and 1990 criminal victimization estimates to future years. Estimates from 1995 and beyond include a small number of victimizations, referred to as series victimizations, using a new counting strategy. High-frequency repeat victimizations, or series victimizations, are six or more similar but separate victimizations that occur with such frequency that the victim is unable to recall each individual event or describe each event in detail. Including series victimizations in national estimates can substantially increase the number and rate of violent victimization; however, trends in violence are generally similar regardless of whether series victimizations are included. See Methods for Counting High-Frequency Repeat Victimizations in the National Crime Victimization Survey, NCJ 237308, BJS web, April 2012 for further discussion of the new counting strategy and supporting research. Due to methodological changes in the 2016 NCVS, use caution when comparing 2016 criminal victimization estimates to other years. See Criminal Victimization, 2016 (BJS Web, NCJ 251150, December, 2017) for more information.

[41] Prior to 1977, the National Prisoners Statistics (NPS) Program reports were based on custody population. Beginning in 1977, the report reoriented to jurisdiction population. Generally, State inmates housed in local jails because of overcrowding are considered to be under State jurisdiction. Most, but not all, States reserve prison for offenders sentenced to a year or more.

[42] For all years, the actuals reflect Active Component only excluding full-time Reserve Component members and RC mobilized to active duty. End Strength for 2017 is preliminary.

[43] Ambient ozone concentrations based on 206 monitoring sites meeting minimum completeness criteria.

[44] Ambient PM2.5 concentrations based on 455 monitoring sites meeting minimum completeness criteria.

[45] The gross emissions indicator does not include sinks, which are processes (sometimes naturally occurring) that remove greenhouse gases from the atmosphere. Gross emissions are therefore more indicative of trends in energy consumption and efficiency than are net emissions.

[46] Percent of the population served by community water systems that receive drinking water that meets all applicable health - based drinking water standards.

[47] Includes net generation from solar thermal and photovoltaic (PV) energy at utility-scale facilities. Does not include distributed (small-scale) solar thermal or photovoltaic generation.

[48] Dry natural gas is also known as consumer-grade natural gas.

Table 5–2. SOURCES FOR SOCIAL INDICATORS

	Indicator	Source
	Economic	
	General Economic Conditions	
1	Real GDP per person (chained 2009 dollars)	Bureau of Economic Analysis, National Economic Accounts Data. http://www.bea.gov/national/
2	Real GDP per person change, 5-year annual average	Bureau of Economic Analysis, National Economic Accounts Data. http://www.bea.gov/national/
3	Consumer Price Index	Bureau of Labor Statistics, BLS Consumer Price Index Program. https://www.bls.gov/cpi/
4	Private goods producing (%)	Bureau of Economic Analysis, National Economic Accounts Data. http://www.bea.gov/national/
5	Private services producing (%)	Bureau of Economic Analysis, National Economic Accounts Data. http://www.bea.gov/national/
6	New business starts (thousands)	U.S. Census Bureau, Business Dynamics Statistics. https://www.census.gov/ces/dataproducts/bds/
7	Business failures (thousands)	U.S. Census Bureau, Business Dynamics Statistics. https://www.census.gov/ces/dataproducts/bds/
8	International trade balance (billions of dollars; + surplus	Bureau of Economic Analysis, International Economics Accounts, https://www.bea.gov/International/index.htm
	Jobs and Unemployment	
9	Labor force participation rate (%)	Bureau of Labor Statistics, Current Population Survey. https://www.bls.gov/cps
10	Employment (millions)	Bureau of Labor Statistics, Current Population Survey. https://www.bls.gov/cps
11	Employment-population ratio (%)	Bureau of Labor Statistics, Current Population Survey. https://www.bls.gov/cps
12	Payroll employment change - December to December, SA (millions)	Bureau of Labor Statistics, Current Employment Statistics program. https://www.bls.gov/ces/
13	Payroll employment change - 5-year annual average, NSA (millions)	Bureau of Labor Statistics, Current Employment Statistics program. https://www.bls.gov/ces/
14	Civilian unemployment rate (%)	Bureau of Labor Statistics, Current Population Survey. https://www.bls.gov/cps
15	Unemployment plus marginally attached and underemployed (%)	Bureau of Labor Statistics, Current Population Survey. https://www.bls.gov/cps
16	Receiving Social Security disabled-worker benefits (% of population)	Social Security Administration, Office of Research, Evaluation, and Statistics, Annual Statistical Supplement to the Social Security Bulletin, (tables 4.C1 and 5.A4). http://www.ssa.gov/policy/docs/statcomps/supplement/
	Infrastructure, Innovation, and Capital Investment	
17	Nonfarm business output per hour (average 5 year % change)	Bureau of Labor Statistics, Major Sector Productivity Program. https://www.bls.gov/lpc/
18	Corn for grain production (million bushels)	National Agricultural Statistics Service, Agricultural Estimates Program. http://www.nass.usda.gov/
19	Real net stock of fixed assets and consumer durable goods (billions of chained 2009 dollars)	Bureau of Economic Analysis, National Economic Accounts Data. http://www.bea.gov/national/
20	Population served by secondary wastewater treatment or better (%)	U.S. Environmental Protection Agency, Clean Watersheds Needs Survey. http://www.epa.gov/cwns
21	Electricity net generation (kWh per capita)	U.S. Energy Information Administration (EIA) calculation from: EIA, Monthly Energy Review (October 2017); and Table 7.2a https://www.eia.gov/totalenergy/data/monthly; and U.S. Census Bureau, Population Division, Vintage 2016 Population Estimates (2010-2016) https://www.census.gov/data/tables/2016/demo/popest/nation-total.html
22	Patents for invention, U.S. origin (per million population)	U.S. Patent and Trademark Office, Patent Technology Monitoring Team, U.S. Patent Statistics Chart, Calendar Years 1963-2015. https://www.uspto.gov/web/offices/ac/ido/oeip/taf/us_stat.htm; and, U.S. Census Bureau, Population Division.
23	Net national saving rate (% of GDP)	Bureau of Economic Analysis, National Economic Accounts Data. http://www.bea.gov/national/
24	R&D spending (% of GDP)	National Science Foundation, National Patterns of R&D Resources. http://www.nsf.gov/statistics/natlpatterns/
	Demographic and Civic	
	Population	
25	Total population (millions)	U.S. Census Bureau, Population Division, Vintage 2017 Population Estimates (2017), Vintage 2016 Population Estimates (2010-2016), 2000-2010 Intercensal Estimates (2000-2005), 1990-1999 Intercensal Estimates (1990-1995), 1980-1990 Intercensal Estimates (1980), 1970-1980 Intercensal Estimates (1970).

TABLE 5–2.   SOURCES FOR SOCIAL INDICATORS—Continued

	Indicator	Source
26	Foreign born population (millions)	U.S. Census Bureau, Population Division, Decennial Census and American Community Survey. http://www.census.gov/prod/www/abs/decennial/ and http://www.census.gov/acs
27	17 years and younger (%)	U.S. Census Bureau, Population Division, Vintage 2017 Population Estimates (2017), Vintage 2016 Population Estimates (2010-2016), 2000-2010 Intercensal Estimates (2000-2005), 1990-1999 Intercensal Estimates (1990-1995), 1980-1990 Intercensal Estimates (1980), 1970-1980 Intercensal Estimates (1970).
28	65 years and older (%)	U.S. Census Bureau, Population Division, Vintage 2017 Population Estimates (2017), Vintage 2016 Population Estimates (2010-2016), 2000-2010 Intercensal Estimates (2000-2005), 1990-1999 Intercensal Estimates (1990-1995), 1980-1990 Intercensal Estimates (1980), 1970-1980 Intercensal Estimates (1970).
29	85 years and older (%)	U.S. Census Bureau, Population Division, Vintage 2017 Population Estimates (2017), Vintage 2016 Population Estimates (2010-2016), 2000-2010 Intercensal Estimates (2000-2005), 1990-1999 Intercensal Estimates (1990-1995), 1980-1990 Intercensal Estimates (1980), 1970-1980 Intercensal Estimates (1970).
	Household Composition	
30	Ever married (% of age 15 and older)	U.S. Census Bureau, Current Population Survey. http://www.census.gov/hhes/families/
31	Average family size	U.S. Census Bureau, Current Population Survey. http://www.census.gov/hhes/families/
32	Births to unmarried women age 15-17 (per 1,000 unmarried women age 15-17)	National Center for Health Statistics, National Vital Statistics System (natality); Births: Final data for 2016 forthcoming.
33	Single parent households (%)	U.S. Census Bureau, Current Population Survey. http://www.census.gov/hhes/families/
	Civic and Cultural Engagement	
34	Average charitable contribution per itemized tax return (2015 dollars)	U.S. Internal Revenue Service, Statistics of Income - Individual Income Tax Returns (IRS Publication 1304). http://www.irs.gov/uac/SOI-Tax-Stats-Individual-Income-Tax-Returns-Publication-1304-(Complete-Report)
35	Voting for President (% of voting age population)	The Office of the Clerk of the U.S. House of Representatives and the U.S. Census Bureau, Current Population Survey. http://www.census.gov/cps/
36	Persons volunteering (% age 16 and older)	Corporation for National and Community Service, Volunteering and Civic Life in America, https://data.nationalservice.gov/Volunteering-and-Civic-Engagement/Volunteering-and-Civic-Life-in-America/spx3-tt2b/data
37	Attendance at visual or performing arts activity, including movie-going (% age 18 and older)	The National Endowment for the Arts, Survey of Public Participation in the Arts & Annual Arts Basic Survey.
38	Reading: Novels or short stories, poetry, or plays (not required for work or school; % age 18 and older)	The National Endowment for the Arts, Survey of Public Participation in the Arts & Annual Arts Basic Survey.
	Socioeconomic	
	Education	
39	High school graduates (% of age 25-34)	U.S. Census Bureau, Decennial Census and American Community Survey. http://www.census.gov/prod/www/decennial.html and http://www.census.gov/acs
40	College graduates (% of age 25-34)	U.S. Census Bureau, Decennial Census and American Community Survey. http://www.census.gov/prod/www/decennial.html and http://www.census.gov/acs
41	Reading achievement score (age 17)	National Center for Education Statistics, National Assessment of Educational Progress. https://nces.ed.gov/nationsreportcard/
42	Math achievement score (age 17)	National Center for Education Statistics, National Assessment of Educational Progress. https://nces.ed.gov/nationsreportcard/
43	Science and engineering graduate degrees (% of total graduate degrees)	National Center for Education Statistics, Integrated Postsecondary Education Data System. http://nces.ed.gov/ipeds/
44	Receiving special education services (% of age 3-21 public school students)	National Center for Education Statistics, Digest of Education Statistics, 2012. http://nces.ed.gov/programs/digest/d12/tables/dt12_046.asp
	Income, Savings, and Inequality	
45	Real median income: all households (2014 dollars)	U.S. Census Bureau, Current Population Survey, Annual Social and Economic Supplements. http://www.census.gov/hhes/www/income/data/historical/household/
46	Real disposable income per capita (chained 2009 dollars)	Bureau of Economic Analysis, National Economic Accounts Data. http://www.bea.gov/national/
47	Adjusted gross income share of top 1% of all taxpayers	U.S. Internal Revenue Service, Statistics of Income. http://www.irs.gov/uac/SOI-Tax-Stats-Individual-Statistical-Tables-by-Tax-Rate-and-Income-Percentile
48	Adjusted gross income share of lower 50% of all taxpayers	U.S. Internal Revenue Service, Statistics of Income. http://www.irs.gov/uac/SOI-Tax-Stats-Individual-Statistical-Tables-by-Tax-Rate-and-Income-Percentile

TABLE 5–2. SOURCES FOR SOCIAL INDICATORS—Continued

	Indicator	Source
49	Personal saving rate (% of disposable personal income)	Bureau of Economic Analysis, National Economic Accounts Data. http://www.bea.gov/national/
50	Foreign remittances (billions of 2016 dollars)	Bureau of Economic Analysis, International Economics Accounts, https://www.bea.gov/International/index.htm
51	Poverty rate (%)	U.S. Census Bureau, Current Population Survey, Annual Social and Economic Supplements. http://www.census.gov/hhes/www/poverty/publications/pubs-cps.html
52	Food-insecure households (% of all households)	Economic Research Service, Household Food Security in the United States report series. http://www.ers.usda.gov/topics/food-nutrition-assistance/food-security-in-the-us/readings.aspx
53	Supplemental Nutrition Assistance Program (% of population on SNAP)	Food and Nutrition Service, USDA
54	Median wealth of households, age 55-64 (in thousands of 2016 dollars)	Board of Governors of the Federal Reserve System, Survey of Consumer Finances 2013 Estimates inflation-adjusted to 2013 dollars (Internal Data) http://www.federalreserve.gov/econresdata/scf/scfindex.htm
	Housing	
55	Homeownership among households with children (%)	U.S. Census Bureau, American Housing Survey (Current Housing Report). Estimated by Housing and Urban Development's Office of Policy Development and Research. http://www.census.gov/housing/ahs
56	Families with children and severe housing cost burden (%)	U.S. Census Bureau, American Housing Survey. Tabulated by Housing and Urban Development's Office of Policy Development and Research. http://www.census.gov/housing/ahs
57	Families with children and inadequate housing (%)	U.S. Census Bureau, American Housing Survey. Tabulated by Housing and Urban Development's Office of Policy Development and Research. http://www.census.gov/housing/ahs
	Health	
	Health Status	
58	Life expectancy at birth (years)	National Center for Health Statistics, National Vital Statistics System: Health, United States 2017 forthcoming, Table 15.
59	Infant mortality (per 1,000 live births)	National Center for Health Statistics, National Vital Statistics System: Health, United States, 2017 forthcoming, Table 11.
60	Low birthweight [<2,500 gms] (% of babies)	National Center for Health Statistics, National Vital Statistics System (natality); Births: Final data for 2016 forthcoming.
61	Disability (% of age 18 and over)	National Center for Health Statistics, National Health Interview Survey, http://www.cdc.gov/nchs/nhis.htm
62	Disability (% of age 65 and over)	National Center for Health Statistics, National Health Interview Survey, http://www.cdc.gov/nchs/nhis.htm
	Health Behavior	
63	Engaged in regular physical activity (% of age 18 and older)	National Center for Health Statistics, National Health Interview Survey, http://www.cdc.gov/nchs/nhis.htm: Health, United States, 2017 forthcoming, Table 57, age adjusted.
64	Obesity (% of age 20-74 with BMI 30 or greater)	National Center for Health Statistics, National Health and Nutrition Examination Survey, http://www.cdc.gov/nchs/nhanes.htm. Health E-stat: http://www.cdc.gov/nchs/data/hestat/obesity_adult_13_14/obesity_adult_13_14.pdf and unpublished data (2016 data), age-adjusted
65	Obesity (% of age 2-19)	National Center for Health Statistics, National Health and Nutrition Examination Survey, http://www.cdc.gov/nchs/nhanes.htm. Health E-stat: http://www.cdc.gov/nchs/data/hestat/obesity_child_13_14/obesity_child_13_14.pdf. Hales CM, Carroll MD, Fryar CD, Ogden CL. Prevalence of obesity among adults and youth: United States, 2015-2016. NCHS data brief, no 288. Hyattsville, MD: National Center for Health Statistics, 2017 (2015 data).
66	Cigarette smokers (% of age 18 and older)	National Center for Health Statistics, National Health Interview Survey, http://www.cdc.gov/nchs/nhis.htm: Health, United States, 2017 forthcoming, Table 47 and unpublished data (1970 and 1980 data), age adjusted.
67	Heavier drinker (% of age 18 and older)	National Center for Health Statistics, National Health Interview Survey, http://www.cdc.gov/nchs/nhis.htm: Health, United States, 2014, Table 58 and unpublished data (2014-2016 data), age adjusted.
	Access to Health Care	
68	Total national health expenditures (% of GDP)	Centers for Medicare and Medicaid Services, National Health Expenditures Data. http://www.cms.gov/Research-Statistics-Data-and-Systems/Statistics-Trends-and-Reports/NationalHealthExpendData/index.html
69	Average total single premium per enrolled employee at private-sector establishments (2016 dollars)	Agency for Healthcare Research and Quality, Medical Expenditure Panel Survey. https://meps.ahrq.gov
70	Average health insurance premium paid by an individual or family (2016 dollars)	Centers for Disease Control and Prevention, National Center for Health Statistics, National Health Interview Survey, 2010-2015, Family Core component.

TABLE 5–2. SOURCES FOR SOCIAL INDICATORS—Continued

	Indicator	Source
71	Persons without health insurance (% of age 18-64)	National Center for Health Statistics, National Health Interview Survey.
72	Persons without health insurance (% of age 17 and younger)	National Center for Health Statistics, National Health Interview Survey.
73	Children age 19-35 months with recommended vaccinations (%)	National Center for Immunization and Respiratory Diseases, National Immunization Survey: http://www.cdc.gov/vaccines/imz-managers/coverage/nis/child/: Health, United States, 2017 forthcoming, Table 66.
	Security and Safety	
	Crime	
74	Property crimes (per 100,000 households)	Bureau of Justice Statistics, National Crime Victimization Survey. http://www.bjs.gov/index.cfm?ty=dcdetail&iid=245
75	Violent crime victimizations (per 100,000 population age 12 or older)	Bureau of Justice Statistics, National Crime Victimization Survey. http://www.bjs.gov/index.cfm?ty=dcdetail&iid=245
76	Murder rate (per 100,000 persons)	Federal Bureau of Investigation, Uniform Crime Reports, Crime in the United States. https://ucr.fbi.gov/ucr
77	Prison incarceration rate (state and federal institutions, rate per 100,000 persons)	U.S. Department of Justice, Bureau of Justice Statistics, National Prisoner Statistics Program. https://www.bjs.gov/index.cfm?ty=dcdetail&iid=269
	National Security	
78	Military personnel on active duty (thousands)	ES actuals for 1960 and 1970 as reported in Table 2-11 of the DoD Selected Manpower Statistics for FY 1997 (DoD WHS, Directorate for Information Operations and Reports). The source for the remaining fiscal year actuals are the Service budget justification books.
79	Veterans (thousands)	U.S. Department of Veterans Affairs. 1960-1999 (Annual Report of the Secretary of Veterans Affairs); 2000-2017 (VetPop16), Predictive Analytics and Actuary. http://www.va.gov/vetdata/Veteran_Population.asp
	Transportation Safety	
80	Safety belt use (%)	National Highway Traffic Safety Administration, National Center for Statistics and Analysis. https://crashstats.nhtsa.dot.gov/Api/Public/ViewPublication/812465
81	Highway fatalities	National Highway Traffic Safety Administration, National Center for Statistics and Analysis. https://crashstats.nhtsa.dot.gov/Api/Public/ViewPublication/812456
	Environment and Energy	
	Air Quality and Greenhouse Gases	
82	Ground level ozone (ppm)	U.S. Environmental Protection Agency, AirTrends Website. https://www.epa.gov/air-trends/ozone-trends
83	Particulate matter 2.5 (ug/m3)	U.S. Environmental Protection Agency, AirTrends Website. https://www.epa.gov/air-trends/particulate-matter-pm25-trends
84	Annual mean atmospheric CO_2 concentration (Mauna Loa, Hawaii; ppm)	National Oceanic and Atmospheric Administration. http://www.esrl.noaa.gov/gmd/ccgg/trends/
85	Gross greenhouse gas emissions (teragrams CO_2 equivalent)	U.S. Environmental Protection Agency (2017). Inventory of U.S. Greenhouse Gas Emissions and Sinks 1990-2015 (EPA Publication No. 431-P-17-001. https://www.epa.gov/ghgemissions/inventory-us-greenhouse-gas-emissions-and-sinks
86	Net greenhouse gas emissions, including sinks (teragrams CO_2 equivalent)	U.S. Environmental Protection Agency (2017). Inventory of U.S. Greenhouse Gas Emissions and Sinks 1990-2015 (EPA Publication No. 431-P-17-001. https://www.epa.gov/ghgemissions/inventory-us-greenhouse-gas-emissions-and-sinks
87	Gross greenhouse gas emissions per capita (metric tons CO_2 equivalent)	U.S. Environmental Protection Agency (2017). Inventory of U.S. Greenhouse Gas Emissions and Sinks 1990-2015 (EPA Publication No. 431-P-17-001. https://www.epa.gov/ghgemissions/inventory-us-greenhouse-gas-emissions-and-sinks
88	Gross greenhouse gas emissions per 2009$ of GDP (kilograms CO_2 equivalent)	U.S. Environmental Protection Agency (2017). Inventory of U.S. Greenhouse Gas Emissions and Sinks 1990-2015 (EPA Publication No. 431-P-17-001. https://www.epa.gov/ghgemissions/inventory-us-greenhouse-gas-emissions-and-sinks
89	Population that receives drinking water in compliance with standards (%)	U.S. Environmental Protection Agency, 2016a. Safe Drinking Water Information System, Federal Version. https://cfpub.epa.gov/roe/indicator.cfm?i=45#1
	Energy	
90	Energy consumption per capita (million Btu)	U.S. Energy Information Administration, Monthly Energy Review (October 2017), Table 1.7 https://www.eia.gov/totalenergy/data/monthly
91	Energy consumption per 2009$ GDP (thousand Btu per 2009$)	U.S. Energy Information Administration, Monthly Energy Review (October 2017), Table 1.7 https://www.eia.gov/totalenergy/data/monthly
92	Electricity net generation from renewable sources, all sectors (% of total)	U.S. Energy Information Administration, Monthly Energy Review (October 2017), Table 7.2a https://www.eia.gov/totalenergy/data/monthly
93	Coal production (million short tons)	U.S. Energy Information Administration, Monthly Energy Review (October 2017), Table 6.1 https://www.eia.gov/totalenergy/data/monthly

TABLE 5–2. SOURCES FOR SOCIAL INDICATORS—Continued

	Indicator	Source
94	Natural gas production (dry) (trillion cubic feet)	U.S. Energy Information Administration, Monthly Energy Review (October 2017), Table 4.1 https://www.eia.gov/totalenergy/data/monthly
95	Petroleum production (million barrels per day)	U.S. Energy Information Administration, Monthly Energy Review (October 2017), Table 3.1 https://www.eia.gov/totalenergy/data/monthly
96	Renewable energy production (quadrillion Btu)	U.S. Energy Information Administration, Monthly Energy Review (October 2017), Table 10.1 https://www.eia.gov/totalenergy/data/monthly

6. BUILDING AND USING EVIDENCE TO IMPROVE GOVERNMENT EFFECTIVENESS

The Administration is committed to a vision for results-driven government that improves mission delivery and directs taxpayer dollars to the most effective and efficient purposes. Achieving this vision means ensuring accountability for results, having the necessary analytical tools, identifying and investing in effective practices, and accessing and using data to transform it into evidence that informs action. With stronger evidence, we can learn from and improve programs to better serve the American people.

The bipartisan Ryan/Murray Commission on Evidence-Based Policymaking was charged with determining how the Federal government could improve how it builds and uses evidence to improve policies and programs, and overcome the current obstacles to doing so. The Commission's September 2017 *final report* articulates its vision of "a future in which rigorous evidence is created efficiently, as a routine part of government operations, and used to construct effective public policy." The Commission identified many barriers to the effective use of government data to generate evidence, and recommended strategies to improve data access in a secure and accountable manner and strengthen Federal capacity to build and use evidence. These strategies recognize the power of data and evidence to improve government while reducing burden on the American public. The Commission concluded that achieving this vision requires Executive Branch leadership, including that of the White House Office of Management and Budget (OMB). The Administration supports the Commission's vision and believes that evidence-based policymaking is a cornerstone of effective and efficient government. As described in this chapter, implementing this vision requires the infrastructure and capacity to credibly build and use evidence and develop a culture of learning and continuous improvement.

Building the Infrastructure for Evidence-based Policymaking

Effective and efficient government requires understanding how well current policies and programs are working, and identifying alternatives for improvements. A variety of considerations go into decision-making, but incorporating evidence is crucial. Multiple forms of evidence—including evaluations, program monitoring, performance measurement, statistics, and other forms of research and analysis—can inform decision-making. For example, statistical indicators examined over time provide context in which policies are set and programs operate, performance data can be used to measure outcomes, and evaluations can inform understanding of program and policy variations and their impacts. The best forms of evidence to use depend on the questions being asked, the current state of knowledge, the context in which a policy or program operates, and practical and methodological considerations.

Routinely creating and using evidence requires a strong infrastructure and commitment. The *President's 2018 Budget* outlined widely accepted principles and practices for evaluation, which, along with similar principles and practices for Federal statistics, provide the foundation to build and use evidence. The 2018 Budget encouraged agencies to think about evidence-building broadly, highlighting how a range of analytic activities can contribute to building and using evidence. To be successful however, agencies need a strong evidence infrastructure, including hiring and deploying trained staff; ensuring independence and rigor in statistics and evaluations; using cost-effective, cutting-edge methods; and bringing evidence to bear in policy and program decisions. This infrastructure will also support agencies in making better use of existing administrative data by ensuring that there are processes and tools in place to use and share data in appropriate and secure ways. This Budget reaffirms and builds upon these evidence principles and practices, and further articulates the Administration's vision for building and using evidence.

Current Federal Landscape

Building and using evidence: Ensuring that evidence can inform policy or program development and implementation requires coordination, agency leadership, available data, robust information technology and other tools, and relevant expertise, among other factors. Using evidence in decision-making entails ongoing coordination between those implementing and managing the operations of a program, including its data, and those responsible for using analysis to determine program effectiveness, opportunities for program improvement, and future policy options. Evidence-based policymaking requires strong leadership from multiple parts of an agency—agency officials, program administrators, performance managers, strategic planners, policy and budget staff, evaluators, analysts, and statisticians—to ensure that data and evidence are developed, analyzed, understood, and acted upon appropriately. Yet, current capacity in Federal agencies to build and use evidence varies widely. While some agencies have made great progress in integrating evidence into policy development, strategic planning, and day-to-day decision-making and operations, in other agencies, the creation and use of evidence is often isolated or limited.

Program evaluation: An important form of evidence-building is program evaluation. Evaluation involves the systematic application of rigorous scientific methods to assess the design, implementation, outcomes, or impact of a policy or program. Evaluation can answer essential questions regarding program effectiveness and cost-efficiency—questions that cannot be answered through performance measurement and monitoring, descriptive statistics, or simple analysis of program data alone. It can answer the questions "did it work and compared to what?" and "would these outcomes have occurred regardless of the program or did the program intervention make the difference?"

However, there is tremendous variation across Federal agencies in their capacity to conduct evaluations, as well as the sophistication and rigor of their evaluation capabilities. Unlike complementary government functions like performance measurement and statistics, there is not a formal, comprehensive infrastructure for Federal evaluation to support consistency across agencies, exchange information, allow for the promulgation of principles and practices, and coordinate and collaborate on areas of common interest. As a result, we lack any evaluation findings for many policies and programs, which greatly limits evidence-based policymaking. A strong infrastructure for Federal evaluation would allow formal coordination and support of evaluation activity across agencies in order to improve evaluation within individual agencies, and enhance the quality, utility, and efficiency of evaluation across government.

Some agencies have impressive evaluation capacity and activity, with independent, centralized evaluation offices working across the agency to conduct rigorous and relevant evaluations. In other cases, agencies have strong evaluation components, but they are in silos that limit their scope and prevent them from leveraging evaluation resources and expertise throughout the agency. Many agencies do not understand or undertake evaluation, or conduct poor-quality evaluation that is of limited utility and may provide misleading or incorrect information. Agencies need to increase their expertise and evaluation capacity to ensure the necessary evidence and understanding to inform program and policy decisions and improvements. One recent successful strategy for increasing agency capacity is the Office of Evaluation Sciences (OES) at the General Services Administration, which pairs experts with Federal agency partners to conduct evaluations that identify cost-effective ways to improve certain policies and programs. OES has had particular success in using existing administrative data at agencies to conduct low-cost evaluations that test no- or very low-cost changes to programs and agency processes. OES complements the evaluation activities at a number of Federal agencies, including bridging gaps at agencies that have limited or no evaluation capacity.

Key Strategies to Strengthen Evidence

A Federal commitment to building and using evidence requires effective strategies. A number of evidence-building strategies are being used across Federal agencies and programs, and new strategies are proposed in this Budget. These strategies vary in their focus and mechanisms, but all serve to enhance how we build and use evidence.

Evaluation principles and practices: The commitment to strengthen Federal evaluation and adhere to key principles and practices was articulated in the President's Budget for 2018. While the process for developing a set of evaluation standards is ongoing, fundamental principles emerge as common themes in established U.S. and international frameworks, as well as several official Federal agency evaluation policies.[1] These principles include rigor, relevance, independence, transparency, and ethics. Principles and practices for evaluation help to ensure that Federal program evaluations meet scientific standards, are relevant and useful, and are conducted and have results disseminated without bias or inappropriate influence. These principles, along with similar ones in place for statistical agencies, provide a foundation for furthering agencies' capacity to routinely build and use high-quality evidence to improve program performance and identify policy options. They also help evaluation offices maintain standards across changes in leadership and personnel. The new guidelines for monitoring and evaluation of foreign assistance, issued in January 2018 as required by the Foreign Aid Transparency and Accountability Act of 2016, also include a set of similar principles.

Designated evaluation officials and offices: For complementary Federal systems, such as performance and statistics, an essential component is having a designated senior official in each agency responsible for coordinating agency activity in the area, providing necessary direction and guiding relevant resources within the agency, serving as a point of contact for other agencies and OMB, and being accountable for agency performance. Agencies with strong evaluation capacity have an independent evaluation office with the organizational standing, resources, independence, and expertise to inform agency leadership, collaborate with policy and program staff, and coordinate with statistical and performance offices. The most effective approach for strengthening Federal program evaluation includes having centralized, independent evaluation offices at agencies, each with a senior career official possessing evaluation expertise and experience given lead responsibility for evaluation at the agency. To minimize budgetary impacts and agency burden, agencies should develop structures most appropriate to their particular context that allow them to make efficient and flexible use of existing resources.

Some agencies already have established centralized evaluation functions, while other agencies are strengthening these functions and are establishing evaluation offices staffed with relevant expertise. For example, the Small Business Administration (SBA) recognized the need to strengthen evidence-based decision-making to support continuous learning and organizational effectiveness and efficiency. The agency recently established a team of evaluation experts in its performance management office, and is building an evidence registry, establishing a community of practice, coordinating an agency-wide learning agenda, and conducting independent evaluations to support their new framework. The SBA will make evaluation results public and incorporate findings into its performance

[1] For example, the Chief Evaluation Office at DOL, the Administration for Children and Families at HHS, the Office of Policy Development and Research at HUD, and Statistical Policy Directive No. 1: Fundamental Responsibilities of Federal Statistical Agencies and Recognized Statistical Units.

management framework. In September 2017, the US Department of Agriculture (USDA) Rural Development Innovation Center established a Data Analytics and Evidence Team that is quickly establishing processes and protocols to conduct independent, rigorous, and relevant program evaluations across rural development programs to build a more robust portfolio of evidence. The 21st Century Cures Act, enacted in 2016, includes provisions to strengthen leadership and accountability for behavioral health at the Federal level and to ensure that mental health and substance abuse programs keep pace with science and technology. The Act requires the Substance Abuse and Mental Health Services Administration (SAMHSA) to disseminate research findings and evidence-based program models to service providers, ensure that grants are evaluated, strengthen the role of the Chief Medical Officer and a new Office of Evaluation, and create a National Mental Health and Substance Use Disorder Policy Laboratory to promote evidence-based practices and services.

Multi-year learning agendas: Learning agendas are a way to allow agencies to plan how to focus evaluation and evidence-building activities over a multi-year period, while enabling them to modify these agendas as needed to reflect changing priorities and new learning. Through collaborative development of such agendas, agencies can identify critical questions and the evidence needed to answer these questions, given agency priorities, available resources, and challenges. Learning agendas should reflect current knowledge and availability of data, identify where new data collection is necessary and how to effectively build evidence, highlight opportunities for cross-agency collaboration and using common tools and resources, and be modified over time to reflect changing priorities and new evidence. The learning that results should be shared with agency leadership, policy and program staff, and key stakeholders in order to facilitate policy and program improvement. For example, the Social Security Administration (SSA) effectively balances comprehensive, long-term research planning in retirement and disability policy with the need to respond to emerging issues and make adjustments given new challenges and information. Through its Retirement Research Consortium and Disability Research Consortium, SSA has cooperative agreements with universities and research organizations. These agreements give SSA access to a pool of independent experts that address priority questions and identify additional issues for consideration, collaborate with SSA researchers to access administrative data and conduct analyses, and quickly respond to unanticipated needs. The resulting portfolio of evidence addresses the priorities of SSA leadership, policy and program staff, Administration officials, Congress, and key stakeholders.

Strengthening interagency coordination: The Federal evidence community is increasingly sharing lessons learned, strategies, tools, and insights from building and using evidence through agency-led trainings, an online Federal community of practice, and dissemination of common standards and metrics. Such coordination is critical for sharing new methods throughout the government and enabling agencies with less experience to learn from more experienced peers. Even for agencies sophisticated in evidence-building, interagency coordination is needed to avoid duplication, highlight service delivery differences, and develop comparable performance measurement systems for analysis and evaluation. A notable example of such interagency coordination is the bipartisan Workforce Innovation and Opportunity Act (WIOA, PL 113-128), which reauthorized the workforce system for the first time in 15 years, improving coordination, collaboration, and service delivery across the six major Departments of Labor (DOL) and Education employment and training programs. For the first time, these core programs were required to conduct joint state planning and report on a standardized set of employment-oriented performance metrics (e.g., participants' placement in a job). In addition to the core WIOA programs, DOL is also aligning performance indicators and data element definitions across most of its other employment and training programs to report on the WIOA performance indicators. States also have the option to fold additional programs or activities into their strategic planning, including the Temporary Assistance for Needy Families (TANF) program, Supplemental Nutrition Assistance Program (SNAP), Community Services Block Grant, and others. In the first round of state planning, 29 states elected to include non-required programs in their plans, indicating states' desire for broader cross-program coordination.

Funding flexibilities and set-asides: Rigorous, independent evaluations and statistical surveys are essential for building evidence. Yet, this inherently complex, dynamic work can span several fiscal years, encompass timing uncertainties, and involve cost variances. For example, the announcement of a new program or policy priority may be delayed, which could postpone procurement of an independent evaluator to study the program's implementation and effectiveness. Similarly, a study's design may need to be altered to respond to natural disasters or factors that were not anticipated. Further, although estimates based on prior work can inform timelines necessary to obtain a sufficient number of study or survey participants, the actual time needed can fluctuate. Many other factors can influence timing and schedule changes during implementation of an evaluation, research, or statistical project such as technological advancements for collecting and analyzing data that may yield significant project efficiencies. Additionally, funding parameters and available Federal procurement strategies and processes often lack the flexibility and agility needed to address the dynamic nature of evaluation and statistical projects. Inflexible appropriations and agency processes may also limit agencies' ability to coordinate on studies of mutual interest and combine funding sources, even though there are important benefits to doing so, including cost efficiencies, burden reduction, and shared learning. In order to improve efficiency of these projects and use of funds, the Budget proposes to leverage existing flexibilities and give agencies the ability to spend funds over longer periods of time. Another proposed flexibility rewards agencies who efficiently and effectively use funds by allowing them to put unused contract funds towards other priority evaluation or statistical activities.

Specifically, the Budget includes a previously enacted general provision (PL 115-31 K, Title II, Sec. 232) allowing the Department of Housing and Urban Development (HUD) to deobligate and then reobligate—in the same fiscal year or the subsequent fiscal year—funds that are unexpended at the time of completion of a contract, grant, or cooperative agreement for research, evaluation, or statistical purposes. A general provision in the Budget will provide this flexibility for other agencies and extend the period of fund availability to five years for funds appropriated or transferred for evaluation, research, and statistical activities in the Department of Labor's Chief Evaluation Office and Bureau of Labor Statistics and Health and Human Services' (HHS) Assistant Secretary for Planning and Evaluation and Administration for Children and Families' (ACF) Office for Planning, Research and Evaluation. These flexibilities will allow agencies to better target evaluation and statistical funds to reflect changing circumstances as a study unfolds.

The Budget also uses set-asides to ensure that agencies have adequate resources to undertake rigorous evaluations. For example, the 2019 Budget enhances research and evaluation on child care supply, demand, and quality through the utilization of the full statutory research and evaluation set-aside of one-half of one percent of funding for the HHS Child Care and Development Fund. As another example of the importance of set-asides, the 2017 Consolidated Appropriations Act included a 0.33 percent set-aside of the TANF program to be used for research, evaluation, and technical assistance. This enabled ACF to develop a demonstration to rigorously evaluate state and local interventions to help low-income persons achieve employment and economic security, with an emphasis on interventions that address opioid dependency, substance abuse, and mental health. The set-aside also allowed ACF to launch a project to improve state-level TANF programs through enhanced use of TANF and related human services data, as well as to develop (in collaboration with the Department of Labor) a database of proven and promising approaches to move TANF recipients into work.

Improving Data Access and Governance for Evidence-Building

Data are a central element for building and using evidence to improve government effectiveness. In order for the Federal government to successfully leverage data as strategic assets, we must address the silos across Federal agencies that can stymie collaboration and result in fragmented services and efforts. Greater coordination is needed among and within agencies, including OMB, to improve how we manage and use data. The government needs a coordinated strategy to ensure that high priority data are collected, and that already-collected data are used to their full extent. A comprehensive data strategy will acknowledge both external and internal needs for data access, recognizing that both have a role to play in addressing the big

questions and challenges of the day, such as solving the opioid epidemic or fueling economic growth.

Congress has already provided OMB with many of the tools needed to implement a coordinated data strategy across agencies. These include the authority to designate single collection authorities for shared data needs, set data quality and classification standards, and manage and coordinate across interagency bodies, among others. These tools rest with multiple statutory offices across the institution. In response, OMB is organizing itself to use these tools together in service of building evidence. This will serve as a model for how agencies can maximize their use of data to build evidence across their own organizational silos. When agencies improve their own use of data for evidence-building, the American people will see improved service delivery, more effective programs, and a more responsive and efficient government.

Data as strategic assets: In undertaking its mission, the Federal government collects large amounts of data, whether for administering a program, assessing or enforcing a regulation, or monitoring contracts and grants. Federal and state administrative data include rich information on labor market outcomes, health care, criminal justice, housing, and other important topics. These data are strategic assets that can be used to meet a number of needs within and outside of government, including to build evidence as the President's 2018 Budget and the Commission on Evidence-Based Policymaking noted. On their own, these data can be used to answer important questions about service delivery, the population served, and the outcomes for an individual program. Yet, these data are often underutilized and do not reach their full potential to evaluate program effectiveness, measure day-to-day performance, and inform the public about how society and the economy are faring. Integrating data systems and linking administrative data across programs or to survey data, where appropriate, provides another opportunity to maximize the power of data for evidence-building and program improvement. Many notable efforts have demonstrated the potential that government data offer to improve internal government operations and increase efficiency, effectiveness, transparency, and accountability, all while reducing the burden on the public and limiting costs from new data collections.

Efforts to better access and use data: Federal agencies are making greater use of their own administrative data for program operations and analytic and statistical activities, including evaluation. Many agencies have data that would be useful to other agencies, other levels of government, and outside researchers, citizens, and businesses. However, systemic legal, policy, and procedural barriers frequently prevent Federal, state, and local agencies from maximizing whether and how they use data. The range of challenges are broad, and include appropriate concerns about confidentiality and privacy, but also restrictive legislative authorities and policies, unclear administrative processes and hurdles, the inability to share data, and, in some cases, lack of sufficient analytic, evaluation, and/or information technology capacity.

Federal law rightly protects some of the most valuable data for building evidence about some of the nation's largest programs, and access must be provided in a secure and confidential manner with appropriate transparency and accountability. Nonetheless, as the Commission's recommendations recognized, the country's laws and practices are not currently optimized to support the use of data for evidence-building, or in a manner that best protects the data. To correct these problems, it recommended using secure technology and cutting-edge statistical methods to blend data in a highly protective manner, building on the tradition of data stewardship and tradition of strong confidentiality of the nation's principal statistical agencies, as discussed in the Strengthening Federal Statistics Chapter of the Budget. The Commission also recommended revising laws, where needed, to enable more consistent, efficient access to data for evidence-building, with appropriate confidentiality and privacy protections in place based on the sensitivity of the data. For example, the access and use of Department of Education (ED) data collected to administer ED student aid programs are governed by a complex, overlapping patchwork of laws that result in inconsistent privacy protections and use restrictions. In addition to inconsistently protecting student privacy, these restrictions make it unnecessarily burdensome for ED to use the data it currently collects to improve the government and public understanding of student loan program costs and improve student aid program effectiveness. A reauthorization of the Higher Education Act should clarify and simplify student aid administrative data use and access restrictions to ensure that student privacy is strongly and consistently protected while allowing the Federal government to efficiently and effectively administer the student aid programs.

To begin to address other statutory barriers, the Budget proposes to provide access to valuable employment and earnings data for certain agencies and programs to achieve government efficiencies. The National Directory of New Hires (NDNH)—a Federal database of new hire, employment, and unemployment insurance data used for administering HHS' Office of Child Support Enforcement programs—is governed by statute that specifies authorized uses of the data and mandates tight controls to protect the data from unauthorized use or disclosure. Entities with the authority to access NDNH are able to use the data to support program administration (e.g., eligibility verification) and evidence-building, subject to the necessary data protections required by law and HHS. In particular, NDNH access allows some programs to eliminate duplicative efforts to collect the same employment and earnings data already in NDNH, improve program integrity, access reliable outcomes data, and create important government efficiencies.

The Budget proposal enables access to NDNH for units within Federal agencies that conduct research, statistical activities, evaluation, and/or performance measurement associated with assessing labor market outcomes. Access to NDNH would enable research and performance measurement that would otherwise require costly surveys or state-by-state or other one-off agreements to obtain

wage data. For example, the proposal would enable the Departments of Labor and Education to use NDNH data to conduct program evaluations on employment and training programs including for WIOA. The proposal would also enable state agencies (designated by each governor with WIOA responsibilities) with the authority to match their data with NDNH for program administration, including program oversight and evaluation of WIOA and other Departments of Labor and Education employment and training programs. Additionally, the proposal would authorize data exchanges between state child support agencies, state agencies that administer workforce programs, and state agencies that administer Adult Education and Vocational Rehabilitation to improve coordination between the programs.

Beyond the evidence-building proposals described, the full proposal on NDNH access includes good government provisions to enable efficiencies for program integrity and eligibility verification. The Budget allows the Department of the Treasury's Do Not Pay Business Center to serve as a pass-through between NDNH and Federal agency programs that are authorized NDNH access for improper payment purposes. The proposal also permits USDA's Rural Housing Service to verify eligibility and validate the income source information provided by means-tested, single family housing loan applicants and multifamily housing project-based tenants. Lastly, the Budget proposes the use of NDNH to establish eligibility for processing Railroad Retirement Board disability benefits in a more efficient manner.

Integrated data systems: Federal agencies also recognize the potential that integrated data systems, which link individual- or household-level data across different programs and services, offer to support evidence-building activities and improve programs. Integrated data systems allow for richer analyses across programs and outcome areas, and enable the use of data for case management and effective service provision, ensuring that programs allocate funds effectively and efficiently. Integrating data systems and linking administrative data often requires that disparate data systems must communicate with one another. Supporting the development of interoperable data systems, which can communicate and exchange data with one another while maintaining the appropriate privacy and security protections, is critical to realize the full potential of shared administrative data. For example, the National Information Exchange Model is a Federally-supported tool that enables interoperability and data exchange at all levels of government across program areas and does so in partnership with private industry stakeholders and state/local partners. This work is done to ensure that technical solutions for data sharing follow the legal requirements.

The Federal government is in a unique position to leverage the data it already collects for a range of evidence-building activities. Using data as strategic assets allows Federal agencies and state, local, and private sector partners to continuously monitor and improve programs, develop evidence on effective approaches and interventions, and ensure that programs and services reach their intended targets.

Using Evidence to Learn and Improve

Evidence should be used as a regular part of decision-making processes. Using the full range of evidence for learning and improvement is especially important for addressing the most pressing policy challenges facing our nation. For example, substantial numbers of individuals with disabilities or serious health conditions have dropped out of the labor market, and in many cases receive disability benefits that consume substantial Federal resources. The Administration is pursuing an ambitious set of demonstration projects to build an evidence base for reforming disability programs to promote employment and self-sufficiency among persons with a disability and to reduce future costs. SSA and DOL are partnering to develop the Retaining Employment and Talent After Injury/Illness Network (RETAIN) demonstration, which will test early interventions to help workers maintain employment after experiencing a work-threatening injury, illness, or disability, thus avoiding the need for disability benefits. The Administration is requesting demonstration authority to test time-limited disability benefits for claimants whose conditions are most likely to be temporary and to enable return to employment. Expanded demonstration authority that allows for universal participation would allow SSA to test new interventions and modified program rules in order to identify effective strategies for helping persons with a disability return to employment. Evaluation findings would be considered by an expert panel in developing recommendations for permanent changes to Federal disability programs.

Another example of an agency building evidence to learn and make critical decisions and improvements in policy is the Health Resources and Services Administration (HRSA), which is beginning a process for a coordinated impact assessment of HRSA programs. Beginning with its largest programs, HRSA will conduct a systematic review of the available research, evaluation, and performance measures—with a focus on compara-

tive effectiveness, patient and population outcomes, and costs—to inform policy decisions, undertake program improvements, prioritize future research and data collection, and better integrate planning, performance, program administration, and evaluation. It is also critical for states to learn and improve their operations, as many Federal dollars pass through to states and localities for administration. As an example, WIOA now requires states to use a portion of their state set-aside funds to conduct evaluations of their programs so that they can learn about effective program strategies and service delivery models. WIOA also requires states to cooperate with Federal evaluations, which will facilitate cross-agency and cross-state learnings.

Conclusion

Policymakers and the American people are rightly concerned with the effectiveness and efficiency of many government programs, yet the evidence base and understanding of these programs are uneven. Some Federal agencies have strong capacity to build and use evidence, while in others that capacity is minimal or the work is siloed. There has been exciting progress in using administrative data for program accountability, learning, and improvement; however, some of the most valuable data sources remain off limits to those who could most benefit from secure access. There is a way forward. A bipartisan consensus has emerged regarding the need to embrace evidence-based policymaking by using available evidence to make decisions and building evidence where it is lacking. Doing so requires leadership and capacity within agencies, adherence to key principles and practices, agency learning agendas, coordination across government, the tools and flexibility necessary for rigorous evidence-building, and strategic use of valuable administrative data. The Administration supports this vision and is prepared to work with Congress to advance evidence-based policymaking. Using evidence to improve government is what taxpayers deserve—carefully and wisely using limited resources to address national priorities and solve pressing problems.

7. STRENGTHENING THE FEDERAL WORKFORCE

Federal employees underpin nearly all the operations of the Government, ensuring the smooth functioning of our democracy. While most Americans will never meet the President or even their Member of Congress, they will interact with the Federal employees who work in their community, keep them safe at airports, or welcome them to a National Park. Regional offices of the Department of Agriculture (USDA) and the Department of Interior (DOI) provide services to farmers and ranchers where they live. When emergencies occur, entities like the Federal Emergency Management Agency, the Coast Guard, and the Small Business Administration help to save and rebuild communities.

Americans expect the Federal Government to keep their food and medication safe, transportation system working, assets protected, and lives spared from natural disaster. Members of the Armed Forces work side-by-side with more than 730,000 civilian counterparts at the Department of Defense (DOD) to help them accomplish their mission. Veterans rely on the more than 350,000 Department of Veterans Affairs (VA) personnel to ensure they receive the medical care and benefits they have earned. More than 20,000 Department of State personnel help safeguard the Nation while serving in posts both foreign and domestic. Federal employees work to cure diseases, explore outer space, and otherwise promote the general welfare. Since Federal workers perform many essential functions, failures can chip away at the citizenry's collective trust in Government.

The cost of employing this workforce is significant. The Federal Government is the single largest direct employer in the Nation. About 1.7 million of the approximately 2.1 million direct Federal employees live outside of the Washington, D.C., metro area. An even larger "indirect" workforce carries out much of the work paid for by Federal funds. These are the Federal contractor personnel, as well as the State, local, and nonprofit employees – many of whose jobs are entirely funded through Federal grants and transfer payments – located all across the Nation, in every state and territory. The size of this broader workforce is unknown, and a subject of dispute.

The Administration is committed to redefining the role of the Federal Government by reprioritizing Federal spending toward those activities that advance the safety and security of the American people. This reassessment includes the cost of Government operations. All too often the basic operating expenses of the Federal Government, including personnel-related expenses such as pay, benefits, and office space, are treated as essentially fixed costs. The Federal Government, with annual civilian personnel costs of almost $300 billion, should always be seeking to ensure it has an optimally sized and skilled workforce operating out of locations best suited to accomplish its various missions. It is important to appropriately compensate personnel based on mission needs and labor market dynamics.

Budgeting for Federal personnel has typically proceeded in the same "incremental" fashion as program budgeting, with proposed staffing and compensation levels determined by annually tweaking prior year totals, instead of reassessing underlying cost drivers and installing a better paradigm. Incremental personnel staff budgeting can perpetuate legacy inefficiencies and perennially forestall investment in the sort of workforce innovations that routinely occur in the private sector.

While pursuing a series of proposals to overhaul Federal compensation and benefits, the Administration also intends to partner with Congress to cull statutory and regulatory rules that have over time created an increasingly incomprehensible and unmanageable civil service system. The Administration will propose changes in hiring and dismissal procedures to empower Federal managers with greater flexibility. Agency managers will be encouraged to restore management prerogatives that have been ceded to Federal labor unions and create a new partnership with these entities that maintains the primacy of each Agency's obligation to efficiently and effectively accomplish its public mission.

Federal Workforce Demographics

The Federal workforce is comprised of approximately 2.1 million non-postal civilian workers and 1.4 million active duty military, in addition to nearly 1 million military reserve personnel, serving throughout the country and the world. As of September 2017, the Federal civilian workforce self-identifies as 62.9 percent White, 18.6 percent Black, 8.9 percent Hispanic of all races, 5.9 percent Asian, 0.5 percent Native Hawaiian/Pacific Islander, 1.6 percent American Indian/Alaska Native, and 1.6 percent more than one race. Men comprise 56.7 percent of all permanent Federal employees and women are 43.3 percent. Veterans are 31.1 percent of the entire Federal workforce, which includes the 13.3 percent of the workforce who are veterans receiving disability compensation. By comparison, veterans comprise approximately 6 percent of the private sector non-agricultural workforce. The Federal workforce continues to age, with more than 600,000 employees older than 55, which is about 40,000 more than in 2013. Roughly 155,000 employees are younger than 30, a decrease of about 20,000 since 2013.

Using data from the Bureau of Labor Statistics (BLS) on full-time, full-year workers, Table 7-1 breaks all Federal and private sector jobs into 22 occupation groups to demonstrate the differences in composition between the Federal and private workforces. Charts 7-1 and 7-2

Chart 7-1. Masters Degree or Above By Year for Federal and Private Sectors

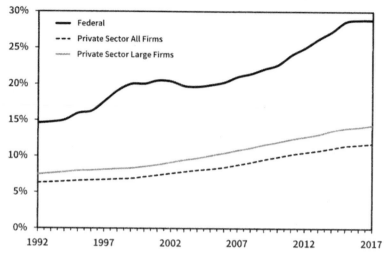

Source: 1992-2017 Current Population Survey, Integrated Public Use Microdata Series.

Notes: Federal excludes the military and Postal Service, but includes all other Federal workers. Private Sector excludes the self-employed. Neither category includes State and local government workers. Large firms have at least 1,000 workers. This analysis is limited to full-time, full-year workers, i.e. those with at least 1,500 annual hours of work and presents five-year averages. Industry is from the year preceding the year on the horizontal axis.

Chart 7-2. High School Graduate or Less By Year for Federal and Private Sectors

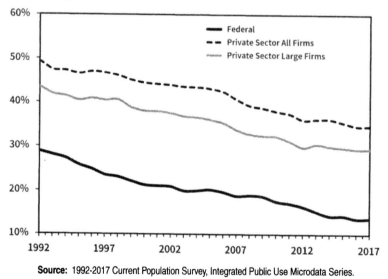

Source: 1992-2017 Current Population Survey, Integrated Public Use Microdata Series.

Notes: Federal excludes the military and Postal Service, but includes all other Federal workers. Private Sector excludes the self-employed. Neither category includes State and local government workers. Large firms have at least 1,000 workers. This analysis is limited to full-time, full-year workers, i.e. those with at least 1,500 annual hours of work and presents five-year averages. Industry is from the year preceding the year on the horizontal axis.

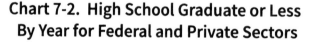

present trends in educational levels for the Federal and private sector workforces over the past two decades. Chart 7-3 shows the trends in average age in both the Federal and private sectors.

When the Administration prepared its Budget request, it did not set specific full-time equivalent (FTE) levels for each Agency. While many agencies plan to reduce FTEs, in some cases, the Administration seeks to increase the workforce. Table 7-2 shows actual Federal civilian FTE levels in the Executive Branch by Agency for 2016 and 2017, with estimates for 2018 and 2019. At the time the Budget was prepared, funding provided for the 2018 annual appropriations bills were operating under a continuing resolution, and FTE estimates reflect this funding. Actual 2018 FTE levels are likely to be different, to account for final appropriations, administrative decisions within agencies, and other factors. Chart 7-4 broadly shows the trends in personnel as a percent of the population in the Federal security related agencies (inclusive of the Departments of Defense, Homeland Security, Justice, State, and Veterans Affairs) and non-security agencies, in comparison to State and local governments and the private sector.

A System Whose Time Has Come - And Gone

Today's Federal personnel system is a relic of an earlier era. The Federal civil service is mired in a job system largely codified in 1949, when the General Schedule (GS) classification system was first created. About two-thirds of Federal civilian employees continue to work under the GS. This antiquated structure hinders the Federal Government's ability to accomplish its mission. The mission and required skills have changed, but the system has not. The competitive personnel system that Civil Service Commissioner Theodore Roosevelt envisioned to elevate the country has fallen into disrepute, criticized from most quarters as a compliance-oriented regime that ill-serves Federal managers, employees, or the Nation at large.

"No Time to Wait," a clarion call to civil service reform, was issued last year by the National Academy of Public Administration. That report questioned whether a "one-size fits all" Federal personnel system is necessary or even effective. The Government Accountability Office regularly includes human capital management on its semiannual High-Risk list of pressing problems facing the Federal Government. The inadequacies of the civil service are chronicled in scores of books and articles. The consensus is that the status quo is unacceptable, and an underlying cause of an array of Government failures rooted in an inability to recruit and manage people.

Back in 2002, the Office of Personnel Management (OPM) issued "A Fresh Start for Federal Pay," a white paper critiquing the Government's pay and job evaluation system as a "system whose time has come - and gone." The paper points out that the workforce "is no longer a government of clerks." It describes the pay system as insensitive to both market forces and individual performance. Fifteen years later, little has changed systemically. When pressing needs arise, statutory fixes are devised to bypass the existing system. Such laws typically allow specific agen-

Table 7-1. OCCUPATIONS OF FEDERAL AND PRIVATE SECTOR WORKFORCES
(Grouped by Average Private Sector Salary)

Occupational Groups	Percent	
	Federal Workers	Private Sector Workers
Highest Paid Occupations Ranked by Private Sector Salary:		
Lawyers and judges	2.3%	0.6%
Engineers	4.4%	1.9%
Scientists and social scientists	5.1%	0.7%
Managers	12.1%	14.0%
Pilots, conductors, and related mechanics	2.2%	0.5%
Doctors, nurses, psychologists, etc.	7.4%	6.4%
Miscellaneous professionals	16.0%	9.1%
Administrators, accountants, HR personnel	6.4%	2.7%
Inspectors	1.2%	0.3%
Total Percentage	**57.1%**	**36.2%**
Medium Paid Occupations Ranked by Private Sector Salary:		
Sales including real estate, insurance agents	1.1%	6.1%
Other miscellaneous occupations	3.2%	4.5%
Automobile and other mechanics	1.6%	3.1%
Law enforcement and related occupations	8.8%	0.7%
Office workers	2.3%	5.7%
Social workers	1.6%	0.6%
Drivers of trucks and taxis	0.9%	3.3%
Laborers and construction workers	3.1%	9.7%
Clerks and administrative assistants	13.2%	10.5%
Manufacturing	2.6%	7.5%
Total Percentage	**38.2%**	**51.6%**
Lowest Paid Occupations Ranked by Private Sector Salary:		
Other miscellaneous service workers	2.5%	5.8%
Janitors and housekeepers	1.4%	2.3%
Cooks, bartenders, bakers, and wait staff	0.8%	4.0%
Total Percentage	**4.7%**	**12.2%**

Source: 2013-2017 Current Population Survey, Integrated Public Use Microdata Series.

Notes: Federal workers exclude the military and Postal Service, but include all other Federal workers in the Executive, Legislative, and Judicial Branches. However, the vast majority of these employees are civil servants in the Executive Branch. Private sector workers exclude the self-employed. Neither category includes state and local government workers. This analysis is limited to full-time, full-year workers, i.e. those with at least 1,500 annual hours of work.

cies to work around intractable parts of the outdated civil service structure. Chart 7-5 is an OPM mapping of the 15 functions and 54 sub-functions comprising the Federal human capital management system.

Complex and outdated, the laws and regulations governing hiring, performance management, pay, and retirement number in the thousands. The rigidity of the system requires human resources specialists to focus on rule-based compliance instead of achieving the best hires. This is in part due to the reality that the civil service system was conceived at a time when the Nation's workforce was much more static than it is today, with employees typically staying with the same job for decades.

The Civil Service Reform Act of 1978 turns 40 this year. It is time to reconsider where that law has succeeded and

Table 7-2.   FEDERAL CIVILIAN EMPLOYMENT IN THE EXECUTIVE BRANCH
(Civilian employment as measured by full-time equivalents (FTE) in thousands, excluding the Postal Service)

Agency	Actual		Estimate		Change: 2018 to 2019	
	2016	2017	2018	2019	FTE	Percent
Cabinet agencies:						
Agriculture	86.8	87.3	88.7	80.9	-7.8	-8.8%
Commerce	40.3	40.9	42.6	51.7	9.1	21.3%
Defense--Military Programs	725.3	726.2	741.5	744.5	3.0	0.4%
Education	4.1	4.1	3.9	3.9	-*	-1.1%
Energy	14.9	14.7	15.4	15.1	-0.2	-1.4%
Health and Human Services	72.6	74.1	75.5	74.9	-0.6	-0.8%
Homeland Security	183.5	182.4	182.0	195.0	13.0	7.2%
Housing and Urban Development	8.0	7.9	7.7	7.5	-0.2	-2.6%
Interior	64.2	64.9	64.4	59.8	-4.6	-7.1%
Justice	114.9	118.2	117.1	116.8	-0.3	-0.3%
Labor	16.5	16.2	15.7	15.8	*	0.3%
State	32.1	27.6	25.7	25.5	-0.2	-0.6%
Transportation	54.3	54.7	55.1	54.7	-0.4	-0.7%
Treasury	93.4	92.5	90.0	88.3	-1.8	-1.9%
Veterans Affairs	345.1	351.6	359.3	366.3	7.0	1.9%
Other agencies—excluding Postal Service:						
Broadcasting Board of Governors	1.6	1.7	1.6	1.6	*	0.3%
Bureau of Consumer Financial Protection	1.6	1.7	1.8	1.8	*	0.9%
Corps of Engineers--Civil Works	21.8	21.7	21.6	21.6	*	*
Environmental Protection Agency	14.7	14.8	15.4	11.6	-3.8	-24.6%
Equal Employment Opportunity Commission	2.2	2.1	2.1	2.0	-*	-0.8%
Federal Communications Commission	1.6	1.5	1.4	1.4	....	....
Federal Deposit Insurance Corporation	6.5	6.1	6.4	6.4	-0.1	-1.0%
Federal Trade Commission	1.2	1.1	1.1	1.1	....	....
General Services Administration	11.2	11.5	11.7	11.9	0.2	1.5%
International Assistance Programs	5.7	5.6	5.5	5.1	-0.3	-6.3%
National Aeronautics and Space Administration	17.1	17.2	17.3	17.2	-0.1	-0.3%
National Archives and Records Administration	2.9	2.9	2.8	2.7	-0.1	-3.0%
National Credit Union Administration	1.2	1.2	1.2	1.2	-*	-1.2%
National Labor Relations Board	1.5	1.5	1.3	1.2	-0.1	-7.2%
National Science Foundation	1.4	1.4	1.4	1.4	....	....
Nuclear Regulatory Commission	3.5	3.2	3.4	3.3	-0.1	-4.4%
Office of Personnel Management	5.1	5.5	5.9	5.8	-0.1	-2.3%
Securities and Exchange Commission	4.6	4.6	4.5	4.5	-0.1	-1.4%
Small Business Administration	3.2	3.4	3.2	3.3	*	0.5%
Smithsonian Institution	4.9	5.0	5.2	5.2	-*	-0.1%
Social Security Administration	63.7	61.4	61.5	60.8	-0.8	-1.2%
Tennessee Valley Authority	10.7	10.1	10.0	9.9	-0.1	-1.1%
All other small agencies	13.4	13.5	13.9	13.4	-0.5	-3.7%
Total, Executive Branch civilian employment	2,057.3	2,062.1	2,085.1	2095.2	10.1	0.5%

* 50 or less.

where it has failed. The private sector continually finds new ways to evolve human capital management programs to maximize the return from their most valuable asset: their people. The Federal Government should do no less.

Federal Workforce Compensation Reform

The civil service salary schedules present an incomplete portrait of Federal pay. Private sector best practice focuses on total compensation, which includes both salary and ben-

efits. Total Federal compensation is summarized in Table 7-3. A Congressional Budget Office (CBO) report issued in April 2017 found that, based on observable characteristics, Federal employees on average received a combined 17 percent higher wage and benefits package than the private sector average over the 2011-2015 period. The disparity is overwhelmingly on the benefits side: CBO found that Federal employees receive on average 47 percent higher benefits and 3 percent higher wages than counterparts in the private sector. These gaps result from disproportion-

Table 7-3. PERSONNEL PAY AND BENEFITS

(In millions of dollars)

Description	2017 Actual	2018 Estimate	2019 Estimate	Change: 2018 to 2019	
				Dollars	Percent
Civilian Personnel Costs:					
Executive Branch (excluding Postal Service):					
Pay	190,243	194,656	198,507	3,851	2.0%
Benefits	82,938	84,587	85,767	1,180	1.4%
Subtotal	273,181	279,243	284,274	5,031	1.8%
Postal Service:					
Pay	37,265	37,328	37,978	650	1.7%
Benefits	13,541	18,113	13,863	-4,250	-23.5%
Subtotal	50,806	55,441	51,841	-3,600	-6.5%
Legislative Branch:					
Pay	2,177	2,234	2,354	120	5.4%
Benefits	690	699	766	67	9.6%
Subtotal	2,867	2,933	3,120	187	6.4%
Judicial Branch:					
Pay	3,207	3,304	3,420	116	3.5%
Benefits	1,069	1,101	1,116	15	1.4%
Subtotal	4,276	4,405	4,536	131	3.0%
Total, Civilian Personnel Costs	331,130	342,022	343,771	1,749	0.5%
Military Personnel Costs:					
Department of Defense—Military Programs:					
Pay	97,263	101,203	105,038	3,835	3.8%
Benefits	43,775	47,038	51,595	4,557	9.7%
Subtotal	141,038	148,241	156,633	8,392	5.7%
All other Executive Branch uniform personnel:					
Pay	3,381	3,387	3,534	147	4.3%
Benefits	715	741	749	8	1.1%
Subtotal	4,096	4,128	4,283	155	3.8%
Total, Military Personnel Costs	145,134	152,369	160,916	8,547	5.6%
Grand total, personnel costs	476,264	494,391	504,687	10,296	2.1%
ADDENDUM					
Former Civilian Personnel:					
Pensions	85,200	86,443	89,861	3,418	4.0%
Health benefits	12,654	12,917	13,642	725	5.6%
Life insurance	43	44	45	1	2.3%
Subtotal	97,897	99,404	103,548	4,144	4.2%
Former Military Personnel:					
Pensions	59,574	60,912	62,618	1,706	2.8%
Health benefits	10,326	10,905	11,451	546	5.0%
Subtotal	69,900	71,817	74,069	2,252	3.1%
Total, Former Personnel	167,797	171,221	177,617	6,396	3.7%

ately high Federal compensation paid to individuals with a bachelor's degree or less; Federal employees with professional degrees are actually undercompensated relative to private sector peers, in CBO's analysis.

The generous benefits package offered by the Federal Government includes a defined benefit annuity plan and retiree health care benefits – both are increasingly rare in the private sector. The Federal defined benefit

Chart 7-3. Average Age by Year for Federal and Private Sectors

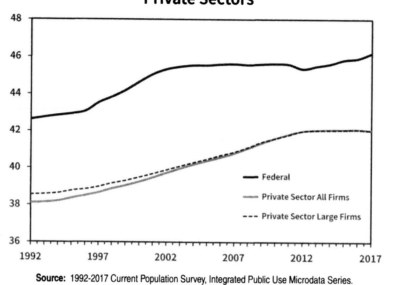

Source: 1992-2017 Current Population Survey, Integrated Public Use Microdata Series.

Notes: Federal excludes the military and Postal Service, but includes all other Federal workers. Private Sector excludes the self-employed. Neither category includes State and local government workers. Large firms have at least 1,000 workers. This analysis is limited to full-time, full-year workers, i.e. those with at least 1,500 annual hours of work and presents five-year averages. Industry is from the year preceding the year on the horizontal axis.

plan, according to CBO, is the single greatest factor contributing to the disparity in total compensation between the Federal and private sector workforce. To better align with the private sector, the Budget reduces

Federal personnel compensation costs, primarily the annuity portion.

The Budget carries forward several FY 2018 Budget proposals, including: increasing employee payments to the Federal Employee Retirement System (FERS) de-

Chart 7-4. Changes from 1975 to 2017 in Employment as a Percent of Population

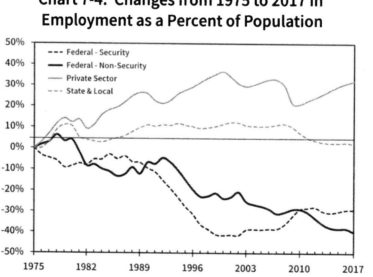

Source: Office of Personnel Management and the Bureau of Labor Statistics.

Notes: Federal excludes the military and Postal Service. Security agencies include the Department of Defense, the Department of Homeland Security, the Department of State, and the Department of Veterans Affairs. Non-Security agencies include the remainder of the Executive Branch. State & Local excludes educational workers.

Maintained by: HRLOB@opm.gov

Chart 7-5
The Human Capital Business Reference Model (HCBRM) functional framework defines Federal Human Capital Management. This map represents the 15 Functions and 54 Sub-functions in the HC lifecycle.

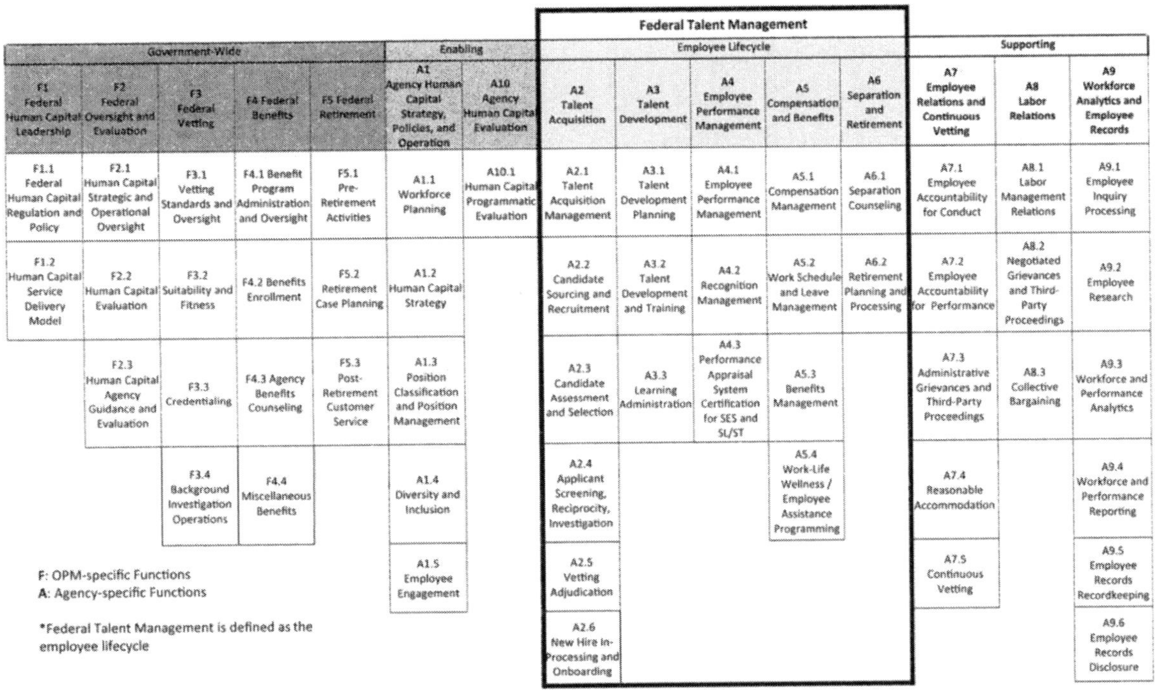

		Government-Wide				Enabling				Federal Talent Management — Employee Lifecycle				Supporting		
F1 Federal Human Capital Leadership	F2 Federal Oversight and Evaluation	F3 Federal Vetting	F4 Federal Benefits	F5 Federal Retirement	A1 Agency Human Capital Strategy, Policies, and Operation	A10 Agency Human Capital Evaluation	A2 Talent Acquisition	A3 Talent Development	A4 Employee Performance Management	A5 Compensation and Benefits	A6 Separation and Retirement	A7 Employee Relations and Continuous Vetting	A8 Labor Relations	A9 Workforce Analytics and Employee Records
F1.1 Federal Human Capital Regulation and Policy	F2.1 Human Capital Strategic and Operational Oversight	F3.1 Vetting Standards and Oversight	F4.1 Benefit Program Administration and Oversight	F5.1 Pre-Retirement Activities	A1.1 Workforce Planning	A10.1 Human Capital Programmatic Evaluation	A2.1 Talent Acquisition Management	A3.1 Talent Development Planning	A4.1 Employee Performance Management	A5.1 Compensation Management	A6.1 Separation Counseling	A7.1 Employee Accountability for Conduct	A8.1 Labor Management Relations	A9.1 Employee Inquiry Processing
F1.2 Human Capital Service Delivery Model	F2.2 Human Capital Evaluation	F3.2 Suitability and Fitness	F4.2 Benefits Enrollment	F5.2 Retirement Case Planning	A1.2 Human Capital Strategy		A2.2 Candidate Sourcing and Recruitment	A3.2 Talent Development and Training	A4.2 Recognition Management	A5.2 Work Schedule and Leave Management	A6.2 Retirement Planning and Processing	A7.2 Employee Accountability for Performance	A8.2 Negotiated Grievances and Third-Party Proceedings	A9.2 Employee Research
	F2.3 Human Capital Agency Guidance and Evaluation	F3.3 Credentialing	F4.3 Agency Benefits Counseling	F5.3 Post-Retirement Customer Service	A1.3 Position Classification and Position Management		A2.3 Candidate Assessment and Selection	A3.3 Learning Administration	A4.3 Performance Appraisal System Certification for SES and SL/ST	A5.3 Benefits Management		A7.3 Administrative Grievances and Third-Party Proceedings	A8.3 Collective Bargaining	A9.3 Workforce and Performance Analytics
		F3.4 Background Investigation Operations	F4.4 Miscellaneous Benefits		A1.4 Diversity and Inclusion		A2.4 Applicant Screening, Reciprocity, Investigation			A5.4 Work-Life Wellness / Employee Assistance Programming		A7.4 Reasonable Accommodation		A9.4 Workforce and Performance Reporting
					A1.5 Employee Engagement		A2.5 Vetting Adjudication					A7.5 Continuous Vetting		A9.5 Employee Records Recordkeeping
							A2.6 New Hire In-Processing and Onboarding							A9.6 Employee Records Disclosure

F: OPM-specific Functions
A: Agency-specific Functions

*Federal Talent Management is defined as the employee lifecycle

Table 7–4. TOTAL FEDERAL EMPLOYMENT
(As measured by Full-Time Equivalents)

Description	2017 Actual	2018 Estimate	2019 Estimate	Change: 2018 to 2019 FTE	Change: 2018 to 2019 Percent
Executive Branch Civilian:					
All Agencies, Except Postal Service	2,062,068	2,085,101	2,095,203	10,102	0.5%
Postal Service [1]	591,179	582,346	583,078	732	0.1%
Subtotal, Executive Branch Civilian	2,653,247	2,667,447	2,678,281	10,834	0.4%
Executive Branch Uniformed Military:					
Department of Defense [2]	1,337,669	1,352,081	1,378,630	26,549	1.9%
Department of Homeland Security (USCG)	41,137	41,503	41,495	–8	–*
Commissioned Corps (DOC, EPA, HHS)	6,792	6,929	7,024	95	1.4%
Subtotal, Uniformed Military	1,385,598	1,400,513	1,427,149	26,636	1.9%
Subtotal, Executive Branch	4,038,845	4,067,960	4,105,430	37,470	0.9%
Legislative Branch [3]	29,640	32,745	33,408	663	2.0%
Judicial Branch	32,810	33,214	33,351	137	0.4%
Grand Total	**4,101,295**	**4,133,919**	**4,172,189**	**38,270**	**0.9%**

[1] Includes Postal Rate Commission.

[2] Includes activated Guard and Reserve members on active duty. Does not include Full-Time Support (Active Guard & Reserve (AGRSs)) paid from Reserve Component appropriations.

[3] FTE data not available for the Senate (positions filled were used for actual year and extended at same level).

* Non-zero less than 0.1%

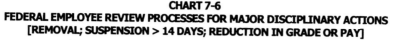

CHART 7-6
FEDERAL EMPLOYEE REVIEW PROCESSES FOR MAJOR DISCIPLINARY ACTIONS
[REMOVAL; SUSPENSION > 14 DAYS; REDUCTION IN GRADE OR PAY]

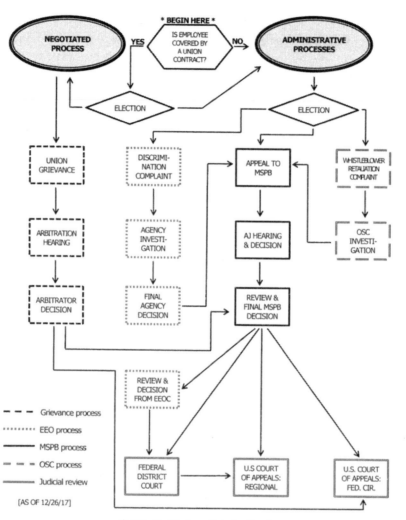

Source: Merit Systems Protection Board

fined benefit plan, so that employees and their employing agency pay an equal share of the employee's annuity cost; and reducing or eliminating cost of living adjustments for existing and future retirees. Increased employee annuity contributions would be phased in at a rate of one percent per year. Also carried forward from the 2018 Budget are proposals to base annuity calculations on employees' "High-5" salary years instead of their "High-3" salary years (a common private sector practice), and the elimination of the FERS Special Retirement Supplement for those employees who retire before their Social Security eligibility age.

This Budget further proposes to modify the "G" fund, an investment vehicle available only through the Thrift Savings Plan (TSP), the defined contribution plan for Federal employees. G fund investors benefit from receiving a medium-term Treasury Bond rate of return on what is essentially a short-term security.

The Budget would instead base the G-fund yield on a short-term T-bill rate. The TSP, one of the largest defined contribution plans in the world, is popular among Federal employees, who appreciate having a pre-tax investment vehicle with low administrative costs and employer matching contributions. The TSP is also taxpayer-friendly, since the program has no unfunded liabilities. In contrast, the Civil Service Retirement and Disability Fund, the Federal defined benefit programs' trust fund, operates like Social Security; it has large, unfunded liabilities backed only by Government IOUs. The TSP is a particularly attractive benefit to young, mobile workers not intending to make a career of Federal service. The Budget, therefore, funds a study to explore the potential benefits, including the recruitment benefit, of creating a defined-contribution only annuity benefit for new Federal workers, and those desiring to transfer out of the existing hybrid system.

Federal employee sick and annual leave benefits are also disproportionate to the private sector. All Federal employees receive 10 paid holidays and up to 13 sick days annually, as well as 13 to 26 vacation days, depending on tenure. This Budget proposes to transition the existing civilian leave system to a model that has worked well in the private sector, which is to grant employees maximum flexibility by combining all leave into one paid time off category. This would reduce total leave days, while adding a short term disability insurance policy to protect employees who experience a serious medical situation.

Across the board pay increases have long-term fixed costs, yet fail to address existing pay disparities, or target mission critical recruitment and retention goals. The Administration therefore proposes a pay freeze for Federal civilian employees for 2019. This Administration believes in pay for performance. The existing Federal salary structure rewards longevity over performance. This is most evident in the tenure-based "step-increase" promotions that white-collar workers receive on a fixed, periodic schedule without regard to whether they are performing at an exceptional level or merely passable (they are granted 99.7 percent of the time). The Budget proposes to slow the frequency of these step increases, while increasing performance-based pay for workers in mission-critical areas.

Separately, the Budget proposes $50 million for a centrally-managed fund to finance innovative approaches to meeting critical recruitment, retention and reskilling needs across the Government. The President's Management Council would designate a board of Federal officials to manage the fund, which would review and select from among agency and cross-agency proposals to pilot innovative and cost-effective ways to strengthen the workforce, to meet future workforce challenges, and to evaluate the impacts in a manner that best informs future policies.

Fixing Hiring and Employee Relations

Federal jobs can take more than a year to fill. The job announcements remain a confusing cipher to applicants. The hiring process – which includes at least 14 steps – is cumbersome and frustrating for Federal hiring managers. As the nature of work changes, the Federal Government requires more term employees. Many individuals are interested in public service but not seeking a career in the civil service. Existing Federal hiring rules make term hiring as difficult as hiring a permanent employee.

Another major hindrance to timely hiring is a massive security investigation inventory. The Administration inherited a significant and growing inventory of background investigations for Federal employment and security clearances. The inventory grew from a steady-state of about 190,000 cases in August 2014 to more than 722,000 by August of last year. It currently stands at more than 706,000. The inventory creates dramatic delays in the hiring process across Government, especially those agencies in need of personnel with a security clearance. Beyond the immediate problem, fundamental reform of the background investigation process is necessary, to both increase efficiency and reduce costs.

Federal Agencies face challenges in effectively implementing information technology (IT) workforce planning and defining cybersecurity staffing needs. Execution of the National Initiative for Cybersecurity Education coding structure is expected to identify critical cyber needs by the end of 2018. IT and cybersecurity recruitment and retention initiatives will continue to focus on mitigation of critical skill gaps and retaining current IT and cybersecurity talent. The Government will experiment in finding new ways to hire the necessary cyber workforce.

As agencies implement new technology and processes, the Administration will invest in reskilling the workforce to meet current needs. Employees who perform transactional work that is phased out can shift to working more directly with customers or on more complex and strategic issues. Current employees can shift from legacy positions into emerging fields in which the Government faces shortages, including data analysis, cybersecurity and other IT disciplines.

Another area of focus is the Senior Executive Service (SES), the roughly 7,000 high-ranking Federal managers who hold many of the most responsible career positions in the Government. SES members are disproportionately retirement-eligible. The Administration is continuing efforts to modernize policies and practices governing the SES, including creating a more robust and effective SES succession pipeline, which could include more recruitment outreach into the private sector.

Many new Federal employees still have paper copies of onboarding documents printed and stored. Employees who move between agencies need to have personnel data, such as basic identifiers or health benefits elections manually re-entered. Electronic personnel files contain scanned copies of old documents, as opposed to being truly digital and interoperable between agencies. The Administration, however, is creating a single electronic identifier for employees that follows them throughout their career and will enable agencies to advance their use of data-driven human resources decisions.

At the end of their careers, a long-standing backlog in Federal retirement claims processing remains an inconvenience to Federal retirees. Paper personnel files on individual employees are maintained in a facility housed in a Pennsylvania mine with 28,000 filing cabinets. Retirement claims may require manual intervention or labor-intensive calculations.

Federal employer-employee relations activities currently consume considerable management time and taxpayer resources, and may negatively impact efficiency, effectiveness, cost of operations, and employee accountability and performance. About 60 percent of Federal employees belong to a union. Federal statute defines the parameters of collective bargaining, which are different than those in the private sector and State or local governments. Federal employees are not allowed to strike and unions must represent all eligible employees regardless of paid membership. Fewer items are negotiable than in the private sector. Yet, collective bargaining contracts can have a significant impact on agency performance, workplace productivity, and employee satisfaction. The Administration sees an opportunity for progress on this front and intends to overhaul labor-management relations. On September 29, 2017, Executive Order 13812 rescinded the requirement for labor-management forums. Agencies were further instructed to remove any internal policies, programs, or guidelines related to existing forums.

Long-term Workforce Planning and Strategies

All agencies are responsible for being good stewards of taxpayer funds. To that end, in M-17-22, "Comprehensive Plan for Reforming the Federal Government and Reducing the Federal Civilian Workforce," the Office of Management and Budget (OMB) required agencies to create short and long term workforce plans to right-size their workforces in keeping with the agency's current mission. The agency plans were used to develop long-term workforce strategies, including the staffing levels proposed in the 2019 Budget.

Agencies will continue to examine their workforces to determine what jobs they need to accomplish their mission, taking into account the impact of technological investments that automate transactional processes, artificial intelligence that can streamline the byzantine compliance and regulatory processes, online and telephone chat-bots to improve customer service, and other such tools that may reduce agency personnel needs. Currently, many professionals are performing tasks that the private sector dispatches via technology tools such as "bots" and artificial intelligence. A Deloitte study used BLS data to show that Federal agencies spend millions of hours performing tasks like documenting and recording paperwork, evaluating information to determine compliance, monitoring resources, and responding to routine questions. The study estimated that VA spent more than 150 million hours on documenting and recording information. It found that Department of Homeland Security (DHS) could save 800,000 hours annually by increasing automation of compliance with standards.

Agencies for too long have devoted too many positions to low-value work. Several agencies are already using shared-service models for mission-support positions, which can also reduce their need for full-time employees. Fewer staff positions may also be needed due to changes in Federal procurement, real estate utilization and administrative processes.

Due to the initial hiring freeze and subsequent efforts, non-security agencies (i.e. USDA, DOI, Treasury, Housing & Urban Development, and Environmental Protection Agency) conducted substantial decreases to the size of their workforce. The 2019 Budget details further proposed reductions in specific agencies. Estimated employment levels for 2019 are higher than the 2017 actual FTE levels and an increase from the 2018 estimates, all of which are slightly less than 2.1 million civilian employees. The Federal workforce increased only modestly in 2017, from 2,057,300 to 2,062,100. From 2018 to 2019, increases occur in 7 of the 24 Chief Financial Officers Act

agencies, primarily in security-related agencies (DOD, VA, and particularly DHS), as well as Commerce as it prepares for the 2020 Census, which requires a large influx of short-term staff. Table 7-4 shows actual 2017 total Federal employment and estimated totals for 2018 and 2019, including the Uniformed Military, Postal Service, Judicial and Legislative branches.

Maximizing Employee Performance

One of the Administration's first priorities was to address poor performers and conduct violators. In lifting the January 23, 2017 hiring freeze, the Administration chose to focus on improving the quality of the current workforce. OMB required all agencies to submit plans to address employee performance. The Administration recognizes that the vast majority of employees uphold their Oath of Office and work diligently. A percentage, however, are simply unable or unwilling to perform at acceptable levels. Their peers in the Federal workforce recognize this issue. Every year, the vast majority of Federal workers surveyed disagree with the statement that, "in my work, steps are taken to deal with a poor performer who cannot or will not improve."

The requirements to successfully remove an employee for misconduct or poor performance are onerous (see Chart 7-6). Employees have a variety of avenues to appeal and challenge actions. Agencies may settle cases to avoid the expense of litigation, regardless of the strength and documentation of a manager's case. Settling can avoid the prospect of an even more costly decision by an arbitrator unaccountable to taxpayers. Federal managers are reluctant to expend the energy necessary to go through the process of dismissing the worst performers and conduct violators. In some cases, the most immediate victims of employee misconduct are fellow employees, who may file claims themselves that they are being harassed, hazed, or threatened by their colleague.

Each year, fewer than one in 200 Federal employees is fired. In contrast, more than 99 percent of employees are rated as fully successful or higher in their evaluations. The failure of Federal performance management systems to adequately differentiate the performance of individuals extends up to the SES cadre, where the modal rating is "exceeds expectations," and at many agencies it is "outstanding." This sort of grade inflation does little to help managers reward high performers or otherwise make necessary distinctions to inform decisions concerning the workforce. This is yet another area where the Federal workforce could benefit from adopting some private sector norms.

The Federal workforce also contains untold numbers of selfless civil servants who perform their jobs in a manner that honors and uplifts their fellow citizens. They are part of the fabric that makes this Nation great. We need reforms that recognize and reward such individuals, and free them from unnecessary red tape so that they can more efficiently and effectively support the mission of Government.

BUDGET CONCEPTS AND BUDGET PROCESS

8. BUDGET CONCEPTS

The budget system of the United States Government provides the means for the President and the Congress to decide how much money to spend, what to spend it on, and how to raise the money they have decided to spend. Through the budget system, they determine the allocation of resources among the agencies of the Federal Government and between the Federal Government and the private sector. The budget system focuses primarily on dollars, but it also allocates other resources, such as Federal employment. The decisions made in the budget process affect the Nation as a whole, State and local governments, and individual Americans. Many budget decisions have worldwide significance. The Congress and the President enact budget decisions into law. The budget system ensures that these laws are carried out.

This chapter provides an overview of the budget system and explains some of the more important budget concepts. It includes summary dollar amounts to illustrate major concepts. Other chapters of the budget documents discuss these amounts and more detailed amounts in greater depth.

The following section discusses the budget process, covering formulation of the President's Budget, action by the Congress, and execution of enacted budget laws. The next section provides information on budget coverage, including a discussion of on-budget and off-budget amounts, functional classification, presentation of budget data, types of funds, and full-cost budgeting. Subsequent sections discuss the concepts of receipts and collections, budget authority, and outlays. These sections are followed by discussions of Federal credit; surpluses, deficits, and means of financing; Federal employment; and the basis for the budget figures. A glossary of budget terms appears at the end of the chapter.

Various laws, enacted to carry out requirements of the Constitution, govern the budget system. The chapter refers to the principal ones by title throughout the text and gives complete citations in the section just preceding the glossary.

THE BUDGET PROCESS

The budget process has three main phases, each of which is related to the others:

1. Formulation of the President's Budget;

2. Action by the Congress; and

3. Execution of enacted budget laws.

Formulation of the President's Budget

The Budget of the United States Government consists of several volumes that set forth the President's fiscal policy goals and priorities for the allocation of resources by the Government. The primary focus of the Budget is on the budget year—the next fiscal year for which the Congress needs to make appropriations, in this case 2019. (Fiscal year 2019 will begin on October 1, 2018, and end on September 30, 2019.) The Budget also covers the nine years following the budget year in order to reflect the effect of budget decisions over the longer term. It includes the funding levels provided for the current year, in this case 2018, which allows the reader to compare the President's Budget proposals with the most recently enacted levels. The Budget also includes data on the most recently completed fiscal year, in this case 2017, so that the reader can compare budget estimates to actual accounting data.

In a normal year, the President begins the process of formulating the budget by establishing general budget and fiscal policy guidelines, usually by the spring of each year, at least nine months before the President transmits the budget to the Congress and at least 18 months before the fiscal year begins. (See the "Budget Calendar" later in this chapter.) Based on these guidelines, the Office of Management and Budget (OMB) works with the Federal agencies to establish specific policy directions and planning levels to guide the preparation of their budget requests.

During the formulation of the budget, the President, the Director of OMB, and other officials in the Executive Office of the President continually exchange information, proposals, and evaluations bearing on policy decisions with the Secretaries of the departments and the heads of the other Government agencies. Decisions reflected in previously enacted budgets, including the one for the fiscal year in progress, reactions to the last proposed budget (which the Congress is considering at the same time the process of preparing the forthcoming budget begins), and evaluations of program performance all influence decisions concerning the forthcoming budget, as do projections of the economic outlook, prepared jointly by the Council of Economic Advisers, OMB, and the Treasury Department.

In early fall, agencies submit their budget requests to OMB, where analysts review them and identify issues that OMB officials need to discuss with the agencies. OMB and the agencies resolve many issues themselves. Others require the involvement of White House policy officials and the President. This decision-making process is usually completed by late December. At that time, the final stage of developing detailed budget data and the preparation of the budget documents begins.

The decision-makers must consider the effects of economic and technical assumptions on the budget estimates. Interest rates, economic growth, the rate of inflation, the unemployment rate, and the number of people eligible for various benefit programs, among other factors, affect Government spending and receipts. Small changes in these assumptions can alter budget estimates by many billions of dollars. (Chapter 2, "Economic Assumptions and Interactions with the Budget," provides more information on this subject.)

Thus, the budget formulation process involves the simultaneous consideration of the resource needs of individual programs, the allocation of resources among the agencies and functions of the Federal Government, and the total outlays and receipts that are appropriate in light of current and prospective economic conditions.

The law governing the President's budget requires its transmittal to the Congress on or after the first Monday in January but not later than the first Monday in February of each year for the following fiscal year, which begins on October 1. The budget is usually scheduled for transmission to the Congress on the first Monday in February, giving the Congress eight months to act on the budget before the fiscal year begins. In years when a Presidential transition has taken place, this timeline for budget release is commonly extended to allow the new Administration sufficient time to take office and formulate its budget policy. While there is no specific timeline set for this circumstance, the detailed budget is usually completed and released in April or May. However, in order to aid the congressional budget process (discussed below), new Administrations often release a budget blueprint that contains broad spending outlines and descriptions of major policies and priorities in February or March.

Congressional Action[1]

The Congress considers the President's budget proposals and approves, modifies, or disapproves them. It can change funding levels, eliminate programs, or add programs not requested by the President. It can add or eliminate taxes and other sources of receipts or make other changes that affect the amount of receipts collected.

The Congress does not enact a budget as such. Through the process of adopting a planning document called a budget resolution (described below), the Congress agrees on targets for total spending and receipts, the size of the deficit or surplus, and the debt limit. The budget resolution provides the framework within which individual congressional committees prepare appropriations bills and other spending and receipts legislation. The Congress provides spending authority—funding—for specified purposes in appropriations acts each year. It also enacts changes each year in other laws that affect spending and receipts. Both

appropriations acts and these other laws are discussed in the following paragraphs.

In making appropriations, the Congress does not vote on the level of outlays (spending) directly, but rather on budget authority, or funding, which is the authority provided by law to incur financial obligations that will result in outlays. In a separate process, prior to making appropriations, the Congress usually enacts legislation that authorizes an agency to carry out particular programs, authorizes the appropriation of funds to carry out those programs, and, in some cases, limits the amount that can be appropriated for the programs. Some authorizing legislation expires after one year, some expires after a specified number of years, and some is permanent. The Congress may enact appropriations for a program even though there is no specific authorization for it or its authorization has expired.

The Congress begins its work on its budget resolution shortly after it receives the President's budget. Under the procedures established by the Congressional Budget Act of 1974, the Congress decides on budget targets before commencing action on individual appropriations. The Act requires each standing committee of the House and Senate to recommend budget levels and report legislative plans concerning matters within the committee's jurisdiction to the Budget Committee in each body. The House and Senate Budget Committees then each design and report, and each body then considers, a concurrent resolution on the budget—a congressional budget plan, or budget resolution. The budget resolution sets targets for total receipts and for budget authority and outlays, both in total and by functional category (see "Functional Classification" later in this chapter). It also sets targets for the budget deficit or surplus and for Federal debt subject to statutory limit.

The congressional timetable calls for the House and Senate to resolve differences between their respective versions of the congressional budget resolution and adopt a single budget resolution by April 15 of each year.

In the report on the budget resolution, the Budget Committees allocate the total on-budget budget authority and outlays set forth in the resolution to the Appropriations Committees and the other committees that have jurisdiction over spending. These committee allocations are commonly known as "302(a)" allocations, in reference to the section of the Congressional Budget Act that provides for them. The Appropriations Committees are then required to divide their 302(a) allocations of budget authority and outlays among their subcommittees. These subcommittee allocations are known as "302(b)" allocations. There are procedural hurdles associated with considering appropriations bills ("discretionary" spending) that would breach or further breach an Appropriations subcommittee's 302(b) allocation. Similar procedural hurdles exist for considering legislation that would cause the 302(a) allocation for any committee to be breached or further breached. The Budget Committees' reports may discuss assumptions about the level of funding for major programs. While these assumptions do not

---

[1] For a fuller discussion of the congressional budget process, see Bill Heniff Jr., Introduction to the Federal Budget Process (Congressional Research Service Report 98–721), and Robert Keith and Allen Schick, Manual on the Federal Budget Process (Congressional Research Service Report 98–720, archived).

bind the other committees and subcommittees, they may influence their decisions.

Budget resolutions may include "reserve funds," which permit adjustment of the resolution allocations as necessary to accommodate legislation addressing specific matters, such as health care or tax reform. Reserve funds are most often limited to legislation that is deficit neutral, including increases in some areas offset by decreases in others.

The budget resolution may also contain "reconciliation directives" (discussed below) to the committees responsible for tax laws and for mandatory spending—programs not controlled by annual appropriation acts—in order to conform the level of receipts and this type of spending to the targets in the budget resolution.

Since the concurrent resolution on the budget is not a law, it does not require the President's approval. However, the Congress considers the President's views in preparing budget resolutions, because legislation developed to meet congressional budget allocations does require the President's approval. In some years, the President and the joint leadership of Congress have formally agreed on plans to reduce the deficit or balance the budget. These agreements were then reflected in the budget resolution and legislation passed for those years.

If the Congress does not pass a budget resolution, the House and Senate typically adopt one or more "deeming resolutions" in the form of a simple resolution or as a provision of a larger bill. A deeming resolution may serve nearly all functions of a budget resolution, except it may not trigger reconciliation procedures in the Senate.

Once the Congress approves the budget resolution, it turns its attention to enacting appropriations bills and authorizing legislation. Appropriations bills are initiated in the House. They provide the budgetary resources for the majority of Federal programs, but only a minority of Federal spending. The Appropriations Committee in each body has jurisdiction over annual appropriations. These committees are divided into subcommittees that hold hearings and review detailed budget justification materials prepared by the Executive Branch agencies within the subcommittee's jurisdiction. After a bill has been draft-

ed by a subcommittee, the full committee and the whole House, in turn, must approve the bill, sometimes with amendments to the original version. The House then forwards the bill to the Senate, where a similar review follows. If the Senate disagrees with the House on particular matters in the bill, which is often the case, the two bodies form a conference committee (consisting of some Members of each body) to resolve the differences. The conference committee revises the bill and returns it to both bodies for approval. When the revised bill is agreed to, first in the House and then in the Senate, the Congress sends it to the President for approval or veto.

Since 1977, when the start of the fiscal year was established as October 1, there have been only three fiscal years (1989, 1995, and 1997) for which the Congress agreed to and enacted every regular appropriations bill by that date. When one or more appropriations bills has not been agreed to by this date, Congress usually enacts a joint resolution called a "continuing resolution" (CR), which is an interim or stop-gap appropriations bill that provides authority for the affected agencies to continue operations at some specified level until a specific date or until the regular appropriations are enacted. Occasionally, a CR has funded a portion or all of the Government for the entire year.

The Congress must present these CRs to the President for approval or veto. In some cases, Congresses have failed to pass a CR or Presidents have rejected CRs because they contained unacceptable provisions. Left without funds, Government agencies were required by law to shut down operations—with exceptions for some limited activities—until the Congress passed a CR the President would approve. Shutdowns have lasted for periods of a day to several weeks.

The Congress also provides budget authority in laws other than appropriations acts. In fact, while annual appropriations acts fund the majority of Federal programs, they account for only about a third of the total spending in a typical year. Authorizing legislation controls the rest of the spending, which is commonly called "mandatory spending." A distinctive feature of these authorizing laws is that they provide agencies with the authority or

BUDGET CALENDAR

The following timetable highlights the scheduled dates for significant budget events during a normal budget year:

Between the 1st Monday in January and the 1st Monday in February	President transmits the budget
Six weeks later	Congressional committees report budget estimates to Budget Committees
April 15	Action to be completed on congressional budget resolution
May 15	House consideration of annual appropriations bills may begin even if the budget resolution has not been agreed to.
June 10	House Appropriations Committee to report the last of its annual appropriations bills.
June 15	Action to be completed on "reconciliation bill" by the Congress.
June 30	Action on appropriations to be completed by House
July 15	President transmits Mid-Session Review of the Budget
October 1	Fiscal year begins

requirement to spend money without first requiring the Appropriations Committees to enact funding. This category of spending includes interest the Government pays on the public debt and the spending of several major programs, such as Social Security, Medicare, Medicaid, unemployment insurance, and Federal employee retirement. This chapter discusses the control of budget authority and outlays in greater detail under "Budget Authority and Other Budgetary Resources, Obligations, and Outlays." Almost all taxes and most other receipts also result from authorizing laws. Article I, Section 7, of the Constitution provides that all bills for raising revenue shall originate in the House of Representatives. In the House, the Ways and Means Committee initiates tax bills; in the Senate, the Finance Committee has jurisdiction over tax laws.

The budget resolution often includes reconciliation directives, which require authorizing committees to recommend changes in laws that affect receipts or mandatory spending. They direct each designated committee to report amendments to the laws under the committee's jurisdiction that would achieve changes in the levels of receipts or reductions in mandatory spending controlled by those laws. These directives specify the dollar amount of changes that each designated committee is expected to achieve, but do not specify which laws are to be changed or the changes to be made. However, the Budget Committees' reports on the budget resolution frequently discuss assumptions about how the laws would be changed. Like other assumptions in the report, they do not bind the committees of jurisdiction but may influence their decisions. A reconciliation instruction may also specify the total amount by which the statutory limit on the public debt is to be changed.

The committees subject to reconciliation directives draft the implementing legislation. Such legislation may, for example, change the tax code, revise benefit formulas or eligibility requirements for benefit programs, or authorize Government agencies to charge fees to cover some of their costs. Reconciliation bills are typically omnibus legislation, combining the legislation submitted by each reconciled committee in a single act.

Such a large and complicated bill would be difficult to enact under normal legislative procedures because it usually involves changes to tax rates or to popular social programs, generally to reduce projected deficits. The Senate considers such omnibus reconciliation acts under expedited procedures that limit total debate on the bill. To offset the procedural advantage gained by expedited procedures, the Senate places significant restrictions on the substantive content of the reconciliation measure itself, as well as on amendments to the measure. Any material in the bill that is extraneous or that contains changes to the Federal Old-Age and Survivors Insurance and the Federal Disability Insurance programs is not in order under the Senate's expedited reconciliation procedures. Non-germane amendments are also prohibited. The House does not allow reconciliation bills to increase mandatory spending in net, but does allow such bills to increase deficits by reducing revenues. Reconciliation acts, together with appropriations acts for the year, are

usually used to implement broad agreements between the President and the Congress on those occasions where the two branches have negotiated a comprehensive budget plan. Reconciliation acts have sometimes included other matters, such as laws providing the means for enforcing these agreements, as described under "Budget Enforcement."

Budget Enforcement

The Federal Government uses three primary enforcement mechanisms to control revenues, spending, and deficits. First, the Statutory Pay-As-You-Go Act of 2010, enacted on February 12, 2010, reestablished a statutory procedure to enforce a rule of deficit neutrality on new revenue and mandatory spending legislation. Second, the Budget Control Act of 2011 (BCA), enacted on August 2, 2011, amended the Balanced Budget and Emergency Deficit Control Act of 1985 (BBEDCA) by reinstating limits ("caps") on the amount of discretionary budget authority that can be provided through the annual appropriations process. Third, the BCA also created a Joint Select Committee on Deficit Reduction that was instructed to develop a bill to reduce the Federal deficit by at least $1.5 trillion over a 10-year period and imposed automatic spending cuts to achieve $1.2 trillion of deficit reduction over 9 years after the Joint Committee process failed to achieve its deficit reduction goal.

BBEDCA divides spending into two types—discretionary spending and direct or mandatory spending. Discretionary spending is controlled through annual appropriations acts. Funding for salaries and other operating expenses of government agencies, for example, is generally discretionary because it is usually provided by appropriations acts. Direct spending is more commonly called mandatory spending. Mandatory spending is controlled by permanent laws. Medicare and Medicaid payments, unemployment insurance benefits, and farm price supports are examples of mandatory spending, because permanent laws authorize payments for those purposes. Receipts are included under the same statutory enforcement rules that apply to mandatory spending because permanent laws generally control receipts.

Discretionary cap enforcement. BBEDCA specifies spending limits ("caps") on discretionary budget authority for 2012 through 2021. Similar enforcement mechanisms were established by the Budget Enforcement Act of 1990 and were extended in 1993 and 1997, but expired at the end of 2002. The caps originally established by the BCA were divided between security and nonsecurity categories for 2012 and 2013, with a single cap for all discretionary spending established for 2014 through 2021. The security category included discretionary budget authority for the Departments of Defense, Homeland Security, and Veterans Affairs, the National Nuclear Security Administration, the Intelligence Community Management account, and all budget accounts in the international affairs budget function (budget function 150). The nonsecurity category included all discretionary budget authority not included in the security category.

As part of the enforcement mechanisms triggered by the failure of the BCA's Joint Committee process, the security and nonsecurity categories were redefined and established for all years through 2021. The "revised security category" includes discretionary budget authority in the defense budget function 050, which primarily consists of the Department of Defense. The "revised nonsecurity category" includes all discretionary budget authority not included in the defense budget function 050. The redefined categories are commonly referred to as the "defense" and "non-defense" categories, respectively, to distinguish them from the original categories.

Since the Joint Committee sequestration that was ordered on March 1, 2013, the Congress and the President have enacted two agreements to provide more resources to discretionary programs than would have been available under the Joint Committee enforcement mechanisms. These increases to the caps were paid for largely with savings in mandatory spending. The Bipartisan Budget Act (BBA) of 2013 set new discretionary caps for 2014 at $520.5 billion for the defense category and $491.8 billion for the non-defense category and for 2015 at $521.3 billion for the defense category and $492.4 billion for the non-defense category. The BBA of 2015 set new discretionary caps for 2016 at $548.1 billion for the defense category and $518.5 for the non-defense category and for 2017 at $551.1 billion for the defense category and $518.5 billion for the non-defense category. In addition, the BBA of 2013 reaffirmed the defense and non-defense category limits through 2021 and the BBA of 2015 left these in place after 2017. However, these limits are still subject to Joint Committee reductions if those procedures remain in place.

BBEDCA requires OMB to adjust the caps each year for: changes in concepts and definitions; appropriations designated by the Congress and the President as emergency requirements; and appropriations designated by the Congress and the President for Overseas Contingency Operations/Global War on Terrorism. BBEDCA also specifies cap adjustments (which are limited to fixed amounts) for: appropriations for continuing disability reviews and redeterminations by the Social Security Administration; the health care fraud and abuse control program at the Department of Health and Human Services; and appropriations designated by Congress as being for disaster relief.

BBEDCA requires OMB to provide cost estimates of each appropriations act in a report to the Congress within 7 business days after enactment of such act and to publish three discretionary sequestration reports: a "preview" report when the President submits the budget; an "update" report in August, and a "final" report within 15 days after the end of a session of the Congress.

The preview report explains the adjustments that are required by law to the discretionary caps, including any changes in concepts and definitions, and publishes the revised caps. The preview report may also provide a summary of policy changes, if any, proposed by the President in the Budget to those caps. The update and final reports revise the preview report estimates to reflect the effects of newly enacted discretionary laws. In addition, the update report must contain a preview estimate of the adjustment for disaster funding for the upcoming fiscal year.

If OMB's final sequestration report for a given fiscal year indicates that the amount of discretionary budget authority provided in appropriations acts for that year exceeds the cap for that category in that year, the President must issue a sequestration order canceling budgetary resources in nonexempt accounts within that category by the amount necessary to eliminate the breach. Under sequestration, each nonexempt account within a category is reduced by a dollar amount calculated by multiplying the enacted level of sequestrable budgetary resources in that account by the uniform percentage necessary to eliminate a breach within that category. BBEDCA specifies special rules for reducing some programs and exempts some programs from sequestration entirely. For example, any sequestration of certain health and medical care accounts is limited to 2 percent. Also, if a continuing resolution is in effect when OMB issues its final sequestration report, the sequestration calculations will be based on the annualized amount provided by that continuing resolution. During the 1990s and so far under the BCA caps, the threat of sequestration proved sufficient to ensure compliance with the discretionary spending limits. In that respect, discretionary sequestration can be viewed first as an incentive for compliance and second as a remedy for noncompliance.

Supplemental appropriations can also trigger spending reductions. From the end of a session of the Congress through the following June 30th, a within-session discretionary sequestration of current-year spending is imposed if appropriations for the current year cause a cap to be breached. In contrast, if supplemental appropriations enacted in the last quarter of a fiscal year (i.e., July 1 through September 30) cause the caps to be breached, the required reduction is instead achieved by reducing the applicable spending limit for the following fiscal year by the amount of the breach, because the size of the potential sequestration in relation to the unused funding remaining for the current year could severely disrupt agencies' operations.

Direct spending enforcement. The Statutory Pay-As-You-Go Act of 2010 requires that new legislation changing mandatory spending or revenue must be enacted on a "pay-as-you-go" (PAYGO) basis; that is, that the cumulative effects of such legislation must not increase projected on-budget deficits. Unlike the budget enforcement mechanism for discretionary programs, PAYGO is a permanent requirement, and it does not impose a cap on spending or a floor on revenues. Instead, PAYGO requires that legislation reducing revenues must be fully offset by cuts in mandatory programs or by revenue increases, and that any bills increasing mandatory spending must be fully offset by revenue increases or cuts in mandatory spending.

This requirement of deficit neutrality is not enforced on a bill-by-bill basis, but is based on two cumulative scorecards that tally the cumulative budgetary effects of PAYGO legislation as averaged over rolling 5- and 10-

year periods starting with the budget year. Any impacts of PAYGO legislation on the current year deficit are counted as budget year impacts when placed on the scorecard. Like the discretionary caps, PAYGO is enforced by sequestration. Within 14 business days after a congressional session ends, OMB issues an annual PAYGO report and determines whether a violation of the PAYGO requirement has occurred. If either the 5- or 10-year scorecard shows net costs in the budget year column, the President is required to issue a sequestration order implementing across-the-board cuts to nonexempt mandatory programs by an amount sufficient to offset those net costs. The PAYGO effects of legislation may be directed in legislation by reference to statements inserted into the *Congressional Record* by the chairmen of the House and Senate Budget Committees. Any such estimates are determined by the Budget Committees and are informed by, but not required to match, the cost estimates prepared by the Congressional Budget Office (CBO). If this procedure is not followed, then the PAYGO effects of the legislation are determined by OMB. During the first year of statutory PAYGO, nearly half the bills included congressional estimates. Subsequently, OMB estimates were used for all but one of the enacted bills due to the absence of a congressional estimate. Provisions of mandatory spending or receipts legislation that are designated in that legislation as an emergency requirement are not scored as PAYGO budgetary effects.

The PAYGO rules apply to the outlays resulting from outyear changes in mandatory programs made in appropriations acts and to all revenue changes made in appropriations acts. However, outyear changes to mandatory programs as part of provisions that have zero net outlay effects over the sum of the current year and the next five fiscal years are not considered PAYGO.

The PAYGO rules do not apply to increases in mandatory spending or decreases in receipts that result automatically under existing law. For example, mandatory spending for benefit programs, such as unemployment insurance, rises when the number of beneficiaries rises, and many benefit payments are automatically increased for inflation under existing laws.

The Senate imposes points of order against consideration of tax or mandatory spending legislation that would violate the PAYGO principle, although the time periods covered by the Senate's rule and the treatment of previously enacted costs or savings may differ in some respects from the requirements of the Statutory Pay-As-You-Go Act of 2010. The House, in contrast, imposes points of order on legislation increasing mandatory spending in net, whether or not those costs are offset by revenue increases, but the House rule does not constrain the size of tax cuts or require them to be offset.

Joint Committee reductions. The failure of the Joint Select Committee on Deficit Reduction to propose, and the Congress to enact, legislation to reduce the deficit by at least $1.2 trillion triggered automatic reductions to discretionary and mandatory spending in fiscal years 2013 through 2021. The reductions are implemented through a combination of sequestration of mandatory spending

and reductions in the discretionary caps. These reductions have already been ordered to take effect for 2013 through 2018, with some modifications as provided for in the American Taxpayer Relief Act of 2012, the BBA of 2013, and the BBA of 2015. Unless any legislative changes are enacted, further reductions will be implemented by pro rata reductions to the discretionary caps from 2019 through 2021, which would be reflected in OMB's discretionary sequestration preview report for those years, and by a sequestration of non-exempt mandatory spending for 2019 onward, which would be ordered when the President's Budget is transmitted to Congress and would take effect beginning October 1 of the upcoming fiscal year.

OMB is required to calculate the amount of the deficit reduction required for 2019 onward as follows:

- The $1.2 trillion savings target is reduced by 18 percent to account for debt service.

- The resulting net savings of $984 billion is divided by nine to spread the reductions in equal amounts across the nine years, 2013 through 2021.

- The annual spending reduction of $109.3 billion is divided equally between the defense and non-defense functions.

- The annual reduction of $54.7 billion for each functional category of spending is divided proportionally between discretionary and direct spending programs, using as the base the discretionary cap, redefined as outlined in the discretionary cap enforcement section above, and the most recent baseline estimate of non-exempt mandatory outlays.

- The resulting reductions in defense and non-defense direct spending are implemented through a sequestration order released with the President's Budget and taking effect the following October 1st. The reductions in discretionary spending are applied as reductions in the discretionary caps, and are enforced through the discretionary cap enforcement procedures discussed earlier in this section.

Subsequent to the enactment of the BCA, the mandatory sequestration provisions were extended beyond 2021 by the BBA of 2013, which extended sequestration through 2023, P.L. 113-82, commonly referred to as the Military Retired Pay Restoration Act, which extended sequestration through 2024, and the BBA of 2015, which extended mandatory sequestration through 2025. Sequestration in these four years is to be applied using the same percentage reductions for defense and non-defense as calculated for 2021 under the procedures outlined above.[2]

The 2019 Budget proposes to remain within the discretionary total of $1,092 billion under current law after

---

[2] The BBA of 2015 specified that, notwithstanding the 2 percent limit on Medicare sequestration in the BCA, in extending sequestration into 2025 the reduction in the Medicare program should be 4.0 percent for the first half of the sequestration period and zero for the second half of the period.

accounting for the discretionary cap reductions for 2019, as ordered in the Joint Committee enforcement report issued simultaneously with the 2019 Budget. However, the Budget would set the 2019 cap for defense programs at $627 billion (up from $562 billion) and the non-defense cap at $465 billion (down from $530 billion). The Budget further proposes new caps for the outyears that would fund defense needs while further reducing the non-defense category. In addition, the Budget proposes that the Joint Committee mandatory sequestration be extended to 2028. For more information on these proposals, see Chapter 10 of this volume, "Budget Process."

Budget Execution

Government agencies may not spend or obligate more than the Congress has appropriated, and they may use funds only for purposes specified in law. The Antideficiency Act prohibits them from spending or obligating the Government to spend in advance of an appropriation, unless specific authority to do so has been provided in law. Additionally, the Act requires the President to apportion the budgetary resources available for most executive branch agencies. The President has delegated this authority to OMB. Some apportionments are by time periods (usually by quarter of the fiscal year), some are by projects or activities, and others are by a combination of both. Agencies may request OMB to reapportion funds during the year to accommodate changing circumstances. This system helps to ensure that funds do not run out before the end of the fiscal year.

During the budget execution phase, the Government sometimes finds that it needs more funding than the Congress has appropriated for the fiscal year because of unanticipated circumstances. For example, more might be needed to respond to a severe natural disaster. Under such circumstances, the Congress may enact a supplemental appropriation.

On the other hand, the President may propose to reduce a previously enacted appropriation. The President may propose to either "cancel" or "rescind" the amount. If the President initiates the withholding of funds while the Congress considers his request, the amounts are apportioned as "deferred" or "withheld pending rescission" on the OMB-approved apportionment form. Agencies are instructed not to withhold funds without the prior approval of OMB. When OMB approves a withholding, the Impoundment Control Act requires that the President transmit a "special message" to the Congress. The historical reason for the special message is to inform Congress that the President has unilaterally withheld funds that were enacted in regular appropriations acts. The notification allows the Congress to consider the proposed rescission in a timely way. The last time the President initiated the withholding of funds was in fiscal year 2000.

COVERAGE OF THE BUDGET

Federal Government and Budget Totals

The budget documents provide information on all Federal agencies and programs. However, because the laws governing Social Security (the Federal Old-Age and Survivors Insurance and the Federal Disability Insurance trust funds) and the Postal Service Fund require that the receipts and outlays for those activities be excluded from the budget totals and from the calculation of the deficit or surplus, the budget presents on-budget and off-budget totals. The off-budget totals include the Federal transactions excluded by law from the budget totals. The on-budget and off-budget amounts are added together to derive the totals for the Federal Government. These are sometimes referred to as the unified or consolidated budget totals.

It is not always obvious whether a transaction or activity should be included in the budget. Where there is a question, OMB normally follows the recommendation of the 1967 President's Commission on Budget Concepts to be comprehensive of the full range of Federal agencies, programs, and activities. In recent years, for example, the budget has included the transactions of the Affordable Housing Program funds, the Universal Service Fund, the Public Company Accounting Oversight Board, the Securities Investor Protection Corporation, Guaranty Agencies Reserves, the National Railroad Retirement Investment Trust, the United Mine Workers Combined Benefits Fund, the Federal Financial Institutions Examination Council, Electric Reliability Organizations (EROs) established pursuant to the Energy Policy Act of 2005, the Corporation for Travel Promotion, and the National Association of Registered Agents and Brokers.

In contrast, the budget excludes tribal trust funds that are owned by Indian tribes and held and managed by the Government in a fiduciary capacity on the tribes' behalf. These funds are not owned by the Government, the Government is not the source of their capital, and the Government's control is limited to the exercise of fiduciary duties. Similarly, the transactions of Government-sponsored enterprises, such as the Federal Home Loan Banks, are not included in the on-budget or off-budget totals. Federal laws established these enterprises for public policy purposes, but they are privately owned and operated corporations. Nevertheless, because of their public charters, the budget discusses them and reports summary financial data in the budget *Appendix* and in some detailed tables.

The budget also excludes the revenues from copyright royalties and spending for subsequent payments to copyright holders where (1) the law allows copyright owners and users to voluntarily set the rate paid for the use of protected material, and (2) the amount paid by users of copyrighted material to copyright owners is related to the frequency or quantity of the material used. The budget excludes license royalties collected and paid out by the

Copyright Office for the retransmission of network broadcasts via cable collected under 17 U.S.C. 111 because these revenues meet both of these conditions. The budget includes the royalties collected and paid out for license fees for digital audio recording technology under 17 U.S.C. 1004, since the amount of license fees paid is unrelated to usage of the material.

The *Appendix* includes a presentation for the Board of Governors of the Federal Reserve System for information only. The amounts are not included in either the on-budget or off-budget totals because of the independent status of the System within the Government. However, the Federal Reserve System transfers its net earnings to the Treasury, and the budget records them as receipts.

Chapter 9 of this volume, "Coverage of the Budget," provides more information on this subject.

Table 8–1. TOTALS FOR THE BUDGET AND THE FEDERAL GOVERNMENT
(In billions of dollars)

	2017 Actual	Estimate	
		2018	2019
Budget authority			
Unified	4,154	4,264	4,571
On-budget	3,349	3,405	3,651
Off-budget	805	859	920
Receipts:			
Unified	3,316	3,340	3,422
On-budget	2,466	2,488	2,517
Off-budget	851	852	905
Outlays:			
Unified	3,982	4,173	4,407
On-budget	3,180	3,316	3,494
Off-budget	801	857	913
Deficit (–) / Surplus (+):			
Unified	–665	–833	–984
On-budget	–715	–828	–977
Off-budget	49	–5	–7

Functional Classification

The functional classification is used to organize budget authority, outlays, and other budget data according to the major purpose served—such as agriculture, transportation, income security, and national defense. There are 20 major functions, 17 of which are concerned with broad areas of national need and are further divided into subfunctions. For example, the Agriculture function comprises the subfunctions Farm Income Stabilization and Agricultural Research and Services. The functional classification meets the Congressional Budget Act requirement for a presentation in the budget by national needs and agency missions and programs. The remaining three functions—Net Interest, Undistributed Offsetting Receipts, and Allowances—enable the functional classification system to cover the entire Federal budget.

The following criteria are used in establishing functional categories and assigning activities to them:

- A function encompasses activities with similar purposes, emphasizing what the Federal Government seeks to accomplish rather than the means of accomplishment, the objects purchased, the clientele or geographic area served (except in the cases of functions 450 for Community and Regional Development, 570 for Medicare, 650 for Social Security, and 700 for Veterans Benefits and Services), or the Federal agency conducting the activity (except in the case of subfunction 051 in the National Defense function, which is used only for defense activities under the Department of Defense—Military).

- A function must be of continuing national importance, and the amounts attributable to it must be significant.

- Each basic unit being classified (generally the appropriation or fund account) usually is classified according to its primary purpose and assigned to only one subfunction. However, some large accounts that serve more than one major purpose are subdivided into two or more functions or subfunctions.

In consultation with the Congress, the functional classification is adjusted from time to time as warranted. Detailed functional tables, which provide information on Government activities by function and subfunction, are available online at *https://www.whitehouse.gov/omb/analytical-perspectives/* and on the *Budget CD-ROM*.

Agencies, Accounts, Programs, Projects, and Activities

Various summary tables in the *Analytical Perspectives* volume of the Budget provide information on budget authority, outlays, and offsetting collections and receipts arrayed by Federal agency. A table that lists budget authority and outlays by budget account within each agency and the totals for each agency of budget authority, outlays, and receipts that offset the agency spending totals is available online at: *https://www.whitehouse.gov/omb/analytical-perspectives/* and on the *Budget CD-ROM*. The *Appendix* provides budgetary, financial, and descriptive information about programs, projects, and activities by account within each agency.

Types of Funds

Agency activities are financed through Federal funds and trust funds.

Federal funds comprise several types of funds. Receipt accounts of the *general fund*, which is the greater part of the budget, record receipts not earmarked by law for a specific purpose, such as income tax receipts. The general fund also includes the proceeds of general borrowing. General fund appropriations accounts record general fund expenditures. General fund appropriations draw from general fund receipts and borrowing collectively and, therefore, are not specifically linked to receipt accounts.

Special funds consist of receipt accounts for Federal fund receipts that laws have designated for specific purposes and the associated appropriation accounts for the expenditure of those receipts.

Public enterprise funds are revolving funds used for programs authorized by law to conduct a cycle of business-type operations, primarily with the public, in which outlays generate collections.

Intragovernmental funds are revolving funds that conduct business-type operations primarily within and between Government agencies. The collections and the outlays of revolving funds are recorded in the same budget account.

Trust funds account for the receipt and expenditure of monies by the Government for carrying out specific purposes and programs in accordance with the terms of a statute that designates the fund as a trust fund (such as the Highway Trust Fund) or for carrying out the stipulations of a trust where the Government itself is the beneficiary (such as any of several trust funds for gifts and donations for specific purposes). *Trust revolving funds* are trust funds credited with collections earmarked by law to carry out a cycle of business-type operations.

The Federal budget meaning of the term "trust," as applied to trust fund accounts, differs significantly from its private-sector usage. In the private sector, the beneficiary of a trust usually owns the trust's assets, which are managed by a trustee who must follow the stipulations of the trust. In contrast, the Federal Government owns the assets of most Federal trust funds, and it can raise or lower future trust fund collections and payments, or change the purposes for which the collections are used, by changing existing laws. There is no substantive difference between a trust fund and a special fund or between a trust revolving fund and a public enterprise revolving fund.

However, in some instances, the Government does act as a true trustee of assets that are owned or held for the benefit of others. For example, it maintains accounts on behalf of individual Federal employees in the Thrift Savings Fund, investing them as directed by the individual employee. The Government accounts for such funds in *deposit funds*, which are not included in the budget. (Chapter 23 of this volume, "Trust Funds and Federal Funds," provides more information on this subject.)

Budgeting for Full Costs

A budget is a financial plan for allocating resources—deciding how much the Federal Government should spend in total, program by program, and for the parts of each program and deciding how to finance the spending. The budgetary system provides a process for proposing policies, making decisions, implementing them, and reporting the results. The budget needs to measure costs accurately so that decision makers can compare the cost of a program with its benefits, the cost of one program with another, and the cost of one method of reaching a specified goal with another. These costs need to be fully included in the budget up front, when the spending decision is made, so that executive and congressional decision makers have the information and the incentive to take the total costs into account when setting priorities.

The budget includes all types of spending, including both current operating expenditures and capital investment, and to the extent possible, both are measured on the basis of full cost. Questions are often raised about the measure of capital investment. The present budget provides policymakers the necessary information regarding investment spending. It records investment on a cash basis, and it requires the Congress to provide budget authority before an agency can obligate the Government to make a cash outlay. However, the budget measures only costs, and the benefits with which these costs are compared, based on policy makers' judgment, must be presented in supplementary materials. By these means, the budget allows the total cost of capital investment to be compared up front in a rough way with the total expected future net benefits. Such a comparison of total costs with benefits is consistent with the formal method of cost-benefit analysis of capital projects in government, in which the full cost of a capital asset as the cash is paid out is compared with the full stream of future benefits (all in terms of present values). (Chapter 17 of this volume, "Federal Investment," provides more information on capital investment.)

RECEIPTS, OFFSETTING COLLECTIONS, AND OFFSETTING RECEIPTS

In General

The budget records amounts collected by Government agencies two different ways. Depending on the nature of the activity generating the collection and the law that established the collection, they are recorded as either:

- *Governmental receipts*, which are compared in total to outlays (net of offsetting collections and offsetting receipts) in calculating the surplus or deficit; or

- *Offsetting collections* or *offsetting receipts*, which are deducted from gross outlays to calculate net outlay figures.

Governmental Receipts

Governmental receipts are collections that result from the Government's exercise of its sovereign power to tax or otherwise compel payment. Sometimes they are called receipts, budget receipts, Federal receipts, or Federal revenues. They consist mostly of individual and corporation income taxes and social insurance taxes, but also include excise taxes, compulsory user charges, regulatory fees, customs duties, court fines, certain license fees, and deposits of earnings by the Federal Reserve System. Total receipts for the Federal Government include both on-budget and off-budget receipts (see Table 8–1, "Totals for the Budget and the Federal Government," which appears earlier in this chapter.) Chapter 11 of this volume, "Governmental Receipts," provides more information on governmental receipts.

Offsetting Collections and Offsetting Receipts

Offsetting collections and offsetting receipts are recorded as offsets to (deductions from) spending, not as additions on the receipt side of the budget. These amounts are recorded as offsets to outlays so that the budget totals represent governmental rather than market activity and reflect the Government's net transactions with the public. They are recorded in one of two ways, based on interpretation of laws and longstanding budget concepts and practice. They are offsetting collections when the collections are authorized by law to be credited to expenditure accounts and are generally available for expenditure without further legislation. Otherwise, they are deposited in receipt accounts and called offsetting receipts; many of these receipts are available for expenditure without further legislation.

Offsetting collections and offsetting receipts result from any of the following types of transactions:

- **Business-like transactions or market-oriented activities with the public**—these include voluntary collections from the public in exchange for goods or services, such as the proceeds from the sale of postage stamps, the fees charged for admittance to recreation areas, and the proceeds from the sale of Government-owned land; and reimbursements for damages. The budget records these amounts as *offsetting collections from non-Federal sources* (for offsetting collections) or as *proprietary receipts* (for offsetting receipts).

- **Intragovernmental transactions**—collections from other Federal Government accounts. The budget records collections by one Government account from another as *offsetting collections from Federal sources* (for offsetting collections) or as *intragovernmental receipts* (for offsetting receipts). For example, the General Services Administration rents office space to other Government agencies and records their rental payments as offsetting collections from Federal sources in the Federal Buildings Fund. These transactions are exactly offsetting and do not affect the surplus or deficit. However, they are an important accounting mechanism for allocating costs to the programs and activities that cause the Government to incur the costs.

- **Voluntary gifts and donations**—gifts and donations of money to the Government, which are treated as offsets to budget authority and outlays.

- **Offsetting governmental transactions**—collections from the public that are governmental in nature and should conceptually be treated like Federal revenues and compared in total to outlays (e.g., tax receipts, regulatory fees, compulsory user charges, custom duties, license fees) but required by law or longstanding practice to be misclassified as offsetting. The budget records amounts from non-Federal sources that are governmental in nature as *offsetting governmental collections* (for offsetting collections) or as *offsetting governmental receipts* (for offsetting receipts).

Offsetting Collections

Some laws authorize agencies to credit collections directly to the account from which they will be spent and, usually, to spend the collections for the purpose of the account without further action by the Congress. Most revolving funds operate with such authority. For example, a permanent law authorizes the Postal Service to use collections from the sale of stamps to finance its operations without a requirement for annual appropriations. The budget records these collections in the Postal Service Fund (a revolving fund) and records budget authority in an amount equal to the collections. In addition to revolving funds, some agencies are authorized to charge fees to defray a portion of costs for a program that are otherwise financed by appropriations from the general fund and usually to spend the collections without further action by the Congress. In such cases, the budget records the offsetting collections and resulting budget authority in the program's general fund expenditure account. Similarly, intragovernmental collections authorized by some laws may be recorded as offsetting collections and budget authority in revolving funds or in general fund expenditure accounts.

Sometimes appropriations acts or provisions in other laws limit the obligations that can be financed by offsetting collections. In those cases, the budget records budget authority in the amount available to incur obligations, not in the amount of the collections.

Offsetting collections credited to expenditure accounts automatically offset the outlays at the expenditure account level. Where accounts have offsetting collections, the budget shows the budget authority and outlays of the account both gross (before deducting offsetting collections) and net (after deducting offsetting collections). Totals for the agency, subfunction, and overall budget are net of offsetting collections.

Offsetting Receipts

Collections that are offset against gross outlays but are not authorized to be credited to expenditure accounts are credited to receipt accounts and are called offsetting receipts. Offsetting receipts are deducted from budget authority and outlays in arriving at total net budget authority and outlays. However, unlike offsetting collections credited to expenditure accounts, offsetting receipts do not offset budget authority and outlays at the account level. In most cases, they offset budget authority and outlays at the agency and subfunction levels.

Proprietary receipts from a few sources, however, are not offset against any specific agency or function and are classified as undistributed offsetting receipts. They are deducted from the Government-wide totals for net budget authority and outlays. For example, the collections of rents and royalties from outer continental shelf lands are undistributed because the amounts are large and for the most part are not related to the spending of the agency that administers the transactions and the subfunction that records the administrative expenses.

Similarly, two kinds of intragovernmental transactions—agencies' payments as employers into Federal employee retirement trust funds and interest received by trust funds—are classified as undistributed offsetting receipts. They appear instead as special deductions in computing total net budget authority and outlays for the Government rather than as offsets at the agency level. This special treatment is necessary because the amounts are so large they would distort measures of the agency's activities if they were attributed to the agency.

User Charges

User charges are fees assessed on individuals or organizations for the provision of Government services and for the sale or use of Government goods or resources. The payers of the user charge must be limited in the authorizing legislation to those receiving special benefits from, or subject to regulation by, the program or activity beyond the benefits received by the general public or broad segments of the public (such as those who pay income taxes or customs duties). Policy regarding user charges is established in OMB Circular A–25, "User Charges." The term encompasses proceeds from the sale or use of Government goods and services, including the sale of natural resources (such as timber, oil, and minerals) and proceeds from asset sales (such as property, plant, and equipment). User charges are not necessarily dedicated to the activity they finance and may be credited to the general fund of the Treasury.

The term "user charge" does not refer to a separate budget category for collections. User charges are classified in the budget as receipts, offsetting receipts, or offsetting collections according to the principles explained previously.

See Chapter 12, "Offsetting Collections and Offsetting Receipts," for more information on the classification of user charges.

BUDGET AUTHORITY, OBLIGATIONS, AND OUTLAYS

Budget authority, obligations, and outlays are the primary benchmarks and measures of the budget control system. The Congress enacts laws that provide agencies with spending authority in the form of budget authority. Before agencies can use these resources—obligate this budget authority—OMB must approve their spending plans. After the plans are approved, agencies can enter into binding agreements to purchase items or services or to make grants or other payments. These agreements are recorded as obligations of the United States and deducted from the amount of budgetary resources available to the agency. When payments are made, the obligations are liquidated and outlays recorded. These concepts are discussed more fully below.

Budget Authority and Other Budgetary Resources

Budget authority is the authority provided in law to enter into legal obligations that will result in immediate or future outlays of the Government. In other words, it is the amount of money that agencies are allowed to commit to be spent in current or future years. Government officials may obligate the Government to make outlays only to the extent they have been granted budget authority.

The budget records new budget authority as a dollar amount in the year when it first becomes available for obligation. When permitted by law, unobligated balances of budget authority may be carried over and used in the next year. The budget does not record these balances as budget authority again. They do, however, constitute a budgetary resource that is available for obligation. In some cases,

a provision of law (such as a limitation on obligations or a benefit formula) precludes the obligation of funds that would otherwise be available for obligation. In such cases, the budget records budget authority equal to the amount of obligations that can be incurred. A major exception to this rule is for the highway and mass transit programs financed by the Highway Trust Fund, where budget authority is measured as the amount of contract authority (described later in this chapter) provided in authorizing statutes, even though the obligation limitations enacted in annual appropriations acts restrict the amount of contract authority that can be obligated.

In deciding the amount of budget authority to request for a program, project, or activity, agency officials estimate the total amount of obligations they will need to incur to achieve desired goals and subtract the unobligated balances available for these purposes. The amount of budget authority requested is influenced by the nature of the programs, projects, or activities being financed. For current operating expenditures, the amount requested usually covers the needs for the fiscal year. For major procurement programs and construction projects, agencies generally must request sufficient budget authority in the first year to fully fund an economically useful segment of a procurement or project, even though it may be obligated over several years. This full funding policy is intended to ensure that the decision-makers take into account all costs and benefits fully at the time decisions are made to provide resources. It also avoids sinking money into a procurement or project without being certain if or when future funding will be available to complete the procurement or project.

Budget authority takes several forms:

- **Appropriations**, provided in annual appropriations acts or authorizing laws, permit agencies to incur obligations and make payment;

- **Borrowing authority**, usually provided in permanent laws, permits agencies to incur obligations but requires them to borrow funds, usually from the general fund of the Treasury, to make payment;

- **Contract authority**, usually provided in permanent law, permits agencies to incur obligations in advance of a separate appropriation of the cash for payment or in anticipation of the collection of receipts that can be used for payment; and

- **Spending authority from offsetting collections**, usually provided in permanent law, permits agencies to credit offsetting collections to an expenditure account, incur obligations, and make payment using the offsetting collections.

Because offsetting collections and offsetting receipts are deducted from gross budget authority, they are referred to as negative budget authority for some purposes, such as Congressional Budget Act provisions that pertain to budget authority.

Authorizing statutes usually determine the form of budget authority for a program. The authorizing statute may authorize a particular type of budget authority to be provided in annual appropriations acts, or it may provide one of the forms of budget authority directly, without the need for further appropriations.

An appropriation may make funds available from the general fund, special funds, or trust funds, or authorize the spending of offsetting collections credited to expenditure accounts, including revolving funds. Borrowing authority is usually authorized for business-like activities where the activity being financed is expected to produce income over time with which to repay the borrowing with interest. The use of contract authority is traditionally limited to transportation programs.

New budget authority for most Federal programs is normally provided in annual appropriations acts. However, new budget authority is also made available through permanent appropriations under existing laws and does not require current action by the Congress. Much of the permanent budget authority is for trust funds, interest on the public debt, and the authority to spend offsetting collections credited to appropriation or fund accounts. For most trust funds, the budget authority is appropriated automatically under existing law from the available balance of the fund and equals the estimated annual obligations of the funds. For interest on the public debt, budget authority is provided automatically under a permanent appropriation enacted in 1847 and equals interest outlays.

Annual appropriations acts generally make budget authority available for obligation only during the fiscal year to which the act applies. However, they frequently allow budget authority for a particular purpose to remain available for obligation for a longer period or indefinitely (that is, until expended or until the program objectives have been attained). Typically, budget authority for current operations is made available for only one year, and budget authority for construction and some research projects is available for a specified number of years or indefinitely. Most budget authority provided in authorizing statutes, such as for most trust funds, is available indefinitely. If budget authority is initially provided for a limited period of availability, an extension of availability would require enactment of another law (see "Reappropriation" later in this chapter).

Budget authority that is available for more than one year and not obligated in the year it becomes available is carried forward for obligation in a following year. In some cases, an account may carry forward unobligated budget authority from more than one prior year. The sum of such amounts constitutes the account's **unobligated balance**. Most of these balances had been provided for specific uses such as the multi-year construction of a major project and so are not available for new programs. A small part may never be obligated or spent, primarily amounts provided for contingencies that do not occur or reserves that never have to be used.

Amounts of budget authority that have been obligated but not yet paid constitute the account's **unpaid obligations**. For example, in the case of salaries and wages, one to three weeks elapse between the time of obligation and the time of payment. In the case of major procurement and construction, payments may occur over a period of several years after the obligation is made. Unpaid obligations (which are made up of accounts payable and undelivered orders) net of the accounts receivable and unfilled customers' orders are defined by law as the **obligated balances**. Obligated balances of budget authority at the end of the year are carried forward until the obligations are paid or the balances are canceled. (A general law provides that the obligated balances of budget authority that was made available for a definite period is automatically cancelled five years after the end of the period.) Due to such flows, a change in the amount of budget authority available in any one year may change the level of obligations and outlays for several years to come. Conversely, a change in the amount of obligations incurred from one year to the next does not necessarily result from an equal change in the amount of budget authority available for that year and will not necessarily result in an equal change in the level of outlays in that year.

The Congress usually makes budget authority available on the first day of the fiscal year for which the appropriations act is passed. Occasionally, the appropriations language specifies a different timing. The language may provide an **advance appropriation**—budget authority that does not become available until one year or more beyond the fiscal year for which the appropriations act is passed. **Forward funding** is budget authority that is made available for obligation beginning in the last quarter of the fiscal year (beginning on July 1) for the financing of ongoing grant programs during the next fiscal year. This kind of funding is used mostly for education programs, so that obligations for education grants can be made prior to the beginning of the next school year. For certain benefit programs funded by annual appropriations, the appropriation provides for *advance funding*—budget authority that is to be charged to the appropriation in the succeeding year, but which authorizes obligations to be incurred in the last quarter of the current fiscal year if necessary to meet benefit payments in excess of the specific amount appropriated for the year. When such authority is used, an adjustment is made to increase the budget authority for the fiscal year in which it is used and to reduce the budget authority of the succeeding fiscal year.

Provisions of law that extend into a new fiscal year the availability of unobligated amounts that have expired or would otherwise expire are called reappropriations. Reappropriations of expired balances that are newly available for obligation in the current or budget year count as new budget authority in the fiscal year in which the balances become newly available. For example, if a 2017 appropriations act extends the availability of unobligated budget authority that expired at the end of 2016, new budget authority would be recorded for 2017. This scorekeeping is used because a reappropriation has exactly the same effect as allowing the earlier appropriation to expire at the end of 2016 and enacting a new appropriation for 2017.

For purposes of BBEDCA and the Statutory Pay-As-You-Go Act of 2010 (discussed earlier under "Budget Enforcement"), the budget classifies budget authority as *discretionary* or *mandatory*. This classification indicates whether an appropriations act or authorizing legislation controls the amount of budget authority that is available. Generally, budget authority is discretionary if provided in an annual appropriations act and mandatory if provided in authorizing legislation. However, the budget authority provided in annual appropriations acts for certain specifically identified programs is also classified as mandatory by OMB and the congressional scorekeepers. This is because the authorizing legislation for these programs entitles beneficiaries—persons, households, or other levels of government—to receive payment, or otherwise legally obligates the Government to make payment and thereby effectively determines the amount of budget authority required, even though the payments are funded by a subsequent appropriation.

Sometimes, budget authority is characterized as current or permanent. Current authority requires the Congress to act on the request for new budget authority for the year involved. Permanent authority becomes available pursuant to standing provisions of law without appropriations action by the Congress for the year involved. Generally, budget authority is current if an annual appropriations act provides it and permanent if authorizing legislation provides it. By and large, the current/permanent distinction has been replaced by the discretionary/mandatory distinction, which is similar but not identical. Outlays are also classified as discretionary or mandatory according to the classification of the budget authority from which they flow (see "Outlays" later in this chapter).

The amount of budget authority recorded in the budget depends on whether the law provides a specific amount or employs a variable factor that determines the amount. It is considered *definite* if the law specifies a dollar amount (which may be stated as an upper limit, for example, "shall not exceed ..."). It is considered *indefinite* if, instead of specifying an amount, the law permits the amount to be determined by subsequent circumstances. For example, indefinite budget authority is provided for interest on the public debt, payment of claims and judgments awarded by the courts against the United States, and many entitlement programs. Many of the laws that authorize collections to be credited to revolving, special, and trust funds make all of the collections available for expenditure for the authorized purposes of the fund, and such authority is considered to be indefinite budget authority because the amount of collections is not known in advance of their collection.

Obligations

Following the enactment of budget authority and the completion of required apportionment action, Government agencies incur obligations to make payments (see earlier discussion under "Budget Execution"). Agencies must record obligations when they enter into binding agreements that will result in immediate or future outlays. Such obligations include the current liabilities for salaries, wages, and interest; and contracts for the purchase of supplies and equipment, construction, and the acquisition of office space, buildings, and land. For Federal credit programs, obligations are recorded in an amount equal to the estimated subsidy cost of direct loans and loan guarantees (see "Federal Credit" later in this chapter).

Outlays

Outlays are the measure of Government spending. They are payments that liquidate obligations (other than most exchanges of financial instruments, of which the repayment of debt is the prime example). The budget records outlays when obligations are paid, in the amount that is paid.

Agency, function and subfunction, and Government-wide outlay totals are stated net of offsetting collections and offsetting receipts for most budget presentations. (Offsetting receipts from a few sources do not offset any specific function, subfunction, or agency, as explained previously, but only offset Government-wide totals.) Outlay totals for accounts with offsetting collections are stated both gross and net of the offsetting collections credited to the account. However, the outlay totals for special and trust funds with offsetting receipts are not stated net of the offsetting receipts. In most cases, these receipts offset the agency, function, and subfunction totals but do not offset account-level outlays. However, when general fund payments are used to finance trust fund outlays to the public, the associated trust fund receipts are netted against the bureau totals to prevent double-counting budget authority and outlays at the bureau level.

The Government usually makes outlays in the form of cash (currency, checks, or electronic fund transfers). However, in some cases agencies pay obligations without disbursing cash, and the budget nevertheless records outlays for the equivalent method. For example, the budget records outlays for the full amount of Federal employees' salaries, even though the cash disbursed to employees is net of Federal and State income taxes withheld, retirement contributions, life and health insurance premiums, and other deductions. (The budget also records receipts for the amounts withheld from Federal employee paychecks for Federal income taxes and other payments to the Government.) When debt instruments (bonds, debentures, notes, or monetary credits) are used in place of cash to pay obligations, the budget records outlays financed by an increase in agency debt. For example, the budget records the acquisition of physical assets through certain types of lease-purchase arrangements as though a cash disbursement were made for an outright purchase. The transaction creates a Government debt, and the cash lease payments are treated as repayments of principal and interest.

The budget records outlays for the interest on the public issues of Treasury debt securities as the interest accrues, not when the cash is paid. A small portion of Treasury debt consists of inflation-indexed securities, which feature monthly adjustments to principal for inflation and semiannual payments of interest on the inflation-adjusted principal. As with fixed-rate securities, the budget records interest outlays as the interest accrues. The monthly adjustment to principal is recorded, simultaneously, as an increase in debt outstanding and an outlay of interest.

Most Treasury debt securities held by trust funds and other Government accounts are in the Government account series. The budget normally states the interest on these securities on a cash basis. When a Government account is invested in Federal debt securities, the purchase price is usually close or identical to the par (face) value of the security. The budget generally records the investment at par value and adjusts the interest paid by Treasury and collected by the account by the difference between purchase price and par, if any.

For Federal credit programs, outlays are equal to the subsidy cost of direct loans and loan guarantees and are recorded as the underlying loans are disbursed (see "Federal Credit" later in this chapter).

The budget records refunds of receipts that result from overpayments by the public (such as income taxes withheld in excess of tax liabilities) as reductions of receipts, rather than as outlays. However, the budget records payments to taxpayers for refundable tax credits (such as earned income tax credits) that exceed the taxpayer's tax liability as outlays. Similarly, when the Government makes overpayments that are later returned to the Government, those refunds to the Government are recorded as offsetting collections or offsetting receipts, not as governmental receipts.

Not all of the new budget authority for 2019 will be obligated or spent in 2019. Outlays during a fiscal year may liquidate obligations incurred in the same year or in prior years. Obligations, in turn, may be incurred against budget authority provided in the same year or against unobligated balances of budget authority provided in prior years. Outlays, therefore, flow in part from budget authority provided for the year in which the money is spent and in part from budget authority provided for prior years.

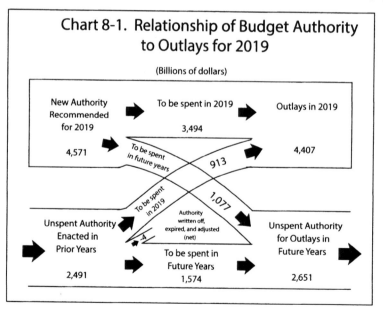

The ratio of a given year's outlays resulting from budget authority enacted in that or a prior year to the original amount of that budget authority is referred to as the outlay rate for that year.

As shown in the accompanying chart, $3,494 billion of outlays in 2019 (79 percent of the outlay total) will be made from that year's $4,571 billion total of proposed new budget authority (a first-year outlay rate of 76 percent). Thus, the remaining $913 billion of outlays in 2019 (21 percent of the outlay total) will be made from budget authority enacted in previous years. At the same time, $1,077 billion of the new budget authority proposed for 2019 (24 percent of the total amount proposed) will not lead to outlays until future years.

As described earlier, the budget classifies budget authority and outlays as discretionary or mandatory. This classification of outlays measures the extent to which actual spending is controlled through the annual appropriations process. About 30 percent of total outlays in 2017 ($1,200 billion) were discretionary and the remaining 70 percent ($2,781 billion in 2017) were mandatory spending and net interest. Such a large portion of total spending is mandatory because authorizing rather than appropriations legislation determines net interest ($263 billion in

2017) and the spending for a few programs with large amounts of spending each year, such as Social Security ($939 billion in 2017) and Medicare ($591 billion in 2017).

The bulk of mandatory outlays flow from budget authority recorded in the same fiscal year. This is not necessarily the case for discretionary budget authority and outlays. For most major construction and procurement projects and long-term contracts, for example, the budget authority covers the entire cost estimated when the projects are initiated even though the work will take place and outlays will be made over a period extending beyond the year for which the budget authority is enacted. Similarly, discretionary budget authority for most education and job training activities is appropriated for school or program years that begin in the fourth quarter of the fiscal year. Most of these funds result in outlays in the year after the appropriation.

FEDERAL CREDIT

Some Government programs provide assistance through direct loans or loan guarantees. A *direct loan* is a disbursement of funds by the Government to a non-Federal borrower under a contract that requires repayment of such funds with or without interest and includes economically equivalent transactions, such as the sale of Federal assets on credit terms. A *loan guarantee* is any guarantee, insurance, or other pledge with respect to the payment of all or a part of the principal or interest on any debt obligation of a non-Federal borrower to a non-Federal lender. The Federal Credit Reform Act of 1990, as amended (FCRA), prescribes the budgetary treatment for Federal credit programs. Under this treatment, the budget records obligations and outlays up front, for the net cost to the Government (subsidy cost), rather than recording the cash flows year by year over the term of the loan. FCRA treatment allows the comparison of direct loans and loan guarantees to each other, and to other methods of delivering assistance, such as grants.

The cost of direct loans and loan guarantees, sometimes called the "subsidy cost," is estimated as the present value of expected payments to and from the public over the term of the loan, discounted using appropriate Treasury interest rates.[3] Similar to most other kinds of programs, agencies can make loans or guarantee loans only if the Congress has appropriated funds sufficient to cover the subsidy costs, or provided a limitation in an appropriations act on the amount of direct loans or loan guarantees that can be made.

The budget records the subsidy cost to the Government arising from direct loans and loan guarantees—the budget authority and outlays—in *credit program accounts*. When a Federal agency disburses a direct loan or when a non-Federal lender disburses a loan guaranteed by a Federal agency, the program account disburses or outlays an amount equal to the estimated present value cost, or

subsidy, to a non-budgetary credit *financing account*. The financing accounts record the actual transactions with the public. For a few programs, the estimated subsidy cost is negative because the present value of expected Government collections exceeds the present value of expected payments to the public over the term of the loan. In such cases, the financing account pays the estimated subsidy cost to the program's negative subsidy receipt account, where it is recorded as an offsetting receipt. In a few cases, the offsetting receipts of credit accounts are dedicated to a special fund established for the program and are available for appropriation for the program.

The agencies responsible for credit programs must reestimate the subsidy cost of the outstanding portfolio of direct loans and loan guarantees each year. If the estimated cost increases, the program account makes an additional payment to the financing account equal to the change in cost. If the estimated cost decreases, the financing account pays the difference to the program's downward reestimate receipt account, where it is recorded as an offsetting receipt. The FCRA provides permanent indefinite appropriations to pay for upward reestimates.

If the Government modifies the terms of an outstanding direct loan or loan guarantee in a way that increases the cost as the result of a law or the exercise of administrative discretion under existing law, the program account records obligations for the increased cost and outlays the amount to the financing account. As with the original subsidy cost, agencies may incur modification costs only if the Congress has appropriated funds to cover them. A modification may also reduce costs, in which case the amounts are generally returned to the general fund, as the financing account makes a payment to the program's negative subsidy receipt account.

Credit financing accounts record all cash flows arising from direct loan obligations and loan guarantee commitments. Such cash flows include all cash flows to and from the public, including direct loan disbursements and repayments, loan guarantee default payments, fees, and

---

[3] Present value is a standard financial concept that considers the time-value of money. That is, it accounts for the fact that a given sum of money is worth more today than the same sum would be worth in the future because interest can be earned.

recoveries on defaults. Financing accounts also record intragovernmental transactions, such as the receipt of subsidy cost payments from program accounts, borrowing and repayments of Treasury debt to finance program activities, and interest paid to or received from the Treasury. The cash flows of direct loans and of loan guarantees are recorded in separate financing accounts for programs that provide both types of credit. The budget totals exclude the transactions of the financing accounts because they are not a cost to the Government. However, since financing accounts record all credit cash flows to and from the public, they affect the means of financing a budget surplus or deficit (see "Credit Financing Accounts" in the next section). The budget documents display the transactions of the financing accounts, together with the related program accounts, for information and analytical purposes.

The FCRA grandfathered the budgetary treatment of direct loan obligations and loan guarantee commitments made prior to 1992. The budget records these on a cash basis in *credit liquidating accounts*, the same as they were recorded before FCRA was enacted. However, this exception ceases to apply if the direct loans or loan guarantees are modified as described above. In that case, the budget records the subsidy cost or savings of the modification, as appropriate, and begins to account for the associated transactions under FCRA treatment for direct loan obligations and loan guarantee commitments made in 1992 or later.

Under the authority provided in various acts, certain activities that do not meet the definition in FCRA of a direct loan or loan guarantee are reflected pursuant to FCRA. For example, the Emergency Economic Stabilization Act of 2008 (EESA) created the Troubled Asset Relief Program (TARP) under the Department of the Treasury, and authorized Treasury to purchase or guarantee troubled assets until October 3, 2010. Under the TARP, Treasury has purchased equity interests in financial institutions. Section 123 of the EESA provides the Administration the authority to treat these equity investments on a FCRA basis, recording outlays for the subsidy as is done for direct loans and loan guarantees. The budget reflects the cost to the Government of TARP direct loans, loan guarantees, and equity investments consistent with the FCRA and Section 123 of EESA, which requires an adjustment to the FCRA discount rate for market risks. Treasury equity purchases under the Small Business Lending Fund are treated pursuant to the FCRA, as provided by the Small Business Jobs Act of 2010. The 2009 increases to the International Monetary Fund (IMF) quota and New Arrangements to Borrow (NAB) enacted in the Supplemental Appropriations Act of 2009 were treated on a FCRA basis through 2015, with a risk adjustment to the discount rate, as directed in that Act. However, pursuant to Title IX of the Department of State, Foreign Operations, and Related Programs Appropriations Act, 2016, these transactions have been restated on a present value basis with a risk adjustment to the discount rate, and the associated FCRA accounts have been closed.

BUDGET DEFICIT OR SURPLUS AND MEANS OF FINANCING

When outlays exceed receipts, the difference is a deficit, which the Government finances primarily by borrowing. When receipts exceed outlays, the difference is a surplus, and the Government automatically uses the surplus primarily to reduce debt. The Federal debt held by the public is approximately the cumulative amount of borrowing to finance deficits, less repayments from surpluses, over the Nation's history.

Borrowing is not exactly equal to the deficit, and debt repayment is not exactly equal to the surplus, because of the other transactions affecting borrowing from the public, or other means of financing, such as those discussed in this section. The factors included in the other means of financing can either increase or decrease the Government's borrowing needs (or decrease or increase its ability to repay debt). For example, the change in the Treasury operating cash balance is a factor included in other means of financing. Holding receipts and outlays constant, increases in the cash balance increase the Government's need to borrow or reduce the Government's ability to repay debt, and decreases in the cash balance decrease the need to borrow or increase the ability to repay debt. In some years, the net effect of the other means of financing is minor relative to the borrowing or debt repayment; in other years, the net effect may be significant.

Borrowing and Debt Repayment

The budget treats borrowing and debt repayment as a means of financing, not as receipts and outlays. If borrowing were defined as receipts and debt repayment as outlays, the budget would always be virtually balanced by definition. This rule applies both to borrowing in the form of Treasury securities and to specialized borrowing in the form of agency securities. The rule reflects the common-sense understanding that lending or borrowing is just an exchange of financial assets of equal value—cash for Treasury securities—and so is fundamentally different from, say, paying taxes, which involve a net transfer of financial assets from taxpayers to the Government.

In 2017, the Government borrowed $498 billion from the public, bringing debt held by the public to $14,665 billion. This borrowing financed the $665 billion deficit in that year, partly offset by the net impacts of the other means of financing, such as changes in cash balances and other accounts discussed below.

In addition to selling debt to the public, the Treasury Department issues debt to Government accounts, primarily trust funds that are required by law to invest in Treasury securities. Issuing and redeeming this debt does not affect the means of financing, because these transactions occur between one Government account and another and thus do not raise or use any cash for the Government as a whole.

(See Chapter 4 of this volume, "Federal Borrowing and Debt," for a fuller discussion of this topic.)

Exercise of Monetary Power

Seigniorage is the profit from coining money. It is the difference between the value of coins as money and their cost of production. Seigniorage reduces the Government's need to borrow. Unlike the payment of taxes or other receipts, it does not involve a transfer of financial assets from the public. Instead, it arises from the exercise of the Government's power to create money and the public's desire to hold financial assets in the form of coins. Therefore, the budget excludes seigniorage from receipts and treats it as a means of financing other than borrowing from the public. The budget also treats proceeds from the sale of gold as a means of financing, since the value of gold is determined by its value as a monetary asset rather than as a commodity.

Credit Financing Accounts

The budget records the net cash flows of credit programs in credit financing accounts. These accounts include the transactions for direct loan and loan guarantee programs, as well as the equity purchase programs under TARP that are recorded on a credit basis consistent with Section 123 of EESA. Financing accounts also record equity purchases under the Small Business Lending Fund consistent with the Small Business Jobs Act of 2010. Credit financing accounts are excluded from the budget because they are not allocations of resources by the Government (see "Federal Credit" earlier in this chapter). However, even though they do not affect the surplus or deficit, they can either increase or decrease the Government's need to borrow. Therefore, they are recorded as a means of financing.

Financing account disbursements to the public increase the requirement for Treasury borrowing in the same way as an increase in budget outlays. Financing account receipts from the public can be used to finance the payment of the Government's obligations and therefore reduce the requirement for Treasury borrowing from the public in the same way as an increase in budget receipts.

Deposit Fund Account Balances

The Treasury uses non-budgetary accounts, called deposit funds, to record cash held temporarily until ownership is determined (for example, earnest money paid by bidders for mineral leases) or cash held by the Government as agent for others (for example, State and local income taxes withheld from Federal employees' salaries and not yet paid to the State or local government or amounts held in the Thrift Savings Fund, a defined contribution pension fund held and managed in a fiduciary capacity by the Government). Deposit fund balances may be held in the form of either invested or uninvested balances. To the

extent that they are not invested, changes in the balances are available to finance expenditures without a change in borrowing and are recorded as a means of financing other than borrowing from the public. To the extent that they are invested in Federal debt, changes in the balances are reflected as borrowing from the public (in lieu of borrowing from other parts of the public) and are not reflected as a separate means of financing.

United States Quota Subscriptions to the International Monetary Fund (IMF)

The United States participates in the IMF through a quota subscription. Financial transactions with the IMF are exchanges of monetary assets. When the IMF temporarily draws dollars from the U.S. quota, the United States simultaneously receives an equal, offsetting, interest-bearing, Special Drawing Right (SDR)-denominated claim in the form of an increase in the U.S. reserve position in the IMF. The U.S. reserve position in the IMF increases when the United States makes deposits in its account at the IMF when the IMF temporarily uses members' quota resources to make loans and decreases when the IMF returns funds to the United States as borrowing countries repay the IMF (and the cash flows from the reserve position to the Treasury letter of credit).

Other exchanges of monetary assets, such as deposits of cash in Treasury accounts at commercial banks, are not included in the Budget. However, Congress has historically expressed interest in showing some kind of budgetary effect for U.S. transactions with the IMF.[4] Most recently, Title IX of the Department of State, Foreign Operations, and Related Programs Appropriations Act, 2016, required the estimated cost of the 2009 and 2016 quota increases and the partial rescission of the new arrangements to borrow (NAB) authorized by the Act to be recorded on a present value basis with a fair value premium added to the Treasury discount rate.[5] As a result, the Budget records budget authority and outlays equal to the estimated present value, including the fair value adjustment to the discount rate, in the year that the quota increase is enacted, i.e., 2016. All concurrent and subsequent transactions between the Treasury and the IMF are treated as a non-budgetary means of financing, which do not directly affect receipts, outlays, or deficits. The only exception is that interest earnings on U.S. deposits in its IMF account are recorded as offsetting receipts. For transparency and to support future decisions concerning the U.S. level of

---

[4] For a more detailed discussion of the history of the budgetary treatment of U.S. participation in the quota and new arrangements to borrow (NAB), see pages 139-141 in the Analytical Perspectives volume of the 2016 Budget. As discussed in that volume, the budgetary treatment of the U.S. participation in the NAB is similar to the quota.

[5] See pages 85-86 of the Analytical Perspectives volume of the 2018 Budget for a more complete discussion of the changes made to the budgetary presentation of quota increases due to Title IX of the Department of State, Foreign Operations, and Related Programs Appropriations Act, 2016.

participation in the IMF quota and the NAB, the Budget Appendix shows supplementary "below-the-lines" information about dollar value of the IMF quota, divided between the portion that is held in a Treasury letter of credit and the amount deposited in the U.S. reserve tranche at the IMF and the NAB. The actual amounts are updated in the Budget to reflect changes in the dollar value of Special Drawing Rights that serve as the unit of measure for countries' level of participation.

FEDERAL EMPLOYMENT

The budget includes information on civilian and military employment. It also includes information on related personnel compensation and benefits and on staffing requirements at overseas missions. Chapter 7 of this volume, "Strengthening the Federal Workforce," provides employment levels measured in full-time equivalents (FTE). Agency FTEs are the measure of total hours worked by an agency's Federal employees divided by the total number of one person's compensable work hours in a fiscal year.

BASIS FOR BUDGET FIGURES

Data for the Past Year

The past year column (2017) generally presents the actual transactions and balances as recorded in agency accounts and as summarized in the central financial reports prepared by the Treasury Department for the most recently completed fiscal year. Occasionally, the budget reports corrections to data reported erroneously to Treasury but not discovered in time to be reflected in Treasury's published data. In addition, in certain cases the Budget has a broader scope and includes financial transactions that are not reported to Treasury (see Chapter 24 of this volume, "Comparison of Actual to Estimated Totals," for a summary of these differences).

Data for the Current Year

The current year column (2018) includes estimates of transactions and balances based on the amounts of budgetary resources that were available when the budget was prepared. In cases where the budget proposes policy changes effective in the current year, the data will also reflect the budgetary effect of those proposed changes.

Data for the Budget Year

The budget year column (2019) includes estimates of transactions and balances based on the amounts of budgetary resources that are estimated to be available, including new budget authority requested under current authorizing legislation, and amounts estimated to result from changes in authorizing legislation and tax laws.

The budget *Appendix* generally includes the appropriations language for the amounts proposed to be appropriated under current authorizing legislation. In a few cases, this language is transmitted later because the exact requirements are unknown when the budget is transmitted. The *Appendix* generally does not include appropriations language for the amounts that will be requested under proposed legislation; that language is usually transmitted later, after the legislation is enacted. Some tables in the budget identify the items for later transmittal and the related outlays separately. Estimates of the total requirements for the budget year include both the amounts requested with the transmittal of the budget and the amounts planned for later transmittal.

Data for the Outyears

The budget presents estimates for each of the nine years beyond the budget year (2020 through 2028) in order to reflect the effect of budget decisions on objectives and plans over a longer period.

Allowances

The budget may include lump-sum allowances to cover certain transactions that are expected to increase or decrease budget authority, outlays, or receipts but are not, for various reasons, reflected in the program details. For example, the budget might include an allowance to show the effect on the budget totals of a proposal that would affect many accounts by relatively small amounts, in order to avoid unnecessary detail in the presentations for the individual accounts.

Baseline

The budget baseline is an estimate of the receipts, outlays, and deficits or surpluses that would occur if no changes were made to current laws and policies during the period covered by the budget. The baseline assumes that receipts and mandatory spending, which generally are authorized on a permanent basis, will continue in the future consistent with current law and policy. The baseline assumes that the future funding for most discretionary programs, which generally are funded annually, will equal the most recently enacted appropriation, adjusted for inflation.

Baseline outlays represent the amount of resources that would be used by the Government over the period covered by the budget on the basis of laws currently enacted.

The baseline serves several useful purposes:

- It may warn of future problems, either for Government fiscal policy as a whole or for individual tax and spending programs.

- It may provide a starting point for formulating the President's Budget.

- It may provide a "policy-neutral" benchmark against which the President's Budget and alternative pro- posals can be compared to assess the magnitude of proposed changes.

The baseline rules in BBEDCA provide that funding for discretionary programs is inflated from the most re- cent enacted appropriations using specified inflation rates. Because the resulting funding would exceed the discretionary caps, the Administration's baseline includes adjustments that reduce overall discretionary funding to levels consistent with the caps. (Chapter 22 of this volume, "Current Services Estimates," provides more information on the baseline.)

PRINCIPAL BUDGET LAWS

The Budget and Accounting Act of 1921 created the core of the current Federal budget process. Before enactment of this law, there was no annual centralized budgeting in the Executive Branch. Federal Government agencies usu- ally sent budget requests independently to congressional committees with no coordination of the various requests in formulating the Federal Government's budget. The Budget and Accounting Act required the President to co- ordinate the budget requests for all Government agencies and to send a comprehensive budget to the Congress. The Congress has amended the requirements many times and portions of the Act are codified in Title 31, United States Code. The major laws that govern the budget process are as follows:

Article 1, section 8, clause 1 of the Constitution, which empowers the Congress to collect taxes.

Article 1, section 9, clause 7 of the Constitution, which requires appropriations in law before money may be spent from the Treasury and the publication of a reg- ular statement of the receipts and expenditures of all public money.

Antideficiency Act (codified in Chapters 13 and 15 of Title 31, United States Code), which prescribes rules and procedures for budget execution.

Balanced Budget and Emergency Deficit Control Act of 1985, as amended, which establishes limits on discretionary spending and provides mechanisms for en- forcing discretionary spending limits.

Chapter 11 of Title 31, United States Code, which prescribes procedures for submission of the President's budget and information to be contained in it.

Congressional Budget and Impoundment Control Act of 1974 (Public Law 93–344), as amended. This Act comprises the:

- *Congressional Budget Act of 1974*, as amended, which prescribes the congressional budget process; and

- *Impoundment Control Act of 1974*, which con- trols certain aspects of budget execution.

- *Federal Credit Reform Act of 1990, as amended (2 USC 661–661f)*, which the Budget Enforcement Act of 1990 included as an amendment to the Con- gressional Budget Act to prescribe the budget treat- ment for Federal credit programs.

Chapter 31 of Title 31, United States Code, which provides the authority for the Secretary of the Treasury to issue debt to finance the deficit and establishes a statu- tory limit on the level of the debt.

Chapter 33 of Title 31, United States Code, which establishes the Department of the Treasury as the author- ity for making disbursements of public funds, with the authority to delegate that authority to executive agencies in the interests of economy and efficiency.

Government Performance and Results Act of 1993 (Public Law 103–62, as amended) which emphasizes managing for results. It requires agencies to prepare strategic plans, annual performance plans, and annual performance reports.

Statutory Pay-As-You-Go Act of 2010, which es- tablishes a budget enforcement mechanism generally requiring that direct spending and revenue legislation enacted into law not increase the deficit.

GLOSSARY OF BUDGET TERMS

Account refers to a separate financial reporting unit used by the Federal Government to record budget author- ity, outlays and income for budgeting or management information purposes as well as for accounting purposes. All budget (and off-budget) accounts are classified as be- ing either expenditure or receipt accounts and by fund group. Budget (and off-budget) transactions fall within either of two fund group: (1) Federal funds and (2) trust funds. (Cf. Federal funds group and trust funds group.)

Accrual method of measuring cost means an ac- counting method that records cost when the liability is incurred. As applied to Federal employee retirement ben- efits, accrual costs are recorded when the benefits are earned rather than when they are paid at some time in the future. The accrual method is used in part to provide data that assists in agency policymaking, but not used in presenting the overall budget of the United States Government.

Advance appropriation means appropriations of new budget authority that become available one or more fiscal years beyond the fiscal year for which the appropriation act was passed.

Advance funding means appropriations of budget authority provided in an appropriations act to be used, if necessary, to cover obligations incurred late in the fiscal year for benefit payments in excess of the amount specifically appropriated in the act for that year, where the budget authority is charged to the appropriation for the program for the fiscal year following the fiscal year for which the appropriations act is passed.

Agency means a department or other establishment of the Government.

Allowance means a lump-sum included in the budget to represent certain transactions that are expected to increase or decrease budget authority, outlays, or receipts but that are not, for various reasons, reflected in the program details.

Balanced Budget and Emergency Deficit Control Act of 1985 (BBEDCA) refers to legislation that altered the budget process, primarily by replacing the earlier fixed targets for annual deficits with a Pay-As-You-Go requirement for new tax or mandatory spending legislation and with caps on annual discretionary funding. The Statutory Pay-As-You-Go Act of 2010, which is a standalone piece of legislation that did not directly amend the BBEDCA, reinstated a statutory pay-as-you-go rule for revenues and mandatory spending legislation, and the Budget Control Act of 2011, which did amend BBEDCA, reinstated discretionary caps on budget authority.

Balances of budget authority means the amounts of budget authority provided in previous years that have not been outlayed.

Baseline means a projection of the estimated receipts, outlays, and deficit or surplus that would result from continuing current law or current policies through the period covered by the budget.

Budget means the Budget of the United States Government, which sets forth the President's comprehensive financial plan for allocating resources and indicates the President's priorities for the Federal Government.

Budget authority (BA) means the authority provided by law to incur financial obligations that will result in outlays. (For a description of the several forms of budget authority, see "Budget Authority and Other Budgetary Resources" earlier in this chapter.)

Budget Control Act of 2011 refers to legislation that, among other things, amended BBEDCA to reinstate discretionary spending limits on budget authority through 2021 and restored the process for enforcing those spending limits. The legislation also increased the statutory debt ceiling; created a Joint Select Committee on Deficit Reduction that was instructed to develop a bill to reduce the Federal deficit by at least $1.5 trillion over a 10-year period; and provided a process to implement alternative spending reductions in the event that legislation achiev-ing at least $1.2 trillion of deficit reduction was not enacted.

Budget resolution—see concurrent resolution on the budget.

Budget totals mean the totals included in the budget for budget authority, outlays, receipts, and the surplus or deficit. Some presentations in the budget distinguish on-budget totals from off-budget totals. On-budget totals reflect the transactions of all Federal Government entities except those excluded from the budget totals by law. Off-budget totals reflect the transactions of Government entities that are excluded from the on-budget totals by law. Under current law, the off-budget totals include the Social Security trust funds (Federal Old-Age and Survivors Insurance and Federal Disability Insurance Trust Funds) and the Postal Service Fund. The budget combines the on- and off-budget totals to derive unified (i.e. consolidated) totals for Federal activity.

Budget year refers to the fiscal year for which the budget is being considered, that is, with respect to a session of Congress, the fiscal year of the government that starts on October 1 of the calendar year in which that session of Congress begins.

Budgetary resources mean amounts available to incur obligations in a given year. The term comprises new budget authority and unobligated balances of budget authority provided in previous years.

Cap means the legal limits for each fiscal year under BBEDCA on the budget authority and outlays (only if applicable) provided by discretionary appropriations.

Cap adjustment means either an increase or a decrease that is permitted to the statutory cap limits for each fiscal year under BBEDCA on the budget authority and outlays (only if applicable) provided by discretionary appropriations only if certain conditions are met. These conditions may include providing for a base level of funding, a designation of the increase or decrease by the Congress, (and in some circumstances, the President) pursuant to a section of the BBEDCA, or a change in concepts and definitions of funding under the cap. Changes in concepts and definitions require consultation with the Congressional Appropriations and Budget Committees.

Cash equivalent transaction means a transaction in which the Government makes outlays or receives collections in a form other than cash or the cash does not accurately measure the cost of the transaction. (For examples, see the section on "Outlays" earlier in this chapter.)

Collections mean money collected by the Government that the budget records as a governmental receipt, an offsetting collection, or an offsetting receipt.

Concurrent resolution on the budget refers to the concurrent resolution adopted by the Congress to set budgetary targets for appropriations, mandatory spending legislation, and tax legislation. These concurrent resolutions are required by the Congressional Budget Act of 1974, and are generally adopted annually.

Continuing resolution means an appropriations act that provides for the ongoing operation of the Government in the absence of enacted appropriations.

Cost refers to legislation or administrative actions that increase outlays or decrease receipts. (Cf. savings.)

Credit program account means a budget account that receives and obligates appropriations to cover the subsidy cost of a direct loan or loan guarantee and disburses the subsidy cost to a financing account.

Current services estimate—see Baseline.

Debt held by the public means the cumulative amount of money the Federal Government has borrowed from the public and not repaid.

Debt held by the public net of financial assets means the cumulative amount of money the Federal Government has borrowed from the public and not repaid, minus the current value of financial assets such as loan assets, bank deposits, or private-sector securities or equities held by the Government and plus the current value of financial liabilities other than debt.

Debt held by Government accounts means the debt the Treasury Department owes to accounts within the Federal Government. Most of it results from the surpluses of the Social Security and other trust funds, which are required by law to be invested in Federal securities.

Debt limit means the maximum amount of Federal debt that may legally be outstanding at any time. It includes both the debt held by the public and the debt held by Government accounts, but without accounting for offsetting financial assets. When the debt limit is reached, the Government cannot borrow more money until the Congress has enacted a law to increase the limit.

Deficit means the amount by which outlays exceed receipts in a fiscal year. It may refer to the on-budget, off-budget, or unified budget deficit.

Direct loan means a disbursement of funds by the Government to a non-Federal borrower under a contract that requires the repayment of such funds with or without interest. The term includes the purchase of, or participation in, a loan made by another lender. The term also includes the sale of a Government asset on credit terms of more than 90 days duration as well as financing arrangements for other transactions that defer payment for more than 90 days. It also includes loans financed by the Federal Financing Bank (FFB) pursuant to agency loan guarantee authority. The term does not include the acquisition of a federally guaranteed loan in satisfaction of default or other guarantee claims or the price support "loans" of the Commodity Credit Corporation. (Cf. loan guarantee.)

Direct spending—see mandatory spending.

Disaster funding means a discretionary appropriation that is enacted that the Congress designates as being for disaster relief. Such amounts are a cap adjustment to the limits on discretionary spending under BBEDCA. The total adjustment for this purpose cannot exceed a ceiling for a particular year that is defined as the total of the average funding provided for disaster relief over the previous 10 years (excluding the highest and lowest years) and the unused amount of the prior year's ceiling (excluding the portion of the prior year's ceiling that was itself due to any unused amount from the year before). Disaster relief is defined as activities carried out pursuant to a de-termination under section 102(2) of the Robert T. Stafford Disaster Relief and Emergency Assistance Act.

Discretionary spending means budgetary resources (except those provided to fund mandatory spending programs) provided in appropriations acts. (Cf. mandatory spending.)

Emergency requirement means an amount that the Congress has designated as an emergency requirement. Such amounts are not included in the estimated budgetary effects of PAYGO legislation under the requirements of the Statutory Pay-As-You-Go Act of 2010, if they are mandatory or receipts. Such a discretionary appropriation that is subsequently designated by the President as an emergency requirement results in a cap adjustment to the limits on discretionary spending under BBEDCA.

Entitlement refers to a program in which the Federal Government is legally obligated to make payments or provide aid to any person who, or State or local government that, meets the legal criteria for eligibility. Examples include Social Security, Medicare, Medicaid, and the Supplemental Nutrition Assistance Program (formerly Food Stamps).

Federal funds group refers to the moneys collected and spent by the Government through accounts other than those designated as trust funds. Federal funds include general, special, public enterprise, and intragovernmental funds. (Cf. trust funds group.)

Financing account means a non-budgetary account (an account whose transactions are excluded from the budget totals) that records all of the cash flows resulting from post-1991 direct loan obligations or loan guarantee commitments. At least one financing account is associated with each credit program account. For programs that make both direct loans and loan guarantees, separate financing accounts are required for direct loan cash flows and for loan guarantee cash flows. (Cf. liquidating account.)

Fiscal year means the Government's accounting period. It begins on October 1st and ends on September 30th, and is designated by the calendar year in which it ends.

Forward funding means appropriations of budget authority that are made for obligation starting in the last quarter of the fiscal year for the financing of ongoing grant programs during the next fiscal year.

General fund means the accounts in which are recorded governmental receipts not earmarked by law for a specific purpose, the proceeds of general borrowing, and the expenditure of these moneys.

Government sponsored enterprises mean private enterprises that were established and chartered by the Federal Government for public policy purposes. They are classified as non-budgetary and not included in the Federal budget because they are private companies, and their securities are not backed by the full faith and credit of the Federal Government. However, the budget presents statements of financial condition for certain Government sponsored enterprises such as the Federal National Mortgage Association. (Cf. off-budget.)

Intragovernmental fund—see Revolving fund.

Liquidating account means a budget account that records all cash flows to and from the Government resulting from pre-1992 direct loan obligations or loan guarantee commitments. (Cf. financing account.)

Loan guarantee means any guarantee, insurance, or other pledge with respect to the payment of all or a part of the principal or interest on any debt obligation of a non-Federal borrower to a non-Federal lender. The term does not include the insurance of deposits, shares, or other withdrawable accounts in financial institutions. (Cf. direct loan.)

Mandatory spending means spending controlled by laws other than appropriations acts (including spending for entitlement programs) and spending for the Supplemental Nutrition Assistance Program, formerly food stamps. Although the Statutory Pay-As-You-Go Act of 2010 uses the term direct spending to mean this, mandatory spending is commonly used instead. (Cf. discretionary spending.)

Means of financing refers to borrowing, the change in cash balances, and certain other transactions involved in financing a deficit. The term is also used to refer to the debt repayment, the change in cash balances, and certain other transactions involved in using a surplus. By definition, the means of financing are not treated as receipts or outlays and so are non-budgetary.

Obligated balance means the cumulative amount of budget authority that has been obligated but not yet outlayed. (Cf. unobligated balance.)

Obligation means a binding agreement that will result in outlays, immediately or in the future. Budgetary resources must be available before obligations can be incurred legally.

Off-budget refers to transactions of the Federal Government that would be treated as budgetary had the Congress not designated them by statute as "off-budget." Currently, transactions of the Social Security trust funds and the Postal Service are the only sets of transactions that are so designated. The term is sometimes used more broadly to refer to the transactions of private enterprises that were established and sponsored by the Government, most especially "Government sponsored enterprises" such as the Federal Home Loan Banks. (Cf. budget totals.)

Offsetting collections mean collections that, by law, are credited directly to expenditure accounts and deducted from gross budget authority and outlays of the expenditure account, rather than added to receipts. Usually, they are authorized to be spent for the purposes of the account without further action by the Congress. They result from business-like transactions with the public, including payments from the public in exchange for goods and services, reimbursements for damages, and gifts or donations of money to the Government and from intragovernmental transactions with other Government accounts. The authority to spend offsetting collections is a form of budget authority. (Cf. receipts and offsetting receipts.)

Offsetting receipts mean collections that are credited to offsetting receipt accounts and deducted from gross budget authority and outlays, rather than added to receipts. They are not authorized to be credited to ex-

penditure accounts. The legislation that authorizes the offsetting receipts may earmark them for a specific purpose and either appropriate them for expenditure for that purpose or require them to be appropriated in annual appropriation acts before they can be spent. Like offsetting collections, they result from business-like transactions or market-oriented activities with the public, including payments from the public in exchange for goods and services, reimbursements for damages, and gifts or donations of money to the Government and from intragovernmental transactions with other Government accounts. (Cf. receipts, undistributed offsetting receipts, and offsetting collections.)

On-budget refers to all budgetary transactions other than those designated by statute as off-budget. (Cf. budget totals.)

Outlay means a payment to liquidate an obligation (other than the repayment of debt principal or other disbursements that are "means of financing" transactions). Outlays generally are equal to cash disbursements, but also are recorded for cash-equivalent transactions, such as the issuance of debentures to pay insurance claims, and in a few cases are recorded on an accrual basis such as interest on public issues of the public debt. Outlays are the measure of Government spending.

Outyear estimates mean estimates presented in the budget for the years beyond the budget year of budget authority, outlays, receipts, and other items (such as debt).

Overseas Contingency Operations/Global War on Terrorism (OCO/GWOT) means a discretionary appropriation that is enacted that the Congress and, subsequently, the President have so designated on an account by account basis. Such a discretionary appropriation that is designated as OCO/GWOT results in a cap adjustment to the limits on discretionary spending under BBEDCA. Funding for these purposes has most recently been associated with the wars in Iraq and Afghanistan.

Pay-as-you-go (PAYGO) refers to requirements of the Statutory Pay-As-You-Go Act of 2010 that result in a sequestration if the estimated combined result of new legislation affecting direct spending or revenue increases the on-budget deficit relative to the baseline, as of the end of a congressional session.

Public enterprise fund—see Revolving fund.

Reappropriation means a provision of law that extends into a new fiscal year the availability of unobligated amounts that have expired or would otherwise expire.

Receipts mean collections that result from the Government's exercise of its sovereign power to tax or otherwise compel payment. They are compared to outlays in calculating a surplus or deficit. (Cf. offsetting collections and offsetting receipts.)

Revolving fund means a fund that conducts continuing cycles of business-like activity, in which the fund charges for the sale of products or services and uses the proceeds to finance its spending, usually without requirement for annual appropriations. There are two types of revolving funds: Public enterprise funds, which conduct business-like operations mainly with the public, and intragovernmental revolving funds, which conduct business-like operations mainly within and between Government agencies. (Cf. special fund and trust fund.)

Savings refers to legislation or administrative actions that decrease outlays or increase receipts. (Cf. cost.)

Scorekeeping means measuring the budget effects of legislation, generally in terms of budget authority, receipts, and outlays, for purposes of measuring adherence to the Budget or to budget targets established by the Congress, as through agreement to a Budget Resolution.

Sequestration means the cancellation of budgetary resources. The Statutory Pay-As-You-Go Act of 2010 requires such cancellations if revenue or direct spending legislation is enacted that, in total, increases projected deficits or reduces projected surpluses relative to the baseline. The Balanced Budget and Emergency Deficit Control Act of 1985, as amended, requires such cancellations if discretionary appropriations exceed the statutory limits on discretionary spending.

Special fund means a Federal fund account for receipts or offsetting receipts earmarked for specific purposes and the expenditure of these receipts. (Cf. revolving fund and trust fund.)

Statutory Pay-As-You-Go Act of 2010 refers to legislation that reinstated a statutory pay-as-you-go requirement for new tax or mandatory spending legislation. The law is a standalone piece of legislation that cross-references BBEDCA but does not directly amend that legislation. This is a permanent law and does not expire.

Subsidy means the estimated long-term cost to the Government of a direct loan or loan guarantee, calculated on a net present value basis, excluding administrative costs and any incidental effects on governmental receipts or outlays.

Surplus means the amount by which receipts exceed outlays in a fiscal year. It may refer to the on-budget, off-budget, or unified budget surplus.

Supplemental appropriation means an appropriation enacted subsequent to a regular annual appropriations act, when the need for additional funds is too urgent to be postponed until the next regular annual appropriations act.

Trust fund refers to a type of account, designated by law as a trust fund, for receipts or offsetting receipts dedicated to specific purposes and the expenditure of these receipts. Some revolving funds are designated as trust funds, and these are called trust revolving funds. (Cf. special fund and revolving fund.)

Trust funds group refers to the moneys collected and spent by the Government through trust fund accounts. (Cf. Federal funds group.)

Undistributed offsetting receipts mean offsetting receipts that are deducted from the Government-wide totals for budget authority and outlays instead of being offset against a specific agency and function. (Cf. offsetting receipts.)

Unified budget includes receipts from all sources and outlays for all programs of the Federal Government, including both on- and off-budget programs. It is the most comprehensive measure of the Government's annual finances.

Unobligated balance means the cumulative amount of budget authority that remains available for obligation under law in unexpired accounts. The term "expired balances available for adjustment only" refers to unobligated amounts in expired accounts.

User charges are charges assessed for the provision of Government services and for the sale or use of Government goods or resources. The payers of the user charge must be limited in the authorizing legislation to those receiving special benefits from, or subject to regulation by, the program or activity beyond the benefits received by the general public or broad segments of the public (such as those who pay income taxes or custom duties).

9. COVERAGE OF THE BUDGET

The Federal budget is the central instrument of national policy making. It is the Government's financial plan for proposing and deciding the allocation of resources to serve national objectives. The budget provides information on the cost and scope of Federal activities to inform decisions and to serve as a means to control the allocation of resources. When enacted, it establishes the level of public goods and services provided by the Government.

Federal Government activities can be either "budgetary" or "non-budgetary." Those activities that involve direct and measurable allocation of Federal resources are budgetary. The payments to and from the public resulting from budgetary activities are included in the budget's accounting of outlays and receipts. Federal activities that do not involve direct and measurable allocation of Federal resources are non-budgetary and are not included in the budget's accounting of outlays and receipts. More detailed information about outlays and receipts may be found in Chapter 8, "Budget Concepts," of this volume.

The budget documents include information on some non-budgetary activities because they can be important instruments of Federal policy and provide insight into the scope and nature of Federal activities. For example, the budget documents show the transactions of the Thrift Savings Program (TSP), a collection of investment funds managed by the Federal Retirement Thrift Investment Board (FRTIB). Despite the fact that the FRTIB is budgetary and one of the TSP funds is invested entirely in Federal securities, the transactions of these funds are non-budgetary because current and retired Federal employees own the funds. The Government manages these funds only in a fiduciary capacity.

The budget also includes information on cash flows that are a means of financing Federal activity, such as for credit financing accounts. However, to avoid double-counting, means of financing amounts are not included in the estimates of outlays or receipts because the costs of the underlying Federal activities are already reflected in the deficit.[1] This chapter provides details about the budgetary and non-budgetary activities of the Federal Government.

Budgetary Activities

The Federal Government has used the unified budget concept—which consolidates outlays and receipts from Federal funds and trust funds, including the Social Security trust funds—since 1968, starting with the 1969 Budget. The 1967 President's Commission on Budget Concepts (the Commission) recommended the change to include the financial transactions of all of the Federal Government's programs and agencies. Thus, the budget includes information on the financial transactions of all 15 Executive departments, all independent agencies (from all three branches of Government), and all Government corporations.[2]

The budget shows outlays and receipts for on-budget and off-budget activities separately to reflect the legal distinction between the two. Although there is a legal distinction between on-budget and off-budget activities, conceptually there is no difference between them. Off-budget Federal activities reflect the same kinds of governmental roles as on-budget activities and result in outlays and receipts. Like on-budget activities, the Government funds and controls off-budget activities. The "unified budget" reflects the conceptual similarity between on-budget and off-budget activities by showing combined totals of outlays and receipts for both.

Many Government corporations are entities with business-type operations that charge the public for services at prices intended to allow the entity to be self-sustaining, although some operate at a loss in order to provide subsidies to specific recipients. Often these entities are more independent than other agencies and have limited exemptions from certain Federal personnel requirements to allow for flexibility.

All accounts in Table 26-1, "Federal Budget by Agency and Account," in the supplemental materials to this volume are budgetary.[3] The majority of budgetary accounts are associated with the departments or other entities that are clearly Federal agencies. Some budgetary accounts reflect Government payments to entities that the Government created or chartered as private or non-Federal entities. Some of these entities receive all or a majority of their funding from the Government. These include the Corporation for Public Broadcasting, Gallaudet University, Howard University, the Legal Services Corporation, the National Railroad Passenger Corporation (Amtrak), the Smithsonian Institution, the State Justice Institute, and the United States Institute of Peace. A related example is the Standard Setting Board, which is not a Federally created entity but since 2003 has received a majority of

---

[1] For more information on means of financing, see the "Budget Deficit or Surplus and Means of Financing" section of Chapter 8, "Budget Concepts," in this volume.

[2] Government corporations are Government entities that are defined as corporations pursuant to the Government Corporation Control Act, as amended (31 U.S.C. 9101), or elsewhere in law. Examples include the Commodity Credit Corporation, the Export-Import Bank of the United States, the Federal Crop Insurance Corporation, the Federal Deposit Insurance Corporation, the Millennium Challenge Corporation, the Overseas Private Investment Corporation, the Pension Benefit Guaranty Corporation, the Tennessee Valley Authority, the African Development Foundation (22 U.S.C. 290h-6), the Inter-American Foundation (22 U.S.C. 290f), the Presidio Trust (16 U.S.C. 460bb note), and the Valles Caldera Trust (16 U.S.C. 698v-4).

[3] Table 26-1 can be found at: *https://www.whitehouse.gov/omb/analytical-perspectives*.

Deposit funds.—Deposit funds are non-budgetary accounts that record amounts held by the Government temporarily until ownership is determined (such as earnest money paid by bidders for mineral leases) or held by the Government as an agent for others (such as State income taxes withheld from Federal employees' salaries and not yet paid to the States). The largest deposit fund is the Government Securities Investment Fund, also known as the G-Fund, which is part of the TSP, the Government's defined contribution retirement plan. The Federal Retirement Thrift Investment Board manages the fund's investment for Federal employees who participate in the TSP (which is similar to private-sector 401(k) plans). The Department of the Treasury holds the G-Fund assets, which are the property of Federal employees, only in a fiduciary capacity; the transactions of the Fund are not resource allocations by the Government and are therefore non-budgetary.[7] For similar reasons, Native American-owned funds that are held and managed in a fiduciary capacity are also excluded from the budget.

Government-Sponsored Enterprises (GSEs).—Government-Sponsored Enterprises are privately owned and therefore distinct from government corporations. The Federal Government has chartered GSEs such as the Federal National Mortgage Association (Fannie Mae), the Federal Home Loan Mortgage Corporation (Freddie Mac), the Federal Home Loan Banks, the Farm Credit System, and the Federal Agricultural Mortgage Corporation to provide financial intermediation for specified public purposes. Although Federally chartered to serve public-policy purposes, GSEs are classified as non-budgetary because they are intended to be privately owned and controlled—with any public benefits accruing indirectly from the GSEs' business transactions. Estimates of the GSEs' activities can be found in a separate chapter of the Budget *Appendix*, and their activities are discussed in Chapter 19 of this volume, "Credit and Insurance."

In September 2008, in response to the financial market crisis, the director of the Federal Housing Finance Agency (FHFA)[8] placed Fannie Mae and Freddie Mac into conservatorship for the purpose of preserving the assets and restoring the solvency of these two GSEs. As conservator, FHFA has broad authority to direct the operations of these GSEs. However, these GSEs remain private companies with board of directors and management responsible for their day-to-day operations. The Budget continues to treat these two GSEs as non-budgetary private entities in conservatorship rather than as Government agencies. By contrast, CBO treats these GSEs as budgetary Federal agencies. Both treatments include budgetary and non-budgetary amounts.

While OMB reflects all of the GSEs' transactions with the public as non-budgetary, the payments from the Treasury to the GSEs are recorded as budgetary outlays and dividends received by the Treasury are recorded as

budgetary receipts. Under CBO's approach, the subsidy costs of Fannie Mae's and Freddie Mac's past credit activities are treated as having already been recorded in the budget estimates; the subsidy costs of future credit activities will be recorded when the activities occur. Lending and borrowing activities between the GSEs and the public apart from the subsidy costs are treated as non-budgetary by CBO, and Treasury payments to the GSEs are intragovernmental transfers (from Treasury to the GSEs) that net to zero in CBO's budget estimates.

Overall, both the budget's accounting and CBO's accounting present Fannie Mae's and Freddie Mac's gains and losses as Government receipts and outlays—which reduce or increase Government deficits. The two approaches, however, reflect the effect of the gains and losses in the budget at different times.

Other Federally-created non-budgetary entities.—In addition to the GSEs, the Federal Government has created a number of other entities that are classified as non-budgetary. These include Federally funded research and development centers (FFRDCs), non-appropriated fund instrumentalities (NAFIs), and other entities; some of these are non-profit entities and some are for-profit entities.[9]

FFRDCs are entities that conduct agency-specific research under contract or cooperative agreement. Some FFRDCs were created to conduct research for the Department of Defense but are administered by colleges, universities, or other non-profit entities. Despite this non-budgetary classification, many FFRDCs receive direct resource allocation from the Government and are included as budget lines in various agencies. Examples of FFRDCs include the Center for Naval Analysis and the Jet Propulsion Laboratory.[10] Even though FFRDCs are non-budgetary, Federal payments to the FFRDC are bud-

---

[7] The administrative functions of the Federal Retirement Thrift Investment Board are carried out by Government employees and included in the budget totals.

[8] FHFA is the regulator of Fannie Mae, Freddie Mac, and the Federal Home Loans Banks.

[9] Although most entities created by the Federal Government are budgetary, as discussed in this section, the GSEs and the Federal Reserve System were created by the Federal Government, but are classified as non-budgetary. In addition, Congress and the President have chartered, but not necessarily created, approximately 100 non-profit entities that are non-budgetary. These include patriotic, charitable, and educational organizations under Title 36 of the U.S. Code and foundations and trusts chartered under other titles of the Code. Title 36 corporations include the American Legion, the American National Red Cross, Big Brothers—Big Sisters of America, Boy Scouts of America, Future Farmers of America, Girl Scouts of the United States of America, the National Academy of Public Administration, the National Academy of Sciences, and Veterans of Foreign Wars of the United States. Virtually all of the non-profit entities chartered by the Government existed under State law prior to the granting of a Government charter, making the Government charter an honorary rather than governing charter. A major exception to this is the American National Red Cross. Its Government charter requires it to provide disaster relief and to ensure compliance with treaty obligations under the Geneva Convention. Although any Government payments (whether made as direct appropriations or through agency appropriations) to these chartered non-profits, including the Red Cross, would be budgetary, the non-profits themselves are classified as non-budgetary. On April 29, 2015, the Subcommittee on Immigration and Border Security of the Committee on the Judiciary in the U.S. House of Representatives adopted a policy prohibiting Congress from granting new Federal charters to private, non-profit organizations. This policy has been adopted by every subcommittee with jurisdiction over charters since the 101st Congress.

[10] The National Science Foundation maintains a list of FFRDCs at *www.nsf.gov/statistics/ffrdc*.

get outlays. In addition to Federal funding, FFRDCs may receive funding from non-Federal sources.

Non-appropriated fund instrumentalities (NAFIs) are entities that support an agency's current and retired personnel. Nearly all NAFIs are associated with the Departments of Defense, Homeland Security (Coast Guard), and Veterans Affairs. Most NAFIs are located on military bases and include the armed forces exchanges (which sell goods to military personnel and their families), recreational facilities, and childcare centers. NAFIs are financed by proceeds from the sale of goods or services and do not receive direct appropriations; thus, they are characterized as non-budgetary but any agency payments to the NAFIs are recorded as budget outlays.

A number of entities created by the Government receive a significant amount of non-Federal funding. Non-Federal individuals or organizations significantly control some of these entities. These entities include Gallaudet University, Howard University, Amtrak, and the Universal Services Administrative Company, among others.[11] Most of these entities receive direct appropriations or other recurring payments from the Government. The appropriations or other payments are budgetary and included in Table 26-1. However, many of these entities are themselves non-budgetary. Generally, entities that receive a significant portion of funding from non-Federal sources but are not controlled by the Government are non-budgetary.

Regulation.—Federal Government regulations often require the private sector or other levels of government to make expenditures for specified purposes that are intended to have public benefits, such as workplace safety and pollution control. Although the budget reflects the Government's cost of conducting regulatory activities, the costs imposed on the private sector as a result of regulation are treated as non-budgetary and not included in the budget. The annual Regulatory Plan and the semi-annual Unified Agenda of Federal Regulatory and Deregulatory Actions describe the Government's regulatory priorities and plans.[12] OMB has published the estimated costs and benefits of Federal regulation annually since 1997.[13]

Monetary policy.— As a fiscal policy tool, the budget is used by elected Government officials to promote eco-nomic growth and achieve other public policy objectives. Monetary policy is another tool that governments use to promote economic policy objectives. In the United States, the Federal Reserve System—which is composed of a Board of Governors and 12 regional Federal Reserve Banks—conducts monetary policy. The Federal Reserve Act provides that the goal of monetary policy is to "maintain long-run growth of the monetary and credit aggregates commensurate with the economy's long run potential to increase production, so as to promote effectively the goals of maximum employment, stable prices, and moderate long-term interest rates."[14] The Full Employment and Balanced Growth Act of 1978, also known as the Humphrey-Hawkins Act, reaffirmed the dual goals of full employment and price stability.[15]

By law, the Federal Reserve System is a self-financing entity that is independent of the Executive Branch and subject only to broad oversight by the Congress. Consistent with the recommendations of the Commission, the effects of monetary policy and the actions of the Federal Reserve System are non-budgetary, with exceptions for the transfer to the Treasury of excess income generated through its operations. The Federal Reserve System earns income from a variety of sources including interest on Government securities, foreign currency investments and loans to depository institutions, and fees for services (e.g., check clearing services) provided to depository institutions. The Federal Reserve System remits to Treasury any excess income over expenses annually. For the fiscal year ending September 2017, Treasury recorded $81.3 billion in receipts from the Federal Reserve System. In addition to remitting excess income to Treasury, current law requires the Federal Reserve to transfer a portion of its excess earnings to the Consumer Financial Protection Bureau (CFPB).[16]

The Board of Governors of the Federal Reserve is a Federal Government agency, but because of its independent status, its budget is not subject to Executive Branch review and is included in the Budget *Appendix* for informational purposes only. The Federal Reserve Banks are subject to Board oversight and managed by boards of directors chosen by the Board of Governors and member banks, which include all national banks and State banks that choose to become members. The budgets of the regional Banks are subject to approval by the Board of Governors and are not included in the Budget *Appendix*.

---

[11] Under section 415(b) of the Amtrak Reform and Accountability Act of 1997, (49 U.S.C. 24304 and note), Amtrak was required to redeem all of its outstanding common stock. Once all outstanding common stock is redeemed, Amtrak will be wholly-owned by the Government and, at that point, its non-budgetary status may need to be reassessed.

[12] The most recent Regulatory Plan and introduction to the Unified Agenda issued by the General Services Administration's Regulatory Information Service Center are available at *www.reginfo.gov* and at *www. gpo.gov*.

[13] In the most recent draft report, OMB indicates that the estimated annual benefits of Federal regulations it reviewed from October 1, 2005, to September 30, 2015, range from $208 billion to $672 billion, while the estimated annual costs range from $57 billion to $85 billion.

[14] See 12 U.S.C. 225a.

[15] See 15 U.S.C. 3101 et seq.

[16] See section 1011 of Public Law 111-203 (12 U.S.C. 5491), (2010). The CFPB is an executive agency, led by a director appointed by the President and reliant on Federal funding, that serves the governmental function of regulating Federal consumer financial laws. Accordingly, it is included in the Budget.

10. BUDGET PROCESS

This chapter addresses two broad categories of budget reform. First, the chapter discusses proposals to improve budgeting and fiscal sustainability with respect to individual programs as well as across Government. These proposals include: an extension of the spending reductions required by the Joint Select Committee on Deficit Reduction; various initiatives to reduce improper payments; funding requests for disaster relief and wildfire suppression; limits on changes in mandatory programs in appropriations Acts; limits on advance appropriations; proposals for the Pell Grant program; changes to capital budgeting for large Federal capital projects; and fast track spending reduction powers. Second, the chapter describes the 2019 Budget proposals for budget enforcement and budget presentation. The budget enforcement proposals include a discussion of the system under the Statutory Pay-As-You-Go Act of 2010 (PAYGO) of scoring legislation affecting receipts and mandatory spending; reforms to account for debt service in cost estimates; administrative PAYGO actions affecting mandatory spending; adjustments in the baseline for Highway Trust Fund spending and the extension of certain expiring tax laws; discretionary spending caps; improvements to how Joint Committee sequestration is shown in the Budget; the budgetary treatment of the housing Government-sponsored enterprises and the United States Postal Service; and using fair value as a method of scoring credit programs. These reforms combine fiscal responsibility with measures to provide citizens a more transparent, comprehensive, and accurate measure of the reach of the Federal budget. Together, the reforms and presentations discussed create a budget more focused on core Government functions and more accountable to the taxpayer.

I. BUDGET REFORM PROPOSALS

Joint Committee Enforcement

In August 2011, as part of the Budget Control Act of 2011 (BCA; Public Law 112-25), bipartisan majorities in both the House and Senate voted to establish the Joint Select Committee on Deficit Reduction to recommend legislation to achieve at least $1.5 trillion of deficit reduction over the period of fiscal years 2012 through 2021. The failure of the Congress to enact such comprehensive deficit reduction legislation to achieve the $1.5 trillion goal triggered a sequestration of discretionary and mandatory spending in 2013, led to reductions in the discretionary caps for 2014 through 2019, and forced additional sequestrations of mandatory spending in each of fiscal years 2014 through 2018. A further sequestration of mandatory spending is scheduled to take effect beginning on October 1 based on the order released with the 2019 Budget.

To date, various enacted legislation has changed the annual reductions required to the discretionary spending limits set in the BCA through 2017. The 2018 caps remain at the levels set in the sequestration preview report that was transmitted with the President's 2018 Budget while the sequestration preview report issued with this Budget reduces the 2019 discretionary caps according to current law. Going forward, the reductions to discretionary spending for fiscal years 2020 and 2021 are to be implemented in the sequestration preview report for each year by reducing the discretionary caps. Future reductions to mandatory programs are to be implemented by a sequestration of non-exempt mandatory budgetary resources in each of fiscal years 2020 through 2025, which is triggered by the transmittal of the President's Budget for each year and take effect on the first day of the fiscal year. The 2019 Budget proposes to continue mandatory sequestration into 2026, 2027, and 2028 to generate an additional $73 billion in deficit reduction.

For discretionary programs, under current law, the 2018 caps remain at $549.1 billion for defense and $515.7 billion for non-defense while, for 2019, the Joint Committee procedures reduce the defense cap from $616 billion to $562.1 billion and the non-defense cap from $566 billion to $530.3 billion. The 2019 Budget continues to illustratively assume its proposed caps for 2018 of $603 billion for defense and $462 billion for non-defense. For 2019, the Budget cancels the Joint Committee reductions made to the defense category and proposes a new defense cap that will support the National Security Strategy goal of preserving peace through strength with a substantial investment that will protect America's vital national interests. This increase is paid for by reducing the cap for non-defense by roughly the same amount. This results in a proposed defense cap of $627 billion for defense programs and a non-defense cap of $465 billion for non-defense programs. After 2019, the Budget sets aside the existing Joint Committee procedures for discretionary programs by proposing new caps for defense and non-defense programs through 2028. These funding levels will enhance the country's national security while maintaining fiscal responsibility by rebalancing the non-defense mission to focus on core Government responsibilities. See Table S–7 in the main *Budget* volume for the proposed annual discretionary caps.

Program Integrity Funding

All Federal programs must be run efficiently and effectively. Therefore, the Administration proposes to make significant investments in activities to ensure that taxpayer dollars are spent correctly by expanding oversight and enforcement activities in the largest benefit programs such as Social Security, Unemployment Insurance, Medicare and Medicaid, and increasing investments in tax compliance related to Internal Revenue Service tax enforcement. In addition, the Administration supports a number of legislative and administrative reforms in order to reduce improper payments. Many of these proposals will yield savings to the Government and taxpayers, and will support Government-wide efforts to improve the management and oversight of Federal resources.

In addition to efforts outlined in the Budget, the Administration will continue to identify areas where it can work with the Congress to further prevent, reduce, and recover improper payments and promote program integrity efforts.

Administrative Funding for Program Integrity.— There is compelling evidence that investments in administrative resources can significantly decrease the rate of improper payments and recoup many times their initial investment. The Social Security Administration (SSA) estimates that continuing disability reviews conducted in 2019 will yield net Federal program savings over the next 10 years of roughly $9 on average per $1 budgeted for dedicated program integrity funding, including the Old Age, Survivors, and Disability Insurance Program (OASDI), Supplemental Security Income (SSI), Medicare and Medicaid program effects. Similarly, for Health Care Fraud and Abuse Control (HCFAC) program integrity efforts, CMS actuaries conservatively estimate approximately $2 is saved or averted for every additional $1 spent.

Enacted Adjustments Pursuant to BBEDCA.— The Balanced Budget and Emergency Deficit Control Act of 1985, as amended (BBEDCA), recognized that a multiyear strategy to reduce the rate of improper payments, commensurate with the large and growing costs of the programs administered by the SSA and the Department of Health and Human Services, is a laudable goal. To support the overall goal, BBEDCA provided for adjustments to the discretionary spending limits through 2021 to allow for additional funding for specific program integrity activities to reduce improper payments in the Social Security programs and in the Medicare and Medicaid programs. Because the additional funding is classified as discretionary and the savings as mandatory, the savings cannot be offset against the funding for budget enforcement purposes. These adjustments to the discretionary caps are made only if appropriations bills increase funding for the specified program integrity purposes above specified minimum, or base levels. This method ensures that the additional funding provided in BBEDCA does not supplant other Federal spending on these activities and that such spending is not diverted to other purposes. The Bipartisan Budget Act of 2015 (BBA) increased the level of such adjustments for Social Security programs by a net $484 million over the 2017-2021 period, and it expanded the uses of cap adjustment funds to include cooperative disability investigation (CDI) units, and special attorneys for fraud prosecutions. To continue support to these important anti-fraud activities, the Budget request provides for SSA to transfer up to $10 million to the SSA Inspector General to fund CDI unit team leaders. This anti-fraud activity is an authorized use of the cap adjustment.

The 2019 Budget supports full funding of the authorized cap adjustments for these programs through 2021 and proposes to extend the cap adjustments through 2028 at the rate of current services inflation assumed in the Budget. The 2019 Budget shows the baseline and policy levels at equivalent amounts. Accordingly, savings generated from such funding levels in the baseline for program integrity activities are reflected in the baselines for Social Security programs, Medicare, and Medicaid.

Social Security Administration Medical Continuing Disability Reviews and Non-Medical Redeterminations of SSI Eligibility.— For the Social Security Administration, the Budget's proposed $1,683 million, the amount authorized in BBEDCA for discretionary funding in 2019 ($273 million in base funding and $1,410 million in cap adjustment funding) will allow SSA to conduct 703,000 full medical CDRs and approximately 2.8 million SSI nonmedical redeterminations of eligibility. Medical CDRs are periodic reevaluations to determine whether disabled OASDI or SSI beneficiaries continue to meet SSA's standards for disability. As a result of the discretionary funding requested in 2019, as well as the fully funded base and cap adjustment amounts in 2020 through 2028, the OASDI, SSI, Medicare and Medicaid programs would recoup about $44 billion in gross Federal savings with additional savings after the 10-year period, according to estimates from SSA's Office of the Chief Actuary and the Centers for Medicare and Medicaid Services' Office of the Actuary. Access to increased cap adjustment amounts and SSA's commitment to fund the fully loaded costs of performing the requested CDR and redetermination volumes would produce net deficit savings of approximately $30 billion in the 10-year window, and additional savings in the outyears. These costs and savings are reflected in Table 10-1.

SSA is required by law to conduct medical CDRs for all beneficiaries who are receiving disability benefits under the OASDI program, as well as all children under age 18 who are receiving SSI. SSI redeterminations are also required by law. However, the frequency of CDRs and redeterminations is constrained by the availability of funds to support these activities. The mandatory savings from the base funding in every year and the enacted discretionary cap adjustment funding assumed for 2018 are included in the BBEDCA baseline, consistent with the levels amended by the BBA of 2015, because the baseline assumes the continued funding of program integrity activities. The Budget shows the savings that would result from the increase in CDRs and redeterminations made possible by the discretionary cap adjustment funding requested in 2019 through 2028. With access to program integrity cap adjustments, SSA is on track to remain current with program integrity workloads throughout the budget window.

As stated above, current estimates indicate that CDRs conducted in 2019 will yield a return on investment (ROI) of about $9 on average in net Federal program savings over 10 years per $1 budgeted for dedicated program integrity funding, including OASDI, SSI, Medicare and Medicaid program effects. Similarly, SSA estimates indicate that non-medical redeterminations conducted in 2019 will yield a ROI of about $4 on average of net Federal program savings over 10 years per $1 budgeted for dedicated program integrity funding, including SSI and Medicaid program effects. The Budget assumes the full cost of performing CDRs to ensure that sufficient resources are available. Additionally, the Budget assumes that SSA will expand how it charges for medical CDRs beginning in 2019 to encompass workloads related to the medical CDR process, as reflected in the annual CDR report to Congress. The savings from one year of program integrity activities are realized over multiple years because some results find that beneficiaries are no longer eligible to receive OASDI or SSI benefits.

Redeterminations are periodic reviews of non-medical eligibility factors, such as income and resources, for the means-tested SSI program and can result in a revision of the individual's benefit level. However, the schedule of savings resulting from redeterminations will be different for the base funding and the cap adjustment funding in 2019 through 2028. This is because redeterminations of eligibility can uncover underpayment errors as well as overpayment errors. SSI recipients are more likely to initiate a redetermination of eligibility if they believe there are underpayments, and these recipient-initiated redeterminations are included in the base. The estimated savings per dollar spent on CDRs and non-medical redeterminations in the baseline reflects an interaction with the state option to expand Medicaid coverage for individuals under age 65 with income less than 133 percent of poverty. As a result of this option, some SSI beneficiaries, who

would otherwise lose Medicaid coverage due to a medical CDR or non-medical redetermination, would continue to be covered. In addition, some of the coverage costs for these individuals will be eligible for the enhanced Federal matching rate, resulting in higher Federal Medicaid costs in those states.

Health Care Fraud and Abuse Program.—The 2019 Budget proposes base and cap adjustment funding levels over the next 10 years and continues the program integrity cap adjustment through 2028. In order to maintain level of effort, the base amount increases annually over the 10-year period. The cap adjustment is set at the levels specified under BBEDCA through 2021 and then increases annually based on inflation from 2022 through 2028. The mandatory savings from both the base and cap adjustment are included in the Medicare and Medicaid baselines.

The discretionary base funding of $311 million plus an additional $5 million adjustment for inflation and cap adjustment of $454 million for HCFAC activities in 2019 are designed to reduce the Medicare improper payment rate, support the Health Care Fraud Prevention & Enforcement Action Team (HEAT) initiative and reduce Medicaid improper payment rates. The investment will also allow CMS to deploy innovative efforts that focus on improving the analysis and application of data, including state-of-the-art predictive modeling capabilities, in order to prevent potentially wasteful, abusive, or fraudulent payments before they occur. The funding is to be allocated among CMS, the Health and Human Services Office of Inspector General, and the Department of Justice.

Over 2019 through 2028, as reflected in Table 10-1, this $5.47 billion investment in HCFAC cap adjustment funding will generate approximately $11.6 billion in savings to Medicare and Medicaid, for new net deficit reduction of $6.1 billion over the 10-year period, reflecting prevention and recoupment of improper payments made to providers, as well as recoveries related to civil and criminal penalties.

Table 10–1. PROGRAM INTEGRITY DISCRETIONARY CAP ADJUSTMENTS, INCLUDING MANDATORY SAVINGS
(Budget authority and outlays in millions of dollars)

	2019	2020	2021	2022	2023	2024	2025	2026	2027	2028	10-year total
Social Security Program Integrity:											
Discretionary Budget Authority (non add)[1]	*1,410*	*1,309*	*1,302*	*1,351*	*1,403*	*1,456*	*1,511*	*1,569*	*1,629*	*1,690*	*14,630*
Discretionary Costs[1]	1,019	1,339	1,303	1,335	1,389	1,441	1,496	1,553	1,612	1,672	14,159
Mandatory Savings[2]	–105	–2,044	–3,092	–4,017	–4,452	–4,751	–5,534	–6,054	–6,580	–7,422	–44,051
Net Savings	914	–705	–1,789	–2,682	–3,063	–3,310	–4,038	–4,501	–4,968	–5,750	–29,892
Health Care Fraud and Abuse Control Program:											
Discretionary Costs[1]	454	475	496	515	534	555	576	598	620	644	5,467
Mandatory Savings[3]	–910	–975	–1,041	–1,106	–1,146	–1,191	–1,236	–1,284	–1,331	–1,382	–11,602
Net Savings	–456	–500	–545	–591	–612	–636	–660	–686	–711	–738	–6,135

[1] The discretionary costs are equal to the outlays associated with the budget authority levels authorized in BBEDCA through 2021; the costs for each of 2022 through 2028 are equal to the outlays associated with the budget authority levels inflated from the 2021 level, using the 2019 Budget assumptions. The levels in baseline are equal to the 2019 Budget policy. The mandatory savings from the cap adjustment funding are included in the baselines for Social Security, Medicare, and Medicaid programs.

[2] This is based on estimates of savings from the Office of the Chief Actuary at SSA and the Office of the Actuary at Centers for Medicare and Medicaid Services.

[3] These savings are based on estimates from the HHS Office of the Actuary for ROI from program integrity activities.

Table 10–2.   PROPOSED PROGRAM INTEGRITY CAP ADJUSTMENT FOR THE INTERNAL REVENUE SERVICE (IRS)

(Budget authority/outlays/receipts in millions of dollars)

	2019	2020	2021	2022	2023	2024	2025	2026	2027	2028	10-year total
Proposed Adjustment Pursuant to the BBEDCA, as amended:											
Enforcement Base (budget authority)	8,784	8,874	8,966	9,058	9,151	9,246	9,341	9,437	9,534	9,632	92,023
Cap Adjustment:											
Budget Authority	362	749	1,098	1,450	1,806	1,893	1,895	1,904	1,912	1,921	14,990
Outlays	320	693	1,040	1,386	1,737	1,850	1,865	1,875	1,885	1,893	14,544
Receipt Increases from Discretionary Program Integrity Base Funding and Cap Adjustments: [1]											
Enforcement Base [2]	−57,000	−57,000	−57,000	−57,000	−57,000	−57,000	−57,000	−57,000	−57,000	−57,000	−570,000
Cap Adjustment [3]	−152	−787	−1,825	−3,033	−4,330	−5,554	−6,416	−6,931	−7,270	−7,505	−43,803
Net Savings from Proposed IRS Cap Adjustment: [1]	168	−94	−785	−1,647	−2,593	−3,704	−4,551	−5,056	−5,385	−5,612	−29,259

[1] Savings for IRS are revenue increases rather than spending reductions. They are shown as negatives for presentation and netting against outlays.

[2] No official estimate for FY 2019 enforcement revenue has been produced, so this figure is an approximation and included only for illustrative purposes.

[3] The IRS cap adjustment funds increases for existing enforcement initiatives and activities and new initiatives. The IRS enforcement program helps maintain the more than $3 trillion in taxes paid each year without direct enforcement measures. The cost increases will help maintain the base revenue while generating additional revenue through targeted program investments. The activities and new initiatives funded out of the cap adjustment will yield more than $43.8 billion in savings over ten years. Aside from direct enforcement revenue, the deterrence impact of these activities suggests the potential for even greater savings.

Proposed Adjustment Pursuant to BBEDCA, Internal Revenue Service (IRS) Program Integrity.— The Budget proposes to establish and fund a new adjustment to the discretionary caps for program integrity activities related to IRS program integrity operations starting in 2019, as shown in Table 10-2. The IRS base appropriation funds current tax administration activities, including all tax enforcement and compliance program activities, in the Enforcement and Operations Support accounts. The additional $362 million cap adjustment in 2019 funds new and continuing investments in expanding and improving the effectiveness and efficiency of the IRS's tax enforcement program. The activities are estimated to generate $44 billion in additional revenue over 10 years and cost approximately $15 billion resulting in an estimated net savings of $29 billion. Once the new enforcement staff are trained and become fully operational these initiatives are expected to generate roughly $4 in additional revenue for every $1 in IRS expenses. Notably, the ROI is likely understated because it only includes amounts received; it does not reflect the effect enhanced enforcement has on deterring noncompliance. This indirect deterrence helps to ensure the continued payment of over $3 trillion in taxes paid each year without direct enforcement measures.

Mandatory Program Integrity Initiatives.— The mandatory and receipt savings from other program integrity initiatives that are included in the 2019 Budget, beyond the expansion in resources resulting from the increases in administrative funding discussed above are shown in table 10-3. These savings total almost $158.4 billion over 10 years. These mandatory proposals to reduce improper payments reflect the importance of these issues to the Administration. Through these and other initiatives outlined in the Budget, the Administration can improve management efforts across the Federal Government.

Unemployment Insurance Program Integrity Package.— The Budget includes proposals aimed at improving integrity in the Unemployment Insurance (UI) program. The proposals would result in $49 million in PAYGO savings over 10 years, and would result in more than $1.8 billion in non-PAYGO savings, including an estimated $709 million reduction in State unemployment taxes, which would reduce revenues from State accounts within the Unemployment Insurance Fund. Included in this package are proposals to: allow for data disclosure to contractors for the Treasury Offset Program; expand State use of the Separation Information Data Exchange System (SIDES), which already improves program integrity by allowing States and employers to exchange information on reasons for a claimant's separation from employment and thereby helping States to determine UI eligibility; mandate the use of the National Directory of New Hires to conduct cross-matches for program integrity purposes; allow the Secretary to set corrective action measures for poor State performance; require States to cross-match claimants against the Prisoner Update Processing System (PUPS), which is currently used by some States; and allow States to retain five percent of overpayment and tax investigation recoveries to fund program integrity activities.

Reemployment Services and Eligibility Assessments (RESEA).— The Budget also includes a mandatory proposal to fund RESEA for one-half of all UI claimants profiled as most likely to exhaust benefits. The related Reemployment and Eligibility Assessment initiative was begun in 2005 to finance in-person interviews at American Job Centers (also known as "One-Stop Career Centers"), to assess UI beneficiaries' need for job finding services and their continued eligibility for benefits. Research, including a random-assignment evaluation, shows that a combination of eligibility reviews and reemployment services reduces the time on UI, increases earnings, and reduces improper payments to claimants

Table 10–3. MANDATORY AND RECEIPT SAVINGS FROM OTHER PROGRAM INTEGRITY INITIATIVES
(Deficit increases (+) or decreases (-) in millions of dollars)

	2019	2020	2021	2022	2023	2024	2025	2026	2027	2028	10-year total
Department of Health and Human Services:											
Cut Waste, Fraud, and Abuse in Medicare, Medicaid, and the Children's Health Insurance Program	-42	-62	-79	-79	-99	-89	-100	-110	-120	-135	-915
Department of Labor:											
Unemployment Insurance Program Integrity Package[1]	-83	-188	-211	-211	-174	-195	-181	-229	-194	-216	-1,882
PAYGO effects	*-11*	*-14*	*-6*	*-6*	*-3*	*-3*	*-2*	*-3*	*-4*	*3*	*-49*
Non-PAYGO effects	*-72*	*-174*	*-205*	*-205*	*-171*	*-192*	*-179*	*-226*	*-190*	*-219*	*-1,833*
Reemployment Services and Eligibility Assessments[1]	....	-73	-465	-440	-417	-445	-413	-346	-413	-277	-3,289
PAYGO effects		*232*	*241*	*251*	*260*	*270*	*280*	*289*	*299*	*310*	*2,432*
Non-PAYGO effects		*-305*	*-706*	*-691*	*-677*	*-715*	*-693*	*-635*	*-712*	*-587*	*-5,721*
Department of the Treasury:											
Increase oversight of paid tax return preparers[1]	-22	-31	-36	-39	-43	-47	-52	-57	-63	-67	-457
Provide more flexible authority for the IRS to address correctable errors[1]	-42	-63	-65	-66	-69	-70	-73	-75	-76	-79	-678
Social Security Administration (SSA):											
Preventing Improper Payments:											
Hold Fraud Facilitators Liable for Overpayments (non-PAYGO)	....	....	....	-1	-1	-1	-1	-1	....	-1	-6
Government Wide Use of CBP Entry/Exit Data to Prevent Improper Payment	....	....	-1	-4	-11	-17	-22	-31	-35	-42	-163
Government Wide Use of CBP Entry/Exit Data to Prevent Improper Payment (non-PAYGO)	....	....		-1	-2	-2	-3	-3	-4	-5	-20
Allow SSA to Use Commercial Databases to Verify Real Property Data in the Supplemental Security Income (SSI) Program	-26	-40	-50	-61	-62	-62	-70	-73	-77	-83	-604
Increase the Overpayment Collection Threshold for OASDI (non-PAYGO)	-11	-72	-91	-102	-124	-148	-167	-219	-233	-231	-1,398
Authorize SSA to Use All Collection Tools to Recover Funds in Certain Scenarios (non-PAYGO)	-1	-2	-2	-4	-4	-5	-6	-7	-7	-7	-45
Simplify the SSI	....	-347	-86	-68	-50	-29	-18	-6	6	19	-579
Improve Collection of Pension Information from States and Localities (non-PAYGO)	18	28	24	-441	-1,058	-1,505	-1,618	-1,534	-1,442	-1,332	-8,860
Additional Debt Collection Authority for Civil and Monetary Penalties and Assessments	....	....	....	....	....	....	....	....	....	....	....
Total SSA, Preventing Improper Payment Effects (PAYGO plus non-PAYGO)	*-20*	*-433*	*-206*	*-682*	*-1,312*	*-1,769*	*-1,905*	*-1,874*	*-1,792*	*-1,682*	*-11,675*
Subtotal, PAYGO effects	*-26*	*-387*	*-137*	*-133*	*-123*	*-108*	*-110*	*-110*	*-106*	*-106*	*-1,346*
Subtotal, Non-PAYGO effects	*6*	*-46*	*-69*	*-549*	*-1,189*	*-1,661*	*-1,795*	*-1,764*	*-1,686*	*-1,576*	*-10,329*
Exclude SSA debts from discharge in bankruptcy	-7	-15	-21	-25	-30	-32	-34	-35	-37	-39	-275
PAYGO effects	....	*-1*	*-2*	*-2*	*-3*	*-3*	*-3*	*-3*	*-4*	*-3*	*-24*
Non-PAYGO effects	*-7*	*-14*	*-19*	*-23*	*-27*	*-29*	*-31*	*-32*	*-33*	*-36*	*-251*
Government-wide:											
Reduce Improper Payments Government-wide (non-PAYGO)	....	-719	-1,482	-2,383	-4,288	-4,549	-9,652	-20,480	-38,024	-57,633	-139,210
Total, Mandatory and Receipt Savings	**-216**	**-1,584**	**-2,565**	**-3,925**	**-6,432**	**-7,196**	**-12,410**	**-23,206**	**-40,719**	**-60,128**	**-158,381**
PAYGO Savings	*-143*	*-326*	*-84*	*-74*	*-80*	*-50*	*-60*	*-69*	*-74*	*-77*	*-458*
Non-PAYGO Savings	*-73*	*-1,258*	*-2,481*	*-3,851*	*-6,352*	*-7,146*	*-12,350*	*-23,137*	*-40,645*	*-60,051*	*-157,344*

[1] The estimate for this proposal includes effects on receipts in addition to changes in outlays; the net effect shown is a decrease in the deficit. Receipt effects by proposal can be seen in table S-6, Mandatory and Receipt Proposals, in the main 2019 Budget volume.

who are not eligible for benefits. Based on this research, the Budget proposes to expand funding for the RESEA initiative to allow States to conduct robust reemployment services along with RESEAs. These reemployment services may include the development of reemployment and work search plans, provision of skills assessments, career counseling, job matching and referrals, and referrals to training as appropriate.

The Budget proposal includes $2.4 billion in PAYGO spending for States to provide RESEA services to focus on UI claimants identified as most likely to exhaust their UI benefits and on newly separated veterans claiming unemployment compensation for ex-service members (UCX), resulting in net non-PAYGO deficit reduction of $5.7 billion. These savings consist of reductions in UI benefit payments of an estimated $7.3 billion, as well as a net reduction in business taxes of $1.4 billion. In total, this proposal is estimated to reduce the deficit by $3.3 billion over 10 years.

Because most unemployment claims are now filed by telephone or online, in-person assessments conducted in the Centers can help determine the continued eligibility for benefits and the adequacy of work search, verify the identity of beneficiaries where there is suspicion of possible identity theft, and provide a referral to reemployment assistance for those who need additional help. The benefit savings from this initiative are short-term because the maximum UI benefit period is limited, typically 26 weeks for regular State UI programs.

Preventing Improper Payments in Social Security.—Overall, the Budget proposes legislation that would avert close to $11.68 billion in improper payments in Social Security over 10 years. While much of this savings is considered off-budget and would be non-PAYGO, about $1.35 billion from various proposals would be PAYGO savings.

- *Hold Fraud Facilitators Liable for Overpayments.* The Budget proposes to hold fraud facilitators liable for overpayments by allowing SSA to recover the overpayment from a third party if the third party was responsible for making fraudulent statements or providing false evidence that allowed the beneficiary to receive payments that should not have been paid. This proposal would result in an estimated $6 million in savings over 10 years.

- *Government-wide Use of Custom and Border Protection (CBP) Entry/Exit Data to Prevent Improper Payments.* The Budget proposes the use of CBP Entry/Exit data to prevent improper OASDI and Supplemental Security Insurance (SSI) payments. Generally, U.S. citizens can receive benefits regardless of residence. Non-citizens may be subject to additional residence requirements depending on the country of residence and benefit type. However, an SSI beneficiary who is outside the United States for 30 consecutive days is not eligible for benefits for that month. These data have the potential to be useful across the Government to prevent improper payments. This proposal would result in an estimated $183 million in savings over 10 years.

- *Allow SSA to Use Commercial Databases to Verify Real Property Data in the SSI Program.* The Budget proposes to reduce improper payments and lessen recipients' reporting burden by authorizing SSA to use private commercial databases to check for ownership of real property (i.e. land and buildings), which could affect SSI eligibility. Consent to allow SSA to access these databases would be a condition of benefit receipt for new beneficiaries and current beneficiaries who complete a determination. All other current due process and appeal rights would be preserved. This proposal would result in savings of $604 million over 10 years.

- *Increase the Overpayment Collection Threshold for OASDI.* The Budget would change the minimum monthly withholding amount for recovery of Social Security benefit overpayments to reflect the

increase in the average monthly benefit since the Agency established the current minimum of $10 in 1960. By changing this amount from $10 to 10% of the monthly benefit payable, SSA would recover overpayments more quickly and better fulfill its stewardship obligations to the combined Social Security Trust Funds. The SSI program already utilizes the 10% rule. Debtors could still pay less if the negotiated amount would allow for repayment of the debt in 36 months. If the beneficiary cannot afford to have his or her full benefit payment withheld because he or she cannot meet ordinary and necessary living expenses, the beneficiary may request partial withholding. To determine a proper partial withholding amount, SSA negotiates (as well as re-negotiates at the overpaid beneficiary's request) a partial withholding rate. This proposal would result in savings of almost $1.4 billion over 10 years.

- *Authorize SSA to Use All Collection Tools to Recover Funds in Certain Scenarios.* The Budget also proposes to allow SSA a broader range of collection tools when someone improperly receives a benefit after the beneficiary has died. Currently, if a spouse cashes a benefit payment (or does not return a directly deposited benefit) for an individual who has died and the spouse is also not receiving benefits on that individual's record, SSA has more limited collection tools available than would be the case if the spouse also receives benefits on the deceased individual's earning record. The Budget proposal would end this disparate treatment of similar types of improper payments and results in an estimated $45 million in savings over 10 years.

- *SSI Simplification.* The Budget proposes changes to simplify the SSI program by incentivizing support from recipients' family and friends, reducing SSA's administrative burden, and streamlining requirements for applicants. SSI benefits are reduced by the amount of food and shelter, or in-kind support and maintenance, a beneficiary receives. The policy is burdensome to administer and is a leading source of SSI improper payments. The Budget proposes to replace the complex calculation of in-kind support and maintenance with a flat rate reduction for adults living with other adults to capture economies of scale. The Budget also proposes to eliminate dedicated accounts for past due benefits and to eliminate the administratively burdensome consideration whether a couple is holding themselves out as married. The proposal saves $579 million over 10 years.

- *Improve Collection of Pension Information from States and Localities.* The Budget proposes a data collection approach designed to provide seed money to the States for them to develop systems that will enable them to report pension payment information to SSA. The proposal would improve reporting for non-covered pensions by including up to $70 million for administrative expenses, $50 million of which would be available to the States, to develop a mechanism so that the Social Security Administration can enforce the current law offsets for the Windfall Elimination Provision and Government Pension Offset, which are a major source of improper payments. The proposal will save $8.86 billion over 10 years.

- *Additional Debt Collection Authority for SSA Civil Monetary Penalties and Assessments.* This proposal would assist SSA with ensuring the integrity of its programs and increase SSA recoveries by establishing statutory authority for the SSA to use the same debt collection tools available for recovery of delinquent overpayments toward recovery of delinquent CMP and assessments.

Cut Waste, Fraud, and Abuse in Medicare, Medicaid, and the Children's Health Insurance Program.—The Budget includes a robust package of Medicare and Medicaid program integrity proposals to help prevent fraud and abuse before they occur; detect fraud and abuse as early as possible; provide greater flexibility to the Secretary of Health and Human Services to implement program integrity activities that allow for efficient use of resources and achieve high return-on-investment; and promote integrity in Federal-State financing. For example, the Budget proposes to strengthen tools available to States and Territories that ensure providers who intend to engage in fraudulent or abusive activities do not enroll in Medicare, Medicaid, or the Children's Health Insurance Program. The Budget also includes several proposals aimed at strengthening the authorities and tools that CMS has to ensure that the Medicare program only pays those providers and suppliers who are eligible and who furnish items and services that are medically necessary to the care of beneficiaries. The package of program integrity proposals will help prevent inappropriate payments, eliminate wasteful Federal and State spending, protect beneficiaries, and reduce time-consuming and expensive "pay and chase" activities. Together, the CMS program integrity authority would net approximately $915 million in savings over 10 years. Additional information on the Medicare and Medicaid program integrity proposals are found in the Major Savings and Reforms volume.

Improving the Prevention of Improper Payments.— The Budget prioritizes focusing on improper payments that result in a monetary loss to the government. Specifically, by 2028 the Budget proposes to increase the prevention of improper payments through a series of actions to improve payment accuracy and financial performance over the budget horizon. Overall, savings are estimated to be approximately $139 billion over 10 years.

Other Program Integrity Initiatives.

Data Analytics to Improve Payment Accuracy.—At the core of Government-wide data analytics to improve payment accuracy is the Treasury Do Not Pay Business Center which includes a system that provides agencies a single-point of entry to access data and matching services

to help detect, prevent, and recover improper payments during the award or payment lifecycle. Additional examples of agencies using data to improve payment accuracy include the Centers for Medicare & Medicaid Services' (CMS) Fraud Prevention System (FPS), a state-of-the-art predictive analytics technology used to identify and prevent fraud in the program; the Department of Defense Business Activity Monitoring tool; and the Department of Labor's Unemployment Insurance (UI) Integrity Center for Excellence, a Federal-State partnership which facilitates the development and implementation of integrity tools that help detect and reduce improper payments in state run programs.

The effective use of data analytics has provided insight into methods of reducing costs and improving performance and decision-making capabilities. The Treasury Do Not Pay Business Center has 56 agencies performing matches against several databases (e.g., Death Master File, System for Award Management, Treasury Debt Check). In 2017, agencies screened over $1.3 trillion payments through the Do Not Pay Business Center using their payment integration function. While the vast majority of these payments were determined to be proper, the Office of Personnel Management alone, for example, stopped over $25 million in improper payments using the system. In addition to the Treasury Do Not Pay Business Center, the agency-specific integrity centers have demonstrated solid returns. Currently, SSA has 23 computer matching agreements that generate over $7 billion in annual savings. During 2016, the Department of Health and Human Services took administrative action against 1,044 providers and suppliers as a result of the CMS FPS, resulting in an estimated $527 million in identified savings. In 2017, DOD's BAM tool prevented $1.4 billion in improper payments in the Department commercial payment systems.

The Administration is continuing to pursue opportunities to improve information sharing by developing or enhancing policy guidance, ensuring privacy protection, and developing legislative proposals to leverage available information and technology in determining benefit eligibility and other opportunities to prevent improper payments.

Amend the Computer Matching Privacy Protection Act for the Department of the Treasury.—Agencies can experience significant bureaucratic challenges when working to implement certain components of the Computer Matching Act. For example, the process of signing an interagency computer matching agreement can take as long as 14 months as multiple levels of leadership sign the agreement. These issues are costly both in terms of improper payments that go undetected as well as the staff time that is needed to resolve them. The Budget proposes legislative changes to exempt the Do Not Pay Business Center at the Department of Treasury from components of the Computer Matching Act for activities designed to help agencies identify, prevent, and reduce improper payments. This proposal will protect citizen privacy while also saving administrative costs and help agencies to more readily leverage data-centric internal controls.

Exclude SSA Debts from Discharge in Bankruptcy.—Debts due to an overpayment of Social Security benefits are generally dischargeable in bankruptcy. The Budget includes a proposal to exclude such debts from discharge in bankruptcy, except when it would result in an undue hardship. This proposal would help ensure program integrity by increasing the amount of overpayments SSA recovers and would save $275 million over the 2019 through 2028 window.

Increase Oversight of Paid Tax Preparers.—This proposal would give the IRS the statutory authority to increase its oversight of paid tax return preparers. As more taxpayers use paid preparers, the quality of the preparers has a dramatic impact on whether taxpayers follow tax laws. Increasing the quality of paid preparers lessens the need for after-the-fact enforcement of tax laws and increases the amount of revenue that the IRS can collect. This proposal saves $457 million over the 2019 through 2028 period.

Provide the IRS with Greater Flexibility to Address Correctable Errors.—The Budget proposes to give the IRS expanded authority to correct errors on taxpayer returns. Current law only allows the IRS to correct errors on returns in certain limited instances, such as basic math errors or the failure to include the appropriate Social Security Number or Taxpayer Identification Number. This proposal would expand the instances in which the IRS could correct a taxpayer's return. For example, with this new authority, the IRS could deny a tax credit that a taxpayer had claimed on a tax return if the taxpayer did not include the required paperwork, or where government databases showed that the taxpayer-provided information was incorrect. This proposal would save $678 million over the 2019 through 2028 window.

Develop Accurate Cost Estimates.—OMB works with Federal agencies and the Congressional Budget Office (CBO) to develop PAYGO estimates for mandatory programs. OMB has issued guidance to agencies for scoring legislation under the statutory PAYGO Act of 2010. This guidance states that agencies must score the effects of program legislation on other programs if the programs are linked by statute. (For example, effects on Medicaid spending that are due to statutory linkages in eligibility for Supplemental Security Income benefits must be scored.) In addition, even when programs are not linked by statute, agencies may score effects on other programs if those effects are significant and well documented. Specifically, the guidance states: "Under certain circumstances, estimates may also include effects in programs not linked by statute where such effects are significant and well documented. For example, such effects may be estimated where rigorous experimental research or past program experience has established a high probability that changes in eligibility or terms of one program will have significant effects on participation in another program."

Disaster Relief Funding

Section 251(b)(2)(D) of BBEDCA includes a provision to adjust the discretionary caps for appropriations that the Congress designates in statute as provided for disaster relief. The law allows for a fiscal year's discretionary cap to be increased by no more than the average funding provided for disaster relief over the previous 10 years, excluding the highest and lowest years. The ceiling for each year's adjustment (as determined by the 10-year average) is then increased by the unused amount of the prior year's ceiling (excluding the portion of the prior year's ceiling that was itself due to any unused amount from the year before). Disaster relief is defined as activities carried out pursuant to a determination under section 102(2) of the Robert T. Stafford Disaster Relief and Emergency Assistance Act (42 U.S.C. 5122(2)) for major disasters declared by the President.

As required by law, OMB included in its Sequestration Update Report for 2018 a preview estimate of the 2018 adjustment for disaster relief. The ceiling for the disaster relief adjustment in 2018 was calculated to be $7,366 million. At the time the Budget was prepared, the Government was operating under a continuing resolution set in the Continuing Appropriations Act, 2018 (division D of Public Law 115-56, as amended by division A of Public Laws 115-90 and 115-96) (the "CR"). The CR had provided for 2018 a continuing appropriation of $6,713 million for the Federal Emergency Management Agency's Disaster Relief Fund (DRF). If final 2018 appropriations affirm this allocation with a final appropriation of $6,713 million for the DRF, this would fall $653 million below the ceiling available in 2018. Table 10-4 shows the statutory cap and the actual appropriations provided from 2012 through the current budget year, 2018.

OMB must include in its Sequestration Update Report for 2019 a preview estimate of the ceiling on the adjustment for disaster relief funding for 2019. This estimate will contain an average funding calculation that incorporates three years (2009 through 2011) using the definition of disaster relief from OMB's September 1, 2011 report and seven years using the funding the Congress designated in 2012 through 2018 for disaster relief pursuant to BBEDCA excluding the highest and lowest years. As noted above, the 2018 appropriation may be $653 million below the ceiling for 2018; therefore, this amount would be carried forward from 2018 into the 2019 preview estimate that will be included in OMB's August 2018 Sequestration Update Report for Fiscal Year 2019. Currently, based on continuing appropriations, OMB estimates the total adjustment available for disaster funding for 2019 at $7,386 million. Any revisions necessary to account for final 2018 appropriations will be included in the 2019 Sequestration Update Report.

At this time, the Administration is requesting $6,652 million in funding for FEMA's DRF in 2019 to cover the costs of Presidentially declared major disasters, including identified costs for previously declared catastrophic events (defined by FEMA as events with expected costs that total more than $500 million) and the predictable an-

Table 10–4. DISASTER RELIEF CAP ADJUSTMENT - HISTORICAL DATA AND CURRENT LAW
(Budget authority in millions of dollars)

	2012	2013	2014	2015	2016	2017	2018
Total Possible Cap Adjustment (statutory cap)	11,252	11,779	12,143	18,430	14,125	8,129	7,366
Annual Appropriations*	10,453	11,779	5,626	6,529	7,643	8,129	6,713
Difference	799	....	6,517	11,901	6,482	....	653

*2018 amount under a Continuing Resolution

nual cost of non-catastrophic events expected to obligate in 2019. For this program, the Budget requests funding for both known needs based on expected costs of prior declared disasters and the typical average expenditures in these programs. This is consistent with past practice of requesting and funding these as part of regular appropriations bills. Also consistent with past practice, the 2019 request level does not seek to pre-fund anticipated needs in other programs arising out of disasters that have yet to occur, nor does the Budget seek funding for potential catastrophic needs. As additional information about the need to fund prior or future disasters becomes available, additional requests, in the form of either 2018 supplemental appropriations (designated as either disaster relief or emergency requirements pursuant to BBEDCA), or amendments to the Budget, may be transmitted.

Under the principles outlined above, the Administration does not have adequate information about known or future requirements necessary to estimate the total amount that will be requested in future years as disaster relief. Accordingly, the Budget does not explicitly request to use the BBEDCA disaster designation in any year after the budget year. Instead, a placeholder for disaster relief is included in each of the outyears that is equal to the current 2019 request. This funding level does not reflect a specific request but a placeholder amount that, along with other outyear appropriations levels, will be decided on an annual basis as part of the normal budget development process. However, as is discussed below, notwithstanding this placeholder, the Administration does propose to address the declining cap under which disaster relief funds are requested.

Declining Disaster Relief Cap Adjustment

As is discussed under the Disaster Relief Funding section above, the Budget Control Act of 2011 established the formula for calculating an annual allowance up to which the discretionary spending limits could be adjusted for disaster-related appropriations, commonly discussed as the disaster cap adjustment. Since then, each Budget has requested Congress provide resources adequate to fund the budget year's: (1) anticipated Federal obligations for previously declared major disasters, (2) estimated obligations for non-catastrophic disasters, and (3) a limited contingency amount in recognition of the risk of an above-average year of disaster activity. During the same period, the allowable adjustment for disaster relief appropriations has declined to levels that approximate the Federal disaster assistance budget request. The annual disaster cap adjustment will soon be insufficient to cover the pro-

jected costs of future major disasters. The decline in the cap adjustment results from relatively modest annual disaster appropriations since 2011 coupled with high-cost response and recovery efforts such as Hurricane Katrina aging out of the rolling 10-year look-back window used in the cap adjustment formula. The extraordinary levels of funding provided for the catastrophic Atlantic hurricanes in 2017 for example, do not contribute to an increase in the cap adjustment under the formula. Inflation, urbanization, and other factors are expected to contribute to increasing future response and recovery costs.

The Administration recommends amending the disaster cap adjustment formula to improve the annual allowance by pegging disaster spending at levels that better reflect the unpredictable nature of disaster response and recovery costs. These steps will ensure that the Federal Government can mount a quick and sustained response to catastrophic disasters while more extensive deliberations over long-term recovery needs take place, an effort that would be frustrated if the allowance falls below projected costs as expected. Two changes will improve the allowance formula in future years: (1) adding all unspent "carryover" balances currently excluded by the formula to future annual cap adjustments until expended, and (2) adding to future annual cap adjustments five percent of emergency appropriations provided for Stafford Act-declared disasters since the creation of the disaster cap formula.

Maintaining unused "carryover" balances would ensure that the annual allowance accurately reflects the unpredictable nature of disasters. Since the pattern of disaster activity is erratic, several years of disaster relief appropriations that were below the calculated allowance have resulted in a drop in future years' projected cap adjustments, even without a reduction in the average magnitude of expected disaster costs. As a result, the funding that will likely be required for future catastrophic disasters will exceed the amounts permitted as a cap adjustment under the current law calculation.

Incorporating five percent of the total spending from emergency supplemental appropriations provided above the disaster cap would further improve the accuracy of the formula by providing a countercyclical stabilizer for the annual disaster cap adjustment. Emergency supplemental appropriations are provided for Stafford Act-declared disasters when the disaster cap adjustment is not sufficient to address the response and recovery needs of a catastrophic disaster. Even though these emergency supplemental appropriations are necessary to address disaster response and recovery needs, under current law they are excluded from the current disaster cap adjustment formula. By adjusting the disaster cap formula to include five percent of emergency supplemental appropriations, the result would better reflect the likely requirements for future disaster response and recovery.

Proposed Adjustments to the Discretionary Spending Limits for Wildfire Suppression Operations at the Departments of Agriculture and the Interior

Wildfires naturally occur on public lands throughout the country. The cost of fighting wildfires has increased due to landscape conditions resulting from drought, pest and disease damage, overgrown forests, expanding residential and commercial development near the borders of public lands, and program management decisions. When these costs exceed the funds appropriated, the Federal Government covers the shortfall through transfers from other land management programs. For example, in 2017, Forest Service wildfire suppression spending reached a record $2.4 billion, necessitating transfers of $527 million from other non-fire programs. Historically, these transfers have been repaid in subsequent appropriations; however, "fire borrowing" impedes the missions of land management agencies to reduce the risk of catastrophic fire and restore and maintain healthy functioning ecosystems.

To resolve concerns about the sufficiency of funding wildfire suppression, the Budget provides funding of $1,553 million under the 2019 discretionary cap to responsibly fund 100 percent of the rolling 10-year average cost for these wildfire suppression activities in the Departments of Agriculture and the Interior within the discretionary budget caps. Similar to how unanticipated funding needs for other natural disasters are addressed, the Budget also proposes to amend BBEDCA and to establish a separate annual cap adjustment for wildfire suppression operations. The Budget requests $1,519 million in additional appropriations from this cap adjustment in 2019 - the full amount that would be authorized under the Administration's proposal - to ensure that adequate resources are available to fight wildland fires, protect communities, and safeguard human life during the most severe wildland fire season. Table 10-5 shows the Administrations proposed statutory cap adjustment of $2,068 million, phased in over nine years. For the years after 2019, the Administration does not have sufficient information about future wildfire suppression needs and, therefore, includes a placeholder for wildfire suppression in each of the outyears that is equal to the current 2019 request. Actual funding levels, up to but not exceeding the proposed cap adjustments, will be decided on an annual basis as part of the normal budget process.

Limits on Changes in Mandatory Spending in Appropriations Acts (CHIMPs)

The discretionary spending caps in place since the enactment of the BCA in 2011 have been circumvented annually in appropriations bills through the use of changes in mandatory programs, or CHIMPs, that have no net outlay savings to offset increases in discretionary spending.

There can be programmatic reasons to make changes to mandatory programs on annual basis in the annual appropriations bills. However, many enacted CHIMPs do not result in actual spending reductions. In some cases, the budget authority reduced in one year may become available again the following year, allowing the same reduction to be taken year after year. In other cases, the reduction comes from a program that never would have spent its funding anyway. In both of these cases, under current scoring rules, reductions in budget authority from such CHIMPs can be used to offset appropriations in other programs, which results in an overall increase in Federal spending. In such cases, CHIMPs are used as a tool to work around the constraints imposed by the discretionary budget enforcement caps.

The Administration supports limiting and ultimately phasing out the use of CHIMPs with no outlay savings. Congress has started to reduce the reliance on such CHIMPs by setting decreasing limits in the budget resolution of $17.0 billion in 2018, $15.0 billion in 2019, and $15.0 billion in 2020. The Budget supports these efforts and limits the use of CHIMPs with no outlay savings to $13.3 billion in 2019.

Limit on Discretionary Advance Appropriations

An advance appropriation first becomes available for obligation one or more fiscal years beyond the year for which the appropriations act is passed. Budget authority is recorded in the year the funds become available for obligation, not in the year the appropriation is enacted.

There are legitimate policy reasons to use advance appropriations to fund programs. However, advance appropriations can also be used in situations that lack a programmatic justification, as a gimmick to make room for expanded funding within the discretionary spending limits on budget authority for a given year under BBEDCA. For example, some education grants are for-

Table 10–5.   PROPOSED WILDFIRE SUPPRESSION OPERATIONS FUND UNITED STATES DEPARTMENTS OF AGRICULTURE AND THE INTERIOR
(Budget authority in millions of dollars)

	2019	2020	2021	2022	2023	2024	2025	2026	2027	2028	10-year total
Proposed Adjustment Pursuant to the BBEDCA, as amended:											
Authorized level, proposed	1,519	1,603	1,683	1,759	1,831	1,898	1,960	2,017	2,068	2,068	18,406

ward funded (available beginning July 1 of the fiscal year) to provide certainty of funding for an entire school year, since school years straddle Federal fiscal years. This funding is recorded in the budget year because the funding is first legally available in that fiscal year. However, $22.6 billion of this funding is advance appropriated (available beginning three months later, on October 1) rather than forward funded. Prior Congresses increased advance appropriations and decreased the amounts of forward funding as a gimmick to free up room in the budget year without affecting the total amount available for a coming school year. This gimmick works because the advance appropriation is not recorded in the budget year but rather the following fiscal year. However, it works only in the year in which funds switch from forward funding to advance appropriations; that is, it works only in years in which the amounts of advance appropriations for such "straddle" programs are increased.

To curtail this gimmick, which allows over-budget funding in the budget year and exerts pressure for increased funding in future years by committing upfront a portion of the total budget authority limits under the discretionary caps in BBEDCA in those years, congressional budget resolutions since 2001 have set limits on the amount of advance appropriations. When the congressional limit equals the amount that had been advance appropriated in the most recent appropriations bill, there is no additional room to switch forward funding to advance appropriations, and so no room for this particular gimmick to operate in that year's budget.

The Budget includes $27,870 million in advance appropriations for 2020 and freezes them at this level in subsequent years. In this way, the Budget does not employ this potential gimmick. Moreover, the Administration supports limiting advance appropriations to the proposed level for 2020, below the limits included in sections 4101 and 5104 for the Senate and the House, respectively, of the Concurrent Resolution on the Budget for Fiscal Year 2018 (H. Con. Res. 71). Those limits apply only to the accounts explicitly specified in the joint explanatory statement of managers accompanying H. Con. Res. 71.

In addition, the Administration would allow discretionary advance appropriations for veterans medical care, as is required by the Veterans Health Care Budget Reform and Transparency Act (P.L. 111-81). The veterans medical care accounts in the Department of Veterans Affairs (VA) currently comprise Medical Services, Medical Support and Compliance, Medical Facilities, and Medical Community Care. The level of advance appropriations funding for veterans medical care is largely determined by the VA's Enrollee Health Care Projection Model. This actuarial model projects the funding requirement for over 90 types of health care services, including primary care, specialty care, and mental health. The remaining funding requirement is estimated based on other models and assumptions for services such as readjustment counseling and special activities. VA has included detailed information in its Congressional Budget Justifications about the overall 2020 veterans medical care funding request.

For a detailed table of accounts that have received discretionary and mandatory advance appropriations since 2017 or for which the Budget requests advance appropriations for 2020 and beyond, please refer to the Advance Appropriations chapter in the *Appendix*.

Pell Grants

The Pell Grant program includes features that make it unlike other discretionary programs including that Pell Grants are awarded to all applicants who meet income and other eligibility criteria. This section provides some background on the unique nature of the Pell Grant program and explains how the Budget accommodates changes in discretionary costs.

Under current law, the Pell program has several notable features:

- The Pell Grant program acts like an entitlement program, such as the Supplemental Nutrition Assistance Program or Supplemental Security Income, in which everyone who meets specific eligibility requirements and applies for the program receives a benefit. Specifically, Pell Grant costs in a given year are determined by the maximum award set in statute, the number of eligible applicants, and the award for which those applicants are eligible based on their needs and costs of attendance. The maximum Pell award for the academic year 2017-2018 is $5,920, of which $4,860 was established in discretionary appropriations and the remaining $1,060 in mandatory funding is provided automatically by the College Cost Reduction and Access Act (CCRAA), as amended. The maximum award for 2018-2019 will be finalized when Congress enacts full year appropriations for 2018.

- The cost of each Pell Grant is funded by discretionary budget authority provided in annual appropriations acts, along with mandatory budget authority provided not only by the CCRAA, as amended, and the BCA, but also by amendments to the Higher Education Act of 1965 contained in the 2011 and 2012 appropriations acts. There is no programmatic difference between the mandatory and discretionary funding.

- If valid applicants are more numerous than expected, or if these applicants are eligible for higher awards than anticipated, the Pell Grant program will cost more than the appropriations provided. If the costs during one academic year are higher than provided for in that year's appropriation, the Department of Education funds the extra costs with the subsequent year's appropriation.[1]

- To prevent deliberate underfunding of Pell costs, in 2006 the congressional and Executive Branch score-

---

[1] This ability to "borrow" from a subsequent appropriation is unique to the Pell program. It comes about for two reasons. First, like many education programs, Pell is "forward-funded"—the budget authority enacted in the fall of one year is intended for the subsequent academic year, which begins in the following July. Second, even though the amount of funding is predicated on the expected cost of Pell during one

keepers agreed to a special scorekeeping rule for Pell. Under this rule, the annual appropriations bill is charged with the full Congressional Budget Office estimated cost of the Pell Grant program for the budget year, plus or minus any cumulative shortfalls or surpluses from prior years. This scorekeeping rule was adopted by the Congress as §406(b) of the Concurrent Resolution on the Budget for Fiscal Year 2006 (H. Con. Res. 95, 109th Congress).

Given the nature of the program, it is reasonable to consider Pell Grants an individual entitlement for purposes of budget analysis and enforcement. The discretionary portion of the award funded in annual appropriations Acts counts against the discretionary spending caps pursuant to section 251 of BBEDCA and appropriations allocations established annually under §302 of the Congressional Budget Act.

The total cost of Pell Grants can fluctuate from year to year, even with no change in the maximum Pell Grant award, because of changes in enrollment, college costs, and student and family resources. In general, the demand for and costs of the program are countercyclical to the economy; more people go to school during periods of higher unemployment, but return to the workforce as the economy improves. In fact, the program experienced a spike in enrollment and costs during the most recent recession, reaching a peak of 9.4 million students in 2011.

---

academic year, the money is made legally available for the full 24-month period covering the current fiscal year and the subsequent fiscal year. This means that, if the funding for an academic year proves inadequate, the following year's appropriation will legally be available to cover the funding shortage for the first academic year. The 2019 appropriation, for instance, will support the 2019-2020 academic year beginning in July 2019 but will become available in October 2018 and can therefore help cover any shortages that may arise in funding for the 2018-2019 academic year.

This spike required temporary mandatory or emergency appropriations to fund the program well above the level that could have been provided as a practical matter by the regular discretionary appropriation. Since 2011, enrollment and costs have continued to decline, and the funding provided has lasted longer than anticipated. In 2018, the Budget proposed and Congress enacted Year-Round Pell, which provides a third semester of Pell Grant support to recipients who have exhausted their eligibility for the award year and wish to enroll in additional coursework. The 2018 Budget projected that this provision would increase program costs by $1.5 billion in 2018. Assuming no changes in current policy, the 2019 Budget baseline expects program costs to stay within available resources, which include the discretionary appropriation, budget authority carried forward from the previous year, and extra mandatory funds, until 2025 (see Table 10-6). These estimates have changed significantly from year to year, which illustrates continuing uncertainty about Pell program costs, and the year in which a shortfall will reemerge.

The 2019 Budget reflects the Administration's commitment to ensuring students receive the maximum Pell Grant for which they are eligible, and to expanding options available to pursuing postsecondary education and training. First, the Budget provides sufficient resources to fully fund Pell Grants in the award years covered by the budget year, and subsequent years, including the funds needed to continue support of year-round Pell grants. The Budget provides $22.5 billion in discretionary budget authority in 2019, the same as the 2017 enacted appropriation. Level-funding Pell in 2019, combined with available budget authority from the previous year and mandatory funding provided in previous legislation, provides $8.1 billion more than is needed to fully fund the program in the 2019-20 award year.

Table 10–6. DISCRETIONARY PELL FUNDING NEEDS
(Dollars in billions)

Discretionary Pell Funding Needs (Baseline)

	2019	2020	2021	2022	2023	2024	2025	2026	2027	2028
Estimated Program Cost for $4,860 Maximum Award ...	24.0	24.3	24.6	25.0	25.4	25.7	26.2	26.6	27.0	27.4
Cumulative Incoming Surplus [1]	8.2	....	....	....	....	....	....	....	....	....
Mandatory Budget Authority Available	1.4	1.4	1.1	1.1	1.1	1.1	1.1	1.1	1.1	1.1
Total Additional Budget Authority Needed	14.4	22.8	23.4	23.8	24.2	24.6	25.0	25.5	25.9	26.3
Fund Pell at 2017 Enacted Level	22.5	22.5	22.5	22.5	22.5	22.5	22.5	22.5	22.5	22.5
Surplus/(Funding Gap) from Prior Year		8.1	7.8	6.8	5.5	3.7	1.6	−0.9	−3.9	−7.3
Cumulative Surplus/Discretionary Funding Gap (−)	8.1	7.8	6.8	5.5	3.7	1.6	−0.9	−3.9	−7.3	−11.2

Effect of 2019 Budget Policies

	2019	2020	2021	2022	2023	2024	2025	2026	2027	2028
Expand Pell to Short-Term Programs	−0.1	−0.1	−0.1	−0.2	−0.2	−0.2	−0.2	−0.2	−0.2	−0.2
Fund Iraq and Afghanistan Service Grants through Pell	....	....	−*	−*	−*	−*	−*	−*	−*	−*
Cancellation of Unobligated Balances	−1.6	....	....	....	....	....	....	....	....	....
Mandatory Funding Shift [2]	−*	−*	−*	−*	−*	−*	−*	−0.1	−0.1	−0.1
Surplus/Funding Gap from Prior Year		6.4	5.9	4.7	3.2	1.2	−1.2	−3.9	−7.2	−10.8
Cumulative Surplus/(Discretionary Funding Gap)	6.4	5.9	4.7	3.2	1.2	−1.2	−3.9	−7.2	−10.8	−14.9

* Less than $50 million.

[1] The 2019 incoming surplus assumes an annualized 2018 appropriation of $22.3 billion, as provided under the Continuing Appropriations Act of 2018.

[2] Some budget authority, provided in previous legislation and classified as mandatory, but used to meet discretionary Pell grant program funding needs, will be shifted to instead fund new costs associated with the mandatory add-on.

In light of these additional resources, the Budget proposes a cancellation of $1.6 billion from the unobligated carryover from 2018. Then, with significant budget authority still available in the program, the Budget also proposes legislative changes to provide more postsecondary pathways by expanding Pell Grant eligibility to high-quality short-term training programs. This will help low-income or out-of-work individuals access training programs that can equip them with skills to secure well-paying jobs in high-demand fields more quickly than traditional 2-year or 4-year degree programs. The Budget also proposes moving Iraq and Afghanistan Service Grants (IASG) into the Pell program, which will exempt those awards from cuts due to sequestration and also streamline the administration of the programs. The expansion of Pell Grants to short-term programs and the costs of incorporating IASG increases future discretionary Pell program costs by $1.7 billion over 10 years (see Table 10–6). With the proposed cancellation and this increase, the Pell program still is expected to have sufficient discretionary funds until 2024; a cancellation of unobligated balances such as that proposed in the 2018 Budget could bring this date forward by one to two years.

Federal Capital Revolving Fund

The structure of the Federal budget and budget enforcement requirements can create hurdles to funding large-dollar capital investments that are handled differently at the States and local government levels. Expenditures for capital investment are combined with operating expenses in the Federal unified budget. Both kinds of expenditures must compete for limited funding within the discretionary caps. Large-dollar Federal capital investments can be squeezed out in this competition, forcing agency managers to turn to operating leases to meet long-term Federal requirements. These alternatives are more expensive than ownership over the long-term because: (1) Treasury can always borrow at lower interest rates; and (2) to avoid triggering scorekeeping and recording requirements for capital leases, agencies sign shorter-term consecutive leases of the same space. For example, the cost of two consecutive 15-year leases for a building can exceed its fair market value by close to 180 percent. Alternative financing proposals typically run up against scorekeeping and recording rules that appropriately measure cost on the basis of the full amount of the Government's obligations under the contract, which further constrains the ability of agency managers to meet capital needs.

In contrast, State and local governments separate capital investment from operating expenses. They are able to evaluate, rank, and finance proposed capital investments in separate capital budgets, which avoids direct competition between proposed capital acquisitions and operating expenses. If capital purchases are financed by borrowing, the associated debt service is an item in the operating budget. This separation of capital spending from operating expenses works well at the State and local government levels because of conditions that do not exist at the Federal level. State and local governments

are required to balance their operating budgets, and their ability to borrow to finance capital spending is subject to the discipline of private credit markets that impose higher interest rates for riskier investments. In addition, State and local governments tend to own capital that they finance. In contrast, the Federal Government does not face a balanced budget requirement, and Treasury debt has historically been considered the safest investment regardless of the condition of the Federal balance sheet. Also, the bulk of Federal funding for capital is in the form of grants to lower levels of Government or to private entities, and it is difficult to see how non-Federally-owned investment can be included in a capital budget.

To deal with the drawbacks of the current Federal approach, the Budget proposes: (1) to create a Federal Capital Revolving Fund (FCRF) to fund large-dollar, Federally-owned, civilian real property capital projects; and (2) provide specific budget enforcement rules for the FCRF that would allow it to function, in effect, like State and local government capital budgets. This proposal incorporates principles that are central to the success of capital budgeting at the State and local level -- a limit on total funding for capital investment, annual decisions on the allocation of funding for capital projects, and spreading the acquisition cost over 15 years in the discretionary operating budgets of agencies that purchase the assets. As part of the overall 2019 Budget infrastructure initiative, the FCRF would be capitalized initially by a $10 billion mandatory appropriation, and scored with anticipated outlays over the 10-year window for the purposes of pay-as-you-go budget enforcement rules. Balances in the FCRF would be available for transfer to purchasing agencies to fund large-dollar capital acquisitions to the extent projects are designated in advance in appropriations Acts and the agency receives a discretionary appropriation for the first of a maximum of 15 required annual repayments. If these two conditions are met, the FCRF would transfer funds to the purchasing agency to cover the full cost to acquire the capital asset. Annual discretionary repayments by purchasing agencies would replenish the FCRF and would become available to fund additional capital projects. Total annual capital purchases would be limited to the lower of $2 billion or the balance in the FCRF.

The flow of funds for the purchase of an office building costing $2.0 billion and the proposed scoring are illustrated in Chart 10–1. Current budget enforcement rules would require the entire $2.0 billion to be scored as discretionary BA in the first year, which would negate the benefit of the FCRF and leave agencies and policy makers facing the same trade-off constraints. As shown in Chart 10–1, under this proposal, transfers from the FCRF to agencies to fund purchases and the actual purchases by agencies would be scored as direct spending (shown as mandatory in Chart 10–1), while agencies would use discretionary appropriations to fund the annual repayments to the FCRF. This proposed allocation of cost between direct spending and discretionary spending would mean that the up-front cost of capital investment would already be reflected in the Budget as direct spending, and would not have to compete with operating expenses in the an-

Chart 10-1. Illustrative Scoring of $2 Billion Purchase using the Federal Capital Revolving Fund

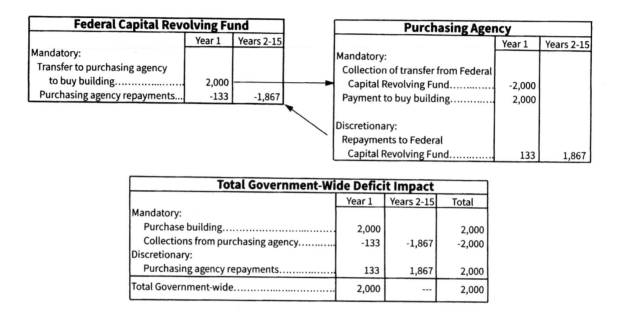

Federal Capital Revolving Fund	Year 1	Years 2-15
Mandatory:		
Transfer to purchasing agency to buy building..................	2,000	
Purchasing agency repayments...	-133	-1,867

Purchasing Agency	Year 1	Years 2-15
Mandatory:		
Collection of transfer from Federal Capital Revolving Fund............	-2,000	
Payment to buy building............	2,000	
Discretionary:		
Repayments to Federal Capital Revolving Fund............	133	1,867

Total Government-Wide Deficit Impact	Year 1	Years 2-15	Total
Mandatory:			
Purchase building..............................	2,000		2,000
Collections from purchasing agency............	-133	-1,867	-2,000
Discretionary:			
Purchasing agency repayments................	133	1,867	2,000
Total Government-wide............................	2,000	---	2,000

nual appropriations process. Instead, the trade off on the discretionary side of the budget would be the incremental annual cost of repaying the FCRF over 15-years. Knowing that future discretionary appropriations will have to be used to repay the FCRF would provide an incentive for agencies, OMB, and the Congress to select projects with the highest mission criticality and returns. OMB would review agencies' proposed projects for inclusion in the President's Budget, and the Appropriations Committees would make final allocations by authorizing projects in annual appropriations Acts and providing the first year of repayment. This approach would allow for a more effective capital planning process, for the Government's largest projects, that is similar to capital budgets used by private companies and State and local governments.

Fast Track Spending Reductions

The Executive Branch has a responsibility to review Federal spending and make recommendations when it is not in the best interest of taxpayers. The President's Budget proposes redirecting funding away from programs

where the goals have been met, or where funds are not being used efficiently to target higher priority needs. In the Budget, the President proposes cancellations, or reductions in budgetary resources. Such cancellations are not subject to the requirements of title X of the Impoundment Control Act of 1974 ("ICA"; 2 U.S.C. 601-88). Amounts proposed for cancellation may not be withheld from obligation pending enactment into law.

Alternatively, the President may propose permanent rescissions of budgetary resources pursuant to the ICA. In such cases, the ICA requires that the President transmit a special message to the Congress. Congress is not required to act on rescissions proposed under the ICA, however. The Administration is interested in working with Congress to enhance the shared goal of reducing Government spending where it no longer serves the interest of taxpayers. For example, the Administration would consider legislative proposals that ease the President's ability to reduce unnecessary spending through expedited rescission procedures.

II. BUDGET ENFORCEMENT AND BUDGET PRESENTATION

Statutory PAYGO

The Statutory Pay-As-You-Go Act of 2010 (the "PAYGO Act") requires that, subject to specific exceptions, all legislation enacted during each session of the Congress

changing taxes or mandatory expenditures and collections not increase projected deficits.

The Act established 5- and 10-year scorecards to record the budgetary effects of legislation; these scorecards are maintained by OMB and are published on the OMB web site. The Act also established special scorekeeping rules that affect whether all estimated budgetary effects of PAYGO bills are entered on the scorecards. Changes to off-budget programs (Social Security and the Postal Service) do not have budgetary effects for the purposes of PAYGO and are not counted. Provisions designated by the Congress in law as emergencies appear on the scorecards, but the effects are subtracted before computing the scorecard totals.

In addition to the exemptions in the PAYGO Act itself, the Congress has enacted laws affecting revenues or direct spending with a provision directing that the budgetary effects of all or part of the law be held off of the PAYGO scorecards. In the most recently completed Congressional session, three pieces of legislation were enacted with such a provision.

The requirement of budget neutrality is enforced by an accompanying requirement of automatic across-the-board cuts in selected mandatory programs if enacted legislation, taken as a whole, does not meet that standard. If the annual report filed by OMB after the end of a Congressional session shows net costs—that is, more costs than savings—in the budget-year column of either the 5- or 10-year scorecard, OMB is required to prepare, and the President is required to issue, a sequestration order implementing across-the-board cuts to non-exempt mandatory programs in an amount sufficient to offset the net costs on the PAYGO scorecards. The list of exempt programs and special sequestration rules for certain programs are contained in sections 255 and 256 of BBEDCA.

As was the case during an earlier PAYGO enforcement regime in the 1990s, the PAYGO sequestration has not been required since the PAYGO Act reinstated the statutory PAYGO requirement. Since PAYGO was reinstated, OMB's annual PAYGO reports showed net savings in the budget year column of both the 5- and 10-year scorecards. For the first session of the 115th Congress, the most recent session, enacted legislation placed costs of $1,089 million in each year of the 5-year scorecard and $653 million in each year of the 10-year scorecard. The new costs lowered the balances of savings from prior sessions of the Congress in the budget year column, and resulted in total net savings of $2,490 million in the 2018 column on the 5-year scorecard, and $13,815 million in the 2018 column on the 10-year scorecard, so no sequestration was required.[2]

There are limitations to Statutory PAYGO's usefulness as a budget enforcement tool. The scorecards have carried large surpluses from year to year, giving Congress little incentive to limit costly spending. Some costs, such as changes to the Postal Service or increases to debt service, are ignored. The frequent exemption of budgetary effects from the PAYGO scorecards by Congress also suggests the PAYGO regime has been ineffective at controlling deficits. In the coming year the Administration looks forward to working with Congress to rein in the deficit by exploring budget enforcement tools, including reforms to PAYGO.

Estimating the Impacts of Debt Service

New legislation that affects direct spending and revenue will also indirectly affect interest payments on the Federal debt. These effects on interest payments can cause a significant budgetary impact; however, they are not captured in cost estimates that are required under the PAYGO Act, nor are they typically included in estimates of new legislation that are produced by the Congressional Budget Office. The Administration believes that cost estimates of new legislation could be improved by incorporating information on the effects of interest payments and looks forward to working with the Congress in making reforms in this area.

Administrative PAYGO

In addition to enforcing budget discipline on enacted legislation, the Administration continues to review potential administrative actions by Executive Branch agencies affecting entitlement programs, so that agencies administering these programs have a requirement to keep costs low. This requirement was codified in a memorandum issued on May 23, 2005, by the Director of the Office of Management and Budget, "Budget Discipline for Agency Administrative Actions." This memo effectively established a PAYGO requirement for administrative actions involving mandatory spending programs. Exceptions to this requirement are only provided in extraordinary or compelling circumstances.

Adjustments to BBEDCA Baseline: Extension of Revenue Provisions and Transportation Spending

In order to provide a more realistic outlook for the deficit under current policies, the Budget presents the Administration's budget proposals relative to a baseline that makes certain adjustments to the statutory baseline defined in BBEDCA. Section 257 of BBEDCA provides the rules for constructing the baseline used by the Executive and Legislative Branches for scoring and other legal purposes. The adjustments made by the Administration are not intended to replace the BBEDCA baseline for these purposes, but rather are intended to make the baseline a more useful benchmark for assessing the deficit outlook and the impact of budget proposals.

Revenue Provisions Extended in Adjusted Baseline.—The Tax Cuts and Jobs Act provided comprehensive tax reform for individuals and corporations. The Administration's adjusted baseline assumes permanent extension of the individual income tax and estate and gift tax provisions enacted in that Act that are currently set to expire at the end of 2025. These expirations were included in the tax bill not because these provisions were intended to be temporary, but in order to comply with reconciliation rules in the Senate. Assuming extension of these provisions in the adjusted baseline presentation results in reductions in governmental receipts and increases in outlays for refundable tax credits of $568.9 billion over the 2026-2028 period relative to the BBEDCA baseline. This yields a more realistic depiction of the outlook for re-

---

[2] OMB's annual PAYGO reports and other explanatory material about the PAYGO Act are available on OMB's website at *https://www.white-house.gov/omb/paygo/*.

ceipts and the deficit than a strictly current law baseline in which these significant tax cuts expire.

Highway Trust Fund (HTF) Spending in the Adjusted Baseline.—Under BBEDCA baseline rules, the Budget shows outlays supported by HTF receipts inflating at the current services level. However, that presentation masks the reality that the HTF has a structural insolvency, one that all stakeholders are aware of, and the source of which is described below. The BBEDCA baseline results in a presentation that overestimates the amount of HTF spending the Government could support. Therefore, beginning in 2022, the Budget presents an adjusted baseline to account for the mismatch between baseline rules that require assuming that spending continues at current levels and the law limiting the spending from the HTF to the level of available balances in the HTF. Under current law, DOT is unable to reimburse States and grantees when the balances in the HTF, largely reflecting the level of incoming receipts, are insufficient to meet their requests. Relative to the BBEDCA baseline levels, reducing outlays from the HTF to the level of receipts in the adjusted baseline presentation results in a reduction in HTF outlays of $122.4 billion over the 2022-2028 window. This adjustment makes the level of spending that could be supported in the HTF absent reforms more apparent.

Surface Transportation Hybrid Budgetary Treatment.— The Highway Revenue Act of 1956 (Public Law 84-627) introduced the HTF to accelerate the development of the Interstate Highway System. In the 1970s, the HTF's scope was expanded to include expenditures on mass transit. In 1982, a permanent Mass Transit Account with the HTF was created. Highway Trust Fund (HTF) programs are treated as hybrids for budget enforcement purposes: contract authority is classified as mandatory, while outlays are controlled by obligation limitations in appropriations acts and are therefore classified as discretionary. Broadly speaking, this framework evolved as a mechanism to ensure that collections into the HTF (e.g., motor fuel taxes) were used to pay only for programs that benefit surface transportation users, and that funding for those programs would generally be commensurate with collections. Deposits to the HTF through the 1990s were historically more than sufficient to meet the surface transportation funding needs.

However, by the 2000s, deposits into the HTF began to level off as vehicle fuel efficiency continued to improve. At the same time, the investment needs continued to rise as the infrastructure, much of which was built in the 1960s and 1970s, deteriorated and required recapitalization. The cost of construction also generally increased. The Federal motor fuel tax rates have stayed constant since 1993. By 2008, balances that had been building in the HTF were spent down. The 2008-2009 recession and rising gasoline prices had led to a reduction in the consumption of fuel resulting in the HTF reaching the point of insolvency for the first time. Congress responded by providing the first in a series of General Fund transfers to the HTF to maintain solvency.

Fixing America's Surface Transportation Act (FAST Act).—The passage of the FAST Act (Public Law 114-94),

shored up the Highway Trust Fund and maintained the hybrid budgetary treatment through 2020. The FAST Act did not significantly amend transportation-related taxes or HTF authorization provisions beyond extending the authority to collect and spend revenue. Congress retained the Federal fuel tax rate at 18.4 cents per gallon for gasoline and 24.4 cents for diesel. To maintain HTF solvency, the FAST Act transferred $70 billion from the General Fund into the HTF. Since 2008, HTF tax revenues have been supplemented by $140 billion in General Fund transfers. For 2019, in policy, the Administration is requesting obligation limitation levels for HTF programs equal to the contract authority levels provided in the FAST Act. For the outyears, those levels are frozen at the 2019 level through 2028. The Budget also reflects the FAST Act contract authority levels for the remainder of the Act, through 2020. Beyond 2020 contract authority is frozen at the 2020 level. Outlays in policy are equal to the adjusted baseline levels, reflecting the need for a long-term solution.

Long-Term Solution Needed.—The fact that the HTF has required $140 billion in General Fund transfers to stay solvent points to the need for a comprehensive re-evaluation of the surface transportation funding regime. The adjusted baseline presentation shows the level of spending expected under current law, without assuming General Fund transfers. While Congress and past Administrations have been unable to find a long-term funding solution to the HTF, many States and localities have raised new revenue sources to finance transportation expenditures. The Administration believes that the Federal Government should incentivize more States and localities to finance their own transportation needs, as they are best equipped to know the right level and mix of infrastructure investments.

Discretionary Spending Limits

The BBEDCA baseline extends enacted or continuing appropriations at the account level assuming current services inflation but allowances are included to bring total base discretionary funding in line with the BBEDCA caps through 2021. Current law requires reductions to those discretionary caps in accordance with Joint Committee enforcement procedures put in place by the BCA. For 2019, the Budget supports maintaining the topline for base discretionary programs at the Joint Committee-enforced level but proposes rebalancing Federal responsibilities by increasing the defense cap under current law by $65 billion while reducing the non-defense cap by about the same amount. After 2019, the Budget proposes new caps that shift resources from non-defense programs by further reducing the non-defense cap over the 2020–2028 window by two percent per year (the "two-penny" plan) while increasing the defense category by an average of three percent per year through 2023 to resource the National Security and National Defense Strategies followed in 2024 through 2028 with inflationary growth of about 2.1 percent per year. The discretionary cap policy levels are reflected in Table S–7 of the main *Budget* volume.

Further adjustments to the proposed discretionary caps

The discretionary non-defense caps proposed in the 2019 Budget are reduced further to account for proposals to remove the air traffic control programs from discretionary spending because of privatization and to reduce the contributions of Federal agencies to the retirement plans of civilian employees. These cap reductions would prevent the savings achieved by these reforms from being redirected to augment existing non-defense programs. Reforms to the retirement plans of Federal civilian employees would also yield savings in the defense category, but the defense caps are not reduced accordingly, in order to allow for those savings to be redirected to critical national security investments within the category.

Air Traffic Control Reform.—The Administration proposes to shift the Federal Aviation Administration's (FAA) air traffic control function into a non-governmental entity beginning in 2022. This proposal reduces the need for discretionary spending in the following FAA accounts: Facilities and Equipment; Research, Engineering, and Development; and Trust Fund Share accounts. The Budget reflects an annual reduction of $10.2 billion in budget authority from 2022 to 2028; this level was determined by measuring the amount allocated as a placeholder in the policy outyears to air traffic control activities under the proposed non-defense category.

Employer-Employee Share of Federal Employee Retirement.—The Budget proposes to reallocate the costs of Federal employee retirement by charging equal shares of employees' accruing retirement costs to employees and employers. The Budget takes the estimated reductions in the share of employee retirement paid by Federal agencies out of the nondefense cap levels starting in 2020. This proposal starts at a reduction of discretionary budget authority of $6.5 billion in 2019 and totals $72.2 billion in reduced discretionary spending over the 2019 to 2028 period.

Gross versus net reductions in Joint Committee sequestration

The net realized savings from Joint Committee mandatory sequestration are less than the intended savings amounts as a result of peculiarities in the BBEDCA sequestration procedures. The 2019 Budget shows the net effect of Joint Committee sequestration reductions by accounting for reductions in 2019 that remain in the sequestered account and become newly available for obligation in the year after sequestration, in accordance with section 256(k)(6) of BBEDCA. The budget authority and outlays from these "pop-up" resources are included in the baseline and policy estimates and amount to a cost of $2.3 billion in 2019. Additionally, the 2019 Budget accounts for $752 million in lost savings that results from the sequestration of certain interfund payments, which produces no net deficit reduction.

Fannie Mae and Freddie Mac

The Budget continues to present Fannie Mae and Freddie Mac, the housing Government-sponsored enterprises (GSEs) currently in Federal conservatorship, as non-Federal entities. However, Treasury equity investments in the GSEs are recorded as budgetary outlays, and the dividends on those investments are recorded as offsetting receipts. In addition, the budget estimates reflect collections from the 10 basis point increase in GSE guarantee fees that was enacted under the Temporary Payroll Tax Cut Continuation Act of 2011 (P.L. 112-78). The baseline also reflects collections from a 4.2 basis point set-aside on each dollar of unpaid principal balance of new business purchases authorized under the Housing and Economic Recovery Act of 2008 (P.L. 111-289) to be remitted to several Federal affordable housing programs; the Budget proposes to eliminate the 4.2 basis point set-aside and discontinue funding for these programs. The GSEs are discussed in more detail in Chapter 20, "Credit and Insurance."

Postal Service Reforms

The Administration proposes reform of the Postal Service, necessitated by the serious financial condition of the Postal Service Fund. The proposals are discussed in the Postal Service and Office of Personnel Management sections of the *Appendix*.

The Postal Service is designated in statute as an off-budget independent establishment of the Executive Branch. This designation and budgetary treatment was most recently mandated in 1989, in part to reflect the policy agreement that the Postal Service should pay for its own costs through its own revenues and should operate more like an independent business entity. Statutory requirements on Postal Service expenses and restrictions that impede the Postal Service's ability to adapt to the ongoing evolution to paperless written communications have made those goals increasingly difficult to achieve. To address its current financial and structural challenges, the Administration proposes reform measures to ensure that the Postal Service funds existing commitments to current and former employees from business revenues, not taxpayer funds. To reflect the Postal Service's practice since 2012 of using defaults to on-budget accounts to continue operations, despite losses, the Administration's baseline now reflects probable defaults to on-budget accounts at the Office of Personnel Management (OPM). This treatment allows for a clearer presentation of the Postal Service's likely actions in the absence of reform and more realistic scoring of reform proposals, with improvements in the Postal Service's finances reflected through lower defaults, and added costs for the Postal Service reflected as higher defaults. Under current scoring rules, savings from reform for the Postal Service affect the unified deficit but do not affect the PAYGO scorecard. Savings to OPM through lower projected defaults affect both the PAYGO scorecard and the unified deficit.

Fair Value for Credit Programs

Fair value is an approach to measuring the cost of Federal direct loan and loan guarantee programs that would align budget estimates with the market value of Federal assistance, typically by including risk premiums observed in the market. Under current budget rules, the cost of Federal credit programs is measured as the net present value of the estimated future cash flows resulting from a loan or loan guarantee discounted at Treasury interest rates. These rules are defined in law by the Federal Credit Reform Act of 1990 (FCRA). In recent years, some analysts have argued that fair value estimates would better capture the true costs imposed on taxpayers from Federal credit programs and would align with private sector standard practices for measuring the value of loans and loan guarantees. The CBO, for instance, has stated that fair value would be a more comprehensive measure of the cost of Federal credit programs. The Concurrent Resolution on the Budget for Fiscal Year 2018 (H. Con. Res. 71) also included language requiring CBO to produce fair value scores alongside FCRA scores upon request. The Administration supports proposals to improve the accuracy of cost estimates and is open to working with Congress to address any conceptual and implementation challenges necessary to implement fair value estimates for Federal credit programs.

FEDERAL RECEIPTS

11. GOVERNMENTAL RECEIPTS

A simpler, fairer, and more efficient tax system is critical to growing the economy and creating jobs. The enactment of the Tax Cuts and Jobs Act (Public Law 115–97) in 2017 reformed the Nation's outdated, overly complex, and burdensome tax system to unleash America's economy, and create millions of new, better-paying jobs that enable American workers to meet their families' needs. This Act, which is the first comprehensive tax reform in a generation, streamlines the tax system and ends special interest tax breaks and loopholes, ensuring that all Americans will be treated fairly by the tax system, not just the wealthy. This chapter presents the Budget's estimates of taxes and governmental receipts including the effects of the Act and other tax legislation enacted in 2017, discusses the provisions of those enacted laws, and explains the Administration's additional receipt proposals.

Table 11–1. RECEIPTS BY SOURCE—SUMMARY
(In billions of dollars)

	2017 Actual	Estimate										
		2018	2019	2020	2021	2022	2023	2024	2025	2026	2027	2028
Individual income taxes	1,587.1	1,660.1	1,687.7	1,790.6	1,918.7	2,052.9	2,201.7	2,353.1	2,510.6	2,707.0	2,890.2	3,069.7
Corporation income taxes	297.0	217.6	225.3	264.8	272.7	314.2	373.8	416.6	434.7	417.4	406.0	413.5
Social insurance and retirement receipts	1,161.9	1,169.7	1,237.6	1,288.5	1,362.8	1,439.0	1,513.7	1,596.3	1,680.7	1,774.1	1,863.4	1,974.7
(On-budget)	(311.3)	(317.4)	(332.4)	(347.1)	(368.4)	(390.1)	(411.2)	(432.2)	(454.7)	(478.3)	(502.5)	(533.0)
(Off-budget)	(850.6)	(852.3)	(905.2)	(941.4)	(994.4)	(1,048.9)	(1,102.6)	(1,164.1)	(1,226.1)	(1,295.8)	(1,360.9)	(1,441.7)
Excise taxes	83.8	108.2	108.4	112.4	118.9	106.3	108.7	111.3	114.2	117.4	121.2	125.5
Estate and gift taxes	22.8	24.7	16.8	18.0	19.4	20.7	22.8	24.4	26.1	27.6	29.1	30.9
Customs duties	34.6	40.4	43.9	46.7	47.8	49.6	50.6	51.5	52.7	54.2	56.0	58.0
Miscellaneous receipts	129.0	119.7	106.0	96.4	100.3	108.8	117.7	125.2	130.5	136.8	143.4	149.3
Allowance for repeal and replacement of Obamacare	....	....	–3.5	–8.6	–2.5	–2.8	–2.9	–3.0	–3.2	–3.5	–3.7	–4.1
Total, receipts	**3,316.2**	**3,340.4**	**3,422.3**	**3,608.9**	**3,838.2**	**4,088.7**	**4,386.1**	**4,675.5**	**4,946.3**	**5,231.1**	**5,505.6**	**5,817.5**
(On-budget)	(2,465.6)	(2,488.1)	(2,517.1)	(2,667.6)	(2,843.8)	(3,039.8)	(3,283.6)	(3,511.4)	(3,720.2)	(3,935.3)	(4,144.7)	(4,375.8)
(Off-budget)	(850.6)	(852.3)	(905.2)	(941.4)	(994.4)	(1,048.9)	(1,102.6)	(1,164.1)	(1,226.1)	(1,295.8)	(1,360.9)	(1,441.7)
Total receipts as a percentage of GDP	17.3	16.7	16.3	16.4	16.5	16.8	17.1	17.4	17.5	17.6	17.7	17.8

ESTIMATES OF GOVERNMENTAL RECEIPTS

Governmental receipts are taxes and other collections from the public that result from the exercise of the Federal Government's sovereign or governmental powers. The difference between governmental receipts and outlays is the surplus or deficit.

The Federal Government also collects income from the public from market-oriented activities. Collections from these activities are subtracted from gross outlays, rather than added to taxes and other governmental receipts, and are discussed in Chapter 12, "Offsetting Collections and Offsetting Receipts," in this volume.

Total governmental receipts (hereafter referred to as "receipts") are estimated to be $3,340.4 billion in 2018, an increase of $24.2 billion or 0.7 percent from 2017. The estimated increase in 2018 is largely due to increases in individual income taxes and excise taxes, partially offset by decreases in taxes on corporate income. Receipts in 2018 are estimated to be 16.7 percent of Gross Domestic Product (GDP), which is lower than in 2017, when receipts were 17.3 percent of GDP.

Receipts are estimated to rise to $3,422.3 billion in 2019, an increase of $81.9 billion or 2.5 percent relative to 2018. Receipts are projected to grow at an average annual rate of 6.4 percent between 2019 and 2023, rising to $4,386.1 billion. Receipts are projected to rise to $5,817.5 billion in 2028, growing at an average annual rate of 5.8 percent between 2023 and 2028. This growth is largely due to assumed increases in incomes resulting from both real economic growth and inflation.

As a share of GDP, receipts are projected to decrease from 16.7 percent in 2018 to 16.3 percent in 2019, and to steadily increase to 17.8 percent of GDP by 2028.

LEGISLATION ENACTED IN 2017 THAT AFFECTS GOVERNMENTAL RECEIPTS

In addition to the Tax Cuts and Jobs Act, two other laws were enacted during 2017 that affect receipts. The major provisions of these laws that have a significant impact on receipts are described below.[1]

DISASTER TAX RELIEF AND AIRPORT AND AIRWAY EXTENSION ACT OF 2017 (Public Law 115–63)

This Act, which was signed into law on September 29, 2017, extended through March 31, 2018, various expiring authorities, programs, and activities of the Federal Aviation Administration in the Department of Transportation, including aviation-related taxes. The Act also modified certain tax provisions for individuals living in areas impacted by Hurricanes Harvey, Irma, and Maria, and tax provisions regarding charitable giving to those areas.

Extend aviation taxes.—The Internal Revenue Code imposes certain aviation-related taxes, including taxes on aviation fuels and ticket taxes on transportation by air of persons and property; and transfers to the Airport and Airway Trust Fund amounts equivalent to the aviation fuel taxes and air transportation ticket taxes received in the Treasury. The Act extended these taxes at their current rates, and extended the exemption under current law on commercial aviation taxes for certain fractional aircraft program flights, both through March 31, 2018.

Impose special disaster-related rules for use of retirement funds.—The Act permits penalty-free withdrawals from eligible retirement plans for individuals whose principal place of abode was located in the Hurricane Harvey, Irma, or Maria disaster areas on the date of disaster and who sustained an economic loss by reason of the hurricane. Individuals can make withdrawals from eligible retirement plans limited to $100,000 over the aggregate amounts treated as qualified hurricane distributions for that individual in all prior taxable years. In addition, individuals who make withdrawals for qualified hurricane relief can, within a three-year period starting on the date of the withdrawal, make contributions back to an eligible retirement plan, not to exceed the amount withdrawn. To qualify, these distributions must be made on or after August 23, 2017, for Hurricane Harvey individuals (September 1, 2017, and September 16, 2017, for Hurricanes Irma and Maria individuals respectively) and before January 1, 2019.

Provide tax credit for disaster-related employment.—The Act allows certain employers who were in business in a Hurricane Harvey, Irma, or Maria disaster zone on the date of the disaster, and before January 1, 2018, whose business is inoperable, to take a tax credit for 40 percent (up to $6,000 per employee) of wages paid during that period to each employee whose principal place of employment with the employer was in a disaster zone.

Temporarily suspend limitations on charitable contributions.—Under current law, individuals and corporations can take itemized deductions for charitable contributions, subject to certain limitations. Individuals may deduct charitable contributions up to 50 percent of adjusted gross income (AGI), further limited by the phase-out of itemized deductions. For corporations, the total deductions for charitable contributions for any taxable year may not exceed 10 percent of a corporation's taxable income. Under the Act, these limitations do not apply to corporate contributions for relief efforts related to Hurricane Harvey, Irma, or Maria, or to any charitable contributions paid by individuals during the period beginning on the date of disaster, and ending on December 31, 2017.

Implement special rules for qualified disaster-related personal casualty losses.—Currently, individual taxpayers are generally allowed to deduct from income any loss sustained during the taxable year and not compensated for by insurance or otherwise. Losses of non-business property may be deducted if they arise from casualty (e.g., fire or storm) or theft. However, these losses are allowed only to the extent that the loss from each casualty or theft exceeds $100. In addition, aggregate net losses from casualties or theft are deductible only to the extent that they exceed 10 percent of an individual taxpayer's AGI. This Act eliminated the 10 percent limitation for losses arising in the Hurricane Harvey, Irma, or Maria disaster areas and attributable to the hurricane; raised the $100 personal loss threshold to $500; and eliminated the requirement that individuals must itemize deductions in order to access the personal casualty loss deduction.

Special rule for determining earned income.—Under current law, eligible taxpayers may receive an earned income tax credit (EITC) and child credits. The EITC is a refundable credit for low-income workers. Taxpayers may claim a refundable child credit of $1,000 for each qualifying child if their AGI is below $75,000 for single filers and $110,000 if married and filing jointly. The Act allows these credits to be determined, at the election of the taxpayer, by substituting the earned income for 2016 for the earned income for 2017. This provision only applies to individuals whose principal place of abode was located, on the date of the disaster, in a Hurricane Harvey, Irma, or Maria disaster zone; or Hurricane Harvey, Irma, or Maria disaster area (but outside the disaster zone) and was displaced due to the hurricane.

TSP MODERNIZATION ACT OF 2017 (Public Law 115–84)

This Act, which was signed into law on November 17, 2017, modifies the rules relating to withdrawals from the Thrift Saving Plan (TSP) accounts of former Federal employees and Members of Congress. Previously, such employees and Members could make only one partial withdrawal upon reaching age 59–1/2 while employed or

---

[1] In the discussions of enacted legislation, years referred to are calendar years, unless otherwise noted.

one such withdrawal after retirement. The Act permits an unlimited number of withdrawals. The Act also eliminates the withdrawal election deadline and the limitation on age-based in-service withdrawals.

AN ACT TO PROVIDE FOR RECONCILIATION PURSUANT TO TITLES II AND V OF THE CONCURRENT RESOLUTION ON THE BUDGET FOR FISCAL YEAR 2018 (Public Law 115–97)

This Act, also referred to as the Tax Cuts and Jobs Act, which was signed into law on December 22, 2017, provided comprehensive tax reform for individuals and corporations, and repealed the individual mandate under the Affordable Care Act. Significant provisions of this Act are described in greater detail below.

Individual tax reform

Consolidate, simplify, and temporarily reduce income tax rates for individuals.—This Act temporarily reduced the individual income tax rates and altered the threshold at which each of the tax rates apply, effective for taxable years beginning after December 31, 2017, and before January 1, 2026. The individual tax rates were reduced to 10 percent, 12 percent, 22 percent, 24 percent, 32 percent, 35 percent, and 37 percent, with the highest rate applying to taxable income over $600,000 for married individuals filing jointly and over $500,000 for single individuals.

Index tax brackets by the chained Consumer Price Index (CPI).—Under prior law, the individual income tax brackets and many other thresholds within the tax code were indexed for inflation using the CPI for all urban consumers, as produced by the Bureau of Labor Statistics (BLS) within the Department of Commerce. This Act revised these indexation provisions to use the chained CPI, an alternative measure of inflation produced by BLS that more accurately measures inflation by better capturing the effects of changes in purchasing patterns on consumer price inflation.

Consolidate and temporarily reduce income tax rates for estates and trusts.—The Act modified the income tax rates for estates and trusts to 10 percent on taxable income below $2,550; 24 percent on taxable income over $2,550 but below $9,150; 35 percent on taxable income over $9,150 but below $12,500; and 37 percent on taxable income over $12,500. The reduced rates apply to taxable years beginning after December 31, 2017, and before January 1, 2026.

Increase the standard deduction.—Individuals who do not elect to itemize deductions may reduce their AGI by the amount of the applicable standard deduction in arriving at their taxable income. The basic standard deduction varies depending upon a taxpayer's filing status. This Act increased the basic standard deduction for individuals in 2018 to be $12,000 for single individuals (from $6,350 in 2017) and $24,000 for married individuals filing a joint return (from $12,700 in 2017). These amounts are indexed for inflation. The increase applies

to taxable years beginning after December 31, 2017, and before January 1, 2026.

Repeal the deduction for personal exemptions.—In determining taxable income, individuals reduce AGI by any personal exemption deductions and either the applicable standard deduction or his or her itemized deductions. Personal exemptions generally are allowed for taxpayers, their spouses, and any dependents. The deduction for the personal exemption is phased out for taxpayers with AGI in excess of $313,800 for married individuals filing jointly and $261,500 for single individuals. The Act repealed the deduction for personal exemptions for tax years beginning after December 31, 2017, through December 31, 2025.

Double the exemption amount for the estate and gift tax.—The Act unified the estate and gift taxes such that a single graduated rate schedule applies to cumulative taxable transfers made by a taxpayer during his or her lifetime and at death. Additionally, in determining one's taxable estate, certain credits are subtracted to determine estate tax liability; the Act doubled the exclusions for estate and gift taxes by increasing the basic exclusion amount from $5 million to $10 million, indexed for inflation occurring after 2011, for tax years beginning after December 31, 2017, through December 31, 2025.

Increase the child tax credit and require valid Social Security number (SSN).—The Act increased the child tax credit from $1,000 to $2,000 per qualifying child, provided $500 for each dependent who does not qualify for the child tax credit, and increased the maximum refundable child tax credit to $1,400 per qualifying child. The Act also increased the threshold for phase-out of the credit to $400,000 for married individuals filing a joint return ($200,000 for all other taxpayers). In addition, the Act required that a taxpayer claiming the child tax credit must include a SSN for each qualifying child for whom the credit is claimed. This additional requirement does not apply to a non-child dependent for whom the $500 non-refundable credit is claimed. These modifications apply to taxable years beginning after December 31, 2017, and before January 1, 2026.

Increase the alternative minimum tax exemption amount and phase-out thresholds.—An alternative minimum tax (AMT) is imposed on an individual, estate, or trust in an amount by which the tentative minimum tax exceeds the regular income tax for the taxable year. If a taxpayer owes more under the AMT calculation than under the regular income tax calculation, the taxpayer must pay the higher amount. A certain amount of income is exempt from the AMT – the so-called "exemption amount." The Act increased the AMT exemption amounts in 2018 to $109,400 for married taxpayers filling a joint return and $70,300 for single filers for taxable years beginning after December 31, 2017, and before January 1, 2026. It also increased the threshold at which this exemption amount is phased out to $1 million for married joint filers and $500,000 for single filers for taxable years beginning after December 31, 2017, and before January 1, 2026. Those amounts are indexed for inflation.

Reduce the threshold for medical expense deduction.—Current law allows for an itemized deduction for unreimbursed medical expenses in excess of 10 percent of a taxpayer's AGI. The Act reduced this floor to 7.5 percent for taxable years beginning after December 31, 2016, and ending before January 1, 2019. The Act made a similar change in calculating the deduction for these expenses under the AMT.

Decrease the mortgage interest deduction limitations.—Prior law allowed for a deduction for interest on certain home mortgages, limited to interest on the first million dollars of debt used for acquiring, constructing, or substantially improving the residence. Prior law also allowed the deduction of interest on up to $100,000 of home equity indebtedness. The Act reduced the limitation to interest on up to $750,000 of acquisition indebtedness and eliminating the deduction for interest on home equity indebtedness for taxable years beginning after December 31, 2017, and before January 1, 2026. In the case of acquisition indebtedness incurred before December 15, 2017, this limitation remains $1,000,000.

Limit State and local tax deduction.—Current law allows for an itemized deduction for State and local income taxes (or, at the taxpayer's election, State and local sales taxes) and property taxes. The Act limited the itemized deduction for State and local taxes to $10,000 for taxable years beginning after December 31, 2017, and before January 1, 2026.

Repeal of deductions and exclusions for moving expenses.—Prior law allowed above-the-line deductions for moving expenses paid by an employee and an exclusion from income for moving expenses reimbursed by an employer. The Act repealed the moving expense deduction and the exclusion of employer-reimbursed moving expense for taxpayers other than members of the Armed Forces, effective for taxable years beginning after December 31, 2017, and before January 1, 2026.

Repeal of deductions for alimony payments.— Prior law allowed above-the-line deductions for payments of alimony and provided that receipt of alimony payments be included as income. Child support payments were not treated as alimony. The Act repealed the alimony deduction and the corresponding inclusion of alimony as income, effective for any divorce or separation instrument executed after December 31, 2018.

Repeal of deduction for personal casualty and theft losses.—Prior law allowed a deduction for any uncompensated loss sustained during the taxable year, provided that the loss was incurred in a business or other profit-seeking activity or arose from theft and certain other casualties. Losses were deductible only above a $100 threshold, and only to the extent that aggregate losses exceeded 10 percent of the taxpayer's AGI. The Act limited the deduction to losses attributable to a Presidentially-declared disaster declared under section 401 of the Robert T. Stafford Disaster Relief and Emergency Assistance Act, effective for losses incurred after December 31, 2017, and before January 1, 2026.

Repeal itemized deductions subject to two percent floor.—Prior law allowed itemized deductions for a number of miscellaneous expenses, as long as the total of those expenses exceeded two percent of the taxpayer's

AGI. Allowable expenses included certain expenses in the production or collection of income, tax preparation expenses, and unreimbursed employee expenses. The Act suspended those itemized deductions subject to the two percent floor for taxable years beginning after December 31, 2017, and before January 1, 2026.

Increase percentage limit for cash contributions to public charities.—Current law limits the deduction of cash contributions to public charities and certain other organizations to 50 percent of the taxpayer's contribution base, generally AGI. The Act increases the limit to 60 percent for taxable years beginning after December 31, 2017, and before January 1, 2026.

Repeal limitation on itemized deductions.—Prior law limited the total amount of most otherwise allowable itemized deductions (other than the deductions for medical expenses, investment interest and casualty, theft or gambling losses) for taxpayers with incomes above certain thresholds. For 2017, the threshold amounts are $261,500 for single taxpayers; $287,650 for heads of household; $313,800 for married couples filing jointly; and $156,900 for married taxpayers filing separately. The Act repealed the limitation on itemized deductions for taxable years beginning after December 31, 2017, and before January 1, 2026.

Allow deduction for certain pass-through income.—Under current law, businesses such as sole proprietorships, partnerships, limited liability companies, and S corporations, are considered to be "pass-through" entities. Pass-through businesses are generally not treated as taxable entities for income tax purposes, but rather income and expenses are passed through to their owners. Income earned by a pass-through entity (whether distributed or not) is taxed to the owners at their own tax rates along with income they may receive from other sources. The Act allows an individual taxpayer to deduct 20 percent of domestic qualified business income from a partnership, S corporation, or sole proprietorship, subject to certain limitations. This provision is effective for tax years beginning after December 31, 2018, through December 31, 2025.

Disallow active pass-through losses in excess of threshold.—Under prior law, active owners of pass-through businesses may use business losses to offset other ordinary income (e.g., wage income) without limit. The Act prohibits taxpayers' use of pass-through losses in excess of certain threshold amounts. Any excess losses that are disallowed are carried forward and can be used to offset future income, subject to limitations. For 2018, the thresholds are $500,000 for married couples filing jointly and $250,000 for all other individuals. This provision is effective for tax years beginning after December 31, 2017, through December 31, 2025.

Business tax reform

Eliminate the corporate income tax graduated rate structure and decrease the corporate tax rate.—Previously, corporate taxable income was subject to tax under a four-step graduated rate structure. The top corporate tax rate was 35 percent on taxable income in excess of $10 million. An additional five-percent tax was imposed on a corporation's taxable income in excess of $100,000, with the maximum additional tax at $11,750. A second additional three-percent tax was imposed on a corporation's taxable income in excess of $15 million. The maximum second additional tax was $100,000. The Act permanently applies a single rate of 21 percent to corporation taxable income, effective for tax years beginning after December 31, 2017.

Repeal the corporate AMT.—Previously, an AMT was imposed on a corporation to the extent the corporation's tentative minimum tax exceeded its regular tax. This tentative minimum tax was computed at the rate of 20 percent on the income covered by the AMT in excess of a $40,000 exemption amount subject to a phase-out. The income taxed under the AMT was the corporation's regular taxable income increased by certain preference items and adjustments. If a corporation was subject to AMT in any year, the amount of AMT is allowed as an AMT credit in any subsequent taxable year to the extent the corporation's regular tax liability exceeded its tentative minimum tax in the subsequent year. The Act repealed the corporate AMT and allowed AMT credits to offset regular tax liability, effective for tax years beginning after December 31, 2017.

Extend, expand, and phase down bonus depreciation.—Businesses can generally recover the cost of certain property over a predetermined period of years. Businesses are allowed to take a first-year bonus depreciation deduction of an additional 50 percent of the cost of assets acquired and placed into service before January 1, 2020, but may elect not to take this additional deduction with respect to certain property. The 50-percent allowance is phased down for property placed in service after December 31, 2017. This Act extends the additional first-year depreciation deduction through December 31, 2026. The 50-percent allowance is increased to 100 percent for property placed in service after September 27, 2017, and before January 1, 2023. The allowance then decreases by 20 percentage points each year before phasing out completely for property placed in service after December 31, 2026.

Limit net interest deduction to 30 percent of adjusted taxable income.—Previously, interest paid or accrued by a business generally was deductible in the computation of taxable income subject to a number of limitations. The Act generally limits the deduction to 30 percent of the adjusted taxable income of the business, but with an exception for certain small businesses. Adjusted taxable income is not reduced for depreciation, amortization, or depletion deductions for taxable years beginning after December 31, 2017, and before January 1, 2022. The excess amount of interest may be carried forward indefinitely to future tax years.

Modify net operating loss deduction.—A net operating loss (NOL) generally means the amount by which the deductions of a business exceed its gross income. Previously, a NOL could be carried back two years and carried forward over 20 years to offset taxable income in such years. The Act limits NOL deductions to 80 percent of taxable income and repeals the ability to carry back NOLs two years, with exceptions for certain businesses. This limitation applies to corporations as well as individuals with pass-through businesses.

Amortize research and experimentation expenditures.—Under current law, businesses may choose to deduct certain research or experimentation expenditures from current income, or to capitalize these expenditures and deduct them over a longer period. The Act requires that these expenditures paid or incurred in taxable years beginning after December 31, 2021, be capitalized and amortized ratably over a five-year period. Certain expenditures which are attributable to research that is conducted outside of the United States are required to be capitalized and amortized ratably over a period of 15 years.

Repeal or limit business-related deductions.—The Act permanently repeals or limits a number of deductions from business income, including eliminating the deduction for income attributable to domestic production activities and limiting the deduction for employee meal, entertainment, and transportation expenses.

International tax reform

Allow deduction of dividends received by domestic corporations from certain foreign corporations.—The Act provides that in the case of any dividend received from a specified 10-percent owned foreign corporation by a domestic corporation which is a United States shareholder with respect to such foreign corporation, a deduction is allowed in an amount equal to the foreign-source portion of such dividend.

Treat deferred foreign income at two-tier rate.—The Act requires that, for the last taxable year of a foreign corporation beginning before January 1, 2018, all U.S. shareholders of any controlled foreign corporation or other foreign corporation (CFC) that is at least 10-percent U.S.-owned but not controlled, include in income their pro rata shares of the accumulated post–1986 deferred foreign income that was not previously taxed. A portion of that pro rata share of deferred foreign income is deductible resulting in a reduced rate of tax of 15.5 percent for the included deferred foreign income held in liquid form and 8 percent for the remaining deferred foreign income.

Include current year global intangible low-taxed income.—The Act requires that U.S. shareholders of any CFC include in gross income its global intangible low-taxed income (GILTI) in a manner generally similar to inclusions of subpart F income. GILTI means, with respect to any U.S. shareholder for the shareholder's taxable year, the excess (if any) of the shareholder's net CFC tested income over the shareholder's net deemed tangible income return. The shareholder's net deemed tangible income return is an amount equal to 10 percent of the aggregate of the shareholder's pro rata share of the qualified business asset investment of each CFC with respect to which it is a U.S. shareholder. Domestic C corporations that are U.S. shareholders of CFCs are given a deduction equal to 50 percent (decreasing to 37.5 percent in 2026) of the GILTI. This results in a pre-credit U.S. effective tax rate on GILTI income of 10.5 percent for 2018 through 2025, and 13.125 percent from 2026 onward. Foreign taxes paid that are attributable to the excess return are creditable against the U.S. tax on GILTI, subject to a 20 percent reduction.

Establish deduction for foreign-derived intangible income.—The Act provides a deduction for domestic corporations based on their foreign-derived intangible income (FDII). FDII is the portion of a domestic corporation's "intangible" income, determined on a formulaic basis, attributable to serving foreign markets. For taxable years beginning after December 31, 2017, and before January 1, 2026, the provision generally allows a deduction equal to 37.5 percent of the corporation's FDII. This deduction reduces the effective tax rate on FDII below the statutory corporate tax rate of 21 percent; for example, the deduction implies a 13.125 percent effective tax rate for FDII in these years. For taxable years beginning after December 31, 2025, the deduction for FDII is reduced to 21.875 percent.

Impose a base erosion and anti-abuse tax.—The Act requires that certain taxpayers compute an alternative minimum tax called the base erosion anti-abuse tax (BEAT). The BEAT is imposed on both domestic and foreign companies with more than $500 million in average annual gross receipts and "base erosion payments" greater than 3 percent of total deductions (2 percent in the case of banks). Base erosion payments are non-cost of goods sold deductible payments made to foreign related parties. The BEAT is computed as the amount by which a company's taxable income computed without regard to base erosion payments exceeds the company's regular corporate tax liability minus certain tax credits. The BEAT rate is 5 percent in 2018, rising to 10 percent in 2019 through 2025, and then to 12.5 percent starting in 2026. Banks are subject to a BEAT rate that is 1 percent higher that applies if the base erosion payments exceed 2 percent of total deductions, but certain payments made with respect to derivatives are excluded from the BEAT.

Other

Permanently repeal the individual mandate tax penalty.—Under the Patient Protection and Affordable Care Act (Public Law 111–148), individuals are required to be covered by a health plan that provides at least minimum essential coverage or be subject to a tax penalty for failure to maintain the coverage (commonly referred to as the "individual mandate"). The tax is imposed for any month that the individual does not have the minimum essential coverage and is equal to the greater of a flat dollar amount or a percentage of income in excess of the filing threshold. This Act permanently repeals the individual mandate tax penalty by decreasing both the individual annual dollar amount and the percentage of income to zero for health coverage in months beginning after December 31, 2018.

Table 11–2.   ADJUSTMENTS TO THE BALANCED BUDGET AND EMERGENCY DEFICIT CONTROL ACT (BBEDCA) BASELINE ESTIMATES OF GOVERNMENTAL RECEIPTS

(In billions of dollars)

	2018	2019	2020	2021	2022	2023	2024	2025	2026	2027	2028	2019–2023	2019–2028
BBEDCA baseline receipts	3,340.5	3,424.3	3,613.3	3,832.9	4,094.7	4,388.9	4,677.8	4,947.7	5,346.1	5,716.9	6,040.3	19,354.1	46,082.9
Adjustments to BBEDCA baseline:													
Extend individual income tax provisions [1]	....	....	....	....	....	....	....	....	–112.7	–194.9	–204.7	....	–512.4
Extend estate and gift tax provisions	....	....	....	....	....	....	....	....	....	–14.2	–15.1	....	–29.2
Total, adjustments to BBEDCA baseline	....	....	....	....	....	....	....	....	–112.7	–209.1	–219.8	....	–541.6
Adjusted baseline receipts	3,340.5	3,424.3	3,613.3	3,832.9	4,094.7	4,388.9	4,677.8	4,947.7	5,233.5	5,507.8	5,820.5	19,354.1	45,541.4

[1] This provision affects both receipts and outlays. Only the receipt effect is shown here. The outlay effects are listed below:

	2018	2019	2020	2021	2022	2023	2024	2025	2026	2027	2028	2019–23	2019–28
Extend individual income tax provisions	....	....	....	....	....	....	....	....	–3.9	15.3	15.9	....	27.3
Total, outlay effects of adjustments to BBEDCA baseline	....	....	....	....	....	....	....	....	–3.9	15.3	15.9	....	27.3

ADJUSTMENTS TO THE BALANCED BUDGET AND EMERGENCY DEFICIT CONTROL ACT (BBEDCA) BASELINE

An important step in addressing the Nation's fiscal problems is to be upfront about them and to establish a baseline that provides a realistic measure of the deficit outlook before new policies are enacted. This Budget does so by adjusting the BBEDCA baseline to reflect the true cost of extending major tax policies that are scheduled to expire but that are likely to be extended. The BBEDCA baseline, which is commonly used in budgeting and is defined in statute, reflects, with some exceptions, the projected receipts level under current law.

However, current law includes a number of scheduled tax changes that the Administration believes are unlikely to occur and that prevent it from serving as a realistic benchmark for judging the effect of new legislation. These tax changes include expiration in 2025 of the individual income and estate and gift tax provisions enacted in the Tax Cuts and Jobs Act. This Budget uses an adjusted baseline that is intended to be more realistic by extending those expiring provisions. This baseline does not reflect the President's policy proposals, but is rather a realistic and fair benchmark from which to measure the effects of those policies.

Extend individual income tax provisions.—The Administration's adjusted baseline projection permanently extends all expiring individual income tax provisions in the Tax Cuts and Jobs Act that are currently set to expire on December 31, 2025.

Extend estate and gift tax provisions.—The Administration's adjusted baseline projection reflects permanent extension of the estate and gift tax parameters and provisions in effect for calendar year 2025.

BUDGET PROPOSALS

The 2019 Budget supports the extension of the individual and estate tax provisions of the Tax Cuts and Jobs Act beyond their expiration in 2025, as described above, to provide certainty for taxpayers and support continued economic growth. The Budget's additional proposals affecting governmental receipts are as follows:

Allow Medicare beneficiaries to contribute to Health Savings Accounts (HSAs) and Medical Savings Accounts (MSAs).—Under current law, workers who are entitled to Medicare are not allowed to contribute to an HSA, even if they are working and are enrolled in a qualifying health plan through their employer. The Administration proposes to allow workers aged 65 or older who have a high-deductible health plan through their employer to contribute to an HSA, even if they are entitled to Medicare. In addition, the Administration proposes to allow beneficiaries enrolled in Medicare MSA Plans to contribute to their MSAs, beginning in 2021, subject to the annual HSA contribution limits as determined by the Internal Revenue Service. Beneficiaries would also be allowed a one-time opportunity to roll over the funds from their private HSAs to their Medicare MSAs. Beneficiaries who elect this plan option would not be allowed to purchase Medigap or other supplemental insurance.

Extend Children's Health Insurance Program (CHIP) funding through 2019.—The Administration proposes to extend CHIP funding through fiscal year 2019. As a result, on net, more children will be enrolled in CHIP and fewer children will be enrolled in Marketplace qualified health plans and employment-based health insurance. This will increase tax revenues and reduce outlays associated with the premium tax credit.

Reform medical liability.—The Administration proposes to reform medical liability beginning in 2019. This proposal has the potential to lower health insurance premiums, increasing taxable income and payroll tax receipts.

Reduce the grace period for Exchange premiums.—The Administration proposes to reduce the 90-day grace period for individuals on Exchange plans to repay any missed premium payments to 30 days. The proposal would decrease premium tax credit outlays and increase governmental receipts.

Provide tax exemption for Indian Health Service (IHS) Health Professions scholarship and loan repayment programs in return for obligatory service requirement.—The Administration proposes to allow scholarship funds for qualified tuition and related expenses received under the IHS Health Professions scholarship to be excluded from income. The Administration also proposes to allow students to exclude from gross income student loan amounts forgiven by the IHS Loan Repayment Program. Under current law, National Health Service Corps programs and Armed Forces Health Professions Scholarships are provided an exception to the general rule that scholarship amounts representing payment for work are considered ordinary income and therefore taxable. Furthermore, certain loans forgiven as part of certain State and profession-based loan programs are provided an exception from the general rule that loan amounts paid on another's behalf are taxable income. Extending the exceptions to IHS programs would provide the IHS programs with comparable treatment to similar programs administered by the National Health Service Corps, the Armed Forces, and certain State programs. Eliminating the current tax burden on scholarship recipients would allow IHS to leverage another tool to bolster its ongoing efforts to recruit and retain qualified healthcare providers.

Establish Electronic Visa Update System (EVUS) user fee.—The Administration proposes to establish a user fee for EVUS, a new U.S. Customs and Border Protection (CBP) program to collect biographic and travel-related information from certain non-immigrant visa holders prior to traveling to the United States. The user fee would fund the costs of establishing, providing, and administering the system.

Eliminate Corporation for Travel Promotion.—The Administration proposes to eliminate funding for the Corporation for Travel Promotion (also known as Brand USA). The Budget extents the authorization for the Electronic System for Travel Authorization (ESTA) surcharge currently deposited in the Travel Promotion Fund and redirects the surcharge to the ESTA account at Customs and Border Protection with a portion to be transferred to the International Trade Administration to administer the Survey of International Air Travelers.

Establish an immigration services surcharge.—The Administration proposes to add a 10 percent surcharge on all requests received by U.S. Citizenship and Immigration Services, including applications for citizenship, adjustment of status, and petitions for temporary workers.

Increase worksite enforcement penalties.—The Administration proposes to increase by 35 percent all penalty amounts against employers who violate Immigration and Nationality Act provisions on the unlawful employment of aliens.

Reinstate the Oil Spill Liability Trust Fund excise tax.—The Administration proposes to reinstate the Oil Spill Liability Trust Fund excise tax, which expired on December 31, 2017. The Trust Fund provides resources for the Federal Government to respond and clean up incidents of oil spills.

Provide paid parental leave benefits.—The Administration proposes establishing a new benefit within the Unemployment Insurance (UI) program to provide up to six weeks paid leave to mothers, fathers, and adoptive parents. States are responsible for adjusting their UI tax structures to maintain sufficient balances in their Unemployment Trust Fund accounts.

Establish Unemployment Insurance (UI) solvency standard.—The Administration proposes to set a minimum solvency standard to encourage States to maintain sufficient balances in their UI trust funds. States that are currently below this minimum standard are expected to increase their State UI taxes to build up their trust fund balances. States that do not build up sufficient reserves will be subject to Federal Unemployment Tax Act credit reductions, increasing Federal UI receipts.

Improve UI Insurance program integrity.—The Administration proposes a package of reforms to the UI program aimed at improving program integrity. These reforms are expected to reduce outlays in the UI program by reducing improper payments. In general, reduced outlays allow States to keep UI taxes lower, reducing overall receipts to the UI trust funds.

Provide for Reemployment Services and Eligibility Assessments (RESEAs).—The Administration proposes mandatory funding to provide RESEAs to the one-half of UI claimants identified as most likely to exhaust benefits. RESEAs have been shown to reduce improper payments and to get claimants back to work more quickly, thereby reducing UI benefit outlays. In general, reduced outlays allow States to keep UI taxes lower, reducing overall receipts to the UI trust funds.

Reform the Essential Air Service (EAS).—The Administration proposes to reform the EAS by reducing discretionary funding and focusing on the remote airports that are most in need of subsidized commercial air service. The proposal will include a mix of reforms, including limits on per-passenger subsidies and higher average daily enplanements. These reforms would affect governmental receipts by reducing aviation overflight fees.

Enact Federal Aviation Administration (FAA) air traffic control reform.—The Administration proposes to shift the FAA's air traffic control function into a nongovernmental entity beginning in 2022. This proposal would reduce the collection of aviation excise taxes. The estimates in the Budget are illustrative of the aviation taxes that would be in place to fund the FAA's Airport Improvement Program.

Provide authority to purchase and construct a new Bureau of Engraving and Printing facility.—The Administration proposes to provide authority to the Bureau of Engraving and Printing to construct a more efficient production facility. This will reduce the cost incurred by the Federal Reserve for printing currency and therefore increase governmental receipts via increased deposits from the Federal Reserve to Treasury.

Subject Financial Research Fund (FRF) to appropriations with reforms to the Financial Stability Oversight Council (FSOC) and Office of Financial Research (OFR).—Expenses of the FSOC and OFR are paid through the FRF, which is funded by assessments on certain bank holding companies with total consolidated assets of $50 billion or greater and nonbank financial companies supervised by the Federal Reserve Board of Governors. The FRF was established by the Dodd-Frank Wall Street Reform and Consumer Protection Act (Public Law 111–203) and is managed by the Department of the Treasury. To improve their effectiveness and ensure greater accountability, the Budget proposes to subject activities of the FSOC and OFR to the annual appropriations process. In so doing, currently authorized assessments would, beginning in fiscal year 2020, be reauthorized as discretionary offsetting collections and set at a level determined by the Congress. The Budget also reflects continued reductions in OFR spending commensurate with the renewed fiscal discipline being applied across the Federal Government.

Provide discretionary funding for Internal Revenue Service (IRS) program integrity cap adjustment.—The Administration proposes to establish and fund a new adjustment to the discretionary caps for IRS program integrity activities starting in 2019. The IRS base funding within the discretionary caps funds current tax administration activities, including all tax enforcement and compliance program activities, in the Enforcement and Operations Support accounts at IRS. The additional $362 million cap adjustment in 2019 will fund new and continuing investments in expanding and improving the effectiveness and efficiency of the IRS's tax enforcement program. The activities are estimated to generate $44 billion in additional revenue over 10 years and cost approximately $15 billion, resulting in an estimated net savings of $29 billion. Once the new staff are trained and become fully operational these initiatives are expected to generate roughly $4 in additional revenue for every $1 in IRS expenses. Notably, the return on investment is likely understated because it only includes amounts received; it does not reflect the effect enhanced enforcement has on deterring noncompliance. This indirect deterrence helps to ensure the continued payment of over $3 trillion in taxes paid each year without direct enforcement measures.

Increase oversight of paid tax return preparers.— Paid tax return preparers have an important role in tax administration because they assist taxpayers in complying with their obligations under the tax laws. Incompetent and dishonest tax return preparers increase collection costs, reduce revenues, disadvantage taxpayers by potentially subjecting them to penalties and interest as a result of incorrect returns, and undermine confidence in the tax system. To promote high quality services from paid tax return preparers, the proposal would explicitly provide that the Secretary of the Treasury has the authority to regulate all paid tax return preparers.

Provide the IRS with greater flexibility to address correctable errors.—The Administration proposes to expand IRS authority to correct errors on taxpayer returns. Current statute only allows the IRS to correct errors on returns in certain limited instances, such as basic math errors or the failure to include the appropriate social security number or taxpayer identification number. This proposal would expand the instances in which the IRS could correct a taxpayer's return including cases where: (1) the information provided by the taxpayer does not match the information contained in Government databases; (2) the taxpayer has exceeded the lifetime limit for claiming a deduction or credit; or (3) the taxpayer has

failed to include with his or her return, certain documentation that is required by statute. The proposal would be effective on the date of enactment.

Reform inland waterways financing.—The Administration proposes to reform the laws governing the Inland Waterways Trust Fund, including establishing a fee to increase the amount paid by commercial navigation users of the inland waterways. In 1986, the Congress provided that commercial traffic on the inland waterways would be responsible for 50 percent of the capital costs of the locks, dams, and other features that make barge transportation possible on the inland waterways. The additional revenue would help finance the users' share of future capital investments as well as 10 percent of the cost of operation and maintenance activities in these wa-

Table 11-3. EFFECT OF BUDGET PROPOSALS

(In millions of dollars)

	2018	2019	2020	2021	2022	2023	2024	2025	2026	2027	2028	2019-2023	2019-2028
Allow Medicare beneficiaries to contribute to Health Savings Accounts (HSAs) and Medical Savings Accounts (MSAs)				−610	−1,071	−1,285	−1,493	−1,599	−1,674	−1,746	−1,807	−2,966	−11,285
Extend Children's Health Insurance Program (CHIP) funding through 2019		388	58									446	446
Reform medical liability		24	222	548	987	1,476	2,067	2,687	3,079	3,290	3,475	3,257	17,855
Reduce the grace period for Exchange premiums		164	55									219	219
Provide tax exemption for Indian Health Service (IHS) Health Professions scholarship and loan repayment programs in return for obligatory service requirement		−5	−12	−13	−14	−14	−14	−14	−15	−17	−19	−58	−137
Establish Electronic Visa Update System (EVUS) user fee		25	28	31	34	38	42	46	52	57	64	156	417
Eliminate Corporation for Travel Promotion				171	177	183	189	196	202	209	216	531	1,543
Establish an immigration services surcharge		453	465	479	493	507	522	538	553	569	587	2,397	5,166
Increase worksite enforcement penalties		13	14	15	15	15	15	15	15	15	15	72	147
Reauthorize the Oil Spill Liability Trust Fund excise tax [1]		354	466	473	480	489	494	500	507	511	511	2,262	4,785
Provide paid parental leave benefits [1]					962	971	1,001	1,194	1,300	1,401	1,495	1,933	8,324
Establish an Unemployment Insurance (UI) solvency standard [1]				633	1,615	2,230	919	1,613	927	1,267	1,907	4,478	11,111
Improve UI program integrity [1]			−1	−9	−21	−72	−66	−98	−69	−127	−105	−103	−568
Provide for Reemployment Services and Eligibility Assessments (RESEAs) [1]			−3	−14	−69	−125	−128	−199	−307	−287	−469	−211	−1,601
Reform the Essential Air Service (EAS)					−152	156	−160	−164	−168	−172	−177	−308	−1,149
Enact Federal Aviation Administration (FAA) air traffic control reform					−15,495	−16,241	−17,027	−17,870	−18,674	−19,497	−20,536	−31,736	−125,340
Provide authority to purchase and construct a new Bureau of Engraving and Printing facility		12	32	3	−89	360	53	−20	3	222	3	318	579
Subject Financial Research Fund (FRF) to appropriations with reforms to the Financial Stability Oversight Council (FSOC) and Office of Financial Research (OFR) [1]		1	−50	−50	−50	−50	−50	−50	−50	−50	−50	−199	−449
Provide discretionary funding for Internal Revenue Service (IRS) program integrity cap adjustment		152	787	1,825	3,033	4,330	5,554	6,416	6,931	7,270	7,505	10,127	43,803
Increase oversight of paid tax return preparers		17	18	21	23	25	28	31	34	38	41	104	276
Provide the IRS with greater flexibility to address correctable errors		7	11	12	12	13	13	14	15	15	16	55	128
Reform inland waterways financing		178	178	178	178	178	178	178	178	178	178	890	1,780
Reduce the Harbor Maintenance Tax [1]		−265	−281	−292	−299	−307	−314	−323	−333	−345	−359	−1,444	−3,118
Increase employee contributions to Federal Employee Retirement System (FERS)			2,267	4,602	6,442	8,068	9,441	9,456	9,470	9,480	9,479	21,379	68,705
Eliminate allocations to the Housing Trust Fund and Capital Magnet Fund		62	74	73	78	82	84	85	87	89	90	369	804
Improve clarity in worker classification and information reporting requirements	−100	−100	100							100	105		205
Repeal and replace Obamacare		−3,452	−8,617	−2,503	−2,829	−2,883	−2,959	−3,192	−3,473	−3,676	−4,092	−20,284	−37,676
Offset overlapping unemployment and disability payments [1]				−3	−6	−7	−14	−18	−25	−29	−31	−16	−133
Expand flexibility and broaden eligibility for Private Activity Bonds (PABs)		−31	−138	−296	−457	−616	−753	−839	−893	−945	−992	−1,538	−5,960
Total, effect of budget proposals	−100	−2,003	−4,327	5,274	−6,023	−2,791	−2,378	−1,417	−2,328	−2,180	−2,950	−9,870	−21,123

[1] Net of income offsets.

terways to support economic growth. The current excise tax on diesel fuel used in inland waterways commerce will not produce sufficient revenue to cover these costs.

Reduce the Harbor Maintenance Tax.—The Administration proposes to reduce the Harbor Maintenance Tax rate to better align estimated annual receipts from this tax with recent appropriation levels for eligible expenditures from the Harbor Maintenance Trust Fund. Reducing this tax would provide greater flexibility for individual ports to establish appropriate fee structures for services they provide, in order to help finance their capital and operating expenses on their own.

Increase employee contributions to Federal Employee Retirement System (FERS).—The Administration proposes to increase Federal employee contributions to FERS, equalizing employee and employer contributions to FERS so that half of the normal cost would be paid by each. For some specific occupations, such as law enforcement officers and firefighters, the cost of their retirement package necessitates a higher normal cost percentage. For those specific occupations, this proposal would increase but not equalize employee contributions. This proposal brings Federal retirement benefits more in line with the private sector. This adjustment will reduce the long term cost to the Federal Government by reducing the Government's contribution rate. To lessen the impact on employees this proposal will be phased in, increasing employee contributions by one percentage point per year until equalized.

Eliminate allocations to the Housing Trust Fund and Capital Magnet Fund.—The Administration proposes to eliminate an assessment on Fannie Mae and Freddie Mac that is used to fund the Housing Trust Fund and Capital Magnet Fund, two Federal programs that support affordable low-income housing. The resulting increase in taxable income at Fannie Mae and Freddie Mac would impact governmental receipts.

Improve clarity in worker classification and information reporting requirements.—The Administration proposes to: (1) establish a new safe harbor that allows a service recipient to classify a service provider as an independent contractor and requires withholding of individual income taxes to this independent contractor at a rate of five percent on the first $20,000 of payments; and (2) raises the reporting threshold for payments to all independent contractors from $600 to $1,000, and reduces the reporting threshold for third-party settlement organizations from $20,000 and 200 transactions per payee to $1,000 without regard to the number of transactions. The proposal increases clarity in the tax code, reduces costly litigation, and raises revenue.

Repeal and replace Obamacare.—The Administration is committed to rescuing Americans from the failures of Obamacare. Repealing and replacing Obamacare would affect governmental receipts by repealing the Premium Tax Credit, the medical device tax, and the HSA tax, and making various other reforms to HSAs.

Offset overlapping unemployment and disability payments.—The Administration proposes to close a loophole that allows individuals to receive both UI and Disability Insurance (DI) benefits for the same period of joblessness. The proposal would offset the DI benefit to account for concurrent receipt of UI benefits. Offsetting the overlapping benefits would discourage some individuals from applying for UI, reducing benefit outlays. The reduction in benefit outlays is accompanied by a reduction in States' UI tax receipts, which are held in the Unemployment Trust Fund.

Expand flexibility and broaden eligibility for private activity bonds (PABs).—As part of the Administration's infrastructure initiative, the Budget proposes to expand flexibility and broaden eligibility for private activity bonds. PABs eligible to finance this broadened definition of "core public infrastructure projects" would not be subject to State volume caps. However, the projects must be either Government-owned or privately-owned but subject to Government regulatory or contractual control and approval such that the facilities are available to the public.

Table 11–4. RECEIPTS BY SOURCE

(In millions of dollars)

Source	2017 Actual	Estimate 2018	2019	2020	2021	2022	2023	2024	2025	2026	2027	2028
Individual income taxes:												
Federal funds	1,587,120	1,660,063	1,687,042	1,789,704	1,917,184	2,050,498	2,197,899	2,347,934	2,504,331	2,700,016	2,882,828	3,062,139
Legislative proposal, not subject to PAYGO	....	....	−14	−29	−65	−175	−206	−129	−175	−134	−156	−188
Legislative proposal, subject to PAYGO	....	....	718	947	1,592	2,626	3,968	5,316	6,428	7,120	7,516	7,797
Total, Individual income taxes	**1,587,120**	**1,660,063**	**1,687,746**	**1,790,622**	**1,918,711**	**2,052,949**	**2,201,661**	**2,353,121**	**2,510,584**	**2,707,002**	**2,890,188**	**3,069,748**
Corporation income taxes:												
Federal funds	297,048	217,648	225,295	264,710	272,706	314,208	373,856	416,627	434,764	417,498	406,137	413,564
Legislative proposal, not subject to PAYGO	....	....	−3	10	10	11	11	10	11	11	11	12
Legislative proposal, subject to PAYGO	....	....	52	40	7	−21	−48	−71	−85	−94	−102	−110
Total, Corporation income taxes	**297,048**	**217,648**	**225,344**	**264,760**	**272,723**	**314,198**	**373,819**	**416,566**	**434,690**	**417,415**	**406,046**	**413,466**
Social insurance and retirement receipts (trust funds):												
Employment and general retirement:												
Old-age survivors insurance (off-budget)	688,048	689,294	762,821	804,675	850,279	897,037	942,951	995,275	1,048,234	1,107,760	1,163,400	1,232,525
Legislative proposal, not subject to PAYGO	....	....	−8	−15	−95	−343	−411	−240	−344	−256	−307	−382
Legislative proposal, subject to PAYGO	....	−43	−80	58	−113	−97	−30	68	194	174	290	311
Disability insurance (off-budget)	162,570	163,035	142,464	136,643	144,388	152,328	160,123	169,009	178,003	188,111	197,558	209,296
Legislative proposal, not subject to PAYGO	....	....	−1	−2	−16	−58	−70	−41	−58	−43	−52	−65
Legislative proposal, subject to PAYGO	....	−7	−14	10	−19	−17	−5	12	33	30	49	53
Hospital Insurance	255,930	259,138	275,214	286,994	304,251	321,942	339,409	358,896	378,617	400,703	421,734	447,540
Legislative proposal, not subject to PAYGO	....	....	−2	−4	−26	−94	−113	−66	−93	−70	−84	−104
Legislative proposal, subject to PAYGO	....	−50	2	120	93	100	126	161	211	334	341	363
Railroad retirement:												
Social security equivalent account	2,213	2,365	2,472	2,536	2,627	2,728	2,835	2,943	3,053	3,167	3,276	3,382
Rail pension & supplemental annuity	3,136	3,187	3,253	3,349	3,464	3,596	3,734	3,876	4,021	4,171	4,512	4,708
Total, Employment and general retirement	1,111,897	1,116,919	1,186,121	1,234,364	1,304,833	1,377,122	1,448,549	1,529,893	1,611,871	1,704,081	1,790,717	1,897,627
On-budget	(261,279)	(264,640)	(280,939)	(292,995)	(310,409)	(328,272)	(345,991)	(365,810)	(385,809)	(408,305)	(429,779)	(455,889)
Off-budget	(850,618)	(852,279)	(905,182)	(941,369)	(994,424)	(1,048,850)	(1,102,558)	(1,164,083)	(1,226,062)	(1,295,776)	(1,360,938)	(1,441,738)
Unemployment insurance:												
Deposits by States [1]	37,551	39,118	39,993	39,936	40,218	39,367	39,907	40,719	41,611	42,983	44,549	47,582
Legislative proposal, not subject to PAYGO	....	....	....	−4	−27	−110	−238	−235	−361	−460	−504	−699
Legislative proposal, subject to PAYGO					−4	1,591	2,172	1,741	2,374	1,950	1,979	2,116
Federal unemployment receipts [1]	8,131	8,811	6,383	6,503	6,629	6,760	6,892	7,037	7,187	7,339	7,499	7,669
Legislative proposal, subject to PAYGO	....	....	....	....	791	1,621	1,814	633	1,100	791	1,305	2,078
Railroad unemployment receipts [1]	126	135	140	146	141	119	116	138	145	138	138	151
Total, Unemployment insurance	45,808	48,064	46,516	46,581	47,748	49,348	50,663	50,033	52,056	52,741	54,966	58,897
Other retirement:												
Federal employees retirement-employee share	4,158	4,681	4,952	5,258	5,623	6,011	6,421	6,850	7,294	7,754	8,233	8,701
Legislative proposal, subject to PAYGO	....	....	....	2,267	4,602	6,442	8,068	9,441	9,456	9,470	9,480	9,479
Non-Federal employees retirement [2]	34	37	39	39	38	38	38	38	38	37	37	37
Total, Other retirement	4,192	4,718	4,991	7,564	10,263	12,491	14,527	16,329	16,788	17,261	17,750	18,217
Total, Social insurance and retirement receipts (trust funds)	**1,161,897**	**1,169,701**	**1,237,628**	**1,288,509**	**1,362,844**	**1,438,961**	**1,513,739**	**1,596,255**	**1,680,715**	**1,774,083**	**1,863,433**	**1,974,741**
On-budget	(311,279)	(317,422)	(332,446)	(347,140)	(368,420)	(390,111)	(411,181)	(432,172)	(454,653)	(478,307)	(502,495)	(533,003)

Table 11–4.   RECEIPTS BY SOURCE—Continued

(In millions of dollars)

Source	2017 Actual	Estimate										
		2018	2019	2020	2021	2022	2023	2024	2025	2026	2027	2028
Off-budget	(850,618)	(852,279)	(905,182)	(941,369)	(994,424)	(1,048,850)	(1,102,558)	(1,164,083)	(1,226,062)	(1,295,776)	(1,360,938)	(1,441,738)
Excise taxes:												
Federal funds:												
Alcohol	9,924	10,208	10,377	10,466	10,576	10,683	10,726	10,833	10,893	10,978	11,183	11,515
Tobacco	13,804	13,669	13,534	13,398	13,263	13,128	12,993	12,857	12,722	12,587	12,451	12,316
Transportation fuels	–3,400	–947	–998	–1,010	–1,013	–1,014	–1,014	–1,016	–1,015	–1,014	–1,015	–1,014
Telephone and teletype services	558	510	463	413	361	308	254	199	143	86	44	23
High-cost health insurance coverage	....	....	....	1,714	5,981	6,919	8,000	9,249	10,671	12,238	14,044	16,105
Health insurance providers	68	14,281	15,026	15,684	16,480	17,374	18,225	19,161	20,149	21,170	22,253	23,391
Indoor tanning services	70	68	67	65	63	61	59	57	55	53	51	49
Medical devices	–202	1,572	2,309	2,489	2,640	2,823	2,992	3,178	3,360	3,556	3,761	3,975
Other Federal fund excise taxes	369	3,159	3,283	3,494	3,635	3,756	3,872	3,995	4,133	4,270	4,418	4,574
Legislative proposal, subject to PAYGO	....	....	....	....	....	–152	–156	–160	–164	–168	–172	–177
Total, Federal funds	21,191	42,520	44,061	46,713	51,986	53,886	55,951	58,353	60,947	63,756	67,018	70,757
Trust funds:												
Transportation	41,020	41,812	42,591	43,244	43,619	43,812	43,934	44,030	44,095	44,254	44,568	44,921
Airport and airway	15,055	15,736	16,538	17,281	18,060	18,845	19,725	20,668	21,678	22,692	23,691	24,915
Legislative proposal, subject to PAYGO	....	....	....	....	....	–15,495	–16,241	–17,027	–17,870	–18,674	–19,497	–20,536
Sport fish restoration and boating safety	559	562	565	569	573	577	583	587	592	597	602	611
Tobacco assessments	3	....	....	....	....	....	....	....	....	....	....	....
Black lung disability insurance	429	473	290	235	234	229	225	221	217	212	207	201
Inland waterway	114	105	104	102	101	98	97	95	94	92	91	92
Oil spill liability	516	137	....	....	....	....	....	....	....	....	....	....
Legislative proposal, subject to PAYGO	....	....	465	612	621	630	641	649	657	666	670	670
Vaccine injury compensation	270	296	303	308	305	308	312	317	316	319	324	329
Leaking underground storage tank	225	215	218	218	219	217	214	212	212	210	208	208
Supplementary medical insurance	4,147	5,997	2,826	2,800	2,800	2,800	2,800	2,800	2,800	2,800	2,800	2,800
Patient-centered outcomes research	294	329	434	366	382	400	418	437	455	475	495	518
Total, Trust funds	62,632	65,662	64,334	65,735	66,914	52,421	52,708	52,989	53,246	53,643	54,159	54,729
Total, Excise taxes	**83,823**	**108,182**	**108,395**	**112,448**	**118,900**	**106,307**	**108,659**	**111,342**	**114,193**	**117,399**	**121,177**	**125,486**
Estate and gift taxes:												
Federal funds	22,768	24,650	16,824	18,042	19,429	20,651	22,848	24,364	26,091	27,635	29,092	30,891
Total, Estate and gift taxes	**22,768**	**24,650**	**16,824**	**18,042**	**19,429**	**20,651**	**22,848**	**24,364**	**26,091**	**27,635**	**29,092**	**30,891**
Customs duties and fees:												
Federal funds	33,097	38,749	42,368	45,150	46,206	47,932	48,852	49,783	50,933	52,360	54,120	56,147
Trust funds:												
Trust funds	1,477	1,688	1,831	1,943	2,018	2,067	2,118	2,165	2,223	2,292	2,292	2,292
Legislative proposal, subject to PAYGO	....	....	–347	–369	–383	–393	–403	–412	–424	–437	–453	–471
Total, Trust funds	1,477	1,688	1,484	1,574	1,635	1,674	1,715	1,753	1,799	1,855	1,839	1,821
Total, Customs duties and fees	**34,574**	**40,437**	**43,852**	**46,724**	**47,841**	**49,606**	**50,567**	**51,536**	**52,732**	**54,215**	**55,959**	**57,968**
Miscellaneous receipts:												
Federal funds:												
Miscellaneous taxes	593	543	544	598	598	599	599	599	599	600	600	600
Deposit of earnings, Federal Reserve System	81,287	72,097	55,102	48,588	52,228	59,130	66,905	72,662	77,280	81,780	86,336	90,854
Legislative proposal, subject to PAYGO	....	....	159	679	665	588	1,054	763	707	747	983	782
Transfers from the Federal Reserve	602	575	632	647	662	677	694	710	727	744	761	779
Legislative proposal, subject to PAYGO	....	....	–147	–647	–662	–677	–694	–710	–727	–744	–761	–779
Fees for permits and regulatory and judicial services	23,911	22,694	22,053	23,258	24,013	25,392	25,955	27,713	27,978	29,372	30,799	31,952

Table 11–4. RECEIPTS BY SOURCE—Continued
(In millions of dollars)

Source	2017 Actual	Estimate										
		2018	2019	2020	2021	2022	2023	2024	2025	2026	2027	2028
Legislative proposal, subject to PAYGO	....	....	478	425	613	636	660	685	712	739	767	799
Fines, penalties, and forfeitures	20,984	22,266	25,236	20,785	20,193	20,462	20,760	21,084	21,435	21,785	22,035	22,417
Legislative proposal, subject to PAYGO	....	....	13	14	15	15	15	15	15	15	15	15
Refunds and recoveries	–50	–50	–50	–50	–50	–50	–50	–50	–50	–50	–50	–50
Total, Federal funds	127,327	118,125	104,020	94,297	98,275	106,772	115,898	123,471	128,676	134,988	141,485	147,369
Trust funds:												
United Mine Workers of America, combined benefit fund	81	17	16	14	13	12	11	10	9	8	7	7
Defense cooperation	375	360	531	697	486	535	232	161	164	167	170	174
Inland waterways (Legislative proposal, subject to PAYGO)	....	....	178	178	178	178	178	178	178	178	178	178
Fines, penalties, and forfeitures	1,169	1,177	1,219	1,259	1,300	1,342	1,383	1,424	1,464	1,505	1,545	1,587
Total, Trust funds	1,625	1,554	1,944	2,148	1,977	2,067	1,804	1,773	1,815	1,858	1,900	1,946
Total, Miscellaneous receipts	**128,952**	**119,679**	**105,964**	**96,445**	**100,252**	**108,839**	**117,702**	**125,244**	**130,491**	**136,846**	**143,385**	**149,315**
Allowance for repeal and replacement of Obamacare	....	....	–3,452	–8,617	–2,503	–2,829	–2,883	–2,959	–3,192	–3,473	–3,676	–4,092
Total, budget receipts	**3,316,182**	**3,340,360**	**3,422,301**	**3,608,933**	**3,838,197**	**4,088,682**	**4,386,112**	**4,675,469**	**4,946,304**	**5,231,122**	**5,505,604**	**5,817,523**
On-budget	(2,465,564)	(2,488,081)	(2,517,119)	(2,667,564)	(2,843,773)	(3,039,832)	(3,283,554)	(3,511,386)	(3,720,242)	(3,935,346)	(4,144,666)	(4,375,785)
Off-budget	(850,618)	(852,279)	(905,182)	(941,369)	(994,424)	(1,048,850)	(1,102,558)	(1,164,083)	(1,226,062)	(1,295,776)	(1,360,938)	(1,441,738)

[1] Deposits by States cover the benefit part of the program. Federal unemployment receipts cover administrative costs at both the Federal and State levels. Railroad unemployment receipts cover both the benefits and administrative costs of the program for the railroads.

[2] Represents employer and employee contributions to the civil service retirement and disability fund for covered employees of Government-sponsored, privately owned enterprises and the District of Columbia municipal government.

12. OFFSETTING COLLECTIONS AND OFFSETTING RECEIPTS

I. INTRODUCTION AND BACKGROUND

The Government records money collected in one of two ways. It is either recorded as a governmental receipt and included in the amount reported on the receipts side of the budget or it is recorded as an offsetting collection or offsetting receipt, which reduces (or "offsets") the amount reported on the outlay side of the budget. Governmental receipts are discussed in the previous chapter, "Governmental Receipts." The first section of this chapter broadly discusses offsetting collections and offsetting receipts. The second section discusses user charges, which consist of a subset of offsetting collections and offsetting receipts and a small share of governmental receipts. The third section describes the user charge proposals in the 2019 Budget.

Offsetting collections and offsetting receipts are recorded as offsets to spending so that the budget totals for receipts and (net) outlays reflect the amount of resources allocated by the Government through collective political choice, rather than through the marketplace.[1] This practice ensures that the budget totals measure the transactions of the Government with the public, and avoids the double counting that would otherwise result when one account makes a payment to another account and the receiving account then spends the proceeds. Offsetting receipts and collections are recorded in the budget in one of two ways, based on interpretation of laws and longstanding budget concepts and practice. They are offsetting collections when the collections are authorized to be credited to expenditure accounts. Otherwise, they are deposited in receipt accounts and called offsetting receipts.

There are two sources of offsetting receipts and offsetting collections: from the public and from other budget accounts. Like governmental receipts, offsetting receipts and offsetting collections from the public reduce the deficit or increase the surplus. In contrast, offsetting receipts and offsetting collections resulting from transactions with other budget accounts, called intragovernmental transactions, exactly offset the payments made by these accounts, with no net impact on the deficit or surplus.[2] In 2017, offsetting receipts and offsetting collections from the public were $546 billion, while receipts and collections from intragovernmental transactions were $1,098 billion, for a total of $1,645 billion government-wide.

As described above, intragovernmental transactions are responsible for the majority of offsetting collections and offsetting receipts, when measured by the magnitude of the dollars collected. Examples of intragovernmental transactions include interest payments to funds that hold Government securities (such as the Social Security trust funds), general fund transfers to civilian and military retirement pension and health benefits funds, and agency payments to funds for employee health insurance and retirement benefits. Although receipts and collections from intragovernmental collections exactly offset the payments themselves, with no effect on the deficit or surplus, it is important to record these transactions in the budget to show how much the Government is allocating to fund various programs. For example, in the case of civilian retirement pensions, Government agencies make accrual payments to the Civil Service Retirement and Disability Fund on behalf of current employees to fund their future retirement benefits; the receipt of these payments to the Fund is shown in a single receipt account. Recording the receipt of these payments is important because it demonstrates the total cost to the Government today of providing this future benefit.

Offsetting receipts and collections from the public comprise approximately 33 percent of total offsetting collections and offsetting receipts, when measured by the magnitude of the dollars collected. Most of the funds collected through offsetting collections and offsetting receipts from the public arise from business-like transactions with the public. Unlike governmental receipts, which are derived from the Government's exercise of its sovereign power, these offsetting collections and offsetting receipts arise primarily from voluntary payments from the public for goods or services provided by the Government. They are classified as offsets to outlays for the cost of producing the goods or services for sale, rather than as governmental receipts. These activities include the sale of postage stamps, land, timber, and electricity; charging fees for services provided to the public (e.g., admission to national parks); and collecting premiums for health care benefits (e.g., Medicare Parts B and D). As described above, treating offsetting collections and offsetting receipts as offsets to outlays ensures the budgetary totals represent governmental rather than market activity.

A relatively small portion ($19.5 billion in 2017) of offsetting collections and offsetting receipts from the public is derived from the Government's exercise of its sovereign power. From a conceptual standpoint, these should be classified as governmental receipts. However, they are classified as offsetting rather than governmental receipts either because this classification has been specified in law or because these collections have traditionally been classi-

---

[1] Showing collections from business-type transactions as offsets on the spending side of the budget follows the concept recommended by the Report of the President's Commission on Budget Concepts in 1967 and is discussed in Chapter 8 of this volume, "Budget Concepts."

[2] For the purposes of this discussion, "collections from the public" include collections from non-budgetary Government accounts, such as credit financing accounts and deposit funds. For more information on these non-budgetary accounts, see Chapter 9, "Coverage of the Budget."

fied as offsets to outlays. Most of the offsetting collections and offsetting receipts in this category derive from fees from Government regulatory services or Government licenses, and include, for example, charges for regulating the nuclear energy industry, bankruptcy filing fees, immigration fees, food inspection fees, passport fees, and patent and trademark fees.[3]

The final source of offsetting collections and offsetting receipts from the public is gifts. Gifts are voluntary contributions to the Government to support particular purposes or reduce the amount of Government debt held by the public.

---

[3] This category of receipts is known as "offsetting governmental receipts." Some argue that regulatory or licensing fees should be viewed as payments for a particular service or for the right to engage in a particular type of business. However, these fees are conceptually much more similar to taxes because they are compulsory, and they fund activities

that are intended to provide broadly dispersed benefits, such as protecting the health of the public. Reclassifying these fees as governmental receipts could require a change in law, and because of conventions for scoring appropriations bills, would make it impossible for fees that are controlled through annual appropriations acts to be scored as offsets to discretionary spending.

Table 12-1. OFFSETTING COLLECTIONS AND OFFSETTING RECEIPTS FROM THE PUBLIC

(In billions of dollars)

	Actual 2017	Estimate	
		2018	2019
Offsetting collections (credited to expenditure accounts):			
User charges:			
Postal Service stamps and other USPS fees (off-budget)	68.7	69.4	72.7
Defense Commissary Agency	4.9	5.0	5.2
Employee contributions for employees and retired employees health benefits funds	15.7	16.7	17.7
Sale of energy:			
Tennessee Valley Authority	47.0	46.4	46.7
Bonneville Power Administration	3.4	3.9	3.9
Pension Benefit Guaranty Corporation fund	10.8	11.4	12.1
Deposit Insurance	12.4	13.7	16.0
All other user charges	47.1	49.1	44.8
Subtotal, user charges	210.1	215.5	219.0
Other collections credited to expenditure accounts:			
Commodity Credit Corporation fund	7.5	9.0	8.8
Supplemental Security Income (collections from the States)	2.6	2.8	2.8
Other collections	36.9	7.8	7.7
Subtotal, other collections	47.0	19.5	19.3
Subtotal, offsetting collections	257.2	235.1	238.3
Offsetting receipts (deposited in receipt accounts):			
User charges:			
Medicare premiums	89.0	100.3	107.4
Spectrum auction, relocation, and licenses	....	5.0	3.8
Outer Continental Shelf rents, bonuses, and royalties	1.8	2.7	2.7
Immigration fees	4.7	5.1	5.8
All other user charges	25.2	24.3	25.5
Subtotal, user charges deposited in receipt accounts	120.7	137.4	145.2
Other collections deposited in receipt accounts:			
Military assistance program sales	31.9	42.0	44.0
Interest received from credit financing accounts	41.6	49.0	51.1
Proceeds, GSE equity related transactions	25.3	6.1	18.7
Student loan receipt of negative subsidy and downward reestimates	19.2	27.1	13.0
All other collections deposited in receipt accounts	50.5	45.5	42.2
Subtotal, other collections deposited in receipt accounts	168.6	169.7	169.1
Subtotal, offsetting receipts	289.2	307.1	314.3
Total, offsetting collections and offsetting receipts from the public	**546.4**	**542.2**	**552.6**
Total, offsetting collections and offsetting receipts excluding off-budget	477.5	472.7	479.9
ADDENDUM:			
User charges that are offsetting collections and offsetting receipts [1]	330.8	353.0	364.2
Other offsetting collections and offsetting receipts from the public	215.6	189.2	188.4

[1] Excludes user charges that are classified on the receipts side of the budget. For total user charges, see Table 12-3.

Table 12–2. SUMMARY OF OFFSETTING RECEIPTS BY TYPE

(In millions of dollars)

Receipt Type	Actual 2017	Estimate					
		2018	2019	2020	2021	2022	2023
Intragovernmental	761,183	774,974	800,348	827,085	869,982	915,124	964,416
Receipts from non-Federal sources:							
Proprietary	275,509	289,350	296,491	304,332	322,676	336,562	350,249
Offsetting governmental	13,736	17,788	17,832	16,692	15,688	16,023	16,651
Total, receipts from non-Federal sources	289,245	307,138	314,323	321,024	338,364	352,585	366,900
Total Offsetting receipts	1,050,428	1,082,112	1,114,671	1,148,109	1,208,346	1,267,709	1,331,316

The spending associated with the activities that generate offsetting collections and offsetting receipts from the public is included in total or "gross outlays." Offsetting collections and offsetting receipts from the public are subtracted from gross outlays to yield "net outlays," which is the most common measure of outlays cited and generally referred to as simply "outlays." For 2017, gross outlays were $5,626 billion, or 29.3 percent of GDP and offsetting collections and offsetting receipts were $1,645 billion, or 8.6 percent of GDP, resulting in net outlays of $3,982 billion or 20.8 percent of GDP. Government-wide net outlays reflect the Government's net disbursements to the public and are subtracted from governmental receipts to derive the Government's deficit or surplus. For 2017, governmental receipts were $3,316 billion, or 17.3 percent of GDP, and the deficit was $665 billion, or 3.5 percent of GDP.

Although both offsetting collections and offsetting receipts are subtracted from gross outlays to derive net outlays, they are treated differently when it comes to accounting for specific programs and agencies. Offsetting collections are usually authorized to be spent for the purposes of an expenditure account and are generally available for use when collected, without further action by the Congress. Therefore, offsetting collections are recorded as offsets to spending within expenditure accounts, so that the account total highlights the net flow of funds.

Like governmental receipts, offsetting receipts are credited to receipt accounts, and any spending of the receipts is recorded in separate expenditure accounts. As a

Table 12–3. GROSS OUTLAYS, USER CHARGES, OTHER OFFSETTING COLLECTIONS AND OFFSETTING RECEIPTS FROM THE PUBLIC, AND NET OUTLAYS

(In billions of dollars)

	Actual 2017	Estimate	
		2018	2019
Gross outlays to the public	4,528.0	4,715.2	4,959.3
Offsetting collections and offsetting receipts from the public:			
User charges [1]	330.8	353.0	364.2
Other	215.6	189.2	188.4
Subtotal, offsetting collections and offsetting receipts from the public	546.4	542.2	552.6
Net outlays	3,981.6	4,173.0	4,406.7

[1] $5.2 billion of the total user charges for 2017 were classified as governmental receipts, and the remainder were classified as offsetting collections and offsetting receipts. $5.5 billion and $5.7 billion of the total user charges for 2018 and 2019 are classified as governmental receipts, respectively.

result, the budget separately displays the flow of funds into and out of the Government. Offsetting receipts may or may not be designated for a specific purpose, depending on the legislation that authorizes their collection. If designated for a particular purpose, the offsetting receipts may, in some cases, be spent without further action by the Congress. When not designated for a particular purpose, offsetting receipts are credited to the general fund, which contains all funds not otherwise allocated and which is used to finance Government spending that is not financed out of dedicated funds. In some cases where the receipts are designated for a particular purpose, offsetting receipts are reported in a particular agency and reduce or offset the outlays reported for that agency. In other cases, the offsetting receipts are "undistributed," which means they reduce total Government outlays, but not the outlays of any particular agency.

Table 12–1 summarizes offsetting collections and offsetting receipts from the public. The amounts shown in the table are not evident in the commonly cited budget measure of outlays, which is already net of these collections and receipts. For 2019, the table shows that total offsetting collections and offsetting receipts from the public are estimated to be $552.6 billion or 2.6 percent of GDP. Of these, an estimated $238.3 billion are offsetting collections and an estimated $314.3 billion are offsetting receipts. Table 12–1 also identifies those offsetting collections and offsetting receipts that are considered user charges, as defined and discussed below.

As shown in the table, major offsetting collections from the public include proceeds from Postal Service sales, electrical power sales, loan repayments to the Commodity Credit Corporation for loans made prior to enactment of the Federal Credit Reform Act, and Federal employee payments for health insurance. As also shown in the table, major offsetting receipts from the public include premiums for Medicare Parts B and D, proceeds from military assistance program sales, rents and royalties from Outer Continental Shelf oil extraction, proceeds from auctions of the electromagnetic spectrum, dividends on holdings of preferred stock of the Government-sponsored enterprises, and interest income.

Tables 12–2 and 12–3 provide further detail about offsetting receipts, including both offsetting receipts from the public (as summarized in Table 12–1) and intragovernmental transactions. Table 12–5, formerly printed in this chapter, and Table 12–6. Offsetting Collections and

Offsetting Receipts, Detail—FY 2019 Budget, which is a complete listing by account, are available on the Internet at *https://www.whitehouse.gov/omb/analytical-perspectives/* and on the Budget CD-ROM. In total, offsetting receipts are estimated to be $1,114.6 billion in 2019; $800.3 billion are from intragovernmental transactions and $314.3 billion are from the public. The offsetting receipts from the public consist of proprietary receipts

($296.5 billion), which are those resulting from business-like transactions such as the sale of goods or services, and offsetting governmental receipts, which, as discussed above, are derived from the exercise of the Government's sovereign power and, absent a specification in law or a long-standing practice, would be classified on the receipts side of the budget ($17.8 billion).

II. USER CHARGES

User charges or user fees[4] refer generally to those monies that the Government receives from the public for market-oriented activities and regulatory activities. In combination with budget concepts, laws that authorize user charges determine whether a user charge is classified as an offsetting collection, an offsetting receipt, or a governmental receipt. Almost all user charges, as defined below, are classified as offsetting collections or offsetting receipts; for 2019, only an estimated 1.4 percent of user charges are classified as governmental receipts. As summarized in Table 12–3, total user charges for 2019 are estimated to be $369.9 billion with $364.2 billion being offsetting collections or offsetting receipts, and accounting for more than half of all offsetting collections and offsetting receipts from the public.

Definition. In this chapter, user charges refer to fees, charges, and assessments levied on individuals or organizations directly benefiting from or subject to regulation by a Government program or activity, where the payers do not represent a broad segment of the public such as those who pay income taxes.

Examples of business-type or market-oriented user charges and regulatory and licensing user charges include those charges listed in Table 12–1 for offsetting collections and offsetting receipts. User charges exclude certain offsetting collections and offsetting receipts from the public, such as payments received from credit programs, interest, and dividends, and also exclude payments from one part of the Federal Government to another. In addition, user charges do not include dedicated taxes (such as taxes paid to social insurance programs or excise taxes on gasoline) or customs duties, fines, penalties, or forfeitures.

Alternative definitions. The definition for user charges used in this chapter follows the definition used in OMB Circular No. A–25, "User Charges," which provides policy guidance to Executive Branch agencies on setting the amount for user charges. Alternative definitions may be used for other purposes. Much of the discussion of user charges below—their purpose, when they should be levied, and how the amount should be set—applies to these alternative definitions as well.

A narrower definition of user charges could be limited to proceeds from the sale of goods and services, excluding the proceeds from the sale of assets, and to proceeds that are dedicated to financing the goods and services being provided. This definition is similar to one the House of Representatives uses as a guide for purposes of committee jurisdiction. (See the Congressional Record, January 3, 1991, p. H31, item 8.) The definition of user charges could be even narrower by excluding regulatory fees and focusing solely on business-type transactions. Alternatively, the user charge definition could be broader than the one used in this chapter by including beneficiary- or liability-based excise taxes.[5]

What is the purpose of user charges? User charges are intended to improve the efficiency and equity of financing certain Government activities. Charging users for activities that benefit a relatively limited number of people reduces the burden on the general taxpayer, as does charging regulated parties for regulatory activities in a particular sector.

User charges that are set to cover the costs of production of goods and services can result in more efficient resource allocation within the economy. When buyers are charged the cost of providing goods and services, they make better cost-benefit calculations regarding the size of their purchase, which in turn signals to the Government how much of the goods or services it should provide. Prices in private, competitive markets serve the same purposes. User charges for goods and services that do not have special social or distributional benefits may also improve equity or fairness by requiring those who benefit from an activity to pay for it and by not requiring those who do not benefit from an activity to pay for it.

When should the Government impose a charge? Discussions of whether to finance spending with a tax or a fee often focus on whether the benefits of the activity accrue to the public in general or to a limited group of people. In general, if the benefits of spending accrue broadly to the public or include special social or distributional benefits, then the program should be financed by taxes paid by the public. In contrast, if the benefits accrue to a limited number of private individuals or organizations

---

[4] In this chapter, the term "user charge" is generally used and has the same meaning as the term "user fee." The term "user charge" is the one used in OMB Circular No. A–11, "Preparation, Submission, and Execution of the Budget"; OMB Circular No. A–25, "User Charges"; and Chapter 8 of this volume, "Budget Concepts." In common usage, the terms "user charge" and "user fee" are often used interchangeably, and in *A Glossary of Terms Used in the Federal Budget Process*, GAO provides the same definition for both terms.

[5] Beneficiary- and liability-based taxes are terms taken from the Congressional Budget Office, *The Growth of Federal User Charges*, August 1993, and updated in October 1995. Gasoline taxes are an example of beneficiary-based taxes. An example of a liability-based tax is the excise tax that formerly helped fund the hazardous substance superfund in the Environmental Protection Agency. This tax was paid by industry groups to finance environmental cleanup activities related to the industry activity but not necessarily caused by the payer of the fee.

and do not include special social or distributional benefits, then the program should be financed by charges paid by the private beneficiaries. For Federal programs where the benefits are entirely public or entirely private, applying this principle can be relatively easy. For example, the benefits from national defense accrue to the public in general, and according to this principle should be (and are) financed by taxes. In contrast, the benefits of electricity sold by the Tennessee Valley Authority accrue primarily to those using the electricity, and should be (and predominantly are) financed by user charges.

In many cases, however, an activity has benefits that accrue to both public and private groups, and it may be difficult to identify how much of the benefits accrue to each. Because of this, it can be difficult to know how much of the program should be financed by taxes and how much by fees. For example, the benefits from recreation areas are mixed. Fees for visitors to these areas are appropriate because the visitors benefit directly from their visit, but the public in general also benefits because these areas protect the Nation's natural and historic heritage now and for posterity. For this reason, visitor recreation fees generally cover only part of the cost to the Government of maintaining the recreation property. Where a fee may be appropriate to finance all or part of an activity, the extent to which a fee can be easily administered must be considered. For example, if fees are charged for entering or using Government-owned land then there must be clear points of entry onto the land and attendants patrolling and monitoring the land's use.

What amount should be charged? When the Government is acting in its capacity as sovereign and where user charges are appropriate, such as for some regulatory activities, current policy supports setting fees equal to the full cost to the Government, including both direct and indirect costs. When the Government is not acting in its capacity as sovereign and engages in a purely business-type transaction (such as leasing or selling goods, services, or resources), market price is generally the basis for establishing the fee.[6] If the Government is engaged in a purely business-type transaction and economic resources are allocated efficiently, then this market price should be equal to or greater than the Government's full cost of production.

Classification of user charges in the budget. As shown in the note to Table 12–3, most user charges are classified as offsets to outlays on the spending side of the budget, but a few are classified on the receipts side of the budget. An estimated $5.2 billion in 2019 of user charges are classified on the receipts side and are included in the governmental receipts totals described in the previous chapter, "Governmental Receipts." They are classified as receipts because they are regulatory charges collected by the Federal Government by the exercise of its sovereign powers. Examples include filing fees in the United States courts and agricultural quarantine inspection fees.

The remaining user charges, an estimated $359.0 billion in 2019, are classified as offsetting collections and offsetting receipts on the spending side of the budget. As discussed above in the context of all offsetting collections and offsetting receipts, some of these user charges are collected by the Federal Government by the exercise of its sovereign powers and conceptually should appear on the receipts side of the budget, but they are required by law or a long-standing practice to be classified on the spending side.

---

[6] Policies for setting user charges are promulgated in OMB Circular No. A–25: "User Charges" (July 8, 1993).

III. USER CHARGE PROPOSALS

As shown in Table 12–1, an estimated $219.0 billion of user charges for 2019 will be credited directly to expenditure accounts and will generally be available for expenditure when they are collected, without further action by the Congress. An estimated $145.2 billion of user charges for 2019 will be deposited in offsetting receipt accounts and will be available to be spent only according to the legislation that established the charges.

As shown in Table 12–4, the Administration is proposing new or increased user charges that would, in the aggregate, increase collections by an estimated $2.4 billion in 2019 and an average of $11.8 billion per year from 2020 through 2028. These estimates reflect only the amounts to be collected; they do not include related spending. Each proposal is classified as either discretionary or mandatory, as those terms are defined in the Balanced Budget and Emergency Deficit Control Act of 1985, as amended. "Discretionary" refers to user charges controlled through annual appropriations acts and generally under the jurisdiction of the appropriations committees in the Congress. "Mandatory" refers to user charges controlled by permanent laws and under the jurisdiction of the authorizing committees. These and other terms are discussed further in this volume in Chapter 8, "Budget Concepts."

A. Discretionary User Charge Proposals

1. Offsetting collections

Department of Agriculture

Establish Federal Grain Inspection Service fee. The Administration proposes establishing a new discretionary user fee to recover the full costs for programs under the Federal Grain Inspection Service (FGIS). Entities that receive marketing benefits from FGIS services should pay for the costs of these programs. For example, grain standards benefit and are used almost solely for the grain industry, and because they facilitate the orderly marketing of grain products, it is industry that should bear the cost.

Establish Agricultural Quarantine Inspection fee. The Administration proposes establishing a new discretionary user fee for the Animal and Plant Health Inspection Service (APHIS) Agricultural Quarantine Inspection

(AQI) pre-departure program. The fees would recover the full costs of APHIS' inspections of passengers and cargo traveling to the continental United States from Hawaii and Puerto Rico to prevent the introduction of non-native agricultural pests and diseases into the mainland.

Department of Health and Human Services

Food and Drug Administration (FDA): Reauthorize Animal Drug User Fee Act. The Budget proposes to reauthorize the Animal Drug User Fee Act (ADUFA), which expires on September 30, 2018. ADUFA fees support FDA's premarket review of new animal drugs.

FDA: Reauthorize Animal Generic Drug User Fee Act. The Budget reauthorizes the Animal Generic Drug User Fee Act (AGDUFA), which expires on September 30, 2018. AGDUFA fees support FDA's premarket review of generic animal drugs.

FDA: Increase export certification user fee cap. Firms exporting products from the United States are often asked by foreign customers or foreign governments to supply a "certificate" for products regulated by the FDA to document the product's regulatory or marketing status. The proposal increases the maximum user fee cap from $175 per export certification to $600 to meet FDA's true cost of issuing export certificates and to ensure better and faster service for American companies that request the service.

FDA: Establish over-the-counter monograph user fee. FDA currently regulates over-the-counter (OTC) products through a three-phase public rulemaking process to establish standards or drug monographs for an OTC therapeutic drug class. The proposal would provide additional resources and authorities to FDA to bring new OTC products into the market faster so that Americans will have greater access to a wider range of safe and effective OTC products.

Centers for Medicare and Medicaid Services (CMS): Establish survey and certification revisit fee. The Budget proposes a revisit user fee to provide CMS with a greater ability to revisit poorly performing health care facilities and build greater accountability by creating an incentive for facilities to correct deficiencies and ensure quality of care.

Health Resources and Services Administration: 340B Program user fee: To improve the administration and oversight of the 340B Drug Discount Program, the Budget includes a new user charge to those covered entities participating in the program.

Department of Homeland Security

Transportation Security Administration (TSA): Increase aviation passenger security fee. Pursuant to the Bipartisan Budget Act (BBA) of 2013, the passenger security fee is $5.60 per one-way trip. The BBA also allocated a portion of the fee revenue to deficit reduction. The 2019 Budget proposes to increase the passenger security fee from $5.60 to $6.60 in FY 2019, and from $6.60 to $8.25 starting in FY 2020 in order to recover the full cost of aviation security from the traveling public. This proposal will increase offsetting collections by an estimated $20.14 billion between 2019 and 2028.

Department of Housing and Urban Development

Federal Housing Administration (FHA): Establish Information technology (IT) fee. The Budget requests authority to charge lenders using FHA mortgage insurance an IT fee, which would generate, through 2022, an estimated $20 million annually in offsetting collections. These additional collections will offset the cost of modernizing FHA's aging IT systems.

Department of State

Establish Diplomacy Center rental fee. This new user fee will enable the Department of State to provide support, on a cost-recovery basis, to outside organizations for programs and conference activities held at the U.S. Diplomacy Center.

Department of Transportation

Federal Railroad Administration (FRA): Establish Railroad Safety Inspection fee. The FRA establishes and enforces safety standards for U.S. railroads. FRA's rail safety inspectors work in the field and oversee railroads' operating and management practices. The Administration is proposing that, starting in 2019, the railroads contribute to partially cover the cost of FRA's field inspections because railroads benefit directly from Government efforts to maintain high safety standards. The proposed fee would be similar to existing charges collected from other industries regulated by Federal safety programs.

Department of the Treasury

Subject Financial Research Fund (FRF) fee to annual appropriations action. Expenses of the Financial Stability Oversight Council (FSOC) and the Office of Financial Research (OFR) are paid through the FRF, which is funded by assessments on certain bank holding companies with total consolidated assets of $50 billion or greater and nonbank financial companies supervised by the Federal Reserve Board of Governors. The FRF was established by the Dodd-Frank Act and is managed by the Department of the Treasury. To improve their effectiveness and ensure greater accountability, the Budget proposes to subject activities of the FSOC and OFR to the appropriations process. In so doing, currently authorized assessments would, beginning in 2020, be reclassified as discretionary offsetting collections and set at a level determined by the Congress. The Budget also reflects continued reductions in OFR spending commensurate with the renewed fiscal discipline being applied across the Federal Government.

Environmental Protection Agency (EPA)

Establish ENERGY STAR fee. The Administration proposes to collect fees to fund EPA's administration of the ENERGY STAR program. Product manufacturers who seek to label their products under the program would pay a modest fee that would recover the full costs of EPA's work to set voluntary energy efficiency standards and to process applications. Fee collections will begin after EPA undertakes a rulemaking process to determine which products would be covered by fees and the level of fees, and to ensure that a fee system would not discourage manufacturers from participating in the program or result in a loss of environmental benefits.

Establish oil and chemical facility compliance assistance fees. The Administration proposes to provide an optional service to oil and chemical facilities to help these facilities identify actions to comply with certain environmental laws and regulations. Upon payment of a fee, EPA would conduct an on-site walk-through of a facility and provide recommendations and best practices regarding how to comply with certain regulations under the Clean Air Act and the Federal Water Pollution Control Act. This service would initially be available to facilities that are responsible for preparing and implementing a Risk Management Plan, Spill Prevention Control and Countermeasure Plan, and/or Facility Response Plan. Facilities choosing to utilize this service would pay a modest fee that would recover the full costs of EPA's work in providing this compliance assistance service to that facility. Fee collections and program implementation will begin after EPA issues procedures for applying for the service and the collection and use of such fees.

Commodity Futures Trading Commission (CFTC)

Establish CFTC user fee. The Budget proposes an amendment to the Commodity Exchange Act authorizing the CFTC to collect user fees to fund the Commission's activities, like other Federal financial and banking regulators. Fee funding would shift the costs of services provided by the CFTC from the general taxpayer to the primary beneficiaries of CFTC oversight. Contingent upon enactment of legislation authorizing the CFTC to collect fees, the Administration proposes that collections begin in 2019 to offset a portion of the CFTC's annual appropriation.

2. *Offsetting receipts*

Department of State

Western Hemisphere Travel Initiative surcharge extension. The Administration proposes to permanently extend the authority for the Department of State to collect the Western Hemisphere Travel Initiative surcharge. The surcharge was initially enacted by the Passport Services Enhancement Act of 2005 (P.L. 109–167) to cover the Department's costs of meeting increased demand for passports, which resulted from the implementation of the Western Hemisphere Travel Initiative.

Border Crossing Card (BCC) fee increase. The Budget includes a proposal to allow the fee charged for BCC minor applicants to be set administratively, rather than statutorily, at one-half the fee charged for processing an adult border crossing card. Administrative fee setting will allow the fee to better reflect the associated cost of service, consistent with other fees charged for consular services. As a result of this change, annual BCC fee collections beginning in 2019 are projected to increase by $13 million (from $3 million to $16 million).

B. Mandatory User Charge Proposals

1. *Offsetting collections*

Department of Labor

Improve Pension Benefit Guaranty Corporation (PBGC) solvency. PBGC acts as a backstop to protect pension payments for workers whose companies have failed. Currently, PBGC's pension insurance programs are underfunded, and its liabilities far exceed its assets. PBGC receives no taxpayer funds and its premiums are currently much lower than what a private financial institution would charge for insuring the same risk. PBGC's multiemployer program, which insures the pension benefits of 10 million workers, is at risk of insolvency by 2025. As an important step to protect the pensions of these hardworking Americans, the Budget proposes to create a variable-rate premium (VRP) and exit premium in the multiemployer program. A multiemployer VRP would require plans to pay additional premiums based on their level of underfunding, up to a cap, as is done in the single-employer program. An exit premium, equal to ten times the VRP cap, would be assessed on employers that withdraw from the system. PBGC would have limited authority to design waivers for some or all of the newly assessed premiums if there is a substantial risk that the payment of premiums will accelerate plan insolvency, resulting in earlier financial assistance to the plan. This proposal would raise approximately $16 billion in premiums over the ten-year window. At this level of receipts, the program is more likely than not to remain solvent over the next 20 years, helping to ensure that there is a safety net available to workers whose multiemployer plans fail.

2. *Offsetting receipts*

Department of Agriculture

Establish Food Safety and Inspection Service (FSIS) user fee. The Administration proposes establishing a Food Safety and Inspection Service (FSIS) user fee to cover the costs of all domestic inspection activity and import re-inspection and most of the central operations costs for Federal, State, and international inspection programs for meat, poultry, and eggs. FSIS inspections benefit the meat, poultry, and egg industries. FSIS personnel are continuously present for all egg processing and domestic slaughter operations, inspect each livestock and poultry carcass, and inspect operations at meat and poultry processing establishments at least once per shift. The inspections cover microbiological and chemical testing as well as cleanliness and cosmetic product defects. The "inspected by USDA" stamp on meat and poultry labels increases consumer confidence in the product which may increase sales. The user fee would not cover Federal functions such as investigation, enforcement, risk analysis, and emergency response. The Administration estimates this fee would increase the cost of meat, poultry, and eggs for consumers by less than one cent per pound.

Establish Packers and Stockyards Program user fee. The Administration proposes establishing a Packers and Stockyards user fee. This would recover the costs of the Packers and Stockyards Program (P&SP) through a licensing fee. The P&SP benefits the livestock, meat, and poultry industries by promoting fair business practices and competitive market environments.

Establish Animal and Plant Health Inspection Service (APHIS) user fee. The Administration proposes establishing three new Animal and Plant Health Inspection Service (APHIS) mandatory user fees to offset costs related to 1) enforcement of the Animal Welfare Act, 2) regulation of biotechnology derived products, and 3) regulation of veterinary biologics products.

Establish Agricultural Marketing Service (AMS) user fee. The Administration proposes establishing an Agricultural Marketing Service (AMS) user fee to cover the full costs of the agency's oversight of Marketing Orders and Agreements. Marketing Orders and Agreements are initiated by industry to help provide stable markets, and are tailored to the specific industry's needs. The industries that substantially benefit from Marketing Orders and Agreements should pay for the oversight of these programs.

Department of Commerce

Lease Shared Secondary Licenses. To promote efficient use of the electromagnetic spectrum, the Administration proposes to require the leasing of Federal spectrum through secondary licenses. Under this proposal, the National Telecommunications and Information Administration (NTIA) would be granted authority to lease access to Federal spectrum for commercial use on a non-interference basis with Federal primary users. Working with other Federal agencies, NTIA would negotiate sharing arrangements on behalf of the Federal Government and would seek to increase the efficiency of spectrum when possible without causing harmful interference to Federal users authorized to operate in the negotiated bands. In addition to Federal spectrum auctions, leases will provide another option for maximizing the economic value of this scarce spectrum resource. Significant resources will be required by NTIA and other Federal agencies to negotiate and manage these spectrum leases. The cost of administering the program will be offset by a portion of the lease revenue. Therefore the proposal is conservatively estimated to generate approximately $700 million in net deficit reduction for taxpayers.

Department of Energy

Reform Power Marketing Administration (PMA) power rates. The PMAs sell wholesale electricity generated at dams owned and operated by the Army Corps of Engineers or the Bureau of Reclamation. The Flood Control Act of 1944 requires the PMAs to generate revenues to recover all costs, including annual operating and maintenance costs and the taxpayers' investment in the power portions of dams and in transmission lines. The PMAs recover these costs by establishing rates, charged to utility customers, based on the cost of providing this electricity. These rates are limited to recovering costs and there is limited regu-

latory or state regulatory oversight to ensure these rates are efficient and justified. Current law permits the PMAs to defer repayment of prior capital investment by the taxpayers and creates economic inefficiencies. The vast majority of the Nation's electricity needs are met through for-profit Investor Owned Utilities, which are subject to state and/or Federal regulatory oversight in the establishment of rates. This proposal would change the statutory requirement that the PMA rates be based on recovering costs to a rate structure that could allow for faster recoupment of taxpayer investment and consideration of rates charged by comparable utilities.

Department of Health and Human Services

Require clearinghouses and billing agents acting on behalf of Medicare providers and suppliers to enroll in the program. The Budget proposes to establish an enrollment and registration process for clearinghouses and billing agents who act on behalf of Medicare providers and suppliers, introducing an application fee to be consistent with program integrity safeguards in place for institutional and individual providers.

Department of Homeland Security

Extend expiring Customs and Border Protection (CBP) fees. The Budget proposes to extend the Merchandise Processing Fee beyond its current expiration date of January 14, 2026 to January 14, 2031. It also proposes to extend COBRA fees (statutorily set under the Consolidated Omnibus Budget Reconciliation Act of 1985) and the Express Consignment Courier Facilities (ECCF) fee created under the Trade Act of 2002 beyond their current expiration date of September 30, 2025 to September 30, 2030.

Increase customs user fees. The Budget proposes to increase COBRA and ECCF fees created under the Trade Act of 2002. COBRA created a series of user fees for air and sea passengers, commercial trucks, railroad cars, private aircraft and vessels, commercial vessels, dutiable mail packages, broker permits, barges and bulk carriers from Canada and Mexico, cruise vessel passengers, and ferry vessel passengers. This proposal would increase the customs inspection fee by $2.10 for certain air and sea passengers and increase other COBRA fees by proportional amounts. The additional revenue raised from increasing the user fees will allow CBP to recover more costs associated with customs related inspections, and reduce waiting times by helping to support the hiring of 840 new CBP Officers. This fee was last adjusted in April 2007, yet international travel volumes have grown since that time and CBP costs for customs inspections continue to increase. As a result, CBP relies on its annually appropriated funds to support the difference between fee collections and the costs of providing customs inspectional services. The Government Accountability Office's most recent review of these COBRA user fees (July 2016) identified that CBP collected $686 million in COBRA/ECCF fees compared to $870 million in operating costs, exhibiting a recovery rate of 78 percent.[7] With the fee increase,

---

[7] GAO–16–443, Enhanced Oversight Could Better Ensure Programs

CBP would potentially collect the same amount it incurs in COBRA/ECCF eligible costs in FY 2019. The proposed legislation will close the gap between costs and collections, enabling CBP to provide improved inspectional services to those who pay this user fee.

Increase immigration user fees. This proposal will increase the Immigration Inspection User Fee (IUF) by $2 and eliminate a partial fee exemption for sea passengers arriving from the United States, Canada, Mexico, or adjacent islands. These two adjustments will result in a total fee of $9 for all passengers, regardless of mode of transportation or point of departure. This fee is paid by passengers and is used to recover some of the costs related to determining the admissibility of passengers entering the U.S. Specifically, the fees collected support immigration inspections, the maintenance and updating of systems to track criminal and illegal aliens in areas with high apprehensions, asylum hearings, and the repair and maintenance of equipment. This fee was last adjusted in November 2001, yet international travel volumes have grown significantly since that time and CBP costs for immigration inspections continue to increase. As a result, CBP relies on annually appropriated funds to support the difference between fee collections and the costs of providing immigration inspection services. The Government Accountability Office's most recent review of IUF (July 2016) identified that CBP collected $728 million in IUF fees compared to $1,003 million in operating costs, exhibiting a recovery rate of 73 percent.[8] To prevent this gap from widening again in the future, the proposal will authorize CBP to adjust the fee without further statutory changes. CBP estimates raising the fee and lifting the exemption could offset the cost of an estimated 1,230 CBP Officers.

Department of the Interior

Reauthorize the Federal Land Transaction Facilitation Act (FLTFA). The Budget proposes to reauthorize the FLTFA, which expired in July 2011, and allow lands identified as suitable for disposal in recent land use plans to be sold using the FLTFA authority. The FLTFA sales revenues would continue to be used to fund the acquisition of environmentally sensitive lands and to cover BLM's administrative costs associated with conducting sales.

Department of Labor

Expand Foreign Labor Certification fees. The Budget proposes authorizing legislation to establish and retain fees to cover the costs of operating the foreign labor certification programs, which ensure that employers proposing to bring in immigrant workers have checked to ensure that American workers cannot meet their needs and that immigrant workers are being compensated appropriately and not disadvantaging American workers. The ability to charge fees for these programs would give the Department

of Labor (DOL) a more reliable, workload-based source of funding for this function (as the Department of Homeland Security has), and would ultimately eliminate the need for discretionary appropriations. The proposal includes the following: 1) charge employer fees for its prevailing wage determinations; 2) charge employer fees for its permanent labor certification program; 3) charge employer fees for H–2B non-agricultural workers; and 4) retain and adjust the H–2A agricultural worker application fees currently deposited into the General Fund. The fee levels would be set via regulation to ensure that the amounts are subject to review. Given the DOL Inspector General's important role in investigating fraud and abuse, the proposal also includes a mechanism to provide funding for the Inspector General's work to oversee foreign labor certification programs.

Department of the Treasury

Increase and extend guarantee fee charged by GSEs. The Temporary Payroll Tax Cut Continuation Act of 2011 (Public Law 112–78) required that Fannie Mae and Freddie Mac increase their credit guarantee fees on single-family mortgage acquisitions between 2012 and 2021 by an average of at least 0.10 percentage points. Revenues generated by this fee increase are remitted directly to the Treasury for deficit reduction. The Budget proposes to increase this fee by 0.10 percentage points for single-family mortgage acquisitions from 2019 through 2021, and then extend the 0.20 percentage point fee for acquisitions through 2023.

Allow District of Columbia Courts to retain bar exam and application fees. Under the 1997 National Capital Revitalization and Self-Government Improvement Act of 1997, all fees collected by the DC courts are deposited into the DC Crime Victims Compensation Fund. Among the various fees collected by the DC courts are bar examination and application fees. Since adopting the Uniform Bar Examination in 2016, DC has seen the number of bar examinees increase by 214%. However, because the associated fees are deposited into the DC Crime Victims Compensation Fund, there has been no correlated increase in the resources available to process the increased number of applications. The proposal would allow the DC courts to retain the bar examination and application fees as offsetting receipts to pay for the processing of exams and applications.

Federal Communications Commission (FCC)

Enact Spectrum License User Fee. To promote efficient use of the electromagnetic spectrum, the Administration proposes to provide the FCC with new authority to use other economic mechanisms, such as fees, as a spectrum management tool. The FCC would be authorized to set charges for unauctioned spectrum licenses based on spectrum-management principles. Fees would be phased in over time as part of an ongoing rulemaking process to determine the appropriate application and level for fees.

Receiving Fees and Other Collections Use Funds Efficiently, *http://www.gao.gov/products/GAO–16–443*

[8] GAO–16–443, Enhanced Oversight Could Better Ensure Programs Receiving Fees and Other Collections Use Funds Efficiently, *http://www.gao.gov/products/GAO–16–443*

C. User Charge Proposals that are Governmental Receipts

Department of Homeland Security

CBP: Establish user fee for Electronic Visa Update System. The Budget proposes to establish a user fee for the Electronic Visa Update System (EVUS), a new CBP program to collect biographic and travel-related information from certain non-immigrant visa holders prior to traveling to the United States. This process will complement the existing visa application process and enhance CBP's ability to make pre-travel admissibility and risk determinations. CBP proposes to establish a user fee to fund the costs of establishing, providing, and administering the system.

Eliminate BrandUSA; make revenue available to CBP. The Administration proposes to eliminate funding for the Corporation for Travel Promotion (also known as Brand USA) as part of the Administration's plans to move the Nation towards fiscal responsibility and to redefine the proper role of the Federal Government. The Budget redirects the Electronic System for Travel Authorization (ESTA) surcharge currently deposited in the Travel Promotion Fund to the ESTA account at Customs and Border Protection with a portion to be transferred to the International Trade Administration.

Make full Electronic System for Travel Authorization (ESTA) receipts available to CBP. The Budget proposes to permanently extend the ESTA receipts and eliminate the $100 million limitation on ESTA receipt transfers from the General Fund, and provide all collections made to CBP's ESTA account. CBP intends to use these resources to support traveler processing, including entry and exit process re-engineering and modernization, staffing and overtime processing of arrivals and departures from the United States, and any other CBP activities related to the processing of passengers including, but not limited to, activities of CBP's National Targeting Center.

Department of the Treasury

Subject Financial Research Fund (FRF) fee to annual appropriations action. As explained above in the section of discretionary use charge proposals, the Budget proposes to subject activities of the Financial Stability Oversight Council (FSOC) and the Office of Financial Research (OFR) to the appropriations process in order to improve their effectiveness and ensure greater accountability. As part of the proposal, currently authorized assessments would be reclassified as discretionary offsetting collections, resulting in a reduction in governmental receipts and an increase in discretionary offsetting collections.

Corps of Engineers—Civil Works

Reform inland waterways funding. The Administration proposes to reform the laws governing the Inland Waterways Trust Fund, including establishing an annual fee to increase the amount paid by commercial navigation users of the inland waterways. In 1986, Congress provided that commercial traffic on the inland waterways would be responsible for 50 percent of the capital costs of the locks, dams, and other features that make barge transportation possible on the inland waterways. The additional revenue would help finance future capital investments, as well as 10 percent of the operation and maintenance cost, in these waterways to support economic growth. The current excise tax on diesel fuel used in inland waterways commerce will not produce the revenue needed to cover these costs.

Reduce harbor maintenance tax. The Administration proposes to reduce the Harbor Maintenance Tax rate to better align estimated annual receipts from this tax with recent appropriation levels for eligible expenditures from the Harbor Maintenance Trust Fund. Reducing this tax would provide greater flexibility for individual ports to establish appropriate fee structures for services they provide, in order to help finance their capital and operating expenses on their own.

Table 12–4. USER CHARGE PROPOSALS IN THE FY 2019 BUDGET [1]

(Estimated collections in millions of dollars)

	2018	2019	2020	2021	2022	2023	2024	2025	2026	2027	2028	2019–2023	2019–2028
OFFSETTING COLLECTIONS AND OFFSETTING RECEIPTS													
DISCRETIONARY:													
Offsetting collections													
Department of Agriculture													
Establish Federal Grain Inspection Service fee	....	20	20	20	20	20	20	20	20	20	20	100	200
Establish Agricultural Quarantine Inspection fee	....	29	30	31	31	32	33	34	35	35	36	153	326
Department of Health and Human Services													
Food and Drug Administration (FDA): Reauthorize Animal Drug User Fee Act	....	25	26	28	29	31	32	34	35	37	39	139	316
FDA: Reauthorize Animal Generic Drug User Fee Act	....	13	14	14	15	16	17	18	18	19	20	72	164
FDA: Increase export certification user fee cap	....	4	4	4	4	5	5	5	5	5	5	21	46
FDA: Establish over-the-counter monograph user fee	....	22	22	25	31	34	36	37	39	41	43	134	330
Centers for Medicare and Medicaid Services: Establish survey and certification revisit fee	....	14	17	28	29	29	30	31	31	32	32	117	273
Health Resources and Services Administration: Establish 340B Program user fee	....	16	16	16	16	16	16	16	16	16	16	80	160
Department of Homeland Security													
Transportation Security Administration: Increase aviation passenger security fee	....	557	2,008	2,048	2,088	2,130	2,173	2,216	2,261	2,306	2,353	8,831	20,140
Department of Housing and Urban Development													
Federal Housing Administration: Establish Information Technology (IT) fee	....	20	20	20	20	....	....	....	....	....	....	80	80
Department of State													
Establish Diplomacy Center Rental Fee	....	*	*	*	*	*	*	*	*	*	*	*	*
Department of Transportation													
Federal Railroad Administration: Establish Railroad Safety Inspection fee	....	50	50	50	50	50	50	50	50	50	50	250	500
Department of the Treasury													
Subject Financial Research Fund fee to annual appropriations action	....	....	68	68	68	68	68	68	68	68	68	272	612
Environmental Protection Agency													
Establish ENERGY STAR fee	....	46	46	46	46	46	46	46	46	46	46	230	460
Establish chemical facility compliance assistance fee	....	20	20	20	20	20	20	20	20	20	20	100	200
Establish oil facility compliance assistance fee	....	10	10	10	10	10	10	10	10	10	10	50	100
Commodity Futures Trading Commission (CFTC)													
Establish CFTC user fee	....	32	32	32	32	32	32	32	32	32	32	160	320
Offsetting receipts													
Department of State													
Extend Western Hemisphere Travel Initiative surcharge	....	465	465	465	465	465	465	465	465	465	465	2,325	4,650
Increase Border Crossing Card Fee	....	13	13	13	13	13	13	13	13	13	13	65	130
Subtotal, discretionary user charge proposals	....	1,356	2,881	2,938	2,987	3,017	3,066	3,115	3,164	3,215	3,268	13,179	29,007
MANDATORY:													
Offsetting collections													
Department of Labor													
Improve Pension Benefit Guaranty Corporation solvency	....	....	1,583	1,670	1,729	1,788	1,821	1,057	2,635	1,875	1,894	6,769	16,051

Table 12–4. USER CHARGE PROPOSALS IN THE FY 2019 BUDGET [1] —Continued
(Estimated collections in millions of dollars)

	2018	2019	2020	2021	2022	2023	2024	2025	2026	2027	2028	2019–2023	2019–2028
Offsetting receipts													
Department of Agriculture													
Establish Food Safety and Inspection Service user fee	....	....	660	660	660	660	660	660	660	660	660	2,640	5,940
Establish Packers and Stockyards Program user fee	....	23	23	23	23	23	23	23	23	23	23	115	230
Establish Animal and Plant Health Inspection Service user fee	....	23	23	23	23	23	23	23	23	23	23	115	230
Establish Agricultural Marketing Service (AMS) user fee	....	20	20	20	20	20	20	20	20	20	20	100	200
Department of Commerce													
Lease Shared Secondary Licenses	....	50	55	55	60	65	70	70	80	80	85	285	670
Department of Energy													
Reform Power Marketing Administration power rates	....	162	169	173	182	188	192	199	206	211	217	874	1,899
Department of Health and Human Services													
Require clearinghouses and billing agents acting on behalf of Medicare providers and suppliers to enroll in the program	....	15	15	16	16	16	17	17	17	18	18	78	165
Department of Homeland Security													
Extend expiring Customs and Border Protection (CBP) fees	....	....	....	....	....	....	....	....	4,159	5,334	5,601	....	15,095
Increase customs user fees	....	312	350	368	388	410	432	456	480	506	507	1,829	4,210
Increase immigration user fees	....	316	328	375	387	478	494	593	614	679	702	1,884	4,966
Department of the Interior													
Reauthorize the Federal Land Transaction Facilitation Act	....	5	10	19	29	29	29	29	29	29	29	92	237
Department of Labor													
Expand Foreign Labor Certification fees	....	1	37	76	79	83	88	92	97	102	108	276	763
Department of the Treasury													
Increase and extend guarantee fee charged by GSEs	....	212	967	1699	2350	3475	4258	4034	3398	2858	2401	8,703	25,652
Allow District of Columbia Courts to retain bar exam and application fees	....	*	*	*	*	*	*	*	*	*	*	2	4
Federal Communications Commission													
Enact Spectrum License User Fee	....	50	150	300	450	500	500	500	500	500	500	1,450	3,950
Subtotal, mandatory user charge proposals	....	1,189	4,390	5,477	6,396	7,758	8,627	7,773	12,941	12,918	12,788	25,210	80,257
Subtotal, user charge proposals that are offsetting collections and offsetting receipts	....	2,545	7,271	8,415	9,383	10,775	11,693	10,888	16,105	16,133	16,056	38,389	109,264
GOVERNMENTAL RECEIPTS													
Department of Homeland Security													
CBP: Establish user fee for Electronic Visa Update System	....	25	28	31	34	38	42	46	52	57	64	156	417
Eliminate BrandUSA; make revenue available to CBP	....	....	....	....	....	....	....	....	....	....	....	....	....
Make full Electronic System for Travel Authorization receipts available to CBP	....	....	....	171	177	183	189	196	202	209	216	531	1,543
Department of the Treasury													
Subject Financial Research Fund fee to annual appropriations action	....	....	–68	–68	–68	–68	–68	–68	–68	–68	–68	–272	–612
Corps of Engineers - Civil Works													
Reform inland waterways funding	....	178	178	178	178	178	178	178	178	178	178	890	1,780
Reduce harbor maintenance fee	....	–347	–369	–383	–393	–403	–412	–424	–437	–453	–471	–1,895	–4,092
Subtotal, governmental receipts user charge proposals	....	–144	–231	–71	–72	–72	–71	–72	–73	–77	–81	–590	–964
Total, user charge proposals	....	2,401	7,040	8,344	9,311	10,703	11,622	10,816	16,032	16,056	15,975	37,799	108,300

[1] A positive sign indicates an increase in collections.
* $500,000 or less

13. TAX EXPENDITURES

The Congressional Budget Act of 1974 (Public Law 93–344) requires that a list of "tax expenditures" be included in the budget. Tax expenditures are defined in the law as "revenue losses attributable to provisions of the Federal tax laws which allow a special exclusion, exemption, or deduction from gross income or which provide a special credit, a preferential rate of tax, or a deferral of tax liability." These exceptions may be viewed as alternatives to other policy instruments, such as spending or regulatory programs.

Identification and measurement of tax expenditures depends crucially on the baseline tax system against which the actual tax system is compared. The tax expenditure estimates presented in this document are patterned on a comprehensive income tax, which defines income as the sum of consumption and the change in net wealth in a given period of time.

An important assumption underlying each tax expenditure estimate reported below is that other parts of the Tax Code remain unchanged. The estimates would be different if tax expenditures were changed simultaneously because of potential interactions among provisions. For that reason, this document does not present a grand total for the estimated tax expenditures.

Tax expenditures relating to the individual and corporate income taxes are estimated for fiscal years 2017–2027 using two methods of accounting: current revenue effects and present value effects. The present value approach provides estimates of the revenue effects for tax expenditures that generally involve deferrals of tax payments into the future.

TAX EXPENDITURES IN THE INCOME TAX

Tax Expenditure Estimates

All tax expenditure estimates and descriptions presented here are based upon current tax law enacted as of July 1, 2017 and reflect the economic assumptions from the Mid-Session Review of the 2017 Budget. In some cases, expired or repealed provisions are listed if their revenue effects occur in fiscal year 2017 or later.

The total revenue effects for tax expenditures for fiscal years 2017–2027 are displayed according to the Budget's functional categories in Table 1. Descriptions of the specific tax expenditure provisions follow the discussion of general features of the tax expenditure concept.

Two baseline concepts—the normal tax baseline and the reference tax law baseline—are used to identify and estimate tax expenditures.[1] For the most part, the two concepts coincide. However, items treated as tax expenditures under the normal tax baseline, but not the reference tax law baseline, are indicated by the designation "normal tax method" in the tables. The revenue effects for these items are zero using the reference tax rules. The alternative baseline concepts are discussed in detail below.

Tables 2A and 2B report separately the respective portions of the total revenue effects that arise under the individual and corporate income taxes. The location of the estimates under the individual and corporate headings does not imply that these categories of filers benefit from the special tax provisions in proportion to the respective tax expenditure amounts shown. Rather, these breakdowns show the form of tax liability that the various provisions affect. The ultimate beneficiaries of corporate tax expenditures could be shareholders, employees, customers, or other providers of capital, depending on economic forces.

Table 3 ranks the major tax expenditures by the size of their 2018–2027 revenue effect. The first column provides the number of the provision in order to cross reference this table to Tables 1, 2A, and 2B, as well as to the descriptions below.

Interpreting Tax Expenditure Estimates

The estimates shown for individual tax expenditures in Tables 1 through 3 do not necessarily equal the increase in Federal revenues (or the change in the budget balance) that would result from repealing these special provisions, for the following reasons.

First, eliminating a tax expenditure may have incentive effects that alter economic behavior. These incentives can affect the resulting magnitudes of the activity or of other tax provisions or Government programs. For example, if capital gains were taxed at ordinary rates, capital gain realizations would be expected to decline, resulting in lower tax receipts. Such behavioral effects are not reflected in the estimates.

Second, tax expenditures are interdependent even without incentive effects. Repeal of a tax expenditure provision can increase or decrease the tax revenues associated with other provisions. For example, even if behavior

---

[1] These baseline concepts are thoroughly discussed in Special Analysis G of the 1985 Budget, where the former is referred to as the pre-1983 method and the latter the post-1982 method.

does not change, repeal of an itemized deduction could increase the revenue costs from other deductions because some taxpayers would be moved into higher tax brackets. Alternatively, repeal of an itemized deduction could lower the revenue cost from other deductions if taxpayers are led to claim the standard deduction instead of itemizing. Similarly, if two provisions were repealed simultaneously, the increase in tax liability could be greater or less than the sum of the two separate tax expenditures, because each is estimated assuming that the other remains in force. In addition, the estimates reported in Table 1 are the totals of individual and corporate income tax revenue effects reported in Tables 2A and 2B, and do not reflect any possible interactions between individual and corporate income tax receipts. For this reason, the estimates in Table 1 should be regarded as approximations.

Present-Value Estimates

The annual value of tax expenditures for tax deferrals is reported on a cash basis in all tables except Table 4. Cash-based estimates reflect the difference between taxes deferred in the current year and incoming revenues that are received due to deferrals of taxes from prior years. Although such estimates are useful as a measure of cash flows into the Government, they do not accurately reflect the true economic cost of these provisions. For example, for a provision where activity levels have changed over time, so that incoming tax receipts from past deferrals are greater than deferred receipts from new activity, the cash-basis tax expenditure estimate can be negative, despite the fact that in present-value terms current deferrals have a real cost to the Government. Alternatively, in the case of a newly enacted deferral provision, a cash-based estimate can overstate the real effect on receipts to the Government because the newly deferred taxes will ultimately be received.

Discounted present-value estimates of revenue effects are presented in Table 4 for certain provisions that involve tax deferrals or other long-term revenue effects. These estimates complement the cash-based tax expenditure estimates presented in the other tables.

The present-value estimates represent the revenue effects, net of future tax payments that follow from activities undertaken during calendar year 2017 which cause the deferrals or other long-term revenue effects. For instance, a pension contribution in 2017 would cause a deferral of tax payments on wages in 2017 and on pension fund earnings on this contribution (e.g., interest) in later years. In some future year, however, the 2017 pension contribution and accrued earnings will be paid out and taxes will be due; these receipts are included in the present-value estimate. In general, this conceptual approach is similar to the one used for reporting the budgetary effects of credit programs, where direct loans and guarantees in a given year affect future cash flows.

Tax Expenditure Baselines

A tax expenditure is an exception to baseline provisions of the tax structure that usually results in a reduction in the amount of tax owed. The 1974 Congressional Budget Act, which mandated the tax expenditure budget, did not specify the baseline provisions of the tax law. As noted previously, deciding whether provisions are exceptions, therefore, is a matter of judgment. As in prior years, most of this year's tax expenditure estimates are presented using two baselines: the normal tax baseline and the reference tax law baseline. Tax expenditures may take the form of credits, deductions, special exceptions and allowances.

The normal tax baseline is patterned on a practical variant of a comprehensive income tax, which defines income as the sum of consumption and the change in net wealth in a given period of time. The normal tax baseline allows personal exemptions, a standard deduction, and deduction of expenses incurred in earning income. It is not limited to a particular structure of tax rates, or by a specific definition of the taxpaying unit.

The reference tax law baseline is also patterned on a comprehensive income tax, but it is closer to existing law. Reference law tax expenditures are limited to special exceptions from a generally provided tax rule that serve programmatic functions in a way that is analogous to spending programs. Provisions under the reference law baseline are generally tax expenditures under the normal tax baseline, but the reverse is not always true.

Both the normal and reference tax baselines allow several major departures from a pure comprehensive income tax. For example, under the normal and reference tax baselines:

- Income is taxable only when it is realized in exchange. Thus, the deferral of tax on unrealized capital gains is not regarded as a tax expenditure. Accrued income would be taxed under a comprehensive income tax.

- There is a separate corporate income tax.

- Tax rates on noncorporate business income vary by level of income.

- Individual tax rates, including brackets, standard deduction, and personal exemptions, are allowed to vary with marital status.

- Values of assets and debt are not generally adjusted for inflation. A comprehensive income tax would adjust the cost basis of capital assets and debt for changes in the general price level. Thus, under a comprehensive income tax baseline, the failure to take account of inflation in measuring depreciation, capital gains, and interest income would be regarded as a negative tax expenditure (i.e., a tax penalty), and failure to take account of inflation in measuring interest costs would be regarded as a positive tax expenditure (i.e., a tax subsidy).

Although the reference law and normal tax baselines are generally similar, areas of difference include:

Tax rates. The separate schedules applying to the various taxpaying units are included in the reference law baseline. Thus, corporate tax rates below the maximum statutory rate do not give rise to a tax expenditure. The normal tax baseline is similar, except that, by convention, it specifies the current maximum rate as the baseline for the corporate income tax. The lower tax rates applied to the first $10 million of corporate income are thus regarded as a tax expenditure under the normal tax. By convention, the Alternative Minimum Tax is treated as part of the baseline rate structure under both the reference and normal tax methods.

Income subject to the tax. Income subject to tax is defined as gross income less the costs of earning that income. Under the reference tax rules, gross income does not include gifts defined as receipts of money or property that are not consideration in an exchange nor does gross income include most transfer payments from the Government.[2] The normal tax baseline also excludes gifts between individuals from gross income. Under the normal tax baseline, however, all cash transfer payments from the Government to private individuals are counted in gross income, and exemptions of such transfers from tax are identified as tax expenditures. The costs of earning income are generally deductible in determining taxable income under both the reference and normal tax baselines.[3]

Capital recovery. Under the reference tax law baseline no tax expenditures arise from accelerated depreciation. Under the normal tax baseline, the depreciation allowance for property is computed using estimates of economic depreciation.

Treatment of foreign income. Both the normal and reference tax baselines allow a tax credit for foreign income taxes paid (up to the amount of U.S. income taxes that would otherwise be due), which prevents double taxation of income earned abroad. Under the normal tax method, however, controlled foreign corporations (CFCs) are not regarded as entities separate from their controlling U.S. shareholders. Thus, the deferral of tax on income received by CFCs is regarded as a tax expenditure under this method. In contrast, except for tax haven activities, the reference law baseline follows current law in treating CFCs as separate taxable entities whose income is not subject to U.S. tax until distributed to U.S. taxpayers. Under this baseline, deferral of tax on CFC income is not a tax expenditure because U.S. taxpayers generally are not taxed on accrued, but unrealized, income.

As illustrated in the Fiscal year 2004 Tax expenditure Budget, provisions defined as tax expenditures in this Budget would be different if a pure comprehensive income tax were employed as the baseline. Similarly, they would also look quite different if a consumption tax were employed; the current income tax can be considered as a hybrid tax with income and consumption tax features. Comprehensive income, also called Haig-Simons income, is the real, inflation adjusted, accretions to wealth, accrued or realized. Using a comprehensive income tax baseline, the tax base can be larger than that considered here. A broad-based consumption tax is a combination of an income tax plus a deduction for net saving, or just consumption plus the change in net worth. Under this baseline, some of the current tax provisions would no longer be considered as tax expenditures (e.g. retirement savings). Because of the dramatic changes in the tax system introduced by the Tax Cuts and Jobs Act of 2017, the Fiscal Year 2020 Budget will update the earlier analysis of 2004 using the new law with its modified tax base and new tax rate structure.

Descriptions of Income Tax Provisions

Descriptions of the individual and corporate income tax expenditures reported on in this document follow. These descriptions relate to current law as of July 1, 2017. The estimates provided below do not reflect the effect of changes introduced by the Tax Cuts and Jobs Act (TCJA), signed into law on December 22, 2017. Given its late date of enactment, these effects will be reflected in the estimates reported in the FY 2020 Budget. Under the Act, a number of provisions were scaled back, expanded, and repealed, or newly introduced. Provisions otherwise untouched directly by the Act were also affected by the modification of the individual tax rate schedule and reduction of corporate tax rates. Below is a brief summary of how TCJA affected tax expenditure provisions, with the Receipts Chapter providing an expanded listing and description.

For individuals, the Act expanded the child tax credit, the deduction for charitable contributions and certain tax preferences for education. It scaled back the deduction for state and local taxes, the mortgage interest deduction, and certain fringe benefits. It also repealed the moving expense deduction and exclusion for non-military taxpayers. For businesses, the Act expanded depreciation allowances and scaled back on the benefit of deferral of gains in like-kind exchanges. It also altered the tax treatment of foreign earnings of US multinational corporations by switching from a global to a territorial tax system. The Act also scaled back the benefit extended to municipal bonds by disallowing advanced refunding, as well as repealing tax credit bonds.

---

[2] Gross income does, however, include transfer payments associated with past employment, such as Social Security benefits.

[3] In the case of individuals who hold "passive" equity interests in businesses, the pro-rata shares of sales and expense deductions reportable in a year are limited. A passive business activity is defined generally to be one in which the holder of the interest, usually a partnership interest, does not actively perform managerial or other participatory functions. The taxpayer may generally report no larger deductions for a year than will reduce taxable income from such activities to zero. Deductions in excess of the limitation may be taken in subsequent years, or when the interest is liquidated. In addition, costs of earning income may be limited under the Alternative Minimum Tax.

Table 13–1.   ESTIMATES OF TOTAL INCOME TAX EXPENDITURES FOR FISCAL YEARS 2017-2027

(In millions of dollars)

	Total from corporations and individuals											
	2017	2018	2019	2020	2021	2022	2023	2024	2025	2026	2027	2018–2027
National Defense:												
1 Exclusion of benefits and allowances to armed forces personnel	12,400	12,830	11,640	11,680	12,040	12,520	13,040	13,590	14,190	14,820	15,490	131,840
International affairs:												
2 Exclusion of income earned abroad by U.S. citizens	6,600	6,930	7,280	7,640	8,020	8,420	8,840	9,290	9,750	10,240	10,750	87,160
3 Exclusion of certain allowances for Federal employees abroad	1,370	1,430	1,510	1,580	1,660	1,740	1,830	1,920	2,020	2,120	2,230	18,040
4 Inventory property sales source rules exception	3,320	3,570	3,840	4,170	4,480	4,760	5,070	5,410	5,780	6,180	6,640	49,900
5 Deferral of income from controlled foreign corporations (normal tax method)	107,200	112,560	118,190	124,100	130,310	136,820	143,660	150,850	158,390	166,310	174,620	1,415,810
6 Deferred taxes for financial firms on certain income earned overseas	16,080	16,880	17,730	18,620	19,550	20,520	21,550	22,630	23,760	24,950	26,190	212,380
General science, space, and technology:												
7 Expensing of research and experimentation expenditures (normal tax method)	8,330	8,340	9,140	10,100	10,910	11,640	12,310	13,040	13,820	14,660	15,540	119,500
8 Credit for increasing research activities	11,500	12,250	13,010	13,820	14,680	15,600	16,580	17,630	18,730	19,900	21,140	163,340
Energy:												
9 Expensing of exploration and development costs, fuels ..	-650	-290	-30	120	200	260	290	290	300	350	370	1,860
10 Excess of percentage over cost depletion, fuels	440	550	600	640	700	830	990	1,110	1,210	1,360	1,510	9,500
11 Exception from passive loss limitation for working interests in oil and gas properties	20	20	20	20	20	30	30	30	30	30	30	260
12 Capital gains treatment of royalties on coal	140	160	150	140	150	150	160	160	170	180	190	1,610
13 Exclusion of interest on energy facility bonds	10	10	10	10	10	10	10	30	30	30	30	180
14 Enhanced oil recovery credit	270	350	400	450	440	460	500	530	510	490	440	4,570
15 Energy production credit [1]	1,590	2,230	2,870	3,430	3,880	4,280	4,600	4,790	4,850	4,750	4,440	40,120
16 Marginal wells credit	70	110	70	30	30	40	100	140	180	210	230	1,140
17 Energy investment credit [1]	1,850	3,410	3,470	3,330	3,330	2,710	1,630	670	80	-120	-150	18,360
18 Alcohol fuel credits [2]	20	0	0	0	0	0	0	0	0	0	0	0
19 Bio-Diesel and small agri-biodiesel producer tax credits [3]	40	0	0	0	0	0	0	0	0	0	0	0
20 Tax credits for clean-fuel burning vehicles and refueling property	590	680	670	490	360	330	280	240	180	130	100	3,460
21 Exclusion of utility conservation subsidies	470	490	520	540	570	590	620	650	680	710	750	6,120
22 Credit for holding clean renewable energy bonds [4]	70	70	70	70	70	70	70	70	70	70	70	700
23 Deferral of gain from dispositions of transmission property to implement FERC restructuring policy	-190	-270	-210	-190	-150	-120	-70	-20	0	0	0	-1,030
24 Credit for investment in clean coal facilities	140	110	100	250	320	190	20	-20	-10	-10	-10	940
25 Temporary 50% expensing for equipment used in the refining of liquid fuels	-1,380	-1,140	-930	-740	-560	-370	-180	-40	0	0	0	-3,960
26 Natural gas distribution pipelines treated as 15-year property	140	150	150	150	120	60	-20	-100	-190	-270	-320	-270
27 Amortize all geological and geophysical expenditures over 2 years	70	60	70	70	70	80	70	60	40	40	50	610
28 Allowance of deduction for certain energy efficient commercial building property	30	-10	-30	-30	-30	-30	-30	-30	-30	-30	-30	-280
29 Credit for construction of new energy efficient homes	170	70	10	0	0	0	0	0	0	0	0	80
30 Credit for energy efficiency improvements to existing homes	290	0	0	0	0	0	0	0	0	0	0	0
31 Credit for residential energy efficient property	1,430	1,380	1,360	1,250	1,060	530	120	20	0	0	0	5,720
32 Qualified energy conservation bonds [5]	30	30	30	30	30	30	30	30	30	30	30	300
33 Advanced Energy Property Credit	50	0	-20	-20	-10	-10	0	0	0	0	0	-60
34 Advanced nuclear power production credit	0	0	170	440	550	550	550	550	550	550	550	4,460
35 Reduced tax rate for nuclear decommissioning funds	210	230	240	260	270	280	290	310	320	340	350	2,890
Natural resources and environment:												
36 Expensing of exploration and development costs, nonfuel minerals	40	50	50	50	50	50	50	50	50	50	50	500
37 Excess of percentage over cost depletion, nonfuel minerals	140	140	150	150	150	150	150	150	140	140	140	1,460
38 Exclusion of interest on bonds for water, sewage, and hazardous waste facilities	420	410	420	420	450	500	540	580	610	650	680	5,260

Table 13–1. ESTIMATES OF TOTAL INCOME TAX EXPENDITURES FOR FISCAL YEARS 2017–2027—Continued

(In millions of dollars)

		Total from corporations and individuals											
		2017	2018	2019	2020	2021	2022	2023	2024	2025	2026	2027	2018–2027
39	Capital gains treatment of certain timber income	140	160	150	140	150	150	160	160	170	180	190	1,610
40	Expensing of multiperiod timber growing costs	340	350	350	360	370	400	400	410	410	420	420	3,890
41	Tax incentives for preservation of historic structures	500	510	520	530	540	550	560	570	590	600	610	5,580
42	Industrial CO_2 capture and sequestration tax credit	190	200	200	0	0	0	0	0	0	0	0	400
43	Deduction for endangered species recovery expenditures	30	30	30	40	50	50	50	50	70	70	80	520
Agriculture:													
44	Expensing of certain capital outlays	190	200	210	220	240	250	260	270	280	290	300	2,520
45	Expensing of certain multiperiod production costs	310	320	330	340	350	370	390	410	420	440	450	3,820
46	Treatment of loans forgiven for solvent farmers	40	50	50	50	50	50	60	60	60	60	70	560
47	Capital gains treatment of certain income	1,360	1,550	1,470	1,450	1,480	1,520	1,580	1,640	1,720	1,800	1,890	16,100
48	Income averaging for farmers	140	150	160	170	180	180	190	200	210	220	230	1,890
49	Deferral of gain on sale of farm refiners	20	20	20	20	20	20	20	20	20	30	30	220
50	Expensing of reforestation expenditures	60	50	60	60	60	70	70	80	80	80	80	690
Commerce and housing:													
	Financial institutions and insurance:												
51	Exemption of credit union income	2,918	2,901	3,053	3,113	3,246	3,450	3,648	3,839	3,967	4,170	4,372	35,759
52	Exclusion of life insurance death benefits	14,750	15,450	16,290	17,210	18,500	19,810	20,970	22,070	23,220	24,420	25,560	203,500
53	Exemption or special alternative tax for small property and casualty insurance companies	50	50	60	60	60	60	70	70	80	80	80	670
54	Tax exemption of insurance income earned by tax-exempt organizations	720	750	790	840	890	920	950	980	1,000	1,030	1,060	9,210
55	Small life insurance company deduction	30	30	30	30	40	40	40	40	40	40	50	380
56	Exclusion of interest spread of financial institutions	160	240	280	290	300	310	320	330	340	350	360	3,120
	Housing:												
57	Exclusion of interest on owner-occupied mortgage subsidy bonds	1,150	1,120	1,150	1,160	1,230	1,360	1,490	1,620	1,710	1,790	1,860	14,490
58	Exclusion of interest on rental housing bonds	1,060	1,040	1,070	1,080	1,140	1,260	1,370	1,490	1,580	1,650	1,710	13,390
59	Deductibility of mortgage interest on owner-occupied homes	65,600	69,130	74,510	81,330	89,030	96,840	104,490	111,810	118,900	125,560	131,630	1,003,230
60	Deductibility of State and local property tax on owner-occupied homes	33,710	35,790	38,190	40,920	43,750	46,600	49,550	52,700	55,940	59,230	62,680	485,350
61	Deferral of income from installment sales	1,590	1,760	1,700	1,690	1,730	1,770	1,830	1,900	1,970	2,050	2,140	18,540
62	Capital gains exclusion on home sales	43,220	43,870	44,550	45,380	46,160	46,870	47,710	48,630	49,500	50,370	51,280	474,320
63	Exclusion of net imputed rental income	121,350	126,000	131,110	136,680	142,590	148,830	155,330	162,180	169,480	177,100	185,370	1,534,670
64	Exception from passive loss rules for $25,000 of rental loss	7,410	7,710	8,060	8,390	8,730	9,080	9,440	9,750	10,100	10,490	10,860	92,610
65	Credit for low-income housing investments	8,310	8,410	8,960	9,090	9,270	9,480	9,720	9,990	10,270	10,600	10,920	96,710
66	Accelerated depreciation on rental housing (normal tax method)	2,090	2,680	3,510	4,370	5,050	5,860	6,660	7,410	8,130	8,810	9,470	61,950
67	Discharge of mortgage indebtedness	310	0	0	0	0	0	0	0	0	0	0	0
	Commerce:												
68	Discharge of business indebtedness	–70	0	10	0	10	30	40	40	40	40	50	260
69	Exceptions from imputed interest rules	60	60	60	70	70	80	80	80	90	90	100	780
70	Treatment of qualified dividends	27,550	29,130	30,700	32,460	34,420	36,580	38,940	41,500	44,310	47,290	50,440	385,770
71	Capital gains (except agriculture, timber, iron ore, and coal)	101,510	115,910	109,880	107,970	110,230	113,500	117,650	122,620	128,280	134,450	141,100	1,201,590
72	Capital gains exclusion of small corporation stock	790	1,020	1,240	1,400	1,520	1,630	1,730	1,830	1,900	1,980	2,050	16,300
73	Step-up basis of capital gains at death	37,910	38,710	39,560	40,160	40,560	41,240	41,860	42,620	43,230	43,820	44,540	416,300
74	Carryover basis of capital gains on gifts	5,190	4,840	4,670	4,560	4,530	4,530	4,560	4,640	4,700	4,730	4,780	46,540
75	Ordinary income treatment of loss from small business corporation stock sale	70	80	80	80	80	80	90	90	90	100	100	870
76	Deferral of gains from like-kind exchanges	7,690	8,080	8,500	8,920	9,360	9,830	10,320	10,840	11,380	11,940	12,490	101,660
77	Depreciation of buildings other than rental housing (normal tax method)	–8,800	–8,970	–9,570	–10,250	–10,770	–11,360	–11,990	–12,690	–13,130	–13,510	–13,980	–116,220
78	Accelerated depreciation of machinery and equipment (normal tax method)	44,300	36,740	26,380	–9,310	–9,550	5,100	14,730	23,590	31,120	37,050	42,050	197,900
79	Expensing of certain small investments (normal tax method)	3,410	3,400	3,710	7,540	7,910	6,970	6,740	6,700	6,770	7,020	7,230	63,990

Table 13–1. ESTIMATES OF TOTAL INCOME TAX EXPENDITURES FOR FISCAL YEARS 2017–2027—Continued

(In millions of dollars)

		Total from corporations and individuals											
		2017	2018	2019	2020	2021	2022	2023	2024	2025	2026	2027	2018–2027
80	Graduated corporation income tax rate (normal tax method)	1,550	1,510	1,440	1,430	1,350	1,330	1,280	1,250	1,180	1,180	1,150	13,100
81	Exclusion of interest on small issue bonds	140	150	140	140	160	180	190	200	220	220	240	1,840
82	Deduction for US production activities	13,520	14,150	14,790	15,500	16,280	17,090	17,950	18,850	19,790	20,790	21,830	177,020
83	Special rules for certain film and TV production	200	110	60	30	0	0	0	0	0	0	0	200
Transportation:													
84	Tonnage tax	80	80	90	90	90	100	100	110	110	120	130	1,020
85	Deferral of tax on shipping companies	20	20	20	20	20	20	20	20	20	20	20	200
86	Exclusion of reimbursed employee parking expenses	3,202	3,319	3,452	3,582	3,731	3,862	3,971	4,117	4,257	4,404	4,571	39,266
87	Exclusion for employer-provided transit passes	1,123	1,192	1,270	1,355	1,446	1,532	1,613	1,719	1,819	1,934	2,054	15,934
88	Tax credit for certain expenditures for maintaining railroad tracks	60	0	0	0	0	0	0	0	0	0	0	0
89	Exclusion of interest on bonds for Highway Projects and rail-truck transfer facilities	200	190	170	170	160	160	140	140	130	130	120	1,510
Community and regional development:													
90	Investment credit for rehabilitation of structures (other than historic)	20	20	20	20	20	20	20	20	20	20	20	200
91	Exclusion of interest for airport, dock, and similar bonds	660	650	660	680	720	790	860	930	990	1,040	1,080	8,400
92	Exemption of certain mutuals' and cooperatives' income	150	150	150	160	160	160	170	170	180	180	190	1,670
93	Empowerment zones	110	50	30	30	10	10	10	0	0	0	0	140
94	New markets tax credit	1,460	1,410	1,320	1,280	1,210	1,090	880	570	290	80	–120	8,010
95	Credit to holders of Gulf Tax Credit Bonds.	240	250	270	300	320	350	380	400	420	430	440	3,560
96	Recovery Zone Bonds [6]	130	140	150	160	180	190	210	220	230	240	250	1,970
97	Tribal Economic Development Bonds	40	40	40	50	50	60	60	70	70	70	80	590
Education, training, employment, and social services:													
	Education:													
98	Exclusion of scholarship and fellowship income (normal tax method)	3,300	3,410	3,490	3,650	3,800	3,970	4,140	4,310	4,500	4,690	4,890	40,850
99	Tax credits and deductions for postsecondary education expenses [7]	16,460	16,360	16,320	16,310	16,290	16,190	16,180	16,170	16,120	16,020	15,980	161,940
100	Education Individual Retirement Accounts	30	30	40	40	40	40	40	40	30	30	30	360
101	Deductibility of student-loan interest	2,340	2,360	2,390	2,500	2,510	2,520	2,610	2,610	2,630	2,650	2,670	25,450
102	Qualified tuition programs	1,950	2,140	2,330	2,530	2,730	2,940	3,150	3,380	3,600	3,830	4,070	30,700
103	Exclusion of interest on student-loan bonds	370	370	370	380	400	440	480	520	550	580	600	4,690
104	Exclusion of interest on bonds for private nonprofit educational facilities	2,250	2,200	2,260	2,280	2,410	2,660	2,900	3,160	3,330	3,510	3,640	28,350
105	Credit for holders of zone academy bonds [8]	170	180	170	150	130	110	90	80	60	50	50	1,070
106	Exclusion of interest on savings bonds redeemed to finance educational expenses	30	30	30	30	40	40	40	40	50	50	50	400
107	Parental personal exemption for students age 19 or over	9,600	9,500	9,490	9,500	9,540	9,590	9,630	9,670	9,700	9,770	9,940	96,330
108	Deductibility of charitable contributions (education)	5,480	5,890	6,330	6,730	7,100	7,490	7,860	8,250	8,630	9,000	9,370	76,650
109	Exclusion of employer-provided educational assistance	900	940	990	1,040	1,100	1,150	1,210	1,270	1,340	1,400	1,480	11,920
110	Special deduction for teacher expenses	200	210	200	210	250	250	250	260	260	260	270	2,420
111	Discharge of student loan indebtedness	100	100	100	110	110	110	110	120	120	120	120	1,120
112	Qualified school construction bonds [9]	650	650	650	650	650	650	650	650	650	650	650	6,500
	Training, employment, and social services:													
113	Work opportunity tax credit	1,320	1,340	1,370	990	490	310	230	180	130	100	70	5,210
114	Employer provided child care exclusion	900	900	940	970	1,000	1,030	1,060	1,100	1,140	1,180	1,220	10,540
115	Employer-provided child care credit	10	10	10	10	10	10	10	10	10	10	10	100
116	Assistance for adopted foster children	590	620	660	690	730	780	820	860	910	950	1,000	8,020
117	Adoption credit and exclusion	620	620	650	620	640	690	690	710	690	710	720	6,740
118	Exclusion of employee meals and lodging (other than military)	4,830	4,990	5,150	5,290	5,440	5,590	5,750	5,910	6,060	6,220	6,380	56,780
119	Credit for child and dependent care expenses	4,600	4,690	4,790	4,890	4,960	5,060	5,140	5,220	5,300	5,370	5,440	50,860
120	Credit for disabled access expenditures	10	10	10	10	10	10	10	10	10	10	10	100
121	Deductibility of charitable contributions, other than education and health	47,760	51,720	55,030	58,590	61,930	65,250	68,510	71,820	75,090	78,270	81,870	668,080
122	Exclusion of certain foster care payments	490	510	530	550	570	590	610	620	640	660	680	5,960

Table 13-1. ESTIMATES OF TOTAL INCOME TAX EXPENDITURES FOR FISCAL YEARS 2017–2027—Continued

(In millions of dollars)

		Total from corporations and individuals											
		2017	2018	2019	2020	2021	2022	2023	2024	2025	2026	2027	2018–2027
123	Exclusion of parsonage allowances	920	970	1,021	1,075	1,132	1,192	1,255	1,322	1,392	1,465	1,543	12,367
124	Indian employment credit	40	20	20	20	20	10	10	10	10	10	10	140
125	Credit for employer differential wage payments	0	0	10	10	10	20	20	20	20	20	20	150
Health:													
126	Exclusion of employer contributions for medical insurance premiums and medical care [10]	214,280	227,880	242,880	257,390	273,180	291,180	309,500	328,620	349,300	370,360	393,430	3,043,720
127	Self-employed medical insurance premiums	8,140	8,170	7,750	8,010	8,460	8,830	9,220	9,640	10,110	10,610	11,170	91,970
128	Medical Savings Accounts / Health Savings Accounts	8,240	9,400	10,650	11,730	12,750	13,820	14,830	15,770	16,720	17,700	18,730	142,100
129	Deductibility of medical expenses	9,720	10,030	10,870	11,850	12,840	13,790	14,790	15,830	16,910	18,090	19,400	144,400
130	Exclusion of interest on hospital construction bonds	3,380	3,310	3,400	3,430	3,630	4,000	4,370	4,740	5,010	5,260	5,470	42,620
131	Refundable Premium Assistance Tax Credit [11]	5,630	6,310	7,100	7,740	8,380	8,910	9,370	10,040	10,590	11,390	12,140	91,970
132	Credit for employee health insurance expenses of small business [12]	90	80	70	50	30	20	10	10	10	10	10	300
133	Deductibility of charitable contributions (health)	5,120	5,530	5,960	6,350	6,710	7,080	7,430	7,790	8,150	8,500	8,860	72,360
134	Tax credit for orphan drug research	2,280	2,760	3,340	4,030	4,880	5,900	7,140	8,630	10,450	12,630	15,290	75,050
135	Special Blue Cross/Blue Shield tax benefits	590	610	630	670	700	740	780	820	870	910	960	7,690
136	Tax credit for health insurance purchased by certain displaced and retired individuals [13]	30	20	10	0	0	0	0	0	0	0	0	30
137	Distributions from retirement plans for premiums for health and long-term care insurance	460	480	500	520	540	560	580	600	620	650	670	5,720
Income security:													
138	Child credit [14]	24,340	24,270	23,960	23,580	23,140	22,690	22,270	21,860	21,410	20,980	20,610	224,770
139	Exclusion of railroad retirement (Social Security equivalent) benefits	290	280	280	270	260	250	240	220	210	190	170	2,370
140	Exclusion of workers' compensation benefits	9,970	10,040	10,110	10,180	10,250	10,320	10,390	10,470	10,540	10,610	10,690	103,600
141	Exclusion of public assistance benefits (normal tax method)	590	600	620	640	670	680	700	730	740	750	660	6,790
142	Exclusion of special benefits for disabled coal miners	20	20	20	20	20	10	10	10	10	10	10	140
143	Exclusion of military disability pensions	170	180	180	190	190	200	200	210	210	220	220	2,000
	Net exclusion of pension contributions and earnings:												
144	Defined benefit employer plans	76,091	76,998	77,341	78,453	77,081	75,678	73,516	71,376	68,657	65,592	61,673	726,365
145	Defined contribution employer plans	69,440	71,270	80,480	87,010	89,310	95,400	112,200	122,030	126,140	130,240	137,820	1,051,900
146	Individual Retirement Accounts	17,320	19,110	20,630	22,180	23,790	25,460	27,100	28,150	29,080	29,880	30,640	256,020
147	Low and moderate income savers credit	1,440	1,470	1,470	1,460	1,440	1,440	1,440	1,440	1,420	1,450	1,430	14,460
148	Self-Employed plans	28,460	26,980	30,010	33,390	36,930	40,280	44,000	48,070	52,400	57,060	62,170	431,290
	Exclusion of other employee benefits:												
149	Premiums on group term life insurance	3,350	3,140	3,250	3,370	3,500	3,630	3,770	3,910	4,070	4,230	4,390	37,260
150	Premiums on accident and disability insurance	330	330	330	330	340	340	340	350	350	350	350	3,410
151	Income of trusts to finance supplementary unemployment benefits	20	30	40	40	50	50	50	50	60	60	60	490
152	Income of trusts to finance voluntary employee benefits associations	1,180	1,240	1,290	1,350	1,420	1,480	1,550	1,630	1,710	1,780	1,860	15,310
153	Special ESOP rules	2,080	2,140	2,210	2,280	2,360	2,430	2,510	2,580	2,660	2,740	2,820	24,730
154	Additional deduction for the blind	30	30	30	30	40	40	40	50	50	60	60	430
155	Additional deduction for the elderly	3,470	3,770	4,050	4,380	4,780	5,090	5,470	5,850	6,290	6,810	7,380	53,870
156	Tax credit for the elderly and disabled	10	10	10	0	0	0	0	0	0	0	0	20
157	Deductibility of casualty losses	330	350	380	400	430	460	500	530	560	590	630	4,830
158	Earned income tax credit [15]	1,760	1,810	3,960	4,100	2,060	2,150	2,250	2,370	2,500	2,570	2,700	26,470
Social Security:													
	Exclusion of social security benefits:												
159	Social Security benefits for retired and disabled workers and spouses, dependents and survivors	34,500	36,110	37,660	39,430	41,430	43,840	46,830	48,780	50,130	53,690	57,850	455,750
160	Credit for certain employer contributions to social security	1,040	1,080	1,130	1,190	1,250	1,310	1,380	1,440	1,520	1,590	1,680	13,570
Veterans benefits and services:													
161	Exclusion of veterans death benefits and disability compensation	7,920	8,620	9,190	9,560	9,910	10,290	10,680	11,090	11,520	11,960	12,440	105,260
162	Exclusion of veterans pensions	480	510	540	560	580	610	630	660	690	720	750	6,250

Table 13–1. ESTIMATES OF TOTAL INCOME TAX EXPENDITURES FOR FISCAL YEARS 2017–2027—Continued

(In millions of dollars)

	Total from corporations and individuals											
	2017	2018	2019	2020	2021	2022	2023	2024	2025	2026	2027	2018–2027
163 Exclusion of GI bill benefits	1,740	1,830	1,910	2,010	2,110	2,220	2,330	2,440	2,570	2,700	2,840	22,960
164 Exclusion of interest on veterans housing bonds	10	10	10	10	10	10	10	30	30	30	30	180
General purpose fiscal assistance:												
165 Exclusion of interest on public purpose State and local bonds	28,560	27,920	28,650	28,950	30,680	33,830	36,880	40,060	42,290	44,470	46,160	359,890
166 Build America Bonds [16]	0	0	0	0	0	0	0	0	0	0	0	0
167 Deductibility of nonbusiness State and local taxes other than on owner-occupied homes	70,420	74,980	80,190	86,220	91,900	97,460	103,350	109,610	116,020	122,310	128,980	1,011,020
Interest:												
168 Deferral of interest on U.S. savings bonds	960	950	940	930	930	920	910	900	890	880	890	9,140
Addendum: Aid to State and local governments:												
Deductibility of:												
Property taxes on owner-occupied homes	33,710	35,790	38,190	40,920	43,750	46,600	49,550	52,700	55,940	59,230	62,680	485,350
Nonbusiness State and local taxes other than on owner-occupied homes	70,420	74,980	80,190	86,220	91,900	97,460	103,350	109,610	116,020	122,310	128,980	1,011,020
Exclusion of interest on State and local bonds for:												
Public purposes	28,560	27,920	28,650	28,950	30,680	33,830	36,880	40,060	42,290	44,470	46,160	359,890
Energy facilities	10	10	10	10	10	10	10	30	30	30	30	180
Water, sewage, and hazardous waste disposal facilities	420	410	420	420	450	500	540	580	610	650	680	5,260
Small-issues	140	150	140	140	160	180	190	200	220	220	240	1,840
Owner-occupied mortgage subsidies	1,150	1,120	1,150	1,160	1,230	1,360	1,490	1,620	1,710	1,790	1,860	14,490
Rental housing	1,060	1,040	1,070	1,080	1,140	1,260	1,370	1,490	1,580	1,650	1,710	13,390
Airports, docks, and similar facilities	660	650	660	680	720	790	860	930	990	1,040	1,080	8,400
Student loans	370	370	370	380	400	440	480	520	550	580	600	4,690
Private nonprofit educational facilities	2,250	2,200	2,260	2,280	2,410	2,660	2,900	3,160	3,330	3,510	3,640	28,350
Hospital construction	3,380	3,310	3,400	3,430	3,630	4,000	4,370	4,740	5,010	5,260	5,470	42,620
Veterans' housing	10	10	10	10	10	10	10	30	30	30	30	180

[1] Firms can take an energy grant in lieu of the energy production credit or the energy investment credit for facilities whose construction began in 2009, 2010, or 2011. The effect of the grant on outlays (in millions of dollars) is as follows: 2017 $1,100; 2018 $50; and $0 thereafter.

[2] The alternative fuel mixture credit results in a reduction in excise tax receipts (in millions of dollars) as follows: 2017 $420 and $0 thereafter.

[3] In addition, the biodiesel producer tax credit results in a reduction in excise tax receipts (in millions of dollars) as follows: 2017 $2,090 and $0 thereafter.

[4] In addition, the credit for holding clean renewable energy bonds has outlay effects of (in millions of dollars) : 2017 $40; 2018 $40; 2019 $40; 2020 $40; 2021 $40; 2022 $40; 2023 $40; 2024 $40; 2025, $40; 2026 $40; and 2027 $40.

[5] In addition, the qualified energy conservation bonds have outlay effects of (in millions of dollars): 2017 $40; 2018 $40; 2019 $40; 2020 $40; 2021 $40; 2022 $40; 2023 $40; 2024 $40; 2025, $40; 2026 $40; and 2027 $40.

[6] In addition, recovery zone bonds have outlay effects (in millions of dollars) as follows: 2017 $290; 2018 $290; 2019 $290; 2020 $290; 2021 $290; 2022 $290; 2023 $290; 2024 $290; 2025, $290; 2026 $290; and 202 $290.

[7] In addition, the tax credits and deductions for postsecondary education expenses have outlay effects of (in millions of dollars): 2017 $5,770; 2018 $5,690; 2019 $5,570; 2020 $5,520; 2021 $5,460; 2022 $5,410; 2023 $5,360; 2024 $5,310; 2025 $5,240; 2026 $5,170; and 2027 $5,100.

[8] In addition, the credit for holders of zone academy bonds has outlay effects of (in millions of dollars) : 2017 $60; 2018 $60; 2019 $60; 2020 $60; 2021 $60; 2022 $60; 2023 $60; 2024 $60; 2025 $60; 2026 $60; and 2027 $60.

[9] In addition, the provision for school construction bonds has outlay effects of (in millions of dollars) : 2017 $740; 2018 $795; 2019 $795; 2020 $795; 2021 $795; 2022 $795; 2023 $795; 2024 $795; 2025 $795; 2026 $795; and 2027 $795.

[10] In addition, the employer contributions for health have effects on payroll tax receipts (in millions of dollars) as follows: 2017 $127,140; 2018 $133,530; 2019 $140,060; 2020 $146,970; 2021 $155,010; 2022 $164,100; 2023 $173,140; 2024 $182,640; 2025 $192,960; 2026 $203,240; and 2027 $214,700.

[11] In addition, the premium assistance credit provision has outlay effects (in millions of dollars) as follows : 2017 $29,730; 2018 $31,890; 2019 $33,840; 2020 $35,720; 2021 $37,770; 2022 $40,010; 2023 $42,110; 2024 $44,400; 2025 $46,790; 2026 $49,340; and 2027 $51,980.

[12] In addition, the small business credit provision has outlay effects (in millions of dollars) as follows : 2017 $20; 2018 $20; 2019 $10; 2020 $10; 2021 $10; 2022 $10; and $0 thereafter.

[13] In addition, the effect of the health coverage tax credit on receipts has outlay effects of (in millions of dollars) 2017 $20; 2018 $30; 2019 $30; 2020 $10; and $0 thereafter.

[14] In addition, the effect of the child tax credit on receipts has outlay effects of (in millions of dollars) : 2017 $29,980; 2018 $30,000; 2019 $30,010; 2020 $30,010; 2021 $30,270; 2022 $30,390; 2023 $30,540; 2024 $30,680; 2025 $30,840; 2026 $31,040; and 2027 $31,150.

[15] In addition, the earned income tax credit on receipts has outlay effects of (in millions of dollars) : 2017 $62,070; 2018 $67,870; 2019 $ 67,120; 2020 $68,500; 2021 $72,630; 2022 $74,420; 2023 $76,390; 2024 $78,260; 2025 $80,240; 2026 $82,240; and 2027 $84,150.

[16] In addition, the Build America Bonds have outlay effects of (in millions of dollars) : 2017 $3,610; 2018 $3,610; 2019 $3,610; 2020 $3,610; 2021 $3,610; 2022 $3,610; 2023 $3,610; 2024 $3,610; 2025, $3,610; 2026 $3,610; and 2027 $3,610.

Note: Provisions with estimates denoted normal tax method have no revenue loss under the reference tax law method.

All estimates have been rounded to the nearest $10 million. Provisions with estimates that rounded to zero in each year are not included in the table.

Table 13–2A. ESTIMATES OF TOTAL CORPORATE INCOME TAX EXPENDITURES FOR FISCAL YEARS 2017-2027

(In millions of dollars)

						Total from corporations						
	2017	2018	2019	2020	2021	2022	2023	2024	2025	2026	2027	2018–2027
National Defense:												
1 Exclusion of benefits and allowances to armed forces personnel	0	0	0	0	0	0	0	0	0	0	0	0
International affairs:												
2 Exclusion of income earned abroad by U.S. citizens	0	0	0	0	0	0	0	0	0	0	0	0
3 Exclusion of certain allowances for Federal employees abroad	0	0	0	0	0	0	0	0	0	0	0	0
4 Inventory property sales source rules exception	3,320	3,570	3,840	4,170	4,480	4,760	5,070	5,410	5,780	6,180	6,640	49,900
5 Deferral of income from controlled foreign corporations (normal tax method)	107,200	112,560	118,190	124,100	130,310	136,820	143,660	150,850	158,390	166,310	174,620	1,415,810
6 Deferred taxes for financial firms on certain income earned overseas	16,080	16,880	17,730	18,620	19,550	20,520	21,550	22,630	23,760	24,950	26,190	212,380
General science, space, and technology:												
7 Expensing of research and experimentation expenditures (normal tax method)	7,620	7,640	8,420	9,290	10,040	10,700	11,320	11,990	12,710	13,480	14,290	109,880
8 Credit for increasing research activities ...	10,520	11,160	11,840	12,560	13,330	14,140	15,010	15,940	16,910	17,940	19,020	147,850
Energy:												
9 Expensing of exploration and development costs,fuels	−470	−210	−20	90	150	190	210	210	220	260	270	1,370
10 Excess of percentage over cost depletion, fuels	350	440	480	510	560	660	790	890	970	1,090	1,210	7,600
11 Exception from passive loss limitation for working interests in oil and gas properties	0	0	0	0	0	0	0	0	0	0	0	0
12 Capital gains treatment of royalties on coal	0	0	0	0	0	0	0	0	0	0	0	0
13 Exclusion of interest on energy facility bonds	0	0	0	0	0	0	0	10	10	10	10	40
14 Enhanced oil recovery credit	220	280	320	360	350	370	400	420	410	390	350	3,650
15 Energy production credit [1]	1,190	1,670	2,150	2,570	2,910	3,210	3,450	3,590	3,640	3,560	3,330	30,080
16 Marginal wells credit	20	30	20	10	10	10	30	40	50	60	70	330
17 Energy investment credit [1]	1,390	2,560	2,600	2,500	2,500	2,030	1,220	500	60	−90	−110	13,770
18 Alcohol fuel credits [2]	0	0	0	0	0	0	0	0	0	0	0	0
19 Bio-Diesel and small agri-biodiesel producer tax credits [3]	10	0	0	0	0	0	0	0	0	0	0	0
20 Tax credits for clean-fuel burning vehicles and refueling property	190	210	180	120	90	80	60	40	30	10	10	830
21 Exclusion of utility conservation subsidies	30	30	30	30	30	30	30	30	30	30	30	300
22 Credit for holding clean renewable energy bonds [4]	20	20	20	20	20	20	20	20	20	20	20	200
23 Deferral of gain from dispositions of transmission property to implement FERC restructuring policy	−190	−270	−210	−190	−150	−120	−70	−20	0	0	0	−1,030
24 Credit for investment in clean coal facilities	130	100	90	230	290	170	20	−20	−10	−10	−10	850
25 Temporary 50% expensing for equipment used in the refining of liquid fuels	−1,380	−1,140	−930	−740	−560	−370	−180	−40	0	0	0	−3,960
26 Natural gas distribution pipelines treated as 15-year property	140	150	150	150	120	60	−20	−100	−190	−270	−320	−270
27 Amortize all geological and geophysical expenditures over 2 years	50	40	50	50	50	60	50	40	30	30	40	440
28 Allowance of deduction for certain energy efficient commercial building property	10	0	−10	−10	−10	−10	−10	−10	−10	−10	−10	−90
29 Credit for construction of new energy efficient homes	50	20	0	0	0	0	0	0	0	0	0	20
30 Credit for energy efficiency improvements to existing homes	0	0	0	0	0	0	0	0	0	0	0	0

Table 13–2A. ESTIMATES OF TOTAL CORPORATE INCOME TAX EXPENDITURES FOR FISCAL YEARS 2017-2027—Continued

(In millions of dollars)

		Total from corporations										
		2017	2018	2019	2020	2021	2022	2023	2024	2025	2026	2027	2018–2027
31	Credit for residential energy efficient property	0	0	0	0	0	0	0	0	0	0	0	0
32	Qualified energy conservation bonds [5]	10	10	10	10	10	10	10	10	10	10	10	100
33	Advanced Energy Property Credit	40	0	–20	–20	–10	–10	0	0	0	0	0	–60
34	Advanced nuclear power production credit	0	0	170	440	550	550	550	550	550	550	550	4,460
35	Reduced tax rate for nuclear decommissioning funds	210	230	240	260	270	280	290	310	320	340	350	2,890
Natural resources and environment:													
36	Expensing of exploration and development costs, nonfuel minerals	40	50	50	50	50	50	50	50	50	50	50	500
37	Excess of percentage over cost depletion, nonfuel minerals	120	120	130	130	130	130	130	130	120	120	120	1,260
38	Exclusion of interest on bonds for water, sewage, and hazardous waste facilities	130	130	130	120	130	140	140	140	140	150	170	1,390
39	Capital gains treatment of certain timber income	0	0	0	0	0	0	0	0	0	0	0	0
40	Expensing of multiperiod timber growing costs	210	220	220	230	230	240	240	250	250	260	260	2,400
41	Tax incentives for preservation of historic structures	430	440	450	460	470	480	490	500	510	520	530	4,850
42	Industrial CO_2 capture and sequestration tax credit	190	200	200	0	0	0	0	0	0	0	0	400
43	Deduction for endangered species recovery expenditures	10	10	10	20	20	20	20	20	30	30	30	210
Agriculture:													
44	Expensing of certain capital outlays	10	10	10	10	20	20	20	20	20	20	20	170
45	Expensing of certain multiperiod production costs	20	20	20	20	20	20	30	30	30	30	30	250
46	Treatment of loans forgiven for solvent farmers	0	0	0	0	0	0	0	0	0	0	0	0
47	Capital gains treatment of certain income	0	0	0	0	0	0	0	0	0	0	0	0
48	Income averaging for farmers	0	0	0	0	0	0	0	0	0	0	0	0
49	Deferral of gain on sale of farm refiners	20	20	20	20	20	20	20	20	20	30	30	220
50	Expensing of reforestation expenditures	20	20	20	20	20	30	30	30	30	30	30	260
Commerce and housing:													
	Financial institutions and insurance:												
51	Exemption of credit union income	2,918	2,901	3,053	3,113	3,246	3,450	3,648	3,839	3,967	4,170	4,372	35,759
52	Exclusion of life insurance death benefits	2,870	2,990	3,130	3,280	3,450	3,620	3,810	4,000	4,200	4,420	4,640	37,540
53	Exemption or special alternative tax for small property and casualty insurance companies	50	50	60	60	60	60	70	70	80	80	80	670
54	Tax exemption of insurance income earned by tax-exempt organizations	720	750	790	840	890	920	950	980	1,000	1,030	1,060	9,210
55	Small life insurance company deduction	30	30	30	30	40	40	40	40	40	40	50	380
56	Exclusion of interest spread of financial institutions	0	0	0	0	0	0	0	0	0	0	0	0
	Housing:												
57	Exclusion of interest on owner-occupied mortgage subsidy bonds	350	360	350	340	350	380	380	400	400	420	460	3,840
58	Exclusion of interest on rental housing bonds	320	340	330	320	330	350	350	370	370	390	420	3,570
59	Deductibility of mortgage interest on owner-occupied homes	0	0	0	0	0	0	0	0	0	0	0	0
60	Deductibility of State and local property tax on owner-occupied homes	0	0	0	0	0	0	0	0	0	0	0	0
61	Deferral of income from installment sales	0	0	0	0	0	0	0	0	0	0	0	0
62	Capital gains exclusion on home sales	0	0	0	0	0	0	0	0	0	0	0	0
63	Exclusion of net imputed rental income	0	0	0	0	0	0	0	0	0	0	0	0

Table 13–2A. ESTIMATES OF TOTAL CORPORATE INCOME TAX EXPENDITURES FOR FISCAL YEARS 2017-2027—Continued

(In millions of dollars)

	Total from corporations											
	2017	2018	2019	2020	2021	2022	2023	2024	2025	2026	2027	2018–2027
64 Exception from passive loss rules for $25,000 of rental loss	0	0	0	0	0	0	0	0	0	0	0	0
65 Credit for low-income housing investments	7,890	7,990	8,510	8,640	8,810	9,010	9,230	9,490	9,760	10,070	10,370	91,880
66 Accelerated depreciation on rental housing (normal tax method)	360	470	580	700	840	990	1,120	1,230	1,350	1,460	1,570	10,310
67 Discharge of mortgage indebtedness												0
Commerce:												
68 Discharge of business indebtedness	0	0	0	0	0	0	0	0	0	0	0	0
69 Exceptions from imputed interest rules	0	0	0	0	0	0	0	0	0	0	0	0
70 Treatment of qualified dividends	0	0	0	0	0	0	0	0	0	0	0	0
71 Capital gains (except agriculture, timber, iron ore, and coal)	0	0	0	0	0	0	0	0	0	0	0	0
72 Capital gains exclusion of small corporation stock	0	0	0	0	0	0	0	0	0	0	0	0
73 Step-up basis of capital gains at death	0	0	0	0	0	0	0	0	0	0	0	0
74 Carryover basis of capital gains on gifts	0	0	0	0	0	0	0	0	0	0	0	0
75 Ordinary income treatment of loss from small business corporation stock sale	0	0	0	0	0	0	0	0	0	0	0	0
76 Deferral of gains from like-kind exchanges	6,000	6,310	6,630	6,960	7,300	7,670	8,050	8,460	8,880	9,320	9,750	79,330
77 Depreciation of buildings other than rental housing (normal tax method)	–3,860	–3,960	–4,150	–4,400	–4,660	–4,920	–5,190	–5,480	–5,670	–5,820	–6,020	–50,270
78 Accelerated depreciation of machinery and equipment (normal tax method)	28,810	24,120	17,490	–3,510	–3,390	5,540	11,460	16,960	21,650	25,380	28,500	144,200
79 Expensing of certain small investments (normal tax method)	290	280	290	1,040	1,120	890	790	730	700	710	710	7,260
80 Graduated corporation income tax rate (normal tax method)	1,550	1,510	1,440	1,430	1,350	1,330	1,280	1,250	1,180	1,180	1,150	13,100
81 Exclusion of interest on small issue bonds	40	50	40	40	50	50	50	50	50	50	60	490
82 Deduction for US production activities	9,930	10,400	10,870	11,390	11,960	12,550	13,180	13,840	14,530	15,260	16,020	130,000
83 Special rules for certain film and TV production	160	90	50	20	0	0	0	0	0	0	0	160
Transportation:												
84 Tonnage tax	80	80	90	90	90	100	100	110	110	120	130	1,020
85 Deferral of tax on shipping companies	20	20	20	20	20	20	20	20	20	20	20	200
86 Exclusion of reimbursed employee parking expenses	0	0	0	0	0	0	0	0	0	0	0	0
87 Exclusion for employer-provided transit passes	0	0	0	0	0	0	0	0	0	0	0	0
88 Tax credit for certain expenditures for maintaining railroad tracks	50	0	0	0	0	0	0	0	0	0	0	0
89 Exclusion of interest on bonds for Highway Projects and rail-truck transfer facilities	50	50	40	40	40	40	30	30	30	30	30	360
Community and regional development:												
90 Investment credit for rehabilitation of structures (other than historic)	10	10	10	10	10	10	10	10	10	10	10	100
91 Exclusion of interest for airport, dock, and similar bonds	200	210	200	200	210	220	220	230	230	250	270	2,240
92 Exemption of certain mutuals' and cooperatives'income	150	150	150	160	160	160	170	170	180	180	190	1,670
93 Empowerment zones	50	20	10	10	0	0	0	0	0	0	0	40
94 New markets tax credit	1,430	1,380	1,290	1,250	1,180	1,070	860	550	280	70	–120	7,810
95 Credit to holders of Gulf Tax Credit Bonds.	70	70	70	70	70	70	70	70	70	70	70	700
96 Recovery Zone Bonds [6]	40	40	40	40	40	40	40	40	40	40	40	400
97 Tribal Economic Development Bonds	10	10	10	10	10	10	10	10	10	10	10	100
Education, training, employment, and social services:												

Table 13–2A. ESTIMATES OF TOTAL CORPORATE INCOME TAX EXPENDITURES FOR FISCAL YEARS 2017-2027—Continued

(In millions of dollars)

		Total from corporations										
		2017	2018	2019	2020	2021	2022	2023	2024	2025	2026	2027	2018–2027
	Education:												
98	Exclusion of scholarship and fellowship income (normal tax method)	0	0	0	0	0	0	0	0	0	0	0	0
99	Tax credits and deductions for postsecondary education expenses [7]	0	0	0	0	0	0	0	0	0	0	0	0
100	Education Individual Retirement Accounts	0	0	0	0	0	0	0	0	0	0	0	0
101	Deductibility of student-loan interest	0	0	0	0	0	0	0	0	0	0	0	0
102	Qualified tuition programs	0	0	0	0	0	0	0	0	0	0	0	0
103	Exclusion of interest on student-loan bonds	110	120	110	110	110	120	120	130	130	140	150	1,240
104	Exclusion of interest on bonds for private nonprofit educational facilities	690	710	690	670	690	740	740	780	780	830	900	7,530
105	Credit for holders of zone academy bonds [8]	170	180	170	150	130	110	90	80	60	50	50	1,070
106	Exclusion of interest on savings bonds redeemed to finance educational expenses	0	0	0	0	0	0	0	0	0	0	0	0
107	Parental personal exemption for students age 19 or over	0	0	0	0	0	0	0	0	0	0	0	0
108	Deductibility of charitable contributions (education)	860	900	950	1,000	1,040	1,100	1,150	1,210	1,270	1,330	1,390	11,340
109	Exclusion of employer-provided educational assistance	0	0	0	0	0	0	0	0	0	0	0	0
110	Special deduction for teacher expenses ...	0	0	0	0	0	0	0	0	0	0	0	0
111	Discharge of student loan indebtedness ...	0	0	0	0	0	0	0	0	0	0	0	0
112	Qualified school construction bonds [9]	160	160	160	160	160	160	160	160	160	160	160	1,600
	Training, employment, and social services:												
113	Work opportunity tax credit	1,000	1,020	1,050	730	380	250	190	150	110	80	60	4,020
114	Employer provided child care exclusion ...	0	0	0	0	0	0	0	0	0	0	0	0
115	Employer-provided child care credit	10	10	10	10	10	10	10	10	10	10	10	100
116	Assistance for adopted foster children	0	0	0	0	0	0	0	0	0	0	0	0
117	Adoption credit and exclusion	0	0	0	0	0	0	0	0	0	0	0	0
118	Exclusion of employee meals and lodging (other than military)	0	0	0	0	0	0	0	0	0	0	0	0
119	Credit for child and dependent care expenses	0	0	0	0	0	0	0	0	0	0	0	0
120	Credit for disabled access expenditures	0	0	0	0	0	0	0	0	0	0	0	0
121	Deductibility of charitable contributions, other than education and health	1,800	1,900	1,930	2,010	2,090	2,170	2,250	2,340	2,430	2,530	2,630	22,280
122	Exclusion of certain foster care payments	0	0	0	0	0	0	0	0	0	0	0	0
123	Exclusion of parsonage allowances	0	0	0	0	0	0	0	0	0	0	0	0
124	Indian employment credit	20	10	10	10	10	0	0	0	0	0	0	40
125	Credit for employer differential wage payments	0	0	10	10	10	10	10	10	10	10	10	90
Health:													
126	Exclusion of employer contributions for medical insurance premiums and medical care [10]	0	0	0	0	0	0	0	0	0	0	0	0
127	Self-employed medical insurance premiums	0	0	0	0	0	0	0	0	0	0	0	0
128	Medical Savings Accounts / Health Savings Accounts	0	0	0	0	0	0	0	0	0	0	0	0
129	Deductibility of medical expenses	0	0	0	0	0	0	0	0	0	0	0	0
130	Exclusion of interest on hospital construction bonds	1,030	1,070	1,040	1,010	1,040	1,110	1,120	1,170	1,170	1,240	1,350	11,320
131	Refundable Premium Assistance Tax Credit [11]	0	0	0	0	0	0	0	0	0	0	0	0
132	Credit for employee health insurance expenses of small business [12]	10	10	10	10	0	0	0	0	0	0	0	30

Table 13-2A. ESTIMATES OF TOTAL CORPORATE INCOME TAX EXPENDITURES FOR FISCAL YEARS 2017-2027—Continued

(In millions of dollars)

		Total from corporations											
		2017	2018	2019	2020	2021	2022	2023	2024	2025	2026	2027	2018–2027
133	Deductibility of charitable contributions (health)	0	0	0	0	0	0	0	0	0	0	0	0
134	Tax credit for orphan drug research	2,240	2,710	3,280	3,960	4,790	5,800	7,020	8,490	10,280	12,440	15,060	73,830
135	Special Blue Cross/Blue Shield tax benefits	590	610	630	670	700	740	780	820	870	910	960	7,690
136	Tax credit for health insurance purchased by certain displaced and retired individuals [13]	0	0	0	0	0	0	0	0	0	0	0	0
137	Distributions from retirement plans for premiums for health and long-term care insurance	0	0	0	0	0	0	0	0	0	0	0	0
Income security:													
138	Child credit [14]	0	0	0	0	0	0	0	0	0	0	0	0
139	Exclusion of railroad retirement (Social Security equivalent) benefits	0	0	0	0	0	0	0	0	0	0	0	0
140	Exclusion of workers' compensation benefits	0	0	0	0	0	0	0	0	0	0	0	0
141	Exclusion of public assistance benefits (normal tax method)	0	0	0	0	0	0	0	0	0	0	0	0
142	Exclusion of special benefits for disabled coal miners	0	0	0	0	0	0	0	0	0	0	0	0
143	Exclusion of military disability pensions	0	0	0	0	0	0	0	0	0	0	0	0
	Net exclusion of pension contributions and earnings:												
144	Defined benefit employer plans	0	0	0	0	0	0	0	0	0	0	0	0
145	Defined contribution employer plans	0	0	0	0	0	0	0	0	0	0	0	0
146	Individual Retirement Accounts	0	0	0	0	0	0	0	0	0	0	0	0
147	Low and moderate income savers credit	0	0	0	0	0	0	0	0	0	0	0	0
148	Self-Employed plans	0	0	0	0	0	0	0	0	0	0	0	0
	Exclusion of other employee benefits:												
149	Premiums on group term life insurance	0	0	0	0	0	0	0	0	0	0	0	0
150	Premiums on accident and disability insurance	0	0	0	0	0	0	0	0	0	0	0	0
151	Income of trusts to finance supplementary unemployment benefits	0	0	0	0	0	0	0	0	0	0	0	0
152	Income of trusts to finance voluntary employee benefits associations	0	0	0	0	0	0	0	0	0	0	0	0
153	Special ESOP rules	1,960	2,020	2,080	2,150	2,220	2,290	2,360	2,430	2,510	2,580	2,660	23,300
154	Additional deduction for the blind	0	0	0	0	0	0	0	0	0	0	0	0
155	Additional deduction for the elderly	0	0	0	0	0	0	0	0	0	0	0	0
156	Tax credit for the elderly and disabled	0	0	0	0	0	0	0	0	0	0	0	0
157	Deductibility of casualty losses	0	0	0	0	0	0	0	0	0	0	0	0
158	Earned income tax credit [15]	0	0	0	0	0	0	0	0	0	0	0	0
Social Security:													
	Exclusion of social security benefits:												
159	Social Security benefits for retired and disabled workers and spouses, dependents and survivors	0	0	0	0	0	0	0	0	0	0	0	0
160	Credit for certain employer contributions to social security	490	510	530	560	590	620	650	680	720	750	790	6,400
Veterans benefits and services:													
161	Exclusion of veterans death benefits and disability compensation	0	0	0	0	0	0	0	0	0	0	0	0
162	Exclusion of veterans pensions	0	0	0	0	0	0	0	0	0	0	0	0
163	Exclusion of GI bill benefits	0	0	0	0	0	0	0	0	0	0	0	0
164	Exclusion of interest on veterans housing bonds	0	0	0	0	0	0	0	10	10	10	10	40
General purpose fiscal assistance:													
165	Exclusion of interest on public purpose State and local bonds	8,710	9,020	8,740	8,530	8,800	9,410	9,450	9,900	9,900	10,510	11,370	95,630

Table 13–2A. ESTIMATES OF TOTAL CORPORATE INCOME TAX EXPENDITURES FOR FISCAL YEARS 2017-2027—Continued

(In millions of dollars)

	Total from corporations											
	2017	2018	2019	2020	2021	2022	2023	2024	2025	2026	2027	2018–2027
166 Build America Bonds [16]	0	0	0	0	0	0	0	0	0	0	0	0
167 Deductibility of nonbusiness State and local taxes other than on owner-occupied homes	0	0	0	0	0	0	0	0	0	0	0	0
Interest:												
168 Deferral of interest on U.S. savings bonds	0	0	0	0	0	0	0	0	0	0	0	0
Addendum: Aid to State and local governments:												
Deductibility of:												
Property taxes on owner-occupied homes	0	0	0	0	0	0	0	0	0	0	0	0
Nonbusiness State and local taxes other than on owner-occupied homes	0	0	0	0	0	0	0	0	0	0	0	0
Exclusion of interest on State and local bonds for:												
Public purposes	8,710	9,020	8,740	8,530	8,800	9,410	9,450	9,900	9,900	10,510	11,370	95,630
Energy facilities	0	0	0	0	0	0	0	10	10	10	10	40
Water, sewage, and hazardous waste disposal facilities	130	130	130	120	130	140	140	140	140	150	170	1,390
Small-issues	40	50	40	40	50	50	50	50	50	50	60	490
Owner-occupied mortgage subsidies	350	360	350	340	350	380	380	400	400	420	460	3,840
Rental housing	320	340	330	320	330	350	350	370	370	390	420	3,570
Airports, docks, and similar facilities	200	210	200	200	210	220	220	230	230	250	270	2,240
Student loans	110	120	110	110	110	120	120	130	130	140	150	1,240
Private nonprofit educational facilities	690	710	690	670	690	740	740	780	780	830	900	7,530
Hospital construction	1,030	1,070	1,040	1,010	1,040	1,110	1,120	1,170	1,170	1,240	1,350	11,320
Veterans' housing	0	0	0	0	0	0	0	10	10	10	10	40

See Table 1 footnotes for specific table information

Table 13-2B. ESTIMATES OF TOTAL INDIVIDUAL INCOME TAX EXPENDITURES FOR FISCAL YEARS 2017-2027

(In millions of dollars)

					Total from individuals							
	2017	2018	2019	2020	2021	2022	2023	2024	2025	2026	2027	2018–2027
National Defense:												
1 Exclusion of benefits and allowances to armed forces personnel	12,400	12,830	11,640	11,680	12,040	12,520	13,040	13,590	14,190	14,820	15,490	131,840
International affairs:												
2 Exclusion of income earned abroad by U.S. citizens ...	6,600	6,930	7,280	7,640	8,020	8,420	8,840	9,290	9,750	10,240	10,750	87,160
3 Exclusion of certain allowances for Federal employees abroad	1,370	1,430	1,510	1,580	1,660	1,740	1,830	1,920	2,020	2,120	2,230	18,040
4 Inventory property sales source rules exception	0	0	0	0	0	0	0	0	0	0	0	0
5 Deferral of income from controlled foreign corporations (normal tax method)	0	0	0	0	0	0	0	0	0	0	0	0
6 Deferred taxes for financial firms on certain income earned overseas	0	0	0	0	0	0	0	0	0	0	0	0
General science, space, and technology:												
7 Expensing of research and experimentation expenditures (normal tax method)	710	700	720	810	870	940	990	1,050	1,110	1,180	1,250	9,620
8 Credit for increasing research activities	980	1,090	1,170	1,260	1,350	1,460	1,570	1,690	1,820	1,960	2,120	15,490
Energy:												
9 Expensing of exploration and development costs,fuels	–180	–80	–10	30	50	70	80	80	80	90	100	490
10 Excess of percentage over cost depletion, fuels	90	110	120	130	140	170	200	220	240	270	300	1,900
11 Exception from passive loss limitation for working interests in oil and gas properties	20	20	20	20	20	30	30	30	30	30	30	260
12 Capital gains treatment of royalties on coal	140	160	150	140	150	150	160	160	170	180	190	1,610
13 Exclusion of interest on energy facility bonds	10	10	10	10	10	10	10	20	20	20	20	140
14 Enhanced oil recovery credit	50	70	80	90	90	90	100	110	100	100	90	920
15 Energy production credit [1]	400	560	720	860	970	1,070	1,150	1,200	1,210	1,190	1,110	10,040
16 Marginal wells credit	50	80	50	20	20	30	70	100	130	150	160	810
17 Energy investment credit [1]	460	850	870	830	830	680	410	170	20	–30	–40	4,590
18 Alcohol fuel credits [2]	20	0	0	0	0	0	0	0	0	0	0	0
19 Bio-Diesel and small agri-biodiesel producer tax credits [3]	30	0	0	0	0	0	0	0	0	0	0	0
20 Tax credits for clean-fuel burning vehicles and refueling property	400	470	490	370	270	250	220	200	150	120	90	2,630
21 Exclusion of utility conservation subsidies	440	460	490	510	540	560	590	620	650	680	720	5,820
22 Credit for holding clean renewable energy bonds [4]	50	50	50	50	50	50	50	50	50	50	50	500
23 Deferral of gain from dispositions of transmission property to implement FERC restructuring policy ...	0	0	0	0	0	0	0	0	0	0	0	0
24 Credit for investment in clean coal facilities	10	10	10	20	30	20	0	0	0	0	0	90
25 Temporary 50% expensing for equipment used in the refining of liquid fuels	0	0	0	0	0	0	0	0	0	0	0	0
26 Natural gas distribution pipelines treated as 15-year property	0	0	0	0	0	0	0	0	0	0	0	0
27 Amortize all geological and geophysical expenditures over 2 years	20	20	20	20	20	20	20	20	10	10	10	170
28 Allowance of deduction for certain energy efficient commercial building property	20	–10	–20	–20	–20	–20	–20	–20	–20	–20	–20	–190
29 Credit for construction of new energy efficient homes ...	120	50	10	0	0	0	0	0	0	0	0	60
30 Credit for energy efficiency improvements to existing homes	290	0	0	0	0	0	0	0	0	0	0	0
31 Credit for residential energy efficient property	1,430	1,380	1,360	1,250	1,060	530	120	20	0	0	0	5,720
32 Qualified energy conservation bonds [5]	20	20	20	20	20	20	20	20	20	20	20	200
33 Advanced Energy Property Credit	10	0	0	0	0	0	0	0	0	0	0	0
34 Advanced nuclear power production credit	0	0	0	0	0	0	0	0	0	0	0	0
35 Reduced tax rate for nuclear decommissioning funds ...	0	0	0	0	0	0	0	0	0	0	0	0
Natural resources and environment:												
36 Expensing of exploration and development costs, nonfuel minerals	0	0	0	0	0	0	0	0	0	0	0	0
37 Excess of percentage over cost depletion, nonfuel minerals	20	20	20	20	20	20	20	20	20	20	20	200

Table 13–2B. ESTIMATES OF TOTAL INDIVIDUAL INCOME TAX EXPENDITURES FOR FISCAL YEARS 2017-2027—Continued
(In millions of dollars)

		Total from individuals											2018–2027
		2017	2018	2019	2020	2021	2022	2023	2024	2025	2026	2027	
38	Exclusion of interest on bonds for water, sewage, and hazardous waste facilities	290	280	290	300	320	360	400	440	470	500	510	3,870
39	Capital gains treatment of certain timber income	140	160	150	140	150	150	160	160	170	180	190	1,610
40	Expensing of multiperiod timber growing costs	130	130	130	130	140	160	160	160	160	160	160	1,490
41	Tax incentives for preservation of historic structures	70	70	70	70	70	70	70	70	80	80	80	730
42	Industrial CO_2 capture and sequestration tax credit	0	0	0	0	0	0	0	0	0	0	0	0
43	Deduction for endangered species recovery expenditures	20	20	20	20	30	30	30	30	40	40	50	310
Agriculture:													
44	Expensing of certain capital outlays	180	190	200	210	220	230	240	250	260	270	280	2,350
45	Expensing of certain multiperiod production costs	290	300	310	320	330	350	360	380	390	410	420	3,570
46	Treatment of loans forgiven for solvent farmers	40	50	50	50	50	50	60	60	60	60	70	560
47	Capital gains treatment of certain income	1,360	1,550	1,470	1,450	1,480	1,520	1,580	1,640	1,720	1,800	1,890	16,100
48	Income averaging for farmers	140	150	160	170	180	180	190	200	210	220	230	1,890
49	Deferral of gain on sale of farm refiners	0	0	0	0	0	0	0	0	0	0	0	0
50	Expensing of reforestation expenditures	40	30	40	40	40	40	40	50	50	50	50	430
Commerce and housing:													
	Financial institutions and insurance:												
51	Exemption of credit union income	0	0	0	0	0	0	0	0	0	0	0	0
52	Exclusion of life insurance death benefits	11,880	12,460	13,160	13,930	15,050	16,190	17,160	18,070	19,020	20,000	20,920	165,960
53	Exemption or special alternative tax for small property and casualty insurance companies	0	0	0	0	0	0	0	0	0	0	0	0
54	Tax exemption of insurance income earned by tax-exempt organizations	0	0	0	0	0	0	0	0	0	0	0	0
55	Small life insurance company deduction	0	0	0	0	0	0	0	0	0	0	0	0
56	Exclusion of interest spread of financial institutions	160	240	280	290	300	310	320	330	340	350	360	3,120
	Housing:												
57	Exclusion of interest on owner-occupied mortgage subsidy bonds	800	760	800	820	880	980	1,110	1,220	1,310	1,370	1,400	10,650
58	Exclusion of interest on rental housing bonds	740	700	740	760	810	910	1,020	1,120	1,210	1,260	1,290	9,820
59	Deductibility of mortgage interest on owner-occupied homes	65,600	69,130	74,510	81,330	89,030	96,840	104,490	111,810	118,900	125,560	131,630	1,003,230
60	Deductibility of State and local property tax on owner-occupied homes	33,710	35,790	38,190	40,920	43,750	46,600	49,550	52,700	55,940	59,230	62,680	485,350
61	Deferral of income from installment sales	1,590	1,760	1,700	1,690	1,730	1,770	1,830	1,900	1,970	2,050	2,140	18,540
62	Capital gains exclusion on home sales	43,220	43,870	44,550	45,380	46,160	46,870	47,710	48,630	49,500	50,370	51,280	474,320
63	Exclusion of net imputed rental income	121,350	126,000	131,110	136,680	142,590	148,830	155,330	162,180	169,480	177,100	185,370	1,534,670
64	Exception from passive loss rules for $25,000 of rental loss	7,410	7,710	8,060	8,390	8,730	9,080	9,440	9,750	10,100	10,490	10,860	92,610
65	Credit for low-income housing investments	420	420	450	450	460	470	490	500	510	530	550	4,830
66	Accelerated depreciation on rental housing (normal tax method)	1,730	2,210	2,930	3,670	4,210	4,870	5,540	6,180	6,780	7,350	7,900	51,640
67	Discharge of mortgage indebtedness	310	0	0	0	0	0	0	0	0	0	0	0
	Commerce:												
68	Discharge of business indebtedness	–70	0	10	0	10	30	40	40	40	40	50	260
69	Exceptions from imputed interest rules	60	60	60	70	70	80	80	80	90	90	100	780
70	Treatment of qualified dividends	27,550	29,130	30,700	32,460	34,420	36,580	38,940	41,500	44,310	47,290	50,440	385,770
71	Capital gains (except agriculture, timber, iron ore, and coal)	101,510	115,910	109,880	107,970	110,230	113,500	117,650	122,620	128,280	134,450	141,100	1,201,590
72	Capital gains exclusion of small corporation stock	790	1,020	1,240	1,400	1,520	1,630	1,730	1,830	1,900	1,980	2,050	16,300
73	Step-up basis of capital gains at death	37,910	38,710	39,560	40,160	40,560	41,240	41,860	42,620	43,230	43,820	44,540	416,300
74	Carryover basis of capital gains on gifts	5,190	4,840	4,670	4,560	4,530	4,530	4,560	4,640	4,700	4,730	4,780	46,540
75	Ordinary income treatment of loss from small business corporation stock sale	70	80	80	80	80	80	90	90	90	100	100	870
76	Deferral of gains from like-kind exchanges	1,690	1,770	1,870	1,960	2,060	2,160	2,270	2,380	2,500	2,620	2,740	22,330
77	Depreciation of buildings other than rental housing (normal tax method)	–4,940	–5,010	–5,420	–5,850	–6,110	–6,440	–6,800	–7,210	–7,460	–7,690	–7,960	–65,950
78	Accelerated depreciation of machinery and equipment (normal tax method)	15,490	12,620	8,890	–5,800	–6,160	–440	3,270	6,630	9,470	11,670	13,550	53,700

Table 13–2B. ESTIMATES OF TOTAL INDIVIDUAL INCOME TAX EXPENDITURES FOR FISCAL YEARS 2017-2027—Continued

(In millions of dollars)

	Total from individuals											
	2017	2018	2019	2020	2021	2022	2023	2024	2025	2026	2027	2018–2027
79 Expensing of certain small investments (normal tax method)	3,120	3,120	3,420	6,500	6,790	6,080	5,950	5,970	6,070	6,310	6,520	56,730
80 Graduated corporation income tax rate (normal tax method)	0	0	0	0	0	0	0	0	0	0	0	0
81 Exclusion of interest on small issue bonds	100	100	100	100	110	130	140	150	170	170	180	1,350
82 Deduction for US production activities	3,590	3,750	3,920	4,110	4,320	4,540	4,770	5,010	5,260	5,530	5,810	47,020
83 Special rules for certain film and TV production	40	20	10	10	0	0	0	0	0	0	0	40
Transportation:												
84 Tonnage tax	0	0	0	0	0	0	0	0	0	0	0	0
85 Deferral of tax on shipping companies	0	0	0	0	0	0	0	0	0	0	0	0
86 Exclusion of reimbursed employee parking expenses	3,202	3,319	3,452	3,582	3,731	3,862	3,971	4,117	4,257	4,404	4,571	39,266
87 Exclusion for employer-provided transit passes	1,123	1,192	1,270	1,355	1,446	1,532	1,613	1,719	1,819	1,934	2,054	15,934
88 Tax credit for certain expenditures for maintaining railroad tracks	10	0	0	0	0	0	0	0	0	0	0	0
89 Exclusion of interest on bonds for Highway Projects and rail-truck transfer facilities	150	140	130	130	120	120	110	110	100	100	90	1,150
Community and regional development:												
90 Investment credit for rehabilitation of structures (other than historic)	10	10	10	10	10	10	10	10	10	10	10	100
91 Exclusion of interest for airport, dock, and similar bonds	460	440	460	480	510	570	640	700	760	790	810	6,160
92 Exemption of certain mutuals' and cooperatives'income	0	0	0	0	0	0	0	0	0	0	0	0
93 Empowerment zones	60	30	20	20	10	10	10	0	0	0	0	100
94 New markets tax credit	30	30	30	30	30	20	20	20	10	10	0	200
95 Credit to holders of Gulf Tax Credit Bonds.	170	180	200	230	250	280	310	330	350	360	370	2,860
96 Recovery Zone Bonds [6]	90	100	110	120	140	150	170	180	190	200	210	1,570
97 Tribal Economic Development Bonds	30	30	30	40	40	50	50	60	60	60	70	490
Education, training, employment, and social services:												
Education:												
98 Exclusion of scholarship and fellowship income (normal tax method)	3,300	3,410	3,490	3,650	3,800	3,970	4,140	4,310	4,500	4,690	4,890	40,850
99 Tax credits and deductions for postsecondary education expenses [7]	16,460	16,360	16,320	16,310	16,290	16,190	16,180	16,170	16,120	16,020	15,980	161,940
100 Education Individual Retirement Accounts	30	30	40	40	40	40	40	40	30	30	30	360
101 Deductibility of student-loan interest	2,340	2,360	2,390	2,500	2,510	2,520	2,610	2,610	2,630	2,650	2,670	25,450
102 Qualified tuition programs	1,950	2,140	2,330	2,530	2,730	2,940	3,150	3,380	3,600	3,830	4,070	30,700
103 Exclusion of interest on student-loan bonds	260	250	260	270	290	320	360	390	420	440	450	3,450
104 Exclusion of interest on bonds for private nonprofit educational facilities	1,560	1,490	1,570	1,610	1,720	1,920	2,160	2,380	2,550	2,680	2,740	20,820
105 Credit for holders of zone academy bonds [8]	0	0	0	0	0	0	0	0	0	0	0	0
106 Exclusion of interest on savings bonds redeemed to finance educational expenses	30	30	30	30	40	40	40	40	50	50	50	400
107 Parental personal exemption for students age 19 or over	9,600	9,500	9,490	9,500	9,540	9,590	9,630	9,670	9,700	9,770	9,940	96,330
108 Deductibility of charitable contributions (education)	4,620	4,990	5,380	5,730	6,060	6,390	6,710	7,040	7,360	7,670	7,980	65,310
109 Exclusion of employer-provided educationalassistance	900	940	990	1,040	1,100	1,150	1,210	1,270	1,340	1,400	1,480	11,920
110 Special deduction for teacher expenses	200	210	200	210	250	250	250	260	260	260	270	2,420
111 Discharge of student loan indebtedness	100	100	100	110	110	110	110	120	120	120	120	1,120
112 Qualified school construction bonds [9]	490	490	490	490	490	490	490	490	490	490	490	4,900
Training, employment, and social services:												
113 Work opportunity tax credit	320	320	320	260	110	60	40	30	20	20	10	1,190
114 Employer provided child care exclusion	900	900	940	970	1,000	1,030	1,060	1,100	1,140	1,180	1,220	10,540
115 Employer-provided child care credit	0	0	0	0	0	0	0	0	0	0	0	0
116 Assistance for adopted foster children	590	620	660	690	730	780	820	860	910	950	1,000	8,020
117 Adoption credit and exclusion	620	620	650	620	640	690	690	710	690	710	720	6,740
118 Exclusion of employee meals and lodging (other than military)	4,830	4,990	5,150	5,290	5,440	5,590	5,750	5,910	6,060	6,220	6,380	56,780

Table 13–2B.   ESTIMATES OF TOTAL INDIVIDUAL INCOME TAX EXPENDITURES FOR FISCAL YEARS 2017-2027—Continued

(In millions of dollars)

		Total from individuals										
		2017	2018	2019	2020	2021	2022	2023	2024	2025	2026	2027	2018–2027
119	Credit for child and dependent care expenses	4,600	4,690	4,790	4,890	4,960	5,060	5,140	5,220	5,300	5,370	5,440	50,860
120	Credit for disabled access expenditures	10	10	10	10	10	10	10	10	10	10	10	100
121	Deductibility of charitable contributions, other than education and health	45,960	49,820	53,100	56,580	59,840	63,080	66,260	69,480	72,660	75,740	79,240	645,800
122	Exclusion of certain foster care payments	490	510	530	550	570	590	610	620	640	660	680	5,960
123	Exclusion of parsonage allowances	920	970	1,021	1,075	1,132	1,192	1,255	1,322	1,392	1,465	1,543	12,367
124	Indian employment credit	20	10	10	10	10	10	10	10	10	10	10	100
125	Credit for employer differential wage payments	0	0	0	0	0	10	10	10	10	10	10	60
Health:													
126	Exclusion of employer contributions for medical insurance premiums and medical care [10]	214,280	227,880	242,880	257,390	273,180	291,180	309,500	328,620	349,300	370,360	393,430	3,043,720
127	Self-employed medical insurance premiums	8,140	8,170	7,750	8,010	8,460	8,830	9,220	9,640	10,110	10,610	11,170	91,970
128	Medical Savings Accounts / Health Savings Accounts	8,240	9,400	10,650	11,730	12,750	13,820	14,830	15,770	16,720	17,700	18,730	142,100
129	Deductibility of medical expenses	9,720	10,030	10,870	11,850	12,840	13,790	14,790	15,830	16,910	18,090	19,400	144,400
130	Exclusion of interest on hospital construction bonds ...	2,350	2,240	2,360	2,420	2,590	2,890	3,250	3,570	3,840	4,020	4,120	31,300
131	Refundable Premium Assistance Tax Credit [11]	5,630	6,310	7,100	7,740	8,380	8,910	9,370	10,040	10,590	11,390	12,140	91,970
132	Credit for employee health insurance expenses of small business [12]	80	70	60	40	30	20	10	10	10	10	10	270
133	Deductibility of charitable contributions (health)	5,120	5,530	5,960	6,350	6,710	7,080	7,430	7,790	8,150	8,500	8,860	72,360
134	Tax credit for orphan drug research	40	50	60	70	90	100	120	140	170	190	230	1,220
135	Special Blue Cross/Blue Shield tax benefits	0	0	0	0	0	0	0	0	0	0	0	0
136	Tax credit for health insurance purchased by certain displaced and retired individuals [13]	30	20	10	0	0	0	0	0	0	0	0	30
137	Distributions from retirement plans for premiums for health and long-term care insurance	460	480	500	520	540	560	580	600	620	650	670	5,720
Income security:													
138	Child credit [14]	24,340	24,270	23,960	23,580	23,140	22,690	22,270	21,860	21,410	20,980	20,610	224,770
139	Exclusion of railroad retirement (Social Security equivalent) benefits	290	280	280	270	260	250	240	220	210	190	170	2,370
140	Exclusion of workers' compensation benefits	9,970	10,040	10,110	10,180	10,250	10,320	10,390	10,470	10,540	10,610	10,690	103,600
141	Exclusion of public assistance benefits (normal tax method)	590	600	620	640	670	680	700	730	740	750	660	6,790
142	Exclusion of special benefits for disabled coal miners ...	20	20	20	20	20	10	10	10	10	10	10	140
143	Exclusion of military disability pensions	170	180	180	190	190	200	200	210	210	220	220	2,000
	Net exclusion of pension contributions and earnings:	0	0	0	0	0	0	0	0	0	0	0	0
144	Defined benefit employer plans	76,091	76,998	77,341	78,453	77,081	75,678	73,516	71,376	68,657	65,592	61,673	726,365
145	Defined contribution employer plans	69,440	71,270	80,480	87,010	89,310	95,400	112,200	122,030	126,140	130,240	137,820	1,051,900
146	Individual Retirement Accounts	17,320	19,110	20,630	22,180	23,790	25,460	27,100	28,150	29,080	29,880	30,640	256,020
147	Low and moderate income savers credit	1,440	1,470	1,470	1,460	1,440	1,440	1,440	1,440	1,420	1,450	1,430	14,460
148	Self-Employed plans	28,460	26,980	30,010	33,390	36,930	40,280	44,000	48,070	52,400	57,060	62,170	431,290
	Exclusion of other employee benefits:	0	0	0	0	0	0	0	0	0	0	0	0
149	Premiums on group term life insurance	3,350	3,140	3,250	3,370	3,500	3,630	3,770	3,910	4,070	4,230	4,390	37,260
150	Premiums on accident and disability insurance	330	330	330	330	340	340	340	350	350	350	350	3,410
151	Income of trusts to finance supplementary unemployment benefits	20	30	40	40	50	50	50	50	60	60	60	490
152	Income of trusts to finance voluntary employee benefits associations	1,180	1,240	1,290	1,350	1,420	1,480	1,550	1,630	1,710	1,780	1,860	15,310
153	Special ESOP rules	120	120	130	130	140	140	150	150	150	160	160	1,430
154	Additional deduction for the blind	30	30	30	30	40	40	40	50	50	60	60	430
155	Additional deduction for the elderly	3,470	3,770	4,050	4,380	4,780	5,090	5,470	5,850	6,290	6,810	7,380	53,870
156	Tax credit for the elderly and disabled	10	10	10	0	0	0	0	0	0	0	0	20
157	Deductibility of casualty losses	330	350	380	400	430	460	500	530	560	590	630	4,830
158	Earned income tax credit [15]	1,760	1,810	3,960	4,100	2,060	2,150	2,250	2,370	2,500	2,570	2,700	26,470
Social Security:													
	Exclusion of social security benefits:												
159	Social Security benefits for retired and disabled workers and spouses, dependents and survivors ...	34,500	36,110	37,660	39,430	41,430	43,840	46,830	48,780	50,130	53,690	57,850	455,750

Table 13–2B.   ESTIMATES OF TOTAL INDIVIDUAL INCOME TAX EXPENDITURES FOR FISCAL YEARS 2017-2027—Continued

(In millions of dollars)

	Total from individuals											
	2017	2018	2019	2020	2021	2022	2023	2024	2025	2026	2027	2018–2027
160 Credit for certain employer contributions to social security	550	570	600	630	660	690	730	760	800	840	890	7,170
Veterans benefits and services:												
161 Exclusion of veterans death benefits and disability compensation	7,920	8,620	9,190	9,560	9,910	10,290	10,680	11,090	11,520	11,960	12,440	105,260
162 Exclusion of veterans pensions	480	510	540	560	580	610	630	660	690	720	750	6,250
163 Exclusion of GI bill benefits	1,740	1,830	1,910	2,010	2,110	2,220	2,330	2,440	2,570	2,700	2,840	22,960
164 Exclusion of interest on veterans housing bonds	10	10	10	10	10	10	10	20	20	20	20	140
General purpose fiscal assistance:												
165 Exclusion of interest on public purpose State and local bonds	19,850	18,900	19,910	20,420	21,880	24,420	27,430	30,160	32,390	33,960	34,790	264,260
166 Build America Bonds [16]	0	0	0	0	0	0	0	0	0	0	0	0
167 Deductibility of nonbusiness State and local taxes other than on owner-occupied homes	70,420	74,980	80,190	86,220	91,900	97,460	103,350	109,610	116,020	122,310	128,980	1,011,020
Interest:												
168 Deferral of interest on U.S. savings bonds	960	950	940	930	930	920	910	900	890	880	890	9,140
Addendum: Aid to State and local governments:												
Deductibility of:												
Property taxes on owner-occupied homes	33,710	35,790	38,190	40,920	43,750	46,600	49,550	52,700	55,940	59,230	62,680	485,350
Nonbusiness State and local taxes other than on owner-occupied homes	70,420	74,980	80,190	86,220	91,900	97,460	103,350	109,610	116,020	122,310	128,980	1,011,020
Exclusion of interest on State and local bonds for:												
Public purposes	19,850	18,900	19,910	20,420	21,880	24,420	27,430	30,160	32,390	33,960	34,790	264,260
Energy facilities	10	10	10	10	10	10	10	20	20	20	20	140
Water, sewage, and hazardous waste disposal facilities	290	280	290	300	320	360	400	440	470	500	510	3,870
Small-issues	100	100	100	100	110	130	140	150	170	170	180	1,350
Owner-occupied mortgage subsidies	800	760	800	820	880	980	1,110	1,220	1,310	1,370	1,400	10,650
Rental housing	740	700	740	760	810	910	1,020	1,120	1,210	1,260	1,290	9,820
Airports, docks, and similar facilities	460	440	460	480	510	570	640	700	760	790	810	6,160
Student loans	260	250	260	270	290	320	360	390	420	440	450	3,450
Private nonprofit educational facilities	1,560	1,490	1,570	1,610	1,720	1,920	2,160	2,380	2,550	2,680	2,740	20,820
Hospital construction	2,350	2,240	2,360	2,420	2,590	2,890	3,250	3,570	3,840	4,020	4,120	31,300
Veterans' housing	10	10	10	10	10	10	10	20	20	20	20	140

See Table 1 footnotes for specific table information

Table 13–3. INCOME TAX EXPENDITURES RANKED BY TOTAL FISCAL YEAR 2018–2027 PROJECTED REVENUE EFFECT

(In millions of dollars)

	Provision	2018	2019	2018–2027
126	Exclusion of employer contributions for medical insurance premiums and medical care [10]	227,880	242,880	3,043,720
63	Exclusion of net imputed rental income	126,000	131,110	1,534,670
5	Deferral of income from controlled foreign corporations (normal tax method)	112,560	118,190	1,415,810
71	Capital gains (except agriculture, timber, iron ore, and coal)	115,910	109,880	1,201,590
145	Defined contribution employer plans	71,270	80,480	1,051,900
167	Deductibility of nonbusiness State and local taxes other than on owner-occupied homes	74,980	80,190	1,011,020
59	Deductibility of mortgage interest on owner-occupied homes	69,130	74,510	1,003,230
144	Defined benefit employer plans	76,998	77,341	726,365
121	Deductibility of charitable contributions, other than education and health	51,720	55,030	668,080
60	Deductibility of State and local property tax on owner-occupied homes	35,790	38,190	485,350
62	Capital gains exclusion on home sales	43,870	44,550	474,320
159	Social Security benefits for retired and disabled workers and spouses, dependents and survivors	36,110	37,660	455,750
148	Self-Employed plans	26,980	30,010	431,290
73	Step-up basis of capital gains at death	38,710	39,560	416,300
70	Treatment of qualified dividends	29,130	30,700	385,770
165	Exclusion of interest on public purpose State and local bonds	27,920	28,650	359,890
146	Individual Retirement Accounts	19,110	20,630	256,020
138	Child credit [14]	24,270	23,960	224,770
6	Deferred taxes for financial firms on certain income earned overseas	16,880	17,730	212,380
52	Exclusion of life insurance death benefits	15,450	16,290	203,500
78	Accelerated depreciation of machinery and equipment (normal tax method)	36,740	26,380	197,900
82	Deduction for US production activities	14,150	14,790	177,020
8	Credit for increasing research activities	12,250	13,010	163,340
99	Tax credits and deductions for postsecondary education expenses [7]	16,360	16,320	161,940
129	Deductibility of medical expenses	10,030	10,870	144,400
128	Medical Savings Accounts / Health Savings Accounts	9,400	10,650	142,100
1	Exclusion of benefits and allowances to armed forces personnel	12,830	11,640	131,840
7	Expensing of research and experimentation expenditures (normal tax method)	8,340	9,140	119,500
161	Exclusion of veterans death benefits and disability compensation	8,620	9,190	105,260
140	Exclusion of workers' compensation benefits	10,040	10,110	103,600
76	Deferral of gains from like-kind exchanges	8,080	8,500	101,660
65	Credit for low-income housing investments	8,410	8,960	96,710
107	Parental personal exemption for students age 19 or over	9,500	9,490	96,330
64	Exception from passive loss rules for $25,000 of rental loss	7,710	8,060	92,610
127	Self-employed medical insurance premiums	8,170	7,750	91,970
131	Refundable Premium Assistance Tax Credit [11]	6,310	7,100	91,970
2	Exclusion of income earned abroad by U.S. citizens	6,930	7,280	87,160
108	Deductibility of charitable contributions (education)	5,890	6,330	76,650
134	Tax credit for orphan drug research	2,760	3,340	75,050
133	Deductibility of charitable contributions (health)	5,530	5,960	72,360
79	Expensing of certain small investments (normal tax method)	3,400	3,710	63,990
66	Accelerated depreciation on rental housing (normal tax method)	2,680	3,510	61,950
118	Exclusion of employee meals and lodging (other than military)	4,990	5,150	56,780
155	Additional deduction for the elderly	3,770	4,050	53,870
119	Credit for child and dependent care expenses	4,690	4,790	50,860
4	Inventory property sales source rules exception	3,570	3,840	49,900
74	Carryover basis of capital gains on gifts	4,840	4,670	46,540
130	Exclusion of interest on hospital construction bonds	3,310	3,400	42,620
98	Exclusion of scholarship and fellowship income (normal tax method)	3,410	3,490	40,850
15	Energy production credit [1]	2,230	2,870	40,120
86	Exclusion of reimbursed employee parking expenses	3,319	3,452	39,266
149	Premiums on group term life insurance	3,140	3,250	37,260
51	Exemption of credit union income	2,901	3,053	35,759
102	Qualified tuition programs	2,140	2,330	30,700
104	Exclusion of interest on bonds for private nonprofit educational facilities	2,200	2,260	28,350
158	Earned income tax credit [15]	1,810	3,960	26,470

Table 13–3. INCOME TAX EXPENDITURES RANKED BY TOTAL FISCAL YEAR 2018–2027 PROJECTED REVENUE EFFECT—Continued

(In millions of dollars)

	Provision	2018	2019	2018–2027
101	Deductibility of student-loan interest	2,360	2,390	25,450
153	Special ESOP rules	2,140	2,210	24,730
163	Exclusion of GI bill benefits	1,830	1,910	22,960
61	Deferral of income from installment sales	1,760	1,700	18,540
17	Energy investment credit [1]	3,410	3,470	18,360
3	Exclusion of certain allowances for Federal employees abroad	1,430	1,510	18,040
72	Capital gains exclusion of small corporation stock	1,020	1,240	16,300
47	Capital gains treatment of certain income	1,550	1,470	16,100
87	Exclusion for employer-provided transit passes	1,192	1,270	15,934
152	Income of trusts to finance voluntary employee benefits associations	1,240	1,290	15,310
57	Exclusion of interest on owner-occupied mortgage subsidy bonds	1,120	1,150	14,490
147	Low and moderate income savers credit	1,470	1,470	14,460
160	Credit for certain employer contributions to social security	1,080	1,130	13,570
58	Exclusion of interest on rental housing bonds	1,040	1,070	13,390
80	Graduated corporation income tax rate (normal tax method)	1,510	1,440	13,100
123	Exclusion of parsonage allowances	970	1,021	12,367
109	Exclusion of employer-provided educational assistance	940	990	11,920
114	Employer provided child care exclusion	900	940	10,540
10	Excess of percentage over cost depletion, fuels	550	600	9,500
54	Tax exemption of insurance income earned by tax-exempt organizations	750	790	9,210
168	Deferral of interest on U.S. savings bonds	950	940	9,140
91	Exclusion of interest for airport, dock, and similar bonds	650	660	8,400
116	Assistance for adopted foster children	620	660	8,020
94	New markets tax credit	1,410	1,320	8,010
135	Special Blue Cross/Blue Shield tax benefits	610	630	7,690
141	Exclusion of public assistance benefits (normal tax method)	600	620	6,790
117	Adoption credit and exclusion	620	650	6,740
112	Qualified school construction bonds [9]	650	650	6,500
162	Exclusion of veterans pensions	510	540	6,250
21	Exclusion of utility conservation subsidies	490	520	6,120
122	Exclusion of certain foster care payments	510	530	5,960
31	Credit for residential energy efficient property	1,380	1,360	5,720
137	Distributions from retirement plans for premiums for health and long-term care insurance	480	500	5,720
41	Tax incentives for preservation of historic structures	510	520	5,580
38	Exclusion of interest on bonds for water, sewage, and hazardous waste facilities	410	420	5,260
113	Work opportunity tax credit	1,340	1,370	5,210
157	Deductibility of casualty losses	350	380	4,830
103	Exclusion of interest on student-loan bonds	370	370	4,690
14	Enhanced oil recovery credit	350	400	4,570
34	Advanced nuclear power production credit	0	170	4,460
40	Expensing of multiperiod timber growing costs	350	350	3,890
45	Expensing of certain multiperiod production costs	320	330	3,820
95	Credit to holders of Gulf Tax Credit Bonds.	250	270	3,560
20	Tax credits for clean-fuel burning vehicles and refueling property	680	670	3,460
150	Premiums on accident and disability insurance	330	330	3,410
56	Exclusion of interest spread of financial institutions	240	280	3,120
35	Reduced tax rate for nuclear decommissioning funds	230	240	2,890
44	Expensing of certain capital outlays	200	210	2,520
110	Special deduction for teacher expenses	210	200	2,420
139	Exclusion of railroad retirement (Social Security equivalent) benefits	280	280	2,370
143	Exclusion of military disability pensions	180	180	2,000
96	Recovery Zone Bonds [6]	140	150	1,970
48	Income averaging for farmers	150	160	1,890
9	Expensing of exploration and development costs, fuels	−290	−30	1,860
81	Exclusion of interest on small issue bonds	150	140	1,840
92	Exemption of certain mutuals' and cooperatives' income	150	150	1,670

Table 13–3. INCOME TAX EXPENDITURES RANKED BY TOTAL FISCAL YEAR 2018–2027 PROJECTED REVENUE EFFECT—Continued

(In millions of dollars)

	Provision	2018	2019	2018–2027
12	Capital gains treatment of royalties on coal	160	150	1,610
39	Capital gains treatment of certain timber income	160	150	1,610
89	Exclusion of interest on bonds for Highway Projects and rail-truck transfer facilities	190	170	1,510
37	Excess of percentage over cost depletion, nonfuel minerals	140	150	1,460
16	Marginal wells credit	110	70	1,140
111	Discharge of student loan indebtedness	100	100	1,120
105	Credit for holders of zone academy bonds [8]	180	170	1,070
84	Tonnage tax	80	90	1,020
24	Credit for investment in clean coal facilities	110	100	940
75	Ordinary income treatment of loss from small business corporation stock sale	80	80	870
69	Exceptions from imputed interest rules	60	60	780
22	Credit for holding clean renewable energy bonds [4]	70	70	700
50	Expensing of reforestation expenditures	50	60	690
53	Exemption or special alternative tax for small property and casualty insurance companies	50	60	670
27	Amortize all geological and geophysical expenditures over 2 years	60	70	610
97	Tribal Economic Development Bonds	40	40	590
46	Treatment of loans forgiven for solvent farmers	50	50	560
43	Deduction for endangered species recovery expenditures	30	30	520
36	Expensing of exploration and development costs, nonfuel minerals	50	50	500
151	Income of trusts to finance supplementary unemployment benefits	30	40	490
154	Additional deduction for the blind	30	30	430
42	Industrial CO_2 capture and sequestration tax credit	200	200	400
106	Exclusion of interest on savings bonds redeemed to finance educational expenses	30	30	400
55	Small life insurance company deduction	30	30	380
100	Education Individual Retirement Accounts	30	40	360
32	Qualified energy conservation bonds [5]	30	30	300
132	Credit for employee health insurance expenses of small business [12]	80	70	300
11	Exception from passive loss limitation for working interests in oil and gas properties	20	20	260
68	Discharge of business indebtedness	0	10	260
49	Deferral of gain on sale of farm refiners	20	20	220
83	Special rules for certain film and TV production	110	60	200
85	Deferral of tax on shipping companies	20	20	200
90	Investment credit for rehabilitation of structures (other than historic)	20	20	200
13	Exclusion of interest on energy facility bonds	10	10	180
164	Exclusion of interest on veterans housing bonds	10	10	180
125	Credit for employer differential wage payments	0	10	150
93	Empowerment zones	50	30	140
124	Indian employment credit	20	20	140
142	Exclusion of special benefits for disabled coal miners	20	20	140
115	Employer-provided child care credit	10	10	100
120	Credit for disabled access expenditures	10	10	100
29	Credit for construction of new energy efficient homes	70	10	80
136	Tax credit for health insurance purchased by certain displaced and retired individuals [13]	20	10	30
156	Tax credit for the elderly and disabled	10	10	20
18	Alcohol fuel credits [2]	0	0	0
19	Bio-Diesel and small agri-biodiesel producer tax credits [3]	0	0	0
30	Credit for energy efficiency improvements to existing homes	0	0	0
67	Discharge of mortgage indebtedness	0	0	0
88	Tax credit for certain expenditures for maintaining railroad tracks	0	0	0
166	Build America Bonds [16]	0	0	0
33	Advanced Energy Property Credit	0	–20	–60
26	Natural gas distribution pipelines treated as 15-year property	150	150	–270
28	Allowance of deduction for certain energy efficient commercial building property	–10	–30	–280
23	Deferral of gain from dispositions of transmission property to implement FERC restructuring policy	–270	–210	–1,030
25	Temporary 50% expensing for equipment used in the refining of liquid fuels	–1,140	–930	–3,960
77	Depreciation of buildings other than rental housing (normal tax method)	–8,970	–9,570	–116,220

See Table 1 footnotes for specific table information

The modified rate structures also have the effect of reducing the cost of most tax expenditures. Statutory individual income tax rates were reduced for most taxpayers. In addition, the expanded standard deduction also had the effect of reducing the benefit of itemized deductions. On the other hand, the repeal of personal exemptions has the effect of increasing the value of tax expenditures as individuals are pushed into higher brackets. The reduction in the corporate tax from 35 to 21 percent also reduces the benefit of tax expenditures as well.

National Defense

1. *Exclusion of benefits and allowances to armed forces personnel.*—Under the baseline tax system, all compensation, including dedicated payments and in-kind benefits, should be included in taxable income because they represent accretions to wealth that do not materially differ from cash wages. As an example, a rental voucher of $100 is (approximately) equal in value to $100 of cash income. In contrast to this treatment, certain housing and meals, in addition to other benefits provided military personnel, either in cash or in kind, as well as certain amounts of pay related to combat service, are excluded from income subject to tax.

International Affairs

2. *Exclusion of income earned abroad by U.S. citizens.*—Under the baseline tax system, all compensation received by U.S. citizens and residents is properly included in their taxable income. It makes no difference whether the compensation is a result of working abroad or whether it is labeled as a housing allowance. In contrast to this treatment, U.S. tax law allows U.S. citizens and residents who live abroad, work in the private sector, and satisfy a foreign residency requirement to exclude up to $80,000, plus adjustments for inflation since 2004, in foreign earned income from U.S. taxes. In addition, if these taxpayers are provided housing by their employers, then they may also exclude the cost of such housing from their income to the extent that it exceeds 16 percent of the earned income exclusion limit. This housing exclusion is capped at 30 percent of the earned income exclusion limit, with geographical adjustments. If taxpayers do not receive a specific allowance for housing expenses, they may deduct housing expenses up to the amount by which foreign earned income exceeds their foreign earned income exclusion.

3. *Exclusion of certain allowances for Federal employees abroad.*—In general, all compensation received by U.S. citizens and residents is properly included in their taxable income. It makes no difference whether the compensation is a result of working abroad or whether it is labeled as an allowance for the high cost of living abroad. In contrast to this treatment, U.S. Federal civilian employees and Peace Corps members who work outside the continental United States are allowed to exclude from U.S. taxable income certain special allowances they

receive to compensate them for the relatively high costs associated with living overseas. The allowances supplement wage income and cover expenses such as rent, education, and the cost of travel to and from the United States.

4. *Inventory property sales source rules exception.*—The United States generally taxes the worldwide income of U.S. persons and business entities. Under the baseline tax system, taxpayers receive a credit for foreign taxes paid which is limited to the pre-credit U.S. tax on the foreign source income. In contrast, the sales source rules for inventory property under current law allow U.S. exporters to use more foreign tax credits by allowing the exporters to attribute a larger portion of their earnings to foreign sources than would be the case if the allocation of earnings was based on actual economic activity.

5. *Deferral of income from controlled foreign corporations (normal tax method).*—Under the baseline tax system, the United States generally taxes the worldwide income of U.S. persons and business entities. In contrast, certain active income of foreign corporations controlled by U.S. shareholders is not subject to U.S. taxation when it is earned. The income becomes taxable only when the controlling U.S. shareholders receive dividends or other distributions from their foreign stockholding. The reference law tax baseline reflects this tax treatment where only realized income is taxed. Under the normal tax method, however, the currently attributable foreign source pre-tax income from such a controlling interest is considered to be subject to U.S. taxation, whether or not distributed. Thus, the normal tax method considers the amount of controlled foreign corporation income not yet distributed to a U.S. shareholder as tax-deferred income.

6. *Deferred taxes for financial firms on certain income earned overseas.*—The United States generally taxes the worldwide income of U.S. persons and business entities. The baseline tax system would not allow the deferral of tax or other relief targeted at particular industries or activities. In contrast, the Tax Code allows financial firms to defer taxes on income earned overseas in an active business.

General Science, Space, and Technology

7. *Expensing of research and experimentation expenditures (normal tax method).*—The baseline tax system allows a deduction for the cost of producing income. It requires taxpayers to capitalize the costs associated with investments over time to better match the streams of income and associated costs. Research and experimentation (R&E) projects can be viewed as investments because, if successful, their benefits accrue for several years. It is often difficult, however, to identify whether a specific R&E project is successful and, if successful, what its expected life will be. Because of this ambiguity, the reference law baseline tax system would allow expensing of R&E expenditures. In contrast, under the normal tax method, the expensing of R&E expenditures is viewed as a tax expenditure. The baseline assumed for the normal

Table 13-4. PRESENT VALUE OF SELECTED TAX EXPENDITURES FOR ACTIVITY IN CALENDAR YEAR 2017

(In millions of dollars)

	Provision	2017 Present Value of Revenue Loss
5	Deferral of income from controlled foreign corporations (normal tax method)	63,630
7	Expensing of research and experimentation expenditures (normal tax method)	3,390
22	Credit for holding clean renewable energy bonds	0
9	Expensing of exploration and development costs - fuels	740
36	Expensing of exploration and development costs - nonfuels	40
40	Expensing of multiperiod timber growing costs	110
45	Expensing of certain multiperiod production costs - agriculture	50
44	Expensing of certain capital outlays - agriculture	30
50	Expensing of reforestation expenditures	20
66	Accelerated depreciation on rental housing	14,080
77	Depreciation of buildings other than rental	−5,300
78	Accelerated depreciation of machinery and equipment	27,200
78	Expensing of certain small investments (normal tax method)	1,320
105	Credit for holders of zone academy bonds	160
65	Credit for low-income housing investments	9,120
102	Qualified tuition programs	3,990
144	Defined benefit employer plans	29,729
145	Defined contribution employer plans	79,310
146	Exclusion of IRA contributions and earnings	1,600
146	Exclusion of Roth earnings and distributions	5,300
146	Exclusion of non-deductible IRA earnings	500
148	Exclusion of contributions and earnings for Self-Employed plans	5,480
165	Exclusion of interest on public-purpose bonds	16,520
	Exclusion of interest on non-public purpose bonds	4,260
170	Deferral of interest on U.S. savings bonds	260

tax method is that all R&E expenditures are successful and have an expected life of five years.

8. *Credit for increasing research activities.*— The baseline tax system would uniformly tax all returns to investments and not allow credits for particular activities, investments, or industries. In contrast, the Tax Code allows an R&E credit of up to 20 percent of qualified research expenditures in excess of a base amount. The base amount of the credit is generally determined by multiplying a "fixed-base percentage" by the average amount of the company's gross receipts for the prior four years. The taxpayer's fixed base percentage generally is the ratio of its research expenses to gross receipts for 1984 through 1988. Taxpayers can elect the alternative simplified credit regime, which equals 14 percent of qualified research expenses that exceed 50 percent of the average qualified research expenses for the three preceding taxable years.

Energy

9. *Expensing of exploration and development costs, fuels.*—Under the baseline tax system, the costs of exploring and developing oil and gas wells and coal mines or other natural fuel deposits would be capitalized and then amortized (or depreciated) over an estimate of the economic life of the property. This insures that the net income from the well or mine is measured appropriately each year.

In contrast to this treatment, current law allows immediate deduction, i.e. expensing, of intangible drilling costs for successful investments in domestic oil and gas wells (such as wages, the cost of using machinery for grading and drilling, and the cost of unsalvageable materials used in constructing wells). Current law also allows immediate deduction of eligible exploration and development costs for domestic coal mines and other natural fuel deposits. Because expensing allows recovery of costs sooner, it is more generous for the taxpayer than amortization. Expensing provisions for exploration expenditures apply only to properties for which a deduction for percentage depletion is allowable. For oil and gas wells, integrated oil companies may deduct only 70 percent of intangible drilling costs and must amortize the remaining 30 percent over five years. Non-integrated oil companies may expense all such costs.

10. *Excess of percentage over cost depletion, fuels.*—The baseline tax system would allow recovery of the costs of developing certain oil, gas, and mineral fuel

properties using cost depletion. Cost depletion is similar in concept to depreciation, in that the costs of developing or acquiring the asset are capitalized and then gradually reduced over an estimate of the asset's economic life, as is appropriate for measuring net income.

In contrast, the Tax Code generally allows independent fuel producers and royalty owners to take percentage depletion deductions rather than cost depletion on limited quantities of output. Under percentage depletion, taxpayers deduct a percentage of gross income from fossil fuel production. In certain cases the deduction is limited to a fraction of the asset's net income. Over the life of an investment, percentage depletion deductions can exceed the cost of the investment. Consequently, percentage depletion offers more generous tax treatment than would cost depletion, which would limit deductions to an investment's cost.

11. *Exception from passive loss limitation for working interests in oil and gas properties.*—The baseline tax system accepts current law's general rule limiting taxpayers' ability to deduct losses from passive activities against nonpassive income (e.g., wages, interest, and dividends). Passive activities generally are defined as those in which the taxpayer does not materially participate, and there are numerous additional considerations brought to bear on the determination of which activities are passive for a given taxpayer. Losses are limited in an attempt to limit tax sheltering activities. Passive losses that are unused may be carried forward and applied against future passive income.

An exception from the passive loss limitation is provided for a working interest in an oil or gas property that the taxpayer holds directly or through an entity that does not limit the liability of the taxpayer with respect to the interest. Thus, taxpayers can deduct losses from such working interests against nonpassive income without regard to whether they materially participate in the activity.

12. *Capital gains treatment of royalties on coal.*—The baseline tax system generally would tax all income under the regular tax rate schedule. It would not allow preferentially low tax rates to apply to certain types or sources of income. For individuals, tax rates on regular income vary from 10 percent to 39.6 percent (plus a 3.8-percent surtax on high income taxpayers), depending on the taxpayer's income. In contrast, current law allows capital gains realized by individuals to be taxed at a preferentially low rate that is no higher than 20 percent (plus the 3.8-percent surtax). Certain sales of coal under royalty contracts qualify for taxation as capital gains rather than ordinary income, and so benefit from the preferentially low 20 percent maximum tax rate on capital gains.

13. *Exclusion of interest on energy facility bonds.*—The baseline tax system generally would tax all income under the regular tax rate schedule. It would not allow preferentially low (or zero) tax rates to apply to certain types or sources of income. In contrast, the Tax Code allows interest earned on State and local bonds used to finance construction of certain energy facilities to be exempt from tax. These bonds are generally subject to the State private-activity-bond annual volume cap.

14. *Enhanced oil recovery credit.*—A credit is provided equal to 15 percent of the taxpayer's costs for enhanced oil recovery on U.S. projects. The credit is reduced in proportion to the ratio of the reference price of oil for the previous calendar year minus $28, adjusted for inflation from 1990, to $6.

15. *Energy production credit.*—The baseline tax system would not allow credits for particular activities, investments, or industries. Instead, it generally would seek to tax uniformly all returns from investment-like activities. In contrast, the Tax Code provides a credit for certain electricity produced from wind energy, biomass, geothermal energy, solar energy, small irrigation power, municipal solid waste, or qualified hydropower and sold to an unrelated party. Wind facilities must have begun construction before January 1, 2020. Facilities that begin construction in 2017 receive 80 percent of the credit, facilities that begin construction in 2018 receive 60 percent of the credit, and facilities that begin construction in 2019 receive 40 percent of the credit. Qualified facilities producing electricity from sources other than wind must begin construction before January 1, 2017. In addition to the electricity production credit, an income tax credit is allowed for the production of refined coal for facilities placed in service before January 1, 2012. The Tax Code also provided an income tax credit for Indian coal facilities. The Indian coal facilities credit expired on December 31, 2016.

16. *Marginal wells credit.*—A credit is provided for crude oil and natural gas produced from a qualified marginal well. A marginal well is one that does not produce more than 1,095 barrel-of-oil equivalents per year, with this limit adjusted proportionately for the number of days the well is in production. The credit is no more than $3.00 per barrel of qualified crude oil production and $0.50 per thousand cubic feet of qualified natural gas production. The credit for natural gas is reduced in proportion to the amount by which the reference price of natural gas at the wellhead for the previous calendar year exceeds $1.67 per thousand cubic feet and is zero for a reference price that exceeds $2.00. The credit for crude oil is reduced in proportion to the amount by which the reference price of oil for the previous calendar year exceeds $15.00 per barrel and is zero for a reference price that exceeds $18.00. All dollar amounts are adjusted for inflation from 2004.

17. *Energy investment credit.*—The baseline tax system would not allow credits for particular activities, investments, or industries. Instead, it generally would seek to tax uniformly all returns from investment-like activities. However, the Tax Code provides credits for investments in solar and geothermal energy property, qualified fuel cell power plants, stationary microturbine power plants, geothermal heat pumps, small wind property and combined heat and power property. A temporary credit of up to 30 percent is available for certain qualified property placed in service before January 1, 2017. For solar energy, a temporary credit is available for property for which construction begins before January 1, 2022, and which is placed in service before January 1, 2024. The credit is 30 percent for property that begins construction

before 2020, 26 percent for property that begins construction in 2020, and 22 percent for property that begins construction in 2021. A permanent 10 percent credit is available for geothermal property placed in service after December 31, 2017 and for qualified solar property for which construction begins after December 31, 2021 or that is placed in service after December 31, 2023. . Owners of renewable power facilities that qualify for the energy production credit may instead elect to take an energy investment credit at a rate specified by law.

18. *Alcohol fuel credits.*—The baseline tax system would not allow credits for particular activities, investments, or industries. Instead, it generally would seek to tax uniformly all returns from investment-like activities. In contrast, the Tax Code provided an income tax credit for qualified cellulosic biofuel production which was renamed the Second generation biofuel producer credit. This provision expired on December 31, 2016.

19. *Bio-diesel and small agri-biodiesel producer tax credits.*—The baseline tax system would not allow credits for particular activities, investments, or industries. Instead, it generally would seek to tax uniformly all returns from investment-like activities. However, the Tax Code allowed an income tax credit for Bio-diesel and for Bio-diesel derived from virgin sources. In lieu of the Bio-diesel credit, the taxpayer could claim a refundable excise tax credit. In addition, small agri-biodiesel producers were eligible for a separate income tax credit for biodiesel production and a separate credit was available for qualified renewable diesel fuel mixtures. This provision expired on December 31, 2016.

20. *Tax credits for clean-fuel burning vehicles and refueling property.*—The baseline tax system would not allow credits for particular activities, investments, or industries. Instead, it generally would seek to tax uniformly all returns from investment-like activities. In contrast, the Tax Code allows credits for plug-in electric-drive motor vehicles, alternative fuel vehicle refueling property, two-wheeled plug-in electric vehicles, and fuel cell motor vehicles. These provisions, except for the plug-in electric-drive motor vehicle credit, expired after December 31, 2016.

21. *Exclusion of utility conservation subsidies.*—The baseline tax system generally takes a comprehensive view of taxable income that includes a wide variety of (measurable) accretions to wealth. In certain circumstances, public utilities offer rate subsidies to non-business customers who invest in energy conservation measures. These rate subsidies are equivalent to payments from the utility to its customer, and so represent accretions to wealth, income that would be taxable to the customer under the baseline tax system. In contrast, the Tax Code exempts these subsidies from the non-business customer's gross income.

22. *Credit for holding clean renewable energy bonds.*—The baseline tax system would uniformly tax all returns to investments and not allow credits for particular activities, investments, or industries. In contrast, the Tax Code provides for the issuance of Clean Renewable Energy Bonds which entitles the bond holder to a Federal income tax credit in lieu of interest. As of March 2010, issuers of the unused authorization of such bonds could opt to receive direct payment with the yield becoming fully taxable.

23. *Deferral of gain from dispositions of transmission property to implement FERC restructuring policy.*—The baseline tax system generally would tax gains from sale of property when realized. It would not allow an exception for particular activities or individuals. However, the Tax Code allowed electric utilities to defer gains from the sale of their transmission assets to a FERC-approved independent transmission company. The sale of property must have been made prior to January 1, 2017.

24. *Credit for investment in clean coal facilities.*—The baseline tax system would uniformly tax all returns to investments and not allow credits for particular activities, investments, or industries. In contrast, the Tax Code provides investment tax credits for clean coal facilities producing electricity and for industrial gasification combined cycle projects.

25. *Temporary 50 percent expensing for equipment used in the refining of liquid fuels.*—The baseline tax system allows the taxpayer to deduct the decline in the economic value of an investment over its economic life. However, the Tax Code provided for an accelerated recovery of the cost of certain investments in refineries by allowing partial expensing of the cost, thereby giving such investments a tax advantage. Qualified refinery property must have been placed in service before January 1, 2014.

26. *Natural gas distribution pipelines treated as 15-year property.*—The baseline tax system allows taxpayers to deduct the decline in the economic value of an investment over its economic life. However, the Tax Code allows depreciation of natural gas distribution pipelines (placed in service between 2005 and 2011) over a 15 year period. These deductions are accelerated relative to deductions based on economic depreciation.

27. *Amortize all geological and geophysical expenditures over two years.*—The baseline tax system allows taxpayers to deduct the decline in the economic value of an investment over its economic life. However, the Tax Code allows geological and geophysical expenditures incurred in connection with oil and gas exploration in the United States to be amortized over two years for non-integrated oil companies, a span of time that is generally shorter than the economic life of the assets.

28. *Allowance of deduction for certain energy efficient commercial building property.*—The baseline tax system would not allow deductions in lieu of normal depreciation allowances for particular investments in particular industries. Instead, it generally would seek to tax uniformly all returns from investment-like activities. In contrast, the Tax Code allows a deduction for certain energy efficient commercial building property. The basis of such property is reduced by the amount of the deduction. This provision expired on December 31, 2016.

29. *Credit for construction of new energy efficient homes.*—The baseline tax system would not allow

credits for particular activities, investments, or industries. Instead, it generally would seek to tax uniformly all returns from investment-like activities. However, the Tax Code allowed contractors a tax credit of $2,000 for the construction of a qualified new energy-efficient home that had an annual level of heating and cooling energy consumption at least 50 percent below the annual consumption under the 2006 International Energy Conservation Code. The credit equaled $1,000 in the case of a new manufactured home that met a 30 percent standard or requirements for EPA's Energy Star homes. This provision expired on December 31, 2016.

30. *Credit for energy efficiency improvements to existing homes.*—The baseline tax system would not allow credits for particular activities, investments, or industries. However, the Tax Code provided an investment tax credit for expenditures made on insulation, exterior windows, and doors that improved the energy efficiency of homes and met certain standards. The Tax Code also provided a credit for purchases of advanced main air circulating fans, natural gas, propane, or oil furnaces or hot water boilers, and other qualified energy efficient property. This provision expired on December 31, 2016.

31. *Credit for residential energy efficient property.*—The baseline tax system would uniformly tax all returns to investments and not allow credits for particular activities, investments, or industries. However, the Tax Code provides a credit for the purchase of a qualified photovoltaic property and solar water heating property, as well as for fuel cell power plants, geothermal heat pumps and small wind property used in or placed on a residence. The credit for qualified solar electric and solar water heating property is 30 percent for property placed in service before January 1, 2020, 26 percent for property placed in service in 2020, and 22 percent for property placed in service in 2021. The credit for fuel cell, small wind, and geothermal heat pump property is 30 percent for property placed in service before January 1, 2017.

32. *Credit for qualified energy conservation bonds.*—The baseline tax system would uniformly tax all returns to investments and not allow credits for particular activities, investments, or industries. However, the Tax Code provides for the issuance of energy conservation bonds which entitle the bond holder to a Federal income tax credit in lieu of interest. As of March 2010, issuers of the unused authorization of such bonds could opt to receive direct payment with the yield becoming fully taxable.

33. *Advanced energy property credit.*—The baseline tax system would not allow credits for particular activities, investments, or industries. However, the Tax Code provides a 30 percent investment credit for property used in a qualified advanced energy manufacturing project. The Treasury Department may award up to $2.3 billion in tax credits for qualified investments.

34. *Advanced nuclear power facilities production credit.*—The baseline tax system would not allow credits or deductions for particular activities, investments, or industries. Instead, it generally would seek to tax uniformly all returns from investment-like activities.

In contrast, the Tax Code allows a tax credit equal to 1.8 cents times the number of kilowatt hours of electricity produced at a qualifying advanced nuclear power facility. A taxpayer may claim no more than $125 million per 1,000 megawatts of capacity. The Treasury Department may allocate up to 6,000 megawatts of credit-eligible capacity.

35. *Reduced tax rate for nuclear decommissioning funds.*—The baseline tax system would uniformly tax all returns to investments and not allow special rates for particular activities, investments, or industries. In contrast, the Tax Code provides a special 20% tax rate for investments made by Nuclear Decommissioning Reserve Funds.

Natural Resources and Environment

36. *Expensing of exploration and development costs, nonfuel minerals.*—The baseline tax system allows the taxpayer to deduct the depreciation of an asset according to the decline in its economic value over time. However, certain capital outlays associated with exploration and development of nonfuel minerals may be expensed rather than depreciated over the life of the asset.

37. *Excess of percentage over cost depletion, nonfuel minerals.*—The baseline tax system allows the taxpayer to deduct the decline in the economic value of an investment over time. Under current law, however, most nonfuel mineral extractors may use percentage depletion (whereby the deduction is fixed as a percentage of revenue) rather than cost depletion, with percentage depletion rates ranging from 22 percent for sulfur to 5 percent for sand and gravel. Over the life of an investment, percentage depletion deductions can exceed the cost of the investment. Consequently, percentage depletion offers more generous tax treatment than would cost depletion, which would limit deductions to an investment's cost.

38. *Exclusion of interest on bonds for water, sewage, and hazardous waste facilities.*—The baseline tax system generally would tax all income under the regular tax rate schedule. It would not allow preferentially low (or zero) tax rates to apply to certain types or sources of income. In contrast, the Tax Code allows interest earned on State and local bonds used to finance construction of sewage, water, or hazardous waste facilities to be exempt from tax. These bonds are generally subject to the State private-activity-bond annual volume cap.

39. *Capital gains treatment of certain timber.*—The baseline tax system generally would tax all income under the regular tax rate schedule. It would not allow preferentially low tax rates to apply to certain types or sources of income. However, under current law certain timber sales can be treated as a capital gain rather than ordinary income and therefore subject to the lower capital-gains tax rate. For individuals, tax rates on regular income vary from 10 percent to 39.6 percent (plus a 3.8-percent surtax on high income taxpayers), depending on the taxpayer's income. In contrast, current law allows capital gains to be taxed at a preferentially low rate that is no higher than 20 percent (plus the 3.8-percent surtax).

40. *Expensing of multi-period timber growing costs.*—The baseline tax system requires the taxpayer to capitalize costs associated with investment property. However, most of the production costs of growing timber may be expensed under current law rather than capitalized and deducted when the timber is sold, thereby accelerating cost recovery.

41. *Tax incentives for preservation of historic structures.*—The baseline tax system would not allow credits for particular activities, investments, or industries. However, expenditures to preserve and restore certified historic structures qualify for an investment tax credit of 20 percent under current law for certified rehabilitation activities. The taxpayer's recoverable basis must be reduced by the amount of the credit.

42. *Industrial CO2 capture and sequestration tax credit.*—The baseline tax system would uniformly tax all returns to investments and not allow credits for particular activities, investments, or industries. In contrast, the Tax Code allows a credit for qualified carbon dioxide captured at a qualified facility and disposed of in secure geological storage. In addition, the provision allows a credit for qualified carbon dioxide that is captured at a qualified facility and used as a tertiary injectant in a qualified enhanced oil or natural gas recovery project. The credit is not allowed after the end of the calendar year in which 75 million metric tons of qualified carbon dioxide are certified as having been taken into account.

43. *Deduction for endangered species recovery expenditures.*—The baseline tax system would not allow deductions in addition to normal depreciation allowances for particular investments in particular industries. Instead, it generally would seek to tax uniformly all returns from investment-like activities. In contrast, under current law farmers can deduct up to 25 percent of their gross income for expenses incurred as a result of site and habitat improvement activities that will benefit endangered species on their farm land, in accordance with site specific management actions included in species recovery plans approved pursuant to the Endangered Species Act of 1973.

Agriculture

44. *Expensing of certain capital outlays.*—The baseline tax system requires the taxpayer to capitalize costs associated with investment property. However, farmers may expense certain expenditures for feed and fertilizer, for soil and water conservation measures and certain other capital improvements under current law.

45. *Expensing of certain multiperiod production costs.*—The baseline tax system requires the taxpayer to capitalize costs associated with an investment over time. However, the production of livestock and crops with a production period greater than two years is exempt from the uniform cost capitalization rules (e.g., for costs for establishing orchards or structure improvements), thereby accelerating cost recovery.

46. *Treatment of loans forgiven for solvent farmers.*—Because loan forgiveness increases a debtors net worth the baseline tax system requires debtors to include the amount of loan forgiveness as income or else reduce their recoverable basis in the property related to the loan. If the amount of forgiveness exceeds the basis, the excess forgiveness is taxable if the taxpayer is not insolvent. For bankrupt debtors, the amount of loan forgiveness reduces carryover losses, unused credits, and then basis, with the remainder of the forgiven debt excluded from taxation. Qualified farm debt that is forgiven, however, is excluded from income even when the taxpayer is solvent.

47. *Capital gains treatment of certain income.*—For individuals, tax rates on regular income vary from 10 percent to 39.6 percent (plus a 3.8-percent surtax on high income taxpayers), depending on the taxpayer's income. The baseline tax system generally would tax all income under the regular tax rate schedule. It would not allow preferentially low tax rates to apply to certain types or sources of income. In contrast, current law allows capital gains to be taxed at a preferentially low rate that is no higher than 20 percent (plus the 3.8-percent surtax). Certain agricultural income, such as unharvested crops, qualify for taxation as capital gains rather than ordinary income, and so benefit from the preferentially low 20 percent maximum tax rate on capital gains.

48. *Income averaging for farmers.*—The baseline tax system generally taxes all earned income each year at the rate determined by the income tax. However, taxpayers may average their taxable income from farming and fishing over the previous three years.

49. *Deferral of gain on sales of farm refiners.*—The baseline tax system generally subjects capital gains to taxes the year that they are realized. However, the Tax Code allows a taxpayer who sells stock in a farm refiner to a farmers' cooperative to defer recognition of the gain if the proceeds are re-invested in a qualified replacement property.

50. *Expensing of reforestation expenditures.*—The baseline tax system requires the taxpayer to capitalize costs associated with an investment over time. In contrast, the Tax Code provides for the expensing of the first $10,000 in reforestation expenditures with 7-year amortization of the remaining expenses.

Commerce and Housing

This category includes a number of tax expenditure provisions that also affect economic activity in other functional categories. For example, provisions related to investment, such as accelerated depreciation, could be classified under the energy, natural resources and environment, agriculture, or transportation categories.

51. *Exemption of credit union income.*—Under the baseline tax system, corporations pay taxes on their profits under the regular tax rate schedule. However, in the Tax Code the earnings of credit unions not distributed to members as interest or dividends are exempt from the income tax.

52. *Exclusion of life insurance death benefits.*—Under the baseline tax system, individuals and

corporations would pay taxes on their income when it is (actually or constructively) received or accrued. Nevertheless, current law excludes from tax amounts received under life insurance contracts if such amounts are paid by reason of the death of the insured.

53. *Exclusion or special alternative tax for small property and casualty insurance companies.*— The baseline tax system would require corporations to pay taxes on their profits under the regular tax rate schedule. It would not allow preferentially low (or zero) tax rates to apply to certain types or sources of income. Under current law, however, stock non-life insurance companies are generally exempt from tax if their gross receipts for the taxable year do not exceed $600,000 and more than 50 percent of such gross receipts consist of premiums. Mutual non-life insurance companies are generally tax-exempt if their annual gross receipts do not exceed $150,000 and more than 35 percent of gross receipts consist of premiums. Also, non-life insurance companies with no more than $2.25 million of annual net written premiums generally may elect to pay tax only on their taxable investment income. Their underwriting income (premiums, less insurance losses and expenses) is excluded from tax.

54. *Tax exemption of insurance income earned by tax-exempt organizations.*—Under the baseline tax system, corporations pay taxes on their profits under the regular tax rate schedule. The baseline tax system would not allow preferentially low (or zero) tax rates to apply to certain types or sources of income. Generally the income generated by life and property and casualty insurance companies is subject to tax, albeit under special rules. However, income from insurance operations conducted by such exempt organizations as fraternal societies, voluntary employee benefit associations, and others are exempt from tax.

55. *Small life insurance company deduction.*— The baseline tax system would require corporations to pay taxes on their profits under the regular tax rate schedule. It would not allow preferentially low (or zero) tax rates to apply to certain types or sources of income. Under current law, small life insurance companies (with gross assets of less than $500 million) can deduct 60 percent of the first $3 million of otherwise taxable income. The deduction phases out for otherwise taxable income between $3 million and $15 million.

56. *Exclusion of interest spread of financial institutions.*—The baseline tax system generally would tax all income under the regular tax rate schedule. It would not allow preferentially low (or zero) tax rates to apply to certain types or sources of income. Consumers pay for some deposit-linked services, such as check cashing, by accepting a below-market interest rate on their demand deposits. If they received a market rate of interest on those deposits and paid explicit fees for the associated services, they would pay taxes on the full market rate and (unlike businesses) could not deduct the fees. The Government thus foregoes tax on the difference between the risk-free market interest rate and below-market interest rates on demand deposits, which under competitive conditions should equal the value added of deposit services.

57. *Exclusion of interest on owner-occupied mortgage subsidy bonds.*—The baseline tax system generally would tax all income under the regular tax rate schedule. It would not allow preferentially low (or zero) tax rates to apply to certain types or sources of income. In contrast, the Tax Code allows interest earned on State and local bonds used to finance homes purchased by first-time, low-to-moderate-income buyers to be exempt from tax. These bonds are generally subject to the State private-activity-bond annual volume cap.

58. *Exclusion of interest on rental housing bonds.*—The baseline tax system generally would tax all income under the regular tax rate schedule. It would not allow preferentially low (or zero) tax rates to apply to certain types or sources of income. In contrast, the Tax Code allows interest earned on State and local government bonds used to finance multifamily rental housing projects to be tax-exempt.

59. *Mortgage interest expense on owner-occupied residences.*—Under the baseline tax system, expenses incurred in earning income would be deductible. However, such expenses would not be deductible when the income or the return on an investment is not taxed. In contrast, the Tax Code allows an exclusion from a taxpayer's taxable income for the value of owner-occupied housing services and also allows the owner-occupant to deduct mortgage interest paid on his or her primary residence and one secondary residence as an itemized non-business deduction. In general, the mortgage interest deduction is limited to interest on debt no greater than the owner's basis in the residence, and is also limited to interest on debt of no more than $1 million. Interest on up to $100,000 of other debt secured by a lien on a principal or second residence is also deductible, irrespective of the purpose of borrowing, provided the total debt does not exceed the fair market value of the residence. As an alternative to the deduction, holders of qualified Mortgage Credit Certificates issued by State or local governmental units or agencies may claim a tax credit equal to a proportion of their interest expense.

60. *Deduction for property taxes on real property.*—Under the baseline tax system, expenses incurred in earning income would be deductible. However, such expenses would not be deductible when the income or the return on an investment is not taxed. In contrast, the Tax Code allows an exclusion from a taxpayer's taxable income for the value of owner-occupied housing services and also allows the owner-occupant to deduct property taxes paid on real property.

61. *Deferral of income from installment sales.*— The baseline tax system generally would tax all income under the regular tax rate schedule. It would not allow preferentially low (or zero) tax rates, or deferral of tax, to apply to certain types or sources of income. Dealers in real and personal property (i.e., sellers who regularly hold property for sale or resale) cannot defer taxable income from installment sales until the receipt of the loan repayment. Nondealers (i.e., sellers of real property used in their business) are required to pay interest on deferred taxes attributable to their total installment obligations in

excess of $5 million. Only properties with sales prices exceeding $150,000 are includable in the total. The payment of a market rate of interest eliminates the benefit of the tax deferral. The tax exemption for nondealers with total installment obligations of less than $5 million is, therefore, a tax expenditure.

62. *Capital gains exclusion on home sales.*—The baseline tax system would not allow deductions and exemptions for certain types of income. In contrast, the Tax Code allows homeowners to exclude from gross income up to $250,000 ($500,000 in the case of a married couple filing a joint return) of the capital gains from the sale of a principal residence. To qualify, the taxpayer must have owned and used the property as the taxpayer's principal residence for a total of at least two of the five years preceding the date of sale. In addition, the exclusion may not be used more than once every two years.

63. *Exclusion of net imputed rental income.*— Under the baseline tax system, the taxable income of a taxpayer who is an owner-occupant would include the implicit value of gross rental income on housing services earned on the investment in owner-occupied housing and would allow a deduction for expenses, such as interest, depreciation, property taxes, and other costs, associated with earning such rental income. In contrast, the Tax Code allows an exclusion from taxable income for the implicit gross rental income on housing services, while in certain circumstances allows a deduction for some costs associated with such income, such as for mortgage interest and property taxes.

64. *Exception from passive loss rules for $25,000 of rental loss.*—The baseline tax system accepts current law's general rule limiting taxpayers' ability to deduct losses from passive activities against nonpassive income (e.g., wages, interest, and dividends). Passive activities generally are defined as those in which the taxpayer does not materially participate and there are numerous additional considerations brought to bear on the determination of which activities are passive for a given taxpayer. Losses are limited in an attempt to limit tax sheltering activities. Passive losses that are unused may be carried forward and applied against future passive income. In contrast to the general restrictions on passive losses, the Tax Code exempts certain owners of rental real estate activities from "passive income" limitations. The exemption is limited to $25,000 in losses and phases out for taxpayers with income between $100,000 and $150,000.

65. *Credit for low-income housing investments.*— The baseline tax system would uniformly tax all returns to investments and not allow credits for particular activities, investments, or industries. However, under current law taxpayers who invest in certain low-income housing are eligible for a tax credit. The credit rate is set so that the present value of the credit is equal to 70 percent for new construction and 30 percent for (1) housing receiving other Federal benefits (such as tax-exempt bond financing), or (2) substantially rehabilitated existing housing. The credit can exceed these levels in certain statutorily defined and State designated areas where project development costs are higher. The credit is allowed in equal amounts over 10 years and is generally subject to a volume cap.

66. *Accelerated depreciation on rental housing.*—Under an economic income tax, the costs of acquiring a building are capitalized and depreciated over time in accordance with the decline in the property's economic value due to wear and tear or obsolescence. This insures that the net income from the rental property is measured appropriately each year. Current law allows depreciation that is accelerated relative to economic depreciation. However, the depreciation provisions of the Tax Code are part of the reference law rules, and thus do not give rise to tax expenditures under reference law. Under normal law, in contrast, depreciation allowances reflect estimates of economic depreciation.

67. *Discharge of mortgage indebtedness.*—Under the baseline tax system, all income would generally be taxed under the regular tax rate schedule. The baseline tax system would not allow preferentially low (or zero) tax rates to apply to certain types or sources of income. In contrast, the Tax Code allowed an exclusion from a taxpayer's taxable income for any discharge of indebtedness of up to $2 million ($1 million in the case of a married individual filing a separate return) from a qualified principal residence. The provision applied to debt discharged after January 1, 2007, and before January 1, 2017.

68. *Discharge of business indebtedness.*—Under the baseline tax system, all income would generally be taxed under the regular tax rate schedule. The baseline tax system would not allow preferentially low (or zero) tax rates to apply to certain types or sources of income. In contrast, the Tax Code allows an exclusion from a taxpayer's taxable income for any discharge of qualified real property business indebtedness by taxpayers other than a C corporation. If the canceled debt is not reported as current income, however, the basis of the underlying property must be reduced by the amount canceled.

69. *Exceptions from imputed interest rules.*— Under the baseline tax system, holders (issuers) of debt instruments are generally required to report interest earned (paid) in the period it accrues, not when received. In addition, the amount of interest accrued is determined by the actual price paid, not by the stated principal and interest stipulated in the instrument. But under current law, any debt associated with the sale of property worth less than $250,000 is exempted from the general interest accounting rules. This general $250,000 exception is not a tax expenditure under reference law but is under normal law. Current law also includes exceptions for certain property worth more than $250,000. These are tax expenditure under reference law and normal law. These exceptions include, sales of personal residences worth more than $250,000, and sales of farms and small businesses worth between $250,000 and $1 million.

70. *Treatment of qualified dividends.*—The baseline tax system generally would tax all income under the regular tax rate schedule. It would not allow preferentially low tax rates to apply to certain types or sources of income. For individuals, tax rates on regular income vary from 10 percent to 39.6 percent (plus a 3.8-percent surtax on high income taxpayers), depending on the taxpayer's income. In contrast, under current law, qualified dividends are taxed at a preferentially low rate that is no higher than 20 percent (plus the 3.8-percent surtax).

71. **Capital gains (except agriculture, timber, iron ore, and coal).**—The baseline tax system generally would tax all income under the regular tax rate schedule. It would not allow preferentially low tax rates to apply to certain types or sources of income. For individuals, tax rates on regular income vary from 10 percent to 39.6 percent (plus a 3.8-percent surtax on high income taxpayers), depending on the taxpayer's income. In contrast, under current law, capital gains on assets held for more than one year are taxed at a preferentially low rate that is no higher than 20 percent (plus the 3.8-percent surtax).

72. **Capital gains exclusion of small corporation stock.**—The baseline tax system would not allow deductions and exemptions, or provide preferential treatment of certain sources of income or types of activities. In contrast, the Tax Code provided an exclusion of 50 percent, applied to ordinary rates with a maximum of a 28 percent tax rate, for capital gains from qualified small business stock held by individuals for more than 5 years; 75 percent for stock issued after February 17, 2009 and before September 28, 2010; and 100 percent for stock issued after September 27, 2010. A qualified small business is a corporation whose gross assets do not exceed $50 million as of the date of issuance of the stock.

73. **Step-up basis of capital gains at death.**—Under the baseline tax system, unrealized capital gains would be taxed when assets are transferred at death. It would not allow for exempting gains upon transfer of the underlying assets to the heirs. In contrast, capital gains on assets held at the owner's death are not subject to capital gains tax under current law. The cost basis of the appreciated assets is adjusted to the market value at the owner's date of death which becomes the basis for the heirs.

74. **Carryover basis of capital gains on gifts.**—Under the baseline tax system, unrealized capital gains would be taxed when assets are transferred by gift. In contrast, when a gift of appreciated asset is made under current law, the donor's basis in the transferred property (the cost that was incurred when the transferred property was first acquired) carries over to the donee. The carryover of the donor's basis allows a continued deferral of unrealized capital gains.

75. **Deferral of capital gains from like-kind exchanges.**—The baseline tax system generally would tax all income under the regular tax rate schedule. It would not allow preferentially low (or zero) tax rates, or deferral of tax, to apply to certain types or sources of income. In contrast, current law allows the deferral of accrued gains on assets transferred in qualified like-kind exchanges.

76. **Ordinary income treatment of loss from small business corporation stock sale.**—The baseline tax system limits to $3,000 the write-off of losses from capital assets, with carryover of the excess to future years. In contrast, the Tax Code allows up to $100,000 in losses from the sale of small business corporate stock (capital-ization less than $1 million) to be treated as ordinary losses and fully deducted.

77. **Depreciation of buildings other than rental housing.**—Under an economic income tax, the costs of acquiring a building are capitalized and depreciated over time in accordance with the decline in the property's economic value due to wear and tear or obsolescence. This insures that the net income from the property is measured appropriately each year. Current law allows depreciation deductions that differ from those under economic depreciation. However, the depreciation provisions of the Tax Code are part of the reference law rules, and thus do not give rise to tax expenditures under reference law. Under normal law, in contrast, depreciation allowances reflect estimates of economic depreciation.

78. **Accelerated depreciation of machinery and equipment.**—Under an economic income tax, the costs of acquiring machinery and equipment are capitalized and depreciated over time in accordance with the decline in the property's economic value due to wear and tear or obsolescence. This insures that the net income from the property is measured appropriately each year. Current law allows depreciation deductions that are accelerated relative to economic depreciation. However, the depreciation provisions of the Tax Code are part of the reference law rules, and thus do not give rise to tax expenditures under reference law. Under normal law, in contrast depreciation allowances reflect estimates of economic depreciation.

79. **Expensing of certain small investments.**—Under the reference law baseline, the costs of acquiring tangible property and computer software would be depreciated using the Tax Code's depreciation provisions. Under the normal tax baseline, depreciation allowances are estimates of economic depreciation. However, the Tax Code allows qualifying investments by small businesses in tangible property and certain computer software to be expensed rather than depreciated over time.

80. **Graduated corporation income tax rate.**—Because the corporate rate schedule is part of reference tax law, it is not considered a tax expenditure under the reference method. A flat corporation income tax rate is taken as the baseline under the normal tax method; therefore the lower rate is considered a tax expenditure under this concept.

81. **Exclusion of interest on small issue bonds.**—The baseline tax system generally would tax all income under the regular tax rate schedule. It would not allow preferentially low (or zero) tax rates to apply to certain types or sources of income. In contrast, the Tax Code allows interest earned on small issue industrial development bonds (IDBs) issued by State and local governments to finance manufacturing facilities to be tax exempt. Depreciable property financed with small issue IDBs must be depreciated, however, using the straight-line method. The annual volume of small issue IDBs is subject to the unified volume cap discussed in the mortgage housing bond section above.

82. **Deduction for U.S. production activities.**—The baseline tax system generally would tax all income under the regular tax rate schedule. It would not allow

preferentially low (or zero) tax rates to apply to certain types or sources of income. In contrast, the Tax Code allows for a deduction equal to a portion of taxable income attributable to domestic production.

83. *Special rules for certain film and TV production.*—The baseline tax system generally would tax all income under the regular tax rate schedule. It would not allow deductions and exemptions or preferentially low (or zero) tax rates to apply to certain types or sources of income. In contrast, the Tax Code allowed taxpayers to deduct up to $15 million per production ($20 million in certain distressed areas) in non-capital expenditures incurred during the year. This provision expired at the end of 2016.

Transportation

84. *Tonnage tax.*—The baseline tax system generally would tax all profits and income under the regular tax rate schedule. U.S. shipping companies may choose to be subject to a tonnage tax based on gross shipping weight in lieu of an income tax, in which case profits would not be subject to tax under the regular tax rate schedule.

85. *Deferral of tax on shipping companies.*—The baseline tax system generally would tax all profits and income under the regular tax rate schedule. It would not allow preferentially low (or zero) tax rates to apply to certain types or sources of income. In contrast, the Tax Code allows certain companies that operate U.S. flag vessels to defer income taxes on that portion of their income used for shipping purposes (e.g., primarily construction, modernization and major repairs to ships, and repayment of loans to finance these investments).

86. *Exclusion of reimbursed employee parking expenses.*—Under the baseline tax system, all compensation, including dedicated payments and in-kind benefits, would be included in taxable income. Dedicated payments and in-kind benefits represent accretions to wealth that do not differ materially from cash wages. In contrast, the Tax Code allows an exclusion from taxable income for employee parking expenses that are paid for by the employer or that are received by the employee in lieu of wages. In 2017, the maximum amount of the parking exclusion is $255 per month. The tax expenditure estimate does not include any subsidy provided through employer-owned parking facilities.

87. *Exclusion for employer-provided transit passes.*—Under the baseline tax system, all compensation, including dedicated payments and in-kind benefits, would be included in taxable income. Dedicated payments and in-kind benefits represent accretions to wealth that do not differ materially from cash wages. In contrast, the Tax Code allows an exclusion from a taxpayer's taxable income for passes, tokens, fare cards, and vanpool expenses that are paid for by an employer or that are received by the employee in lieu of wages to defray an employee's commuting costs. Due to a parity to parking provision, the maximum amount of the transit exclusion is $255 per month in 2017.

88. *Tax credit for certain expenditures for maintaining railroad tracks.*—The baseline tax system would not allow credits for particular activities, investments, or industries. However, the Tax Code allowed eligible taxpayers to claim a credit equal to the lesser of 50 percent of maintenance expenditures and the product of $3,500 and the number of miles of track owned or leased. This provision applies to maintenance expenditures in taxable years beginning before January 1, 2017.

89. *Exclusion of interest on bonds for Highway Projects and rail-truck transfer facilities.*—The baseline tax system generally would tax all income under the regular tax rate schedule. It would not allow preferentially low (or zero) tax rates to apply to certain types or sources of income. In contrast, the Tax Code provides for $15 billion of tax-exempt bond authority to finance qualified highway or surface freight transfer facilities.

Community and Regional Development

90. *Investment credit for rehabilitation of structures.*—The baseline tax system would uniformly tax all returns to investments and not allow credits for particular activities, investments, or industries. However, the Tax Code allows a 10-percent investment tax credit for the rehabilitation of buildings that are used for business or productive activities and that were erected before 1936 for other than residential purposes. The taxpayer's recoverable basis must be reduced by the amount of the credit.

91. *Exclusion of interest for airport, dock, and similar bonds.*—The baseline tax system generally would tax all income under the regular tax rate schedule. It would not allow preferentially low (or zero) tax rates to apply to certain types or sources of income. In contrast, the Tax Code allows interest earned on State and local bonds issued to finance high-speed rail facilities and Government-owned airports, docks, wharves, and sport and convention facilities to be tax-exempt. These bonds are not subject to a volume cap.

92. *Exemption of certain mutuals' and cooperatives' income.*—Under the baseline tax system, corporations pay taxes on their profits under the regular tax rate schedule. In contrast, the Tax Code provides for the incomes of mutual and cooperative telephone and electric companies to be exempt from tax if at least 85 percent of their revenues are derived from patron service charges.

93. *Empowerment zones.*—The baseline tax system generally would tax all income under the regular tax rate schedule. It would not allow preferentially low tax rates to apply to certain types or sources of income, tax credits, and write-offs faster than economic depreciation. In contrast, the Tax Code allowed qualifying businesses in designated economically depressed areas to receive tax benefits such as an employment credit, increased expensing of investment in equipment, special tax-exempt financing, and certain capital gains incentives. A taxpayer's ability to accrue new tax benefits for empowerment zones expired on December 31, 2016.

94. New markets tax credit.—The baseline tax system would not allow credits for particular activities, investments, or industries. However, the Tax Code allowed taxpayers who made qualified equity investments in a community development entity (CDE), which then made qualified investments in low-income communities, to be eligible for a tax credit that is received over 7 years. The total equity investment available for the credit across all CDEs is $3.5 billion for each calendar year 2010 through 2019, the last year for which credit allocations are authorized.

95. Credit to holders of Gulf and Midwest Tax Credit Bonds.—The baseline tax system would not allow credits for particular activities, investments, or industries. Instead, under current law taxpayers that own Gulf and Midwest Tax Credit bonds receive a non-refundable tax credit rather than interest. The credit is included in gross income.

96. Recovery Zone Bonds.—The baseline tax system would not allow credits for particular activities, investments, or industries. In addition, it would tax all income under the regular tax rate schedule. It would not allow preferentially low (or zero) tax rates to apply to certain types or sources of income. In contrast, the Tax Code allowed local governments to issue up $10 billion in taxable Recovery Zone Economic Development Bonds in 2009 and 2010 and receive a direct payment from Treasury equal to 45 percent of interest expenses. In addition, local governments could issue up to $15 billion in tax exempt Recovery Zone Facility Bonds. These bonds financed certain kinds of business development in areas of economic distress.

97. Tribal Economic Development Bonds.—The baseline tax system generally would tax all income under the regular tax rate schedule. It would not allow preferentially low (or zero) tax rates to apply to certain types or sources of income. In contrast, the Tax Code was modified in 2009 to allow Indian tribal governments to issue tax exempt "tribal economic development bonds." There is a national bond limitation of $2 billion on such bonds.

Education, Training, Employment, and Social Services

98. Exclusion of scholarship and fellowship income.—Scholarships and fellowships are excluded from taxable income to the extent they pay for tuition and course-related expenses of the grantee. Similarly, tuition reductions for employees of educational institutions and their families are not included in taxable income. From an economic point of view, scholarships and fellowships are either gifts not conditioned on the performance of services, or they are rebates of educational costs. Thus, under the baseline tax system of the reference law method, this exclusion is not a tax expenditure because this method does not include either gifts or price reductions in a taxpayer's gross income. The exclusion, however, is considered a tax expenditure under the normal tax method, which includes gift-like transfers of Government funds in gross income (many scholarships are derived directly or indirectly from Government funding).

99. Tax credits and deductions for post-secondary education expenses.—The baseline tax system would not allow credits for particular activities, investments, or industries. Under current law in 2017, however, there were two credits for certain post-secondary education expenses. A deduction for post-secondary expenses expired at the end of 2016. The American Opportunity Tax Credit allows a partially refundable credit of up to $2,500 per eligible student for qualified tuition and related expenses paid during each of the first four years of the student's post-secondary education. The credit is phased out for taxpayers with modified adjusted gross income between $160,000 and $180,000 if married filing jointly ($80,000 and $90,000 for other taxpayers), not indexed. The Lifetime Learning Credit allows a non-refundable credit for 20 percent of an eligible student's qualified tuition and fees, up to a maximum credit per return of $2,000. In 2017, the credit is phased out ratably for taxpayers with modified AGI between $112,000 and $132,000 if married filing jointly ($56,000 and $66,000 for other taxpayers), indexed. The credit can be claimed in any year in which post-secondary education expenses are incurred. The deduction for post-secondary education expenses provides a maximum deduction of $4,000 for qualified post-secondary education expenses for taxpayers with modified adjusted gross income up to $130,000 if married filing jointly ($65,000 for other taxpayers). Taxpayers with modified adjusted gross income up to $160,000 if married filing jointly ($80,000 for other taxpayers) could deduct up to $2,000 of qualified post-secondary education expenses. This provision expired on December 31, 2016.

100. Education Individual Retirement Accounts (IRA).—The baseline tax system generally would tax all income under the regular tax rate schedule. It would not allow preferentially low (or zero) tax rates to apply to certain types or sources of income. While contributions to an education IRA are not tax-deductible under current law, investment income earned by education IRAs is not taxed when earned, and investment income from an education IRA is tax-exempt when withdrawn to pay for a student's education expenses. The maximum contribution to an education IRA in 2017 is $2,000 per beneficiary. In 2017, the maximum contribution is phased down ratably for taxpayers with modified AGI between $190,000 and $220,000 if married filing jointly ($95,000 and $110,000 for other taxpayers).

101. Deductibility of student loan interest.—The baseline tax system accepts current law's general rule limiting taxpayers' ability to deduct non-business interest expenses. In contrast, taxpayers may claim an above-the-line deduction of up to $2,500 on interest paid on an education loan. In 2017, the maximum deduction is phased down ratably for taxpayers with modified AGI between $135,000 and $165,000 if married filing jointly ($65,000 and $80,000 for other taxpayers).

102. Qualified tuition programs.—The baseline tax system generally would tax all income under the regular tax rate schedule. It would not allow preferentially low (or zero) tax rates to apply to certain types or sources of income. Some States have adopted prepaid tuition plans, prepaid room and board plans, and college savings plans, which allow persons to pay in advance or save for college expenses for designated beneficiaries. Under current law, investment income, or the return on prepayments, is not taxed when earned, and is tax-exempt when withdrawn to pay for qualified expenses.

103. *Exclusion of interest on student-loan bonds.*—The baseline tax system generally would tax all income under the regular tax rate schedule. It would not allow preferentially low (or zero) tax rates to apply to certain types or sources of income. In contrast, interest earned on State and local bonds issued to finance student loans is tax-exempt under current law. The volume of all such private activity bonds that each State may issue annually is limited.

104. *Exclusion of interest on bonds for private nonprofit educational facilities.*—The baseline tax system generally would tax all income under the regular tax rate schedule. It would not allow preferentially low (or zero) tax rates to apply to certain types or sources of income. In contrast, under current law interest earned on State and local Government bonds issued to finance the construction of facilities used by private nonprofit educational institutions is not taxed.

105. *Credit for holders of zone academy bonds.*— The baseline tax system would not allow credits for particular activities, investments, or industries. Under current law, however, financial institutions that own zone academy bonds receive a non-refundable tax credit rather than interest. The credit is included in gross income. Proceeds from zone academy bonds may only be used to renovate, but not construct, qualifying schools and for certain other school purposes. The total amount of zone academy bonds that may be issued was limited to $1.4 billion in 2009 and 2010. As of March 2010, issuers of the unused authorization of such bonds could opt to receive direct payment with the yield becoming fully taxable. An additional $0.4 billion of these bonds with a tax credit was authorized to be issued each year in 2011 through 2016.

106. *Exclusion of interest on savings bonds redeemed to finance educational expenses.*—The baseline tax system generally would tax all income under the regular tax rate schedule. It would not allow preferentially low (or zero) tax rates to apply to certain types or sources of income. Under current law, however, interest earned on U.S. savings bonds issued after December 31, 1989 is tax-exempt if the bonds are transferred to an educational institution to pay for educational expenses. The tax exemption is phased out for taxpayers with AGI between $117,250 and $147,250 if married filing jointly ($78,150 and $93,150 for other taxpayers) in 2017.

107. *Parental personal exemption for students age 19 or over.*—Under the baseline tax system, a personal exemption would be allowed for the taxpayer, as well as for the taxpayer's spouse and dependents who do not claim a personal exemption on their own tax returns. To be considered a dependent, a child would have to be under age 19. In contrast, the Tax Code allows taxpayers to claim personal exemptions for children aged 19 to 23, as long as the children are full-time students and reside with the taxpayer for over half the year (with exceptions for temporary absences from home, such as for school attendance).

108. *Charitable contributions to educational institutions.*—The baseline tax system would not allow a deduction for personal expenditures. In contrast, the Tax Code provides taxpayers a deduction for contributions to nonprofit educational institutions that are similar to personal expenditures. Moreover, taxpayers who donate capital assets to educational institutions can deduct the asset's current value without being taxed on any appreciation in value. An individual's total charitable contribution generally may not exceed 50 percent of adjusted gross income; a corporation's total charitable contributions generally may not exceed 10 percent of pre-tax income.

109. *Exclusion of employer-provided educational assistance.*—Under the baseline tax system, all compensation, including dedicated payments and in-kind benefits, should be included in taxable income because they represent accretions to wealth that do not materially differ from cash wages. Under current law, however, employer-provided educational assistance is excluded from an employee's gross income, even though the employer's costs for this assistance are a deductible business expense. The maximum exclusion is $5,250 per taxpayer.

110. *Special deduction for teacher expenses.*— The baseline tax system would not allow a deduction for personal expenditures. In contrast, the Tax Code allowed educators in both public and private elementary and secondary schools, who worked at least 900 hours during a school year as a teacher, instructor, counselor, principal or aide, to subtract up to $250 of qualified expenses, indexed to 2014, when determining their adjusted gross income (AGI).

111. *Discharge of student loan indebtedness.*— Under the baseline tax system, all compensation, including dedicated payments and in-kind benefits, should be included in taxable income. In contrast, the Tax Code allows certain professionals who perform in underserved areas or specific fields, and as a consequence have their student loans discharged, not to recognize such discharge as income.

112. *Qualified school construction bonds.*—The baseline tax system would not allow credits for particular activities, investments, or industries. Instead, it generally would seek to tax uniformly all returns from investment-like activities. In contrast, the Tax Code was modified in 2009 to provide a tax credit in lieu of interest to holders of qualified school construction bonds. The national volume limit is $22.4 billion over 2009 and 2010. As of March 2010, issuers of such bonds could opt to receive direct payment with the yield becoming fully taxable.

113. *Work opportunity tax credit.*—The baseline tax system would not allow credits for particular activities, investments, or industries. Instead, it generally would seek to tax uniformly all returns from investment-like activities. In contrast, the Tax Code provides employers with a tax credit for qualified wages paid to individuals.

The credit applies to employees who began work on or before December 31, 2019 and who are certified as members of various targeted groups. The amount of the credit that can be claimed is 25 percent of qualified wages for employment less than 400 hours and 40 percent for employment of 400 hours or more. Generally, the maximum credit per employee is $2,400 and can only be claimed on the first year of wages an individual earns from an employer. However, the credit for long-term welfare recipients can be claimed on second year wages as well and has a $9,000 maximum. Also, certain categories of veterans are eligible for a higher maximum credit of up to $9,600. Employers must reduce their deduction for wages paid by the amount of the credit claimed.

114. *Employer-provided child care exclusion.*—Under the baseline tax system, all compensation, including dedicated payments and in-kind benefits, should be included in taxable income. In contrast, under current law up to $5,000 of employer-provided child care is excluded from an employee's gross income even though the employer's costs for the child care are a deductible business expense.

115. *Employer-provided child care credit.*—The baseline tax system would not allow credits for particular activities, investments, or industries. In contrast, current law provides a credit equal to 25 percent of qualified expenses for employee child care and 10 percent of qualified expenses for child care resource and referral services. Employer deductions for such expenses are reduced by the amount of the credit. The maximum total credit is limited to $150,000 per taxable year.

116. *Assistance for adopted foster children.*—Under the baseline tax system, all compensation, including dedicated payments and in-kind benefits, should be included in taxable income. Taxpayers who adopt eligible children from the public foster care system can receive monthly payments for the children's significant and varied needs and a reimbursement of up to $2,000 for nonrecurring adoption expenses; special needs adoptions receive the maximum benefit even if that amount is not spent. These payments are excluded from gross income under current law.

117. *Adoption credit and exclusion.*—The baseline tax system would not allow credits for particular activities. In contrast, taxpayers can receive a tax credit for qualified adoption expenses under current law. Taxpayers may also exclude qualified adoption expenses provided or reimbursed by an employer from income, subject to the same maximum amounts and phase-out as the credit. The same expenses cannot qualify for tax benefits under both programs; however, a taxpayer may use the benefits of the exclusion and the tax credit for different expenses.

118. *Exclusion of employee meals and lodging.*—Under the baseline tax system, all compensation, including dedicated payments and in-kind benefits, should be included in taxable income. In contrast, under current law employer-provided meals and lodging are excluded from an employee's gross income even though the employer's costs for these items are a deductible business expense.

119. *Credit for child and dependent care expenses.*—The baseline tax system would not allow credits for particular activities or targeted at specific groups. In contrast, the Tax Code provides parents who work or attend school and who have child and dependent care expenses a tax credit. Expenditures up to a maximum $3,000 for one dependent and $6,000 for two or more dependents are eligible for the credit. The credit is equal to 35 percent of qualified expenditures for taxpayers with incomes of up to $15,000. The credit is reduced to a minimum of 20 percent by one percentage point for each $2,000 of income in excess of $15,000.

120. *Credit for disabled access expenditures.*—The baseline tax system would not allow credits for particular activities, investments, or industries. In contrast, the Tax Code provides small businesses (less than $1 million in gross receipts or fewer than 31 full-time employees) a 50-percent credit for expenditures in excess of $250 to remove access barriers for disabled persons. The credit is limited to $5,000.

121. *Deductibility of charitable contributions, other than education and health.*—The baseline tax system would not allow a deduction for personal expenditures including charitable contributions. In contrast, the Tax Code provides taxpayers a deduction for contributions to charitable, religious, and certain other nonprofit organizations. Taxpayers who donate capital assets to charitable organizations can deduct the assets' current value without being taxed on any appreciation in value. An individual's total charitable contribution generally may not exceed 50 percent of adjusted gross income; a corporation's total charitable contributions generally may not exceed 10 percent of pre-tax income.

122. *Exclusion of certain foster care payments.*—The baseline tax system generally would tax all income under the regular tax rate schedule. It would not allow preferentially low (or zero) tax rates to apply to certain types or sources of income. Foster parents provide a home and care for children who are wards of the State, under contract with the State. Under current law, compensation received for this service is excluded from the gross incomes of foster parents; the expenses they incur are nondeductible.

123. *Exclusion of parsonage allowances.*—Under the baseline tax system, all compensation, including dedicated payments and in-kind benefits, would be included in taxable income. Dedicated payments and in-kind benefits represent accretions to wealth that do not differ materially from cash wages. In contrast, the Tax Code allows an exclusion from a clergyman's taxable income for the value of the clergyman's housing allowance or the rental value of the clergyman's parsonage.

124. *Indian employment credit.*—The baseline tax system would not allow credits for particular activities, investments, or industries. Instead, it generally would seek to tax uniformly all returns from investment-like activities. In contrast, the Tax Code provides employers with a tax credit for qualified wages paid to employees

who are enrolled members of Indian tribes. The amount of the credit that could be claimed is 20 percent of the excess of qualified wages and health insurance costs paid by the employer in the current tax year over the amount of such wages and costs paid by the employer in 1993. Qualified wages and health insurance costs with respect to any employee for the taxable year could not exceed $20,000. Employees have to live on or near the reservation where he or she work to be eligible for the credit. Employers must reduce their deduction for wages paid by the amount of the credit claimed. The credit does not apply to taxable years beginning after December 31, 2016.

125. Credit for employer differential wage payments.—The baseline tax system would not allow credits for particular activities, investments, or industries. In contrast, the Tax Code provides employers with a 20 percent tax credit for eligible differential wages paid to employees who are members of the uniformed services while on active duty for more than 30 days. The amount of eligible differential wage payments made to a qualified employee in a taxable year is capped at $20,000. Employers must reduce their deduction for wages paid by the amount of the credit claimed.

Health

126. **Exclusion of employer contributions for medical insurance premiums and medical care.**—Under the baseline tax system, all compensation, including dedicated payments and in-kind benefits, should be included in taxable income. In contrast, under current law, employer-paid health insurance premiums and other medical expenses (including long-term care) are not included in employee gross income even though they are deducted as a business expense by the employee.

127. **Self-employed medical insurance premiums.**—Under the baseline tax system, all compensation and remuneration, including dedicated payments and in-kind benefits, should be included in taxable income. In contrast, under current law self-employed taxpayers may deduct their family health insurance premiums. Taxpayers without self-employment income are not eligible for this special deduction. The deduction is not available for any month in which the self-employed individual is eligible to participate in an employer-subsidized health plan and the deduction may not exceed the self-employed individual's earned income from self-employment.

128. **Medical Savings Accounts and Health Savings Accounts.**—Under the baseline tax system, all compensation, including dedicated payments and in-kind benefits, should be included in taxable income. Also, the baseline tax system would not allow a deduction for personal expenditures and generally would tax investment earnings. In contrast, individual contributions to Archer Medical Savings Accounts (Archer MSAs) and Health Savings Accounts (HSAs) are allowed as a deduction in determining adjusted gross income whether or not the individual itemizes deductions. Employer contributions to Archer MSAs and HSAs are excluded from income and employment taxes. Archer MSAs and HSAs require that

the individual have coverage by a qualifying high deductible health plan. Earnings from the accounts are excluded from taxable income. Distributions from the accounts used for medical expenses are not taxable. The rules for HSAs are generally more flexible than for Archer MSAs and the deductible contribution amounts are greater (in 2017, $3,350 for taxpayers with individual coverage and $6,750 for taxpayers with family coverage). Thus, HSAs have largely replaced MSAs.

129. **Deductibility of medical expenses.**—The baseline tax system would not allow a deduction for personal expenditures. In contrast, under current law personal expenditures for medical care (including the costs of prescription drugs) exceeding 7.5 percent of the taxpayer's adjusted gross income are deductible. For tax years beginning after 2012, only medical expenditures exceeding 10 percent of the taxpayer's adjusted gross income are deductible. However, for the years 2013, 2014, 2015 and 2016, if either the taxpayer or the taxpayer's spouse turns 65 before the end of the taxable year, the threshold remains at 7.5 percent of adjusted income. Beginning in 2017, the 10-percent threshold will apply to all taxpayers, including those over 65.

130. **Exclusion of interest on hospital construction bonds.**—The baseline tax system generally would tax all income under the regular tax rate schedule. It would not allow preferentially low (or zero) tax rates to apply to certain types or sources of income. In contrast, under current law interest earned on State and local government debt issued to finance hospital construction is excluded from income subject to tax.

131. **Refundable Premium Assistance Tax Credit.**—The baseline tax system would not allow credits for particular activities or targeted at specific groups. In contrast, for taxable years ending after 2013, the Tax Code provides a premium assistance credit to any eligible taxpayer for any qualified health insurance purchased through a Health Insurance Exchange. In general, an eligible taxpayer is a taxpayer with annual household income between 100% and 400% of the Federal poverty level for a family of the taxpayer's size and that does not have access to affordable minimum essential health care coverage. The amount of the credit equals the lesser of (1) the actual premiums paid by the taxpayer for such coverage or (2) the difference between the cost of a statutorily-identified benchmark plan offered on the exchange and a required payment by the taxpayer that increases with income.

132. **Credit for employee health insurance expenses of small business.**—The baseline tax system would not allow credits for particular activities or targeted at specific groups. In contrast, the Tax Code provides a tax credit to qualified small employers that make a certain level of non-elective contributions towards the purchase of certain health insurance coverage for its employees. To receive a credit, an employer must have fewer than 25 full-time-equivalent employees whose average annual full-time-equivalent wages from the employer are less than $50,000 (indexed for taxable years after 2013). However, to receive a full credit, an employer

must have no more than 10 full-time employees, and the average wage paid to these employees must be no more than $25,000 (indexed for taxable years after 2013). A qualifying employer may claim the credit for any taxable year beginning in 2010, 2011, 2012, and 2013 and for up to two years for insurance purchased through a Health Insurance Exchange thereafter. For taxable years beginning in 2010, 2011, 2012, and 2013, the maximum credit is 35 percent of premiums paid by qualified taxable employers and 25 percent of premiums paid by qualified tax-exempt organizations. For taxable years beginning in 2014 and later years, the maximum tax credit increases to 50 percent of premiums paid by qualified taxable employers and 35 percent of premiums paid by qualified tax-exempt organizations.

133. *Deductibility of charitable contributions to health institutions.*—The baseline tax system would not allow a deduction for personal expenditures including charitable contributions. In contrast, the Tax Code provides individuals and corporations a deduction for contributions to nonprofit health institutions. Tax expenditures resulting from the deductibility of contributions to other charitable institutions are listed under the education, training, employment, and social services function.

134. *Tax credit for orphan drug research.*—The baseline tax system would not allow credits for particular activities, investments, or industries. In contrast, under current law drug firms can claim a tax credit of 50 percent of the costs for clinical testing required by the Food and Drug Administration for drugs that treat rare physical conditions or rare diseases.

135. *Special Blue Cross/Blue Shield tax benefits.*—The baseline tax system generally would tax all profits under the regular tax rate schedule using broadly applicable measures of baseline income. It would not allow preferentially low tax rates to apply to certain types or sources of income. In contrast, certain Blue Cross and Blue Shield (BC/BS) health insurance providers and certain other health insurers are provided with special tax benefits, provided that their percentage of total premium revenue expended on reimbursement for clinical services provided to enrollees or for activities that improve health care quality is not less than 85 percent for the taxable year. Qualifying insurers may take as a deduction 100 percent of any net increase in their unearned premium reserves, instead of the 80 percent allowed other insurers. Qualifying insurers are also allowed a special deduction equal to the amount by which 25 percent of an insurer's health-claim expenses exceeds its beginning-of-the-year accounting surplus. The deduction is limited to the insurer's taxable income determined without the special deduction.

136. *Tax credit for health insurance purchased by certain displaced and retired individuals.*—The baseline tax system would not allow credits for particular activities, investments, or industries. In contrast, the Tax Code provides a refundable tax credit of 72.5 percent for the purchase of health insurance coverage by individuals eligible for Trade Adjustment Assistance and certain

Pension Benefit Guarantee Corporation pension recipients. This provision will expire on December 31, 2019.

137. *Distributions from retirement plans for premiums for health and long-term care insurance.*—Under the baseline tax system, all compensation, including dedicated and deferred payments, should be included in taxable income. In contrast, the Tax Code provides for tax-free distributions of up to $3,000 from governmental retirement plans for premiums for health and long term care premiums of public safety officers.

Income Security

138. *Child credit.*—The baseline tax system would not allow credits for particular activities or targeted at specific groups. Under current law, however, taxpayers with children under age 17 can qualify for a $1,000 partially refundable per child credit. Any unclaimed credit due to insufficient tax liability may be refundable – taxpayers may claim a refund for 15 percent of earnings in excess of a $3,000 floor, up to the amount of unused credit. Alternatively, taxpayers with three or more children may claim a refund of the amount of payroll taxes paid in excess of the Earned Income Tax Credit received (up to the amount of unused credit) if this results in a larger refund. The credit is phased out for taxpayers at the rate of $50 per $1,000 of modified AGI above $110,000 ($75,000 for single or head of household filers and $55,000 for married taxpayers filing separately).

139. *Exclusion of railroad Social Security equivalent benefits.*—Under the baseline tax system, all compensation, including dedicated and deferred payments, should be included in taxable income. In contrast, the Social Security Equivalent Benefit paid to railroad retirees is not generally subject to the income tax unless the recipient's gross income reaches a certain threshold under current law. See provision number 158, Social Security benefits for retired workers, for discussion of the threshold.

140. *Exclusion of workers' compensation benefits.*—Under the baseline tax system, all compensation, including dedicated payments and in-kind benefits, should be included in taxable income. However, workers compensation is not subject to the income tax under current law.

141. *Exclusion of public assistance benefits.*—Under the reference law baseline tax system, gifts and transfers are not treated as income to the recipients. In contrast, the normal tax method considers cash transfers from the Government as part of the recipients' income, and thus, treats the exclusion for public assistance benefits under current law as a tax expenditure.

142. *Exclusion of special benefits for disabled coal miners.*—Under the baseline tax system, all compensation, including dedicated payments and in-kind benefits, should be included in taxable income. However, disability payments to former coal miners out of the Black Lung Trust Fund, although income to the recipient, are not subject to the income tax.

143. *Exclusion of military disability pensions.*—Under the baseline tax system, all compensation,

including dedicated payments and in-kind benefits, should be included in taxable income. In contrast, most of the military disability pension income received by current disabled military retirees is excluded from their income subject to tax.

144. *Defined benefit employer plans.*—Under the baseline tax system, all compensation, including deferred and dedicated payments, should be included in taxable income. In addition, investment income would be taxed as earned. In contrast, under current law certain contributions to defined benefit pension plans are excluded from an employee's gross income even though employers can deduct their contributions. In addition, the tax on the investment income earned by defined benefit pension plans is deferred until the money is withdrawn.

145. *Defined contribution employer plans.*—Under the baseline tax system, all compensation, including deferred and dedicated payments, should be included in taxable income. In addition, investment income would be taxed as earned. In contrast, under current law individual taxpayers and employers can make tax-preferred contributions to employer-provided 401(k) and similar plans (e.g. 403(b) plans and the Federal Government's Thrift Savings Plan). In 2017, an employee could exclude up to $18,000 of wages from AGI under a qualified arrangement with an employer's 401(k) plan. Employees age 50 or over could exclude up to $24,000 in contributions. The defined contribution plan limit, including both employee and employer contributions, is $54,000 in 2017. The tax on contributions made by both employees and employers and the investment income earned by these plans is deferred until withdrawn.

146. *Individual Retirement Accounts (IRAs).*—Under the baseline tax system, all compensation, including deferred and dedicated payments, should be included in taxable income. In addition, investment income would be taxed as earned. In contrast, under current law individual taxpayers can take advantage of traditional and Roth IRAs to defer or otherwise reduce the tax on the return to their retirement savings. The IRA contribution limit is $5,500 in 2017; taxpayers age 50 or over are allowed to make additional "catch-up" contributions of $1,000. Contributions to a traditional IRA are generally deductible but the deduction is phased out for workers with incomes above certain levels who, or whose spouses, are active participants in an employer-provided retirement plan. Contributions and account earnings are includible in income when withdrawn from traditional IRAs. Roth IRA contributions are not deductible, but earnings and withdrawals are exempt from taxation. Income limits also apply to Roth IRA contributions.

147. *Low and moderate-income savers' credit.*—The baseline tax system would not allow credits for particular activities or targeted at specific groups. In contrast, the Tax Code provides an additional incentive for lower-income taxpayers to save through a nonrefundable credit of up to 50 percent on IRA and other retirement contributions of up to $2,000. This credit is in addition to any deduction or exclusion. The credit is completely phased out by $62,000 for joint filers, $46,500 for head of household filers, and $31,000 for other filers in 2017.

148. *Self-employed plans.*—Under the baseline tax system, all compensation, including deferred and dedicated payments, should be included in taxable income. In addition, investment income would be taxed as earned. In contrast, under current law self-employed individuals can make deductible contributions to their own retirement plans equal to 25 percent of their income, up to a maximum of $54,000 in 2017. Total plan contributions are limited to 25 percent of a firm's total wages. The tax on the investment income earned by self-employed SEP, SIMPLE, and qualified plans is deferred until withdrawn.

149. *Premiums on group term life insurance.*—Under the baseline tax system, all compensation, including deferred and dedicated payments, should be included in taxable income. In contrast, under current law employer-provided life insurance benefits are excluded from an employee's gross income (to the extent that the employer's share of the total costs does not exceed the cost of $50,000 of such insurance) even though the employer's costs for the insurance are a deductible business expense.

150. *Premiums on accident and disability insurance.*—Under the baseline tax system, all compensation, including dedicated payments and in-kind benefits, should be included in taxable income. In contrast, under current law employer-provided accident and disability benefits are excluded from an employee's gross income even though the employer's costs for the benefits are a deductible business expense.

151. *Exclusion of investment income from Supplementary Unemployment Benefit Trusts.*—Under the baseline tax system, all compensation, including dedicated payments and in-kind benefits, should be included in taxable income. In addition, investment income would be taxed as earned. Under current law, employers may establish trusts to pay supplemental unemployment benefits to employees separated from employment. Investment income earned by such trusts is exempt from taxation.

152. *Exclusion of investment income from Voluntary Employee Benefit Associations trusts.*—Under the baseline tax system, all compensation, including dedicated payments and in-kind benefits, should be included in taxable income. Under current law, employers may establish associations, or VEBAs, to pay employee benefits, which may include health benefit plans, life insurance, and disability insurance, among other employee benefits. Investment income earned by such trusts is exempt from taxation.

153. *Special ESOP rules.*—ESOPs are a special type of tax-exempt employee benefit plan. Under the baseline tax system, all compensation, including dedicated payments and in-kind benefits, should be included in taxable income. In addition, investment income would be taxed as earned. In contrast, employer-paid contributions (the value of stock issued to the ESOP) are deductible by the employer as part of employee compensation costs. They are not included in the employees' gross income for tax purposes, however, until they are paid out as benefits.

In addition, the following special income tax provisions for ESOPs are intended to increase ownership of corporations by their employees: (1) annual employer contributions are subject to less restrictive limitations than other qualified retirement plans; (2) ESOPs may borrow to purchase employer stock, guaranteed by their agreement with the employer that the debt will be serviced by his payment (deductible by him) of a portion of wages (excludable by the employees) to service the loan; (3) employees who sell appreciated company stock to the ESOP may defer any taxes due until they withdraw benefits; (4) dividends paid to ESOP-held stock are deductible by the employer; and (5) earnings are not taxed as they accrue.

154. *Additional deduction for the blind.*—Under the baseline tax system, the standard deduction is allowed. An additional standard deduction for a targeted group within a given filing status would not be allowed. In contrast, the Tax Code allows taxpayers who are blind to claim an additional $1,550 standard deduction if single, or $1,250 if married in 2017.

155. *Additional deduction for the elderly.*— Under the baseline tax system, the standard deduction is allowed. An additional standard deduction for a targeted group within a given filing status would not be allowed. In contrast, the Tax Code allows taxpayers who are 65 years or older to claim an additional $1,550 standard deduction if single, or $1,250 if married in 2017.

156. *Tax credit for the elderly and disabled.*— Under the baseline tax system, a credit targeted at a specific group within a given filing status or for particular activities would not be allowed. In contrast, the Tax Code allows taxpayers who are 65 years of age or older, or who are permanently disabled, to claim a non-refundable tax credit equal to 15 percent of the sum of their earned and retirement income. The amount to which the 15-percent rate is applied is limited to no more than $5,000 for single individuals or married couples filing a joint return where only one spouse is 65 years of age or older or disabled, and up to $7,500 for joint returns where both spouses are 65 years of age or older or disabled. These limits are reduced by one-half of the taxpayer's adjusted gross income over $7,500 for single individuals and $10,000 for married couples filing a joint return.

157. *Deductibility of casualty losses.*—Under the baseline tax system, neither the purchase of property nor insurance premiums to protect the property's value are deductible as costs of earning income. Therefore, reimbursement for insured loss of such property is not included as a part of gross income, and uninsured losses are not deductible. In contrast, the Tax Code provides a deduction for uninsured casualty and theft losses of more than $100 each, to the extent that total losses during the year exceed 10 percent of the taxpayer's adjusted gross income.

158. *Earned income tax credit (EITC).*—The baseline tax system would not allow credits for particular activities or targeted at specific groups. In contrast, the Tax Code provides an EITC to low-income workers at a maximum rate of 45 percent of income. For a family with one qualifying child, the credit is 34 percent of the first $10,000 of earned income in 2017. The credit is 40 percent of the first $14,040 of income for a family with two qualifying children, and it is 45 percent of the first $14,040 of income for a family with three or more qualifying children. Low-income workers with no qualifying children are eligible for a 7.65-percent credit on the first $6,670 of earned income. The credit is phased out at income levels and rates which depend upon how many qualifying children are eligible and marital status. In 2017, the phase-down for married filers begins at incomes $5,590 greater than for otherwise similar unmarried filers. Earned income tax credits in excess of tax liabilities owed through the individual income tax system are refundable to individuals.

Social Security

159. *Social Security benefits for retired and disabled workers and spouses, dependents, and survivors.*—The baseline tax system would tax Social Security benefits to the extent that contributions to Social Security were not previously taxed. Thus, the portion of Social Security benefits that is attributable to employer contributions and to earnings on employer and employee contributions (and not attributable to employee contributions which are taxed at the time of contribution) would be subject to tax. In contrast, the Tax Code may not tax all of the Social Security benefits that exceed the beneficiary's contributions from previously taxed income. Actuarially, previously taxed contributions generally do not exceed 15 percent of benefits, even for retirees receiving the highest levels of benefits. Therefore, up to 85 percent of recipients' Social Security and Railroad Social Security Equivalent retirement benefits are included in (phased into) the income tax base if the recipient's provisional income exceeds certain base amounts. (Provisional income is equal to other items included in adjusted gross income plus foreign or U.S. possession income, tax-exempt interest, and one half of Social Security and Railroad Social Security Equivalent retirement benefits.) The untaxed portion of the benefits received by taxpayers who are below the income amounts at which 85 percent of the benefits are taxable is counted as a tax expenditure. Benefits paid to disabled workers and to spouses, dependents, and survivors are treated in a similar manner. Railroad Social Security Equivalent benefits are treated like Social Security benefits. See also provision number 138, Exclusion of railroad Social Security equivalent benefits.

160. *Credit for certain employer social security contributions.*—Under the baseline tax system, employer contributions to Social Security represent labor cost and are deductible expenses. Under current law, however, certain employers are allowed a tax credit, instead of a deduction, against taxes paid on tips received from customers in connection with the providing, delivering, or serving of food or beverages for consumption, The tip credit equals the full amount of the employer's share of FICA taxes paid on the portion of tips, when added to the employee's non-tip wages, in excess of $5.15 per hour. The credit is available only with respect to FICA taxes paid on tips.

Veterans Benefits and Services

161. *Exclusion of veterans death benefits and disability compensation.*—Under the baseline tax system, all compensation, including dedicated payments and in-kind benefits, should be included in taxable income because they represent accretions to wealth that do not materially differ from cash wages. In contrast, all compensation due to death or disability paid by the Veterans Administration is excluded from taxable income under current law.

162. *Exclusion of veterans pensions.*—Under the baseline tax system, all compensation, including dedicated payments and in-kind benefits, should be included in taxable income because they represent accretions to wealth that do not materially differ from cash wages. Under current law, however, pension payments made by the Veterans Administration are excluded from gross income.

163. *Exclusion of G.I. Bill benefits.*—Under the baseline tax system, all compensation, including dedicated payments and in-kind benefits, should be included in taxable income because they represent accretions to wealth that do not materially differ from cash wages. Under current law, however, G.I. Bill benefits paid by the Veterans Administration are excluded from gross income.

164. *Exclusion of interest on veterans housing bonds.*—The baseline tax system generally would tax all income under the regular tax rate schedule. It would not allow preferentially low (or zero) tax rates to apply to certain types or sources of income. In contrast, under current law, interest earned on general obligation bonds issued by State and local governments to finance housing for veterans is excluded from taxable income.

General Government

165. *Exclusion of interest on public purpose State and local bonds.*—The baseline tax system generally would tax all income under the regular tax rate schedule. It would not allow preferentially low (or zero) tax rates to apply to certain types or sources of income. In contrast, under current law interest earned on State and local government bonds issued to finance public-purpose construction (e.g., schools, roads, sewers), equipment acquisition, and other public purposes is tax-exempt. Interest on bonds issued by Indian tribal governments for essential governmental purposes is also tax-exempt.

166. *Build America Bonds.*—The baseline tax system would not allow credits for particular activities or targeted at specific group. In contrast, the Tax Code in 2009 allowed State and local governments to issue taxable bonds through 2010 and receive a direct payment from Treasury equal to 35 percent of interest expenses. Alternatively, State and local governments could issue taxable bonds and the private lenders receive the 35-percent credit which is included in taxable income.

167. *Deductibility of nonbusiness State and local taxes other than on owner-occupied homes.*—Under the baseline tax system, a deduction for personal consumption expenditures would not be allowed. In contrast, the Tax Code allows taxpayers who itemize their deductions to claim a deduction for State and local income taxes (or, at the taxpayer's election, State and local sales taxes) and property taxes, even though these taxes primarily pay for services that, if purchased directly by taxpayers, would not be deductible. (The estimates for this tax expenditure do not include the estimates for the deductibility of State and local property tax on owner-occupied homes. See item 59.)

Interest

168. *Deferral of interest on U.S. savings bonds.*—The baseline tax system would uniformly tax all returns to investments and not allow an exemption or deferral for particular activities, investments, or industries. In contrast, taxpayers may defer paying tax on interest earned on U.S. savings bonds until the bonds are redeemed.

APPENDIX

Performance Measures and the Economic Effects of Tax Expenditures

The Government Performance and Results Act of 1993 (GPRA) directs Federal agencies to develop annual and strategic plans for their programs and activities. These plans set out performance objectives to be achieved over a specific time period. Most of these objectives are achieved through direct expenditure programs. Tax expenditures – spending programs implemented through the tax code by reducing tax obligations for certain activities -- contribute to achieving these goals in a manner similar to direct expenditure programs.

Tax expenditures by definition work through the tax system and, particularly, the income tax. Thus, they may be relatively advantageous policy approaches when the benefit or incentive is related to income and is intended to be widely available. Because there is an existing public administrative and private compliance structure for the tax system, income-based programs that require little oversight might be efficiently run through the tax system. In addition, some tax expenditures actually simplify the operation of the tax system (for example, the exclusion for up to $500,000 of capital gains on home sales). Tax expenditures also implicitly subsidize certain activities in a manner similar to direct expenditures. For example, exempting employer-sponsored health insurance from income taxation is equivalent to a direct spending subsidy equal to the forgone tax obligations for this type of compensation. Spending, regulatory or tax-disincentive policies can also modify behavior, but may have different economic effects. Finally, a variety of tax expenditure tools can be used, e.g., deductions; credits; exemptions; deferrals; floors; ceilings; phase-ins; phase-outs; and these can be dependent on income, expenses, or demographic characteristics (age, number of family members, etc.). This wide range of policy instruments means that tax expenditures can be flexible and can have very different economic effects.

Tax expenditures also have limitations. In many cases they add to the complexity of the tax system, which raises both administrative and compliance costs. For example, personal exemptions, deductions, credits, and phase-outs can complicate filing and decision-making. The income tax system may have little or no contact with persons who have no or very low incomes, and does not require information on certain characteristics of individuals used in some spending programs, such as wealth or duration of employment. These features may reduce the effectiveness of tax expenditures for addressing socioeconomic disparities. Tax expenditures also generally do not enable the same degree of agency discretion as an outlay program. For example, grant or direct Federal service delivery programs can prioritize activities to be addressed with specific resources in a way that is difficult to emulate with tax expenditures.

Outlay programs have advantages where the direct provision of government services is particularly warranted, such as equipping and maintaining the armed forces or administering the system of justice. Outlay programs may also be specifically designed to meet the needs of low-income families who would not otherwise be subject to income taxes or need to file a tax return. Outlay programs may also receive more year-to-year oversight and fine tuning through the legislative and executive budget process. In addition, many different types of spending programs include direct Government provision; credit programs; and payments to State and local governments, the private sector, or individuals in the form of grants or contracts provide flexibility for policy design. On the other hand, certain outlay programs may rely less directly on economic incentives and private-market provision than tax incentives, thereby reducing the relative efficiency of spending programs for some goals. Finally, spending programs, particularly on the discretionary side, may respond less rapidly to changing activity levels and economic conditions than tax expenditures.

Regulations may have more direct and immediate effects than outlay and tax-expenditure programs because regulations apply directly and immediately to the regulated party (i.e., the intended actor), generally in the private sector. Regulations can also be fine-tuned more quickly than tax expenditures because they can often be changed as needed by the Executive Branch without legislation. Like tax expenditures, regulations often rely largely on voluntary compliance, rather than detailed inspections and policing. As such, the public administrative costs tend to be modest relative to the private resource costs associated with modifying activities. Historically, regulations have tended to rely on proscriptive measures, as opposed to economic incentives. This reliance can diminish their economic efficiency, although this feature can also promote full compliance where (as in certain safety-related cases) policymakers believe that trade-offs with economic considerations are not of paramount importance. Also, regulations generally do not directly affect Federal outlays or receipts. Thus, like tax expenditures, they may escape the degree of scrutiny that outlay programs receive. Some policy objectives are achieved using multiple approaches. For example, minimum wage legislation, the earned income tax credit, and the food stamp program (SNAP) are regulatory, tax expenditure, and direct outlay programs, respectively, all having the objective of improving the economic welfare of low-wage workers and families.

A Framework for Evaluating the Effectiveness of Tax Expenditures

Across all major budgetary categories - from housing and health to space, technology, agriculture, and national defense - tax expenditures make up a significant portion of Federal activity and affect every area of the economy. For these reasons, a comprehensive evaluation framework that examines incentives, direct results, and spillover effects will benefit the budgetary process by informing decisions on tax expenditure policy.

As described above, tax expenditures, like spending and regulatory programs, have a variety of objectives and economic effects. These include: encouraging certain types of activities (e.g., saving for retirement or investing in certain sectors); increasing certain types of after-tax income (e.g., favorable tax treatment of Social Security income); and reducing private compliance costs and Government administrative costs (e.g., the exclusion for up to $500,000 of capital gains on home sales). Some of these objectives are well suited to quantitative measurement and evaluation, while others are less well suited.

Performance measurement is generally concerned with inputs, outputs, and outcomes. In the case of tax expenditures, the principal input is usually the revenue effect. Outputs are quantitative or qualitative measures of goods and services, or changes in income and investment, directly produced by these inputs. Outcomes, in turn, represent the changes in the economy, society, or environment that are the ultimate goals of programs. Evaluations assess whether programs are meeting intended goals, but may also encompass analyzing whether initiatives are superior to other policy alternatives.

The Administration is working towards examining the objectives and effects of the wide range of tax expenditures in our budget, despite challenges related to data availability, measurement, and analysis. Evaluations include an assessment of whether tax expenditures are achieving intended policy results in an efficient manner, with minimal burdens on individual taxpayers, consumers, and firms; and an examination of possible unintended effects and their consequences.

As an illustration of how evaluations can inform budgetary decisions, consider education, and research investment credits.

Education. There are millions of individuals taking advantage of tax credits designed to help pay for educational expenses. There are a number of different credits available as well as other important forms of Federal support for higher education such as subsidized loans and grants. An evaluation would explore the possible relationships between use of the credits and the use of loans and grants, seeking to answer, for example, whether the use of credits reduce or increase the likelihood of the students applying for loans. Such an evaluation would allow stakeholders to determine the most effective program – whether it is a tax credit, a subsidized loan, or a grant.

Investment. A series of tax expenditures reduce the cost of investment, both in specific activities such as research and experimentation, extractive industries, and certain financial activities and more generally throughout the economy, through accelerated depreciation for plant and equipment. These provisions can be evaluated along a number of dimensions. For example, it is useful to consider the strength of the incentives by measuring their effects on the cost of capital (the return which investments must yield to cover their costs) and effective tax rates. The impact of these provisions on the amounts of corresponding forms of investment (e.g., research spending, exploration activity, equipment) might also be estimated. In some cases, such as research, there is evidence that the investment can provide significant positive externalities—that is, economic benefits that are not reflected in the market transactions between private parties. It could be useful to quantify these externalities and compare them with the size of tax expenditures. Measures could also indicate the effects on production from these investments such as numbers or values of patents, energy production and reserves, and industrial production. Issues to be considered include the extent to which the preferences increase production (as opposed to benefiting existing output) and their cost-effectiveness relative to other policies. Analysis could also consider objectives that are more difficult to measure but still are ultimate goals, such as promoting the Nation's technological base, energy security, environmental quality, or economic growth. Such an assessment is likely to involve tax analysis as well as consideration of non-tax matters such as market structure, scientific, and other information (such as the effects of increased domestic fuel production on imports from various regions, or the effects of various energy sources on the environment).

The tax proposals subject to these analyses include items that indirectly affect the estimated value of tax expenditures (such as changes in income tax rates), proposals that make reforms to improve tax compliance and administration, as well as proposals which would change, add, or delete tax expenditures.

Barriers to Evaluation. Developing a framework that is sufficiently comprehensive, accurate, and flexible is a significant challenge. Evaluations are constrained by the availability of appropriate data and challenges in economic modeling:

- Data availability. Data may not exist, or may not exist in an analytically appropriate form, to conduct rigorous evaluations of certain types of expenditures. For example, measuring the effects of tax expenditures designed to achieve tax neutrality for individuals and firms earning income abroad, and foreign firms could require data from foreign governments or firms which are not readily available.

- Analytical constraints. Evaluations of tax expenditures face analytical constraints even when data are available. For example, individuals might have access to several tax expenditures and programs aimed at improving the same outcome. Isolating the effect of a single tax credit is challenging absent a well-specified research design.

- Resources. Tax expenditure analyses are seriously constrained by staffing considerations. Evaluations typically require expert analysts who are often engaged in other more competing areas of work related to the budget.

The Executive Branch is focused on addressing these challenges to lay the foundation for the analysis of tax expenditures comprehensively, alongside evaluations of the effectiveness of direct spending initiatives.

SPECIAL TOPICS

14. AID TO STATE AND LOCAL GOVERNMENTS

The analysis in this chapter focuses on Federal spending that is provided to State and local governments, U.S. territories, and American Indian Tribal governments to help fund programs administered by those entities and provide economic support. This type of Federal spending is known as Federal grants-in-aid. Grants in aid are the most direct form of Federal support to State and local governments, but the Federal Government provides other important forms of support as well, including direct payments to State residents, direct intervention in times of natural disaster, and tax expenditures benefiting States and localities.[1] Finally, the Federal Government's efforts to promote economic growth are critical to maintaining a healthy tax base for States and local governments and creating jobs for State residents.

Under our Nation's federalist structure, States are sovereign entities and generally have the authority to legislate on all activity within their borders "concerning the promotion and regulation of safety, health, welfare, and economic activity."[2] The Federal Government's role is limited under the U.S. Constitution to the enumerated powers, and, under the Tenth Amendment, all of the authorities not given to the Federal Government are reserved to the States and their people.[3] However, the Spending Clause of the Constitution has been interpreted to allow the Federal Government to provide funds to States (and other non-Federal entities) and to specify the terms and conditions that accompany acceptance of those funds.[4]

In the 19th century, most Federal grants came in the form of land and were used for canals, waterways, railroads, and land grant colleges.[5] During the Great Depression (1929-1939), the reach of Federal grants-in-aid expanded to meet income security and other social welfare needs. The Federal Emergency Relief Act of 1933 was the first piece of legislation that specifically provided fiscal relief to States through grants.[6] Federal grants, however, did not become a significant portion of Federal Government expenditures until after World War II. During the middle of the 20th century, the Eisenhower Administration made large investments in the National infrastructure system through the creation of the Interstate Highway program. Since the 1960s, there have been significant increases in grant spending for education, training, employment, and social services; income security; and health (primarily Medicaid). In the 1980s, there was an effort to control grant spending and reduce the number of Federal grants by combining programs into block grants.[7]

Today, 16, or two-thirds, of Executive Branch agencies and 13 independent agencies provide grants to State and local governments, and grant spending has increased from 1.3 percent of GDP in 1960 to 3.5 percent of GDP in 2017. Over many decades, the increasing number of grants and size of grants has created overlap between programs, and complexity for grantees, and has made it difficult to compare program performance and conduct oversight.[8] The multiple layers of grants administration can increase the cost of administration and create inefficiencies and duplication.[9] Less Federal control gives State and local recipients more flexibility to use their knowledge of local conditions and needs to administer programs and projects more efficiently.[10] The 2019 Budget takes steps toward limiting the Federal role, and reducing spending.

Federal grants are authorized by the Congress in statute, which establishes the purpose of the grant and how it is awarded. Federal grants generally fall into one of two broad categories—block grants or categorical grants—depending on the requirements of the grant program. Block grants give States and localities more flexibility to define the use and distribution of the funding and are awarded on a formula basis specified in law. Categorical grants provide less flexibility than block grants. Categorical grants have a narrowly defined purpose and may be awarded on a formula basis or as a project grant. Project grants, a type of categorical grant, are the least flexible, are often awarded competitively, and are typified by a predetermined end product or duration. Project grants can include grants for research, training, evaluation, planning, technical assistance, survey work, and construction. In addition, grants may be characterized by how the funding is awarded, such as by formula, by project, or by matching State and local funds.

---

[1] Historical Federal spending for grants and direct payments for individuals may be found in the Budget's historical tables in tables 6.1, 11.1, 11.2, and 11.3 at *https://www.whitehouse.gov/omb/historical-tables/*. Information on Federal credit programs targeted to States and localities may be found in Chapter 19, "Credit and Insurance," in this volume. Chapter 13, "Tax Expenditures," in this volume, discusses this topic and includes a display of tax expenditures that particularly aid State and local governments at the end of Tables 13-1 and 13-2.

[2] Yeh, Brian T. "The Federal Government's Authority to Impose Conditions on Grant Funds." Congressional Research Service, the Library of Congress. March 23, 2017. p. 3.

[3] Ibid., p. 1-2.

[4] Ibid., p. 4.

[5] Canada, Ben. "Federal Grants to State and Local Governments: A Brief History. Congressional Research Service, the Library of Congress. February 19, 2003.

[6] Ibid.

[7] "Block Grants: Characteristics, Experience, and Lessons Learned." U.S. General Accounting Office. February 1995.

[8] Keegan, Natalie. "Federal Grants-in-Aid Administration: A Primer." Congressional Research Service, the Library of Congress. October 3, 2012. p. 2.

[9] "Federal Grants to State and Local Governments." Congressional Budget Office. March 2013, p. 8.

[10] Ibid., p. 2.

Most often Federal grants-in-aid are awarded as direct cash assistance, but Federal grants-in-aid can also include payments for grants-in-kind—non-monetary aid, such as commodities purchased for the National School Lunch Program. Federal revenues shared with State and local governments, such as funds distributed to State and local law enforcement agencies from Federal asset forfeiture programs, are also considered grants-in-aid.

Federal grants-in-aid are an important part of State budgets. It is estimated that 31.3 percent of total State spending in State fiscal year[11] 2017, which is estimated to reach nearly $2 trillion, will have come from Federal funds.[12] Federal funds aid States particularly because many States have requirements in law or State constitutions to enact balanced budgets, limiting debt or debt service, and limiting carrying over deficits. These restrictions create fiscal discipline, but also give States few options when facing shortfalls. State budgets are formulated based on revenue projections and when actual revenues come in lower than expected States may enact mid-year budget cuts or tap budget stabilization (rainy day) funds. Only some States may carry over a deficit under certain circumstances.

In its Fiscal Survey of States, the National Association of State Budget Officers (NASBO) looks at enacted State budgets to make projections for the coming year and at general fund[13] spending as an indication of State fiscal health. General funds are the largest category of total State spending, accounting for an estimated 40.3 percent of State spending in 2017, followed by Federal funds.[14] According to the most recent report, State 2018 budgets reflect caution after two years of lower-than-expected revenue growth and increase overall by only 2.3 percent over

2017.[15] However, the report suggests that States are forecasting modest improvements in revenue collections in 2018.[16] This is bolstered by a December report from the U.S. Census Bureau, which reported that third quarter 2017 tax revenues for the four largest State and local government tax categories increased 3.1 percent over 2016.[17] Many States are continuing to build back up rainy day funds after the recession in 2009. Fiscal year 2018 enacted budgets suggest 25 States are projecting total rainy day fund balances higher than last year.[18]

Also affecting State revenues and budgets is the Tax Cuts and Jobs Act, Public Law 115-97, enacted in December 2017, which will prompt States to look at their own tax laws. There are many differences across States as to whether or how their tax codes tie or conform to the Federal tax code. Each State will need to assess how the new Federal tax changes will affect future revenues and what adjustments they want to make.

The 2019 Budget refocuses Federal grants to State and local governments on the highest priority areas for Federal support, and recognizes a greater role for State and local governments, and the private sector as part of the Budget's proposals to restore Federal fiscal responsibility. This Budget slows the growth of grant spending over the 10-year budget window and, in particular, starts to rein in the growth of Medicaid, which accounts for 55 percent of total grant spending to State and local governments. The Budget provides $749 billion in outlays for aid to State and local governments in 2019, an increase of 3 percent from 2018. The increase is entirely due to spending for the Administration's infrastructure initiative; all grant spending other than for Medicaid and the infrastructure initiative will decline by 11 percent in 2019. Total Federal grant spending to State and local governments is estimated to be 3.6 percent of GDP in 2019 and 17 percent of total Federal outlays. Below are highlights from the Budget listed by function followed by Table 14-1 which shows the Budget's funding level for grants in every budget account, organized by functional category and by Federal agency.

---

[11] According to "The Fiscal Survey of States" published by the National Association of State Budget Officers (Fall 2017), "Forty-six states begin their fiscal years in July and end them in June. The exceptions are New York, which starts its fiscal year on April 1; Texas, with a September 1 start date; and Alabama and Michigan, which start their fiscal years on October 1."

[12] "The Fiscal Survey of States." National Association of State Budget Officers, Fall 2017. p. 1.

[13] A State general fund is "the predominant fund for financing a state's operations. Revenues are received from broad-based state taxes. However, there are differences in how specific functions are financed from state to state." State Expenditure Report, Examining Fiscal 2015-2017 State Spending. The National Association of State Budget Officers. 2017. p. 5.

[14] "The Fiscal Survey of States." National Association of State Budget Officers, Fall 2017. p. 1.

[15] Ibid. p. VII-1.

[16] Ibid.

[17] United States Census Bureau. Quarterly Summary of State and Local Government Tax Revenue for 2017: Q3. *https://www.census.gov/library/publications/2017/econ/g17-qtax3.html*

[18] "The Fiscal Survey of States." National Association of State Budget Officers, Fall 2017. p. IX.

HIGHLIGHTS

Natural Resources and Environment

To expand hunting opportunities, the Budget invests $34 million in North American Wetlands Conservation Act grants, a program that finances conservation of wetlands and associated uplands habitat to benefit waterfowl. The Budget includes elimination of discretionary Abandoned Mine Land grants that overlap with existing mandatory grants, aid for National Heritage Areas that are more appropriately funded locally, and National Wildlife Refuge fund payments to local governments that are duplicative of other payment programs.

States are the primary implementers of many Federal environmental statutes and critical partners in protecting the Nation's environment and human health. The States have long sought flexibility to direct grant resources to their individual priorities, rather than receiving funding only through grants dedicated to specific programs. This Budget recognizes and responds to this need by providing $27 million for "Multipurpose Grants" within EPA's Categorical Grant portfolio totaling $597 million. States would be able to spend this funding on any statutorily mandated delegated duty. This proposal would enable each State to set its own environmental priorities and quickly respond to new threats as they arise.

The Budget funds water infrastructure through the State Revolving Funds. The 2019 capitalization of the State Revolving Funds would supplement the approximately $80 billion currently revolving at the State level.

The 2019 Budget prioritizes funding for Brownfields site assessment grants in order to accelerate investment in local communities. The EPA Brownfields program provides competitive grants to local communities to address sites where redevelopment is challenged by the presence or potential presence of contamination. EPA's Brownfields program site assessment grants provide useful information to communities about the extent of contamination at a property. Real estate developers use this information to estimate future cleanup costs and to plan for redevelopment of the property. EPA brownfields grantees report that approximately 30 percent of brownfield properties that are assessed using EPA Brownfields funding do not require remediation for the intended reuse of the property; although, in some cases, institutional controls may be required. Finding that remediation is not necessary for the intended reuse of the site means faster redevelopment and the return of the property to productive use.

Community and Regional Development

The Budget eliminates programs that are duplicative or have failed to demonstrate effectiveness, such as the Community Development Block Grant (CDBG) program, and devolves responsibility for community and economic development to State and local governments that are better equipped to respond to local conditions.

The Budget also eliminates the Economic Development Administration, which provides small grants with limited measurable impacts and duplicates other Federal programs, such as Rural Utilities Service grants at the Department of Agriculture and formula grants to States from the Department of Transportation.

The Budget continues to invest in key areas, including $30 million to fund broadband grants and $24 million to fund distance learning and telemedicine grants to provide rural communities with modern information access. A new program of Rural Infrastructure grants is included as part of the Budget's infrastructure initiative. See that section below for more details.

Lead paint in housing presents a significant threat to the health, safety, and future productivity of America's next generation. The Budget continues to make progress to promote healthy and lead-safe homes by providing $145 million, equal to the 2017 enacted level, for the mitigation of lead-based paint and other hazards in low-income homes, especially those in which children reside. This funding level also includes resources for enforcement, education, and research activities to further support this

goal. Research suggests that this program generates high returns on investment due to higher wages and reduced medical costs.

The Budget requests $1.9 billion for the Federal Emergency Management Agency (FEMA) for its programs that award grants to State and local governments. These funds help equip emergency responders so they can be prepared for natural or manmade disasters. Responding to and recovering from any disaster is a community-wide effort that relies on the strength of Federal agencies, such as FEMA, State, local, and tribal governments, as well as non-governmental entities and individuals. The Budget also supports efforts by communities to invest their own resources by establishing a non-Federal cost share for certain FEMA grant programs, and proposing to eliminate the National Domestic Preparedness Consortium.

Education, Training, Employment, and Social Services

The Budget maintains funding for essential formula grant programs that support the Nation's neediest students, including those in low-income communities and students with disabilities. The Budget also streamlines and refocuses the Federal investment in K-12 education by eliminating funding for 17 programs totaling $4.4 billion that are duplicative, ineffective, or more appropriately supported through State, local, or private funds. The Budget requests $500 million to establish a new school choice grant program to support a wide range of innovative approaches to school choice. These might include expanding existing private school choice programs to serve more low-income and at-risk students, developing new private school choice models, or supporting school districts' efforts to adopt student-based budgeting and open enrollment policies that enable Federal, State and local funding to follow the student to the public school of his or her choice.

To support State and local education agencies in providing high-quality special education services to more than 6.8 million children with disabilities, the Budget maintains the Federal investment in the Individuals with Disabilities Education Act (IDEA) formula and discretionary grant programs. The Budget invests $12.8 billion for IDEA formula grants to States to support special education and early intervention services. In addition, the Budget requests $222 million for discretionary grants to States, institutions of higher education, and other non-profit organizations to support research, demonstrations, technical assistance and dissemination, and personnel preparation and development. These investments would ensure that high-quality special education and related services would meet the unique needs of children with disabilities and their families.

The Budget invests $43 million for School Climate Transformation grants to help school districts implement multi-tiered, evidence-based strategies to prevent opioid-misuse and address associated behavioral and academic challenges through interventions such as trauma counselling, violence prevention and targeted academic support. This funding would also support technical assistance centers that develop and provide opioid abuse prevention and treatment resources that would be publicly available to all schools and postsecondary institutions.

The Budget proposes to restructure and streamline the TRIO and GEAR UP programs by consolidating them into a $550 million State formula grant. These grants would support evidence-based postsecondary preparation programs designed to help low-income students progress from middle school to postsecondary opportunities. The Budget supports STEM education through a variety of programs including those that test and replicate what works in education and a new, $20 million grant program for STEM-focused career and technical education programs.

Eliminations in the Budget include Supporting Effective Instruction State Grants, and 21st Century Community Learning Centers.

Health

The Budget includes a new Market-Based Health Care Grant Program for States, as part of its two-part approach to repeal and replace Obamacare. The Market-Based Health Care Grant Program would provide more equitable and sustainable funding to States to develop affordable healthcare options. The block grant program will promote structural reforms to improve the functioning of the healthcare market through greater choice, and competition, with States and consumers in charge rather than the Washington bureaucracy. The Budget would allow States to use the block grant for a variety of approaches in order to help their citizens, including those with high cost medical needs, afford quality healthcare services. The block grant approach also reflects the Administration's view that Federal Government subsidies are better targeted directly to States and consumers rather than funneled through insurance companies as is the case under Obamacare. In addition, the Budget also includes $5 billion over five years to combat the opioid epidemic as part of the repeal and replacement effort.

Medicaid financing reform would empower States to design individual, State-based solutions that prioritize Medicaid dollars for the most vulnerable and support innovations such as community engagement initiatives for able-bodied adults. National healthcare spending trends are unsustainable in the long term and the Budget includes additional proposals to build on the Graham Cassidy Heller Johnson bill to make the system more efficient, including proposals to align the Market-Based Health Care Grant Program, Medicaid per capita cap and block grant growth rates with the Consumer Price Index (CPI-U).

In addition to the program flexibilities included in the Budget proposal to repeal and replace Obamacare, the Budget proposes to empower States to further modernize Medicaid benefits and eligibility. The Budget would give States additional flexibility around benefits and cost-sharing, allow States to consider savings and other assets when determining Medicaid eligibility, and would reduce waste by counting lottery winnings as income for Medicaid eligibility. These proposals enable the Federal and State Governments to be partners in greater fiscal responsibility, which would preserve and protect the Medicaid program for Americans who truly need it.

The Budget maintains funding for the Community Mental Health Services Block Grant, which requires States to support services for first episode psychosis, which is vitally important to ensuring that individuals with serious mental illness receive appropriate treatment in a timely manner.

The Ryan White HIV/AIDS Program provides a comprehensive system of primary medical care, treatment, and supportive services to over half a million people living with HIV, which is more than half of the people in the United States who have been diagnosed with HIV. The Budget supports reauthorizing the Ryan White Program to ensure Federal funds are allocated to address the changing landscape of HIV across the United States. Reauthorization of the Ryan White Program should include data-driven programmatic changes as well as simplifying and standardizing certain requirements and definitions. These changes would ensure Federal funds may be allocated to populations experiencing high or increasing levels of HIV infections/diagnoses while continuing to support Americans already living with HIV across the Nation.

Income Security

The Budget invests in a better future for Americans with a fully paid-for proposal to provide six weeks of paid family leave to new mothers and fathers, including adoptive parents, so all families can afford to take time to recover from childbirth and bond with a new child. Using the Unemployment Insurance system as a base, the proposal would allow States to establish paid parental leave programs in a way that is most appropriate for their workforce and economy. The Administration looks forward to working with the Congress to advance policies that would make paid parental leave a reality for families across the Nation.

The Budget provides $33.8 billion across the Department of Housing and Urban Development's (HUD's) rental assistance programs, a decrease of 11 percent relative to the 2017 enacted level. To address the increasing and unsustainable Federal costs of rental assistance, the Budget requests legislative reforms that would produce significant cost savings. In addition to these reforms, the Budget proposes one-time offsets in the Housing Voucher and Public Housing programs. These funding levels should support currently assisted households while gradually decreasing the Federal footprint of HUD's rental assistance programs over time.

The Budget does not request funding for the Public Housing Capital Fund, as the provision of affordable housing should be a responsibility more fully shared with State and local governments.

The Budget also eliminates the HOME Investment Partnerships Program, which has not been authorized since 1994. The Budget devolves responsibility to State and local governments, which are better positioned to assess local community needs and address unique market challenges.

The Budget provides investments and statutory authorities to facilitate a shift from the Public Housing funding platform to Housing Vouchers and Project-Based Rental Assistance (PBRA). The Voucher and PBRA programs benefit from greater private sector involvement and are able to leverage private financing to modernize their units, generally resulting in higher quality housing for assisted low-income families. To further this objective, the Budget requests $100 million for the Rental Assistance Demonstration, which supports the redevelopment of Public Housing units through conversion to the Housing Voucher and PBRA funding platforms. Additional authorities in the Public Housing program, such as tenant protection vouchers and the strategic release of certain public housing assets, would also assist in this effort.

The Budget provides $2.4 billion for the Homeless Assistance Grants (HAG) program, equal to the 2017 enacted level. HAG primarily funds the Continuum of Care program, which is designed to prevent and address homelessness through a coordinated community-based network of programs. HUD uses its annual grant competition to encourage grantees to allocate funds to evidence-based and cost-effective strategies. These policies have encouraged communities to increasingly support evidence-based interventions such as permanent supportive housing rather than models like transitional housing that have been proven less effective. The Budget also provides $255 million for Emergency Solutions Grants, which enable municipalities to support emergency shelter, rapid rehousing, and homelessness prevention.

The Budget proposes to provide $5.8 billion to serve all projected participants in the Special Supplemental Nutrition Program for Women, Infants, and Children (WIC), which provides for nutritious supplemental food packages, nutrition education and counseling, and health and immunization referrals to low-income and nutritionally at-risk pregnant and postpartum women, infants, and children. The Budget promotes using data to improve efficiency and integrity in State operations of the Supplemental Nutrition Assistance Program (SNAP), and proposes to encourage State innovation in developing pathways to self-sufficiency through work among able-bodied adults.

The Budget continues to invest in programs that help American families and children thrive. The Budget supports States in providing key services to children and youth by increasing State flexibilities and reducing administrative burdens in foster care. The Budget also helps working families afford and access child care by maintaining funding for key HHS child care programs and using these investments to leverage additional State support for child care.

The Budget continues the 2018 Budget proposals to eliminate low-performing or ineffective programs, such as the Low Income Home Energy Assistance Program (LIHEAP) and the Community Services Block Grant (CSBG).

Administration of Justice

The Budget includes $103 million for opioid-related State and local assistance including: $20 million for the Comprehensive Opioid Abuse Program to support a variety of activities such as treatment and recovery support services, diversion, and alternative to incarceration programs; $59 million for Drug Courts, Mental Health Courts, and Veterans Treatment Courts; $12 million for Residential Substance Abuse Treatment; and $12 million for Prescription Drug Monitoring Programs. The Budget also supports key State and local assistance programs, including $333 million for the Byrne Justice Assistance Grants (JAG) Program, which provides State and local governments with crucial Federal funding to prevent and control crime. These resources also contribute to important officer safety programs serving State and local law enforcement such as the Bulletproof Vest program. Additionally, $70 million is provided for the Violent Gang and Gun Crime Reduction Program/Project Safe Neighborhoods (PSN). This program will reinvigorate and build on DOJ's ongoing PSN Initiative to create safer neighborhoods through sustained reductions in gang violence and gun crime. This program relies on partnerships of Federal, State, and local agencies led by U.S. Attorneys to enhance the effectiveness of its crime and violence reduction efforts.

The Budget also supports $230 million for State and local juvenile justice programs, including programs aimed at delinquency prevention, intervention, and making improvements to the juvenile justice system. Another $5 million is set aside to support the Public Safety Partnership program, which leverages DOJ resources to reduce violence in cities with the highest violent crime rates in the Nation. The Budget provides $486 million to reinforce efforts to combat and respond to violent crimes against women, including $215 million for the STOP Violence Against Women Formula Grant Program.

Transportation

The Budget provides $2.6 billion to the Federal Highway Administration's (FHWA) Highway Safety Improvement Program, to assist States in the implementation of their safety plans. The request also funds other FHWA, National Highway Traffic Safety Administration (NHTSA), and Federal Motor Carriers Safety Administration (FMCSA) safety programs, to prevent highway fatalities. The Budget requests $57.4 billion in mandatory funds and obligation limitation to improve the Nation's highways, bridges and transit systems. This request includes $46 billion for highway infrastructure and safety programs, $9.9 billion for transit infrastructure, and $1.4 billion for NHTSA and FMCSA safety programs. These levels match the authorized amounts in the Fixing America's Surface Transportation Act of 2015 (FAST Act).

The Budget also eliminates funding for the unauthorized TIGER discretionary grant program, which awards grants to projects that are generally eligible for funding under existing surface transportation formula grant and loan programs. In addition, DOT's Infrastructure for Rebuilding America grant program, authorized by the FAST Act, supports larger highway and multimodal freight projects with demonstrable national or regional benefits. The Budget also proposes to wind down the Federal Transit Administration's Capital Investment Grant program (New Starts), by limiting funding to projects with existing full funding grant agreements only.

Infrastructure Initiative

The Administration's infrastructure initiative includes three new grant programs: Incentive Grants, Transformative Project Grants, and Rural Infrastructure Grants.

Incentive Grants are competitive grants that encourage increased State, local, and private infrastructure investment by awarding incentives to project sponsors for demonstrating innovative approaches that would generate new revenue streams, prioritize maintenance, modernize procurement practices, and generate a social and economic return on investment. The Budget provides $1 billion in outlays for this program in 2019 and $100 billion in total through 2028.

Transformative Project Grants will act to support bold, innovative, and transformative infrastructure projects that can significantly improve existing infrastructure conditions and services. Funding would be awarded on a competitive basis for commercially viable projects that are capable of generating revenue, provide net public benefits, and would have a significant positive impact on the Nation, a region, State, or metropolitan area. The Budget provides $15 million in outlays in 2019 and $20 billion in total through 2028.

The Rural Infrastructure Grants would address the significant need for investment in rural infrastructure, including broadband internet service. Federal funding would be made available to States and territories via formula distribution, along with a bonus competition based on State performance in achieving goals outlined in State-developed rural infrastructure plans. Within this amount, funding is set aside for Federally recognized Tribes. The Budget provides $41 billion in outlays in 2019 and $50 billion in total through 2028.

The grant programs in the Administration's infrastructure initiative cut across multiple budget functions and proposals within it may be found under the Community and Regional Development, and Allowances functions in Table 14-1.

Table 14–1. FEDERAL GRANTS TO STATE AND LOCAL GOVERNMENTS—BUDGET AUTHORITY AND OUTLAYS

(In millions of dollars)

Function, Category, Agency and Program	Budget Authority			Outlays		
	2017 Actual	2018 Estimate	2019 Estimate	2017 Actual	2018 Estimate	2019 Estimate
Energy						
Discretionary:						
Department of Energy:						
Energy Programs:						
Energy Efficiency and Renewable Energy	275	275	....	250	250	210
Mandatory:						
Tennessee Valley Authority:						
Tennessee Valley Authority Fund	524	510	512	524	510	512
Total, Energy	**799**	**785**	**512**	**774**	**760**	**722**
Natural Resources and Environment						
Discretionary:						
Department of Agriculture:						
Farm Service Agency:						
Grassroots Source Water Protection Program	7	7	....	7	7	....
Natural Resources Conservation Service:						
Watershed Rehabilitation Program	27	15	....	33	10	....
Watershed and Flood Prevention Operations	172	356	....	57	117	....
Forest Service:						
State and Private Forestry	143	164	162	158	169	192
Department of Commerce:						
National Oceanic and Atmospheric Administration:						
Operations, Research, and Facilities	90	....	....	88	....	....
Pacific Coastal Salmon Recovery	65	65	....	58	66	63
Department of the Interior:						
Office of Surface Mining Reclamation and Enforcement:						
Regulation and Technology	69	68	52	62	69	62

Table 14–1. FEDERAL GRANTS TO STATE AND LOCAL GOVERNMENTS—BUDGET AUTHORITY AND OUTLAYS—Continued
(In millions of dollars)

Function, Category, Agency and Program	Budget Authority			Outlays		
	2017 Actual	2018 Estimate	2019 Estimate	2017 Actual	2018 Estimate	2019 Estimate
Abandoned Mine Reclamation Fund	132	131	20	34	46	40
United States Geological Survey:						
Surveys, Investigations, and Research	6	6	....	6	6	....
United States Fish and Wildlife Service:						
Cooperative Endangered Species Conservation Fund	53	53	....	44	56	55
State Wildlife Grants	63	62	31	61	74	67
Landowner Incentive Program	....	....	....	1	....	....
National Park Service:						
National Recreation and Preservation	63	62	32	61	66	48
Land Acquisition and State Assistance	4	109	....	47	70	76
Historic Preservation Fund	81	80	33	66	101	78
Environmental Protection Agency:						
State and Tribal Assistance Grants	3,566	3,442	2,402	3,453	3,439	2,284
Hazardous Substance Superfund	18	19	16	217	220	218
Leaking Underground Storage Tank Trust Fund	80	80	42	80	80	60
Total, discretionary	**4,639**	**4,719**	**2,790**	**4,533**	**4,596**	**3,243**
Mandatory:						
Department of Commerce:						
National Oceanic and Atmospheric Administration:						
Gulf Coast Ecosystem Restoration Science, Observation, Monitoring, and Technology	8	6	6	2	5	5
Department of the Interior:						
Bureau of Land Management:						
Miscellaneous Permanent Payment Accounts	43	39	28	39	39	30
Office of Surface Mining Reclamation and Enforcement:						
Payments to States in Lieu of Coal Fee Receipts	....	....	....	29	30	30
Abandoned Mine Reclamation Fund	135	194	211	166	174	185
United States Fish and Wildlife Service:						
Federal Aid in Wildlife Restoration	787	817	909	700	746	852
Cooperative Endangered Species Conservation Fund	76	75	73	76	75	73
Coastal Impact Assistance	....	....	....	142	3	2
Sport Fish Restoration	435	439	470	446	465	487
National Park Service:						
Land Acquisition and State Assistance	....	63	89	1	14	27
Departmental Offices:						
National Forests Fund, Payment to States	6	8	9	6	8	9
Leases of Lands Acquired for Flood Control, Navigation, and Allied Purposes	14	48	51	14	48	51
States Share from Certain Gulf of Mexico Leases	1	188	268	1	188	268
Corps of Engineers--Civil Works:						
South Dakota Terrestrial Wildlife Habitat Restoration Trust Fund	2	2	3	....	3	3
Total, mandatory	**1,507**	**1,879**	**2,117**	**1,622**	**1,798**	**2,022**
Total, Natural Resources and Environment	**6,146**	**6,598**	**4,907**	**6,155**	**6,394**	**5,265**
Agriculture						
Discretionary:						
Department of Agriculture:						
National Institute of Food and Agriculture:						
Extension Activities	418	447	399	388	594	545
Research and Education Activities	336	334	326	308	341	341
Agricultural Marketing Service:						
Payments to States and Possessions	1	1	1	1	1	1

Table 14–1. FEDERAL GRANTS TO STATE AND LOCAL GOVERNMENTS—BUDGET AUTHORITY AND OUTLAYS—Continued

(In millions of dollars)

Function, Category, Agency and Program	Budget Authority			Outlays		
	2017 Actual	2018 Estimate	2019 Estimate	2017 Actual	2018 Estimate	2019 Estimate
Farm Service Agency:						
State Mediation Grants	4	4	3	4	2	3
Total, discretionary	**759**	**786**	**729**	**701**	**938**	**890**
Mandatory:						
Department of Agriculture:						
Payments to States and Possessions	67	85	85	62	68	73
Total, Agriculture	**826**	**871**	**814**	**763**	**1,006**	**963**
Commerce and Housing Credit						
Discretionary:						
Department of Commerce:						
National Oceanic and Atmospheric Administration:						
Fisheries Disaster Assistance	....	....	....	8	16	....
Mandatory:						
Department of Commerce:						
National Telecommunications and Information Administration:						
State and Local Implementation Fund	....	....	....	20	9	12
Department of the Treasury:						
Departmental Offices:						
State Small Business Credit Initiative	....	....	....	28	25	....
Federal Communications Commission:						
Universal Service Fund	1,416	1,697	1,971	2,199	2,360	2,261
Total, mandatory	**1,416**	**1,697**	**1,971**	**2,247**	**2,394**	**2,273**
Total, Commerce and Housing Credit	**1,416**	**1,697**	**1,971**	**2,255**	**2,410**	**2,273**
Transportation						
Discretionary:						
Department of Transportation:						
Office of the Secretary:						
National Infrastructure Investments	479	477	....	357	667	561
Federal Aviation Administration:						
Grants-in-aid for Airports (Airport and Airway Trust Fund)	....	....	....	3,129	3,291	3,314
Grants-in-aid for Airports (Airport and Airway Trust Fund) (non-add obligation limitations)[1]	*3,350*	*3,327*	*3,350*	....	....	....
Federal Highway Administration:						
Emergency Relief Program	1,532	....	....	515	611	496
Highway Infrastructure Programs	....	....	....	3	....	....
Appalachian Development Highway System	....	....	−46	1	4	4
Federal-aid Highways	107	105	110	42,498	42,592	43,782
Federal-aid Highways (non-add obligation limitations)[1]	*40,328*	*41,573*	*43,969*	....	....	....
Miscellaneous Appropriations	....	....	−112	27	31	22
Miscellaneous Highway Trust Funds	....	....	−59	11	12	7
Federal Motor Carrier Safety Administration:						
Motor Carrier Safety Grants	....	....	....	277	336	373
Motor Carrier Safety Grants (non-add obligation limitations)[1]	*367*	*365*	*382*	....	....	....
National Highway Traffic Safety Administration:						
Highway Traffic Safety Grants	....	....	....	621	629	635
Highway Traffic Safety Grants (non-add obligation limitations)[1]	*585*	*680*	*610*	....	....	....
Federal Railroad Administration:						
Northeast Corridor Improvement Program	....	....	....	....	1	3
Capital and Debt Service Grants to the National Railroad Passenger Corporation	....	....	....	263	62	5
Restoration and Enhancement Grants	5	5	....	....	....	....
Railroad Safety Grants	....	....	....	....	16	14

Table 14–1. FEDERAL GRANTS TO STATE AND LOCAL GOVERNMENTS—BUDGET AUTHORITY AND OUTLAYS—Continued

(In millions of dollars)

Function, Category, Agency and Program	Budget Authority			Outlays		
	2017 Actual	2018 Estimate	2019 Estimate	2017 Actual	2018 Estimate	2019 Estimate
Grants to the National Railroad Passenger Corporation	....	....	....	11	5	9
Intercity Passenger Rail Grant Program	....	....	....	....	21	2
Rail Line Relocation and Improvement Program	....	....	–2	3	4	1
Capital Assistance for High Speed Rail Corridors and Intercity Passenger Rail Service	....	....	–53	2,567	302	82
Northeast Corridor Grants to the National Railroad Passenger Corporation	326	325	199	321	325	199
National Network Grants to the National Railroad Passenger Corporation	1,160	1,153	535	1,160	1,152	538
Federal-State Partnership for State of Good Repair	25	25	....	....	....	....
Consolidated Rail Infrastructure and Safety Improvements	68	68	....	....	....	....
Federal Transit Administration:						
Washington Metropolitan Area Transit Authority	150	149	120	204	150	105
Formula Grants	....	....	–47	19	33	25
Grants for Energy Efficiency and Greenhouse Gas Reductions	....	....	....	16	9	....
Capital Investment Grants	2,413	2,396	1,000	1,907	2,100	2,100
Public Transportation Emergency Relief Program	....	....	....	518	1,053	834
Transit Formula Grants	....	....	....	9,460	9,786	9,985
Transit Formula Grants (non-add obligation limitations) [1]	*11,170*	*10,968*	*11,239*	....	....	....
Pipeline and Hazardous Materials Safety Administration:						
Pipeline Safety	51	47	47	40	54	54
Trust Fund Share of Pipeline Safety	8	8	8	9	8	8
Total, discretionary	**6,324**	**4,758**	**1,700**	**63,937**	**63,254**	**63,158**
Total, obligation limitations (non-add) [1]	*55,800*	*56,913*	*59,550*	....	....	....
Mandatory:						
Department of Homeland Security:						
United States Coast Guard:						
Boat Safety	105	107	115	106	109	122
Department of Transportation:						
Federal Aviation Administration:						
Grants-in-aid for Airports (Airport and Airway Trust Fund) [1]	3,196	3,197	3,189	....	....	....
Federal Highway Administration:						
Federal-aid Highways [1]	41,125	42,249	44,243	738	742	743
Miscellaneous Appropriations	2	251	....	2	251	....
Federal Motor Carrier Safety Administration:						
Motor Carrier Safety Grants [1]	367	375	382	....	....	....
National Highway Traffic Safety Administration:						
Highway Traffic Safety Grants [1]	624	635	547	....	....	....
Federal Transit Administration:						
Transit Formula Grants [1]	11,170	11,005	11,211	....	....	....
Total, mandatory	**56,589**	**57,819**	**59,687**	**846**	**1,102**	**865**
Total, Transportation	**62,913**	**62,577**	**61,387**	**64,783**	**64,356**	**64,023**
Community and Regional Development						
Discretionary:						
Department of Agriculture:						
Rural Utilities Service:						
Distance Learning, Telemedicine, and Broadband Program	141	64	58	123	46	59
Rural Water and Waste Disposal Program Account	516	556	–34	493	502	661
Rural Housing Service:						
Rural Community Facilities Program Account	47	47	145	40	50	197
Rural Business_Cooperative Service:						
Rural Business Program Account	65	65	....	71	87	57
Department of Commerce:						
Economic Development Administration:						

Table 14–1. FEDERAL GRANTS TO STATE AND LOCAL GOVERNMENTS—BUDGET AUTHORITY AND OUTLAYS—Continued

(In millions of dollars)

Function, Category, Agency and Program	Budget Authority			Outlays		
	2017 Actual	2018 Estimate	2019 Estimate	2017 Actual	2018 Estimate	2019 Estimate
Economic Development Assistance Programs	227	225	–40	249	299	296
Department of Homeland Security:						
Federal Emergency Management Agency:						
Federal Assistance	2,687	2,669	1,981	84	1,518	1,626
State and Local Programs	–11	–4	....	2,119	1,479	1,047
Disaster Relief Fund	11,779	17,642	4,067	5,348	20,076	10,340
National Flood Insurance Fund	11	10	10	11	10	10
Department of Housing and Urban Development:						
Community Planning and Development:						
Community Development Fund	12,666	3,039	....	5,616	7,094	8,004
Community Development Loan Guarantees Program Account	....	....	....	1	3	3
Brownfields Redevelopment	....	....	....	....	3	3
Office of Lead Hazard Control and Healthy Homes:						
Lead Hazard Reduction	145	144	145	102	104	118
Department of the Interior:						
Bureau of Indian Affairs and Bureau of Indian Education:						
Operation of Indian Programs	150	159	159	146	88	149
Indian Guaranteed Loan Program Account	9	8	7	6	10	7
Appalachian Regional Commission	146	145	144	78	114	116
Delta Regional Authority	25	22	....	14	35	25
Denali Commission	15	15	....	18	12	20
Total, discretionary	**28,618**	**24,806**	**6,642**	**14,519**	**31,530**	**22,738**
Mandatory:						
Department of Homeland Security:						
Federal Emergency Management Agency:						
National Flood Insurance Fund	175	157	157	196	200	200
Department of Housing and Urban Development:						
Community Planning and Development:						
Community Development Loan Guarantees Program Account	1	....	....	1	4	....
Neighborhood Stabilization Program	....	....	....	30	58	58
Department of the Interior:						
Bureau of Indian Affairs and Bureau of Indian Education:						
Indian Guaranteed Loan Program Account	2	9	....	2	9	....
Department of the Treasury:						
Fiscal Service:						
Gulf Coast Restoration Trust Fund	295	176	335	49	115	120
Infrastructure Initiative:						
Rural Infrastructure	....	....	50,000	....	....	41,350
Total, mandatory	**473**	**342**	**50,492**	**278**	**386**	**41,728**
Total, Community and Regional Development	**29,091**	**25,148**	**57,134**	**14,797**	**31,916**	**64,466**
Education, Training, Employment, and Social Services						
Discretionary:						
Department of Education:						
Office of Elementary and Secondary Education:						
Indian Education	160	157	158	131	176	159
Impact Aid	1,323	1,315	730	1,495	1,223	850
Safe Schools and Citizenship Education	151	150	43	195	215	173
Education for the Disadvantaged	16,094	15,986	15,036	16,186	16,276	16,011
School Improvement Programs	4,279	4,257	2,320	4,295	4,211	4,243
Office of Innovation and Improvement:						
Innovation and Improvement	719	625	1,098	1,109	1,495	858

Table 14–1. FEDERAL GRANTS TO STATE AND LOCAL GOVERNMENTS—BUDGET AUTHORITY AND OUTLAYS—Continued

(In millions of dollars)

Function, Category, Agency and Program	Budget Authority			Outlays		
	2017 Actual	2018 Estimate	2019 Estimate	2017 Actual	2018 Estimate	2019 Estimate
Office of English Language Acquisition:						
English Language Acquisition	689	684	689	703	741	690
Office of Special Education and Rehabilitative Services:						
Special Education	12,869	12,742	11,989	12,479	12,845	12,759
Rehabilitation Services	92	91	64	82	91	77
Office of Career, Technical, and Adult Education:						
Career, Technical and Adult Education	1,700	1,688	1,604	1,726	1,635	1,678
Office of Postsecondary Education:						
Higher Education	340	336	....	302	381	329
Institute of Education Sciences	32	32	....	24	39	32
Department of Health and Human Services:						
Administration for Children and Families:						
Promoting Safe and Stable Families	60	37	58	54	51	48
Children and Families Services Programs	10,897	10,860	9,966	10,232	11,673	10,587
Administration for Community Living:						
Aging and Disability Services Programs	1,912	1,906	1,781	1,869	1,937	1,903
Department of the Interior:						
Bureau of Indian Affairs and Bureau of Indian Education:						
Operation of Indian Programs	75	75	75	71	73	71
Department of Labor:						
Employment and Training Administration:						
Training and Employment Services	2,850	2,905	1,681	2,783	3,002	2,123
State Unemployment Insurance and Employment Service Operations	293	88	88	62	64	275
Unemployment Trust Fund	939	933	685	920	918	880
Corporation for National and Community Service:						
Operating Expenses	483	478	31	238	228	9
Corporation for Public Broadcasting	495	492	15	495	492	15
District of Columbia:						
District of Columbia General and Special Payments:						
Federal Payment for Resident Tuition Support	40	40	....	40	40	....
Federal Payment for School Improvement	45	45	45	45	45	45
Institute of Museum and Library Services:						
Office of Museum and Library Services: Grants and Administration	214	215	....	212	224	155
National Endowment for the Arts:						
Grants and Administration	48	47	....	45	47	42
Total, discretionary	**56,799**	**56,184**	**48,156**	**55,793**	**58,122**	**54,012**
Mandatory:						
Department of Education:						
Office of Special Education and Rehabilitative Services:						
Rehabilitation Services	3,164	3,225	3,522	3,210	3,278	3,356
Department of Health and Human Services:						
Administration for Children and Families:						
Promoting Safe and Stable Families	452	316	529	403	436	394
Social Services Block Grant	1,662	1,588	....	1,661	1,621	307
Department of Labor:						
Employment and Training Administration:						
TAA Community College and Career Training Grant Fund	....	....	....	257	96	64
Federal Unemployment Benefits and Allowances	391	450	300	229	223	218
Total, mandatory	**5,669**	**5,579**	**4,351**	**5,760**	**5,654**	**4,339**
Total, Education, Training, Employment, and Social Services	**62,468**	**61,763**	**52,507**	**61,553**	**63,776**	**58,351**

Table 14–1. FEDERAL GRANTS TO STATE AND LOCAL GOVERNMENTS—BUDGET AUTHORITY AND OUTLAYS—Continued

(In millions of dollars)

Function, Category, Agency and Program	Budget Authority			Outlays		
	2017 Actual	2018 Estimate	2019 Estimate	2017 Actual	2018 Estimate	2019 Estimate
Health						
Discretionary:						
Department of Agriculture:						
Food Safety and Inspection Service:						
Salaries and Expenses	51	51	51	51	51	51
Department of Health and Human Services:						
Health Resources and Services Administration:						
Health Resources and Services	2,857	2,827	2,720	4,838	4,092	1,754
Indian Health Service:						
Contract Support Costs	712	795	797	716	843	797
Centers for Disease Control and Prevention:						
CDC-wide Activities and Program Support	3,440	3,388	1,888	1,189	1,236	1,000
Substance Abuse and Mental Health Services Administration	3,505	3,488	2,927	2,903	3,170	3,091
Departmental Management:						
Public Health and Social Services Emergency Fund	255	253	227	255	453	244
Department of Labor:						
Occupational Safety and Health Administration:						
Salaries and Expenses	111	110	100	111	110	100
Mine Safety and Health Administration:						
Salaries and Expenses	9	9	9	9	9	9
Total, discretionary	**10,940**	**10,921**	**8,719**	**10,072**	**9,964**	**7,046**
Mandatory:						
Department of Health and Human Services:						
Health Resources and Services Administration:						
Maternal, Infant, and Early Childhood Home Visiting Programs	372	400	400	416	388	389
Centers for Medicare and Medicaid Services:						
Rate Review Grants	....	....	....	23	26	13
Affordable Insurance Exchange Grants	18	13	....	147	135	24
Cost-sharing Reductions [2]	....	820	589	....	820	589
Grants to States for Medicaid	389,350	408,317	402,875	374,682	400,388	412,033
Children's Health Insurance Fund	15,026	8,602	11,754	16,224	17,120	11,424
State Grants and Demonstrations	−682	80	87	502	583	578
Child Enrollment Contingency Fund	574	1,739	−1,812	27	198	....
Departmental Management:						
Pregnancy Assistance Fund	23	25	25	23	24	23
Payment to the State Response to the Opioid Abuse Crisis Account, CURES Act	500	500	....	500	500	....
Department of the Treasury:						
Internal Revenue Service:						
Refundable Premium Tax Credit and Cost Sharing Reductions [2]	4,330	3,289	3,585	4,330	3,289	3,585
Payment Where Small Business Health Insurance Tax Credit Exceeds Liability for Tax [2]	....	1	1	....	1	1
Total, mandatory	**409,511**	**423,786**	**417,504**	**396,874**	**423,472**	**428,659**
Total, Health	**420,451**	**434,707**	**426,223**	**406,946**	**433,436**	**435,705**
Income Security						
Discretionary:						
Department of Agriculture:						
Food and Nutrition Service:						
Commodity Assistance Program	318	317	55	277	317	176
Special Supplemental Nutrition Program for Women, Infants, and Children (WIC)	5,500	5,463	5,535	5,698	5,803	5,522
Department of Health and Human Services:						
Administration for Children and Families:						

Table 14–1.   FEDERAL GRANTS TO STATE AND LOCAL GOVERNMENTS—BUDGET AUTHORITY AND OUTLAYS—Continued

(In millions of dollars)

Function, Category, Agency and Program	Budget Authority			Outlays		
	2017 Actual	2018 Estimate	2019 Estimate	2017 Actual	2018 Estimate	2019 Estimate
Low Income Home Energy Assistance	3,390	3,367	....	3,183	3,271	1,079
Refugee and Entrant Assistance	629	687	515	662	648	515
Payments to States for the Child Care and Development Block Grant	2,834	2,825	2,548	2,781	2,839	2,632
Department of Homeland Security:						
Federal Emergency Management Agency:						
Federal Assistance	120	119	....	....	83	109
Emergency Food and Shelter	....	....	....	141	61	26
Department of Housing and Urban Development:						
Public and Indian Housing Programs:						
Public Housing Operating Fund	4,290	4,245	2,675	4,316	4,246	3,099
Revitalization of Severely Distressed Public Housing (HOPE VI)	....	....	−1	56	45	4
Native Hawaiian Housing Block Grant	2	2	....	6	6	6
Tenant Based Rental Assistance	20,375	20,258	19,393	20,584	20,748	19,902
Public Housing Capital Fund	1,906	1,895	....	1,755	1,892	1,822
Native American Housing Block Grant	654	650	600	620	627	533
Housing Certificate Fund	....	....	....	94	97	97
Choice Neighborhoods Initiative	138	137	−137	36	150	12
Family Self-Sufficiency	75	74	75	73	61	85
Rental Assistance Demonstration	....	....	100	....	....	100
Community Planning and Development:						
Homeless Assistance Grants	1,271	1,262	1,271	1,056	1,214	1,244
Home Investment Partnership Program	950	944	....	1,104	938	937
Housing Opportunities for Persons with AIDS	356	354	330	306	311	353
Rural Housing and Economic Development	....	....	....	2	2	....
Permanent Supportive Housing	....	....	....	....	5	....
Housing Programs:						
Project-based Rental Assistance	241	235	245	241	235	245
Department of Labor:						
Employment and Training Administration:						
Unemployment Trust Fund	2,711	2,690	2,511	3,016	2,869	3,062
Total, discretionary	**45,760**	**45,524**	**35,715**	**46,007**	**46,468**	**41,560**
Mandatory:						
Department of Agriculture:						
Agricultural Marketing Service:						
Funds for Strengthening Markets, Income, and Supply (section 32)	789	1,040	1,070	743	1,020	1,072
Food and Nutrition Service:						
Supplemental Nutrition Assistance Program	7,135	7,405	6,929	6,954	7,355	7,020
Commodity Assistance Program	20	20	21	17	20	21
Child Nutrition Programs	22,951	24,280	23,153	22,445	24,019	23,486
Department of Health and Human Services:						
Administration for Children and Families:						
Payments to States for Child Support Enforcement and Family Support Programs	4,311	4,326	4,398	4,075	4,206	4,334
Contingency Fund	608	608	....	567	626	64
Payments for Foster Care and Permanency	8,357	8,468	8,756	7,712	8,267	8,615
Child Care Entitlement to States	2,917	2,917	3,588	2,905	3,010	3,442
Temporary Assistance for Needy Families	16,737	16,736	15,136	15,972	16,328	15,353
Department of Housing and Urban Development:						
Public and Indian Housing Programs:						
Native American Housing Block Grant	3	2	....	3	2	....
Total, mandatory	**63,828**	**65,802**	**63,051**	**61,393**	**64,853**	**63,407**
Total, Income Security	**109,588**	**111,326**	**98,766**	**107,400**	**111,321**	**104,967**

Table 14–1. FEDERAL GRANTS TO STATE AND LOCAL GOVERNMENTS—BUDGET AUTHORITY AND OUTLAYS—Continued
(In millions of dollars)

Function, Category, Agency and Program	Budget Authority			Outlays		
	2017 Actual	2018 Estimate	2019 Estimate	2017 Actual	2018 Estimate	2019 Estimate
Social Security						
Mandatory:						
Social Security Administration:						
Federal Disability Insurance Trust Fund	47	14	14	10	19	14
Veterans Benefits and Services						
Discretionary:						
Department of Veterans Affairs:						
Veterans Health Administration:						
Medical Community Care	1,253	1,237	....	1,253	1,237	....
Medical Services	559	592	1,895	559	592	1,895
Departmental Administration:						
Grants for Construction of State Extended Care Facilities	90	89	150	139	109	105
Grants for Construction of Veterans Cemeteries	45	45	45	41	24	68
Total, discretionary	**1,947**	**1,963**	**2,090**	**1,992**	**1,962**	**2,068**
Total, Veterans Benefits and Services	**1,947**	**1,963**	**2,090**	**1,992**	**1,962**	**2,068**
Administration of Justice						
Discretionary:						
Department of Housing and Urban Development:						
Fair Housing and Equal Opportunity:						
Fair Housing Activities	65	65	62	64	65	66
Department of Justice:						
Legal Activities and U.S. Marshals:						
Assets Forfeiture Fund	21	–482	–653	18	16	20
Drug Enforcement Administration:						
High Intensity Drug Trafficking Areas Program [3]	....	....	254	....	....	64
Office of Justice Programs:						
Research, Evaluation, and Statistics	75	69	17	117	354	9
State and Local Law Enforcement Assistance [4]	968	953	605	947	1,313	1,049
Juvenile Justice Programs	222	238	214	256	274	358
Community Oriented Policing Services [4]	150	161	....	195	177	32
Violence against Women Prevention and Prosecution Programs	450	446	452	418	485	479
Equal Employment Opportunity Commission:						
Salaries and Expenses	29	29	29	47	60	47
Federal Drug Control Programs:						
High Intensity Drug Trafficking Areas Program [3]	235	252	....	228	300	151
State Justice Institute:						
Salaries and Expenses	5	5	7	5	6	5
Total, discretionary	**2,220**	**1,736**	**987**	**2,295**	**3,050**	**2,280**
Mandatory:						
Department of Justice:						
Legal Activities and U.S. Marshals:						
Assets Forfeiture Fund	400	250	250	179	217	322
Office of Justice Programs:						
Crime Victims Fund	2,270	2,246	2,065	1,404	3,786	2,862
Department of the Treasury:						
Departmental Offices:						
Treasury Forfeiture Fund	95	89	106	95	89	106
Total, mandatory	**2,765**	**2,585**	**2,421**	**1,678**	**4,092**	**3,290**
Total, Administration of Justice	**4,985**	**4,321**	**3,408**	**3,973**	**7,142**	**5,570**

Table 14–1.   FEDERAL GRANTS TO STATE AND LOCAL GOVERNMENTS—BUDGET AUTHORITY AND OUTLAYS—Continued

(In millions of dollars)

Function, Category, Agency and Program	Budget Authority			Outlays		
	2017 Actual	2018 Estimate	2019 Estimate	2017 Actual	2018 Estimate	2019 Estimate
General Government						
Discretionary:						
Department of the Interior:						
United States Fish and Wildlife Service:						
National Wildlife Refuge Fund	13	13	....	13	13	....
Insular Affairs:						
Assistance to Territories	64	64	53	56	82	79
Department-Wide Programs:						
Payments in Lieu of Taxes	465	462	397	465	462	397
District of Columbia:						
District of Columbia Courts:						
Federal Payment to the District of Columbia Courts	275	273	245	263	262	246
Federal Payment for Defender Services in District of Columbia Courts	50	51	46	46	57	54
District of Columbia General and Special Payments:						
Federal Support for Economic Development and Management Reforms in the District	22	22	8	22	22	8
Election Assistance Commission:						
Election Reform Programs	....	....	....	2	....	....
Total, discretionary	**889**	**885**	**749**	**867**	**898**	**784**
Mandatory:						
Department of Agriculture:						
Forest Service:						
Forest Service Permanent Appropriations	90	77	77	90	77	77
Department of Energy:						
Energy Programs:						
Payments to States under Federal Power Act	4	4	5	8	4	5
Department of the Interior:						
Office of Surface Mining Reclamation and Enforcement:						
Payments to States in Lieu of Coal Fee Receipts	47	106	117	173	115	156
United States Fish and Wildlife Service:						
National Wildlife Refuge Fund	8	8	9	11	10	9
Departmental Offices:						
Mineral Leasing and Associated Payments	1,407	1,656	1,834	1,407	1,656	1,834
National Petroleum Reserve, Alaska	2	21	24	2	21	24
Geothermal Lease Revenues, Payment to Counties	3	4	....	3	4	....
Insular Affairs:						
Assistance to Territories	28	28	28	37	16	4
Payments to the United States Territories, Fiscal Assistance	328	302	302	328	302	302
Department of the Treasury:						
Alcohol and Tobacco Tax and Trade Bureau:						
Internal Revenue Collections for Puerto Rico	365	379	391	365	379	391
Corps of Engineers--Civil Works:						
Permanent Appropriations	4	4	4	....	....	....
District of Columbia:						
District of Columbia Courts:						
District of Columbia Crime Victims Compensation Fund	12	6	6	8	6	6
Total, mandatory	**2,298**	**2,595**	**2,797**	**2,432**	**2,590**	**2,808**
Total, General Government	**3,187**	**3,480**	**3,546**	**3,299**	**3,488**	**3,592**

Table 14–1. FEDERAL GRANTS TO STATE AND LOCAL GOVERNMENTS—BUDGET AUTHORITY AND OUTLAYS—Continued

(In millions of dollars)

Function, Category, Agency and Program	Budget Authority			Outlays		
	2017 Actual	2018 Estimate	2019 Estimate	2017 Actual	2018 Estimate	2019 Estimate
Allowances						
Mandatory:						
Infrastructure Initiative:						
Transformative Projects	....	....	20,040	....	....	15
Infrastructure Incentives	....	....	100,000	....	....	1,000
Total, mandatory	....	....	120,040	....	....	1,015
Total, Allowances	....	....	120,040	....	....	1,015
Total, Grants	703,864	715,250	833,319	674,700	727,986	748,994
Discretionary	159,170	152,557	108,277	200,974	221,048	197,989
Transportation obligation limitations (non-add)[1]	55,800	56,913	59,550	....	....	....
Mandatory	544,694	562,693	725,042	473,726	506,938	551,005

[1] Mandatory contract authority provides budget authority for these programs, but program levels are set by discretionary obligation limitations in appropriations bills and outlays are recorded as discretionary. This table shows the obligation limitations as non-additive items to avoid double counting.

[2] Reflects budget authority and outlays for the Basic Health Program, under which a State may offer standard health plans to eligible individuals in lieu of offering such individuals coverage through an Exchange, and/or budget authority and outlays for State Innovation Waivers, as appropriate.

[3] For 2019, the Budget proposes to transfer the High Intensity Drug Trafficking Areas Program from the Office of National Drug Control Policy to the Department of Justice. Budget authority for the High Intensity Drug Trafficking Areas Program in 2019 is included under the Drug Enforcement Administration heading.

[4] For 2019, the Budget proposes to transfer the Community Oriented Policing Services account to the State and Local Law Enforcement Assistance account.

Table 14-2, below, shows Federal grants-in-aid spending by decade, actual spending in 2017, and estimated spending in 2018 and 2019. The Federal budget classifies grants-in-aid by general area or function. Of the total proposed grant spending in 2019, 58 percent is for health programs, with most of the funding going to Medicaid. Beyond health programs, 14 percent of Federal aid is estimated to go to income security programs; 9 percent to Community and Regional Development, which includes the Rural Grants portion of the Infrastructure Initiative; 9 percent to transportation; 8 percent to education, training, and social services; and 3 percent for all other functions.

The Federal budget also classifies grant spending by BEA category—discretionary and mandatory.[19] Funding for discretionary grant programs is determined annually through appropriations acts. Outlays for discretionary grant programs account for 26 percent of total grant spending. Funding for mandatory programs is provided directly in authorizing legislation that establishes eligibility criteria or benefit formulas; funding for mandatory programs usually is not limited by the annual appropriations process. Outlays for mandatory grant programs account for 74 percent of total grant spending. Section B of Table 14-1 shows the distribution of grants between mandatory and discretionary spending.

In 2019, grants-in-aid provided from discretionary funding are estimated to have outlays of $198 billion, a decrease of 10 percent from 2018. The three largest discretionary programs in 2019 are estimated to be Federal-aid Highways programs, with outlays of $44 billion; Tenant Based Rental Assistance, with outlays of $20

billion; and Education for the Disadvantaged, with outlays of $16 billion.[20]

In 2019, outlays for mandatory grant programs are estimated to be $551 billion, a 9 percent increase from 2018. $42 billion of that increase is for the infrastructure initiative proposal, without which outlays for mandatory grants would be $2 billion higher than 2018. Medicaid is by far the largest mandatory grant program with estimated outlays of $412 billion in 2019. After Medicaid, the three largest mandatory grant programs by outlays in 2019 are estimated to be Rural Infrastructure grants (part of the infrastructure initiative), $41 billion; Child Nutrition programs, which include the School Breakfast Program, the National School Lunch Program and others, $23 billion; and the Temporary Assistance for Needy Families program, $15 billion.[21]

Federal grant spending by State for major grants may be found on the OMB web site at *www.whitehouse.gov/ omb/Analytical-Perspectives/* and on the Budget CD-ROM. This supplemental material includes two tables that summarize State-by-State spending for selected grant programs, one summarizing obligations for each program by agency and bureau, and another summarizing total obligations across all programs for each State, followed by 35 individual tables showing State-by-State obligation data for each grant program. The programs shown in these State-by-State tables cover almost 90 percent of total grants-in-aid to State and local governments.

[19] For more information on these categories, see Chapter 8, "Budget Concepts," in this volume.

[20] Obligation data by State for programs in each of these budget accounts may be found in the State-by-State tables included with other budget materials on the OMB web site and Budget CD-ROM.

[21] Obligation data by State for programs in each of these budget accounts may be found in the State-by-State tables included with other budget materials on the OMB web site and Budget CD-ROM.

Table 14–2. TRENDS IN FEDERAL GRANTS TO STATE AND LOCAL GOVERNMENTS

(Outlays in billions of dollars)

	Actual									Estimate	
	1960	1970	1980	1990	2000	2005	2010	2015	2017	2018	2019
A. Distribution of grants by function:											
Natural resources and environment	0.1	0.4	5.4	3.7	4.6	5.9	9.1	7.0	6.2	6.4	5.3
Agriculture	0.2	0.6	0.6	1.1	0.7	0.9	0.8	0.7	0.8	1.0	1.0
Transportation	3.0	4.6	13.0	19.2	32.2	43.4	61.0	60.8	64.8	64.4	64.0
Community and regional development	0.1	1.8	6.5	5.0	8.7	20.2	18.9	14.4	14.8	31.9	64.5
Education, training, employment, and social services	0.5	6.4	21.9	21.8	36.7	57.2	97.6	60.5	61.6	63.8	58.4
Health	0.2	3.8	15.8	43.9	124.8	197.8	290.2	368.0	406.9	433.4	435.7
Income security	2.6	5.8	18.5	36.9	68.7	90.9	115.2	101.1	107.4	111.3	105.0
Administration of justice	....	0.0	0.5	0.6	5.3	4.8	5.1	3.7	4.0	7.1	5.6
General government	0.2	0.5	8.6	2.3	2.1	4.4	5.2	3.8	3.3	3.5	3.6
Other	0.0	0.1	0.7	0.8	2.1	2.6	5.3	4.3	5.0	5.2	6.1
Total	**7.0**	**24.1**	**91.4**	**135.3**	**285.9**	**428.0**	**608.4**	**624.4**	**674.7**	**728.0**	**749.0**
B. Distribution of grants by BEA category:											
Discretionary	N/A	10.2	53.4	63.5	116.7	182.3	247.4	189.6	201.0	221.0	198.0
Mandatory	N/A	13.9	38.0	71.9	169.2	245.7	361.0	434.7	473.7	506.9	551.0
Total	**7.0**	**24.1**	**91.4**	**135.3**	**285.9**	**428.0**	**608.4**	**624.4**	**674.7**	**728.0**	**749.0**
C. Composition:											
Current dollars:											
Payments for individuals [1]	2.6	9.1	33.1	77.4	186.5	278.8	391.4	463.4	508.0	538.0	535.2
Physical capital [1]	3.3	7.1	22.6	27.2	48.7	60.8	93.3	77.2	79.5	81.0	122.9
Other grants	1.1	7.9	35.8	30.7	50.7	88.4	123.7	83.7	87.3	109.0	90.9
Total	**7.0**	**24.1**	**91.4**	**135.3**	**285.9**	**428.0**	**608.4**	**624.4**	**674.7**	**728.0**	**749.0**
Percentage of total grants:											
Payments for individuals [1]	37.4%	37.7%	36.2%	57.2%	65.3%	65.1%	64.3%	74.2%	75.3%	73.9%	71.5%
Physical capital [1]	47.3%	29.3%	24.7%	20.1%	17.0%	14.2%	15.3%	12.4%	11.8%	11.1%	16.4%
Other grants	15.3%	33.0%	39.1%	22.7%	17.7%	20.7%	20.3%	13.4%	12.9%	15.0%	12.1%
Total	**100.0%**	**100.0%**	**100.0%**	**100.0%**	**100.0%**	**100.0%**	**100.0%**	**100.0%**	**100.0%**	**100.0%**	**100.0%**
Constant (FY 2009) dollars:											
Payments for individuals [1]	15.0	41.4	76.8	116.1	225.9	304.1	385.3	422.4	449.9	466.1	454.9
Physical capital [1]	23.8	38.2	54.7	45.7	68.6	74.2	93.7	69.8	69.8	69.4	102.6
Other grants	12.7	62.2	133.1	62.7	71.9	102.3	120.1	73.0	73.7	89.7	72.9
Total	**51.5**	**141.8**	**264.6**	**224.5**	**366.4**	**480.6**	**599.1**	**565.2**	**593.5**	**625.2**	**630.3**
D. Total grants as a percent of:											
Federal outlays:											
Total	7.6%	12.3%	15.5%	10.8%	16.0%	17.3%	17.6%	16.9%	16.9%	17.4%	17.0%
Domestic programs [2]	18.0%	23.2%	22.2%	17.1%	22.0%	23.5%	23.4%	21.2%	21.3%	22.2%	22.1%
State and local expenditures	14.3%	19.6%	27.3%	18.7%	21.8%	23.5%	26.3%	25.1%	26.8%	N/A	N/A
Gross domestic product	1.3%	2.3%	3.3%	2.3%	2.8%	3.3%	4.1%	3.5%	3.5%	3.6%	3.6%
E. As a share of total State and local gross investments:											
Federal capital grants	24.1%	24.6%	34.5%	21.0%	21.2%	21.3%	26.4%	22.4%	22.6%	N/A	N/A
State and local own-source financing	75.9%	75.4%	65.5%	79.0%	78.8%	78.7%	73.6%	77.6%	77.4%	N/A	N/A
Total	**100.0%**	**100.0%**	**100.0%**	**100.0%**	**100.0%**	**100.0%**	**100.0%**	**100.0%**	**100.0%**		

N/A: Not available at publishing.

[1] Grants that are both payments for individuals and capital investment are shown under capital investment.

[2] Excludes national defense, international affairs, net interest, and undistributed offsetting receipts.

OTHER SOURCES OF INFORMATION ON FEDERAL GRANTS-IN-AID

A number of other sources provide State-by-State spending data and other information on Federal grants, but may use a broader definition of grants beyond what is included in this chapter.

The website *Grants.gov* is a primary source of information for communities wishing to apply for grants and other domestic assistance. *Grants.gov* hosts all open notices of opportunities to apply for Federal grants.

The *Catalog of Federal Domestic Assistance* hosted by the General Services Administration contains detailed listings of grant and other assistance programs; discussions of eligibility criteria, application procedures, and estimated obligations; and related information. The *Catalog* is available on the Internet at *www.cfda.gov*.

Current and updated grant receipt information by State and local governments and other non-Federal entities can be found on *USASpending.gov*. This public website also contains contract and loan information and is updated twice per month.

The Federal Audit Clearinghouse maintains an online database *(https://harvester.census.gov/facweb/)* that provides access to summary information about audits conducted under OMB guidance located at 2 CFR part 200, Uniform Administrative Requirements, Cost Principles, and Audit Requirements for Federal Awards. Information is available for each audited entity, including the amount of Federal money expended by program and whether there were audit findings.

The Bureau of Economic Analysis, in the Department of Commerce, produces the monthly *Survey of Current Business*, which provides data on the national income and product accounts (NIPA), a broad statistical concept encompassing the entire economy. These accounts, which are available at *bea.gov/national*, include data on Federal grants to State and local governments.

In addition, information on grants and awards can be found through individual Federal agencies' web sites:

- USDA Current Research Information System, *https://cris.nifa.usda.gov/*

- DOD Medical Research Programs, *http://cdmrp.army.mil/search.aspx*

- Department of Education, Institute of Education Sciences, Funded Research Grants and Contracts, *https://www2.ed.gov/fund/grants-apply.html*

- Department of Health and Human Services (HHS) Grants, *https://www.hhs.gov/grants/grants/index.html*

- HHS Tracking Accountability in Government Grants System (TAGGS), *http://taggs.hhs.gov/AdvancedSearch.cfm*

- National Institutes of Health (NIH) Grants and Funding, *https://grants.nih.gov/funding/index.htm*

- Department of Housing and Urban Development Grants, *https://www.hud.gov/program-offices/spm/geomgmt/grantsinfe*

- Department of Justice Grants, *https://www.justice.gov/grants*

- Department of Labor Employment and Training Administration (ETA), Grants Awarded, *http://www.doleta.gov/grants/grants_awarded.cfm*

- Department of Transportation Grants, *https://www.transportation.gov/grants*

- Environmental Protection Agency (EPA), *https://www.epa.gov/grants*

- National Library of Medicine (NLM), Health Services Research Projects in Progress (HSRProj), *https://wwwcf.nlm.nih.gov/hsr_project/home_proj.cfm*

- National Science Foundation (NSF) Awards, *http://www.nsf.gov/awardsearch/*

- Small Business Innovation Research (SBIR) and Small Business Technology Transfer (STTR) Awards, *https://www.sbir.gov/sbirsearch/award/all*

15. STRENGTHENING FEDERAL STATISTICS

The Federal Government's statistical agencies and programs play a vital role in generating the data that citizens, businesses, and governments need to make informed decisions. Timely, accurate, and relevant statistical data are the foundation of evidence-based decision-making. Citizens use statistical information in their daily lives, such as information on education, commuting, health, crime, or aging in their communities. These data are displayed on internet search engines, incorporated into popular applications, or downloaded from agency websites to support in-depth research on relevant policy topics. The Federal Statistical System has informed the nation about its population, condition and progress since its founding, beginning with the first constitutionally-mandated Census in 1790. Today, these statistical indicators contribute to our nation's ability to grow the economy, create jobs, measure our progress, and increase the effectiveness and efficiency of the government. Businesses depend on reliable statistical information that is nationally consistent to locate and grow their businesses, better serve customers, and link workers to jobs across our nation, including data on current and potential markets, international trade, the labor force, and changing economic conditions. State and local governments rely on Federal data to improve the lives of their citizens through better planning and delivery of essential services.

The mission of the Federal Statistical System is to collect data, transform them into useful, objective information; and make that information readily and equitably accessible to government decision makers and the public. There are thirteen Principal Statistical Agencies (PSAs—see Table 15.1) and almost 100 smaller units spread across the Executive Branch that generate statistics on such topics as the economy, Veterans, housing, crime, transportation, agriculture, energy, health, and education. The PSAs are responsible for modeling best practices in data stewardship and statistical practice.

As our society evolves, several challenges compel the Federal Statistical System to modernize and adopt new 21st century methods to continue to meet the growing needs of data users. Declining response rates to surveys raise data collection costs and harm data quality. Needed innovations that incorporate computer and data science techniques require staff with skills that are difficult for agencies to retain and keep current. Legal and organizational barriers to increased data sharing that would increase efficiency while still protecting data confidentiality make it difficult for statistical agencies to coordinate, improve data quality and utility, reduce respondent burden, and share best practices. Meanwhile, stakeholders and consumers of statistical products expect more granular and specific information to be delivered faster without compromising quality.

The Federal Statistical System works hard to meet these challenges and to remain the trusted provider of independent and accurate information amidst proliferating sources of information that often lack transparency, dependability, and proof of quality. By exploring the use of new data sources, including reusing data the government already collects as it administers programs, the PSAs and other statistical programs strengthen existing capacity and develop new methods to supplement or replace more burdensome surveys. These non-survey data sources can help agencies counter falling levels of cooperation from the public; increase the accuracy, timeliness, and relevance of their statistical products; and save money.

Outlined below are some examples of the many recent activities designed to address these challenges.

The *Bureau of the Census* conducts the Economic Census and the Census of Governments every five years, which are integral to the Bureau of Economic Analysis (BEA) estimates of gross domestic product (GDP), industry inputs and outputs, and the economic activities of more than 90,000 state and local governments. Together, these programs measure the structure and functioning of nearly the entire U.S. economy. For the most recent Economic Census and Census of Governments the Census Bureau is collecting data electronically, replacing paper-based methods used in past censuses, thereby reducing response burden, costs, and processing times.

The *Bureau of Economic Analysis* embarked on research to harness big data on housing and credit card transactions to improve statistics of consumer spending, housing investment, and regional prices and to reduce revisions to the early gross domestic product (GDP) estimates.

The *Bureau of Justice Statistics* linked a decade of data on sentences served by state prisoners in the National Corrections Reporting Program (NCRP) to other administrative datasets to inform post-prison mortality, pre- and post-prison use of subsidized housing, and post-prison enrollment in Medicaid.

The *Economic Research Service* partnered with the Census Bureau to expand the use of State-level administrative data by linking it with American Community survey data to inform key policy decisions for USDA's Food and Nutrition Assistance programs. The linked data provided new insights into these programs such as the share of people estimated to be eligible for Supplemental Nutrition Assistance Programs (SNAP) who actually participate in the program (by congressional district) and the number of SNAP participants by annual income relative to the poverty line. The public can access the data through an interactive tool on the Census website.

The *National Agricultural Statistics Service* (NASS) developed a modern, responsive web form to improve data quality and reduce respondent burden for the Census of

Agriculture, conducted every five years. NASS has also developed the operational capacity to produce acreage assessments throughout the growing season using mid-resolution satellite imagery and verified administrative ground reference data to produce a product called the Cropland Data Layer (CDL).

The *National Center for Health Statistics* initiated a program to release monthly provisional national and state level counts of drug overdose deaths to facilitate more timely release of critical indicators for public health surveillance of one of the fastest growing and most serious health concerns in the US. The Center also released data products with survey records linked to Medicare administrative enrollment and claims records, providing new opportunities for researchers to study changes in health status, health care utilization, and expenditures for survey participants with matched Medicare records.

The *National Center for Veterans Analysis and Studies*, a statistical unit within the Veterans Administration, initiated the Veterans Voices Project, an application prototype that runs sentiment analysis and applies artificial intelligence against organic real-time big data streams of public content and key measures in order to develop real-time insights on the experiences of veterans.

There are also several cross-cutting initiatives underway to modernize and strengthen the Federal Statistical System. The bipartisan Commission on Evidence-Based Policymaking was charged with determining how the Federal Government could effectively and routinely build and use evidence to improve policies and programs, and overcome the current obstacles to doing so. The Commission's 2017 final report identified many barriers to the effective use of administrative data to generate statistics and other forms of evidence and suggested ways to overcome them. These include a series of legal barriers to accessing and using administrative data for statistical purposes, as discussed in Chapter 6, Building and Using Evidence to Improve Government Effectiveness.

The Commission described coordination and capacity challenges and emphasized the need for greater coordination within and across agencies to ensure that the highest priority data are collected, and that already-collected data are used to their fullest extent. To address these challenges, the Commission recommended an expanded role for the PSAs in managing a department's data resources in support of Federal evidence building. Beyond enabling the PSAs to access and use administrative data in their own statistical programs, this expanded data stewardship role would facilitate evaluator and researcher access to these same data assets within the strong data stewardship laws and practices intrinsic to the PSAs. The Commission noted that PSAs vary in their readiness to take on this greater and essential role for achieving a coordinated and efficient evidence-building effort within departments.

The Office of Management and Budget (OMB) is charged with coordination of the evidence-building functions of the government, including the Federal Statistical System. OMB is organizing itself to leverage its statutory and other tools in a more integrated manner to improve the use of data for evidence building. One important aspect of this is to provide data users with important information on statistical data quality in order to determine whether the data are appropriate for the purposes intended. Both a large body of knowledge and OMB standards exist on maintaining and assessing the quality of data collected through surveys and censuses. However, increasing combination of survey data with administrative records and other data sources results in new statistical data, and data quality aspects of importance to users both within and outside of government need to be measured and described consistently and transparently by the agencies producing these data products. Tools available to OMB include setting statistical standards to address data quality questions that arise when blending survey and non-survey datasets, and facilitating agency development and use of learning agendas.

Executive Order 13781, "Comprehensive Plan for Reorganizing the Executive Branch," directs agencies to develop plans to modernize and streamline their operations. To increase cost-effectiveness, improve data quality, and reduce respondent burden, the Administration is planning a review on how it can streamline Federal statistical functions across multiple Federal agencies. The results of these analyses will be included in the Comprehensive Plan when it is released later this year. The 2019 Budget also provides a framework for streamlining statistical services by targeting funding for the Economic Research Service on its core mission and examining the potential benefits of consolidating the Economic Research Service with the National Agricultural Statistical Service in fiscal year 2020.

Highlights of 2019 Program Budget Proposals

Excluding cyclical funding for the decennial census, approximately 40 percent of the total budget for these programs provides resources for 13 agencies or units that have statistical activities as their principal mission (see Table 16–1). The remaining funding supports work in approximately 94 agencies or units that carry out statistical activities in conjunction with other missions such as providing services, conducting research, or implementing regulations. More comprehensive budget and program information about the Federal statistical system, including its core programs, will be available in OMB's annual report, Statistical Programs of the United States Government, Fiscal Year 2018, when it is published later this year. The following highlights the Administration's proposals for the programs of the PSAs, giving particular attention to new initiatives and to other program changes.

Bureau of the Census (Census Bureau), Department of Commerce: Funding is requested to provide continued support for ongoing Census Bureau programs and to: (1) begin major field operations for the 2020 Census, including the nationwide in-field address canvassing operation, as well as final preparations for the collection of 2020 Census respondent data in FY 2020; (2) continue development and refinement of capabilities for the Census Enterprise Data Collection and Processing

System in support of the 2020 Census; (3) complete data collection and begin processing and dissemination for the 2017 Economic Census and Census of Governments; and (4) support further transformation of Census Bureau data dissemination through the Center for Enterprise Data Services and Consumer Information.

Bureau of Economic Analysis (BEA), Department of Commerce: Funding is requested to provide support for core programs including the production of some of the Nation's most critical economic statistics including GDP and to continue: (1) exploration of new and nontraditional data sources to improve the accuracy and coverage of official statistics; (2) research on expanding the geographic detail of GDP to over 3,100 U.S. counties; and (3) work to accelerate key data sources for the initial estimates of GDP to achieve more accurate early reads of U.S. economic growth.

Bureau of Justice Statistics (BJS), Department of Justice: Funding is requested to maintain BJS's portfolio of statistical programs and to: (1) continue to support the redesign efforts of the National Crime Victimization Survey and its supplements and field redesigned surveys in 2020; (2) use criminal history records to support various projects to assess criminal histories and recidivism rates of persons admitted to state prisons, compare the attributes of U.S. criminal history record systems to other industrialized countries, and continue to identify and work with states to improve the quality, accuracy, and comprehensiveness of their criminal history records; (3) continue redesign efforts on the Survey of Inmates in Local Jails to collect information on individual characteristics of jail inmates, current offenses and detention status, characteristics of victims, criminal histories, family background, gun possession and use, prior opiate and alcohol use and treatment, medical and mental health, personal characteristics, and programs and services provided in jail; (4) expand the use of administrative records to support various projects, such as using criminal history records to examine prisoner and probationer recidivism, explore the feasibility of building a national collection of arrest booking statistics, and expanding record linkages among survey, administrative, and operational records from the Census Bureau, other Office of Justice (OJP) components, and other Federal agencies to support research on various topics; and (5) provide continued support to OJP components and other Federal agencies through BJS's statistical infrastructure to examine program outcomes and improve measures to better understand the U.S. justice system, for example by looking at how the flow of Bureau of Justice Assistance Byrne/Justice Assistance Grant funds impacts changes in crime rate at the jurisdiction level and assisting the Office of Victims of Crime's efforts to collect more geographic data on victimization.

Bureau of Labor Statistics (BLS), Department of Labor: Funding is requested to explore methods to incorporate questions from the Telephone Point of Purchase Survey (TPOPS) into the Consumer Expenditure (CE) Survey. The BLS could improve survey efficiencies by incorporating the unique TPOPS questions into the CE Survey, thereby eliminating TPOPS as a stand-alone survey, as well as its overhead costs, addressing the critical need for a cost-effective alternative to TPOPS, and reducing global respondent burden. Funding is also requested to determine the feasibility of expanding collection capabilities for additional Current Employment Statistics (CES) and Quarterly Census of Employment and Wages (QCEW) information by adding a new Electronic Data Interchange (EDI) Center. Expanding the EDI operation would allow for more efficient data collection and reduce respondent burden for these programs.

Bureau of Transportation Statistics (BTS), Department of Transportation: Funding is requested to initiate a major research program to develop methods and new data sources for supplementing and enhancing portions of the Freight Analysis Framework and reducing respondent burden for the Commodity Flow Survey.

Economic Research Service (ERS), Department of Agriculture: Funding is requested for ERS's core programs of research, data analysis, and market outlook. Proposals for ERS budget priorities include research that: 1) builds on unique or confidential data sources or investments at the Federal level; (2) provides coordination for a national perspective or framework; (3) requires sustained investment and large teams; (4) directly serves the U.S. Government's or USDA's long-term national goals; and (5) addresses questions with short-run payoff or that have immediate policy implications. ERS also seeks to cover the breadth of USDA programs (except forestry) and provide funding to ensure sustained expertise in the analysis of farming, commodity markets and trade, natural resources and the environment, rural communities, food safety, food markets, and nutrition.

Energy Information Administration (EIA), Department of Energy: Funding is requested for EIA to maintain recent program enhancements, continue most core statistical and analysis activities, and follow through on planned cybersecurity initiatives. At the requested level, EIA would continue to (1) enhance its energy modeling program, including planned IT maintenance and upgrades to the National Energy Modeling System (NEMS), the nation's preeminent tool for developing long-term projections of U.S. energy production, consumption, prices, and technologies; and (2) conduct the Commercial Buildings Energy Consumption Survey (CBECS) on schedule, which is the only statistically reliable source of information on energy consumption, expenditures, and end-uses in U.S. commercial buildings. EIA would delay expansion on two programs: EIA-930 collection survey that provides near real-time supply and demand electricity data for the United States; and National Oil and Gas Gateway to include well-level oil and gas data for additional states.

National Agricultural Statistics Service (NASS), Department of Agriculture: Funding is requested to support the Census of Agriculture (COA) to obtain agricultural statistics for each County, State, and the Nation. Additional funding requested for the geospatial program would be used to integrate the Decision Support System (DSS) into NASS processes and to move production of the Cropland Data Layer (CDL) and derivative products into a secure cloud environment. The DSS integrates weather, climate and crop information, customized to match the time-frame for NASS's weekly Crop Progress and Condition Reports (CPCR). Processing the data using a cloud-based service would create efficiencies and enable research to move rapidly to produce estimates for smaller geographical areas and for more commodities, especially specialty crops. The Budget also request $5 million in additional funding to conduct the Farm Labor Survey (FLS). The survey instrument is undergoing modifications and cognitive testing to ensure that the wage rate is reflecting current trends in the industry. Additionally, the granularity of data published is under review in an effort to continue to meet stakeholder needs. In FY 2019, NASS will publish the first FLS results that are based on the improved survey instrument at increased levels of granularity.

National Center for Education Statistics (NCES), Department of Education: Funding is requested to provide support for NCES ongoing activities and to: (1) support operations of the National Assessment of Education Progress (NAEP) which is the only source of nationally comparable information about students' knowledge and skills across a wide range of academic topics; (2) support U.S. participation in the 2019 Trends in International Mathematics and Science Study (TIMSS) in grades 4 and 8 – essential for evaluating how U.S. students compare to students in many of the nation's primary economic competitors; (3) support development of the next high school longitudinal study scheduled for national collection starting in 2020 with a nationally representative cohort of 9th grade students; (4) support for evaluation of approaches to integrate NAEP information about students and National Teacher and Principal Survey (NTPS) information about teachers to both improve operational efficiency and increase available information; (5) support completion of the first administrative record driven collection of the National Postsecondary Student Aid Study (NPSAS-AC) to provide more regular data on how students are financing college education; and (6) evaluate new approaches to improve response rates and efficiency of the National Household Education Surveys (NHES).

National Center for Health Statistics (NCHS), Department of Health and Human Services: Funding is requested to provide support for ongoing NCHS programs and to: (1) enhance the agency's data linkage program which creates new information products through linkages of survey records and administrative data to maximize the utility of NCHS data; (2) continue the expansion and modernization of electronic death reporting to provide more timely information to decision makers and the public on deaths significant for public health; (3) enhance the quality and usability of surveys that are widely-used for health policy and program development, such as the National Health Interview Survey and the National Health and Nutrition Examination Survey; (4) further reduce the turnaround time associated with research access to NCHS-compiled birth and death data with continued support of the Vital Statistics Rapid Release program and the new monthly drug overdose death reports; (5) test and implement modules to the National Health and Nutrition

Examination Survey to address emerging health topics and adopt new methods and technologies for the survey's examination and laboratory components; and (6) advance research and innovation to address survey response rate issues and improve metrics for assessing data quality.

National Center for Science and Engineering Statistics (NCSES), National Science Foundation: Funding is requested to maintain NCSES ongoing activities measuring research and development trends, the science and engineering workforce, U.S. competitiveness, and the condition and progress of STEM education. NCSES seeks to preserve recent gains in coverage and data quality and to explore and develop more cost-efficient measures of innovation, entrepreneurship, and competitiveness utilizing non-survey data in these areas: (1) the impact of open source software on the economy, (2) non-traditional pathways to working in STEM, and (3) innovation through company administrative data.

Office of Research and Evaluation Statistics (ORES), Social Security Administration: Funding is requested to continue our efforts to ensure that policymakers and the public have access to objective, scientific and methodologically sound data and analysis as the dialogue on how to strengthen and reform Social Security continues. In support of this effort, we intend to consolidate the current Retirement Research Consortium and Disability Research Consortium into a single program with a scope equivalent to the two currently existing programs. This single program will address issues related to Supplemental Security Income, and Retirement, Survivors, and Disability Insurance. By funding the combined Retirement and Disability Research Consortium, we will continue to maintain our capability to produce policy relevant research on retirement, to address a shortage of disability policy research, and foster collaborative research with other Federal agencies.

Statistics of Income (SOI), Treasury Department: Funding is requested to provide support for ongoing SOI programs and to: (1) provide continued opportunities to study the impacts of tax law and economic changes on tax administration by further integrating existing administrative data with edited data to allow for improved data linkages across sectors, building on existing efforts that have reduced cost and improved timeliness by streamlining data processing, thus reducing the number of, or eliminating the need for, fields to be transcribed; (2) continue evaluation of sample designs for major programs, and implement changes to the designs to expand population coverage and improve estimation; (3) expand geographic data releases to provide the public with extensive small-area estimates for the filing population of individual taxpayers; (4) support innovative research with the potential to improve tax administration by working with experts within and outside Government; (5) ensure timely data releases to reflect the impact of legislative changes on the tax system; (6) work with other agencies to develop new products, insights, and/or methods for expanding access to data for research purposes while protecting individual taxpayer privacy; (7) conduct holistic assessments of projects to identify opportunities to further develop relationships between SOI products, thus providing more comprehensive and statistically useful data to customers; (8) continue efforts to modernize SOI's public communications by developing extensive data visualizations, conducting social media outreach, and continue redesigning the public Tax Stats web pages; and (9) continue efforts to address the impact of IRS' con-solidation of its Submission Processing Centers, working to minimize the effects of the center closures on the quality and timeliness of SOI's statistical products. 8 Includes funds for salaries and expenses. The FY 2018 Analytical Perspectives report did not include funds for salaries and expenses.

Table 15–1.   2017–2019 BUDGET AUTHORITY FOR PRINCIPAL STATISTICAL AGENCIES[1]

(In millions of dollars)

Agency	Actual 2017	Estimate 2018[2]	Estimate 2019
Bureau of Economic Analysis	104	97	98
Bureau of Justice Statistics[3]	91	89	78
Bureau of Labor Statistics	609	605	609
Bureau of Transportation Statistics	26	26	26
Bureau of the Census[4]	1,497	1,488	3,827
Salaries and Expenses/Current Surveys and Programs	276	274	279
Periodic Censuses and Programs	1,210	1,202	3,548
Economic Research Service	87	77	45
Energy Information Administration	122	118	118
National Agricultural Statistics Service[5]	171	170	165
National Center for Education Statistics[6]	295	301	299
Statistics	110	109	113
Assessment	149	148	149
National Assessment Governing Board	8	8	8
National Center for Health Statistics	160	159	155
National Center for Science and Engineering Statistics, NSF[7]	60	57	46
Office of Research, Evaluation, and Statistics, SSA	24	32	31
Statistics of Income Division, IRS[8]	34	34	35

[1] Reflects any rescissions and sequestration.

[2] FY 2018 amounts reflect the annualized continuing resolution levels.

[3] Includes directly appropriated funds as well as funds transferred to BJS for research and statistical services; management and administrative (M&A) costs; and assessments for rescissions.

[4] Amounts include discretionary and mandatory funds. 2018 estimate does not include a budget adjustment of $187M

[5] Includes funds for the periodic Census of Agriculture of $43, $42, and $45 million in 2017, 2018, and 2019, respectively.

[6] Includes funds for salaries and expenses of $18, $18, and $18 million in 2017, 2018, and 2019, respectively, which are displayed in the Budget Appendix under the Institute of Education Sciences (IES). In addition, the National Center for Education Statistics manages the IES grant program for the State Longitudinal Data System which is funded at $5 million and $6 million 2017 and 2018, respectively, and the EDFacts Initiative which is funded at $5 million, $12 million, and $11 million in 2017, 2018, and 2019 respectively.

[7] Includes funds for salaries and expenses of $8.5, $8.7, and $8.7 million in 2017, 2018, and 2019, respectively.

[8] Includes funds for salaries and expenses. The FY 2018 Analytical Perspectives report did not include funds for salaries and expenses.

16. INFORMATION TECHNOLOGY

Every day millions of Americans rely on Federal information technology (IT) to engage with Federal services and information. The President proposes spending nearly $45.8 billion on IT investments at major civilian agencies, which will be used to acquire, develop, and implement modern technologies that enhance digital service delivery. This budget also supports the forthcoming President's Management Agenda (PMA), OMB policies, and Federal laws that enable agency technology planning, oversight, funding, and accountability practices. It will also support the consolidation of common agency services; migration to secure, cost-effective commercial cloud solutions; and the modernization of antiquated and often unsecured legacy systems. This investment will, in alignment with the PMA, focus on addressing root structural, process, and capability challenges in government technology service delivery. The analysis in this chapter excludes the Department of Defense and classified spending which in FY 2018 was $42.5 billion, or 44 percent of the IT budget for that year.

OVERVIEW OF FEDERAL INFORMATION TECHNOLOGY

Federal Spending on IT

As shown in Table 16-1, the Federal Government Budget for civilian IT is estimated to be $45.8 billion in FY 2019.[1] This figure is a decrease from the reported civilian value for FY 2018, largely due to a change in reporting guidance for Federal IT spending. In previous years, the IT budget included grants made by two Federal agencies to state and local governments for IT systems used to administer Federal benefits. In FY 2018, these grants were estimated

<hr>

[1] Based on agencies represented on the IT Dashboard, located at *https://www.itdashboard.gov*.

to be $9.0 billion, making up 10 percent of the IT budget. Not including these grants in FY 2019 affects the IT budgets reported for the Department of Agriculture (USDA) and the Department of Health and Human Services (HHS), as these agencies account for all of the aforementioned grants spending. While USDA and HHS typically set requirements for State and local government use of these funds, it is the State or local government that is responsible for development and maintenance of the systems, so the revised time series excluding these grants effectively presents the spending for which Federal Chief Information Officers (CIOs) can be fairly held accountable. Chart 16-1 shows historical estimates of the annual IT budget since FY 2011, with an additional estimate where these grants have been removed[2] in order to maintain continuity with current reporting guidance. It should be noted that the total agency budgets presented elsewhere in the budget do include these IT grants.

Table 16–1.   FEDERAL IT SPENDING
(In millions of dollars)

	2017	2018	2019
Non-Defense	44,924	45,554	45,775
Total	**44,924**	**45,554**	**45,775**

The analysis in this chapter excludes the Department of Defense and classified spending.

There is significant variation in spending on IT among Executive Branch Departments and Agencies, as shown in Table 16-2, which displays IT spending by agency. The

<hr>

[2] Investments labeled as 'Part 06 – Grants to State and Local IT Investments' were excluded from FY 2011 – 2015 figures and investments labeled 'Part 04 - Grants and Other Transferred Funding' were excluded in FY 2016 – 2017 figures. FY 2018 – 2019 estimates did not collect these investments.

Chart 16-1. Trends in Federal IT Spending Grants Spending Removal Comparison

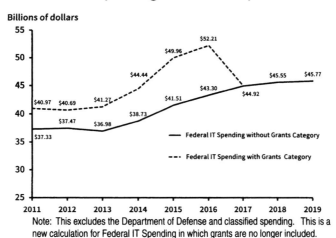

Note: This excludes the Department of Defense and classified spending. This is a new calculation for Federal IT Spending in which grants are no longer included.

Table 16–2. ESTIMATED FY 2019 FEDERAL IT SPENDING AND PERCENTAGE BY AGENCY
(In millions of dollars)

Agency	FY 2019	Percent of Total
Department of Homeland Security	$6,844	15.0%
Department of Health and Human Services	$5,472	12.0%
Department of the Treasury	$4,649	10.2%
Department of Veterans Affairs	$4,281	9.4%
Department of Transportation	$3,306	7.2%
Department of Commerce	$3,008	6.6%
Department of Justice	$2,878	6.3%
Department of State	$2,429	5.3%
Department of Energy	$2,331	5.1%
Department of Agriculture	$2,034	4.4%
Social Security Administration	$1,671	3.7%
National Aeronautics and Space Administration	$1,645	3.6%
Department of the Interior	$1,195	2.6%
Department of Education	$741	1.6%
Department of Labor	$690	1.5%
General Services Administration	$667	1.5%
U.S. Army Corps of Engineers	$468	1.0%
Environmental Protection Agency	$342	0.7%
Department of Housing and Urban Development	$338	0.7%
Nuclear Regulatory Commission	$169	0.4%
U.S. Agency for International Development	$154	0.3%
Office of Personnel Management	$147	0.3%
National Archives and Records Administration	$120	0.3%
National Science Foundation	$105	0.2%
Small Business Administration	$90	0.2%
Total	**$45,775**	**100.0%**

The analysis in this chapter excludes the Department of Defense and classified spending.

Department of Homeland Security is the largest civilian agency in IT spending, while the bottom 5 agencies only spend 1.3 percent of Federal IT spending.

IT Investments Overview

The FY 2019 budget includes funding for 4,113 IT investments at major civilian agencies. These investments support three main functions: mission delivery; IT infrastructure, IT security, and IT management; and administrative services and support systems (see Chart 16-2). As Chart 16-3 shows, IT investments can vary widely in size and scope. As a result, the largest 100 investments account for 45 percent of Federal IT spending.

Of those 4,113 IT investments, 507 are major IT investments. Agencies determine if an IT investment is classified as major based on whether the associated investment has significant program or policy implications; has high executive visibility; has high development, operating, or maintenance costs; or requires special management attention because of its importance to the mission or function of the agency. For all major IT investments, agencies are required to submit Business Cases, which provide additional transparency regarding the cost, schedule, and performance data related to its spending.

OMB requires that agency CIOs provide risk ratings for all major IT investments on the IT Dashboard website on a continuous basis and assess how risks for major development efforts are being addressed and mitigated. The Agency CIO rates each investment based on his or her best judgment, using a set of pre-established criteria. As a rule, the evaluation should reflect the CIO's assessment of the investment's ability to accomplish its goals. Chart 16-4 summarizes the latest CIO risk ratings for all major IT investments government-wide.

The IT Dashboard shows slight decreases in the general health of IT investments across government, as denoted by the decreased proportion of CIO-rated "Green" ("Low Risk" to "Moderately Low Risk") investments on the IT Dashboard, which comprised 58 percent of all rated investments in 2018 compared to 79 percent in 2012 (assessments based on total life cycle of investments).

Chart 16-2. 2019 IT Investment Portfolio Summary

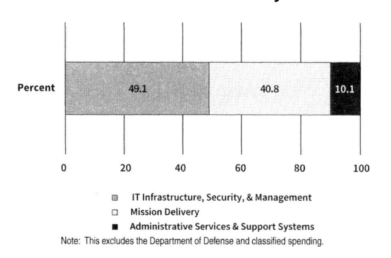

Note: This excludes the Department of Defense and classified spending.

Chart 16-3. Percentage of 2019 IT Spending by Number of Investments

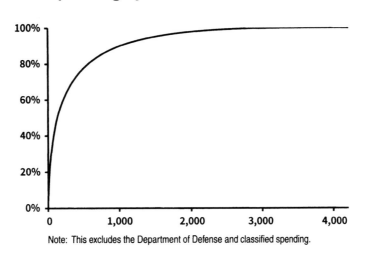

Note: This excludes the Department of Defense and classified spending.

Legacy IT Spending

Historically, the Federal government has had a poor record in acquiring, developing, and managing Federal IT investments. Frequently too many Federal IT projects ran over budget, fell behind schedule, or failed to deliver the intended results. Moreover, the Federal government plans to spend more than 80 percent of the total amount budgeted for IT on Operations & Maintenance (O&M). This spending includes aging legacy systems, which pose efficiency, cybersecurity, and mission risk issues, such as ever-rising costs to maintain them and an inability to meet current or expected mission requirements. Legacy systems may also operate with known security vulnerabilities that are either technically difficult or prohibitively expensive to address and thus may hinder agencies' ability to comply with critical cybersecurity statutory and policy requirements.

Chart 16-5 displays the percent of the government-wide IT funding going toward new capabilities (referred to as Development, Modernization, and Enhancement or DME) and O&M.

IT Modernization

Federal agencies have struggled with appropriately planning and budgeting for continuous modernization of their legacy IT systems, upgrading their underlying infrastructure, and investing in high quality, lower cost service delivery technology. Further, transition to provisioned services, such as cloud and shared services, remains slow. The lack of proactive adoption of cloud and shared services has resulted in agencies accumulating a backlog of technology maintenance work. The FY 2019 President's Budget requires agencies to identify and budget for the modernization of specific high-risk legacy IT systems, with

Chart 16-4. CIO Risk Ratings for Investments

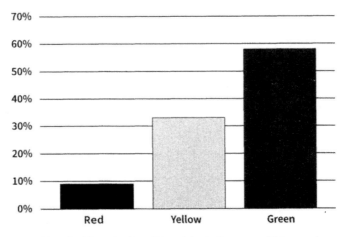

Note: As of December 2017. This excludes the Department of Defense and classified spending.

Chart 16-5. IT Spending by DME and O&M

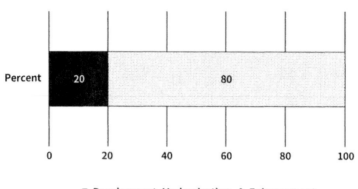

■ Development, Modernization, & Enhancement

□ Operations and Maintenance

Note: This excludes the Department of Defense and classified spending.

a particular focus on transitioning these systems to cloud and shared services. Doing so will improve the quality and efficiency of the Government's critical citizen-facing services by migrating to commercial cloud solutions, consolidating common agency services, and modernizing agencies' legacy systems.

The forthcoming PMA will prominently feature IT modernization as one of the foundational pillars on which the Executive Branch will focus its time, resources, and attention. Detailed below are key elements of this Administration's IT modernization strategy under the PMA.

Technology Modernization Fund

The FY 2019 President's Budget includes $210 million for the Technology Modernization Fund (TMF). The TMF was established as a key component of the Modernizing Government Technology provisions in the Fiscal Year 2018 National Defense Authorization Act (NDAA). The FY 2019 funding will complement any initial seed funding provided in FY 2018, when discretionary appropriations are finalized, and will help grow the revolving fund to a sustained level that will allow the TMF to tackle more complex government-wide IT modernization efforts.

The TMF pioneers a new model for Federal technology modernization projects. Agencies must apply to and compete for TMF funds. Effective evaluation, selection, and monitoring of approved projects by the TMF Board will provide strong incentives for agencies to develop comprehensive, high quality modernization plans. Agencies will provide plans that meet key criteria defined by the TMF Board, which will likely include: having a high probability of success, a strong team, and a substantial impact on mission and citizen service delivery. Funds will be distributed in an incremental manner, tied to milestones and objectives. Agencies that receive funds from the TMF will work with the General Services Administration (GSA) and the Office of Management and Budget (OMB) to ensure that projects make maximum use of commercial products and

services in their planning and execution and have a high likelihood of success.

TMF funds will be repaid over a period not to exceed five years, aided through cost savings and avoidance, subject to a written agreement and the availability of out-year agency appropriations. In addition, incremental funds transfers will be tied to successful delivery of products. Successful projects will operate as proofs of concept and will provide valuable insights to the Board, which may recommend prioritizing the selection of more comprehensive modernization projects that can serve the interests of the Executive Branch as a whole.

Cybersecurity

Strengthening the cybersecurity of Federal networks, systems, and data is one of the most important challenges we face as a nation. Risk management assessments carried out under the President's Executive Order 13800[3], Strengthening the Cybersecurity of Federal Networks and Critical Infrastructure, demonstrated that the majority of Federal agencies could not appropriately manage their cybersecurity risk. These assessments found enterprise-wide gaps in network visibility, IT tool standardization, and common operating procedures, all of which negatively affect Federal cybersecurity and put our nation at risk. Bold approaches are needed to improve government-wide governance processes and implement cybersecurity capabilities "commensurate with risk and magnitude of the harm"[4] that a compromise of Federal information systems and information would entail. As part of the larger

---

[3]   *https://www.whitehouse.gov/presidential-actions/presidential-executive-order-strengthening-cybersecurity-federal-networks-critical-infrastructure/*

[4] FISMA requires agencies to implement information security protections commensurate with the risk and magnitude of the harm resulting from the unauthorized access, use, disclosure, disruption, modification, or destruction of "information collected or maintained by or on behalf of [an] agency" and "information systems used or operated by an agency or by a contractor of an agency or other organization on behalf of an agency". 44 U.S.C. § 3554.

effort to utilize modern solutions to drive more effective and efficient IT, the Federal Government will move to better utilize threat information in its decision-making processes, implement improved baseline security capabilities, and enhance accountability for the management of information security risks. Additionally, to protect privacy, prevent fraud, and mitigate high impact data breaches of Personally Identifiable Information (PII) (such as the 2016 Equifax breach) the Federal Government will move to better implement modern digital identity management processes, technologies, and remediation techniques.

For the first time, this budget includes information on discrete cyber investments at Federal agencies to help drive progress and accountability in the active management of cybersecurity risk. This information will allow more in-depth assessments of agency cybersecurity budgeting activities. In future years, this information will be aligned with the NIST Framework for Improving Critical Infrastructure Cybersecurity, also known as the NIST Cybersecurity Framework, which all agencies were directed to adopt under Executive Order 13800 and to which existing performance metrics are also aligned. Additional details on this Administration's cybersecurity efforts can be found in the Analytical Perspectives Chapter on Cybersecurity Funding.

Modern Public-Facing Services

Americans expect and deserve their interactions with the Federal Government to be simple, fast, and helpful. The FY 2019 President's Budget provides IT funding for major Federal civilian agencies to focus on providing better services to the American public. Specifically, the President's Budget continues to fund the United States Digital Service (USDS). USDS recruits some of the country's top technical talent, partnering directly with Federal agencies to enhance the Federal Government's most critical public-facing digital services. USDS uses design and technology expertise to deliver better services, including IT systems that will ensure veterans can easily access the benefits and services they have earned, small business owners can compete for government contracts, and doctors and clinicians are rewarded for the quality, not quantity, of care. Modernization efforts not only provide the public with better digital services, but also help streamline agency processes and save taxpayer dollars.

Cloud Adoption/Email Migration

Email and collaboration tools are essential to the day-to-day operations of Federal agencies, yet too few Federal agencies have basic collaboration tools like real-time web-based collaboration tools or video conferencing. In many cases, the tools being used by agencies are more than a decade old and run on legacy systems with growing maintenance costs. This situation is a hidden tax on productivity: it wastes time, creates missed opportunities, and slows coordination and creativity.

The majority of agencies that moved to cloud-based collaboration solutions experienced cost savings after just a few years of investment. These cost savings ranged from $500,000 per year for smaller agencies to $10 million per year for larger agencies. For example, the National Oceanic and Atmospheric Administration (NOAA) was able to migrate to cloud-based email within six months and decommission its legacy servers over the next two years to achieve a total of $3.1 million dollars of cost savings per year.

Migrating the remaining Federal agencies from agency owned-and-operated email systems to cloud-based email will result in significant cost savings, improved security, and greater productivity.

Improving Data Analytics and IT Portfolio Management

Data, accountability, and transparency provide the tools to deliver visibly better results to the public and hold agencies accountable to taxpayers. The Administration is focusing on improving the quality of IT spending data that will increase the government's ability to make data-driven decisions and analyze trade-offs among cost, quality, and value. To better understand and utilize Federal IT spending data, the Federal Government needs to better integrate data collection efforts, standardize reporting data, and find new opportunities to simplify, automate, and consolidate reporting.

Federal adoption of the Technology Business Management (TBM) framework will improve the consistency, granularity, and quality of Federal IT spending information. The TBM framework is an industry best practice and open data standard widely leveraged by private and public sector organizations.

In FY 2019, the Administration will continue driving Federal Government-wide adoption of the TBM framework and release implementation guidance to agencies. This will increase the strategic value of IT and empower CIOs to better support agency missions through more effective IT management. The TBM framework is a powerful tool that can enhance Federal Information Technology Reform Act (FITARA) implementation by helping agency CIOs better understand, manage, and demonstrate value from the money spent on IT resources. This will also help the Government benchmark IT spending, improve acquisitions and procurement practices, and better understand IT investment costs, providing an opportunity to improve budgeting for IT.

Improving the IT Workforce

A high-caliber IT workforce is key to achieving lasting success in each of the Administration's technology initiatives. Well-intentioned, yet unnecessarily restrictive rules, coupled with outdated technology and ineffective outreach to prospective employees have left the Federal Government struggling to attract the best talent, to hire quickly, or to hold workers and leaders accountable. To date, Federal agencies have faced challenges in effectively implementing IT workforce planning and defining cybersecurity staffing needs. As part of the broader PMA, we will modernize processes and practices to bring out the best in employees and enable the Federal workforce to more effectively deliver on mission. Execution of the National Initiative for Cybersecurity Education (NICE) coding structure is expected to identify critical cyber needs by the end of FY 2018. IT and cybersecurity recruitment and retention initiatives will continue to focus on mitigation of critical skill gaps and retaining current IT and cybersecurity talent. This past year the CIO Council, OMB, and the Office of Personnel Management held the first-ever government-wide tech and cyber hiring and recruitment event that attracted almost 2,000 attendees.

Increasing Buying Power

The Federal Government is the world's largest buyer, yet does not adequately leverage its buying power or price information to get the best value for the taxpayer. Significant contract duplication means that agencies award multiple contracts for similar goods and services, and experience significant price variance for the exact same item. At the same time, acquisition processes remain slow and complicated, reflecting strategies that were designed more than a half-century ago that fail to leverage modern technologies and private sector practices.

In FY 2019, the Administration will drive adoption of Category Management strategies, which enable Federal agencies to buy products and services in a coordinated and collaborative manner using Best in Class solutions and practices to the maximum extent practicable. Modernization will be supported with: (1) the adoption of government-wide standards; (2) using the standards to reduce contract duplication for IT and professional services; and (3) leveraging common solutions, shared services, and innovative commercial and government practices to bring spending under management control, with continued strong small business participation.

Implementation of these strategies has the potential to drive numerous benefits, including generating savings and administrative cost avoidance, increasing the Federal Government's ability to rapidly deploy best-in-class industry solutions, and enhancing cybersecurity.

17. FEDERAL INVESTMENT

Federal investment is the portion of Federal spending intended to yield long-term benefits for the economy and the country. It promotes improved efficiency within Federal agencies, as well as growth in the national economy by increasing the overall stock of capital. Investment spending can take the form of direct Federal spending or of grants to State and local governments.[1] It can be designated for physical capital, which creates a tangible asset that yields a stream of services over a period of years. It also can be for research and development, education, or

[1] For more information on Federal grants to State and local governments see Chapter 14, "Aid to State and Local Governments," in this volume.

training, all of which are intangible, but still increase income in the future or provide other long-term benefits.

Most presentations in this volume combine investment spending with spending intended for current use. This chapter focuses solely on Federal and Federally financed investment. It provides a comprehensive picture of Federal investment spending for physical capital, research and development, and education and training, but because it disregards spending for non-investment activities, it provides only a partial picture of Federal support for specific national needs, such as defense and transportation.

DESCRIPTION OF FEDERAL INVESTMENT

The distinction between investment spending and current outlays is a matter of judgment. The budget has historically employed a relatively broad classification of investment, encompassing physical investment, research, development, education, and training. The budget further classifies investments into those that are grants to State and local governments, such as grants for highways, and all other investments, or "direct Federal programs." This "direct Federal" category consists primarily of spending for assets owned by the Federal Government, such as weapons systems and buildings, but also includes grants to private organizations and individuals for investment, such as capital grants to Amtrak or higher education loans directly to individuals.

The definition of investment in a particular presentation can vary depending on specific considerations:

- Taking the approach of a traditional balance sheet would limit investment to only those physical assets owned by the Federal Government, excluding capital financed through grants and intangible assets such as research and education.

- Focusing on the role of investment in improving national productivity and enhancing economic growth would exclude items such as national defense assets, the direct benefits of which enhance national security rather than economic growth.

- Examining the efficiency of Federal operations would confine the coverage to investments that reduce costs or improve the effectiveness of internal Federal agency operations, such as computer systems.

- Considering a "social investment" perspective would broaden the coverage of investment beyond what is included in this chapter to include programs such as maternal health, certain nutrition programs, and

substance abuse treatment, which are designed in part to prevent more costly health problems in future years.

This analysis takes the relatively broad approach of including all investment in physical assets, research and development, and education and training, regardless of ultimate ownership of the resulting asset or the purpose it serves. It does not include "social investment" items like health care or social services where it is difficult to separate out the degree to which the spending provides current versus future benefits. The definition of investment used in this section provides consistency over time (historical figures on investment outlays back to 1940 may be found in the Budget's historical tables).[2]

In addition to this basic issue of definition, there are two technical problems in the classification of investment data: the treatment of grants to State and local governments, and the classification of spending that could be shown in multiple categories.

First, for some grants to State and local governments it is the recipient jurisdiction, not the Federal Government, which ultimately determines whether the money is used to finance investment or current purposes. This analysis classifies all of the outlays into the category in which the recipient jurisdictions are expected to spend a majority of the money. General purpose fiscal assistance is classified as current spending, although in practice, some may be spent by recipient jurisdictions on investment.

Second, some spending could be classified in more than one category of investment. For example, outlays for construction of research facilities finance the acquisition of physical assets, but they also contribute to research and development. To avoid double counting, the outlays are classified hierarchically in the category that is most com-

[2] The historical tables are available at *https://www.whitehouse.gov/omb/historical-tables/* and on the Budget CD-ROM.

monly recognized as investment: physical assets, followed by research and development, followed by education and training. Consequently, outlays for the conduct of research and development do not include outlays for the construction of research facilities, because these outlays are included in the category for investment in physical assets.

Additionally, in this analysis, Federal investment includes credit programs that are for investment purposes. When direct loans and loan guarantees are used to fund investment, the subsidy value is included as investment. The subsidies are classified according to their program purpose, such as construction or education and training. For more information about the treatment of Federal credit programs, refer to the section on Federal credit in Chapter 8, "Budget Concepts," in this volume.

This discussion presents spending for gross investment, without adjusting for depreciation.

Composition of Federal Investment Outlays

Major Federal Investment

The composition of major Federal investment outlays is summarized in Table 17–1. The categories include major public physical investment, the conduct of research and development, and the conduct of education and training. Total major Federal investment outlays were $528.1 billion in 2017. Federal investment outlays are estimated to decrease 5.5 percent to $498.8 billion in 2018, and increase by 13.6 percent to $566.7 billion in 2019. In 2019, defense investment outlays are estimated to increase by $26.0 billion, while nondefense investment outlays are expected to increase by $42.0 billion. The major factors contributing to these changes are described below.

Major Federal investment outlays will comprise an estimated 12.0 percent of total Federal outlays in 2019 and 2.7 percent of the Nation's gross domestic product. Budget authority and outlays for major Federal investment by subcategory may be found in Table 17–2 at the end of this chapter.

Physical investment. Outlays for major public physical capital investment (hereafter referred to as "physical investment outlays") are estimated to increase by 21.2 percent in 2019 to $322.8 billion, primarily driven by increases in funding to support the Administration's infrastructure initiative. Physical investment outlays are for construction and renovation, the purchase of major equipment, and the purchase or sale of land and structures. Almost two-thirds of these outlays are for direct physical investment by the Federal Government, with the remainder being grants to State and local governments for physical investment.

Direct physical investment outlays by the Federal Government are primarily for national defense. Defense outlays for physical investment are estimated to be

Table 17–1. COMPOSITION OF FEDERAL INVESTMENT OUTLAYS

(In billions of dollars)

Federal Investment	Actual 2017	Estimate	
		2018	2019
Major public physical capital investment:			
Direct Federal:			
National defense	134.0	144.7	159.9
Nondefense	38.4	40.6	40.0
Subtotal, direct major public physical capital investment	172.4	185.4	199.9
Grants to State and local governments	79.5	81.0	122.9
Subtotal, major public physical capital investment	251.9	266.3	322.8
Conduct of research and development:			
National defense	51.3	49.6	60.3
Nondefense	64.3	67.2	63.0
Subtotal, conduct of research and development	115.6	116.7	123.3
Conduct of education and training:			
Grants to State and local governments	57.5	60.0	55.9
Direct Federal	103.1	55.8	64.7
Subtotal, conduct of education and training	160.6	115.8	120.6
Total, major Federal investment outlays	**528.1**	**498.8**	**566.7**
MEMORANDUM			
Major Federal investment outlays:			
National defense	185.3	194.3	220.2
Nondefense	342.8	304.6	346.5
Total, major Federal investment outlays	528.1	498.8	566.7
Miscellaneous physical investment:			
Commodity inventories	–0.8	–0.8	–1.0
Other physical investment (direct)	2.6	2.8	2.9
Total, miscellaneous physical investment	1.7	2.0	1.9
Total, Federal investment outlays, including miscellaneous physical investment	529.8	500.8	568.6

$159.9 billion in 2019, $15.2 billion higher than in 2018. Approximately 94 percent of defense physical investment outlays, or an estimated $149.9 billion, are for the procurement of weapons and other defense equipment, and the remainder is primarily for construction on military bases, family housing for military personnel, and Department of Energy defense facilities.

Outlays for direct physical investment for nondefense purposes are estimated to be $40.0 billion in 2019. Outlays for 2019 include $21.5 billion for construction and renovation. This amount includes funds for construction and renovation of veterans' hospitals and Indian Health Service hospitals and clinics; water, power, and natural resources projects of the Corps of Engineers, and the Bureau of Reclamation within the Department of the Interior, energy projects of the Power Marketing Administrations within the Department of Energy, and the Tennessee Valley Authority; construction of office buildings by the General Services Administration; construction for the administration of justice programs (largely in Customs and Border Protection within the Department of Homeland Security); construction for embassy security; facilities for space and science programs of the National Aeronautics and Space Administration, Department of Energy, and National Science Foundation; and Postal Service facilities. Outlays for this category are estimated to decrease by $0.6 billion in 2019. The new Federal Capital Revolving Fund, proposed as part of the Administration's infrastructure initiative, increases outlays by $1.9 billion relative to 2018. However, this increase is offset by decreases resulting from one-time upward re-estimates of credit subsidy in 2018 in the Federal Housing Administration and decreases in capital spending in 2019 in the Department of Energy's Western Area Power Administration (WAPA). The Budget proposes to repeal WAPA's authority to borrow from Treasury to fund transmission projects that are best carried out by the private sector.

Outlays for grants to State and local governments for physical investment are estimated to be $122.9 billion in 2019, a 51.8 percent increase over the 2018 estimate of $81.0 billion. Grants for physical investment fund transportation programs, sewage treatment plants, community and regional development, public housing, and other State and tribal assistance. The increase in 2019 is mostly accounted for by the Administration's infrastructure initiative, which will begin to rebuild and modernize the Nation's physical infrastructure, help create jobs, maintain America's economic competitiveness, and connect communities and people to more opportunities. While the Administration continues to work with the Congress, States, localities, and other infrastructure stakeholders to finalize the suite of Federal programs that will support this effort, the 2019 Budget allocates $200 billion for the infrastructure initiative. The majority of this initiative is classified as grants to State and local governments, with $42.4 billion in outlays estimated to occur in 2019.

Conduct of research and development. Outlays for the conduct of research and development are estimated to be $123.3 billion in 2019, a $6.6 billion or 5.7 percent increase from 2018. Nearly half of research and development outlays are for national defense. Much of this year's increase is due to a $10.7 billion increase in research and development within military programs accompanied by smaller increases in defense-related research and development at the Department of Energy and Department of Homeland Security. Physical investment for research and development facilities and equipment is included in the physical investment category.

Non-defense outlays for the conduct of research and development are estimated to be $63.0 billion in 2019, a $4.2 billion or 6.2 percent decrease from 2018. Most investments in this area are funded through programs in the National Institutes of Health, the National Aeronautics and Space Administration, the Department of Energy, and the National Science Foundation.

A discussion of research and development funding can be found in Chapter 18, "Research and Development," in this volume.

Conduct of education and training. Outlays for the conduct of education and training were $160.6 billion in 2017. Outlays are estimated to decrease to $115.8 billion in 2018, and increase in 2019 to $120.6 billion. Grants to State and local governments for this category are estimated to be $55.9 billion in 2019, 46.3 percent of the total. They include education programs for the disadvantaged and individuals with disabilities, early care and education programs, training programs in the Department of Labor, and other education programs. Direct Federal education and training outlays in 2019 are estimated to be $64.7 billion, which is an increase of $8.9 billion, or 15.9 percent, from 2018. Programs in this category primarily consist of aid for higher education through student financial assistance, loan subsidies, and veterans' education, training, and rehabilitation. The decrease in outlays for the conduct of education and training from 2017 to 2018, and the increase from 2018 to 2019 are largely the result of annual re-estimates of subsidies to the Federal Direct Student Loan Program, which increased outlays in 2017 by $28.4 billion but reduced outlays by $11.4 billion in 2018. Another factor raising 2019 outlays is a $4.1 billion increase in the Student Financial Assistance account at the Department of Education.

This category does not include outlays for education and training of Federal civilian and military employees. Outlays for education and training that are for physical investment and for research and development are in the categories for physical investment and the conduct of research and development.

Miscellaneous Physical Investment

In addition to the categories of major Federal investment, several miscellaneous categories of investment outlays are shown at the bottom of Table 17–1. These items, all for physical investment, are generally unrelated to improving Government operations or enhancing economic activity.

Outlays for commodity inventories are for the purchase or sale of agricultural products pursuant to farm price support programs and other commodities. Sales are estimated to exceed purchases by $1.0 billion in 2019.

Outlays for other miscellaneous physical investment are estimated to be $2.9 billion in 2019. This category consists entirely of direct Federal outlays and includes primarily conservation programs.

Detailed Table on Investment Spending

Table 17-2 provides data on budget authority as well as outlays for major Federal investment, divided according to grants to State and local governments and direct Federal spending. Miscellaneous investment is not included because it is generally unrelated to improving Government operations or enhancing economic activity. The majority of funding for the Administration's infrastructure initiative may be found under the grants to State and local governments section of the table on the "community and regional development" line and the "other" line under the "other construction and rehabilitation" heading.

Table 17-2. FEDERAL INVESTMENT BUDGET AUTHORITY AND OUTLAYS: GRANT AND DIRECT FEDERAL PROGRAMS

(In millions of dollars)

Description	Budget Authority			Outlays		
	2017 Actual	2018 Estimate	2019 Estimate	2017 Actual	2018 Estimate	2019 Estimate
GRANTS TO STATE AND LOCAL GOVERNMENTS						
Major public physical investment:						
Construction and rehabilitation:						
Transportation:						
Highways	42,510	42,350	43,872	43,644	44,094	44,898
Mass transportation	13,733	13,550	12,284	12,124	13,131	13,049
Rail transportation	1,579	1,571	679	4,325	1,888	853
Air and other transportation	3,675	3,674	3,189	3,486	3,958	3,875
Subtotal, transportation	61,497	61,145	60,024	63,579	63,071	62,675
Other construction and rehabilitation:						
Pollution control and abatement	2,920	2,821	1,959	3,055	3,050	2,126
Community and regional development	13,775	4,182	50,285	6,667	8,296	50,837
Housing assistance	3,653	3,630	462	3,582	3,667	3,314
Other	809	1,166	120,673	687	912	1,849
Subtotal, other construction and rehabilitation	21,157	11,799	173,379	13,991	15,925	58,126
Subtotal, construction and rehabilitation	82,654	72,944	233,403	77,570	78,996	120,801
Other physical assets	1,990	2,192	2,032	1,881	1,958	2,122
Subtotal, major public physical investment	84,644	75,136	235,435	79,451	80,954	122,923
Conduct of research and development:						
Agriculture	336	334	326	308	341	341
Other	188	183	173	108	104	92
Subtotal, conduct of research and development	524	517	499	416	445	433
Conduct of education and training:						
Elementary, secondary, and vocational education	38,087	37,707	33,770	38,427	38,927	37,527
Higher education	380	376		342	421	329
Research and general education aids	789	786	15	776	802	244
Training and employment	3,241	3,355	1,981	3,269	3,321	2,405
Social services	12,464	12,721	12,097	11,854	13,292	12,358
Agriculture	418	447	399	388	594	545
Other	1,702	1,952	2,209	2,448	2,629	2,494
Subtotal, conduct of education and training	57,081	57,344	50,471	57,504	59,986	55,902
Subtotal, grants for investment	**142,249**	**132,997**	**286,405**	**137,371**	**141,385**	**179,258**
DIRECT FEDERAL PROGRAMS						
Major public physical investment:						
Construction and rehabilitation:						
National defense:						
Military construction and family housing	6,798	6,994	9,877	6,278	7,917	9,487
Atomic energy defense activities and other	534	524	626	390	466	578

Table 17-2. FEDERAL INVESTMENT BUDGET AUTHORITY AND OUTLAYS: GRANT AND DIRECT FEDERAL PROGRAMS—Continued

(In millions of dollars)

Description	Budget Authority			Outlays		
	2017 Actual	2018 Estimate	2019 Estimate	2017 Actual	2018 Estimate	2019 Estimate
Subtotal, national defense	7,332	7,518	10,503	6,668	8,383	10,065
Nondefense:						
International affairs	2,416	2,328	980	943	1,412	1,626
General science, space, and technology	1,396	1,290	1,158	1,280	1,260	1,410
Water resources projects	3,401	3,129	1,920	3,130	3,346	3,206
Other natural resources and environment	1,156	1,266	927	1,069	1,297	1,113
Energy	3,491	3,783	−2,568	3,521	2,846	2,242
Postal service	500	575	607	507	486	518
Transportation	185	160	201	136	217	263
Veterans hospitals and other health facilities	2,632	3,278	4,236	2,726	4,155	3,633
Administration of justice	1,571	1,437	2,178	921	1,459	1,607
GSA real property activities	900	876	2,461	1,256	1,456	2,147
Other construction	6,466	3,656	2,817	6,452	4,263	3,774
Subtotal, nondefense	24,114	21,778	14,917	21,941	22,197	21,539
Subtotal, construction and rehabilitation	31,446	29,296	25,420	28,609	30,580	31,604
Acquisition of major equipment:						
National defense:						
Department of Defense	147,865	155,025	178,363	126,912	135,906	149,398
Atomic energy defense activities	485	567	594	432	471	469
Subtotal, national defense	148,350	155,592	178,957	127,344	136,377	149,867
Nondefense:						
General science and basic research	365	358	293	357	340	332
Postal service	877	1,533	4,976	837	1,432	2,250
Air transportation	3,383	3,703	3,030	2,927	3,784	3,381
Water transportation (Coast Guard)	1,174	1,192	1,012	1,383	1,269	1,237
Hospital and medical care for veterans	1,783	1,857	2,802	1,375	1,582	2,150
Federal law enforcement activities	1,318	1,423	1,394	1,359	1,710	1,401
Department of the Treasury (fiscal operations)	317	322	144	396	245	190
National Oceanic and Atmospheric Administration	2,022	2,062	1,476	1,766	1,916	1,751
Other	4,962	5,019	5,181	5,557	5,815	5,430
Subtotal, nondefense	16,201	17,469	20,308	15,957	18,093	18,122
Subtotal, acquisition of major equipment	164,551	173,061	199,265	143,301	154,470	167,989
Purchase or sale of land and structures:						
National defense	−33	−38	−37	−36	−31	−31
Natural resources and environment	388	295	52	265	275	163
General government	....	....	13	....	....	4
Other	149	159	159	283	67	170
Subtotal, purchase or sale of land and structures	504	416	187	512	311	306
Subtotal, major public physical investment	196,501	202,773	224,872	172,422	185,361	199,899
Conduct of research and development:						
National defense:						
Defense military	49,036	43,564	57,102	45,431	43,271	53,965
Atomic energy and other	6,209	6,211	6,430	5,913	6,286	6,371
Subtotal, national defense	55,245	49,775	63,532	51,344	49,557	60,336
Nondefense:						
International affairs	289	322	117	290	266	266
General science, space, and technology:						
NASA	10,135	9,713	10,109	10,066	9,525	10,016
National Science Foundation	5,517	5,591	3,948	5,279	5,258	5,010
Department of Energy	4,657	4,456	3,253	4,338	4,456	3,253
Subtotal, general science, space, and technology	20,309	19,760	17,310	19,683	19,239	18,279
Energy	2,994	3,237	1,603	2,911	3,410	3,189
Transportation:						

Table 17–2. FEDERAL INVESTMENT BUDGET AUTHORITY AND OUTLAYS: GRANT AND DIRECT FEDERAL PROGRAMS—Continued

(In millions of dollars)

Description	Budget Authority			Outlays		
	2017 Actual	2018 Estimate	2019 Estimate	2017 Actual	2018 Estimate	2019 Estimate
Department of Transportation	720	745	639	690	745	703
NASA	517	508	488	462	494	471
Other transportation	41	41	40	24	40	39
Subtotal, transportation	1,278	1,294	1,167	1,176	1,279	1,213.
Health:						
National Institutes of Health	32,419	32,233	23,540	30,021	33,282	31,295
Other health	2,066	1,796	1,454	2,610	1,436	1,455
Subtotal, health	34,485	34,029	24,994	32,631	34,718	32,750
Agriculture	1,751	1,660	1,436	1,646	1,848	1,592
Natural resources and environment	2,369	2,359	1,708	2,378	2,317	1,834
National Institute of Standards and Technology	615	612	497	618	629	551
Hospital and medical care for veterans	1,346	1,338	1,454	1,188	1,314	1,372
All other research and development	1,633	1,615	1,479	1,365	1,713	1,526
Subtotal, nondefense	67,069	66,226	51,765	63,886	66,733	62,572
Subtotal, conduct of research and development	122,314	116,001	115,297	115,230	116,290	122,908
Conduct of education and training:						
Elementary, secondary, and vocational education	1,426	1,552	1,265	1,436	1,241	1,417
Higher education	83,052	35,641	35,765	79,673	31,246	39,219
Research and general education aids	2,353	2,300	2,132	2,403	2,237	2,201
Training and employment	2,267	2,227	1,826	2,099	2,461	2,485
Health	1,746	1,746	939	1,735	1,803	1,644
Veterans education, training, and rehabilitation	16,642	14,003	12,147	13,520	13,968	15,439
General science and basic research	902	887	634	814	943	901
National defense	....	....	....	1	3	....
International affairs	650	646	171	645	844	483
Other	836	942	721	742	1,056	891
Subtotal, conduct of education and training	109,874	59,944	55,600	103,068	55,802	64,680
Subtotal, direct Federal investment	**428,689**	**378,718**	**395,769**	**390,720**	**357,453**	**387,487**
Total, Federal investment	**570,938**	**511,715**	**682,174**	**528,091**	**498,838**	**566,745**

18. RESEARCH AND DEVELOPMENT

Innovation in science and technology has been a cornerstone of America's economic progress since the founding of this nation. The most recent estimate of total U.S. research and development (R&D) spending was about $495 billion, an amount greater than any other country and more than a quarter of the global total.[1] While the private sector funds and performs the majority of U.S. R&D, the Federal government has an important role in funding R&D in areas that industry does not have a strong incentive to invest in and in areas of critical importance to national and economic security. The Federal government has been the leading source of support for basic research and provides more than 25 times the amount funded by state and local governments in total R&D.[2] Prior Federally funded R&D has greatly advanced human knowledge, and applications of that knowledge permeate our lives—from the phones we carry, to the cars we drive, to the medicines that return us to health. Recognizing the critical importance

of fostering innovation to promote America's interests, including competitiveness, economic and job growth, and national security, the 2019 Budget continues support of investments in basic research, early-stage applied research, and technology transfer efforts that will lead to the breakthroughs of the future.

The President's 2019 Budget provides $118.1 billion for Federal R&D, including the conduct of R&D and investments in R&D facilities and equipment (see Table 18-2). This figure applies a change to the R&D definitions introduced in July 2016 per OMB Circular A-11. Under the former R&D definitions, the President's 2019 Budget provides $156.8 billion for R&D, a $2.8 billion (or 2%) increase over the FY 2018[3] level, and includes an $18.1 billion increase for Defense-related R&D. Detailed R&D definitions and a discussion of the definition change are available in Section II. Table 18-1 shows a breakout of FY 2019 R&D funding by major funding agencies at the bureau or account level.

---

[1] National Science Board. 2018 Science and Engineering Indicators. January 2018.

[2] NSF National Center for Science and Engineering Statistics (Dec. 2017). InfoBrief - NSF 18-306.

---

[3] Because an appropriation for FY 2018 was not passed by the time this chapter went to print, the chapter calculates FY 2018 estimates using an annualized version of the FY 2018 Continuing Resolution.

Table 18–1. TOTAL FEDERAL R&D FUNDING BY AGENCY AT THE BUREAU OR ACCOUNT LEVEL

(Mandatory and discretionary budget authority [1,2], dollar amounts in millions)

	2017 Actual	2018 Annualized CR	2019 Proposed	Dollar Change: 2018 to 2019	Percent Change: 2018 to 2019
By Agency					
Agriculture	2,585	2,487	1,914	–573	–23%
Agriculture Research Service	1,298	1,289	855	–434	–34%
Animal and Plant Health Inspection Service	40	39	34	–5	–13%
Economic Research Service	87	86	45	–41	–48%
Forest Service	282	281	235	–46	–16%
National Agricultural Statistics Service	9	9	9	0	0%
National Institute of Food and Agriculture	869	783	736	–47	–6%
Commerce	1,794	1,833	1,361	–472	–26%
Bureau of the Census	232	237	165	–72	–30%
National Institute of Standards and Technology	750	746	564	–182	–24%
National Oceanic and Atmospheric Administration	804	839	619	–220	–26%
National Telecommunications and Information Administration	8	11	13	2	18%
Defense[3]	49,197	43,616	57,156	13,540	31%
Military Construction	155	37	53	16	43%
Military Personnel	410	439	455	16	4%
Defense Health Program	1,452	336	362	26	8%
Research, Development, Test, and Evaluation	47,180	42,804	56,286	13,482	31%
Education	254	243	240	–3	–1%
Institute of Education Sciences	226	219	216	–3	–1%
Office of Postsecondary Education	3	0	0	0	0%
Office of Special Education and Rehabilitative Services	23	24	24	0	0%
Office of Career, Technical, and Adult Education	2	0	0	0	0%

Table 18–1.   TOTAL FEDERAL R&D FUNDING BY AGENCY AT THE BUREAU OR ACCOUNT LEVEL—Continued

(Mandatory and discretionary budget authority [1,2], dollar amounts in millions)

	2017 Actual	2018 Annualized CR	2019 Proposed	Dollar Change: 2018 to 2019	Percent Change: 2018 to 2019
Energy	14,896	15,006	12,685	–2,321	–15%
Fossil Energy Research and Development	399	419	292	–127	–30%
Science	5,438	5,307	4,127	–1,180	–22%
Electricity Delivery	144	144	46	–98	–68%
Nuclear Energy	764	955	754	–201	–21%
Energy Efficiency and Renewable Energy	1,445	1,492	524	–968	–65%
Advanced Research Projects Agency--Energy	306	295	0	–295	–100%
Cybersecurity, Energy Security, and Emergency Response	0	0	40	40	n/a
Defense Environmental Cleanup	28	28	28	0	0%
National Nuclear Security Administration	6,357	6,351	6,859	508	8%
Power Marketing Administration	15	15	15	0	0%
Environmental Protection Agency	497	496	269	–227	–46%
Science and Technology	481	480	256	–224	–47%
Hazardous Substance Superfund	15	15	12	–3	–20%
Inland Oil Spill Programs	1	1	1	0	0%
Health and Human Services	34,222	33,772	24,742	–9,030	–27%
Administration for Children and Families	16	5	89	84	1680%
Centers for Disease Control and Prevention	511	464	296	–168	–36%
Centers for Medicare and Medicaid Services	278	19	17	–2	–11%
Departmental Management	116	131	158	27	21%
Food and Drug Administration	390	410	410	0	0%
Health Resources and Services Administration	30	30	22	–8	–27%
National Institutes of Health [4]	32,881	32,713	23,750	–8,963	–27%
Homeland Security	724	672	548	–124	–18%
National Protection and Programs Directorate	6	6	48	42	700%
Science and Technology	597	527	371	–156	–30%
Transportation Security Administration	5	5	21	16	320%
United States Coast Guard	38	38	21	–17	–45%
United States Secret Service	3	2	3	1	50%
Management Directorate	3	3	3	0	0%
Countering Weapons of Mass Destruction Office	72	91	81	–10	–11%
Interior	953	964	759	–205	–21%
Bureau of Indian Affairs and Bureau of Indian Education	5	5	5	0	0%
Bureau of Land Management	23	23	23	0	0%
Bureau of Reclamation	72	104	83	–21	–20%
Bureau of Safety and Environmental Enforcement	27	27	21	–6	–22%
Department-Wide Programs	6	3	0	–3	–100%
National Park Service	27	26	24	–2	–8%
Office of Surface Mining Reclamation and Enforcement	1	1	1	0	0%
United States Fish and Wildlife Service	32	15	15	0	0%
United States Geological Survey	687	683	503	–180	–26%
Bureau of Ocean Energy Management	73	77	84	7	9%
National Aeronautics and Space Administration	10,704	10,243	10,651	408	4%
Science	5,668	5,666	5,820	154	3%
Aeronautics	517	508	488	–20	–4%
Low Earth Orbit and Spaceflight Operations	2,542	2,166	1,727	–439	–20%
Safety, Security and Mission Services	269	262	257	–5	–2%
Deep Space Exploration Systems	976	937	1,392	455	49%
Construction and Environmental Compliance and Restoration	52	22	54	32	145%
Exploration Research and Technology	680	682	913	231	34%
National Science Foundation	5,938	6,030	4,177	–1,853	–31%
Research and Related Activities	5,314	5,412	3,821	–1,591	–29%
Education and Human Resources	409	410	290	–120	–29%
Major Research Equipment and Facilities Construction	215	208	66	–142	–68%
Patient-Centered Outcomes Research Trust Fund	463	501	622	121	24%

Table 18–1.   TOTAL FEDERAL R&D FUNDING BY AGENCY AT THE BUREAU OR ACCOUNT LEVEL—Continued

(Mandatory and discretionary budget authority [1,2], dollar amounts in millions)

	2017 Actual	2018 Annualized CR	2019 Proposed	Dollar Change: 2018 to 2019	Percent Change: 2018 to 2019
Transportation	904	929	826	–103	–11%
Federal Aviation Administration	433	439	351	–88	–20%
Federal Highway Administration	317	311	334	23	7%
Federal Motor Carrier Safety Administration	11	9	9	0	0%
Federal Railroad Administration	43	43	24	–19	–44%
Federal Transit Administration	0	28	22	–6	–21%
Maritime Administration	0	1	0	–1	–100%
National Highway Traffic Safety Administration	63	60	62	2	3%
Office of the Secretary	17	17	13	–4	–24%
Pipeline and Hazardous Materials Safety Administration	20	21	11	–10	–48%
Smithsonian Institution	251	242	271	29	12%
Veterans Affairs	1,346	1,338	1,345	7	1%
Medical Services	673	669	618	–51	–8%
Medical and Prosthetic Research	673	669	727	58	9%

[1] This table shows funding levels for Departments or Independent agencies with more than $200 million in R&D activities in 2019.

[2] The Experimental Development definition is used in this table across all three fiscal years.

[3] Unlike previous years, totals for Experimental Development spending in FY 2017-2019 do not include the DOD Budget Activity 07 (Operational System Development) due to changes in the definition of development. These funds are requested in the FY 2019 Budget request and support the development efforts to upgrade systems that have been fielded or have received approval for full rate production and anticipate production funding in the current or subsequent fiscal year.

[4] The FY 2019 Budget proposes to consolidate the activities of the Agency for Healthcare Research and Quality (AHRQ) within NIH. The NIH total includes R&D funding that previously occurred in AHRQ.

I. PRIORITIES FOR FEDERAL RESEARCH AND DEVELOPMENT

The President's Budget provides support for Federal R&D to enhance our national security, increase American economic prosperity, create well-paying American jobs, and improve the national science and technology enterprise. This section highlights key areas of R&D funding in the 2019 Budget.

Protecting the Homeland against Physical and Cyber Attacks

Worldwide advances in technology mean that the threats to our national security are changing. Nations best able to employ precision-guided weapons, track enemy movements in real-time, disrupt communications, and work seamlessly in the fight will prevail. The President's National Security Strategy affirms the importance of peace through strength, reiterating that U.S. military strength remains a vital component of our nation's security, and renewing calls for American military overmatch. Historically, Federal R&D investments in military technology have led to the development of breakthrough technologies with tremendously useful civil applications, and the President's 2019 Budget encourages programs with dual-use potential to be leveraged for Federal non-military advancements.

The Department of Defense (DOD) will invest more than $84 billion in research, engineering, and prototyping activities in 2019 to maintain technical superiority and promote U.S. national security innovation. For example,

DOD is the centerpiece of a government-wide effort to out-innovate competitors and bolster the U.S. engineering and design communities in the area of trusted microelectronics, semiconductors, and future computing. Electronics, such as computer chips and their integrated circuits, are in everything from cell phones to jet aircraft. The Defense Advanced Research Projects Agency (DARPA) announced its Electronics Resurgence Initiative, investing more than $150 million per year —not including matching funds from industry – toward chip innovation. In addition, DOD is investing in hypersonics research for non-nuclear weapons, which can deter our potential adversaries and are able to strike any point on the globe within an hour. DOD will also support intelligence, surveillance, and reconnaissance along with kinetic and non-kinetic technologies that will disrupt and defeat missiles prior to launch. The 2019 Budget provides $6.8 billion for R&D efforts at the Missile Defense Agency to develop missile defeat, detection, and defense capabilities to protect the United States, our deployed forces, allies, and partners from missile attacks.

Beyond DOD, the 2019 Budget also supports a number of critical investments to protect the homeland at the Department of Homeland Security (DHS) and the Department of Health and Human Services (HHS). In particular, at DHS, the President's Budget requests $80.4 million in R&D funding to detect radiological and nuclear threats in order to defend against weapons of mass destruction, $25 million for biodefense-related R&D, $71.1 million in R&D to improve border surveillance and law enforcement capabilities to detect and interdict illegal activity, including the smuggling of contraband, and $70.6 million for cybersecurity R&D. In alignment with the President's National Security Strategy call to bolster transportation security, the 2019 Budget will also invest $20.6 million in R&D at the Transportation Security Administration to counter emerging threats to our aviation, surface, and intermodal transportation systems. At HHS, the Budget also provides $1 billion to develop enhanced medical countermeasures to respond to potential public health emergencies.

Improving Preparedness for and Response to Natural Disasters

In the wake of natural disasters, including a devastating hurricane season and catastrophic forest fires, it is more important than ever to invest in the tools necessary to predict, protect against, mitigate, respond to, and recover from natural disasters. The Budget supports investments in high-priority Earth observations that contribute to the nation's ability to predict the weather and respond to natural disasters. Within the National Aeronautics and Space Administration (NASA), the Budget provides $1.8 billion to maintain progress toward satellite missions and research that will improve our understanding of the Earth, including natural hazards. The joint NASA-Indian Space Research Organization Synthetic Aperture Radar (NISAR) mission will provide unprecedented, detailed views of Earth and will enhance our understanding and response to hazards such as earthquakes, tsunamis, and landslides. The Budget also supports National Oceanic and Atmospheric Administration (NOAA) research on seasonal to subseasonal atmospheric behavior to improve our ability to understand, predict and communicate information associated with hazardous weather. The Budget also funds the U.S. Geological Survey to conduct research to quantify earthquake likelihoods and to develop a nationwide capability to release aftershock advisories during major earthquake sequences. The Budget also continues to support space weather-related R&D, since space weather can affect not just the nation's satellites and space explorers, but can potentially cause significant damage to our electrical grid and electronic systems.

Expanding Human Exploration and Commercialization of Space

The Budget supports more innovative and sustainable approaches for exploration with commercial and international partners to enable the return of humans to the Moon for long-term exploration and utilization, followed by human missions to Mars and other destinations. As it pioneers the space frontier, NASA will support growth of the nation's space economy, increase understanding of the universe and our place in it, and advance America's aerospace technology.

This Budget continues investments to once again launch Americans into space from American soil. Additionally, it initiates new industry partnerships for landing robotic missions on the surface of the Moon in the next few years, paving the way for a return of our astronauts—this time not just to visit, but to lay the foundation for further journeys of exploration and the expansion of our economy into space. The Budget supports a space exploration program that we can be proud of—one that reflects American ingenuity, ambition, and leadership. One key to an affordable and dynamic exploration program is the development of new technologies and the Budget spends over $750 million on exploration technology. The Budget also provides $150 million for a program to expand commercial activities in low Earth orbit, with a focus on developing and deploying commercial space stations that can be used by NASA and other customers as a successor to the International Space Station.

Harnessing Artificial Intelligence and High Performance Computing

The development of artificial intelligence (AI) is advancing at a rapid pace, and the 2019 Budget invests in fundamental AI research and computing infrastructure to maintain U.S. leadership in this field. AI holds the potential to transform the lives of Americans through improved technology integration in the workplace and enhanced standards of living at home. The Budget funds basic research related to AI at the National Science Foundation and applied R&D in the Department of Transportation for the further development of autonomous and unmanned systems. In defense applications, DOD is working to deliver AI-driven algorithms to warfighting systems, which can rapidly turn volumes of data into decision-quality insights. And in the health realm, NIH is supporting the use of high performance computing to analyze large data sets to drive cancer research forward.

The Budget also funds high performance computing through supporting investments in computing infrastructure, which hold the potential for AI technology use and other purposes. The Budget provides $811 million to the Department of Energy's Advanced Scientific Computing Research Program to support research and facility upgrades to supercomputing infrastructure at Argonne and Oak Ridge National Laboratories, including the development of exascale high performance computers. These supercomputers will rank among the fastest and most powerful in the world, and will leverage strong partnerships with industry and academia in their development and use.

Combating Drug Abuse and the Opioid Overdose Epidemic

The Administration is committed to combating drug abuse and the opioid overdose epidemic, which poses an urgent threat to public safety and public health. The Administration's declaration of a nationwide public health emergency on October 26, 2017 highlighted the need for improved R&D to prevent and treat drug addiction. The President's Commission on Combating Drug Addiction and the Opioid Crisis provided recommendations for related research to the President. In addition, the White House Office of Science and Technology Policy is convening an interagency body to facilitate efforts across agencies on health science and technology in response to the opioid crisis, and to develop an R&D roadmap designed to enhance the national opioid response.

The 2019 Budget supports a number of important R&D efforts at agencies to understand and fight this critical problem. For instance, the Budget invests in research into the biological and social-behavioral basis of drug addiction to improve the fundamental understanding of opioid addiction, and in the development of technologies to measure brain function, which can potentially improve our understanding of addictive behavior, brain systems, and related phenomena. In addition, NIH has launched an initiative in partnership with innovator companies and the Food and Drug Administration (FDA) to address the urgent need for non-addictive alternatives to opioids for pain relief. With the 2019 Budget's investment of $100 million, this public-private partnership will facilitate the development of new treatments for addiction, overdose-reversal, and non-addictive therapies for pain. Furthermore, the 2019 Budget supports R&D at DHS to develop cost-effective detection systems to rapidly collect information useful for detecting opioids and fentanyls at land borders and international mail handling facilities - enhancing efforts to prevent illicit drugs from entering the country.

Stimulating Biomedical Innovation for American Health

Encouraging biomedical innovation is key to preventing, treating, and defeating disease and maintaining America's global leadership in healthcare. Achieving these goals requires effective and efficient transfer of research results from bench to bedside. To ensure that the work of the National Institutes of Health (NIH) continues to drive biomedical innovation that improves health, the 2019 Budget supports the expansion of policies that promote technology transfer, including policies that encourage investigators to seek intellectual property protection for their inventions. The Budget also supports the highest priority research at NIH to continue to make progress on finding cures for major diseases and illnesses.

Integrating Autonomous and Unmanned Systems into the Transportation Network

Autonomous and unmanned systems, such as drones and self-driving cars, can provide novel, low-cost capabilities across a broad range of commercial sectors, including transportation. In order to leverage these benefits, research is needed on how these systems and technologies can be safely integrated into the existing transportation network.

The 2019 Budget provides $17.3 million to the Federal Aviation Administration for R&D related to the integration of unmanned aircraft systems (UAS) into the national airspace system. The Budget will also provide $57 million to NASA for research on further development of the UAS traffic management system and UAS operating standards. This funding will allow NASA to complete its current UAS-related projects, which will contribute to the integration of UAS into the national aerospace system. The Budget also proposes accelerating the start of advanced autonomous systems research to ensure the safe integration of autonomous vehicle systems, such as advanced UAS and passenger-carrying urban air mobility aircraft, into the national airspace.

The Budget provides $10 million to the National Highway Transportation Safety Administration's Automated Driving Systems program for critical research that will assist the agency in the development of an advanced regulatory approach for a new generation of transportation technologies. The Budget also provides $100 million to the Federal Highway Administration's Intelligent Transportation Systems program to support R&D on connected and autonomous vehicles and related technologies.

Leveraging Biotechnologies for Agriculture and Rural Prosperity

The report from the President's Interagency Task Force on Agriculture and Rural Prosperity called for an increased focus on leveraging agricultural biotechnology to further improve agricultural efficiency and the quality of food products. Therefore, the Budget prioritizes the U.S. Department of Agriculture (USDA) research portfolio by providing formula funding at the FY 2017 Enacted level for research and extension activities at land-grant universities and competitive research through the Department's flagship competitive research grant program, the Agriculture and Food Research Initiative. The Budget also proposes over $800 million for in-house basic and applied research conducted by the Agriculture Research Service.

The Budget also proposes to transfer operational responsibility of the National Bio-and Agro-Defense Facility (NBAF) from the Department of Homeland Security to USDA. NBAF is a laboratory facility designed to study diseases that threaten the animal agricultural industry and public health, and given that USDA is already responsible for the research programs that will be conducted at this facility once construction is completed, it makes sense for USDA to manage the facility itself.

Unleashing an Era of Energy Dominance through Strategic Support for Innovation

The United States has among the most abundant and diverse energy resources in the world, including oil, gas, coal, nuclear, and renewables. The ability of our entrepreneurs and businesses to commercialize technologies that take full advantage of those resources is paramount to promoting U.S. economic growth, security, and competitiveness. That is why the Budget invests approximately $1.7 billion across the applied energy offices at the Department of Energy (DOE) for early-stage research and development that will enable the private sector to deploy the next generation of technologies and energy services that usher in a more secure, resilient, and integrated energy system. Through balanced support across generation types and fuel sources, the Budget helps usher in a new era of US energy dominance.

II. FEDERAL R&D DATA

R&D is the collection of efforts directed toward gaining greater knowledge or understanding and applying knowledge toward the production of useful materials, devices, and methods. R&D investments can be characterized as basic research, applied research, development, R&D equipment, or R&D facilities. The Office of Management and Budget (OMB) has used those or similar categories in its collection of R&D data since 1949. Starting with the FY 2018 Budget, OMB implemented a refinement to the categories by more narrowly defining "development" as "experimental development" to better align with the data collected by the National Science Foundation on its multiple R&D surveys, and to be consistent with international standards. An explanation of this change is included below. Please note that R&D cross-cuts in specific topical areas as mandated by law will be reported separately in forthcoming Supplements to the President's 2019 Budget.

Background on Federal R&D Funding

More than 20 Federal agencies fund R&D in the United States. The character of the R&D that these agencies fund depends on the mission of each agency and on the role of R&D in accomplishing it. Table 18-2 shows agency-by-agency spending on basic research, applied research, experimental development, and R&D equipment and facilities.

Basic research is systematic study directed toward a fuller knowledge or understanding of the fundamental aspects of phenomena and of observable facts without specific applications towards processes or products in mind. Basic research, however, may include activities with broad applications in mind.

Applied research is systematic study to gain knowledge or understanding necessary to determine the means by which a recognized and specific need may be met.

Experimental development is creative and systematic work, drawing on knowledge gained from research and practical experience, which is directed at producing new products or processes or improving existing products or processes. Like research, experimental development will result in gaining additional knowledge.

Research and development equipment includes acquisition or design and production of movable equipment, such as spectrometers, research satellites, detectors, and other instruments. At a minimum, this category includes programs devoted to the purchase or construction of R&D equipment.

Research and development facilities include the acquisition, design, and construction of, or major repairs or alterations to, all physical facilities for use in R&D activities. Facilities include land, buildings, and fixed capital equipment, regardless of whether the facilities are to be used by the Government or by a private organization, and regardless of where title to the property may rest. This category includes such fixed facilities as reactors, wind tunnels, and particle accelerators.

Comprehensive government-wide efforts are currently underway to increase the accuracy and consistency of the R&D budget via a collaborative community of practice of Federal agencies which have been working to identify best practices and standards for the most accurate classification and reporting of R&D activities. For example, to better align with National Science Foundation R&D surveys and international standards, starting with the FY 2018 Budget OMB has narrowed the definition of development to "experimental development." This definition, unlike the previous definition of development, excludes user demonstrations of a system for a specific use case and pre-production development (i.e., non-experimental work on a product or system before it goes into full production). Because of this recent change, the experimental development amounts reported are significantly lower than the development amounts shown in past Budgets. In particular, the change in definition of experimental development reduces R&D spending compared to what it would have been under the previous definition by approximately $38.7 billion in FY 2019.

III. OTHER SOURCES OF FEDERAL SUPPORT FOR R&D

The President's 2019 Budget seeks to build on strong private sector R&D investment by prioritizing Federal resources on areas that industry is not likely to support over later-stage applied research and development

Table 18–2.   FEDERAL RESEARCH AND DEVELOPMENT SPENDING
(Mandatory and discretionary budget authority [1], dollar amounts in millions)

	2017 Actual	2018 Annualized CR	2019 Proposed	Dollar Change: 2018 to 2019	Percent Change: 2018 to 2019
By Agency					
Defense [3]	49,197	43,616	57,156	13,540	31%
Health and Human Services	34,222	33,772	24,742	–9,030	–27%
Energy	14,896	15,006	12,685	–2,321	–15%
NASA	10,704	10,243	10,651	408	4%
National Science Foundation	5,938	6,030	4,177	–1,853	–31%
Agriculture	2,585	2,487	1,914	–573	–23%
Veterans Affairs	1,346	1,338	1,345	7	1%
Commerce	1,794	1,833	1,361	–472	–26%

Table 18-2. FEDERAL RESEARCH AND DEVELOPMENT SPENDING—Continued

(Mandatory and discretionary budget authority [1], dollar amounts in millions)

	2017 Actual	2018 Annualized CR	2019 Proposed	Dollar Change: 2018 to 2019	Percent Change: 2018 to 2019
Transportation	904	929	826	-103	-11%
Interior	953	964	759	-205	-21%
Patient-Centered Outcomes Research Trust Fund	463	501	622	121	24%
Homeland Security	724	672	548	-124	-18%
Smithsonian Institution	251	242	271	29	12%
Environmental Protection Agency	497	496	269	-227	-46%
Education	254	243	240	-3	-1%
Other	561	629	490	-139	-22%
TOTAL [2]	125,289	119,001	118,056	-945	-1%
Total (using the former definition of Development)	*154,983*	*153,932*	*156,777*	*2,845*	*2%*
Basic Research					
Defense	2,215	2,244	2,284	40	2%
Health and Human Services	16,701	16,859	12,114	-4,745	-28%
Energy	4,802	4,601	3,398	-1,203	-26%
NASA	3,607	3,713	4,150	437	12%
National Science Foundation	4,739	4,818	3,402	-1,416	-29%
Agriculture	1,119	1,038	921	-117	-11%
Veterans Affairs	538	538	540	2	0%
Commerce	234	232	197	-35	-15%
Transportation	....	....	....	....	....
Interior	54	54	40	-14	-26%
Patient-Centered Outcomes Research Trust Fund	....	....	....	....	....
Homeland Security	49	53	31	-22	-42%
Smithsonian Institution	224	220	225	5	2%
Environmental Protection Agency	....	....	....	....	....
Education	34	28	28	0	0%
Other	11	11	11	0	0%
SUBTOTAL	34,327	34,409	27,341	-7,068	-21%
Applied Research					
Defense	5,276	5,101	5,239	138	3%
Health and Human Services	17,356	16,685	12,348	-4,337	-26%
Energy	6,491	6,693	5,885	-808	-12%
NASA	2,476	2,517	2,713	196	8%
National Science Foundation	778	773	546	-227	-29%
Agriculture	1,070	1,055	904	-151	-14%
Veterans Affairs	780	774	779	5	1%
Commerce	979	961	733	-228	-24%
Transportation	594	602	497	-105	-17%
Interior	745	744	580	-164	-22%
Patient-Centered Outcomes Research Trust Fund	463	501	622	121	24%
Homeland Security	184	179	125	-54	-30%
Smithsonian Institution	....	....	....	....	....
Environmental Protection Agency	420	418	228	-190	-45%
Education	133	135	132	-3	-2%
Other	403	421	317	-104	-25%
SUBTOTAL	38,148	37,559	31,648	-5,911	-16%
Experimental Development [2]					
Defense [3]	41,545	36,219	49,579	13,360	37%
Health and Human Services	27	35	35	0	0%
Energy	2,488	2,533	1,865	-668	-26%
NASA	4,569	3,991	3,734	-257	-6%
National Science Foundation	....	....	....	....	....
Agriculture	174	173	163	-10	-6%
Veterans Affairs	28	26	26	0	0%
Commerce	303	322	191	-131	-41%

Table 18–2.   FEDERAL RESEARCH AND DEVELOPMENT SPENDING—Continued

(Mandatory and discretionary budget authority [1], dollar amounts in millions)

	2017 Actual	2018 Annualized CR	2019 Proposed	Dollar Change: 2018 to 2019	Percent Change: 2018 to 2019
Transportation	275	293	296	3	1%
Interior	152	164	137	–27	–16%
Patient-Centered Outcomes Research Trust Fund	....	....	....	....	....
Homeland Security	491	440	392	–48	–11%
Smithsonian Institution	....	....	....	....	....
Environmental Protection Agency	75	75	41	–34	–45%
Education	87	80	80	0	0%
Other	149	199	157	–42	–21%
SUBTOTAL	50,363	44,550	56,696	12,146	27%
Subtotal (using the former definition of Development)	*80,057*	*79,481*	*95,417*	*15,936*	*20%*
Facilities and Equipment					
Defense	161	52	54	2	4%
Health and Human Services	138	193	245	52	27%
Energy	1,115	1,179	1,537	358	30%
NASA	52	22	54	32	145%
National Science Foundation	421	439	229	–210	–48%
Agriculture	222	221	–74	–295	–133%
Veterans Affairs	....	....	....	....	....
Commerce	278	318	240	–78	–25%
Transportation	35	34	33	–1	–3%
Interior	2	2	2	0	0%
Patient-Centered Outcomes Research Trust Fund	....	....	....	....	....
Homeland Security	....	....	....	....	....
Smithsonian Institution	27	22	46	24	109%
Environmental Protection Agency	2	3	0	–3	–100%
Education	....	....	....	....	....
Other	–2	–2	5	7	–350%
SUBTOTAL	**2,451**	**2,483**	**2,371**	**–112**	**–5%**

[1] This table shows funding levels for Departments or Independent agencies with more than $200 million in R&D activities in 2019.

[2] The total uses the new Experimental Development definition across the three fiscal years.

[3] The totals for Experimental Development spending in FY 2017-2019 do not include the DOD Budget Activity 07 (Operational System Development) due to changes in the definition of development. These funds are requested in the FY 2019 Budget request and support the development efforts to upgrade systems that have been fielded or have received approval for full rate production and anticipate production funding in the current or subsequent fiscal year.

that the private sector is better equipped to pursue. A key means of stimulating private sector investment and bridging Federal government research with industry development is through the transfer of technology. Federal technology transfer seeks to help enable domestic companies to develop and commercialize products derived from government-funded R&D, which can lead to greater productivity from U.S. R&D investments and ultimately promote the nation's economic growth. Recognizing the benefits of this mechanism, the 2019 Budget sustains funding for technology transfer efforts where appropriate. The Administration will also be launching a new initiative to enable and enhance the Federal government's transition of discoveries from laboratory to market as a Cross-Agency Priority Goal.

Because much of the Federally funded R&D is conducted outside of the government, the Administration seeks to reduce the associated burdens to funding recipients and partners in order to promote greater effectiveness and efficiency in our Federal spending. A significant effort to reduce the administrative and regulatory burdens associated with Federal R&D funding is currently underway through new interagency groups. One of these, an interagency working group on research regulation (as required by the Research and Development Efficiency Act), is examining ways to reduce the administrative burden on those performing Federally funded research. The Administration remains committed to reducing administrative burdens for all Federal grant recipients - not just those for R&D. Specifically, OMB plans to take actions on

the recommendations outlined in the DATA Act Section 5 Pilot report, which identified specific opportunities to reduce recipient reporting burden.

The Federal Government also stimulates private investment in R&D through tax preferences. Historically, dating back to the 1950s, the private sector has performed the majority of U.S. R&D. As of 2015, businesses performed 72% of total U.S. R&D.[4] The research and experimentation (R&E) tax credit, which was made permanent through the Protecting Americans from Tax Hikes Act of 2015 (P.L. 114-113) and modified in the Tax Cut and Jobs Act of 2017 (P.L. 115-97), essentially provides a credit to qualified research expenses. R&E tax credit claims have at least doubled over the past two decades, growing from an estimated $4.4 billion in 1997 to $11.3 billion in 2013.[5] The manufacturing and the professional, scientific and technical services sectors account for about 70% of total claims in 2013.

[4] NSF National Center for Science and Engineering Statistics (Dec. 2017). InfoBrief - NSF 18-306.

[5] IRS Statistics of Income Division (August 2017). 1990-2013 Corporate Returns Data.

19. CREDIT AND INSURANCE

The Federal Government offers direct loans and loan guarantees to support a wide range of activities including home ownership, student loans, small business, farming, energy, infrastructure investment, and exports. In addition, Government-sponsored enterprises (GSEs) operate under Federal charters for the purpose of enhancing credit availability for targeted sectors. Through its insurance programs, the Federal Government insures deposits at depository institutions, guarantees private-sector de-fined-benefit pensions, and insures against some other risks such as flood and terrorism.

This chapter discusses the roles of these diverse programs. The first section discusses individual credit programs and GSEs. The second section reviews Federal deposit insurance, pension guarantees, disaster insurance, and insurance against terrorism and other security-related risks.

I. CREDIT IN VARIOUS SECTORS

Housing Credit Programs

Through housing credit programs, the Federal Government promotes homeownership among various target groups, including low- and moderate-income people, veterans, and rural residents. In times of economic crisis, the Federal Government's role and target market can expand dramatically.

Federal Housing Administration

The Federal Housing Administration (FHA) guarantees mortgage loans to provide access to homeownership for people who may have difficulty obtaining a conventional mortgage. FHA has been a primary facilitator of mortgage credit for first-time and minority buyers, a pioneer of products such as the 30-year self-amortizing mortgage, and a vehicle to enhance credit for many low- to moderate-income households. One of the major benefits of an FHA-insured mortgage is that it provides a homeownership option for borrowers who can make only a modest down-payment, but show that they are creditworthy and have sufficient income to afford the house they want to buy.

In addition to traditional single-family "forward" mortgages, FHA insures "reverse" mortgages for seniors and loans for the construction, rehabilitation, and refinancing of multifamily housing, hospitals and other health care facilities.

FHA and the Single-Family Mortgage Market

In the early 2000s, FHA's market presence diminished greatly as low interest rates increased the affordability of mortgage financing and more borrowers used emerging non-prime mortgage products, including subprime and Alt-A mortgages. Many of these products had risky and hard-to-understand features such as low "teaser rates" offered for periods as short as the first two years of the mortgage, high loan-to-value ratios (with some mortgages exceeding the value of the house), and interest-only loans with balloon payments that require full payoff at a set future date. The Alt-A mortgage made credit easily available by waiving documentation of income or assets. This competition eroded the market share of FHA's single-family purchase and refinance loans, reducing it from 9 percent in 2000 to less than 2 percent in 2005.

During the financial crisis, starting at the end of 2007, the availability of credit guarantees from the FHA and Government National Mortgage Association (which supports the secondary market for Federally-insured housing loans by guaranteeing securities backed by mortgages guaranteed by FHA, VA, and USDA) was an important factor countering the tightening of private-sector credit. The annual volume of FHA's single-family mortgages soared from $52 billion in 2006 to a high of $330 billion in 2009.

Although loan volume has declined since its 2009 peak, FHA continued to experience strong demand in 2017 as mortgage rates remained low and the improving economy brought new home buyers into the market. FHA's single-family origination loan volume in 2017 was $251 billion, and FHA's market share of home financing by dollar volume was 15 percent. For 2019, the Budget projects FHA volume will be $230 billion.

FHA Home Equity Conversion Mortgages

Home Equity Conversion Mortgages (HECMs) are designed to support aging in place by enabling elderly homeowners to borrow against the equity in their homes without having to make repayments during their lifetime (unless they move, refinance or fail to meet certain requirements). A HECM is also known as a "reverse" mortgage because the change in home equity over time is generally the opposite of a forward mortgage. While a traditional forward mortgage starts with a small amount of equity and builds equity with amortization of the loan, a HECM starts with a large equity cushion that declines over time as the loan accrues interest and premiums. The risk of HECMs therefore is weighted toward the end of the mortgage, while forward mortgage risk is concentrated in the first 10 years. FHA recently took steps, including lowering the share of home equity a homeowner can borrow against (the "principal limit factors"), to mitigate the risk of losses on HECMs, and FHA is exploring additional risk mitigation measures for 2019. HECM origination volume was $18 billion in 2017, and the Budget projects $12 billion in 2019.

FHA Mutual Mortgage Insurance (MMI) Fund

FHA guarantees for forward and reverse mortgages are administered under the Mutual Mortgage Insurance (MMI) Fund. At the end of 2017, the MMI Fund had $1,227 billion in total mortgages outstanding and a capital ratio of 2.09%, remaining above the 2% statutory minimum for the third straight year but declining from the 2016 level of 2.35%. The HECM portfolio continues to have a negative impact on the MMI Fund, offsetting the positive capital position of the forward mortgage portfolio. While the 2017 capital ratio for forward mortgages was 3.33%, the HECM portfolio had a capital ratio of –19.84%. For more information on the financial status of the MMI Fund, please see the *Annual Report to Congress Regarding the Financial Status of the FHA Mutual Mortgage Insurance Fund, Fiscal Year 2017.*

FHA Multifamily and Healthcare Guarantees

In addition to the single-family mortgage insurance provided through the MMI Fund, FHA's General Insurance and Special Risk Insurance (GISRI) loan programs continue to facilitate the construction, rehabilitation, and refinancing of multifamily housing, hospitals and other health care facilities. The credit enhancement provided by FHA enables borrowers to obtain long-term, fixed-rate financing, which mitigates interest rate risk and facilitates lower monthly mortgage payments. This can improve the financial sustainability of multifamily housing and healthcare facilities and may also translate into more affordable rents/lower healthcare costs for consumers.

GISRI's new origination loan volume for all programs in 2017 was $21 billion and the Budget projects $21 billion for 2019. Total mortgages outstanding in the FHA GISRI Fund were $158 billion at the end of 2017.

VA Housing Program

The Department of Veterans Affairs (VA) assists veterans, members of the Selected Reserve, and active duty personnel in purchasing homes in recognition of their service to the Nation. The housing program effectively substitutes the Federal guarantee for the borrower's down payment, making the lending terms more favorable than loans without a VA guarantee. VA does not guarantee the entire mortgage loan to veterans, but provides a 100 percent guarantee on the first 25 percent of losses upon default. The number of loans that VA guaranteed reached a new record level in 2017, as mortgage rates remained low and the improving economy provided opportunities for returning veterans to purchase homes. The continued historically low interest rate environment of 2017 allowed 190,914 Veteran borrowers to lower interest rates on their home mortgages through refinancing. VA provided approximately $47 billion in guarantees to assist 740,389 borrowers in 2017. This followed $45 billion and 705,474 borrowers in 2016.

Approximately 4 percent of active VA-guaranteed loans were delinquent at any time during 2017. VA, in cooperation with VA-guaranteed loan servicers, also assists borrowers through home retention options and alternatives to foreclosure. VA intervenes when needed to help veterans and service members avoid foreclosure through loan modifications, special forbearances, repayment plans, and acquired loans, as well as assistance to complete compromise sales or deeds-in-lieu of foreclosure. These joint efforts helped resolve over 85 percent of defaulted VA-guaranteed loans and assisted over 97,000 Veterans retain homeownership and/or avoid foreclosure in 2017. These actions resulted in $2.7B in avoided guaranteed claim payments.

Rural Housing Service

The Rural Housing Service (RHS) at the U.S. Department of Agriculture (USDA) offers direct and guaranteed loans to help very-low- to moderate-income rural residents buy and maintain adequate, affordable housing. RHS housing loans and loan guarantees differ from other Federal housing loan programs in that they are means-tested, making them more accessible to low-income, rural residents. The single family housing guaranteed loan program is designed to provide home loan guarantees for moderate-income rural residents whose incomes are between 80 percent and 115 percent (maximum for the program) of area median income.

Historically, RHS has offered both direct and guaranteed homeownership loans. In recent years, the portfolio has shifted to more efficient loan guarantees, an indication the direct loan program has achieved its goal of graduating borrowers to commercial credit and lowering costs to the taxpayer. The single family housing guaranteed loan program was authorized in 1990 at $100 million and has grown into a $24 billion loan program annually. The shift to guaranteed lending is in part attributable to the mortgage banking industry offering historically low mortgage rates, resulting in instances where the average 30-year fixed commercial mortgage rate has been at or below the average borrower rate for the RHS single family direct loan. Furthermore, financial markets have become more efficient and have increased the reach of mortgage credit to lower credit qualities and incomes. The number of rural areas isolated from broad credit availability has shrunk as access to high speed broadband has increased and correspondent lending has grown.

Education Credit Programs

The Department of Education (ED) direct student loan program is one of the largest Federal credit programs with $999 billion in Direct Loan principal outstanding at the end of 2017. The Federal student loan programs provide students and their families with the funds to help meet postsecondary education costs. Because funding for the loan programs is provided through mandatory budget authority, student loans are considered separately for budget purposes from other Federal student financial assistance programs (which are largely discretionary), but should be viewed as part of the overall Federal effort to expand access to higher education.

Loans for higher education were first authorized under the William D. Ford program—which was included in the Higher Education Act of 1965. The direct loan program was authorized by the Student Loan Reform Act of 1993 (Public Law 103–66). The enactment of the Student Aid and Fiscal Responsibility Act (SAFRA) of 2010 (Public Law 111–152) ended the guaranteed loan program (FFEL). On July 1, 2010, ED became the sole originator of Federal student loans through the Direct Loan program.

Under the current direct loan program, the Federal Government provides loan capital directly to over 6,000 institutions, which then disburse loan funds to students. Loans are available to students and parents of students regardless of income. There are three types of Direct Loans: Federal Direct Subsidized Stafford Loans, Federal Direct Unsubsidized Stafford Loans, and Federal Direct PLUS Loans, each with different terms. The Federal Government does not charge interest while the borrowers are in school and during certain deferment periods for Direct Subsidized Stafford loans—which are available only to undergraduate borrowers from low and moderate income families.

The Direct Loan program offers a variety of repayment plans including income-driven ones for all student borrowers, regardless of the type of loan. Depending on the plan, monthly payments are capped at no more than between 10 and 15 percent of borrower discretionary income and balances remaining after 20 to 25 years are forgiven. In addition, under current law, borrowers who work in public service professions while making 10 years of qualifying payments are eligible for Public Service Loan Forgiveness (PSLF).

The 2019 President's Budget includes several policy proposals for this program. For a detailed description of these proposals, please see the Federal Direct Student Loan Program Account section of the Budget Appendix.

Small Business and Farm Credit Programs

The Government offers direct loans and loan guarantees to small businesses and farmers, who may have difficulty obtaining credit elsewhere. It also provides guarantees of debt issued by certain investment funds that invest in small businesses. Two GSEs, the Farm Credit System and the Federal Agricultural Mortgage Corporation, increase liquidity in the agricultural lending market.

Small Business Administration

Congress created the U.S. Small Business Administration (SBA) in 1953 as an independent agency of the Federal Government to aid, counsel, assist and protect the interests of small business concerns; preserve free competitive enterprise; and maintain and strengthen the overall economy of the Nation. The SBA began making direct business loans and guaranteeing bank loans to small business owners, and providing inexpensive and immediate disaster relief to those hard-hit by natural disasters. By 1958, The Investment Company Act had established the Small Business Investment Company (SBIC) Program, under which the SBA continues to license, regulate, and guarantee funds for privately-owned and operated venture capital investment firms. To this day, the SBA continues to complement credit markets by guaranteeing access to affordable credit provided by private lenders for those that cannot attain it elsewhere.

The SBA has grown significantly since its creation, both in terms of its total assistance provided and its array of programs offered to micro-entrepreneurs and small business owners. With its headquarters located in Washington, DC, it leverages its field personnel and diverse network of private sector and nonprofit partners across each U.S. State and territory to ensure that America's small businesses have the tools and resources needed to start and develop their operations, drive U.S. competitiveness, help grow the economy, and promote economic security.

In 2017, the SBA provided $25.4 billion in loan guarantees to assist small business owners with access to affordable capital through its largest program, the 7(a) General Business Loan Guarantee program. This program provides access to financing for general business operations, such as operating and capital expenses. Through the 504 Certified Development Company (CDC) and Refinance Programs, the SBA also supported $5.0 billion in guaranteed loans for fixed-asset financing and the opportunity for small businesses to refinance existing 504 CDC loans. These programs enable small businesses to secure financing for assets such as machinery and equipment, construction, and commercial real estate, and to take advantage of current low interest rates and free up resources for expansion.

The SBA also creates opportunities for very small and emerging businesses to grow. Through the 7(m) Direct Microloan program, which supports non-profit intermediaries that provide loans of up to $50,000 to rising entrepreneurs, the SBA provided $68 million in direct lending to the smallest of small businesses and startups. By supporting innovative financial instruments such as the SBA's SBIC program that partners with private investors to finance small businesses through professionally managed investment funds, the SBA leveraged $2.0 billion in long-term, guaranteed loans to support $5.7 billion in venture capital investments in small businesses in 2017.

SBA continues to be a valuable source for American communities who need access to low-interest loans to recovery quickly in the wake of disaster. In 2017 alone, the SBA delivered $1.6 billion in disaster relief lending to businesses, homeowners, renters, and property owners.

The 2019 President's Budget includes several policy proposals for this program. For a detailed description of these proposals, please see the SBA Business Loans Program Account section of the Budget Appendix.

Community Development Financial Institutions

Since its creation in 1994, the Department of the Treasury's Community Development Financial Institutions (CDFI) Fund has—through different grant, loan, and tax credit programs—worked to expand the availability of credit, investment capital, and financial services for underserved people and communities by supporting the growth and capacity of a national network of CDFIs, investors, and financial service providers. Today, there are over 1,100 Certified CDFIs nationwide, including a variety of loan funds, community development banks, credit unions, and venture capital funds.

Unlike other CDFI Fund programs, the CDFI Bond Guarantee Program (BGP)—enacted through the Small Business Jobs Act of 2010—does not offer grants, but is instead a Federal credit program designed to function at no cost to taxpayers. The BGP was designed to provide CDFIs greater access to low-cost, long-term, fixed-rate capital, and incentivize and empower them to finance large community and economic development projects in low-income or underserved urban, rural, and Native areas.

Under the BGP, the Secretary of the Treasury provides a 100-percent guarantee on long-term bonds of at least $100 million issued to qualified CDFIs, with a maximum maturity of 30 years. To date, Treasury has issued $1.4 billion in bond guarantee commitments to 26 CDFIs, over $505 million of which has been disbursed to help finance affordable housing, charter schools, commercial real estate, and community healthcare facilities in 16 States and the District of Columbia.

Farm Service Agency

Farm operating loans were first offered in 1937 (by the newly created Farm Security Administration) to assist family farmers who were unable to obtain credit from a commercial source to buy equipment, livestock, or seed. Farm ownership loans were authorized in 1961 to provide family farmers with financial assistance to purchase farmland. Presently, the Farm Service Agency (FSA) assists low-income family farmers in starting and maintaining viable farming operations. Emphasis is placed on aiding beginning and socially disadvantaged farmers. Legislation mandates that a portion of appropriated funds are set aside for exclusive use by underserved groups (beginning, minority, and women farmers).

FSA offers operating loans and ownership loans, both of which may be either direct or guaranteed loans. Operating loans provide credit to farmers and ranchers for annual production expenses and purchases of livestock, machinery, and equipment, while farm ownership loans assist producers in acquiring and developing their farming or ranching operations. As a condition of eligibility for direct loans, borrowers must be unable to obtain private credit at reasonable rates and terms. As FSA is the "lender of last resort," default rates on FSA direct loans are generally higher than those on private-sector loans. FSA-guaranteed farm loans are made to more creditworthy borrowers who have access to private credit

markets. The subsidy rates for the direct programs fluctuate largely because of changes in the interest component of the subsidy rate.

In 2017, FSA provided loans and loan guarantees to more than 38,000 family farmers totaling $6.0 billion. Direct and guaranteed loan programs provided assistance totaling $2.6 billion to beginning farmers during 2017. Loans for socially disadvantaged farmers totaled $832 million, of which $437 million was in the farm ownership program and $395 million in the farm operating program. The majority of assistance provided in the operating loan program during 2017 was to beginning farmers as well.

Following a downturn in the agricultural economy, in recent years FSA assistance has been at historically high levels. Though overall loan totals were slightly lower in 2017 compared to 2016, the amount of direct and guaranteed operating and farm ownership loan assistance provided in 2017 was the second highest total in agency history. Demand for FSA loans—both direct and guaranteed—continues to be high. More conservative credit standards in the private sector continue to drive applicants from commercial credit to FSA direct programs. Low grain prices and uncertainty over interest rates continue to cause lenders to force their marginal borrowers to FSA for credit.

Lending to beginning farmers was strong during 2017. FSA provided direct or guaranteed loans to more than 21,000 beginning farmers. The number of beginning farmer loans decreased slightly by one percent. Sixty-two percent of direct operating loans were made to beginning farmers. Overall, as a percentage of funds available, lending to beginning farmers was only 1 percentage point below record-breaking 2016 levels. Lending to minority and women farmers was a significant portion of overall assistance provided, with $832 million in loans and loan guarantees provided to more than 8,700 farmers. Though loan assistance provided to beginning and socially disadvantaged farmers decreased slightly in 2017 compared to 2016, the trend in lending to underserved groups has remained relatively stable as a percentage of total loans made. Continued outreach efforts by FSA field offices to reach out to beginning and minority farmers and promote FSA funding have resulted in increased lending to these groups.

FSA continues to evaluate the farm loan programs in order to improve their effectiveness. FSA recently released a new microloan program to increase lending to small niche producers and minorities. This program has been expanded to include guaranteed as well as direct loans. This program dramatically simplifies application procedures for small loans, and implements more flexible eligibility and experience requirements. The demand for the micro-loan program continues to grow while delinquencies and defaults remain at or below those of the regular FSA operating loan program. FSA has also developed a nationwide continuing education program for its loan officers to ensure that they remain experts in agricultural lending, and it has transitioned information technology applications for direct loan servicing into a single, web-based application that expands on existing capabilities including special servicing options. Its implementation allows FSA to better service its delinquent and financially distressed borrowers.

FSA farm loan (direct and guaranteed) programs have had a considerable impact on rural communities – not just with farm families who have received needed credit for their farming business but also main street businesses. FSA assistance is enabling farm families with the credit needed to sustain and grow their farming organization and become contributing members of rural communities.

Energy and Infrastructure Credit Programs

The Department of Energy (DOE) administers two credit programs: Title XVII (a loan guarantee program to support innovative energy technologies) and the Advanced Technology Vehicle Manufacturing loan program (a direct loan program to support advanced automotive technologies).Title XVII of the Energy Policy Act of 2005 (Public Law 109–58) authorizes DOE to issue loan guarantees for projects that employ innovative technologies to reduce air pollutants or man-made greenhouse gases. Congress provided DOE $4 billion in loan volume authority in 2007, and the 2009 Consolidated Appropriations Act provided an additional $47 billion in loan volume authority, allocated as follows: $18.5 billion for nuclear power facilities, $2 billion for "front-end" nuclear enrichment activities, $8 billion for advanced fossil energy technologies, and $18.5 billion for energy efficiency, renewable energy, and transmission and distribution projects. The 2011 appropriations reduced the available loan volume authority for energy efficiency, renewable energy, and transmission and distribution projects by $17 billion and provided $170 million in credit subsidy to support renewable energy or energy efficient end-use energy technologies. From 2014 to 2015, DOE issued three loan guarantees totaling over $8 billion to support the construction of two new commercial nuclear power reactors. DOE has not issued any Title XVII loan guarantees since 2015.

The American Reinvestment and Recovery Act of 2009 (Public Law 111–5) amended the program's authorizing statute and provided $2.5 billion in credit subsidy to support loan guarantees on a temporary basis for commercial or advanced renewable energy systems, electric power transmission systems, and leading edge biofuel projects. Authority for the temporary program to extend new loans expired September 30, 2011. Prior to expiration, DOE issued loan guarantees to 28 projects totaling over $16 billion in loan volume. Four projects withdrew prior to any disbursement of funds.

Section 136 of the Energy Independence and Security Act of 2007 (Public Law 110–140) authorizes DOE to issue loans to support the development of advanced technology vehicles and qualifying components. In 2009, Congress appropriated $7.5 billion in credit subsidy to support a maximum of $25 billion in loans under ATVM. From 2009 to 2011, DOE issued 5 loans totaling over $8 billion to support the manufacturing of advanced technology vehicles. DOE has not issued any ATVM loans since 2011.

Electric and Telecommunications Loans

Rural Utilities Service (RUS) programs of the USDA provide grants and loans to support the distribution of rural electrification, telecommunications, distance learning, and broadband infrastructure systems.

In 2017, RUS delivered $4.2 billion in direct electrification loans, $428 million in direct telecommunications loans and $24 million in direct broadband loans.

USDA Rural Infrastructure and Business Development Programs

USDA, through a variety of Rural Development (RD) programs, provides grants, direct loans, and loan guarantees to communities for constructing facilities such as healthcare clinics, police stations, and water systems, as well as to assist rural businesses and cooperatives in creating new community infrastructure (e.g., educational and healthcare networks) and to diversify the rural economy and employment opportunities.

In 2017, RD provided $2.6 billion in Community Facility (CF) direct loans, which are for communities of 20,000 or less. The CF programs have the flexibility to finance more than 100 separate types of essential community infrastructure that ultimately improve access to healthcare, education, public safety and other critical facilities and services. In 2017 RD also provided $1.3 billion in water and wastewater direct loans.

Water Infrastructure

The Environmental Protection Agency's (EPA) new Water Infrastructure Finance and Innovation Act (WIFIA) program accelerates investment in the Nation's water infrastructure by providing long-term, low-cost supplemental loans for projects of regional or national significance. During 2017, EPA solicited the first loans, selecting twelve entities with projects in nine States to apply for more than $2 billion in WIFIA loans. Those first twelve projects will leverage more than $1 billion in private capital, in addition other funding sources, to help finance a total of over $5 billion in water infrastructure investments. The selected projects demonstrate the broad range of project types that the WIFIA program can finance, including wastewater, drinking water, stormwater, and water recycling projects.

Transportation Infrastructure

Federal credit programs offered through the Department of Transportation (DOT) fund critical transportation infrastructure projects, often using innovative financing methods. The two predominant programs are the Transportation Infrastructure Finance and Innovation Act (TIFIA) and the Railroad Rehabilitation and Improvement Financing (RRIF) loan programs, both managed in DOT's Build America Bureau. The Bureau combines the TIFIA and RRIF loan programs, Private Activity Bonds (PABs), and the Nationally Significant Freight and Highway Projects (INFRA) grant program all under one roof. The Bureau serves as the single point of contact and coordination for States, municipalities, and project sponsors looking to utilize Federal transportation expertise, apply for Federal transportation credit and grant programs, and explore ways to access private capital in public-private partnerships.

Established by the Transportation Equity Act of the 21st century (TEA–21) (Public Law 105–178) in 1998, the TIFIA program is designed to fill market gaps and leverage substantial private co-investment by providing supplemental and subordinate capital to projects of national or regional significance. Through TIFIA, DOT provides three types of Federal credit assistance to highway, transit, rail, and intermodal projects: direct loans, loan guarantees, and lines of credit.

TIFIA can help advance qualified, large-scale projects that otherwise might be delayed or deferred because of size, complexity, or uncertainty over the timing of revenues at a relatively low budgetary cost. Each dollar of subsidy provided for TIFIA can provide approximately $14 in credit assistance, and leverage additional non-Federal transportation infrastructure investment. The Fixing America's Surface Transportation (FAST) Act of 2015 (Public Law 114–94) authorizes TIFIA at $300 million in 2019.

DOT has also provided direct loans and loan guarantees to railroads since 1976 for facilities maintenance, rehabilitation, acquisitions, and refinancing. Federal assistance was created to provide financial assistance to the financially-challenged portions of the rail industry. However, following railroad deregulation in 1980, the industry's financial condition began to improve, larger railroads were able to access private credit markets, and interest in Federal credit support began to decrease.

Also established by TEA–21 in 1998, the RRIF program may provide loans or loan guarantees with an interest rate equal to the Treasury rate for similar-term securities. TEA–21 also stipulates that non-Federal sources pay the subsidy cost of the loan, thereby allowing the program to operate without Federal subsidy appropriations. The RRIF program assists projects that improve rail safety, enhance the environment, promote economic development, or enhance the capacity of the national rail network. While refinancing existing debt is an eligible use of RRIF proceeds, capital investment projects that would not occur without a RRIF loan are prioritized. Since its inception, over $5.1 billion in direct loans have been made under the RRIF program.

The FAST Act included programmatic changes to enhance the RRIF program to mirror the qualities of TIFIA, including broader eligibility, a loan term that can be as long as 35 years from project completion, and a fully subordinated loan under certain conditions. Additionally, in 2016 Congress appropriated $1.96 million to assist Class II and Class III Railroads in preparing and applying for direct loans and loan guarantees.

International Credit Programs

Currently, seven Federal agencies—USDA, the Department of Defense, the Department of State, the Department of the Treasury, the Agency for International Development (USAID), the Export-Import Bank (ExIm), and the Overseas Private Investment Corporation (OPIC)—provide direct loans, loan guarantees, and insurance to a variety of private and sovereign borrowers. These programs are intended to level the playing field for U.S. exporters, deliver robust support for U.S. goods and services, stabilize international financial markets, enhance security, and promote sustainable development.

Federal export credit programs counter official financing that foreign governments around the world, largely in Europe and Japan, but also increasingly in emerging markets such as China and Brazil, provide their exporters, usually through export credit agencies (ECAs). The U.S. Government has worked since the 1970's to constrain official credit support through a multilateral agreement in the Organization for Economic Cooperation and Development (OECD). This agreement has established standards for Government-backed financing of exports. In addition to ongoing work in keeping these OECD standards up-to-date, the U.S. Government established the International Working Group (IWG) on Export Credits to set up a new framework that will include China and other non-OECD countries, which until now have not been subject to export credit standards. The process of establishing these new standards, which is not yet complete, advances a Congressional mandate to reduce subsidized export financing programs.

Export Support Programs

When the private sector is unable or unwilling to provide financing, the Export-Import Bank, the U.S. ECA, fills the gap for American businesses by equipping them with the financing support necessary to level the playing field against foreign competitors. ExIm support includes direct loans and loan guarantees for creditworthy foreign buyers to help secure export sales from U.S. exporters, as well as working capital guarantees and export credit insurance to help U.S. exporters secure financing for overseas sales. USDA's Export Credit Guarantee Programs (also known as GSM programs) similarly help to level the playing field. Like programs of other agricultural exporting nations, GSM programs guarantee payment from countries and entities that want to import U.S. agricultural products but cannot easily obtain credit.

Exchange Stabilization Fund

Consistent with U.S. obligations in the International Monetary Fund regarding global financial stability, the Exchange Stabilization Fund managed by the Department of the Treasury may provide loans or credits to a foreign entity or government of a foreign country. A loan or credit may not be made for more than six months in any 12-month period unless the President gives the Congress a written statement that unique or emergency circumstances require that the loan or credit be for more than six months.

Sovereign Lending and Guarantees

The U.S. Government, through USAID, can extend short-to-medium-term loan guarantees that cover potential losses that might be incurred by lenders if a country defaults on its borrowings; for example, the U.S. may guarantee another country's sovereign bond issuance. The purpose of this tool is to provide the Nation's sovereign international partners access to necessary, urgent, and relatively affordable financing during temporary periods of strain when they cannot access such financing in international financial markets, and to support critical reforms that will enhance long term fiscal sustainability, often in concert with support from international financial institutions such as the International Monetary Fund. The long term goal of sovereign loan guarantees is to help lay the economic groundwork for the Nation's international partners to graduate to an unenhanced bond issuance in the international capital markets. For example, as part of the U.S. response to fiscal crises, the U.S. Government has extended sovereign loan guarantees to Tunisia, Jordan, Ukraine, and Iraq to enhance their access to capital markets, while promoting economic policy adjustment.

Development Programs

Credit is an important tool in U.S. bilateral assistance to promote sustainable development. USAID's Development Credit Authority (DCA) allows USAID to use a variety of credit tools to support its development activities abroad. DCA provides non-sovereign loan guarantees in targeted cases where credit serves more effectively than traditional grant mechanisms to achieve sustainable development. DCA is intended to mobilize host country private capital to finance sustainable development in line with USAID's strategic objectives. Through the use of partial loan guarantees and risk sharing with the private sector, DCA stimulates private-sector lending for financially viable development projects, thereby leveraging host-country capital and strengthening sub-national capital markets in the developing world.

Established in 1971, OPIC provides businesses with the tools to manage the risks associated with foreign direct investment, fosters economic development in emerging market countries, and advances U.S. foreign policy and national security priorities. OPIC helps American businesses gain footholds in new markets, catalyzes new revenues and contributes to jobs and growth opportunities both at home and abroad. OPIC fulfills its mission by providing businesses with financing, political risk insurance, and advocacy, and by partnering with private equity investment fund managers.

The Budget includes policy proposals involving development credit programs. For a discussion of those proposals, please see the Department of State and Other International Programs chapter of the main Budget volume.

The Government-Sponsored Enterprises (GSEs)

Fannie Mae and Freddie Mac

The Federal National Mortgage Association, or Fannie Mae, created in 1938, and the Federal Home Loan Mortgage Corporation, or Freddie Mac, created in 1970, were established to support the stability and liquidity of a secondary market for residential mortgage loans. Fannie Mae's and Freddie Mac's public missions were later broadened to promote affordable housing. The Federal Home Loan Bank (FHLB) System, created in 1932, is comprised of eleven individual banks with shared liabilities. Together they lend money to financial institutions—mainly banks and thrifts—that are involved in mortgage financing to varying degrees, and they also finance some mortgages using their own funds. The mission of the FHLB System is broadly defined as promoting housing finance, and the System also has specific requirements to support affordable housing.

Together these three GSEs currently are involved, in one form or another, with approximately half of residential mortgages outstanding in the U.S. today.

History of the Conservatorship of Fannie Mae and Freddie Mac and Budgetary Effects

Growing stress and losses in the mortgage markets in 2007 and 2008 seriously eroded the capital of Fannie Mae and Freddie Mac. Legislation enacted in July 2008 strengthened regulation of the housing GSEs through the creation of the Federal Housing Finance Agency (FHFA), a new independent regulator of housing GSEs, and provided the Treasury Department with authorities to purchase securities from Fannie Mae and Freddie Mac.

On September 6, 2008, FHFA placed Fannie Mae and Freddie Mac under Federal conservatorship. In its Strategic Plan for the Conservatorships of Fannie Mae and Freddie Mac, released in 2014, FHFA outlined three key goals for conservatorship: 1) maintain, in a safe and sound manner, foreclosure prevention activities and credit availability for new and refinanced mortgages to foster liquid, efficient, competitive and resilient national housing finance markets; 2) reduce taxpayer risk through increasing the role of private capital in the mortgage market; and 3) build a new single-family securitization infrastructure for use by Fannie Mae and Freddie Mac and adaptable for use by other participants in the secondary market in the future.

On September 7, 2008, the U.S. Treasury launched various programs to provide temporary financial support to Fannie Mae and Freddie Mac under the temporary authority to purchase securities. Treasury entered into agreements with Fannie Mae and Freddie Mac to make investments in senior preferred stock in each GSE in order to ensure that each company maintains a positive net worth. Based on the financial results reported by each company as of December 31, 2012, the cumulative funding commitment through these Preferred Stock Purchase Agreements (PSPAs) with Fannie Mae and Freddie Mac was set at $445.5 billion. In total, as of December 31,

2017, $187.5 billion has been invested in Fannie Mae and Freddie Mac, and this amount is projected to increase, based on publicly available information available through year-end 2017, by approximately $5.1 billion in 2018 due to an accounting-related write-down of deferred tax assets resulting from the enactment of tax reform legislation.

The PSPAs also require that Fannie Mae and Freddie Mac pay quarterly dividends to Treasury, equal to the GSE's positive net worth above a capital reserve amount. The capital reserve amount for each company was initially set at $3 billion for calendar year 2013, and set to decline by $600 million each year until reaching zero on January 1, 2018. However, in December 2017, the PSPAs were amended to reinstate the $3 billion reserve per GSE. Through December 31, 2017, the GSEs have paid a total of $278.8 billion in dividend payments to Treasury on the senior preferred stock. The Budget estimates additional dividend receipts of $184.7 billion from January 1, 2018, through 2028.

The Temporary Payroll Tax Cut Continuation Act of 2011 (Public Law 112–78) required that Fannie Mae and Freddie Mac increase their credit guarantee fees on single-family mortgage acquisitions between 2012 and 2021 by an average of at least 0.10 percentage points. Revenues generated by this fee increase are remitted directly to the Treasury for deficit reduction and are not included in the PSPA amounts. The Budget proposes to increase this fee by 0.10 percentage points for single-family mortgage acquisitions from 2019 through 2021, and then extend the 0.20 percentage point fee for acquisitions through 2023. This proposal will increase compensation to the Federal Government for its ongoing and unprecedented support of the GSEs, while at the same time helping to level the playing field for private lenders seeking to compete with Fannie Mae and Freddie Mac. With this proposal, combined with the existing authority under the Temporary Pay-roll Tax Cut Continuation Act, the Budget estimates resulting deficit reductions of $78.6 billion from 2012 through 2028.

In addition, in 2014 FHFA directed Fannie Mae and Freddie Mac to set aside 0.042 percentage points for each dollar of the unpaid principal balance of new business purchases (including but not limited to mortgages purchased for securitization) in each year to fund several Federal affordable housing programs created by Housing and Economic Recovery act of 2008, including the Housing Trust Fund and the Capital Magnet Fund. These set-asides were suspended by FHFA in November 2008 and reinstated effective January 1, 2015. Based on FHFA's stated policy the Budget assumes that no funds will be remitted to the programs in 2018 as a result of the anticipated draw on Treasury's funding commitments. Thereafter, the 2019 Budget again proposes to eliminate the 0.042 percentage point set-aside and discontinue funding for these funds, resulting in an increase to the estimated PSPA dividends.

Future of Fannie Mae and Freddie Mac

The Administration has publicly expressed its desire to work with members of Congress to facilitate a more sustainable housing finance system. Any reform of the housing system likely will impact the cash flows attributable to the Fannie Mae and Freddie Mac in the 2019 Budget projections in ways that cannot be estimated at this time.

The Farm Credit System (Banks and Associations)

The Farm Credit System (FCS or System) is a Government-sponsored enterprise composed of a nationwide network of borrower-owned cooperative lending institutions originally authorized by Congress in 1916. The FCS's mission is providing sound and dependable credit to American farmers, ranchers, producers or harvesters of aquatic products, their cooperatives, and farm-related businesses. In addition, the System serves rural America by providing financing for rural residential real estate, rural communication, energy and water infrastructure, and agricultural exports. In addition, maintaining special policies and programs for the extension of credit to young, beginning, and small farmers and ranchers is a legislative mandate for the System.

The financial condition of the System's banks and associations remains fundamentally sound. The ratio of capital to assets has remained stable at 17.3 percent on September 30, 2017, compared with 16.7 percent on September 30, 2016. Capital consisted of $50.8 billion in unrestricted capital and $4.7 billion in restricted capital in the Farm Credit Insurance Fund, which is held by the Farm Credit System Insurance Corporation (FCSIC). For the first nine months of calendar year 2017, net income equaled $3.7 billion compared with $3.6 billion for the same period of the previous year.

Over the 12-month period ending September 30, 2017, nonperforming loans as a percentage of total loans outstanding increased from 0.82 percent to 0.81 percent. System assets grew 2.3 percent during the year ending September 30, 2017, primarily due to increases in real estate mortgage loans and agribusiness loans. Real estate mortgage loans increased due to continued demand from new and existing customers.

Over the 12-month period ending September 30, 2017, the System's loans outstanding grew by $9.0 billion, or 3.7 percent, while over the past three years they grew by $43.1 billion, or 20.7 percent. As required by law, borrowers are also stockholder-owners of System banks and associations. As of September 30, 2017, System institutions had 525,309 of these stockholders-owners.

The number of FCS institutions continues to decrease because of consolidation. As of September 30, 2017, the System consisted of four banks and 70 associations, compared with seven banks and 104 associations in September 2002. Of the 73 FCS banks and associations rated (one association was not rated because it merged into another association on Oct 1, 2017), 69 of them had one of the top two examination ratings (1 or 2 on a 1 to 5 scale) and accounted for 98.5 percent of gross Systems assets. Four FCS institutions had a rating of 3.

In 2016, the pace of new lending to young, beginning, and small farmers remained relatively flat. In terms of dollar volume, the pace of young, beginning, and small farmers (YBS) lending slightly exceeded the pace of overall farm lending by FCS institutions. In terms of loan numbers, the pace of YBS lending lagged slightly behind the pace of overall farm lending. The number of loans made in 2016 to young, beginning and small farmers decreased by 0.2 percent, 0.6 percent and 0.2 percent respectively from 2015, while overall the number of farm loans made by the System grew by 0.5 percent. Loans to young, beginning, and small farmers and ranchers represented 17.0 percent, 21.7 percent, and 41.1 percent, respectively, of the total new farm loans made in 2016.

From 2015 to 2016, the dollar volume of new loans made to small farmers rose 3.3 percent, while the dollar volume of new loans to young and beginning farmers declined by 1.9 percent and 0.3 percent, respectively. However, since the dollar volume of the FCS's overall farm lending declined by 5.4 percent in 2016, the proportion of the System's dollar volume going to every YBS category actually increased slightly. Loans to young, beginning, and small farmers and ranchers represented 11.7 percent, 16.0 percent, and 15.4 percent, respectively, of the total dollar volume of all new farm loans made in 2016. Young, beginning, and small farmers are not mutually exclusive groups and, thus, cannot be added across categories.

The System, while continuing to record strong earnings and capital growth, remains exposed to a variety of risks associated with its portfolio concentration in agriculture and rural America. In 2017, continued downward pressure on grain prices due to large supplies relative to demand following bumper crops in recent years has stressed less efficient producers and those renting a large share of their acreage. Low grain and oilseed prices have helped control feed costs for livestock, poultry, and dairy farmers, and they have benefited from relatively strong demand. Nevertheless, robust production in the livestock sector will likely lead to lower prices and profit margins in coming months. The general economy continues to expand and mortgage interest rates remain at historically low levels. This has benefited the housing sector, which should translate into improved credit conditions for the housing-related sectors such as timber and nurseries. Overall, the agricultural sector remains subject to risks such as a farmland price decline, which has been underway since 2015 in the Midwest, rising interest rates, continued volatility in commodity prices, weather-related catastrophes, and long-term environmental risks related to climate change.

The FCSIC, an independent Government-controlled corporation, ensures the timely payment of principal and interest on FCS obligations on which the System banks are jointly and severally liable. On September 30, 2017, the assets in the Insurance Fund totaled $4.7 billion. As of September 30, 2017, the Insurance Fund as a percentage of adjusted insured debt was 2.11 percent. This was slightly above the statutory secure base amount of 2 percent. During the first nine months of calendar year 2017, outstanding insured System obligations remained essentially flat, compared with that of December 31, 2016.

Federal Agricultural Mortgage Corporation (Farmer Mac)

Farmer Mac was established in 1988 as a Federally chartered instrumentality of the United States and an institution of the FCS to facilitate a secondary market for farm real estate and rural housing loans. Farmer Mac is not liable for any debt or obligation of the other System institutions, and no other System institutions are liable for any debt or obligation of Farmer Mac. The Farm Credit System Reform Act of 1996 expanded Farmer Mac's role from a guarantor of securities backed by loan pools to a direct purchaser of mortgages, enabling it to form pools to securitize. In May 2008, the Food, Conservation and Energy Act of 2008 (2008 Farm Bill) expanded Farmer Mac's program authorities by allowing it to purchase and guarantee securities backed by rural utility loans made by cooperatives.

Farmer Mac continues to meet core capital and regulatory risk-based capital requirements. As of September 30, 2017, Farmer Mac's total outstanding program volume (loans purchased and guaranteed, standby loan purchase commitments, and AgVantage bonds purchased and guaranteed) amounted to $18.6 billion, which represents an increase of 8.1 percent from the level a year ago. Of total program activity, $14.8 billion were on-balance sheet loans and guaranteed securities, and $3.8 billion were off-balance-sheet obligations. Total assets were $17.7 billion, with non-program investments (including cash and cash equivalents) accounting for $2.6 billion of those assets. Farmer Mac's net income attributable to common stockholders ("net income") for the first three quarters of calendar year 2017 was $54.6 million. Net income increased compared to the same period in 2016 during which Farmer Mac reported net income of $38.7 million.

II. INSURANCE PROGRAMS

Deposit Insurance

Federal deposit insurance promotes stability in the U.S. financial system. Prior to the establishment of Federal deposit insurance, depository institution failures often caused depositors to lose confidence in the banking system and rush to withdraw deposits. Such sudden withdrawals caused serious disruption to the economy. In 1933, in the midst of the Great Depression, a system of Federal deposit insurance was established to protect depositors and to prevent bank failures from causing widespread disruption in financial markets.

Today, the Federal Deposit Insurance Corporation (FDIC) insures deposits in banks and savings associations (thrifts) using the resources available in its Deposit Insurance Fund (DIF). The National Credit Union Administration (NCUA) insures deposits (shares) in most credit unions through the National Credit Union Share

Insurance Fund (SIF). (Some credit unions are privately insured.) As of September 30, 2017, the FDIC insured $7.1 trillion of deposits at 5,746 commercial banks and thrifts, and the NCUA insured nearly $1.1 trillion of shares at 5,642 credit unions.

Recent Reforms

Since its creation, the Federal deposit insurance system has undergone many reforms. As a result of the 2008 financial crisis, several reforms were enacted to protect both the immediate and longer-term integrity of the Federal deposit insurance system. The Helping Families Save Their Homes Act of 2009 (P.L. 111–22) provided NCUA with tools to protect the Share Insurance Fund and the financial stability of the credit union system. Notably, the Helping Families Save Their Homes Act:

- Established the Temporary Corporate Credit Union Stabilization Fund (TCCUSF), allowing NCUA to segregate the losses of corporate credit unions and providing a mechanism for assessing those losses to Federally-insured credit unions over an extended period of time;

- Provided flexibility to the NCUA Board by permitting use of a restoration plan to spread insurance premium assessments over a period of up to eight years, or longer in extraordinary circumstances, if the SIF equity ratio fell below 1.2 percent; and

- Permanently increased the Share Insurance Fund's borrowing authority to $6 billion.

The Dodd-Frank Wall Street Reform and Consumer Protection (Dodd-Frank) Act of 2010 (Public Law 111–203) established new DIF reserve ratio requirements. The Act requires the FDIC to achieve a minimum DIF reserve ratio (ratio of the deposit insurance fund balance to total estimated insured deposits) of 1.35 percent by 2020, up from 1.15 percent in 2016. In addition to raising the minimum reserve ratio, the Dodd-Frank Act also:

- Eliminated the FDIC's requirement to rebate premiums when the DIF reserve ratio is between 1.35 and 1.5 percent;

- Gave the FDIC discretion to suspend or limit rebates when the DIF reserve ratio is 1.5 percent or higher, effectively removing the 1.5 percent cap on the DIF; and

- Required the FDIC to offset the effect on small insured depository institutions (defined as banks with assets less than $10 billion) when setting assessments to raise the reserve ratio from 1.15 to 1.35 percent.

In implementing the Dodd-Frank Act, the FDIC issued a final rule setting a long-term (i.e., beyond 2028) reserve ratio target of 2 percent, a goal that FDIC considers necessary to maintain a positive fund balance during economic crises while permitting steady long-term assess-ment rates that provide transparency and predictability to the banking sector.

The Dodd-Frank Act also permanently increased the insured deposit level to $250,000 per account at banks or credit unions insured by the FDIC or NCUA.

Recent Fund Performance

As of September 30, 2017, the FDIC DIF balance stood at $90.5 billion, a one-year increase of $9.8 billion. The growth in the DIF balance is primarily a result of assessment revenue inflows. The reserve ratio on September 30, 2017, was 1.28 percent.

As of September 30, 2017, the number of insured institutions on the FDIC's "problem list" (institutions with the highest risk ratings) totaled 104, which represented a decrease of more than 88 percent from December 2010, the peak year for bank failures during the financial crisis. Furthermore, the assets held by problem institutions decreased by nearly 95 percent.

The NCUA SIF ended September 2017 with assets of $13.7 billion and an equity ratio of 1.25 percent. On September 28, 2017, NCUA raised the normal operating level of the SIF equity ratio to 1.39 percent. If the ratio exceeds the normal operating level, a distribution is normally paid to insured credit unions to reduce the equity ratio. On October 1, 2017, NCUA transferred the funds, property, and assets of the TCCUSF to the SIF. This action also moved present and contingent liabilities, any receivables from insolvent corporate credit unions, and future income associated with guaranty fees from the NCUA Guaranteed Notes Program from the TCCUSF to the SIF. The transfer from the TCCUSF to the SIF raised liquid assets in the SIF by nearly $1.9 billion. The Budget estimates that this transfer will result in the SIF equity ratio exceeding the normal operating level in 2018, resulting in a distribution of capital to credit unions.

The health of the credit union industry has markedly improved since the financial crisis. As of September 30, 2017, the SIF had set aside $286 million in reserves to cover potential losses, an increase of 56 percent from the $183 million set-aside as of September 30, 2016. The ratio of insured shares in problem institutions to total insured shares decreased slightly from 0.86 percent in September 2016 to 0.84 percent in September 2017. However, this is still a significant reduction from a high of 5.7 percent in December 2009.

Restoring the Deposit Insurance Funds

Pursuant to the Dodd-Frank Act, the restoration period for the FDIC's DIF reserve ratio to reach 1.35 percent was extended to 2020. (Prior to the Act, the DIF reserve ratio was required to reach the minimum target of 1.15 percent by the end of 2016.) On March 25, 2016, the FDIC published a final rule to implement this requirement no later than 2019. The Act also placed the responsibility for the cost of increasing the reserve ratio to 1.35 percent on large banks (generally, those with $10 billion or more in assets). The final rule would lower overall regular assessment rates for all banks but also impose a 4.5 basis point surcharge on the assessment base (with certain adjustments) of large banks. The reduction in regular rates and large bank surcharges would begin the quarter after the DIF reserve ratio reaches 1.15 percent. The reserve ratio surpassed 1.15 percent on June 30, 2016, with lower regular assessment rates and large bank surcharges commencing in the July-September quarter. Surcharges on large banks will continue until the reserve ratio reaches 1.35 percent. The Budget estimates reflect these assessment rates.

NCUA continues to seek compensation from the parties that created and sold troubled assets to the failed corporate credit unions. As of September 30, 2017, NCUA's gross recoveries from securities underwriters totaled more than $5.1 billion, helping to minimize losses and future assessments on Federally-insured credit unions.

Budget Outlook

The Budget estimates DIF net outlays of -$69.6 billion over the current 10-year budget window (2019–2028). This $69.6 billion in net inflows to the DIF is $7.8 billion lower than estimated over the previous 10-year window (2018–2027) for the 2018 President's Budget. The latest public data on the banking industry led to a reduction in projections of failed assets, reducing receivership proceeds, resolution outlays, and premiums necessary to reach the minimum Dodd-Frank Act DIF reserve ratio of 1.35 percent relative to MSR. The Budget estimates reflects a DIF reserve ratio of at least 1.35 percent in 2019. Although the FDIC has authority to borrow up to $100 billion from Treasury to maintain sufficient DIF balances, the Budget does not anticipate FDIC utilizing its borrowing authority because the DIF is projected to maintain positive operating cash flows over the entire 10-year budget horizon.

Pension Guarantees

The Pension Benefit Guaranty Corporation (PBGC) insures the pension benefits of workers and retirees in covered defined-benefit pension plans. PBGC operates two legally distinct insurance programs: single-employer plans and multiemployer plans.

Single-Employer Program

Under the single-employer program, PBGC pays benefits, up to a guaranteed level, when a company's plan closes without enough assets to pay future benefits. PBGC's claims exposure is the amount by which qualified benefits exceed assets in insured plans. In the near term, the risk of loss stems from financially distressed firms with underfunded plans. In the longer term, loss exposure results from the possibility that well-funded plans become underfunded due to inadequate contributions, poor investment results, or increased liabilities, and that the healthy firms sponsoring those plans become distressed.

PBGC monitors companies with underfunded plans and acts to protect the interests of the pension insurance program's stakeholders where possible. Under its Early Warning Program, PBGC works with companies to strengthen plan funding or otherwise protect the insurance program from avoidable losses. However, PBGC's authority to manage risks to the insurance program is limited. Most private insurers can diversify or reinsure their catastrophic risks as well as flexibly price these risks. Unlike private insurers, Federal law does not allow PBGC to deny insurance coverage to a defined-benefit plan or adjust premiums according to risk. Both types of PBGC premiums—the flat rate (a per person charge paid by all plans) and the variable rate (paid by some underfunded plans) are set in statute.

Claims against PBGC's insurance programs are highly variable. One large pension plan termination may result in a larger claim against PBGC than the termination of many smaller plans. The future financial health of the PBGC will continue to depend largely on the termination of a limited number of very large plans.

Single employer plans generally provide benefits to the employees of one employer. When an underfunded single employer plan terminates, usually through the bankruptcy process, PBGC becomes trustee of the plan, applies legal limits on payouts, and pays benefits. The amount of benefit paid is determined after taking into account (a) the benefit that a beneficiary had accrued in the terminated plan, (b) the availability of assets from the terminated plan to cover benefits, and (c) the legal maximum benefit level set in statute. In 2018, the maximum annual payment guaranteed under the single-employer program was $65,045 for a retiree aged 65. This limit is indexed for inflation.

Since 2000, PBGC's single-employer program has incurred substantial losses from underfunded plan terminations. Nine of the ten largest plan termination losses were concentrated between 2001 and 2009. The other occurred in the early 1990s.

Multiemployer Plans

Multiemployer plans are collectively bargained pension plans maintained by one or more labor unions and more than one unrelated employer, usually within the same or related industries. PBGC's role in the multiemployer program is more like that of a re-insurer; if a company sponsoring a multiemployer plan fails, its liabilities are assumed by the other employers in the collective bargaining agreement, not by PBGC, although employers can withdraw from a plan for an exit fee. PBGC becomes responsible for insurance coverage when the plan runs out of money to pay benefits at the statutorily guaranteed level, which usually occurs after all contributing employers have withdrawn from the plan, leaving the plan without a source of income. PBGC provides insolvent multiemployer plans with financial assistance in the form of loans sufficient to pay guaranteed benefits and administrative expenses. Since multiemployer plans do not receive PBGC assistance until their assets are fully depleted, financial assistance is almost never repaid. Benefits under the multiemployer program are calculated based on the benefit that a participant would have received under the insolvent plan, subject to the legal multiemployer maximum set in statute. The maximum guaranteed amount depends on the participant's years of service and the rate at which benefits are accrued. For example, for a participant with 30 years of service, PBGC guarantees 100 percent of the pension benefit up to a yearly amount of $3,960. If the pension exceeds that amount, PBGC guarantees 75 percent of the rest of the pension benefit up to a total maximum guarantee of $12,870 per year. This limit has been in place since 2011 and is not adjusted for inflation or cost-of-living increases.

In recent years, many multiemployer pension plans have become severely underfunded as a result of unfavorable investment outcomes, employers withdrawing from plans, and demographic challenges. In 2001, only 15 plans covering about 80,000 participants were under 40 percent funded using estimated market rates. By 2011, this had grown to almost 200 plans covering almost 1.5 million participants. While many plans have benefited from an improving economy and will recover, a small number of plans are severely underfunded and, absent any changes, projected to become insolvent within ten years.

As of November 15, 2017, the single-employer and multi-employer programs reported long-term actuarial deficits of $10.9 billion and $65.1 billion, respectively. While both programs have significant deficits, the challenges facing the multiemployer program are more immediate. In its 2017 Annual Report, PBGC reported that it had just $2 billion in accumulated assets from premium payments made by multiemployer plans, which it projected would be depleted by 2025. If the program runs out of cash, the only funds available to support benefits would be the premiums that continue to be paid by remaining plans; this could result in benefits being cut much more deeply, to a small fraction of current guarantee levels.

To address the problems facing the multiemployer program and the millions of Americans who rely on those plans for their retirement security, the Congress passed The Multiemployer Pension Reform Act, which was included in the Consolidated and Further Continuing Appropriations Act signed on December 16, 2014. The law includes significant reforms to the multiemployer pension plan system, including provisions that allow trustees of multiemployer plans facing insolvency to apply to the Department of Treasury to reduce benefits by temporarily or permanently suspending benefits. The law does not allow suspensions for individuals over age 80 or for those receiving a disability retirement benefit. A participant or beneficiary's monthly benefit cannot be reduced below 110 percent of the PBGC guarantee. It also increases PBGC premiums from $12 per person to $26 beginning in 2015 and indexes premiums to inflation thereafter. While the legislation is an important first step, it will not be enough to improve PBGC's solvency for more than a very short period of time. PBGC projects that it is likely to become insolvent by 2025, extending its projected insolvency date by three years compared to the 2013 projection.

In addition, Congress enacted premium increases in the single-employer program as part of the Bipartisan Budget Act of 2015 (BBA). By increasing both the flat-rate and variable-rate premiums, the Act will raise an estimated $4 billion over the 10-year budget window. This additional revenue will improve the financial outlook for the single-employer program, which was already projected to see a large reduction in its deficit over the next 10 years.

Premiums

Both programs are underfunded, with combined liabilities exceeding assets by $76 billion at the end of 2017. While the single-employer program's financial position is projected to improve over the next 10 years, in part because Congress has raised premiums in that program several times in recent years, the multiemployer program is projected to run out of funds in 2025. Particularly in the multiemployer program, premium rates remain much lower than what a private financial institution would charge for insuring the same risk and well below what is needed to ensure PBGC's solvency.

The Budget includes a policy proposal to add additional PBGC premiums. For an in-depth discussion of that proposal, please see the Labor chapter of the Budget Appendix.

Disaster Insurance

Flood Insurance

The Federal Government provides flood insurance through the National Flood Insurance Program (NFIP), which is administered by the Federal Emergency Management Agency (FEMA) of the Department of Homeland Security (DHS). Flood insurance is available to homeowners and businesses in communities that have adopted and enforce appropriate floodplain management measures. Coverage is limited to buildings and their contents. At the end of 2017, the program had over five million policies worth $1.25 trillion in force in 22,286 communities.

The NFIP was established in 1968 to make flood insurance coverage widely available, to combine a program of insurance with flood mitigation measures to reduce the nation's risk of loss from floods, and to reduce Federal disaster-assistance expenditures on flood losses. The NFIP requires participating communities to adopt certain building standards and take other mitigation efforts to reduce flood-related losses, and operates a flood hazard-mapping program to quantify geographic variation in the risk of flooding. These efforts have resulted in substantial reductions in the risk of flood-related losses nationwide. However, structures built prior to flood mapping and NFIP floodplain management requirements are eligible for reduced premiums. Currently, 20 percent of the total policies in force pay less than fully actuarial rates while continuing to be at relatively high risk of flooding.

To complement flood insurance, FEMA has a multipronged strategy for reducing future flood damage. The NFIP offers flood mitigation assistance grants to assist flood disaster survivors to rebuild to current building codes, including higher base flood elevations, thereby reducing the likelihood of future flood damage. In particular, flood mitigation assistance grants targeted toward repetitive and severe repetitive loss properties not only help owners of high-risk property, but also reduce the disproportionate drain these properties cause on the National Flood Insurance Fund, through acquisition, relocation, or elevation of select structures. Further, through the Community Rating System, FEMA adjusts premium rates to encourage community and State mitigation activities beyond those required by the NFIP. These efforts, in addition to the minimum NFIP requirements for floodplain management, save over $1.9 billion annually in avoided flood damage claims.

A major goal of the NFIP is to expand flood insurance coverage in the United States in order to reduce risk for more homeowners. The agency's strategy aims to increase the number of Americans insured against flood losses and improve retention of policies among existing customers. The strategy includes:

1. Providing financial incentives to private insurers that sell and service flood policies for the Federal Government to expand the flood insurance business.

2. Conducting a national campaign to inform the public about the NFIP and attract new policyholders.

3. Fostering lender compliance with flood insurance requirements through training, guidance materials, and regular communication with lending regulators and the lending community.

4. Conducting NFIP training for insurance agents via instructor-led seminars, online training modules, and other vehicles.

5. Seeking opportunities to simplify and clarify NFIP processes and products to make it easier for agents to sell and for consumers to buy flood insurance.

These strategies resulted in steady policy growth for many years, peaking in 2010 at 5.61 million policies. Subsequently, however, policy growth was hampered by the lingering effects of the Great Recession and by premium increases.

Due to the catastrophic nature of flooding, with hurricanes Harvey, Katrina and Sandy as notable examples, insured flood damages can far exceed premium revenue and deplete the program's reserves. On those occasions, the NFIP exercises its borrowing authority through the Treasury to meet flood insurance claim obligations. While the program needed appropriations in the early 1980s to repay the funds borrowed during the 1970's, it was able to repay all borrowed funds with interest using only premium dollars between 1986 and 2004. In 2005, however, Hurricanes Katrina, Rita, and Wilma generated more flood insurance claims than the cumulative number of claims paid from 1968 to 2004. Hurricane Sandy in 2012 generated $8.5 billion in flood insurance claims. As a result, in 2013 Congress increased the borrowing authority for the fund to $30.425 billion. After the estimated $2.4 billion and $670 million in flood insurance claims generated

by the Louisiana flooding of August 2016 and Hurricane Matthew in October 2016, respectively, the NFIP used its borrowing authority again, bringing the total outstanding debt to Treasury to $24.6 billion.

In fall 2017, Hurricanes Harvey and Irma struck the southern coast of the United States, resulting in catastrophic flood damage across Texas, Louisiana, and Florida. Congress provided $16 billion in debt forgiveness to the National Flood Insurance Program, bringing its total borrowing to $20.525 billion. To pay Hurricane Harvey flood claims, NFIP also received $1 billion in reinsurance payments as a result of transferring risk to the private reinsurance market at the beginning of 2017. FEMA plans to expand its reinsurance program and transfer additional risk to the private market in 2018 and beyond.

In July 2012, resulting largely from experiences during Hurricanes Katrina, Rita, and Wilma in 2005, the Biggert Waters Flood Insurance Reform Act of 2012 (Public Law 112–141; BW–12) was signed into law. In addition to reauthorizing the NFIP for five years, the bill required the NFIP generally to move to full risk-based premium rates and strengthened the NFIP financially and operationally. In 2013, the NFIP began phasing in risk-based premiums for certain properties, as required by the law. In 2014, when policy premiums were increased in compliance with the Biggert-Waters legislation, policy counts dropped 4.3 percent to 5.3 million.

In March 2014, largely in reaction to premium increases initiated by BW–12, the Homeowner Flood Insurance Affordability Act of 2014 (HFIAA) was signed into law, further reforming the NFIP and revising many sections of BW–12. Notably, HFIAA repealed many of the major premium increases introduced by BW–12 and required retroactive refunds of collected BW–12 premium increases, introduced a phase-in to higher full-risk premiums for structures newly mapped into the Special Flood Hazard Area, and created an Office of the Flood Insurance Advocate. In 2015, when a surcharge on all policyholders was introduced in compliance with HFIAA, policy counts dropped an additional 3.8 percent to 5.1 million. At the end of 2017, policies in force totaled 5.1 million.

Crop Insurance

Subsidized Federal crop insurance, administered by USDA's Risk Management Agency (RMA) on behalf of the Federal Crop Insurance Corporation (FCIC), assists farmers in managing yield and revenue shortfalls due to bad weather or other natural disasters. The program is a cooperative partnership between the Federal Government and the private insurance industry. Private insurance companies sell and service crop insurance policies. The Federal Government, in turn, pays private companies an administrative and operating (A&O) expense subsidy to cover expenses associated with selling and servicing these policies. The Federal Government also provides reinsurance through the Standard Reinsurance Agreement (SRA) and pays companies an "underwriting gain" if they have a profitable year. For the 2019 Budget, the payments to the companies are projected to be $2.5 billion in combined subsidies. The Federal Government also subsidizes premiums for farmers as a way to encourage farmers to participate in the program.

The most basic type of crop insurance is catastrophic coverage (CAT), which compensates the farmer for losses in excess of 50 percent of the individual's average yield at 55 percent of the expected market price. The CAT premium is entirely subsidized, and farmers pay only an administrative fee. Higher levels of coverage, called "buy-up," are also available. A portion of the premium for buy-up coverage is paid by FCIC on behalf of producers and varies by coverage level – generally, the higher the coverage level, the lower the percent of premium subsidized. The remaining (unsubsidized) premium amount is owed by the producer and represents an out-of-pocket expense.

For 2017, the 10 principal crops (barley, corn, cotton, grain sorghum, peanuts, potatoes, rice, soybeans, tobacco, and wheat) accounted for over 77 percent of total liability, and approximately 86 percent of the total U.S. planted acres of those 10 crops were covered by crop insurance. Producers can purchase both yield and revenue-based insurance products which are underwritten on the basis of a producer's actual production history (APH). Revenue insurance programs protect against loss of revenue resulting from low prices, low yields, or a combination of both. Revenue insurance has enhanced traditional yield insurance by adding price as an insurable component.

In addition to price and revenue insurance, FCIC has made available other plans of insurance to provide protection for a variety of crops grown across the United States. For example, "area plans" of insurance offer protection based on a geographic area (most commonly, a county), and do not directly insure an individual farm. Often, the loss trigger is based on an index, such as a rainfall or vegetative index, which is established by a Government entity (for example, NOAA or USGS). One such plan is the pilot Rainfall and Vegetation Index plan, which insures against a decline in an index value covering Pasture, Rangeland, and Forage. These pilot programs meet the needs of livestock producers who purchase insurance for protection from losses of forage produced for grazing or harvested for hay. In 2017, there were 25,150 Rainfall and Vegetation Index policies earning premiums, covering over 75 million acres of pasture, rangeland and forage. In 2017, there was about $1.9 billion in liability, with $251 million in indemnities paid to livestock producers who purchased coverage.

A crop insurance policy also contains coverage compensating farmers when they are prevented from planting their crops due to weather and other perils. When an insured farmer is unable to plant the planned crop within the planting time period because of excessive drought or moisture, the farmer may file a prevented planting claim, which pays the farmer a portion of the full coverage level. It is optional for the farmer to plant a second crop on the acreage. If the farmer does, the prevented planting claim on the first crop is reduced and the farmer's APH is recorded for that year. If the farmer does not plant a second crop, the farmer gets the full prevented planting claim, and the farmer's APH is held harmless for premium cal-

culation purposes the following year. In November 2017, RMA's actuarial documents were updated to remove the 10 percent buy-up coverage option on prevented planting coverage. This coverage represented the most expensive form of prevented planting coverage. Removing this coverage is expected to save the taxpayers $414 million over 10 years.

RMA is continuously working to develop new products and to expand or improve existing products in order to cover more agricultural commodities. Under section 508(h) of the Federal Crop Insurance Act, RMA may advance payment of up to 50 percent of expected reasonable research and development costs for FCIC Board-approved Concept Proposals prior to the complete submission of the policy or plan of insurance. Numerous private products have been approved through the 508(h) authority, including Downed Rice Endorsement, Machine Harvested Cucumbers, ARPI Popcorn, Clary Sage, Hybrid Seed Rice, Specialty Trait Soybean, and Malting Barley.

For more information and additional crop insurance program details, please reference RMA's web site (*https://www.rma.usda.gov/*).

Insurance against Security-Related Risks

Terrorism Risk Insurance

The Terrorism Risk Insurance Program (TRIP) was authorized under P.L. 107–297 to help ensure the continued availability of property and casualty insurance following the terrorist attacks of September 11, 2001. TRIP's initial three-year authorization enabled the Federal Government to establish a system of shared public and private compensation for insured property and casualty losses arising from certified acts of foreign terrorism.

TRIP was originally intended to be temporary, but has been extended three times, and is currently set to expire on December 31, 2020. The most recent reauthorization, the Terrorism Risk Insurance Extension Act of 2015 (P.L. 114–1), made several program changes to reduce potential Federal liability. Over the first five extension years, the loss threshold that triggers Federal assistance is increased by $20 million each year to $200 million in 2020, and the Government's share of losses above the deductible decreases from 85 to 80 percent over the same period. The 2015 extension also requires Treasury to recoup 140 percent of all Federal payments made under the program up to a mandatory recoupment amount, which increases by $2 billion each year until 2019 when the threshold is set at $37.5 billion. Effective January 1, 2020, the mandatory recoupment amount will be indexed to a running three-year average of the aggregate insurer deductible of 20 percent of direct-earned premiums. Each successive reauthorization has included programmatic reforms to limit the Federal Government's risk exposure and the 2015 reauthorization will facilitate, over the longer term, full transition of support for terrorism risk insurance to the private sector.

The Budget baseline includes the estimated Federal cost of providing terrorism risk insurance, reflecting the

2015 extension. Using market data synthesized through a proprietary model, the Budget projects annual outlays and recoupment for TRIP. While the Budget does not forecast any specific triggering events, the Budget includes estimates representing the weighted average of TRIP payments over a full range of possible scenarios, most of which include no notional terrorist attacks (and therefore no TRIP payments), and some of which include notional terrorist attacks of varying magnitudes. On this basis, the Budget projects net spending of $252 million over the 2019–2023 period and $332 million over the 2019–2028 period.

Aviation War Risk Insurance

In December 2014, Congress sunset the premium aviation war risk insurance program, thereby sending U.S. air carriers back to the commercial aviation insurance market for all of their war risk insurance coverage. The non-premium program is authorized through December 31, 2018. It provides aviation insurance coverage for aircraft used in connection with certain Government contract operations by a department or agency that agrees to indemnify the Secretary of Transportation for any losses covered by the insurance.

Chart 19-1. Face Value of Federal Credit Outstanding

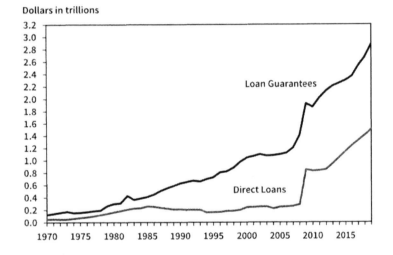

Table 19–1.   ESTIMATED FUTURE COST OF OUTSTANDING DIRECT LOANS AND LOAN GUARANTEES [1]

(In billions of dollars)

Program	Outstanding 2016	Estimated Future Costs of 2016 Outstanding [2]	Outstanding 2017	Estimated Future Costs of 2017 Outstanding [2]
Direct Loans: [2]				
Federal Student Loans	943	15	1,038	39
Education Temporary Student Loan Purchase Authority	70	–7	63	–3
Farm Service Agency, Rural Development, Rural Housing	55	4	57	4
Rural Utilities Service and Rural Telephone Bank	52	2	52	2
Housing and Urban Development	24	12	27	15
Export-Import Bank	24	1	22	1
Advanced Technology Vehicle Manufacturing, Title 17 Loans	16	2	14	1
Transportation Infrastructure Finance and Innovation Act Loans	13	1	13	*
Disaster Assistance	6	1	6	1
State Housing Finance Authority Direct Loans	7	1	5	1
International Assistance	3	1	6	1
Public Law 480	3	1	2	1
Small Business Lending Fund (SBLF) [3]	*	–*	*	–*
Troubled Asset Relief Program (TARP) [3]	1	*	*	*
Other direct loan programs [3]	20	7	19	6
Total direct loans	1,239	41	1,328	70
Guaranteed Loans: [2]				
FHA Mutual Mortgage Insurance Fund	1,153	–4	1,228	13
Department of Veterans Affairs (VA) Mortgages	525	10	604	11
Federal Student Loan Guarantees	197	1	176	4
FHA General and Special Risk Insurance Fund	149	3	156	8
Farm Service Agency, Rural Development, Rural Housing	140	2	145	1
Small Business Administration (SBA) Business Loan Guarantees [4]	113	2	121	3
Export-Import Bank	56	1	56	1
International Assistance	24	2	24	2
Title 17 Loan Guarantees	3	*	3	*
Commodity Credit Corporation Export Loan Guarantees	2	*	2	*
Other guaranteed loan programs [3]	14	2	15	3
Total guaranteed loans [4]	2,375	20	2,529	44
Total Federal credit	**3,614**	**61**	**3,857**	**114**

* $500 million or less.

[1] Future costs represent balance sheet estimates of allowance for subsidy cost, liabilities for loan guarantees, and estimated uncollectible principal and interest.

[2] Excludes loans and guarantees by deposit insurance agencies and programs not included under credit reform, such as Tennessee Valley Authority loan guarantees. Defaulted guaranteed loans that result in loans receivable are included in direct loan amounts.

[3] As authorized by the statute, table includes TARP and SBLF equity purchases. Future costs for TARP are calculated using the discount rate required by the Federal Credit Reform Act adjusted for market risks, as directed in legislation.

[4] To avoid double-counting, outstandings for GNMA and SBA secondary market guarantees, and TARP FHA Letter of Credit program are excluded from the totals.

Table 19–2. DIRECT LOAN SUBSIDY RATES, BUDGET AUTHORITY, AND LOAN LEVELS, 2017–2019

(Dollar amounts in millions)

Agency and Program Account	2017 Actual			2018 Estimated			2019 Proposed		
	Subsidy rate [1]	Subsidy budget authority	Loan levels	Subsidy rate [1]	Subsidy budget authority	Loan levels	Subsidy rate [1]	Subsidy budget authority	Loan levels
Agriculture:									
Agricultural Credit Insurance Fund Program Account	1.75	42	2,353	0.22	8	3,248	1.13	36	3,152
Farm Storage Facility Loans Program Account	−1.30	−3	215	−1.30	−4	309	−0.53	−2	309
Rural Electrification and Telecommunications Loans Program Account	−4.24	−198	4,658	−3.89	−208	5,339	−4.09	−165	4,034
Distance Learning, Telemedicine, and Broadband Program	16.64	4	24	16.75	7	41	19.53	9	45
Rural Water and Waste Disposal Program Account	4.34	57	1,311	0.17	2	1,334	−0.27	−3	1,200
Rural Community Facilities Program Account	−2.56	−67	2,600	−8.10	−211	2,600	−7.61	−266	3,500
Multifamily Housing Revitalization Program Account	57.01	14	25	51.86	24	46	....	....	....
Rural Housing Insurance Fund Program Account	8.36	90	1,091	5.37	61	1,115	−2.42	....	2
Rural Microenterprise Investment Program Account	12.40	1	8	9.98	1	8	0.00	....	1
Intermediary Relending Program Fund Account	28.99	6	19	23.09	6	24	....	....	....
Rural Economic Development Loans Program Account	14.23	6	39	12.92	7	56	....	....	....
Commerce:									
Fisheries Finance Program Account	−0.35	−*	72	−10.37	−13	124	−9.31	−12	124
Education:									
College Housing and Academic Facilities Loans Program Account	7.14	13	175	6.42	20	314	3.48	20	580
TEACH Grant Program Account	14.97	15	100	23.06	30	131	28.45	40	140
Federal Direct Student Loan Program Account	−0.75	−1,179	157,883	−2.20	−3,500	158,883	−5.24	−8,535	163,028
Energy:									
Title 17 Innovative Technology Loan Guarantee Program	....	....	....	−2.89	−107	3,703	....	....	....
Homeland Security:									
Disaster Assistance Direct Loan Program Account	91.03	12	14	95.73	4,754	4,966	90.71	75	83
Housing and Urban Development:									
FHA-Mutual Mortgage Insurance Program Account	....	....	....	0.00	....	5	0.00	....	5
FHA-General and Special Risk Program Account	−11.19	−104	922	−8.18	−107	1,308	....	....	....
State:									
Repatriation Loans Program Account	53.42	1	2	53.26	1	2	40.45	1	2
Transportation:									
Federal-aid Highways	5.28	202	3,851	[2]6.64	249	3,751	[2]6.3	249	3,945
Railroad Rehabilitation and Improvement Program	....	....	....	0.00	....	600	0.00	....	600
Treasury:									
Community Development Financial Institutions Fund Program Account	−2.41	−6	252	[2]0.51	3	525	[2]0.00	....	500
Veterans Affairs:									
Veterans Housing Benefit Program Fund	1.92	*	6	−25.37	−70	276	−5.12	−16	333
Native American Veteran Housing Loan Program Account	−12.89	−1	7	−16.92	−2	13	−9.92	−1	14
Environmental Protection Agency:									
Water Infrastructure Finance and Innovation Program Account	....	....	....	[2]1.55	25	1,613	[2]0.98	25	2,554
International Assistance Programs:									
Foreign Military Financing Loan Program Account	....	....	....	13.55	150	1,105	[2]6.60	75	1,135
Overseas Private Investment Corporation Program Account	−10.03	−53	535	[2]−10.88	−65	600	....	....	....
Development Finance Institution, Program Account	....	....	....	....	....	....	[2]−12.83	−77	600
Small Business Administration:									
Disaster Loans Program Account	14.42	187	1,297	12.54	138	1,100	12.29	135	1,100
Business Loans Program Account	9.08	4	44	8.91	4	44	8.77	4	42
Infrastructure Initiative:									
Infrastructure Credit Programs Program Account	....	....	....	....	....	....	[2]10.00	2,800	28,000
Export-Import Bank of the United States:									
Export-Import Bank Loans Program Account	0.00	....	6	....	....	....	....	....	....
Total	**N/A**	**−957**	**177,509**	**N/A**	**1,203**	**193,183**	**N/A**	**−5,608**	**215,028**

N/A = Not applicable

*$500,000 or less

[1] Additional information on credit subsidy rates is contained in the Federal Credit Supplement.

[2] Rate reflects notional estimate. Estimates will be determined at the time of execution and will reflect the terms of the contracts and other characteristics.

Table 19–3. LOAN GUARANTEE SUBSIDY RATES, BUDGET AUTHORITY, AND LOAN LEVELS, 2017–2019
(Dollar amounts in millions)

Agency and Program Account	2017 Actual			2018 Estimated			2019 Proposed		
	Subsidy rate[1]	Subsidy budget authority	Loan levels	Subsidy rate[1]	Subsidy budget authority	Loan levels	Subsidy rate[1]	Subsidy budget authority	Loan levels
Agriculture:									
Agricultural Credit Insurance Fund Program Account	0.36	14	3,646	0.32	16	4,777	0.22	10	4,500
Commodity Credit Corporation Export Loans Program Account	−0.24	−4	1,582	−0.43	−23	5,500	−0.43	−24	5,500
Rural Water and Waste Disposal Program Account	0.48	*	5	0.00	....	16	....	....	....
Rural Community Facilities Program Account	2.24	3	150	3.27	4	137	....	....	....
Rural Housing Insurance Fund Program Account	−0.79	−153	19,457	−0.72	−124	17,312	−0.72	−136	18,945
Rural Business Program Account	3.83	54	1,417	4.06	48	1,172	....	....	....
Rural Energy for America Program	4.64	17	372	3.87	23	601	....	....	....
Biorefinery Assistance Program Account	18.46	59	322	21.24	64	300	....	....	....
Health and Human Services:									
Health Resources and Services	....	....	....	2.69	*	3	2.71	....	3
Housing and Urban Development:									
Indian Housing Loan Guarantee Fund Program Account	0.55	4	674	0.37	3	880	0.26	3	880
Native Hawaiian Housing Loan Guarantee Fund Program Account	−0.27	−*	15	−0.28	....	23	−0.32	−*	23
Native American Housing Block Grant	11.20	1	10	11.50	2	17	11.26	2	17
Community Development Loan Guarantees Program Account	0.00	....	39	0.00	....	150	....	....	....
FHA-Mutual Mortgage Insurance Program Account	−4.15	−11,150	268,664	−3.02	−7,641	252,800	[2] −3.04	−7,360	242,110
FHA-General and Special Risk Program Account	−3.40	−696	20,440	−3.62	−763	21,079	−3.08	−648	21,060
Interior:									
Indian Guaranteed Loan Program Account	6.32	7	106	6.50	7	106	5.34	6	106
Transportation:									
Maritime Guaranteed Loan (Title XI) Program Account	9.90	42	424	....	....	....	....	....	....
Treasury:									
Troubled Asset Relief Program, Housing Programs[3]	0.80	*	8	....	....	....	....	....	....
Veterans Affairs:									
Veterans Housing Benefit Program Fund	0.51	891	174,746	0.27	434	160,620	0.08	210	156,824
International Assistance Programs:									
Loan Guarantees to Israel Program Account	....	....	....	0.00	....	1,000	0.00	....	1,000
MENA Loan Guarantee Program Account	25.53	255	1,000	....	....	....	....	....	....
Development Credit Authority Program Account	3.37	24	712	4.19	12	287	....	....	....
Overseas Private Investment Corporation Program Account	−6.87	−139	2,033	[2] −8.95	−242	2,700	....	....	....
Development Finance Institution, Program Account	....	....	....	....	....	....	[2] −7.09	−250	3,531
Small Business Administration:									
Business Loans Program Account	0.00	....	30,958	0.00	....	46,103	−0.35	−150	42,500
Export-Import Bank of the United States:									
Export-Import Bank Loans Program Account	−0.08	−2	3,425	−3.02	−604	20,024	−5.61	−929	16,574
Total	N/A	−10,773	530,205	N/A	−8,784	535,607	N/A	−9,269	513,573
ADDENDUM: SECONDARY GUARANTEED LOAN COMMITMENT LIMITATIONS									
Government National Mortgage Association:									
Guarantees of Mortgage-backed Securities Loan Guarantee Program Account	−0.37	−2,016	504,575	−0.40	−1,696	424,000	−0.44	−1,914	435,000
Small Business Administration:									
Secondary Market Guarantee Program	0.00	....	9,301	0.00	....	11,919	−0.04	−5	12,000
Total, secondary guarantee loan commitments	N/A	−2,016	513,875	N/A	−1,696	435,919	N/A	−1,919	447,000

N/A = Not applicable.

* $500,000 or less

[1] Additional information on credit subsidy rates is contained in the Federal Credit Supplement.

[2] Rate reflects notional estimate. Estimates will be determined at the time of execution and will reflect the terms of the contracts and other characteristics.

[3] Amounts reflect the Troubled Asset Relief Program, FHA Refinance Letter of Credit. Subsidy costs for the program are calculated using the discount rate under the Federal Credit Reform Act adjusted for market risks, consistent with the Emergency Economic Stabilization Act of 2008.

Table 19–4. SUMMARY OF FEDERAL DIRECT LOANS AND LOAN GUARANTEES [1]

(In billions of dollars)

	Actual								Estimate	
	2010	2011	2012	2013	2014	2015	2016	2017	2018	2019
Direct Loans:										
Obligations	246.0	296.3	191.1	174.4	174.0	181.3	175.6	180.0	193.2	215.0
Disbursements	218.9	186.7	170.0	157.5	155.4	161.4	158.5	164.4	174.3	175.6
Budget authority:										
New subsidy budget authority [2]	−9.2	−15.7	−27.2	−29.8	−22.4	4.9	−9.0	−1.0	1.3	−5.6
Reestimated subsidy budget authority [2,3]	−125.1	−66.8	16.8	−19.7	−0.8	10.1	8.0	32.5	−10.3	....
Total subsidy budget authority	**−134.3**	**−82.5**	**−10.4**	**−49.4**	**−23.2**	**15.1**	**−1.1**	**31.5**	**−9.0**	**−5.6**
Loan guarantees:										
Commitments [4]	507.3	446.7	479.7	536.6	350.8	478.3	537.6	530.2	535.6	513.6
Lender disbursements [4]	494.8	384.1	444.3	491.3	335.6	461.6	517.6	520.6	485.4	510.6
Budget authority:										
New subsidy budget authority [2]	−4.9	−7.4	−6.9	−17.9	−13.7	−11.9	−7.5	−8.8	−7.1	−7.4
Reestimated subsidy budget authority [2,3]	7.6	−4.0	−4.9	20.8	1.2	−1.1	−13.6	16.8	9.4	....
Total subsidy budget authority	**2.7**	**−11.4**	**−11.8**	**2.8**	**−12.5**	**−13.1**	**−21.1**	**8.0**	**2.3**	**−7.4**

[1] As authorized by statute, table includes TARP and SBLF equity purchases, and International Monetary Fund (IMF) transactions resulting from the 2009 Supplemental Appropriations Act.

[2] Credit subsidy costs for TARP and IMF transactions are calculated using the discount rate required by the Federal Credit Reform Act adjusted for market risks, as directed in legislation.

[3] Includes interest on reestimate.

[4] To avoid double-counting, the face value of GNMA and SBA secondary market guarantees and the TARP FHA Letter of Credit program are excluded from the totals.

20. BUDGETARY EFFECTS OF THE TROUBLED ASSET RELIEF PROGRAM

This chapter reports on the cost and budgetary effects of Treasury's Troubled Asset Relief Program (TARP), consistent with Sections 202 and 203 of the Emergency Economic Stabilization Act (EESA) of 2008 (P.L. 110–343), as amended. The cost estimates in this report reflect transactions as of September 30, 2017, and expected future transactions as reflected in the Budget and required under EESA. Where noted, a descriptive analysis of additional transactions that occurred after September 30, 2017, is provided. For information on subsequent TARP program developments, please consult the Treasury Department's TARP Monthly Reports to Congress. EESA authorized Treasury to purchase or guarantee troubled assets and other financial instruments to restore liquidity and stability to the financial system of the United States while protecting taxpayers. On October 3, 2010, Treasury's general authority to make new TARP commitments expired. Treasury continues to manage existing investments and is authorized to expend previously-committed TARP funds pursuant to obligations entered into prior to October 3, 2010. Subsequently, in December 2015, the Consolidated Appropriations Act, 2016 (P.L. 114-113) granted Treasury limited authority to make an additional $2.0 billion in commitments through the TARP Hardest Hit Fund (HHF).

Treasury's current estimate of TARP's lifetime deficit cost for its $454.5 billion in cumulative obligations is $32.3 billion (see Tables 20–1 and 20–6). Section 123 of EESA requires TARP costs to be estimated on a net present value basis, adjusted to reflect a premium for market risk. As investments are liquidated, their actual costs (including any market risk effects) become known and are reflected in reestimates. It is likely that the total cost of TARP to taxpayers will eventually be marginally lower than current estimates as the forecast market risk premiums and estimates are replaced by actual costs, but the total cost will not be fully known until all TARP investments have been extinguished.

A description of the market impact of TARP programs, followed by a detailed analysis of the assets purchased through TARP, is provided at the end of this report.

Method for Estimating the Cost of TARP Transactions

Under EESA, Treasury has purchased different types of financial instruments with varying terms and conditions. The Budget reflects the costs of these instruments using the methodology as provided by Section 123 of EESA.

The estimated costs of each transaction reflect the underlying structure of the instrument. TARP financial instruments have included direct loans, structured loans, equity, loan guarantees, and direct incentive payments. The costs of equity purchases, loans, guarantees, and loss sharing are the net present value of cash flows to and from the Government over the life of the instrument, per the Federal Credit Reform Act (FCRA) of 1990; as amended (2 U.S.C. 661 et seq.), with an EESA-required adjustment to the discount rate for market risks. Costs for the incentive payments under TARP housing programs, other than loss sharing under the Federal Housing Administration (FHA) Refinance program, involve financial instruments

Table 20–1. CHANGE IN PROGRAMMATIC COSTS OF TROUBLED ASSET RELIEF PROGRAM

(In billions of dollars)

TARP Programs	2018 Budget		2019 Budget		Change from 2018 Budget to 2019 Budget	
	TARP Obligations[1]	Estimated Cost (+) / Savings (–)	TARP Obligations[1]	Estimated Cost (+) / Savings (–)	TARP Obligations[1]	Estimated Cost (+) / Savings (–)
Equity Programs	335.8	5.8	335.8	5.7	....	–*
Structured and Direct Loan Programs	76.2	16.7	76.2	16.7	....	–*
Guarantee Programs[2]	5.0	–3.9	5.0	–3.9	....	
TARP Housing Programs[3]	37.4	32.6	37.4	32.5	–*	–0.1
Total programmatic costs[4]	**454.5**	**51.2**	**454.5**	**51.1**	**–***	**–0.1**
Memorandum:						
Deficit impact with interest on reestimates[5]		*32.4*		*32.3*		*–0.1*

*$50 million or less.
[1] TARP obligations are net of cancellations.
[2] The total assets supported by the Asset Guarantee Program were $301 billion.
[3] TARP obligations include FHA Refinance Letter of Credit first loss coverage of eligible FHA insured mortgages.
[4] Total programmatic costs of TARP exclude interest on reestimates.
[5] The total deficit impact of TARP as of November 30, 2017 includes $17.43 billion in subsidy cost for TARP investments in AIG. Additional proceeds of $17.55 billion resulting from Treasury holdings of non-TARP shares in AIG are not included.

Table 20–2. TROUBLED ASSET RELIEF PROGRAM CURRENT VALUE [1]

(In billions of dollars)

	Actual									Estimate										
	2009	2010	2011	2012	2013	2014	2015	2016	2017	2018	2019	2020	2021	2022	2023	2024	2025	2026	2027	2028
Financing Account Balances:																				
Troubled Asset Relief Program Equity Purchase Financing Account	105.4	76.9	74.9	13.6	6.6	0.9	0.4	0.4	0.2	0.1	0.1	0.1	*	*	*	*	*	*	*	*
Troubled Asset Relief Program Direct Loan Financing Account	23.9	42.7	28.5	17.9	3.1	–0.2	–0.1	*	–*	–*	–*	–*	–*	–*	–*	–*	–*	–*	–*	–*
Troubled Assets Insurance Financing Fund Guaranteed Loan Financing Account	0.6	2.4	0.8	0.8	....	....	....	....	....	....	....									
Troubled Assets Relief Program FHA Refinance Letter of Credit Financing Account	....	....	–*	–*	–*	–*	–*	–*	–*	–*	....	*	*	*	*	*	*	*	*	*
Total Financing Account Balances	129.9	122.0	104.1	32.2	9.7	0.7	0.3	0.4	0.1	0.1	0.1	0.1	*	*	*	*	*	*	*	*

* $50 million or less.

[1] Current value as reflected in the 2019 Budget. Amounts exclude housing activity under the Making Home Affordable program and the Hardest Hit Fund as these programs are reflected on a cash basis.

without any provision for future returns and are recorded on a cash basis.[1]

For each of these instruments, cash flow models[2] are used to estimate future cash flows to and from the Government over the life of a program or facility. Consistent with the requirement under FCRA to reflect the lifetime present value cost, subsidy cost estimates are reestimated every year an instrument is outstanding, with a final closing reestimate once an instrument is fully liquidated. Reestimates update the cost for actual transactions, and updated future expectations. When all investments in a given cohort are liquidated, their actual costs (including any market risk effects) become known and are reflected in final closing reestimates.

TARP Program Costs and Current Value of Assets

This section provides the special analysis required under Sections 202 and 203 of EESA, including estimates of the cost to taxpayers and the budgetary effects of TARP transactions as reflected in the Budget.[3] This section also explains the changes in TARP costs, and includes alternative estimates as prescribed under EESA. Additionally, this section includes a comparison of the current cost estimates with previous estimates provided by OMB and by the Congressional Budget Office (CBO).

Table 20–1 summarizes the cumulative and anticipated activity under TARP, and the estimated lifetime budgetary cost reflected in the Budget, compared to estimates from the 2018 Budget. The direct impact of TARP on the deficit is projected to be $32.3 billion, down $0.1 billion from the $32.4 billion estimate in the 2018 Budget. The total programmatic cost represents the lifetime net present value cost of TARP obligations from the date of disbursement, which is now estimated to be $51.1 billion, a figure that excludes interest on reestimates.[4] The final subsidy cost of TARP is likely to be marginally lower than the current estimate because projected cash flows are discounted using a risk adjustment to the discount rate as required by EESA. This requirement adds a premium to current estimates of TARP costs on top of other risks already reflected in the estimated cash flows with the public. Over time, the added risk premium for uncertainty on future estimated TARP cash flows is returned to the General Fund through subsidy reestimates as actual cash flows become known. TARP's overall cost to taxpayers will not be fully known until all TARP investments are extinguished.

Current Value of Assets

The current value of future cash flows related to TARP transactions can also be measured by the balances in the program's non-budgetary credit financing accounts. Under the FCRA budgetary accounting structure, the net debt or cash balances in non-budgetary credit financing accounts at the end of each fiscal year reflect the present value of anticipated cash flows to and from the public.[5] Therefore, the net debt or cash balances reflect the expected present

---

[1] Section 123 of EESA provides Treasury the authority to record TARP equity purchases pursuant to FCRA, with required adjustments to the discount rate for market risks. The HHF and Making Home Affordable (MHA) program involve the purchase of financial instruments that have no provision for repayment or other return on investment, and do not constitute direct loans or guarantees under FCRA. Therefore these purchases are recorded on a cash basis. Administrative expenses for TARP are recorded under the Office of Financial Stability and the Special Inspector General for TARP on a cash basis, consistent with other Federal administrative costs, but are recorded separately from TARP program costs.

[2] The basic methods for each of these models are outlined in chapter 21 of the *Analytical Perspectives* volume of the 2015 Budget, "Financial Stabilization Efforts and Their Budgetary Effects."

[3] The analysis does not assume the effects on net TARP costs of a recoupment proposal required by Section 134 of EESA.

[4] With the exception of MHA and HHF, all the other TARP investments are reflected on a present value basis pursuant to FCRA and EESA.

[5] For example, to finance a loan disbursement to a borrower, a direct loan financing account receives the subsidy cost from the program account, and borrows from the Treasury the difference between the face value of the loan and the subsidy cost. As loan and interest payments from the public are received, the value is realized and these amounts are used to repay the financing account's debt to Treasury.

value of the asset or liability. Future collections from the public—such as proceeds from stock sales, or payments of principal and interest—are financial assets, just as future payments to the public are financial liabilities. The current year reestimates true-up assets and liabilities, setting the net debt or cash balance in the financing account equal to the present value of future cash flows.[6]

Table 20–2 shows the actual balances of TARP financing accounts as of the end of each fiscal year through 2017, and projected balances for each subsequent year through 2028.[7] Based on actual net balances in financing accounts at the end of 2009, the value of TARP assets totaled $129.9 billion. As of September 30, 2017, total TARP net asset value has decreased to $0.1 billion as repayments, repurchases, and other liquidations have reduced the inventory of TARP assets. Estimates in 2018 and beyond reflect estimated TARP net asset values over time, and future anticipated transactions. The overall balance of the financing accounts is estimated to continue falling over the next few years, as TARP investments continue to wind down.

The value of TARP equity purchases reached a high of $105.4 billion in 2009, and has since declined significantly with the wind down of American International Group (AIG) funding and repayments from large financial institutions. Remaining equity investments are concentrated in only two programs, the Capital Purchase Program (CPP) and the Community Development Capital Initiative (CDCI). The value of the TARP equity portfolio is anticipated to continue declining as participants repurchase stock and assets are sold. TARP direct loans were fully liquidated in 2014. The FHA Refinance Letter of Credit financing account reflects net cash balances, showing the reserves set aside to cover TARP's share of default claims for FHA Refinance mortgages over the life of the letter of credit facility which expires in December 2022. These reserves are projected to fall as claims are paid and as TARP coverage expires.

Estimate of the Deficit, Debt Held by the Public, and Gross Federal Debt, Based on the EESA Methodology

The estimates of the deficit and debt in the Budget reflect the impact of TARP as estimated under FCRA and Section 123 of EESA. The deficit estimates include the budgetary costs for each program under TARP, administrative expenses, certain indirect interest effects of credit programs, and the debt service cost to finance the program. As shown in Table 20–3, direct activity under TARP is expected to increase the 2018 deficit by $3.2 billion. This reflects estimated TARP programmatic and administrative outlays of $2.8 billion, and $0.4 billion in interest effects. The estimates of U.S. Treasury debt attributable to TARP include borrowing to finance both the deficit impacts of TARP activity and the cash flows to and from

the Government reflected as a means of financing in the TARP financing accounts. Estimated debt due to TARP at the end of 2018 is $31.8 billion.

Debt held by the public net of financial assets reflects the cumulative amount of money the Government has borrowed from the public for the program and not repaid, minus the current value of financial assets acquired with the proceeds of this debt, such as loan assets, or equity held by the Government. While debt held by the public is one useful measure for examining the impact of TARP, it provides incomplete information on the program's effect on the Government's financial condition. Debt held by the public net of financial assets provides a more complete picture of the Government's financial position because it reflects the net change in the Government's balance sheet due to the program.

Debt net of financial assets due to TARP is estimated to be $31.7 billion as of the end of 2018. This matches the projected debt held net of financial assets for 2018 that was reflected in the 2018 Budget. However, debt net of financial assets is anticipated to continue increasing annually, as debt is incurred to finance TARP housing program costs and debt service.

Under FCRA, the financing account earns and pays interest on its Treasury borrowings at the same interest rate used to discount cash flows for the credit subsidy cost. Section 123 of EESA requires an adjustment to the discount rate used to value TARP subsidy costs to account for market risks. However, actual cash flows as of September 30, 2017, already reflect the effect of any incurred market risks to that point, and therefore actual financing account interest transactions reflect the FCRA Treasury interest rates, with no additional risk adjustment.[8] Future cash flows reflect a risk adjusted discount rate and the corresponding financing account interest rate, consistent with the EESA requirement. For ongoing TARP credit programs, the risk adjusted discount rates on future cash flows result in subsidy costs that are higher than subsidy costs estimated under FCRA.

Estimates on a Cash Basis

The value to the Federal Government of the assets acquired through TARP is the same whether the costs of acquiring the assets are recorded in the Budget on a cash basis, or a credit basis. As noted above, the Budget records the cost of equity purchases, direct loans, and guarantees as the net present value cost to the Government, discounted at the rate required under FCRA and adjusted for market risks as required under Section 123 of EESA. Therefore, the net present value cost of the assets is reflected on-budget, and the gross value of these assets is reflected in the financing accounts.[9] If these purchases

---

[6] For a full explanation of FCRA budgetary accounting, please see chapter 8, "Budget Concepts," in this volume.

[7] Reestimates for TARP are calculated using actual data through September 30, 2017, and updated projections of future activity. Thus, the full impacts of TARP reestimates are reflected in the 2018 financing account balances.

[8] As TARP transactions wind down, the final lifetime cost estimates under the requirements of Section 123 of EESA will reflect no adjustment to the discount rate for market risks, as these risks have already been realized in the actual cash flows. Therefore, the final subsidy cost for TARP transactions will equal the cost per FCRA, where the net present value costs are estimated by discounting cash flows using Treasury rates.

[9] For MHA programs and HHF, Treasury's purchases of financial

were instead presented in the Budget on a cash basis, the Budget would reflect outlays for each disbursement (whether a purchase, a loan disbursement, or a default claim payment), and offsetting collections as cash is received from the public, with no obvious indication of whether the outflows and inflows leave the Government in a better or worse financial position, or what the net value of the transaction is.

instruments do not result in the acquisition of assets with potential for future cash flows, and therefore are recorded on a cash basis.

Revised Estimate of the Deficit, Debt Held by the Public, and Gross Federal Debt Based on the Cash-basis Valuation

The estimated effects of TARP transactions on the deficit and debt, as calculated on a cash basis, are reflected in Table 20–4. For comparison, the estimates in Table 20–3 reflect TARP transactions' effects as calculated consistent with FCRA and Section 123 of EESA.

If TARP transactions were reported on a cash basis, the annual budgetary effects would include the full amount of Government disbursements for activities such as equity purchases and direct loans, offset by cash inflows from dividend payments, redemptions, and loan repayments occurring in each year. For loan guarantees, the deficit would show fees, claim payouts, or other cash transac-

Table 20–3. TROUBLED ASSET RELIEF PROGRAM EFFECTS ON THE DEFICIT AND DEBT [1]
(Dollars in billions)

	Actual									Estimate										
	2009	2010	2011	2012	2013	2014	2015	2016	2017	2018	2019	2020	2021	2022	2023	2024	2025	2026	2027	2028
Deficit Effect:																				
Programmatic and administrative expenses ...	151.3	−109.6	−37.3	24.6	−8.5	−3.6	2.9	4.3	4.1	2.8	1.9	1.1	0.7	0.5	0.4	0.1	*	*	*	....
Interest effects [2,3]	*	*	*	*	*	*	*	*	*	0.1	0.2	0.4	0.6	1.1	1.1	1.2	1.2	1.3	1.3	1.4	1.4	1.5
Total deficit impact	**151.3**	**−109.6**	**−37.3**	**24.7**	**−8.5**	**−3.6**	**2.9**	**4.3**	**4.3**	**3.2**	**2.5**	**2.1**	**1.8**	**1.7**	**1.6**	**1.4**	**1.3**	**1.4**	**1.4**	**1.5**
Debt held by the public:																				
Deficit impact	151.3	−109.6	−37.3	24.7	−8.5	−3.6	2.9	4.3	4.3	3.2	2.5	2.1	1.8	1.7	1.6	1.4	1.3	1.4	1.4	1.5
Net disbursements of credit financing accounts	129.9	−7.9	−17.8	−71.9	−22.5	−9.0	−0.4	0.1	−0.3	−*	−*	−*	−*	−*	−*	....	....	....		
Total change in debt held by the public	281.2	−117.5	−55.1	−47.2	−31.0	−12.6	2.5	4.5	4.0	3.2	2.5	2.1	1.8	1.7	1.6	1.4	1.3	1.4	1.4	1.5
Debt held by the public	**281.2**	**163.6**	**108.5**	**61.3**	**30.3**	**17.6**	**20.2**	**24.6**	**28.7**	**31.8**	**34.3**	**36.4**	**38.2**	**39.9**	**41.5**	**42.9**	**44.2**	**45.6**	**47.1**	**48.5**
As a percent of GDP	2.0%	1.1%	0.7%	0.4%	0.2%	0.1%	0.1%	0.1%	0.1%	0.2%	0.2%	0.2%	0.2%	0.2%	0.2%	0.2%	0.2%	0.2%	0.2%	0.1%
Debt held by the public	281.2	163.6	108.5	61.3	30.3	17.6	20.2	24.6	28.7	31.8	34.3	36.4	38.2	39.9	41.5	42.9	44.2	45.6	47.1	48.5
Less financial assets net of liabilities	129.9	122.0	104.1	32.2	9.7	0.7	0.3	0.4	0.1	0.1	0.1	0.1	*	*	*	*	*	....	....	....
Debt held by the public net of financial assets	**151.3**	**41.6**	**4.4**	**29.0**	**20.5**	**17.0**	**19.9**	**24.2**	**28.5**	**31.7**	**34.2**	**36.4**	**38.2**	**39.9**	**41.4**	**42.8**	**44.2**	**45.6**	**47.1**	**48.5**

* $50 million or less.

[1] Table reflects the deficit effects of the TARP program, including administrative costs and interest effects.

[2] Projected Treasury interest transactions with credit financing accounts are based on the market-risk adjusted rates. Actual credit financing account interest transactions reflect the appropriate Treasury rates under the FCRA.

[3] Includes estimated debt service effects of all TARP transactions that affect borrowing from the public.

Table 20–4. TROUBLED ASSET RELIEF PROGRAM EFFECTS ON THE DEFICIT AND DEBT CALCULATED ON A CASH BASIS [1]
(Dollars in billions)

	Actual									Estimate										
	2009	2010	2011	2012	2013	2014	2015	2016	2017	2018	2019	2020	2021	2022	2023	2024	2025	2026	2027	2028
Deficit Effect:																				
Programmatic and administrative expenses	278.4	−122.3	−58.1	−48.9	−31.6	−12.8	2.5	4.4	3.8	2.7	1.8	1.0	0.6	0.5	0.3	*	−*	*	−0.1	....
Debt service [2]	2.8	4.7	3.0	1.7	0.6	0.2	*	0.1	0.2	0.5	0.8	1.1	1.2	1.2	1.3	1.3	1.4	1.4	1.4	1.5
Total deficit impact	**281.2**	**−117.5**	**−55.1**	**−47.2**	**−31.0**	**−12.6**	**2.5**	**4.5**	**4.0**	**3.1**	**2.5**	**2.1**	**1.8**	**1.7**	**1.6**	**1.4**	**1.3**	**1.4**	**1.4**	**1.5**

* $50 million or less.

[1] Table reflects deficit effect of budgetary costs, substituting estimates calculated on a cash basis for estimates calculated under FCRA and Sec. 123 of EESA.

[2] Includes estimated debt service effects of all TARP transactions affecting borrowing from the public.

tions associated with the guarantees as they occurred. Updates to estimates of future performance would affect the deficit in the year that they occur, and there would not be credit reestimates.

Under cash basis reporting, TARP would decrease the deficit in 2018 by an estimated $0.1 billion, so if this ba-sis was used the 2018 deficit would be $0.1 billion lower than the $3.2 billion estimate now reflected in the Budget. Under FCRA, the marginal change in the present value attributable to better-than-expected future inflows from the public would be recognized up front in a downward reestimate, in contrast to a cash-based treatment that

Table 20-5. TROUBLED ASSET RELIEF PROGRAM REESTIMATES

(In billions of dollars)

TARP Program and Cohort Year	Original subsidy rate	Current reestimate rate	Current reestimate amount	Net lifetime reestimate amount, excluding interest	TARP disbursements as of 09/30/2017
Equity Programs:					
Automotive Industry Financing Program (AIFP) - Equity:					
2009	54.52%	2.39%	....	−6.5	12.5
2010	30.25%	−16.81%	....	−1.6	3.8
Capital Purchase Program (CPP):				....	
2009	26.99%	−6.84%	−*	−65.8	204.6
2010	5.77%	1.95%	−*	−*	0.3
AIG Investment Program (AIG):				....	
2009	82.78%	21.88%	....	−38.5	67.8
Public-Private Investment Program (PPIP) - Equity:				....	
2009	34.62%	−20.41%	....	−0.3	0.7
2010	22.97%	−51.03%	−*	−3.7	5.5
Targeted Investment Program (TIP):				....	
2009	48.85%	−8.47%	....	−23.2	40.0
Community Development Capital Initiative (CDCI):				....	
2010	48.06%	15.01%	−*	−0.2	0.6
Subtotal Equity Programs			−*	−139.8	335.8
Structured and Direct Loan Programs:					
Automotive Industry Financing Program (AIFP) - Debt:					
2009	58.75%	21.71%	−*	−19.9	63.4
Public Private Investment Program (PPIP) - Debt:				....	
2009	−2.52%	−0.29%	....	*	1.4
2010	−10.85%	1.84%	....	1.3	11.0
Small Business 7(a) program (SBA 7(a)):				....	
2010	0.48%	−1.35%	....	−*	0.4
Term-Asset Backed Securities Loan Facility (TALF):[1]				....	
2009	−104.23%	−605.59%	....	−0.4	0.1
Subtotal Structured and Direct Loan Programs			−*	−18.9	76.2
Guarantee Programs:[2]					
Asset Guarantee Program (AGP):[3]					
2009	−0.25%	−1.20%	....	−1.4	301.0
FHA Refinance Letter of Credit:[4]				....	
2011	1.26%	0.13%	−*	−*	0.1
2012	4.00%	0.64%	−*	−*	0.2
2013	2.48%	0.56%	−*	−*	0.2
2015	1.64%	0.71%	−*	−*	0.1
2017[5]	0.80%	0.93%	*	*	0.2
Subtotal Guarantee Program			−*	−1.4	301.8
Total TARP			−*	−160.1	713.9

* $50 million or less.

[1] The Term-Asset Backed Securities Loan Facility original subsidy rate reflects the anticipated collections for Treasury's $20 billion commitment, as a percent of estimated lifetime disbursements of roughly $0.1 billion.

[2] Disbursement amounts for Guarantee Programs reflect the face value of the assets supported by the guarantees.

[3] The TARP obligation for this program was $5 billion, the maximum contingent liability while the guarantee was in force.

[4] The FHA Refinance Letter of Credit, which is considered a TARP Housing Program, is also a guarantee program subject to FCRA.

[5] The FHA Refinance Letter of Credit 2017 cohort was only open from September 30, 2016 to December 31, 2016.

Table 20–6. DETAILED TARP PROGRAM LEVELS AND COSTS

(In billions of dollars)

Program	2018 Budget		2019 Budget	
	TARP Obligations	Subsidy Costs	TARP Obligations	Subsidy Costs
Equity Purchases:				
Capital Purchase Program (CPP)	204.9	–8.4	204.9	–8.4
AIG Investment Program (AIG)	67.8	17.4	67.8	17.4
Targeted Investment Program (TIP)	40.0	–3.6	40.0	–3.6
Automotive Industry Financing Program (AIFP) - Equity	16.3	2.8	16.3	2.8
Public-Private Investment Program (PPIP) - Equity	6.2	–2.5	6.2	–2.5
Community Development Capital Initiative (CDCI).	0.6	0.1	0.6	0.1
Subtotal equity purchases	335.8	5.8	335.8	5.7
Structured and Direct Loan Programs:				
Automotive Industry Financing Program (AIFP) - Debt	63.4	17.1	63.4	17.1
Term Asset-Backed Securities Loan Facility (TALF)	0.1	–0.6	0.1	–0.6
Public-Private Investment Program (PPIP) - Debt	12.4	0.1	12.4	0.1
Small Business 7(a) Program (SBA 7(a))	0.4	*	0.4	*
Subtotal direct loan programs	76.2	16.7	76.2	16.7
Guarantee Programs:				
Asset Guarantee Program (AGP) [1]	5.0	–3.9	5.0	–3.9
Subtotal asset guarantees	5.0	–3.9	5.0	–3.9
TARP Housing Programs:				
Making Home Affordable (MHA) Programs	27.8	23.0	27.8	22.9
Hardest Hit Fund (HHF)	9.6	9.6	9.6	9.6
Subtotal non-credit programs	37.4	32.6	37.4	32.5
FHA Refinance Letter of Credit	*	*	*	*
Subtotal TARP housing programs	37.4	32.6	37.4	32.5
Totals	**454.5**	**51.2**	**454.5**	**51.1**
Memorandum:				
Interest on reestimates		–18.8		–18.8
Deficit impact with interest on reestimates [2]		*32.4*		*32.3*

* $50 million or less.

[1] The total assets supported by the Asset Guarantee Program were $301 billion.

[2] Total programmatic costs of TARP exclude interest on reestimates of $18.8 billion in both the 2018 Budget and the 2019 Budget. Interest on reestimates is an adjustment that accounts for the time between the original subsidy costs and current estimates; such adjustments impact the deficit but are not direct programmatic costs.

would show the annual marginal changes in cash flows. However, the impact of TARP on the Federal debt, and on debt held net of financial assets, is the same on a cash basis as under FCRA. Because debt held by the public and debt net of financial assets are the same on a cash and present value basis, these data are not repeated in Table 20–4.

Portion of the Deficit Attributable to TARP, and the Extent to Which the Deficit Impact is Due to a Reestimate

Table 20–3 shows the portion of the deficit attributable to TARP transactions. The major components of TARP's $3.2 billion deficit effects in 2018 are as follows:

- Outlays for TARP housing programs are estimated at $2.6 billion in 2018, which includes outlays under MHA and HHF. Outlays for TARP housing programs are estimated to decline gradually through 2024.

- Administrative expense outlays for TARP are estimated at $117 million in 2018, and are expected to

decrease annually thereafter as TARP winds down. Outlays for the Special Inspector General for TARP are estimated at $39 million in 2018.

- TARP reestimates and interest on reestimates will decrease the deficit by $14.6 million in 2018.

- Interest transactions with credit financing accounts include interest paid to Treasury on borrowing by the financing accounts, offset by interest paid by Treasury on the financing accounts' uninvested balances. Although the financing accounts are non-budgetary, Treasury payments to these accounts and receipt of interest from them are budgetary transactions and therefore affect net outlays and the deficit. For TARP financing accounts, projected interest transactions are based on the market risk adjusted rates used to discount the cash flows. The projected net financing account interest paid to Treasury at market risk adjusted rates is $15 million in 2018 and declines over time as the financing accounts repay borrowing from Treasury through investment sale proceeds and repayments on TARP equity purchases and direct loans.

The full impact of TARP on the deficit includes the estimated cost of Treasury borrowing from the public—debt service—for the outlays listed above. Debt service is estimated at $452 million for 2018 and then expected to increase to $1.5 billion by 2028, largely due to outlays for TARP housing programs. Total debt service will continue over time after TARP winds down, due to the financing of past TARP costs.

Analysis of TARP Reestimates

The costs of outstanding TARP assistance are re-estimated annually by updating cash flows for actual experience and new assumptions, and adjusting for any changes by either recording additional subsidy costs (an upward technical and economic reestimate) or by reducing subsidy costs (a downward reestimate). The re-estimated dollar amounts to be recorded in 2018 reflect TARP disbursements through September 30, 2017, while reestimated subsidy rates reflect the full lifetime costs, including anticipated future disbursements.[10] Detailed information on upward and downward reestimates to program costs is reflected in Table 20–5.

The current reestimate of -$15 million reflects a decrease in estimated TARP costs from the 2018 Budget. This decrease was due in large part to improved market conditions and continued progress winding down TARP investments over the past year.

Differences Between Current and Previous OMB Estimates

As shown in Table 20–6, the 2019 Budget reflects a total TARP deficit impact of $32.3 billion. This is a decrease of $0.1 billion from the 2018 Budget projection of $32.4 billion. This decrease is predominantly due to reduced estimated outlays within TARP housing programs.

The estimated 2019 TARP deficit impact reflected in Table 20–6 differs from the programmatic cost of $51.1 billion in the Budget because the deficit impact includes $18.8 billion in cumulative downward adjustments for interest on subsidy reestimates. See footnote 2 in Table 20–6.

Differences Between OMB and CBO Estimates

Table 20–7 compares the OMB estimate for TARP's deficit impact to the deficit impact estimated by CBO in its "Report on the Troubled Asset Relief Program—June 2017."[11]

CBO estimates the total cost of TARP at $33 billion, based on estimated lifetime TARP disbursements of $445 billion. The Budget reflects a total deficit cost of $32 billion, based estimated disbursements of $444.3 billion. CBO and OMB cost estimates for TARP have converged over time as TARP equity programs have wound down, differences in assumptions for the future performance of equity investments in the program have been eliminated, and divergent assumptions regarding estimated demand and participation rates in TARP housing programs have been replaced by actuals.

---

[10] The current reestimated dollar amounts also include the $0.5 million PPIP post-closure recovery received in December 2017.

[11] Available at: *www.cbo.gov/system/files/115th-congress-2017-2018/reports/52840-tarp.pdf*

Table 20–7.   COMPARISON OF CBO AND OMB TARP COSTS

(In billions of dollars)

Program	Estimates of Deficit Impact[1]	
	CBO Cost Estimate[2]	OMB Cost Estimate
Capital Purchase Program	−16	−16
Targeted Investment Program & Asset Guarantee Program	−8	−8
AIG assistance	15	15
Automotive Industry Financing Program	12	12
Term Asset-Backed Securities Loan Facility	−1	−1
Public-Private Investment Programs[3]	−3	−3
Other programs[4]	*	*
TARP housing programs	33	33
Total	**33**	**32**

* Amounts round to less than $1 billion.

[1] Totals include interest on reestimates.

[2] CBO estimates from June 2017, available at *www.cbo.gov/system/files/115th-congress-2017-2018/reports/52840-tarp.pdf*

[3] Includes both debt and equity purchases.

[4] "Other programs" reflects an aggregate cost for CDCI and small business programs.

TARP Market Impact

TARP provided support to the financial sector through the Capital Purchase Program, Targeted Investment Program, Asset Guarantee Program, and the Community Development Capital Initiative which strengthened the financial position of the Nation's financial institutions. TARP's intervention in the auto industry through the Automotive Industry Financing Program was effectively wound down in 2014; however, Treasury retains the right to receive proceeds from Chrysler and General Motors (GM) liquidation trusts. TARP housing programs provided assistance to millions of homeowners including more than 1.7 million borrowers who received permanent mortgage modifications through the Home Affordable Modification Program (HAMP) as of November 30, 2017.

Description of Assets Purchased Through TARP, by Program

Capital Purchase Program (CPP): Pursuant to EESA, Treasury created the CPP in October 2008 to restore confidence throughout the financial system by ensuring that the Nation's financial institutions had a sufficient capital cushion against potential future losses and to support lending to creditworthy borrowers. Treasury purchased $204.9 billion in preferred stock in 707 financial institutions under CPP. As of November 30, 2017, Treasury had received approximately $199.7 billion in principal repayments and $27.1 billion in revenues from dividends, interest, warrants, gains/other interest and fees. CPP cash proceeds of $226.8 billion now exceed Treasury's initial investment by $21.9 billion. As of November 30, 2017, $48 million remained outstanding under the program among 6 remaining CPP institutions.

Community Development Capital Initiative (CDCI): The CDCI program provided lower-cost capital to Community Development Financial Institutions (CDFIs), which operate in markets underserved by traditional financial institutions. In February 2010, Treasury released program terms for the CDCI program, under which participating institutions received capital investments of up to 5 percent of risk-weighted assets and pay dividends to Treasury of as low as 2 percent per annum. The dividend rate increases to 9 percent after eight years. TARP capital of $570 million has been committed to this program. As of November 30, 2017, Treasury has received $540 million in cash back on its CDCI investments and $68 million remains outstanding.

Capital Assistance Program (CAP): In 2009, Treasury worked with Federal banking regulators to develop a comprehensive "stress test" to assess the health of the nation's 19 largest bank holding companies. Treasury also announced it would provide capital under TARP through the Capital Assistance Program (CAP) to institutions that participated in the stress tests as well as others. Only one TARP institution (Ally Financial) required additional funds under the stress tests, but it received them through AIFP, not CAP. CAP closed on November 9, 2009, without making any investments and did not incur any losses to taxpayers. Following the release of the stress test results, banks were able to raise hundreds of billions of dollars in private capital.

American International Group (AIG) Investments: During the financial crisis, the Federal Reserve Bank of New York (FRBNY) and Treasury provided financial support to AIG in order to mitigate broader systemic risks that would have resulted from the disorderly failure of the company. In September 2008, prior to the enactment of TARP, the FRBNY provided an $85 billion line of credit to AIG and received preferred shares that entitled it to 79.8 percent of the voting rights of AIG's common stock. After TARP was enacted, FRBNY and Treasury continued to work to facilitate AIG's execution of its plan to sell certain of its businesses in an orderly manner, promote market stability, and protect the interests of the U.S. Government and taxpayers. As of December 31, 2008, when purchases ended, Treasury had purchased $40 billion in preferred shares from AIG through TARP and later extended a $29.8 billion line of credit, of which AIG drew down $27.8 billion, in exchange for additional preferred stock. The remaining $2 billion obligation was canceled.

AIG executed a recapitalization plan with FRBNY, Treasury, and the AIG Credit Facility Trust in 2011 that allowed for the acceleration of the Government's exit from its 92 percent ownership stake in AIG.[12] Following the restructuring, Treasury executed a multi-year process of liquidating its position, and fully exited its investment in AIG in 2013.[13] In total, TARP's AIG commitments totaled $67.8 billion and, with the program closed, yielded $55.3 billion in total cash back. Treasury also collected net proceeds of $17.6 billion for its non-TARP shares in AIG. Total AIG-related proceeds exceeded disbursements by $5.0 billion for Treasury as a whole.

Targeted Investment Program (TIP): The goal of TIP was to stabilize the financial system by making investments in institutions that are critical to the functioning of the financial system. Under TIP, Treasury purchased $20 billion in preferred stock from Citigroup and $20 billion in preferred stock from Bank of America. Treasury also received stock warrants from each company. Both Citigroup and Bank of America repaid their TIP investments in full in December 2009. In total, TARP's TIP commitments totaled $40 billion and, with the program closed, yielded $44.4 billion in total cash back.

Asset Guarantee Program (AGP): The AGP was created to provide Government assurances for assets held by financial institutions that were critical to the functioning of the Nation's financial system. Under the AGP, Treasury and FDIC committed to provide support to two institutions – Bank of America and Citigroup. Bank of America, however, ultimately decided not to participate, and paid TARP a termination fee of $276 million. TARP, in conjunction with the Federal Reserve, and the FDIC agreed to share potential losses on a $301.0 billion pool of Citigroup's covered assets. As a premium for the guaran-

---

[12] Treasury's investment in AIG common shares consisted of shares acquired in exchange for preferred stock purchased with TARP funds (TARP shares) and shares received from the trust created by FRBNY for the benefit of Treasury as a result of its loan to AIG (non-TARP shares).

[13] A summary of the deal terms and transactions can be found in the *Analytical Perspectives* volume of the 2014 Budget.

tee to Citigroup, TARP received $4.0 billion of Citigroup preferred stock, which was reduced by $1.8 billion upon early termination of the agreement. TARP completed the wind-down of the AGP in 2013, and received more than $4.1 billion in proceeds from the AGP without disbursing any claim payments.

Automotive Industry Support Programs: In December 2008, Treasury established several programs to prevent the collapse of the domestic automotive industry. Through the Automotive Industry Financing Program (AIFP), TARP made emergency loans to Chrysler, Chrysler Financial, and GM. Additionally, TARP bought equity in Ally Financial, formerly GMAC, and assisted Chrysler and GM during their bankruptcy proceedings.

Treasury has liquidated its AIFP holdings and AIFP is effectively wound down. In total, of the $12.4 billion committed to Chrysler, TARP was repaid $11.1 billion in total cash back.[14] In December 2013, TARP sold its last remaining shares in GM, recouping a total of $39.0 billion from TARP's $49.5 billion investment in GM.[15] In total, Treasury recovered $19.6 billion on its investment in Ally Financial, roughly $2.4 billion more than the original investment of $17.2 billion. Through the Auto Supplier Support Program (Supplier Program) and the Auto Warranty Commitment Program (Warranty Program), Treasury disbursed $1.1 billion in direct loans to GM and Chrysler to support auto parts manufacturers and suppliers. Both the Supplier and Warranty Programs have closed and, in aggregate, these investments yielded $1.2 billion in total cash back. TARP's AIFP disbursements—including the GM, Chrysler, Ally (GMAC), Supplier, and Warranty Programs—totaled $79.7 billion and, with all programs effectively wound down, AIFP yielded $70.5 billion in total cash back.

TARP maintains an interest in the ongoing bankruptcy proceedings of the automotive entities it invested in. In November 2016, TARP received a payment of $5.0 million from the GM bankruptcy proceedings. Additional future payments are possible, but not anticipated.

Term Asset-Backed Securities Loan Facility (TALF): The TALF was a joint initiative with the Federal Reserve that provided financing loans to private investors to facilitate the restoration of secondary credit markets. Treasury provided protection to the Federal Reserve through a loan to TALF's special purpose vehicle (SPV), which was originally available to purchase up to $20 billion in assets that would be acquired in the event of default on Federal Reserve financing. In March 2009 Treasury disbursed $0.1 billion of this amount to the TALF SPV to implement the program and the loss-coverage was subsequently reduced. In 2013, Treasury and the Federal Reserve determined that Treasury's commitment was no longer necessary because the accumulated fees collected through TALF exceeded the total principal

amount of TALF loans outstanding. In total, Treasury had accumulated income of $685 million from TALF and the program is closed.

Small Business 7(a) Program (SBA 7(a)): In March 2009, Treasury and the Small Business Administration (SBA) announced a Treasury program to purchase SBA-guaranteed securities (pooled certificates) to re-start the secondary market in these loans. Through a pilot program, Treasury purchased 31 SBA-guaranteed securities with an aggregate face value of approximately $368 million. In 2012, Treasury completed the final disposition of its SBA 7(a) securities portfolio. The SBA 7(a) Program received total proceeds of $376 million, representing a gain of approximately $8 million to taxpayers.

Public Private Investment Program (PPIP): Treasury announced the Legacy Securities Public-Private Investment Partnership (PPIP) on March 23, 2009, to help restart the market for legacy mortgage-backed securities. Under the Program, Public-Private Investment Funds (PPIFs) were established by private sector fund managers for the purchase of eligible legacy securities from banks, insurance companies, mutual funds, pension funds, and other eligible sellers as defined under EESA. In total, after obligating $18.6 billion, and with all PPIFs closed, PPIP investments yielded $22.5 billion in total cash back. In December 2017, TARP received a payment of $0.5 million from a PPIP-related legal settlement. Additional future payments are possible, but not anticipated.

TARP Housing Programs: In February 2009 Treasury created three housing programs utilizing up to $50 billion in TARP funding. The Government-Sponsored Enterprises, Fannie Mae and Freddie Mac, participated in the housing programs both as Treasury's financial agents, and by implementing similar policies for their own mortgage portfolios. Following the enactment of the 2010 Dodd-Frank Wall Street Reform Act, Treasury reduced its commitments to TARP housing programs to $45.6 billion. These programs are:

- Making Home Affordable (MHA);

- Housing Finance Agency (HFA) Hardest-Hit Fund (HHF); and

- Federal Housing Administration (FHA) Refinance Program.[16]

Making Home Affordable (MHA): Programs under MHA included the Home Affordable Modification Program (HAMP), FHA-HAMP, the Second Lien Modification Program, and Rural Development-HAMP.[17] MHA also included the Home Affordable Foreclosure Alternatives Program, which provided short sale and deed-in-lieu of foreclosure opportunities to borrowers, as well as assistance to borrowers who are unemployed or underwater (owe more than their home is worth). On December 31, 2016 the application window for MHA

---

[14] Chrysler repayments of $11.1 billion include $560 million in proceeds from the sale of Treasury's 6 percent fully diluted equity interest in Chrysler to Fiat and Treasury's interest in an agreement with the United Automobile Worker's retiree trust that were executed on July 21, 2011.

[15] This excludes the $884 million loan to GM that was converted to GMAC common stock.

[16]The FHA Refinance Program is supported by Treasury through TARP via a letter of credit to cover a share of any losses on these particular FHA Refinance loans. This program has also been referred to as the FHA Short Refinance Program or Option in other reporting.

[17]For additional information on MHA programs, visit: *https://www. makinghomeaffordable.gov/pages/default.aspx.*

closed. As of November 30, 2017, TARP has paid $18.2 billion in MHA-related incentive payments and an additional $5.3 billion in TARP funds have been committed but not yet disbursed.

HFA Hardest-Hit Fund (HHF): The $9.6 billion HHF provides the eligible entities of HFAs from 18 states and the District of Columbia with flexible funding to implement programs to prevent foreclosures and bring stability to local housing markets. In December 2015, P.L. 114-113 provided limited authority for Treasury to obligate up to $2 billion in additional HHF funds through December 31, 2017; Treasury allocated $2 billion in additional HHF funds to eighteen currently participating jurisdictions in 2016. Participating jurisdictions have until 2020 to utilize HHF funds.

FHA Refinance Program: FHA administers this program with TARP's support. The Program was initiated in September 2010 to allow eligible borrowers who were current on their mortgages but owed more than their home was worth, to refinance into an FHA-guaranteed loan if the lender wrote off at least 10 percent of the existing loan. Treasury committed $27 million through a letter of credit agreement to cover a share of any losses on the loans and administrative expenses. The Program eligibility window closed on December 31, 2016, and the letter of credit expires in December 2022.

21. CYBERSECURITY FUNDING

Section 630 of the Consolidated Appropriations Act, 2017 (Pub. L. No. 115-31) amended 31 U.S.C. § 1105 (a) (35) to require that a cybersecurity funding analysis be incorporated into the President's Budget. This analysis addresses that legislative requirement and covers cybersecurity activities and funding for all Federal agencies, not just those carried out by the Department of Homeland Security (DHS) and Department of Defense (DOD). Cybersecurity is an important component of the Administration's IT modernization efforts, and the President remains dedicated to securing the Federal enterprise from cyber-related threats. An assessment of the Federal Government's overall cybersecurity risk found the Federal enterprise to be at risk. Cybersecurity budgetary priorities will continue to seek to reduce this risk based on data-driven, risk-based assessments of the threat environment and the current Federal cybersecurity posture.

Data Collection Methodology and Adjustments

The Federal spending estimates in this analysis utilize funding and programmatic information collected on the Executive Branch's cybersecurity efforts. Agencies provide funding data at a level of detail sufficient to consolidate information to determine total governmental spending on cybersecurity. OMB provided the following guidance to agencies regarding the reporting of cybersecurity budget information for each fiscal year (FY): FY 2017 Actual levels should reflect the actual budgetary resources available for that year; FY 2018 Estimate levels should reflect the estimated budgetary resources available that year, assuming the annualized amounts provided in the Continuing Appropriations Act, 2018 (Divisions D of P.L. 115-56)(CR); and FY 2019 President's Budget levels should reflect final policy decisions included in the President's Budget. Agencies were directed to coordinate responses between their Chief Financial Officers, Chief Information Officers, and Chief Information Security Officers.

OMB analyzed the cybersecurity activity spending reported by agencies through the initial FY 2019 cybersecurity budget submission and compared those submissions to cybersecurity spending reported by agencies in their Capital Planning and Investment Control (CPIC) IT Portfolio submissions. The CPIC process captures cybersecurity-related IT investment information, but does not provide information at the account level. It also does not capture non-IT cybersecurity investments. The FY 2019 cybersecurity budget submission captures these non-IT cybersecurity investments. In addition to the comparison to CPIC, submissions were assessed against prior cybersecurity budget submissions and historical security performance.

The Administration will continue to refine definitions and cybersecurity initiatives over time based on additional analysis or changes in the way specific activities are characterized, aggregated, or disaggregated.

Federal Budget Authority

The FY 2019 President's Budget includes $15 billion of budget authority for cybersecurity-related activities, a $583.4 million (4.1 percent) increase above the FY 2018 Estimate. Due to the sensitive nature of some activities, this amount does not represent the entire cyber budget. The DOD was the largest contributor to this total. In particular, DOD reported $8.5 billion in cybersecurity funding in FY 2019, a $340 million (4.2 percent) increase above the FY 2018 Estimate. At an aggregate level, civilian cybersecurity spending increased 3.9 percent in the FY 2019 President's Budget. Most of this change was among the civilian Chief Financial Officer (CFO) Act agencies, for whom cybersecurity spending increased 4.1 percent from the FY 2018 Estimate to the FY 2019 President's Budget. While some non-CFO Act agencies reported significant increases in their cybersecurity spending, non-CFO Act agencies as a whole reported a less than 1 percent change in cybersecurity spending from the FY 2018 Estimate.

A total of 76 civilian agencies, plus DOD, reported cybersecurity budget authority in FY 2019, reflecting the fact that every agency is ultimately responsible for protecting its information and assets commensurate with the potential impact of its loss or compromise. However, a number of agencies also have cybersecurity-related spending that is not dedicated to the protection of their own networks, serving instead a broader cybersecurity mission. For instance, to ensure a consistent baseline level of information security, there are a number of programs that provide tools and capabilities government-wide, such as DHS's Continuous Diagnostics and Mitigation (CDM) program. Additionally, numerous programs exist that further enhance national and Federal cybersecurity but are focused on areas such as standards, research, and the investigation of cyber crimes rather than specific technical capabilities. Budgets for these areas are captured in the totals in Chart 21-1 below.

Chart 21-2 provides a more detailed view of the information presented in Chart 21-1. In addition to total cybersecurity budget amounts, the table provides amounts at the bureau level as well as the account level to give greater insight into the structure of agency cybersecurity budgets. Chart 21-2 also includes budget function codes for each account as well as the designation of each account as mandatory, discretionary, or split use. Due to the sensitivity of the information, the cybersecurity budget information for DOD has not been broken out in this way.

Table 21–1. AGENCY CYBERSECURITY FUNDING TOTALS
(In millions of dollars)

Agency	FY 2017 Actual	FY 2018 Estimate	FY 2019 Budget
CFO Act Agencies			
Department of Agriculture	114.6	125.7	129.5
Department of Commerce	273.8	292.7	291.2
Department of Defense [1]	7,224.0	8,157.0	8,497.0
Department of Education	74.1	103.0	135.3
Department of Energy	370.6	379.0	464.9
Department of Health & Human Services	319.7	309.9	352.6
Department of Homeland Security	1,614.3	1,722.2	1,724.6
Department of Housing & Urban Development	15.2	16.6	18.7
Department of the Interior	84.0	90.3	96.9
Department of Justice	735.0	703.6	721.4
Department of Labor	83.4	73.7	73.8
Department of State	254.3	270.5	263.1
Department of the Treasury	458.4	529.4	500.1
Department of Transportation	140.2	157.3	168.7
Department of Veterans Affairs	385.8	360.0	418.4
Environmental Protection Agency	25.1	34.7	42.0
General Services Administration	65.9	65.6	67.9
National Aeronautics & Space Administration	148.4	182.4	185.8
National Science Foundation	182.7	167.6	153.3
Nuclear Regulatory Commission	22.7	24.1	32.3
Office of Personnel Management	37.6	38.5	45.6
Small Business Administration	19.5	18.8	17.4
Social Security Administration	156.3	177.1	190.6
U.S. Agency for International Development	36.5	45.1	37.3
Non-CFO Act Agencies			
Access Board	0.2	0.2	....
African Development Foundation	0.6	1.0	0.0
American Battle Monuments Commission	1.3	1.7	1.5
Barry Goldwater Scholarship and Excellence in Education Foundation	*	*	....
Broadcasting Board of Governors	4.3	4.9	5.6
Chemical Safety and Hazard Investigation Board	0.1	0.1	0.1
Commission on Civil Rights	0.4	0.5	....
Commodity Futures Trading Commission	7.0	6.4	7.0
Consumer Product Safety Commission	2.4	2.3	2.3
Corporation for National and Community Service	9.6	9.6	0.0
Council of the Inspectors General on Integrity and Efficiency	*	0.4	0.3
Court Services and Offender Supervision Agency for the District	6.3	4.9	5.0
Defense Nuclear Facilities Safety Board	0.8	0.9	0.8
Equal Employment Opportunity Commission	3.9	4.1	4.5
Export-Import Bank of the United States	3.4	2.5	2.6
Farm Credit Administration	2.8	3.0	3.0
Federal Communications Commission	13.0	7.4	8.3
Federal Deposit Insurance Corporation	61.5	98.0	109.8
Federal Election Commission	1.0	....	....
Federal Financial Institutions Examination Council	*	....	....
Federal Labor Relations Authority	0.2	0.2	0.2
Federal Maritime Commission	0.5	0.3	0.3
Federal Retirement Thrift Investment Board	41.0	21.6	21.4
Federal Trade Commission	11.5	14.6	13.4
Gulf Coast Ecosystem Restoration Council	*	....	....
Institute of Museum and Library Services	0.3	0.0	....
Inter-American Foundation	0.4	0.4	0.0
International Trade Commission	2.5	3.3	3.3
Marine Mammal Commission	*	*	....

Table 21–1.   AGENCY CYBERSECURITY FUNDING TOTALS—Continued

(In millions of dollars)

Agency	FY 2017 Actual	FY 2018 Estimate	FY 2019 Budget
Merit Systems Protection Board	0.2	0.9	1.0
Morris K. Udall and Stewart L. Udall Foundation	*	*	*
National Archives and Records Administration	6.6	8.3	8.5
National Credit Union Administration	4.1	5.0	8.2
National Endowment for the Arts	0.5	1.3	0.6
National Endowment for the Humanities	0.2	0.2	0.0
National Labor Relations Board	1.6	1.6	....
National Transportation Safety Board	0.8	1.8	2.3
Nuclear Waste Technical Review Board	0.2	0.3	0.3
Occupational Safety and Health Review Commission	1.2	1.3	2.2
Office of Government Ethics	0.3	0.2	0.4
Office of Special Counsel	0.4	0.8	0.6
Overseas Private Investment Corporation	3.0	3.1	3.5
Peace Corps	10.0	10.4	10.9
Presidio Trust	0.7	0.7	0.6
Privacy and Civil Liberties Oversight Board	0.9	0.8	0.9
Securities and Exchange Commission	42.2	63.0	59.4
Selective Service System	1.0	0.9	1.4
Smithsonian Institution	5.1	5.6	6.8
Tennessee Valley Authority	30.3	30.2	28.8
Trade and Development Agency	0.3	0.3	1.0
U.S. Army Corps of Engineers	23.3	23.8	25.2
United States Holocaust Memorial Museum	1.3	1.3	1.3
United States Institute of Peace	0.3	....	....
Grand Total	**13,152.0**	**14,399.9**	**14,983.3**

* $50 thousand or less

[1] These amounts represent estimates as of the time of publication.

Non-Federal Cybersecurity Spending

The most recent and comprehensive study of state-level cybersecurity spending revealed that the majority of states allocate between zero and two percent of their total IT budgets to cybersecurity.[1,2] It also revealed that cybersecurity spending has not increased to meet increasing cybersecurity challenges, with the majority of respondents reporting such budgets remaining flat or increasing less than five percent since 2014. Recent research also indicates that state and local governments rely heavily on inter-agency collaboration and Federal programs to fund their cybersecurity activities, with 49 percent of state CISOs reporting they seek alternative funding sources from intra-state agencies or programs, and 47 percent reporting a heavy reliance on DHS-specific programs.[3] According to the Federal Emergency Management Administration (FEMA)'s 2017 National Preparedness Report, 82 percent of states report that cybersecurity is a high priority but only 13 percent rate themselves as proficient, which marks a three percent decline from 2012.[4] However, states also report cybersecurity as the biggest growth area for IT spending moving forward.[5]

While it is difficult to estimate how much the U.S. private sector spends on cybersecurity, the research firm Gartner releases routine estimates of cybersecurity spending globally and forecasts that cybersecurity spending is anticipated to rise eight percent in 2018 to $96.3 billion. A similar report from Gartner in early 2017 noted that private entities are moving away from a prevention-only focus and moving toward a defense-in-depth approach by enhancing capabilities to detect and respond to cybersecurity incidents. The International Data Corporation predicts that spending will continue to grow, and at a faster rate than overall IT spending, reaching $101.6 billion in 2020.[6]

[1] OMB does not collect any cybersecurity expenditure data from State, local, or private entities directly.

[2] Source: Doug Robinson and Srini Subramanian, 2016 Deloitte-NASCIO Cybersecurity Study, "State Governments at Risk: Turning Strategy and Awareness into Progress," September 20, 2016, at *https://www.nascio.org/Portals/0/Publications/Documents/2016/2016-Deloitte-NASCIO-Cybersecurity-Study.pdf*.

[3] Source: Robinson and Subramanian.

[4] Source: Federal Emergency Management Agency, Department of Homeland Security, 2017 National Preparedness Report, at: www.fema.gov/media-library-data/1503926640648-0b64216b808eb42a93ba96fe8888d113/2017NationalPreparednessReport_508_COMPLIANT.pdf.

[5] Source: Paul Lipman, "4 Critical Challenges to State and Local Government Cybersecurity Efforts (Industry Perspective)," July 17, 2015, at *http://www.govtech.com/opinion/4-Critical-Challenges-to-State-and-Local-Government-Cybersecurity-Efforts.html*.

[6] Source: International Data Corporation, "Worldwide Semiannual Security Spending Guide," October 12, 2016, at www.idc.com/getdoc.jsp?containerId=prUS41851116.

Additional Information

The Budget is also required to include an analysis of fee-based cybersecurity costs as well as gross and net appropriations or obligational authority and outlays. Agencies have not historically reported their cybersecurity budgets in this manner, and OMB continues to work with the broader Federal community to capture this information in a way that is helpful to both agencies and Congress. Moreover, future years will array agency cy-bersecurity information against the National Institute of Standards and Technology Framework for Improving Critical Infrastructure Cybersecurity (Cybersecurity Framework). The incorporation of the Cybersecurity Framework, to which cybersecurity performance metrics and risk management assessments are already aligned, will provide a more structured manner for discussing Federal cybersecurity budgets and how they strategically address areas of noted risk.

Table 21–2. CIVILIAN AGENCY CYBERSECURITY FUNDING BY ACCOUNT
(In millions of dollars)

Organization	FY 2017 Actual	FY 2018 Estimate	FY 2019 Budget
Access Board			
Access Board			
Access Board (310-00-3200-751), Discretionary	0.2	0.2	....
American Battle Monuments Commission			
American Battle Monuments Commission			
American Battle Monuments Commission (MULTIPLE ACCOUNTS-705), Split	1.3	1.7	1.5
Barry Goldwater Scholarship and Excellence in Education Foundation			
Barry Goldwater Scholarship and Excellence in Education Foundation			
Barry Goldwater Scholarship and Excellence in Education Foundation (MULTIPLE ACCOUNTS-502), Mandatory	*	*	....
Broadcasting Board of Governors			
Broadcasting Board of Governors			
Broadcasting Board of Governors (MULTIPLE ACCOUNTS-999), Discretionary	4.3	4.9	5.6
Chemical Safety and Hazard Investigation Board			
Chemical Safety and Hazard Investigation Board			
Chemical Safety and Hazard Investigation Board (MULTIPLE ACCOUNTS-304), Discretionary	0.1	0.1	0.1
Commission on Civil Rights			
Commission on Civil Rights			
Commission on Civil Rights (326-00-1900-751), Discretionary	0.4	0.5	....
Commodity Futures Trading Commission			
Commodity Futures Trading Commission			
Commodity Futures Trading Commission (MULTIPLE ACCOUNTS-376), Split	7.0	6.4	7.0
Consumer Product Safety Commission			
Consumer Product Safety Commission			
Consumer Product Safety Commission (343-00-0100-554), Discretionary	2.4	2.3	2.3
Corporation for National and Community Service			
Corporation for National and Community Service			
Corporation for National and Community Service (MULTIPLE ACCOUNTS-506), Discretionary	9.6	9.6	....
Council of the Inspectors General on Integrity and Efficiency			
Council of the Inspectors General on Integrity and Efficiency			
Council of the Inspectors General on Integrity and Efficiency (542-00-4592-808), Mandatory	*	0.4	0.3
Court Services and Offender Supervision Agency for the District			
Court Services and Offender Supervision Agency for the District			
Court Services and Offender Supervision Agency for the District (511-001734-752), Discretionary	6.3	4.9	5.0
Defense Nuclear Facilities Safety Board			
Defense Nuclear Facilities Safety Board			
Defense Nuclear Facilities Safety Board (347-00-3900-999), Discretionary	0.8	0.9	0.8
Department of Agriculture			
Agricultural Marketing Service			
Marketing Services (005-45-2500-352), Split	0.1	0.1	0.1

Table 21–2. CIVILIAN AGENCY CYBERSECURITY FUNDING BY ACCOUNT—Continued

(In millions of dollars)

Organization	FY 2017 Actual	FY 2018 Estimate	FY 2019 Budget
Expenses and Refunds, Inspection and Grading of Farm Products (005-45-8015-352), Mandatory	0.7	0.7	0.2
Funds for Strengthening Markets, Income, and Supply (005-45-5209-605), Mandatory	*	*	*
Agricultural Research Service			
Salaries and Expenses (005-18-1400-352), Discretionary	2.5	2.5	2.5
Animal & Plant Health Inspection Service			
Salaries and Expenses (005-32-1600-352), Split	1.4	1.5	1.5
Departmental Management			
OCIO Working Capital Fund (005-14-4609-352), Discretionary	16.6	17.9	17.9
Office of the Chief Information Officer (005-12-0013-352), Discretionary	35.7	45.9	46.0
Economic Research Service			
Economic Research Service (005-13-1701-352), Discretionary	*	0.1	0.1
Executive Operations			
Office of the Chief Economist (005-04-0123-352), Split	0.2	0.2	0.2
Farm Service Agency			
Salaries and Expenses (005-49-0600-351), Discretionary	8.1	8.8	8.0
Food and Nutrition Service			
Supplemental Nutrition Assistance Program (005-84-3505-605), Split	2.8	2.9	2.9
Nutrition Programs Administration (005-84-3508-605), Discretionary	1.0	1.0	1.0
Food Safety & Inspection Services			
Expenses and Refunds, Inspection and Grading of Farm Products (005-35-8137-352), Mandatory	7.1	7.4	7.5
Foreign Agricultural Service			
FAS Commodity Credit Corporation Fund (005-49-4336-999), Mandatory	0.8	1.2	1.0
Salaries and Expenses (005-68-2900-352), Split	0.2	0.4	0.3
Forest Service			
National Forest System (005-96-1106-302), Discretionary	15.7	14.1	14.1
Wildland Fire Management (005-96-1115-302), Discretionary	0.7	0.7	0.6
Grain Inspection, Packers & Stockyards			
Salaries and Expenses (005-37-2400-352), Discretionary	0.5	0.5	0.5
National Agricultural Statistics Service			
National Agricultural Statistics Service (005-15-1801-352), Discretionary	1.9	1.9	1.6
National Institute of Food and Agriculture			
Research and Education Activities (005-20-1500-352), Split	0.6	0.6	0.6
Natural Resources Conservation			
Private Lands Conservation Operations (005-53-1000-302), Discretionary	1.5	0.6	0.1
Farm Security and Rural Investment Programs (005-53-1004-302), Mandatory	4.2	4.1	5.6
Office of Chief Economist			
Office of the Chief Economist (005-09-0123-352), Split	0.2	0.2	0.2
Office of Inspector General			
Office of Inspector General (005-08-0900-352), Discretionary	0.5	0.5	0.7
Office of the Secretary			
OFCO Working Capital Fund (005-04-4609-352), Discretionary	5.4	5.2	5.4
Office of the Secretary (005-03-9913-999), Split	0.0	0.0	0.0
Risk Management Agency			
RMA Salaries and Expenses (005-47-2707-351), Split	1.0	1.0	1.1
Federal Crop Insurance Corporation Fund (005-47-4085-351), Mandatory	1.0	1.0	1.0
Rural Development			
Salaries and Expenses (005-55-0403-452), Discretionary	4.3	4.4	8.4
Department of Commerce			
Bureau of Industry and Security			
Operations and Administration (006-30-0300-999), Discretionary	2.5	3.5	3.5
Bureau of the Census			

Table 21–2. CIVILIAN AGENCY CYBERSECURITY FUNDING BY ACCOUNT—Continued

(In millions of dollars)

Organization	FY 2017 Actual	FY 2018 Estimate	FY 2019 Budget
Census Working Capital Fund (006-07-4512-376), Discretionary	13.5	30.4	30.4
Periodic Censuses and Programs (006-07-0450-376), Discretionary	5.0	5.7	10.4
Current Surveys and Programs (006-07-0401-376), Split	1.1	1.1	1.5
Departmental Management			
Salaries and Expenses (006-05-0120-376), Discretionary	7.0	6.7	6.7
Working Capital Fund (006-05-4511-376), Discretionary	20.6	20.1	20.1
Office of the Inspector General (006-05-0126-376), Discretionary	1.0	1.0	1.0
Economic and Statistical Analysis			
Salaries and Expenses (006-08-1500-376), Discretionary	1.7	2.3	2.4
International Trade Administration			
Operations and Administration (006-25-1250-376), Discretionary	6.7	7.0	7.1
National Institution of Standards & Technology			
Industrial Technology Services (006-55-0525-376), Discretionary	0.2	0.2	....
Working Capital Fund (006-55-4650-376), Discretionary	20.4	20.8	19.0
Scientific and Technical Research and Services (006-55-0500-376), Discretionary	84.4	78.7	78.3
National Oceanic & Atmospheric Administration			
Operations, Research, and Facilities (006-48-1450-306), Split	66.4	66.3	66.3
National Technical Information Service			
NTIS Revolving Fund (006-54-4295-376), Discretionary	6.1	5.8	2.5
National Telecom/Information Administration			
Salaries and Expenses (006-60-0550-376), Discretionary	3.1	2.7	2.7
US Patent and Trademark Office			
Salaries and Expenses (006-51-1006-376), Discretionary	34.0	40.3	39.1
Department of Education			
Departmental Management			
Program Administration (018-80-0800-503), Discretionary	20.3	30.1	34.1
Institute of Education Science			
Institute of education science (018-50-1100-503), Discretionary	2.3	4.2	4.1
Office of Federal Student Aid			
Student Aid Administration (018-45-0202-502), Split	51.5	68.7	97.2
Department of Energy			
Departmental Administration			
Chief Financial Officer (019-60-0228-276), Discretionary	1.2	1.2	1.2
Chief Information Officer (019-60-0228-276), Discretionary	69.0	83.0	87.1
Energy Programs			
Geothermal Resources Development Fund (019-20-0206-271), Discretionary	0.9	0.9	0.9
Nuclear Energy (019-20-0319-999), Discretionary	20.0	18.5	22.7
Science (019-20-0222-251), Discretionary	27.5	28.9	30.5
Fossil Energy Research and Development (019-20-0213-271), Discretionary	2.6	4.0	4.1
Strategic Petroleum Reserve (019-20-0218-274), Discretionary	2.6	2.1	3.2
Electricity Delivery (019-20-0318-271), Discretionary	62.0	43.3	79.8
Energy Efficiency and Renewable Energy (019-20-0321-270), Discretionary	5.3	5.7	5.8
Environment & Other Defense Activities			
Defense Environmental Cleanup (019-10-0251-53), Discretionary	28.8	33.3	46.2
Enterprise Assessments (019-10-0243-999), Discretionary	3.8	5.3	5.9
Environment, Health, Safety and Security (019-10-0243-999), Discretionary	4.3	4.3	4.2
Legacy Management (019-10-0243-999), Discretionary	1.1	1.3	1.3
National Nuclear Security Administration			
Weapons Activities (019-05-0240-53), Discretionary	122.9	126.8	149.2
Power Marketing Administration			
O&M Western Area Power Administration (019-50-5068-271), Discretionary	6.5	7.4	8.8
O&M Southwestern Power Administration (019-50-0303-271), Discretionary	1.9	1.9	1.9

Table 21–2. CIVILIAN AGENCY CYBERSECURITY FUNDING BY ACCOUNT—Continued

(In millions of dollars)

Organization	FY 2017 Actual	FY 2018 Estimate	FY 2019 Budget
Bonneville Power Administration Fund (019-50-4045-271), Mandatory	9.7	10.7	11.8
O&M Southeastern Power Administration (019-50-0302-271), Discretionary	0.3	0.4	0.4
Department of Health & Human Services			
Administration for Children & Families			
Refugee and Entrant Assistance (009-70-1503-609), Discretionary	0.1	0.4	0.4
Children and Families Services Programs (009-70-1536-506), Split	1.4	6.0	6.3
Children's Research and Technical Assistance (009-70-1553-609), Mandatory	0.2	1.1	1.1
Administration on Aging			
Aging and Disability Services Programs (009-75-0142-506), Split	0.7	0.9	0.7
Agency for Healthcare Research			
Healthcare Research and Quality (009-33-1700-552), Split	1.5	1.5	1.5
Centers for Disease Control			
CDC-wide Activities and Program Support (009-20-0943-999), Split	30.7	33.4	36.5
Centers for Medicare and Medicaid Services			
Program Management (009-38-0511-550), Split	33.1	33.7	34.7
Departmental Management			
Nonrecurring Expenses Fund (009-90-0125-551), Discretionary	23.7	....	....
Prevention and Public Health Fund (009-90-0116-551), Mandatory	1.5	1.9	2.3
Public Health and Social Services Emergency Fund (009-90-0140-551), Discretionary	50.9	50.5	68.1
Food and Drug Administration			
Salaries and Expenses (009-10-9911-554), Split	29.2	31.0	43.9
Revolving Fund for Certification and Other Services (009-10-4309-554), Mandatory	20.8	20.5	20.5
Health Resources & Services Administration			
Health Resources and Services (009-15-0350-550), Split	6.1	6.3	10.0
Indian Health Service			
Indian Health Services (009-17-0390-551), Split	4.2	14.8	14.8
National Institutes of Health			
National Institutes of Health (009-25-9915-552), Split	73.9	73.3	76.7
Office of Inspector General			
Office of Inspector General (009-92-0128-551), Split	1.9	2.1	2.3
Program Support Center			
HHS Service and Supply Fund (009-91-9941-551), Split	32.1	30.3	30.3
Substance Abuse and Mental Health Administration			
Substance Abuse and Mental Health Services Administration (009-30-1362-551), Split	7.6	2.2	2.6
Department of Homeland Security			
Customs and Border Protection			
Operations and Support (024-58-0530-751), Split	24.5	25.4	25.4
Department of Homeland Security			
Immigration Examination Fee (024-00-508810-751), Mandatory	41.9	52.7	46.8
Department of Management and Operations			
OUSM Operations and Support (024-10-0112-999), Discretionary	88.8	109.9	128.4
OUSM Procurement, Construction, and Improvements (024-10-0406-751), Discretionary	0.8	7.6	7.6
Working Capital Fund (024-10-4640-751), Discretionary	10.5	9.4	9.4
Domestic Nuclear Detection Office			
Operations and Support (024-85-0861-999), Discretionary	3.0	3.4	3.4
Federal Emergency Management Agency			
Operations and Support (024-70-0700-999), Discretionary	27.5	24.9	42.9
Federal Law Enforcement Training Center			
Operations and Support (024-49-0509-751), Discretionary	1.0	1.0	1.0
Immigration and Customs Enforcement			
Operations and Support (024-55-0540-751), Split	73.7	79.7	89.4

Table 21–2.   CIVILIAN AGENCY CYBERSECURITY FUNDING BY ACCOUNT—Continued

(In millions of dollars)

Organization	FY 2017 Actual	FY 2018 Estimate	FY 2019 Budget
National Protection and Program Directorate			
Operations and Support (024-65-0566-999), Discretionary	590.6	669.6	785.8
Procurement, Construction, and Improvements (024-65-0412-999), Discretionary	299.2	297.1	167.6
Research and Development (024-65-0805-54), Discretionary	2.0	2.0	41.4
Office of Inspector General			
Operations and Support (024-20-0200-751), Discretionary	2.9	3.7	3.7
Science and Technology			
Operations and Support (024-80-0800-751), Discretionary	2.7	2.7	2.8
Research and Development (024-80-0803-751), Discretionary	93.5	93.5	22.8
Transportation Security Administration			
Operations and Support (024-45-0550-400), Split	96.6	96.8	96.8
United States Coast Guard			
Operations and Support (024-60-0610-999), Discretionary	160.1	160.1	165.7
United States Secret Service			
Operations and Support (024-40-0400-751), Discretionary	94.7	82.6	83.5
Research and Development (024-40-0804-751), Discretionary	0.3	0.3	0.3
Department of Housing & Urban Development			
Management and Administration			
Information Technology Fund (025-35-4586-451), Discretionary	15.2	16.6	18.7
Department of the Interior			
Bureau of Indian Affairs			
Department-wide working capital fund (010-95-4523-306), Discretionary	2.4	3.1	4.1
Operation of Indian Programs (010-76-2100-999), Discretionary	5.2	5.2	5.2
Bureau of Land Management			
Department-wide working capital fund (010-95-4523-306), Discretionary	3.9	4.5	6.1
Wildland Fire Management (010-95-1125-302), Discretionary	0.1	....	....
Oregon and California Grant Lands (010-04-1116-302), Discretionary	0.2	....	....
Management of Lands and Resources (010-04-1109-302), Discretionary	2.5	3.5	3.7
Bureau of Ocean Energy Management			
Department-wide working capital fund (010-95-4523-306), Discretionary	0.2	0.2	0.2
Ocean Energy Management (010-06-1917-302), Discretionary	0.6	0.2	0.5
Bureau of Reclamation			
Department-wide working capital fund (010-95-4523-306), Discretionary	2.0	2.2	3.0
Policy and Administration (010-10-5065-301), Discretionary	2.4	2.4	....
Water and Related Resources (010-10-0680-301), Split	1.0	1.0	1.0
Working Capital Fund (010-10-4524-301), Discretionary	8.6	9.8	7.6
Colorado River Dam Fund, Boulder Canyon Project (010-10-5656-301), Discretionary	0.4	0.4	0.4
Bureau of Safety Environmental Enforcement			
Department-wide working capital fund (010-95-4523-306), Discretionary	0.7	0.9	1.0
Offshore Safety and Environmental Enforcement (010-22-1700-302), Discretionary	0.8	0.3	0.8
Departmental Offices			
Salaries and Expenses (010-84-0102-306), Discretionary	0.8	0.2	0.7
Department-Wide Programs			
Department-wide working capital fund (010-95-4523-306), Discretionary	19.1	22.3	23.1
Wildland Fire Management (010-95-1125-302), Discretionary	0.1	0.1	0.1
Central Hazardous Materials Fund (010-95-1121-304), Discretionary	*	*	*
National Park Service			
Department-wide working capital fund (010-95-4523-306), Discretionary	8.1	9.0	12.1
Wildland Fire Management (010-95-1125-302), Discretionary	*	*	*
Operation of the National Park System (010-24-1036-303), Discretionary	6.6	4.7	4.7
Recreation Fee Permanent Appropriations (010-24-9928-303), Mandatory	0.6	0.6	0.6
Office of Inspector General			

Table 21–2. CIVILIAN AGENCY CYBERSECURITY FUNDING BY ACCOUNT—Continued

(In millions of dollars)

Organization	FY 2017 Actual	FY 2018 Estimate	FY 2019 Budget
Department-wide working capital fund (010-95-4523-306), Discretionary	0.2	0.2	0.2
Office of Insular Affairs			
Department-wide working capital fund (010-95-4523-306), Discretionary	*	*	*
Assistance to Territories (010-85-0412-808), Split	*	*	....
Office of Surface Mining Reclamation			
Department-wide working capital fund (010-95-4523-306), Discretionary	0.5	0.5	0.6
Regulation and Technology (010-08-1801-302), Discretionary	1.2	1.2	1.0
Abandoned Mine Reclamation Fund (010-08-5015-999), Split	*	*	....
Office of the Solicitor			
Department-wide working capital fund (010-95-4523-306), Discretionary	0.4	1.2	1.3
Salaries and Expenses (010-86-0107-306), Discretionary	0.5	0.4	0.4
Office of the Special Trustee for American Indians			
Department-wide working capital fund (010-95-4523-306), Discretionary	0.3	0.3	0.4
Federal Trust Programs (010-90-0120-808), Discretionary	0.4	0.5	0.4
US Fish and Wildlife Service			
Department-wide working capital fund (010-95-4523-306), Discretionary	3.1	3.8	4.8
Resource Management (010-18-1611-302), Discretionary	3.6	3.4	3.3
US Geological Survey			
Department-wide working capital fund (010-95-4523-306), Discretionary	3.1	3.6	4.8
Surveys, Investigations, and Research (010-12-0804-306), Discretionary	4.2	4.4	4.9
Department of Justice			
Bureau of Alcohol, Tobacco, Firearms, and Explosives			
Salaries and Expenses (011-14-0700-751), Discretionary	10.4	11.5	9.0
Drug Enforcement Administration			
Salaries and Expenses (011-12-1100-751), Discretionary	22.2	14.6	20.6
Federal Bureau of Investigation			
Salaries and Expenses (011-10-0200-999), Split	577.8	543.7	547.0
Federal Prison System			
Salaries and Expenses (011-20-1060-753), Discretionary	9.2	9.2	9.2
General Administration			
Working Capital Fund (011-03-4526-751), Discretionary	35.9	42.5	43.0
Justice Information Sharing Technology (011-03-0134-751), Discretionary	7.5	7.8	3.6
Legal Activities & US Marshals			
Salaries and Expenses, General Legal Activities (011-05-0128-999), Discretionary	35.4	35.9	49.4
Salaries and Expenses, United States Attorneys (011-05-0322-752), Discretionary	23.3	23.2	23.2
Salaries and Expenses, United States Marshals Service (011-05-0324-752), Discretionary	6.2	7.3	7.4
United States Trustee System Fund (011-05-5073-752), Discretionary	1.5	2.2	2.3
National Security Division			
Salaries and Expenses (011-08-1300-751), Discretionary	0.7	0.8	1.6
Office of Justice Programs			
Salaries and Expenses, Office of Justice Programs (011-21-0420-754), Discretionary	4.9	4.9	5.0
Department of Labor			
Bureau of Labor Statistics			
Salaries and Expenses (012-20-0200-505), Discretionary	8.7	8.9	8.9
Departmental Management			
Office of Inspector General (012-25-0106-505), Discretionary	0.2	0.2	0.2
Salaries and Expenses (012-25-0165-505), Discretionary	3.4	3.6	3.6
Working Capital Fund (012-25-4601-505), Discretionary	34.8	26.1	24.9
Information Technology Modernization (012-25-0162-505), Discretionary	0.3	*	*
Veterans Employment and Training (012-25-0164-702), Discretionary	0.7	0.4	0.4
Office of Disability Employment Policy (012-25-0166-505), Discretionary	0.4	0.5	0.1
Employee Benefits Security Administration			

Table 21–2.   CIVILIAN AGENCY CYBERSECURITY FUNDING BY ACCOUNT—Continued
(In millions of dollars)

Organization	FY 2017 Actual	FY 2018 Estimate	FY 2019 Budget
Salaries and Expenses (012-11-1700-601), Discretionary	4.7	3.1	3.1
Employment & Training Administration			
Program Administration (012-05-0172-504), Discretionary	1.2	1.3	1.5
Training and Employment Services (012-05-0174-504), Split	0.1	0.2	0.3
State Unemployment Insurance and Employment Service Operations (012-05-0179-999), Split	0.5	0.7	0.6
Job Corps (012-05-0181-504), Discretionary	3.0	3.1	3.1
Mine Safety and Health Administration			
Salaries and Expenses (012-19-1200-554), Discretionary	1.3	1.4	1.3
Occupation Safety & Health Administration			
Salaries and Expenses (012-18-0400-554), Discretionary	2.9	2.9	2.9
Office of Federal Contract Compliance Programs			
Salaries and Expenses (012-22-0148-505), Discretionary	0.9	0.9	0.9
Office of Labor Management Standards			
Salaries and Expenses (012-23-0150-505), Discretionary	0.1	0.1	0.1
Office of Workers' Compensation			
Salaries and Expenses (012-15-0163-505), Discretionary	0.8	0.7	0.7
Special Benefits (012-15-1521-600), Mandatory	0.9	0.7	0.7
Administrative Expenses, Energy Employees Occupational Illness Compensation Fund (012-15-1524-53), Mandatory	0.6	0.6	0.6
Black Lung Disability Trust Fund (012-15-8144-601), Mandatory	0.2	0.2	0.2
Pension Benefit Guaranty Corporation			
Pension Benefit Guaranty Corporation Fund (012-12-4204-601), Mandatory	16.8	17.5	19.0
Wage and Hour Division			
Salaries and Expenses (012-16-0143-505), Discretionary	0.7	0.6	0.9
Department of State			
Administration of Foreign Affairs			
Working Capital Fund (014-05-4519-153), Discretionary	4.8	3.7	5.7
Diplomatic and Consular Programs (014-05-0113-153), Split	246.4	263.6	254.6
Embassy Security, Construction, and Maintenance (014-05-0535-153), Discretionary	1.9	2.4	2.0
Department of State			
International Litigation Fund (014-00-517710-153), Mandatory	0.6	0.4	0.4
Other			
International Litigation Fund (014-25-5177-153), Discretionary	0.6	0.4	0.4
Department of the Treasury			
Alcohol & Tobacco Tax and Trade Bureau			
Salaries and Expenses (015-13-1008-803), Discretionary	5.0	4.1	4.5
Bureau of Engraving and Printing			
Bureau of Engraving and Printing Fund (015-20-4502-803), Discretionary	5.5	8.1	8.5
Comptroller of the Currency			
Assessment Funds (015-57-8413-373), Mandatory	33.4	35.0	36.1
Departmental Offices			
Community Development Financial Institutions Fund (015-05-1881-451), Split	0.2	0.2	0.1
Cybersecurity Enhancement Account (015-05-1855-808), Discretionary	8.4	66.6	25.2
Office of Inspector General (015-05-0106-803), Discretionary	0.1	0.1	0.1
Salaries and Expenses (015-05-0101-803), Discretionary	9.9	9.4	10.3
Treasury Inspector General for Tax Administration (015-05-0119-803), Discretionary	2.9	3.2	5.4
Treasury Franchise Fund (015-05-4560-803), Discretionary	70.4	70.4	70.4
Financial Research Fund (015-05-5590-376), Mandatory	0.9	....	....
Financial Crimes Enforcement Network			
Salaries and Expenses (015-04-0173-751), Discretionary	6.3	6.1	5.3
Fiscal Service			
Salaries and Expenses (015-12-0520-803), Split	6.1	5.2	5.7
Federal Reserve Bank Reimbursement Fund (015-12-1884-803), Mandatory	15.6	18.6	15.3

Table 21–2. CIVILIAN AGENCY CYBERSECURITY FUNDING BY ACCOUNT—Continued

(In millions of dollars)

Organization	FY 2017 Actual	FY 2018 Estimate	FY 2019 Budget
Internal Revenue Service			
Enforcement (015-45-0913-999), Discretionary	10.9	10.8	19.0
Operations Support (015-45-0919-803), Discretionary	267.7	266.6	270.1
Taxpayer Services (015-45-0912-803), Discretionary	6.6	11.0	10.9
United States Mint			
United States Mint Public Enterprise Fund (015-25-4159-803), Discretionary	8.5	14.1	13.1
Department of Transportation			
Federal Aviation Administration			
Operations (021-12-1301-402), Discretionary	50.6	83.4	90.3
Administrative Services Franchise Fund (021-12-4562-402), Discretionary	3.5	3.5	3.5
Facilities and Equipment (Airport and Airway Trust Fund) (021-12-8107-402), Split	40.2	29.9	32.4
Federal Highway Administration			
Federal-aid Highways (021-15-8083-401), Split	2.2	2.3	2.4
Federal Motor Carrier Safety Administration			
Motor Carrier Safety Operations and Programs (021-17-8159-401), Split	3.1	3.2	3.3
Federal Railroad Administration			
Safety and Operations (021-27-0700-401), Discretionary	1.7	1.7	1.6
Federal Transit Administration			
Administrative Expenses (021-36-1120-401), Discretionary	1.1	0.9	1.0
Maritime Administration			
Operations and Training (021-70-1750-403), Discretionary	1.8	1.8	2.6
National Highway Traffic Safety Administration			
Highway Traffic Safety Grants (021-18-8020-401), Split	....	....	0.8
Operations and Research (021-18-0650-401), Discretionary	....	....	0.9
Operations and Research (Highway Trust Fund) (021-18-8016-401), Split	4.0	3.6	3.0
Office of Inspector General			
Salaries and Expenses (021-56-0130-407), Discretionary	0.5	0.6	0.8
Office of the Secretary			
Cybersecurity Initiatives (021-04-0159-407), Discretionary	15.0	10.0	12.8
Office of Civil Rights (021-04-0118-407), Discretionary	0.1	0.1	....
Salaries and Expenses (021-04-0102-407), Discretionary	2.2	2.0	3.5
Working Capital Fund (021-04-4520-407), Discretionary	13.5	13.4	6.2
Working Capital Fund, Volpe National Transportation Systems Center (021-04-4522-407), Discretionary			2.7
Essential Air Service and Rural Airport Improvement Fund (021-04-5423-402), Mandatory	0.2	0.1	....
Pipeline and Hazardous Materia			
Operational Expenses (021-50-1400-407), Discretionary	0.5	0.7	0.9
St Lawrence Seaway Develop Corporation			
Saint Lawrence Seaway Development Corporation (021-40-4089-403), Mandatory	0.1	0.1	0.1
Department of Veterans Affairs			
Departmental Administration			
Information Technology Systems (029-40-0167-705), Discretionary	385.8	360.0	418.4
Environmental Protection Agency			
Environmental Protection Agency			
Hazardous Substance Superfund (020-00-8145-304), Split	5.4	5.5	8.9
Inland Oil Spill Programs (020-00-8221-304), Discretionary	....	....	*
Office of Inspector General (020-00-0112-304), Discretionary	0.4	0.4	1.3
Science and Technology (020-00-0107-304), Discretionary	5.6	0.9	3.6
Environmental Programs and Management (020-00-0108-304), Discretionary	13.6	27.8	28.1
Hazardous Waste Electronic Manifest System Fund (020-00-4330-304), Discretionary	0.1	0.1	....
State and Tribal Assistance Grants (020-00-0103-304), Discretionary	....	....	0.1
Leaking Underground Storage Tank Trust Fund (020-00-8153-999), Discretionary	....	....	*
Equal Employment Opportunity Commission			

Table 21–2. CIVILIAN AGENCY CYBERSECURITY FUNDING BY ACCOUNT—Continued

(In millions of dollars)

Organization	FY 2017 Actual	FY 2018 Estimate	FY 2019 Budget
Equal Employment Opportunity Commission			
Equal Employment Opportunity Commission (MULTIPLE ACCOUNTS-751), Split	3.9	4.1	4.5
Export-Import Bank of the United States			
Export-Import Bank of the United States			
Export-Import Bank of the United States (MULTIPLE ACCOUNTS-150), Split	3.4	2.5	2.6
Farm Credit Administration			
Farm Credit Administration			
Farm Credit Administration (352-00-4131-351), Mandatory	2.8	3.0	3.0
Federal Communications Commission			
Federal Communications Commission			
Federal Communications Commission (MULTIPLE ACCOUNTS-376), Mandatory	13.0	7.4	8.3
Federal Deposit Insurance Corporation			
Federal Deposit Insurance Corporation			
Federal Deposit Insurance Corporation (MULTIPLE ACCOUNTS-373), Split	61.5	98.0	109.8
Federal Election Commission			
Federal Election Commission			
Federal Election Commission (360-00-1600-808), Discretionary	1.0	....	....
Federal Financial Institutions Examination Council			
Federal Financial Institutions Examination Council			
Federal Financial Institutions Examination Council (MULTIPLE ACCOUNTS-376), Mandatory	*	....	....
Federal Labor Relations Authority			
Federal Labor Relations Authority			
Federal Labor Relations Authority (365-00-0100-805), Discretionary	0.2	0.2	0.2
Federal Maritime Commission			
Federal Maritime Commission			
Federal Maritime Commission (366-000100-403), Discretionary	0.5	0.3	0.3
Federal Retirement Thrift Investment Board			
Federal Retirement Thrift Investment Board			
Federal Retirement Thrift Investment Board (369-00-5290-602), Mandatory	41.0	21.6	21.4
Federal Trade Commission			
Federal Trade Commission			
Federal Trade Commission (370-00-0100-376), Discretionary	11.5	14.6	13.4
General Services Administration			
General Activities			
Government-wide Policy (023-30-0401-804), Discretionary	0.2	0.2	0.3
Working Capital Fund (023-30-4540-804), Discretionary	42.0	37.4	36.8
Federal Citizen Services Fund (023-30-4549-376), Discretionary	12.0	12.5	14.7
Acquisition Workforce Training Fund (023-30-5381-804), Mandatory	*	*	*
Real Property Activities			
Federal Buildings Fund (023-05-4542-804), Discretionary	0.1	0.1	0.1
Supply & Technology Activities			
Acquisition Services Fund (023-10-4534-804), Mandatory	11.6	15.4	15.9
Gulf Coast Ecosystem Restoration Council			
Gulf Coast Ecosystem Restoration Council			
Gulf Coast Ecosystem Restoration Council (586-00-1770-452), Mandatory	0.1	....	....
Institute of Museum and Library Services			
Institute of Museum and Library Services			
Institute of Museum and Library Services (474-00-0300-503), Discretionary	0.3	....	....
International Trade Commission			

Table 21–2. CIVILIAN AGENCY CYBERSECURITY FUNDING BY ACCOUNT—Continued

(In millions of dollars)

Organization	FY 2017 Actual	FY 2018 Estimate	FY 2019 Budget
International Trade Commission			
International Trade Commission (378-00-0100-153), Discretionary	2.5	3.3	3.3
Marine Mammal Commission			
Marine Mammal Commission			
Marine Mammal Commission (387-00-2200-302), Discretionary	0.1	*	....
Merit Systems Protection Board			
Merit Systems Protection Board			
Merit Systems Protection Board (389-00-0100-805), Discretionary	0.2	0.9	1.0
Morris K. Udall and Stewart L. Udall Foundation			
Morris K. Udall and Stewart L. Udall Foundation			
Morris K. Udall and Stewart L. Udall Foundation (MULTIPLE ACCOUNTS-999), Split	*	*	*
National Aeronautics & Space Administration			
National Aeronautics & Space Administration			
Aeronautics (026-00-0126-402), Discretionary	0.7	1.3	1.3
Education (026-00-0128-252), Discretionary	*	....	....
Science (026-00-0120-252), Discretionary	14.3	25.1	25.6
Working Capital Fund (026-00-4546-252), Discretionary	26.8	20.3	20.8
LEO and Spaceflight Operations (026-00-0115-252), Discretionary	12.0	21.1	21.6
Safety, Security and Mission Services (026-00-0122-252), Discretionary	89.7	106.3	108.1
Deep Space Exploration Systems (026-00-0124-252), Discretionary	4.5	7.8	8.0
Construction and Environmental Compliance and Restoration (026-00-0130-252), Discretionary	0.1	0.1	0.1
Exploration Research and Technology (026-00-0131-252), Discretionary	0.2	0.4	0.4
National Archives and Records Administration			
National Archives and Records Administration			
National Archives and Records Administration (MULTIPLE ACCOUNTS-804), Split	6.6	8.3	8.5
National Credit Union Administration			
National Credit Union Administration			
National Credit Union Administration (MULTIPLE ACCOUNTS-300), Split	4.1	5.0	8.2
National Endowment for the Arts			
National Endowment for the Arts			
National Endowment for the Arts (MULTIPLE ACCOUNTS-503), Split	0.5	1.3	0.6
National Endowment for the Humanities			
National Endowment for the Humanities			
National Endowment for the Humanities (MULTIPLE ACCOUNTS-503), Split	0.2	0.2	....
National Labor Relations Board			
National Labor Relations Board			
National Labor Relations Board (420-00-0100-505), Discretionary	1.6	1.6	....
National Science Foundation			
National Science Foundation			
Agency Operations and Award Management (422-00-0180-251), Discretionary	7.7	8.3	7.7
Education and Human Resources (422-00-0106-251), Split	1.7	1.3	1.6
Research and Related Activities (422-00-0100-999), Discretionary	173.3	158.0	144.1
National Transportation Safety Board			
National Transportation Safety Board			
National Transportation Safety Board (MULTIPLE ACCOUNTS-407), Discretionary	0.8	1.8	2.3
Nuclear Regulatory Commission			
Nuclear Regulatory Commission			
Office of Inspector General (429-00-0300-276), Discretionary	0.4	0.4	0.7
Salaries and Expenses (429-00-0200-276), Discretionary	22.3	23.6	31.6
Nuclear Waste Technical Review Board			
Nuclear Waste Technical Review Board			
Nuclear Waste Technical Review Board (431-00-0500-271), Discretionary	0.2	0.3	0.3

Table 21–2. CIVILIAN AGENCY CYBERSECURITY FUNDING BY ACCOUNT—Continued

(In millions of dollars)

Organization	FY 2017 Actual	FY 2018 Estimate	FY 2019 Budget
Occupational Safety and Health Review Commission			
Occupational Safety and Health Review Commission			
Occupational Safety and Health Review Commission (432-00-2100-554), Discretionary	1.2	1.3	2.2
Office of Government Ethics			
Office of Government Ethics			
Office of Government Ethics (434-00-1100-805), Discretionary	0.3	0.2	0.4
Office of Personnel Management			
Office of Personnel Management			
Office of Inspector General (027-00-0400-805), Discretionary	4.3	5.2	7.8
Revolving Fund (027-00-4571-805), Mandatory	14.0	14.8	14.6
Salaries and Expenses (027-00-0100-805), Discretionary	19.2	18.4	23.2
Office of Special Counsel			
Office of Special Counsel			
Office of Special Counsel (436-00-0100-805), Discretionary	0.4	0.8	0.6
Presidio Trust			
Presidio Trust			
Presidio Trust (512-00-4331-303), Discretionary	0.7	0.7	0.6
Privacy and Civil Liberties Oversight Board			
Privacy and Civil Liberties Oversight Board			
Privacy and Civil Liberties Oversight Board (535-002724-54), Discretionary	0.9	0.8	0.9
Securities and Exchange Commission			
Securities and Exchange Commission			
SEC Reserve Fund (449-00-5566-376), Mandatory	8.0	5.1	1.4
SEC S&E (449-00-0100-376), Discretionary	34.2	63.0	59.4
Selective Service System			
Selective Service System			
Selective Service System (200-45-0400-54), Discretionary	1.0	0.9	1.4
Small Business Administration			
Small Business Administration			
Business Loans Program Account (028-00-1154-376), Split	1.8	1.8	1.3
Disaster Loans Program Account (028-00-1152-453), Split	3.3	3.1	2.5
Salaries and Expenses (028-00-0100-376), Discretionary	14.4	13.9	13.6
Smithsonian Institution			
Smithsonian Institution			
Smithsonian Institution (MULTIPLE ACCOUNTS-503), Discretionary	5.1	5.6	6.8
Social Security Administration			
Social Security Administration			
Limitation on Administrative Expenses (016-00-8704-651), Discretionary	156.3	177.1	190.6
Tennessee Valley Authority			
Tennessee Valley Authority			
Tennessee Valley Authority (455-00-4110-999), Split	30.3	30.2	28.8
U.S. Agency for International Development			
Agency for International Development			
Operating Expenses of the Agency for International Development (184-15-1000-151), Discretionary	36.5	45.1	37.3
U.S. Army Corps of Engineers			
Corps of Engineers--Civil Works			
Corps of Engineers--Civil Works (MULTIPLE ACCOUNTS-999), Split	23.3	23.8	25.2
United States Holocaust Memorial Museum			
United States Holocaust Memorial Museum			
United States Holocaust Memorial Museum (456-00-3300-503), Discretionary	1.3	1.3	1.3
United States Institute of Peace			

Table 21–2.   CIVILIAN AGENCY CYBERSECURITY FUNDING BY ACCOUNT—Continued

(In millions of dollars)

Organization	FY 2017 Actual	FY 2018 Estimate	FY 2019 Budget
United States Institute of Peace			
United States Institute of Peace (458-00-1300-153), Discretionary	0.3	....	....
African Development Foundation			
African Development Foundation			
African Development Foundation (MULTIPLE ACCOUNTS-151), Split	0.6	1.0	....
Inter-American Foundation			
Inter-American Foundation			
Inter-American Foundation (184-40-1300-151), Discretionary	0.4	0.4	....
Overseas Private Investment Corporation			
Overseas Private Investment Corporation			
Overseas Private Investment Corporation (MULTIPLE ACCOUNTS-151), Split	3.0	3.1	3.5
Peace Corps			
Peace Corps			
Peace Corps (MULTIPLE ACCOUNTS-151), Split	10.0	10.4	10.9
Trade and Development Agency			
Trade and Development Agency			
Trade and Development Agency (184-25-1001-151), Discretionary	0.3	0.3	1.0
Grand Total	5,928.0	6,242.9	6,486.3

* $50 thousand or less.

22. FEDERAL DRUG CONTROL FUNDING

The FY 2019 Budget supports $29.9 billion for National Drug Control Program agencies to implement the Administration's drug control policies. The funding requested by each Department and agency in the National Drug Control Program is included in the table below.

Table 22–1.   DRUG CONTROL FUNDING FY 2017—FY 2019
(Budget authority, in millions of dollars)

Department/Agency	FY 2017 Final	FY 2018 CR	FY 2019 President's Budget
Department of Agriculture:			
U.S. Forest Service	12.30	12.22	14.80
Court Services and Offender Supervision Agency for D.C.:	57.41	56.35	57.15
Department of Defense:			
Drug Interdiction and Counterdrug Activities [1] (incl. OPTEMPO, DSCA, and OCO)	1,280.15	1,273.07	1,154.54
Defense Health Program	80.03	77.14	77.01
Total DOD	1,360.18	1,350.21	1,231.55
Department of Education:			
Office of Elementary and Secondary Education	48.89	48.68	43.00
Federal Judiciary:	1,041.09	1,053.47	1,083.31
Department of Health and Human Services: [2]			
Administration for Children and Families	18.62	18.62	60.00
Centers for Disease Control and Prevention	125.40	124.73	225.58
Centers for Medicare and Medicaid Services [3]	7,050.00	7,400.00	7,690.00
Drug Prevention and Treatment Activities	0.00	0.00	85.00
Health Resources and Services Administration	173.00	173.00	238.00
Indian Health Service	114.37	109.96	159.61
National Institute on Alcohol Abuse and Alcoholism	50.64	50.16	36.53
National Institute on Drug Abuse	1,070.81	1,083.45	839.82
Substance Abuse and Mental Health Services Administration (incl. DFC in FY 2019) [4,5]	3,033.11	3,012.54	3,144.71
Total HHS	11,635.95	11,972.45	12,479.24
Department of Homeland Security:			
Customs and Border Protection	2,799.66	2,799.66	3,207.34
Federal Emergency Management Agency	8.25	8.25	6.19
Federal Law Enforcement Training Center	43.58	43.24	53.45
Immigration and Customs Enforcement	534.42	623.87	587.99
U.S. Coast Guard	1,343.96	1,483.76	1,246.33
Total DHS	4,729.86	4,958.77	5,101.29
Department of Housing and Urban Development:			
Office of Community Planning and Development	513.61	494.22	542.20
Department of the Interior:			
Bureau of Indian Affairs	9.72	9.72	11.29
Bureau of Land Management	5.10	5.10	5.10
National Park Service	3.30	3.30	2.96
Total DOI	18.12	18.12	19.35

Table 22–1. DRUG CONTROL FUNDING FY 2017—FY 2019—Continued
(Budget authority, in millions of dollars)

Department/Agency	FY 2017 Final	FY 2018 CR	FY 2019 President's Budget
Department of Justice:			
Assets Forfeiture Fund	222.64	231.70	231.97
Bureau of Prisons	3,345.36	3,344.59	3,346.62
Criminal Division	40.27	40.09	40.00
Drug Enforcement Administration (incl. HIDTA in FY 2019)[6]	2,457.94	2,478.67	2,862.16
Organized Crime Drug Enforcement Task Force	517.00	513.49	521.56
Office of Justice Programs	210.48	228.80	167.12
U.S. Attorneys	75.86	78.10	78.85
Unites States Marshals Service	787.15	776.00	810.74
Total DOJ	**7,656.70**	**7,691.43**	**8,059.03**
Department of Labor:			
Employment and Training Administration	**6.00**	**6.00**	**6.00**
Office of National Drug Control Policy:			
Operations	19.27	19.14	17.40
High Intensity Drug Trafficking Areas Program[6]	254.00	252.28	0.00
Other Federal Drug Control Programs[5]	114.87	114.09	11.84
Total ONDCP	**388.15**	**385.51**	**29.24**
Department of State:[7]			
Bureau of International Narcotics and Law Enforcement Affairs	392.93	390.27	288.96
United States Agency for International Development	107.93	107.20	70.52
Total DOS	**500.87**	**497.47**	**359.49**
Department of the Transportation:			
Federal Aviation Administration	29.29	33.06	33.63
National Highway Traffic Safety Administration	3.45	2.72	2.72
Total DOT	**32.74**	**35.78**	**36.35**
Department of the Treasury:			
Internal Revenue Service	**60.26**	**60.26**	**60.26**
Department of Veterans Affairs:			
Veterans Health Administration	**750.44**	**778.83**	**806.91**
Total Federal Drug Budget[8]	**$28,812.56**	**$29,419.75**	**$29,929.15**

[1] Due to statutory changes included in the FY 2017 National Defense Authorization Act that consolidated the Department of Defense's (DOD) security sector assistance authorities, funding for building foreign partner counter-drug enforcement capacities is now included in DOD's Defense Security Cooperation Agency's budget request.

[2] FY 2019 HHS funding levels include $1 billion in new funding to combat the opioid epidemic as part of the Budget proposal to repeal and replace Obamacare.

[3] The estimates for the Centers for Medicare & Medicaid Services reflect Medicaid and Medicare benefit outlays for substance abuse treatment; they do not reflect budget authority. The estimates were developed by the CMS Office of the Actuary.

[4] Includes budget authority and funding through evaluation set-aside authorized by Section 241 of the Public Health Service (PHS) Act.

[5] The FY 2019 funding level for SAMHSA includes $100 million for the Drug-Free Communities (DFC) program. For FY 2017 and FY 2018, DFC is included under the Office of National Drug Control Policy heading.

[6] The FY 2019 funding level for DEA includes $254 million for the High Intensity Drug Trafficking Areas (HIDTA) program. For FY 2017 and FY 2018, HIDTA is included under the Office of National Drug Control Policy heading.

[7] Funding for FY 2018 is a mechanical calculation that does not reflect decisions on funding priorities.

[8] Detail may not sum to total due to rounding.

TECHNICAL BUDGET ANALYSES

23. CURRENT SERVICES ESTIMATES

Current services, or "baseline," estimates are designed to provide a benchmark against which budget proposals can be measured. A baseline is not a prediction of the final outcome of the annual budget process, nor is it a proposed budget. It can be a useful tool in budgeting, however. It can be used as a benchmark against which to measure the magnitude of the policy changes in the President's Budget or other budget proposals, and it can also be used to warn of future problems if policy is not changed, either for the Government's overall fiscal health or for individual tax and spending programs.

Ideally, a current services baseline would provide a projection of estimated receipts, outlays, deficits or surpluses, and budget authority reflecting this year's enacted policies and programs for each year in the future. Defining this baseline is challenging because funding for many programs in operation today expires within the 10-year budget window. Most significantly, funding for discretionary programs is provided one year at a time in annual appropriations acts. Mandatory programs are not generally subject to annual appropriations, but many operate under multi-year authorizations that expire within the budget window. The framework used to construct the baseline must address whether and how to project forward the funding for these programs beyond their scheduled expiration dates.

Since the early 1970s, when the first requirements for the calculation of a "current services" baseline were enacted, the baseline has been constructed using a variety of concepts and measures. Throughout the 1990s, the baseline was calculated using a detailed set of rules enacted through amendments to the Balanced Budget and Emergency Deficit Control Act of 1985 (BBEDCA) made by the Budget Enforcement Act of 1990 (BEA). The BBEDCA baseline rules lapsed after the enforcement provisions of the BEA expired in 2002, but even after the lapse they were largely adhered to in practice until they were

Table 23–1. CATEGORY TOTALS FOR THE ADJUSTED BASELINE
(In billions of dollars)

	2017	2018	2019	2020	2021	2022	2023	2024	2025	2026	2027	2028
Receipts	3,316	3,340	3,424	3,613	3,833	4,095	4,389	4,678	4,948	5,233	5,508	5,820
Outlays:												
Discretionary:												
Defense	590	611	637	668	678	690	705	719	737	755	774	793
Non-defense	610	661	656	659	670	669	676	689	705	721	738	756
Subtotal, discretionary	1,200	1,271	1,293	1,327	1,349	1,359	1,381	1,408	1,442	1,476	1,512	1,549
Mandatory:												
Social Security	939	987	1,047	1,109	1,174	1,245	1,319	1,398	1,480	1,566	1,656	1,752
Medicare	591	582	640	688	743	845	876	902	1,005	1,103	1,196	1,353
Medicaid and CHIP	391	415	426	445	469	496	524	555	588	630	667	706
Other mandatory	597	605	618	631	656	700	704	709	738	802	824	878
Subtotal, mandatory	2,519	2,588	2,731	2,873	3,042	3,286	3,423	3,564	3,811	4,100	4,343	4,689
Net interest	263	310	364	447	515	577	636	684	727	772	815	859
Total, outlays	3,982	4,170	4,388	4,647	4,906	5,222	5,439	5,656	5,980	6,348	6,670	7,098
Unified deficit(+)/surplus(–)	665	829	964	1,033	1,073	1,127	1,051	978	1,032	1,115	1,162	1,277
(On-budget)	(715)	(824)	(955)	(1,000)	(1,029)	(1,070)	(975)	(887)	(925)	(1,003)	(1,035)	(1,142)
(Off-budget)	(–49)	(5)	(9)	(33)	(44)	(57)	(76)	(91)	(107)	(112)	(127)	(135)
Memoranda:												
BBEDCA baseline deficit	665	829	964	1,033	1,073	1,139	1,067	996	1,052	1,026	954	1,052
Extension of expiring tax provisions	....	....	....	....	....	....	....	....	....	109	224	236
Assume Highway Trust Fund outlays conform to Highway Trust Fund revenues	....	....	....	....	....	–12	–16	–17	–18	–19	–20	–21
Related debt service	....	....	....	....	....	–*	–1	–1	–2	–1	4	10
Adjusted baseline deficit	665	829	964	1,033	1,073	1,127	1,051	978	1,032	1,115	1,162	1,277
Adjusted baseline totals with pre-policy economic assumptions:												
Receipts	3,316	3,340	3,419	3,597	3,804	4,051	4,329	4,600	4,850	5,115	5,366	5,650
Outlays	3,982	4,170	4,388	4,647	4,906	5,223	5,442	5,661	5,986	6,357	6,682	7,113
Deficit	665	829	969	1,049	1,103	1,173	1,114	1,061	1,136	1,242	1,316	1,462

* Less than $500 million.

officially reinstated through amendments to BBEDCA enacted in the Budget Control Act of 2011 (BCA).

The Administration believes adjustments to the BBEDCA baseline are needed to better represent the deficit outlook under current policy and to serve as a more appropriate benchmark against which to measure policy changes. These adjustments, which affect tax receipts and the Highway Trust Fund, allow the baseline to provide a more realistic outlook for receipts and for the highway program than a baseline following the BBEDCA rules. These baseline adjustments are discussed in more detail below. Table 23–1 shows estimates of receipts, outlays, and deficits under the Administration's adjusted baseline for 2017 through 2028.[1] The table also shows the Administration's estimates by major component of the budget. The estimates are based on the economic assumptions underlying the Budget, which, as discussed later in this chapter, were developed on the assumption that the Administration's budget proposals will be enacted. A memorandum bank details the adjustments made to the BBEDCA baseline to produce the adjusted baseline, and also shows estimates of the adjusted baseline totals under "pre-policy" economic assumptions that do not include the economic impact of the Administration's proposals.

Conceptual Basis for Estimates

Receipts and outlays are divided into two categories that are important for calculating the baseline: those controlled by authorizing legislation (receipts and direct or mandatory spending) and those controlled through the annual appropriations process (discretionary spending). Different estimating rules apply to each category.

Direct spending and receipts.—Direct spending includes the major entitlement programs, such as Social Security, Medicare, Medicaid, Federal employee retirement, unemployment compensation, and the Supplemental Nutrition Assistance Program (SNAP). It also includes such programs as deposit insurance and farm price and income supports, where the Government is legally obligated to make payments under certain conditions. Taxes and other receipts are like direct spending in that they involve ongoing activities that generally operate under permanent or long-standing authority, and the underlying statutes generally specify the tax rates or benefit levels that must be collected or paid, and who must pay or who is eligible to receive benefits.

The baseline generally—but not always—assumes that receipts and direct spending programs continue in the future as specified by current law.[2] The budgetary effects of anticipated regulatory and administrative actions that are permissible under current law are also reflected in the estimates. BBEDCA requires several exemptions to this general rule, and the Administration's adjusted baseline

also provides exceptions to produce a more realistic deficit outlook. Exceptions in BBEDCA and the Administration's adjusted baseline are described below:

- Expiring excise taxes dedicated to a trust fund are assumed to be extended at the rates in effect at the time of expiration. During the projection period of 2018 through 2028, the taxes affected by this exception are:

  — taxes deposited in the Airport and Airway Trust Fund, which expire on March 31, 2018;

  — taxes deposited in the Patient-Centered Outcomes Research Trust Fund, which expire on September 30, 2019;

  — taxes deposited in the Sport Fish Restoration and Boating Resources Trust Fund, which expire on September 30, 2020; and

  — taxes deposited in the Highway Trust Fund and the Leaking Underground Storage Tank Trust Fund, which expire on September 30, 2022.

- While BBEDCA requires the extension of trust fund excise taxes, it otherwise bases the receipt estimates on current law. Individual income tax and estate tax provisions of the recently enacted Tax Cuts and Jobs Act that expire after tax year 2025 are assumed to expire according to current law in the BBEDCA baseline. However, the Administration's adjusted baseline extends these provisions permanently. This results in a more realistic outlook for receipts and the deficit, reflecting the likely extension of these provisions.

- Expiring authorizations for direct spending programs that were enacted on or before the date of enactment of the Balanced Budget Act of 1997 are assumed to be extended if their current year outlays exceed $50 million. For example, even though the Environmental Quality Incentives Program, which was authorized prior to the Balanced Budget Act of 1997, continues only through 2018 under current law, the baseline estimates assume continuation of this program through the projection period, because the program's current year outlays exceed the $50 million threshold.[3]

Discretionary spending.—Discretionary programs differ in one important aspect from direct spending programs: the Congress provides spending authority for almost all discretionary programs one year at a time. The spending authority is normally provided in the form of annual appropriations. Absent appropriations of additional funds in the future, discretionary programs would cease to operate after existing balances were spent. If the baseline were intended strictly to reflect current law, then a baseline would reflect only the expenditure of remaining balances from appropriations laws already enacted.

---

[1] The estimates are shown on a unified budget basis; i.e., the off-budget receipts and outlays of the Social Security trust funds and the Postal Service Fund are added to the on-budget receipts and outlays to calculate the unified budget totals.

[2] The Budget estimates were finalized prior to enactment of Public Law 115-120, so do not include the reauthorization of the Children's Health Insurance Program and amendments to the tax code in that law.

[3] For programs enacted after the Balanced Budget Act of 1997, programs that are explicitly temporary in nature expire in the baseline as provided by current law even if their current year outlays exceed the $50 million threshold.

Instead, the BBEDCA baseline provides a mechanical definition to reflect the continuing costs of discretionary programs. Under BBEDCA, the baseline estimates for discretionary programs in the current year are based on that year's enacted appropriations, or on the annualized levels provided by a continuing resolution if final full-year appropriations have not been enacted.[4] For the budget year and beyond, the spending authority in the current year is adjusted for inflation, using specified inflation rates.[5] The definition attempts to keep discretionary spending for each program roughly level in real terms.

BBEDCA also imposes caps through 2021 on budget authority for the defense function and for the aggregate of the non-defense functions. These caps were initially established by the BCA, and subsequent legislation later amended the caps through 2017. The baseline includes allowances that bring the inflated baseline calculated for individual discretionary accounts down to the level of the defense and non-defense caps. After 2021, these allowances assume that discretionary spending grows with inflation from the 2021 cap levels.

BBEDCA allows for adjustments to the discretionary caps for disaster relief spending, emergency requirements, Overseas Contingency Operations (OCO), and certain program integrity activities. The adjustments are permitted provided that such funding is designated in legislation by the Congress and, where appropriate, subsequently so by the President. Current adjustments include the following:

- Disaster relief and emergency requirements.—The BBEDCA baseline projects forward the $6.7 billion of continuing disaster relief funding for disasters pursuant to Stafford Act declarations for the Department of Homeland Security in 2018. This funding is increased thereafter by the BBEDCA inflation rates but held at the projected funding ceiling for such appropriations determined by a formula included in BBEDCA. The baseline also inflates the $23.6 billion of enacted emergency funding provided to the Departments of Agriculture, Defense, Homeland Security, and the Interior for missile defense and emergency response and recovery efforts to natural disasters, including Hurricanes Harvey, Irma, Maria, and the 2017 wildfires. The baseline does not reflect the pending request of $44 billion that the Administra-

tion transmitted on November 17, 2017 for continuing response and recovery efforts.

- OCO.—The BBEDCA baseline reflects the annualized level of OCO appropriations included in the 2018 continuing resolution inflated at the BBEDCA inflation rates.

- Program integrity activities.—The baseline assumes annualized levels provided in the 2018 continuing resolution and full funding for the program integrity cap adjustments authorized in BBEDCA through 2021, and inflates those amounts after the cap adjustments expire in 2021. Additionally, the baseline assumes savings in mandatory benefit payments from enacting the program integrity cap adjustments at their full levels after 2018.

In addition to the cap adjustments specified in BBEDCA, the 21st Century CURES Act permitted funds to be appropriated each year and not count towards the discretionary caps so long as the appropriations were specified for the authorized purposes. These amounts are included in the baseline outside of the discretionary cap totals and adjusted for inflation in the budget year and beyond.

As noted above, the Administration believes an adjustment to the BBEDCA baseline for the Highway Trust Fund is needed to better represent the outlook for the program under current law. Under the BBEDCA baseline, obligation limitations for the Highway Trust Fund are inflated from the annualized level in the Continuing Appropriations Act, 2018 (Division D of PL, 115-56), as amended, resulting in outlays that exceed available balances in the fund starting in 2022. By contrast, the Administration's adjusted baseline assumes Highway Trust Fund outlays are limited starting in 2022 to levels that can be supported with existing Highway Trust Fund tax receipts. This presentation shows a reduction in total Highway Trust Fund outlays of $121 billion over the 2022-2028 window as would be required by law.

Joint Committee Enforcement.—The Joint Select Committee process under the BCA stipulated that, absent intervening legislation, enforcement procedures would be invoked annually to reduce the levels of discretionary and mandatory spending to accomplish certain deficit reduction. The BBEDCA baseline includes the effects of the across-the-board reductions ("sequestration") already invoked by Joint Committee sequestration orders for 2013 through 2018, as well as the discretionary cap reductions and mandatory sequestration order for 2019 issued with the transmittal of the 2019 Budget.[6] Further Joint Committee enforcement—consisting of mandatory sequestration and discretionary cap reductions for 2020 and 2021—is reflected in the BBEDCA baseline in the form

---

[4] As of the preparation of the baseline for the 2019 Budget, most discretionary appropriations were operating under the Continuing Appropriations Act, 2018 (Division D of P.L. 115-56), as amended. See the note at the beginning of this volume for additional details.

[5] The Administration's baseline uses the same inflation rates for discretionary spending as required by BBEDCA, despite the fact that this allows for an overcompensation for Federal pay inherent in the BBEDCA definition. At the time the BEA was enacted, it failed to account for the nearly contemporaneous enactment of the Federal Employees Compensation Act of 1991 that shifted the effective date of Federal employee pay raises from October to January. This oversight was not corrected when the baseline definition was reinstated by the BCA amendments to BBEDCA. Correcting for this error would have only a small effect on the discretionary baseline.

[6] The effects of past sequestration reductions are reflected in the detailed schedules for the affected budget accounts, while the 2019 reductions are reflected in allowance accounts due to the timing of the preparation of the detailed budget estimates and the issuance of the 2019 sequestration order. See Chapter 10, "Budget Process," of this volume for a more thorough discussion of the Joint Committee sequestration procedures.

Table 23–2. SUMMARY OF ECONOMIC ASSUMPTIONS

(Fiscal years; in billions of dollars)

	2017	2018	2019	2020	2021	2022	2023	2024	2025	2026	2027	2028
Gross Domestic Product (GDP):												
Levels, in billions of dollars:												
Current dollars	19,177	20,029	21,003	22,069	23,194	24,369	25,605	26,900	28,253	29,647	31,089	32,602
Real, chained (2009) dollars	16,986	17,467	18,015	18,585	19,154	19,729	20,321	20,930	21,550	22,167	22,788	23,426
Percent change, year over year:												
Current dollars	3.8	4.4	4.9	5.1	5.1	5.1	5.1	5.1	5.0	4.9	4.9	4.9
Real, chained (2009) dollars	2.1	2.8	3.1	3.2	3.1	3.0	3.0	3.0	3.0	2.9	2.8	2.8
Inflation measures (percent change, year over year):												
GDP chained price index	1.7	1.6	1.7	1.9	2.0	2.0	2.0	2.0	2.0	2.0	2.0	2.0
Consumer price index (all urban)	2.1	2.1	1.9	2.1	2.3	2.3	2.3	2.3	2.3	2.3	2.3	2.3
Unemployment rate, civilian (percent)	4.5	4.0	3.8	3.7	3.9	4.0	4.2	4.3	4.5	4.6	4.8	4.8
Interest rates (percent):												
91-day Treasury bills	0.7	1.4	2.1	2.8	3.0	3.0	2.9	2.9	2.9	2.9	2.9	2.9
10-year Treasury notes	2.3	2.5	3.0	3.3	3.6	3.7	3.7	3.7	3.7	3.6	3.6	3.6
MEMORANDUM:												
Related program assumptions:												
Automatic benefit increases (percent):												
Social security and veterans pensions	0.3	2.0	2.4	2.0	2.2	2.3	2.3	2.3	2.3	2.3	2.3	2.3
Federal employee retirement	0.3	2.0	2.4	2.0	2.2	2.3	2.3	2.3	2.3	2.3	2.3	2.3
Supplemental Nutrition Assistance Program	....	....	0.8	2.0	2.2	2.3	2.3	2.3	2.3	2.3	2.3	2.3
Insured unemployment rate	1.4	1.3	1.3	1.3	1.3	1.3	1.3	1.3	1.3	1.4	1.4	1.4

of allowances in the amount of the required reductions. As with the allowances to reach the unreduced BBEDCA caps, after 2021, the allowances for the Joint Committee cap reductions assume that the reduced level of discretionary spending grows with inflation from the 2021 levels. Pursuant to subsequent legislation, the BBEDCA baseline also includes the extension of mandatory sequestration through 2025 at the rate required for 2021 by the BCA.[7]

Economic Assumptions

As discussed above, an important purpose of the baseline is to serve as a benchmark against which policy proposals are measured. By convention, President's Budgets construct baseline and policy estimates under the same set of economic and technical assumptions. These assumptions are developed on the basis that the President's Budget proposals will be enacted.

While this estimating approach has the virtue of simplicity, it offers an incomplete view of the effects of proposals, because it fails to capture the fact that the economy and the budget interact. Government tax and spending policies can influence prices, economic growth, consumption, savings, and investment. In turn, changes

in economic conditions due to the enactment of proposals affect tax receipts and spending, including for unemployment benefits, entitlement payments that receive automatic cost-of-living adjustments (COLAs), income support programs for low-income individuals, and interest on the Federal debt.

Because of these interactions, it would be reasonable, from an economic perspective, to assume different economic paths for the baseline projection and the President's Budget. However, this would greatly complicate the process of producing the Budget, which normally includes a large number of proposals that could have potential economic feedback effects. Agencies would have to produce two sets of estimates for programs sensitive to economic assumptions even if those programs were not directly affected by any proposal in the Budget. Using different economic assumptions for baseline and policy estimates would also diminish the value of the baseline estimates as a benchmark for measuring proposed policy changes, because it would be difficult to separate the effects of proposed policy changes from the effects of different economic assumptions. Using the same economic assumptions for the baseline and the President's Budget eliminates this potential source of confusion.

The economic assumptions underlying the Budget and the Administration's baseline are summarized in Table 23–2. The economic outlook underlying these assumptions is discussed in greater detail in Chapter 2 of this volume.

---

[7] The Bipartisan Budget Act of 2013 (P.L. 113-67) extended mandatory sequestration through 2023, at the rate required for 2021 by the BCA. The Military Retired Pay Restoration Act (P.L. 113-82) extended mandatory sequestration through 2024. The Bipartisan Budget Act of 2015 (P.L. 114-74) further extended mandatory sequestration through 2025. This Act also specified for 2025 that the Medicare program should be reduced by 4.0 percent for the first half of the sequestration period and zero for the second half of the period.

Table 23–3. BASELINE BENEFICIARY PROJECTIONS FOR MAJOR BENEFIT PROGRAMS
(Annual average, in thousands)

	Actual 2017	Estimate										
		2018	2019	2020	2021	2022	2023	2024	2025	2026	2027	2028
Farmers receiving Federal payments	1,052	1,047	1,042	1,036	1,031	1,026	1,021	1,016	1,011	1,006	1,001	996
Federal direct student loans	8,696	8,785	8,884	8,955	8,999	9,041	9,084	9,167	9,220	9,273	9,314	9,364
Federal Pell Grants	7,168	7,399	7,544	7,705	7,894	8,064	8,217	8,358	8,503	8,649	8,796	8,940
Medicaid/Children's Health Insurance Program [1]	79,051	79,674	79,955	81,446	82,602	83,575	84,441	85,179	85,918	86,648	87,388	88,138
Medicare-eligible military retiree health benefits	2,358	2,380	2,400	2,419	2,438	2,461	2,484	2,508	2,532	2,532	2,532	2,532
Medicare: [2]												
Hospital insurance	57,636	59,096	60,708	62,460	64,245	66,047	67,823	69,551	71,292	73,019	74,676	76,274
Supplementary medical insurance:												
Part B	53,137	54,443	55,853	57,481	59,130	60,798	62,466	64,061	65,675	67,297	68,837	70,328
Part D	44,130	45,567	47,143	48,805	50,465	52,079	53,592	54,983	56,358	57,726	59,038	60,303
Prescription Drug Plans and Medicare:												
Advantage Prescription Drug Plans	42,403	44,129	45,974	47,857	49,550	51,138	52,626	53,991	55,342	56,685	57,973	59,216
Retiree Drug Subsidy	1,727	1,438	1,170	948	915	941	966	991	1,016	1,041	1,065	1,088
Managed Care Enrollment [3]	19,453	20,764	21,819	22,680	23,557	24,458	25,350	26,209	27,051	27,882	28,680	29,441
Railroad retirement	517	513	509	503	497	491	483	476	468	460	452	445
Federal civil service retirement	2,678	2,704	2,730	2,758	2,786	2,815	2,843	2,867	2,890	2,915	2,939	2,962
Military retirement	2,280	2,293	2,304	2,314	2,324	2,335	2,345	2,375	2,380	2,384	2,385	2,385
Unemployment insurance	5,828	5,592	5,843	5,946	6,071	6,207	6,288	6,374	6,468	6,557	6,662	6,693
Supplemental Nutrition Assistance Program (formerly Food Stamps)	42,165	42,164	40,818	39,187	38,879	38,675	38,489	38,320	38,168	38,083	38,026	37,697
Child nutrition	34,821	35,281	35,708	36,138	36,501	36,797	37,096	37,399	37,706	38,017	38,332	38,651
Foster care, Adoption Assistance and Guardianship Assistance	611	667	704	744	786	826	868	912	956	1,000	1,044	1,090
Supplemental security income (SSI):												
Aged	1,114	1,121	1,126	1,135	1,145	1,158	1,171	1,187	1,205	1,224	1,243	1,261
Blind/disabled	6,986	6,922	6,893	6,929	6,963	6,997	7,036	7,082	7,133	7,173	7,208	7,242
Total, SSI	8,100	8,042	8,019	8,064	8,108	8,154	8,208	8,269	8,338	8,397	8,451	8,503
Child care and development fund (CCDF) [4]	1,816	1,692	1,525	1,477	1,432	1,391	1,351	1,311	1,273	1,236	1,199	1,165
Social security (OASDI):												
Old age and survivors insurance	50,597	52,104	53,708	55,360	56,935	58,487	60,063	61,667	63,230	64,774	66,271	67,856
Disability insurance	10,563	10,463	10,421	10,437	10,519	10,622	10,711	10,786	10,892	11,000	11,112	11,140
Total, OASDI	61,161	62,567	64,129	65,797	67,454	69,109	70,774	72,453	74,122	75,774	77,383	78,996
Veterans compensation:												
Veterans	4,456	4,656	4,850	5,039	5,206	5,361	5,512	5,661	5,806	5,947	6,083	6,215
Survivors (non-veterans)	406	421	432	445	459	475	491	509	527	547	567	587
Total, Veterans compensation	4,862	5,077	5,283	5,485	5,665	5,835	6,003	6,169	6,333	6,493	6,650	6,802
Veterans pensions:												
Veterans	282	274	269	266	265	265	266	267	269	270	271	273
Survivors (non-veterans)	202	201	200	201	202	204	206	209	211	213	215	217
Total, Veterans pensions	483	474	469	467	468	470	473	476	479	483	486	490

[1] Medicaid enrollment excludes territories.

[2] Medicare figures (Hospital Insurance, Part B, and Part D) do not sum to total Medicare enrollment due to enrollment in multiple programs.

[3] Enrollment figures include only beneficiaries who receive both Part A and Part B services through managed care.

[4] These levels include children served through CCDF (including Temporary Assistance for Needy Families (TANF) transfers) and through funds spent directly on child care in the Social Services Block Grant and TANF programs.

Major Programmatic Assumptions

A number of programmatic assumptions must be made to calculate the baseline estimates. These include assumptions about annual cost-of-living adjustments in the indexed programs and the number of beneficiaries who will receive payments from the major benefit programs. Assumptions about various automatic cost-of-living-adjustments are shown in Table 23–2, and assumptions about baseline caseload projections for the major benefit programs are shown in Table 23–3. These assumptions affect baseline estimates of direct spending for each of these programs, and they also affect estimates of the discretionary baseline for a limited number of programs. For the administrative expenses for Medicare, Railroad

Table 23–5. RECEIPTS BY SOURCE IN THE PROJECTION OF ADJUSTED BASELINE
(In billions of dollars)

	2017 Actual	Estimate										
		2018	2019	2020	2021	2022	2023	2024	2025	2026	2027	2028
Individual income taxes	1,587.1	1,660.1	1,687.0	1,789.7	1,917.2	2,050.5	2,197.9	2,347.9	2,504.3	2,700.0	2,882.8	3,062.1
Corporation income taxes	297.0	217.6	225.3	264.7	272.7	314.2	373.9	416.6	434.8	417.5	406.1	413.6
Social insurance and retirement receipts	1,161.9	1,169.8	1,237.7	1,286.1	1,357.7	1,429.9	1,502.4	1,584.8	1,668.2	1,762.2	1,850.9	1,961.6
(On-budget)	(311.3)	(317.5)	(332.4)	(344.8)	(363.0)	(380.6)	(399.4)	(420.5)	(442.0)	(466.3)	(490.0)	(519.8)
(Off-budget)	(850.6)	(852.3)	(905.3)	(941.3)	(994.7)	(1,049.4)	(1,103.1)	(1,164.3)	(1,226.2)	(1,295.9)	(1,361.0)	(1,441.8)
Excise taxes	83.8	108.2	107.9	111.8	118.3	121.3	124.4	127.9	131.6	135.6	140.2	145.5
Estate and gift taxes	22.8	24.7	16.8	18.0	19.4	20.7	22.8	24.4	26.1	27.6	29.1	30.9
Customs duties	34.6	40.4	44.2	47.1	48.2	50.0	51.0	51.9	53.2	54.7	56.4	58.4
Miscellaneous receipts	129.0	119.7	105.3	95.8	99.4	108.1	116.5	124.3	129.6	135.9	142.2	148.3
Total, receipts	**3,316.2**	**3,340.5**	**3,424.3**	**3,613.3**	**3,832.9**	**4,094.7**	**4,388.9**	**4,677.8**	**4,947.7**	**5,233.5**	**5,507.8**	**5,820.5**
(On-budget)	(2,465.6)	(2,488.1)	(2,519.0)	(2,671.9)	(2,838.3)	(3,045.3)	(3,285.8)	(3,513.6)	(3,721.5)	(3,937.6)	(4,146.8)	(4,378.7)
(Off-budget)	(850.6)	(852.3)	(905.3)	(941.3)	(994.7)	(1,049.4)	(1,103.1)	(1,164.3)	(1,226.2)	(1,295.9)	(1,361.0)	(1,441.8)

Retirement, and unemployment insurance, the discretionary baseline is increased (or decreased) for changes in the number of beneficiaries in addition to the adjustments for inflation described earlier. Although these adjustments are applied at the account level, they have no effect in the aggregate because discretionary baseline levels are constrained to the BBEDCA caps, as reduced for Joint Committee enforcement.

It is also necessary to make assumptions about the continuation of expiring programs and provisions. As explained above, in the baseline estimates provided here, expiring excise taxes dedicated to a trust fund are extended at current rates. In general, mandatory programs with spending of at least $50 million in the current year are also assumed to continue, unless the programs are explicitly temporary in nature. Table 23–4, available on the Internet at *https://www.whitehouse.gov/omb/analytical-perspectives/* and on the Budget CD-ROM, provides a listing of mandatory programs and taxes assumed to continue in the baseline after their expiration.[8] Many other important assumptions must be made in order to calculate the baseline estimates. These include assumptions about the timing and substance of regulations that will be issued over the projection period, the use of administrative discretion provided under current law, and other assumptions about the way programs operate, including actions under OMB Memorandum M-05-13, "Budget Discipline for Agency Administrative Actions." Table 23–4

lists many of these assumptions and their effects on the baseline estimates. It is not intended to be an exhaustive listing; the variety and complexity of Government programs are too great to provide a complete list. Instead, some of the more important assumptions are shown.

Current Services Receipts, Outlays, and Budget Authority

Receipts.—Table 23–5 shows the Administration's baseline receipts by major source. Table 23–6 shows the scheduled increases in the Social Security taxable earnings base, which affect both payroll tax receipts for the program and the initial benefit levels for certain retirees.

Outlays.—Table 23–7 shows the growth from 2018 to 2019 and average annual growth over the five-year and ten-year periods for certain discretionary and major mandatory programs. Tables 23–8 and 23–9 show the Administration's baseline outlays by function and by agency, respectively. A more detailed presentation of these outlays (by function, category, subfunction, and program) is available on the Internet as part of Table 23–12 at *https://www.whitehouse.gov/omb/analytical-perspectives/* and on the Budget CD-ROM.

Budget authority.—Tables 23–10 and 23–11 show estimates of budget authority in the Administration's baseline by function and by agency, respectively. A more detailed presentation of this budget authority with program-level estimates is also available on the Internet as part of Table 23–12 at *https://www.whitehouse.gov/omb/analytical-perspectives/* and on the Budget CD-ROM.

---

[8] All discretionary programs with continuing or enacted appropriations in the current year, including costs for overseas contingency operations in Iraq and Afghanistan and other recurring international activities, are assumed to continue, and are therefore not presented in Table 23-4.

Table 23–6.   EFFECT ON RECEIPTS OF CHANGES IN THE SOCIAL SECURITY TAXABLE EARNINGS BASE

(In billions of dollars)

	2019	2020	2021	2022	2023	2024	2025	2026	2027	2028
Social security (OASDI) taxable earnings base increases:										
$128,400 to $132,300 on Jan. 1, 2019	2.1	5.2	5.8	6.4	7.1	7.9	8.8	9.8	10.8	11.9
$132,300 to $135,900 on Jan. 1, 2020	....	2.0	5.0	5.6	6.2	6.9	7.7	8.5	9.4	10.4
$135,900 to $140,700 on Jan. 1, 2021	....	....	2.7	7.0	7.7	8.6	9.5	10.7	11.8	13.1
$140,700 to $146,700 on Jan. 1, 2022	....	....	....	3.5	8.9	9.9	11.0	12.3	13.6	15.1
$146,700 to $153,600 on Jan. 1, 2023	....	....	....	....	4.1	10.5	11.6	12.9	14.3	15.9
$153,600 to $161,400 on Jan. 1, 2024	....	....	....	....	....	4.7	11.9	13.2	14.6	16.3
$161,400 to $169,500 on Jan. 1, 2025	....	....	....	....	....	....	4.9	12.4	13.7	15.3
$169,500 to $177,900 on Jan. 1, 2026	....	....	....	....	....	....	....	5.1	12.9	14.3
$177,900 to $186,900 on Jan. 1, 2027	....	....	....	....	....	....	....	....	5.4	13.9
$186,900 to $196,500 on Jan. 1, 2028	....	....	....	....	....	....	....	....	....	5.9

Table 23–7.   CHANGE IN OUTLAY ESTIMATES BY CATEGORY IN THE ADJUSTED BASELINE

(In billions of dollars)

	2018	2019	2020	2021	2022	2023	2024	2025	2026	2027	2028	Change 2018 to 2019[1]		Change 2018 to 2023[1]		Change 2018 to 2028[1]	
												Amount	Percent	Amount	Average annual rate	Amount	Average annual rate
Outlays:																	
Discretionary:																	
Defense	611	637	668	678	690	705	719	737	755	774	793	26	4.3%	94	2.9%	183	2.7%
Non-defense	661	656	659	670	669	676	689	705	721	738	756	–5	–0.7%	16	0.5%	95	1.4%
Subtotal, discretionary	1,271	1,293	1,327	1,349	1,359	1,381	1,408	1,442	1,476	1,512	1,549	22	1.7%	109	1.7%	278	2.0%
Mandatory:																	
Farm programs	20	15	14	18	18	18	17	17	17	17	17	–5	–22.9%	–2	–2.6%	–3	–1.8%
GSE support	–5	–22	–23	–23	–22	–21	–21	–21	–21	–21	–21	–17	367.8%	–16	34.7%	–16	16.0%
Medicaid	402	420	439	464	490	519	549	583	624	661	701	18	4.5%	117	5.2%	299	5.7%
Other health care	118	95	95	98	101	106	110	116	122	128	135	–23	–19.2%	–11	–2.0%	17	1.4%
Medicare	582	640	688	743	845	876	902	1,005	1,103	1,196	1,353	58	10.1%	294	8.5%	772	8.8%
Federal employee retirement and disability	140	149	154	159	169	169	169	180	185	191	202	9	6.6%	29	3.8%	63	3.8%
Unemployment compensation ..	29	29	30	31	33	35	37	39	42	45	47	*	–0.5%	6	3.5%	18	5.0%
Other income security programs	261	279	282	290	302	306	308	317	333	335	346	18	7.0%	45	3.2%	85	2.9%
Social Security	987	1,047	1,109	1,174	1,245	1,319	1,398	1,480	1,566	1,656	1,752	60	6.1%	333	6.0%	765	5.9%
Veterans programs	101	116	123	129	146	143	140	159	167	175	200	15	15.1%	43	7.3%	99	7.1%
Other mandatory programs ..	56	63	62	60	63	59	61	58	74	74	76	7	12.2%	3	1.0%	20	3.0%
Undistributed offsetting receipts	–102	–100	–100	–101	–104	–105	–107	–121	–112	–115	–118	2	–1.5%	–3	0.6%	–16	1.5%
Subtotal, mandatory	2,588	2,731	2,873	3,042	3,286	3,423	3,564	3,811	4,100	4,343	4,689	143	5.5%	835	5.8%	2,101	6.1%
Net interest	310	364	447	515	577	636	684	727	772	815	859	54	17.3%	325	15.4%	549	10.7%
Total, outlays	4,170	4,388	4,647	4,906	5,222	5,439	5,656	5,980	6,348	6,670	7,098	219	5.2%	1,270	5.5%	2,928	5.5%

*Less than $500 million.

[1] Not adjusted for timing shifts. Includes 11 benefit payments in 2018, 12 benefit payments in 2019 and 2023, and 13 benefit payments in 2023.

Table 23–8. OUTLAYS BY FUNCTION IN THE ADJUSTED BASELINE
(In billions of dollars)

Function	2017 Actual	Estimate										
		2018	2019	2020	2021	2022	2023	2024	2025	2026	2027	2028
National Defense:												
Department of Defense—Military	568.9	589.7	616.6	647.6	657.2	668.9	683.2	696.2	713.3	731.4	749.7	768.3
Other	29.8	30.3	30.7	31.7	32.6	32.8	32.9	33.6	34.3	35.1	35.8	36.1
Total, National Defense	598.7	620.0	647.4	679.3	689.8	701.7	716.1	729.7	747.6	766.5	785.6	804.5
International Affairs	46.3	47.3	70.9	63.8	64.4	66.2	64.1	66.8	65.0	70.6	70.5	73.3
General Science, Space, and Technology	30.4	31.7	33.7	32.9	34.0	34.4	35.3	35.0	36.2	36.9	37.8	38.6
Energy	3.9	4.0	3.9	4.0	3.9	2.8	2.3	2.0	1.9	4.3	4.5	4.8
Natural Resources and Environment	37.9	40.4	43.1	45.9	46.0	45.6	47.1	48.2	48.4	49.6	50.0	50.9
Agriculture	18.9	26.9	22.2	20.9	25.3	24.9	24.9	25.1	25.0	24.9	25.1	25.0
Commerce and Housing Credit	−26.8	4.9	−22.6	−20.2	−17.4	−15.3	−13.8	−12.4	−11.9	−10.3	−9.5	−8.5
(On-Budget)	(−24.6)	(2.4)	(−21.8)	(−20.7)	(−18.6)	(−15.6)	(−14.1)	(−12.6)	(−12.1)	(−11.5)	(−10.6)	(−9.7)
(Off-Budget)	(−2.3)	(2.5)	(−0.8)	(0.5)	(1.3)	(0.2)	(0.2)	(0.2)	(0.2)	(1.2)	(1.1)	(1.1)
Transportation	93.6	94.4	95.8	97.3	98.7	88.1	85.9	87.1	88.2	90.7	92.8	94.6
Community and Regional Development	24.9	54.3	39.2	39.0	40.2	37.3	36.8	37.1	37.4	38.2	39.0	40.0
Education, Training, Employment, and Social Services	144.0	98.6	111.3	117.2	119.0	126.3	128.7	131.2	133.5	135.5	137.5	139.9
Health	533.1	589.1	580.9	599.7	627.8	658.0	692.9	728.5	769.0	818.2	862.8	910.7
Medicare	597.3	588.3	646.4	694.6	749.8	852.4	882.8	909.1	1,012.7	1,110.5	1,204.5	1,361.4
Income Security	503.5	498.8	526.8	535.2	551.2	576.0	583.0	588.7	612.9	638.2	650.2	676.1
Social Security	944.9	992.5	1,052.6	1,114.7	1,180.2	1,250.9	1,325.6	1,404.3	1,486.2	1,572.3	1,662.5	1,758.8
(On-Budget)	(37.4)	(35.8)	(37.0)	(41.3)	(45.3)	(49.3)	(53.5)	(58.0)	(62.8)	(75.9)	(84.8)	(92.1)
(Off-Budget)	(907.5)	(956.7)	(1,015.6)	(1,073.4)	(1,134.9)	(1,201.5)	(1,272.1)	(1,346.3)	(1,423.4)	(1,496.4)	(1,577.7)	(1,666.7)
Veterans Benefits and Services	176.5	177.2	194.1	204.5	212.6	231.2	231.4	230.6	251.9	263.0	274.3	301.4
Administration of Justice	57.9	68.5	69.8	67.1	67.4	68.0	67.0	68.6	70.4	75.9	78.8	80.9
General Government	23.9	26.3	27.4	28.2	27.4	29.0	29.2	30.1	31.5	31.5	32.3	33.2
Net Interest	262.6	310.3	363.9	446.9	514.5	577.2	635.5	684.4	727.4	771.7	815.2	859.3
(On-Budget)	(349.1)	(394.0)	(445.6)	(526.5)	(592.1)	(651.2)	(707.3)	(753.1)	(794.4)	(836.9)	(880.5)	(923.6)
(Off-Budget)	(−86.5)	(−83.7)	(−81.7)	(−79.6)	(−77.6)	(−74.1)	(−71.8)	(−68.8)	(−67.0)	(−65.3)	(−65.3)	(−64.3)
Allowances	....	−2.1	−18.4	−24.1	−27.5	−29.5	−30.2	−31.0	−31.8	−28.5	−29.2	−29.4
Undistributed Offsetting Receipts:												
Employer share, employee retirement (on-budget)	−67.5	−74.6	−73.8	−74.9	−76.9	−77.3	−78.4	−79.2	−79.9	−81.6	−83.4	−85.3
Employer share, employee retirement (off-budget)	−17.5	−18.3	−18.8	−19.5	−20.2	−21.1	−21.8	−22.5	−23.6	−24.5	−25.5	−26.7
Rents and royalties on the Outer Continental Shelf	−3.1	−4.1	−4.1	−4.2	−4.3	−5.2	−5.0	−5.2	−5.7	−5.6	−5.7	−5.9
Sale of major assets	....	....	....	....	....	....	....	....	....	....	....	....
Other undistributed offsetting receipts	−1.8	−5.0	−3.7	−1.8	−0.1	....	−0.1	−0.1	−12.3	....	....	....
Total, Undistributed Offsetting Receipts	−89.8	−102.0	−100.5	−100.3	−101.5	−103.7	−105.2	−107.0	−121.4	−111.6	−114.6	−117.8
(On-Budget)	(−72.3)	(−83.7)	(−81.6)	(−80.8)	(−81.3)	(−82.6)	(−83.4)	(−84.5)	(−97.9)	(−87.1)	(−89.1)	(−91.1)
(Off-Budget)	(−17.5)	(−18.3)	(−18.8)	(−19.5)	(−20.2)	(−21.1)	(−21.8)	(−22.5)	(−23.6)	(−24.5)	(−25.5)	(−26.7)
Total	**3,981.6**	**4,169.6**	**4,388.1**	**4,646.5**	**4,905.6**	**5,221.5**	**5,439.5**	**5,656.2**	**5,980.0**	**6,348.1**	**6,670.0**	**7,097.6**
(On-Budget)	(3,180.4)	(3,312.3)	(3,473.8)	(3,671.7)	(3,867.2)	(4,114.9)	(4,260.7)	(4,400.9)	(4,646.9)	(4,940.3)	(5,182.1)	(5,520.7)
(Off-Budget)	(801.2)	(857.2)	(914.2)	(974.8)	(1,038.4)	(1,106.6)	(1,178.7)	(1,255.3)	(1,333.1)	(1,407.8)	(1,487.9)	(1,576.9)

Table 23–9. OUTLAYS BY AGENCY IN THE ADJUSTED BASELINE
(In billions of dollars)

Agency	2017 Actual	Estimate										
		2018	2019	2020	2021	2022	2023	2024	2025	2026	2027	2028
Legislative Branch	4.5	5.2	4.8	5.0	5.1	5.2	5.4	5.5	5.7	5.9	6.0	6.2
Judicial Branch	7.6	8.2	7.9	8.2	8.5	8.7	9.0	9.3	9.6	9.9	10.2	10.5
Agriculture	127.6	145.8	142.7	142.1	150.0	152.7	156.0	159.5	162.5	166.4	168.3	169.5
Commerce	10.3	9.9	11.2	11.6	11.6	11.8	10.7	10.9	11.2	11.5	11.8	12.1
Defense—Military Programs	568.9	591.1	618.4	650.3	660.3	672.3	687.1	700.3	717.9	736.3	755.3	774.5
Education	111.7	63.9	76.9	82.6	84.1	91.1	92.9	94.8	96.5	97.9	99.6	101.4
Energy	25.8	28.3	29.0	30.4	30.3	29.4	28.7	29.1	29.6	32.2	32.8	33.5
Health and Human Services	1,116.8	1,162.9	1,217.2	1,294.1	1,376.7	1,508.3	1,572.1	1,631.6	1,782.0	1,901.6	2,030.4	2,230.5
Homeland Security	50.5	83.1	64.5	65.9	69.3	67.6	69.3	71.2	73.0	79.7	83.1	85.5
Housing and Urban Development	55.5	54.9	43.0	42.3	42.4	42.3	42.2	42.9	43.5	44.6	45.5	46.4
Interior	12.2	14.4	15.1	15.5	15.8	15.9	16.3	16.5	16.6	16.9	17.2	17.6
Justice	31.0	38.5	41.3	38.4	38.1	38.2	36.4	37.3	38.3	39.2	40.2	41.2
Labor	40.1	39.4	39.7	40.7	43.7	46.5	49.0	52.0	52.6	62.8	63.4	66.2
State	27.1	30.6	34.3	35.0	35.3	35.4	34.4	35.1	36.0	36.8	37.7	38.5
Transportation	79.4	79.7	81.2	82.2	83.3	72.6	69.8	70.5	71.1	71.9	72.8	74.0
Treasury	546.4	606.6	657.3	742.4	813.8	882.2	947.8	1,002.7	1,050.2	1,093.6	1,160.6	1,210.9
Veterans Affairs	176.1	176.8	193.7	204.1	212.2	230.8	231.0	230.3	251.5	262.6	273.9	300.9
Corps of Engineers—Civil Works	6.5	6.8	7.7	8.1	7.8	7.9	7.9	8.1	8.2	8.2	7.8	7.7
Other Defense Civil Programs	58.7	55.9	62.3	62.9	64.5	71.8	68.7	65.6	74.0	78.7	78.4	86.5
Environmental Protection Agency	8.2	7.9	6.7	7.5	7.9	8.3	8.6	9.0	9.2	9.5	9.7	10.0
Executive Office of the President	0.4	0.4	0.4	0.4	0.4	0.5	0.5	0.5	0.5	0.5	0.5	0.5
General Services Administration	−0.7	−0.1	0.6	0.6	−0.2	0.1	0.2	0.2	0.2	0.2	0.2	0.2
International Assistance Programs	18.9	16.3	36.0	28.0	28.0	29.6	28.5	30.4	27.6	32.4	31.4	33.3
National Aeronautics and Space Administration	18.7	19.3	21.5	20.2	20.7	21.1	21.6	22.1	22.6	23.1	23.6	24.2
National Science Foundation	7.2	7.3	7.4	7.8	8.2	8.2	8.5	7.8	8.4	8.5	8.7	8.9
Office of Personnel Management	95.5	99.7	103.7	107.6	111.7	115.9	120.3	125.1	129.6	135.0	140.2	146.3
Small Business Administration	0.4	−0.6	1.0	0.8	0.9	0.9	0.9	1.0	1.0	1.0	1.0	1.1
Social Security Administration	1,000.8	1,045.8	1,111.2	1,174.7	1,241.8	1,318.9	1,390.8	1,466.2	1,555.1	1,643.3	1,735.4	1,839.6
(On-Budget)	(93.3)	(89.1)	(95.6)	(101.3)	(106.9)	(117.4)	(118.7)	(119.9)	(131.7)	(146.9)	(157.8)	(172.9)
(Off-Budget)	(907.5)	(956.7)	(1,015.6)	(1,073.4)	(1,134.9)	(1,201.5)	(1,272.1)	(1,346.3)	(1,423.4)	(1,496.4)	(1,577.7)	(1,666.7)
Other Independent Agencies	12.5	20.9	21.0	23.3	27.8	29.1	31.0	32.4	33.2	35.1	36.2	36.8
(On-Budget)	(14.8)	(18.4)	(21.8)	(22.8)	(26.5)	(28.9)	(30.8)	(32.1)	(32.9)	(33.9)	(35.1)	(35.7)
(Off-Budget)	(−2.3)	(2.5)	(−0.8)	(0.5)	(1.3)	(0.2)	(0.2)	(0.2)	(0.2)	(1.2)	(1.1)	(1.1)
Allowances	....	−3.6	−25.5	−41.3	−46.1	−50.0	−52.6	−54.5	−65.4	−38.9	−34.6	−35.6
Undistributed Offsetting Receipts	−236.9	−245.8	−243.9	−245.2	−248.1	−251.8	−253.5	−256.9	−272.0	−258.3	−277.5	−281.4
(On-Budget)	(−132.9)	(−143.7)	(−143.4)	(−146.1)	(−150.4)	(−156.6)	(−159.9)	(−165.7)	(−181.4)	(−168.5)	(−186.7)	(−190.5)
(Off-Budget)	(−104.0)	(−102.0)	(−100.6)	(−99.1)	(−97.8)	(−95.2)	(−93.6)	(−91.3)	(−90.5)	(−89.8)	(−90.8)	(−91.0)
Total	**3,981.6**	**4,169.5**	**4,388.1**	**4,646.5**	**4,905.6**	**5,221.6**	**5,439.5**	**5,656.2**	**5,980.0**	**6,348.1**	**6,670.0**	**7,097.6**
(On-Budget)	(4,181.2)	(4,358.1)	(4,585.1)	(4,846.4)	(5,108.9)	(5,433.8)	(5,651.5)	(5,867.1)	(6,202.0)	(6,583.6)	(6,917.6)	(7,360.3)
(Off-Budget)	(801.2)	(857.2)	(914.2)	(974.8)	(1,038.4)	(1,106.6)	(1,178.7)	(1,255.3)	(1,333.1)	(1,407.8)	(1,487.9)	(1,576.9)

Table 23–10. BUDGET AUTHORITY BY FUNCTION IN THE ADJUSTED BASELINE
(In billions of dollars)

Function	2017 Actual	Estimate										
		2018	2019	2020	2021	2022	2023	2024	2025	2026	2027	2028
National Defense:												
Department of Defense—Military	626.2	616.3	632.2	647.8	662.9	679.2	695.6	712.6	730.2	748.4	766.9	785.9
Other	30.1	29.6	30.6	31.2	31.8	32.5	33.2	33.9	34.6	35.4	36.2	37.0
Total, National Defense	656.3	646.0	662.8	679.0	694.8	711.7	728.7	746.5	764.9	783.8	803.1	822.9
International Affairs	66.7	78.9	61.7	65.1	64.7	67.9	72.7	72.4	74.1	76.2	76.9	80.6
General Science, Space, and Technology	32.2	31.7	32.3	33.0	33.7	34.4	35.2	35.9	36.7	37.5	38.4	39.2
Energy	5.9	4.7	3.9	3.8	3.8	3.2	3.1	2.2	2.4	4.9	5.1	5.4
Natural Resources and Environment	44.4	41.7	42.6	43.3	44.3	44.4	46.2	47.3	47.9	49.2	50.4	51.5
Agriculture	14.2	20.7	24.4	24.8	25.1	24.8	25.0	24.9	24.9	25.1	25.1	25.1
Commerce and Housing Credit	–14.2	6.5	–3.2	–2.1	–1.8	0.7	3.7	4.5	5.1	6.0	6.9	7.9
(On-Budget)	(–14.5)	(6.3)	(–3.4)	(–2.3)	(–2.0)	(0.5)	(3.4)	(4.2)	(4.9)	(5.8)	(6.7)	(7.6)
(Off-Budget)	(0.3)	(0.3)	(0.3)	(0.2)	(0.2)	(0.2)	(0.2)	(0.2)	(0.2)	(0.2)	(0.2)	(0.2)
Transportation	92.3	91.4	95.0	89.7	98.3	99.4	100.5	101.6	102.8	105.7	107.0	108.3
Community and Regional Development	43.2	42.7	37.9	38.8	39.7	40.9	42.0	42.9	43.9	44.9	45.8	47.0
Education, Training, Employment, and Social Services	148.4	100.7	112.7	119.5	124.5	129.5	131.5	134.0	136.2	138.3	140.4	142.8
Health	556.0	573.9	568.8	609.4	629.7	661.4	696.5	733.1	773.8	823.3	867.7	915.7
Medicare	607.1	623.7	688.3	694.6	749.6	852.2	882.9	908.2	1,009.8	1,116.3	1,204.7	1,361.6
Income Security	514.2	503.7	532.8	544.2	559.6	578.5	591.0	602.1	623.1	641.7	656.5	675.4
Social Security	946.2	997.1	1,057.7	1,120.1	1,185.9	1,257.0	1,332.0	1,411.0	1,493.3	1,579.7	1,670.4	1,767.0
(On-Budget)	(37.4)	(35.8)	(37.0)	(41.3)	(45.3)	(49.3)	(53.5)	(58.0)	(62.8)	(75.9)	(84.8)	(92.1)
(Off-Budget)	(908.8)	(961.3)	(1,020.7)	(1,078.7)	(1,140.6)	(1,207.6)	(1,278.5)	(1,353.1)	(1,430.5)	(1,503.8)	(1,585.6)	(1,674.9)
Veterans Benefits and Services	179.3	182.6	189.5	203.9	214.2	223.3	233.8	244.5	256.1	266.4	277.9	291.1
Administration of Justice	65.7	58.2	75.2	62.3	63.9	65.6	67.3	69.1	70.9	76.1	79.2	81.4
General Government	23.5	25.1	27.6	28.1	28.7	30.2	30.3	30.8	32.1	32.6	33.4	34.3
Net Interest	262.5	310.3	363.9	446.9	514.5	577.2	635.5	684.4	727.4	771.7	815.2	859.3
(On-Budget)	(349.0)	(394.0)	(445.6)	(526.5)	(592.1)	(651.2)	(707.3)	(753.1)	(794.4)	(836.9)	(880.5)	(923.6)
(Off-Budget)	(–86.5)	(–83.7)	(–81.7)	(–79.6)	(–77.6)	(–74.1)	(–71.8)	(–68.8)	(–67.0)	(–65.3)	(–65.3)	(–64.3)
Allowances	....	–3.5	–29.1	–27.8	–29.7	–30.4	–31.1	–31.7	–32.4	–27.5	–29.2	–29.7
Undistributed Offsetting Receipts:												
Employer share, employee retirement (on-budget)	–67.5	–74.6	–73.8	–74.9	–76.9	–77.3	–78.4	–79.2	–79.9	–81.6	–83.4	–85.3
Employer share, employee retirement (off-budget)	–17.5	–18.3	–18.8	–19.5	–20.2	–21.1	–21.8	–22.5	–23.6	–24.5	–25.5	–26.7
Rents and royalties on the Outer Continental Shelf	–3.1	–4.1	–4.1	–4.2	–4.3	–5.2	–5.0	–5.2	–5.7	–5.6	–5.7	–5.9
Sale of major assets	....	....	....	....	....	....	....	....	....	....	....	....
Other undistributed offsetting receipts	–1.8	–5.0	–3.7	–1.8	–0.1	....	–0.1	–0.1	–12.3	....	....	....
Total, Undistributed Offsetting Receipts	–89.8	–102.0	–100.5	–100.3	–101.5	–103.7	–105.2	–107.0	–121.4	–111.6	–114.6	–117.8
(On-Budget)	(–72.3)	(–83.7)	(–81.6)	(–80.8)	(–81.3)	(–82.6)	(–83.4)	(–84.5)	(–97.9)	(–87.1)	(–89.1)	(–91.1)
(Off-Budget)	(–17.5)	(–18.3)	(–18.8)	(–19.5)	(–20.2)	(–21.1)	(–21.8)	(–22.5)	(–23.6)	(–24.5)	(–25.5)	(–26.7)
Total	**4,153.9**	**4,234.0**	**4,444.1**	**4,676.1**	**4,942.0**	**5,268.2**	**5,521.7**	**5,756.6**	**6,071.5**	**6,440.2**	**6,760.1**	**7,169.1**
(On-Budget)	(3,348.9)	(3,374.5)	(3,523.8)	(3,696.2)	(3,898.9)	(4,155.4)	(4,336.5)	(4,494.6)	(4,731.3)	(5,025.9)	(5,265.1)	(5,584.9)
(Off-Budget)	(805.0)	(859.5)	(920.3)	(979.9)	(1,043.1)	(1,112.7)	(1,185.2)	(1,262.0)	(1,340.2)	(1,414.3)	(1,495.0)	(1,584.2)
MEMORANDUM												
Discretionary Budget Authority:												
National Defense	634.1	637.3	652.0	667.8	683.7	700.5	717.8	735.6	753.8	772.6	791.7	811.3
International Affairs	59.5	59.0	60.1	61.4	62.7	64.1	65.4	66.8	68.3	69.8	71.3	72.9
Domestic	526.4	505.9	520.4	532.5	545.3	559.2	573.5	588.2	603.3	618.8	634.7	650.9
Total, Discretionary	1,220.0	1,202.2	1,232.4	1,261.6	1,291.7	1,323.7	1,356.7	1,390.6	1,425.4	1,461.2	1,497.6	1,535.1

Table 23–11. BUDGET AUTHORITY BY AGENCY IN THE ADJUSTED BASELINE

(In billions of dollars)

Agency	2017 Actual	Estimate										
		2018	2019	2020	2021	2022	2023	2024	2025	2026	2027	2028
Legislative Branch	4.7	4.7	4.8	5.0	5.1	5.3	5.4	5.6	5.7	5.9	6.1	6.3
Judicial Branch	7.8	7.7	8.0	8.3	8.6	8.9	9.1	9.4	9.7	10.0	10.2	10.5
Agriculture	136.5	143.6	147.1	148.0	153.0	155.8	159.5	162.9	166.0	170.5	172.0	173.0
Commerce	9.5	9.4	9.8	10.0	10.3	10.5	10.8	11.1	11.4	11.7	12.0	12.3
Defense—Military Programs	626.2	618.6	634.5	650.0	666.1	682.8	699.6	717.0	735.1	753.7	772.9	792.5
Education	114.8	67.3	78.3	84.7	89.2	93.8	95.3	97.2	98.8	100.2	101.9	103.7
Energy	27.5	28.5	28.3	29.3	29.2	29.2	29.6	29.6	30.4	33.0	33.7	34.3
Health and Human Services	1,144.0	1,183.0	1,249.0	1,304.0	1,378.0	1,511.1	1,575.3	1,635.0	1,786.5	1,906.6	2,035.3	2,236.1
Homeland Security	62.3	72.2	68.1	69.7	71.6	73.6	75.7	77.7	79.7	86.8	90.1	92.6
Housing and Urban Development	60.7	47.9	47.6	49.0	50.2	51.2	52.3	53.5	54.6	55.7	56.6	57.6
Interior	13.9	14.2	14.9	15.2	15.4	15.7	16.0	16.1	16.5	16.8	17.3	17.8
Justice	37.0	31.6	46.3	33.8	34.7	35.6	36.5	37.4	38.4	39.3	40.4	41.5
Labor	44.9	43.8	43.8	45.0	46.8	48.3	50.6	53.0	55.9	59.1	62.6	65.1
State	31.5	31.6	32.2	32.9	33.6	34.3	35.1	35.9	36.7	37.5	38.4	39.2
Transportation	78.3	77.3	80.6	74.9	83.0	83.6	84.2	84.9	85.5	86.2	86.9	87.6
Treasury	548.9	599.0	657.7	742.7	814.8	883.8	949.4	1,004.3	1,051.6	1,095.4	1,162.4	1,212.8
Veterans Affairs	178.8	182.3	189.1	203.5	213.9	223.0	233.5	244.1	255.7	266.0	277.5	290.7
Corps of Engineers—Civil Works	7.1	5.9	6.1	6.2	6.3	6.5	6.6	6.8	6.9	7.1	7.3	7.4
Other Defense Civil Programs	58.7	60.1	62.5	63.1	64.7	66.9	68.9	71.0	74.3	79.0	78.7	80.7
Environmental Protection Agency	8.3	8.0	8.1	8.3	8.5	8.7	8.9	9.2	9.4	9.6	9.9	10.2
Executive Office of the President	0.4	0.4	0.4	0.4	0.4	0.5	0.5	0.5	0.5	0.5	0.5	0.6
General Services Administration	−1.3	−1.0	0.2	0.2	0.2	0.2	0.3	0.3	0.3	0.3	0.3	0.3
International Assistance Programs	34.3	46.1	28.0	30.6	29.4	31.7	35.7	34.5	35.4	36.6	36.4	39.2
National Aeronautics and Space Administration	19.8	19.5	19.9	20.4	20.8	21.3	21.8	22.3	22.8	23.4	23.9	24.4
National Science Foundation	7.6	7.6	7.7	7.8	8.0	8.1	8.3	8.5	8.6	8.8	9.0	9.2
Office of Personnel Management	98.7	100.4	104.8	109.2	113.7	118.4	123.3	128.1	133.1	138.2	143.5	149.1
Small Business Administration	0.7	−0.8	0.8	0.9	0.9	0.9	0.9	1.0	1.0	1.0	1.1	1.1
Social Security Administration	1,001.5	1,047.9	1,115.7	1,180.1	1,247.5	1,324.8	1,397.3	1,473.3	1,562.3	1,650.8	1,743.4	1,847.5
(On-Budget)	(92.7)	(86.6)	(95.0)	(101.3)	(106.9)	(117.2)	(118.7)	(120.2)	(131.8)	(147.0)	(157.8)	(172.6)
(Off-Budget)	(908.8)	(961.3)	(1,020.7)	(1,078.7)	(1,140.6)	(1,207.6)	(1,278.5)	(1,353.1)	(1,430.5)	(1,503.8)	(1,585.6)	(1,674.9)
Other Independent Agencies	27.8	29.1	32.1	32.8	34.8	36.5	38.4	39.2	40.2	41.4	42.6	43.5
(On-Budget)	(27.5)	(28.9)	(31.9)	(32.5)	(34.6)	(36.2)	(38.2)	(38.9)	(39.9)	(41.2)	(42.4)	(43.3)
(Off-Budget)	(0.3)	(0.3)	(0.3)	(0.2)	(0.2)	(0.2)	(0.2)	(0.2)	(0.2)	(0.2)	(0.2)	(0.2)
Allowances	....	−6.0	−38.1	−44.4	−48.4	−51.1	−53.7	−55.5	−69.4	−32.7	−35.1	−36.2
Undistributed Offsetting Receipts	−236.9	−245.8	−243.9	−245.2	−248.1	−251.8	−253.5	−256.9	−272.0	−258.3	−277.5	−281.4
(On-Budget)	(−132.9)	(−143.7)	(−143.4)	(−146.1)	(−150.4)	(−156.6)	(−159.9)	(−165.7)	(−181.4)	(−168.5)	(−186.7)	(−190.5)
(Off-Budget)	(−104.0)	(−102.0)	(−100.6)	(−99.1)	(−97.8)	(−95.2)	(−93.6)	(−91.3)	(−90.5)	(−89.8)	(−90.8)	(−91.0)
Total	**4,153.9**	**4,234.0**	**4,444.1**	**4,676.1**	**4,942.0**	**5,268.2**	**5,521.7**	**5,756.6**	**6,071.5**	**6,440.2**	**6,760.1**	**7,169.1**
(On-Budget)	(3,348.9)	(3,374.5)	(3,523.8)	(3,696.2)	(3,898.9)	(4,155.4)	(4,336.5)	(4,494.6)	(4,731.3)	(5,025.9)	(5,265.1)	(5,584.9)
(Off-Budget)	(805.0)	(859.5)	(920.3)	(979.9)	(1,043.1)	(1,112.7)	(1,185.2)	(1,262.0)	(1,340.2)	(1,414.3)	(1,495.0)	(1,584.2)

24. TRUST FUNDS AND FEDERAL FUNDS

As is common for State and local government budgets, the budget for the Federal Government contains information about collections and expenditures for different types of funds. This chapter presents summary information about the transactions of the two major fund groups used by the Federal Government, trust funds and Federal funds. It also presents information about the income and outgo of the major trust funds and certain Federal funds that are financed by dedicated collections in a manner similar to trust funds.

The Federal Funds Group

The Federal funds group includes all financial transactions of the Government that are not required by law to be recorded in trust funds. It accounts for a larger share of the budget than the trust funds group.

The Federal funds group includes the "general fund," which is used for the general purposes of Government rather than being restricted by law to a specific program. The general fund is the largest fund in the Government and it receives all collections not dedicated for some other fund, including virtually all income taxes and many excise taxes. The general fund is used for all programs that are not supported by trust, special, or revolving funds.

The Federal funds group also includes special funds and revolving funds, both of which receive collections that are dedicated by law for specific purposes. Where the law requires that Federal fund collections be dedicated to a particular program, the collections and associated disbursements are recorded in special fund receipt and expenditure accounts.[1] An example is the portion of the Outer Continental Shelf mineral leasing receipts deposited into the Land and Water Conservation Fund. Money in special fund receipt accounts must be appropriated before it can be obligated and spent. The majority of special fund collections are derived from the Government's power to impose taxes or fines, or otherwise compel payment, as in the case of the Crime Victims Fund. In addition, a significant amount of collections credited to special funds is derived from certain types of business-like activity, such as the sale of Government land or other assets or the use of Government property. These collections include receipts from timber sales and royalties from oil and gas extraction.

Revolving funds are used to conduct continuing cycles of business-like activity. Revolving funds receive proceeds from the sale of products or services, and these proceeds finance ongoing activities that continue to provide products or services. Instead of being deposited in receipt accounts, the proceeds are recorded in revolving fund expenditure accounts. The proceeds are generally available for obligation and expenditure without further legislative action. Outlays for programs with revolving funds are reported both gross and net of these proceeds; gross outlays include the expenditures from the proceeds and net program outlays are derived by subtracting the proceeds from gross outlays. Because the proceeds of these sales are recorded as offsets to outlays within expenditure accounts rather than receipt accounts, the proceeds are known as "offsetting collections."[2] There are two classes of revolving funds in the Federal funds group. Public enterprise funds, such as the Postal Service Fund, conduct business-like operations mainly with the public. Intragovernmental funds, such as the Federal Buildings Fund, conduct business-like operations mainly within and between Government agencies.

The Trust Funds Group

The trust funds group consists of funds that are designated by law as trust funds. Like special funds and revolving funds, trust funds receive collections that are dedicated by law for specific purposes. Many of the larger trust funds are used to budget for social insurance programs, such as Social Security, Medicare, and unemployment compensation. Other large trust funds are used to budget for military and Federal civilian employees' retirement benefits, highway and transit construction and maintenance, and airport and airway development and maintenance. There are a few trust revolving funds that are credited with collections earmarked by law to carry out a cycle of business-type operations. There are also a few small trust funds that have been established to carry out the terms of a conditional gift or bequest.

There is no substantive difference between special funds in the Federal funds group and trust funds, or between revolving funds in the Federal funds group and trust revolving funds. Whether a particular fund is designated in law as a trust fund is, in many cases, arbitrary. For example, the National Service Life Insurance Fund is a trust fund, but the Servicemen's Group Life Insurance Fund is a Federal fund, even though both receive dedicated collections from veterans and both provide life insurance payments to veterans' beneficiaries.

The Federal Government uses the term "trust fund" differently than the way in which it is commonly used. In common usage, the term is used to refer to a private fund that has a beneficiary who owns the trust's income and may also own the trust's assets. A custodian or trustee

---

[1] There are two types of budget accounts: expenditure (or appropriation) accounts and receipt accounts. Expenditure accounts are used to record outlays and receipt accounts are used to record governmental receipts and offsetting receipts. For further detail on expenditure and receipt accounts, see Chapter 8, "Budget Concepts," in this volume.

[2] See Chapter 12 in this volume for more information on offsetting collections and offsetting receipts.

manages the assets on behalf of the beneficiary according to the terms of the trust agreement, as established by a trustor. Neither the trustee nor the beneficiary can change the terms of the trust agreement; only the trustor can change the terms of the agreement. In contrast, the Federal Government owns and manages the assets and the earnings of most Federal trust funds and can unilaterally change the law to raise or lower future trust fund collections and payments or change the purpose for which the collections are used. Only a few small Federal trust funds are managed pursuant to a trust agreement whereby the Government acts as the trustee; even then the Government generally owns the funds and has some ability to alter the amount deposited into or paid out of the funds.

Deposit funds, which are funds held by the Government as a custodian on behalf of individuals or a non-Feder-

al entity, are similar to private-sector trust funds. The Government makes no decisions about the amount of money placed in deposit funds or about how the proceeds are spent. For this reason, these funds are not classified as Federal trust funds, but are instead considered to be non-budgetary and excluded from the Federal budget.[3]

The income of a Federal Government trust fund must be used for the purposes specified in law. The income of some trust funds, such as the Federal Employees Health Benefits fund, is spent almost as quickly as it is collected. In other cases, such as the Social Security and Federal civilian employees' retirement trust funds, the trust fund income is not spent as quickly as it is collected. Currently, these funds do not use all of their annual income (which includes intragovernmental interest income). This sur-

[3] Deposit funds are discussed briefly in Chapter 9 of this volume, "Coverage of the Budget."

Table 24–1. RECEIPTS, OUTLAYS AND SURPLUS OR DEFICIT BY FUND GROUP
(In billions of dollars)

	2017 Actual	Estimate					
		2018	2019	2020	2021	2022	2023
Receipts:							
Federal funds cash income:							
From the public	2,465.5	2,448.3	2,465.1	2,626.8	2,765.1	2,963.1	3,193.3
From trust funds	1.1	1.0	0.9	1.0	1.0	1.0	1.1
Total, Federal funds cash income	2,466.6	2,449.3	2,466.0	2,627.8	2,766.1	2,964.1	3,194.4
Trust funds cash income:							
From the public	1,397.1	1,434.3	1,509.8	1,568.1	1,656.7	1,729.9	1,816.6
From Federal funds:							
Interest	147.1	143.8	143.8	145.9	148.9	151.9	153.7
Other	573.7	586.3	614.2	636.3	674.6	714.5	760.0
Total, Trust funds cash income	2,117.9	2,164.4	2,267.8	2,350.3	2,480.2	2,596.3	2,730.4
Offsetting collections from the public and offsetting receipts:							
Federal funds	–378.1	–347.5	–349.1	–376.8	–361.2	–370.5	–378.3
Trust funds	–890.2	–925.8	–962.4	–992.4	–1,046.8	–1,101.1	–1,160.4
Total, offsetting collections from the public and offsetting receipts	–1,268.3	–1,273.4	–1,311.5	–1,369.2	–1,408.1	–1,471.7	–1,538.7
Unified budget receipts:							
Federal funds	2,088.6	2,101.8	2,116.9	2,251.0	2,404.8	2,593.6	2,816.1
Trust funds	1,227.6	1,238.6	1,305.4	1,358.0	1,433.4	1,495.1	1,570.0
Total, unified budget receipts	3,316.2	3,340.4	3,422.3	3,608.9	3,838.2	4,088.7	4,386.1
Outlays:							
Federal funds cash outgo	3,285.6	3,425.6	3,553.7	3,694.9	3,757.7	3,897.6	4,022.1
Trust funds cash outgo	1,964.2	2,020.8	2,164.5	2,270.1	2,404.5	2,570.6	2,681.2
Offsetting collections from the public and offsetting receipts:							
Federal funds	–378.1	–347.5	–349.1	–376.8	–361.2	–370.5	–378.3
Trust funds	–890.2	–925.8	–962.4	–992.4	–1,046.8	–1,101.1	–1,160.4
Total, offsetting collections from the public and offsetting receipts	–1,268.3	–1,273.4	–1,311.5	–1,369.2	–1,408.1	–1,471.7	–1,538.7
Unified budget outlays:							
Federal funds	2,907.5	3,078.1	3,204.6	3,318.1	3,396.5	3,527.0	3,643.9
Trust funds	1,074.0	1,094.9	1,202.1	1,277.7	1,357.6	1,469.5	1,520.8
Total, unified budget outlays	3,981.6	4,173.0	4,406.7	4,595.9	4,754.1	4,996.5	5,164.6
Surplus or deficit(–):							
Federal funds	–819.0	–976.3	–1,087.7	–1,067.2	–991.6	–933.5	–827.7
Trust funds	153.6	143.7	103.3	80.2	75.7	25.7	49.2
Total, unified surplus/deficit(–)	–665.4	–832.6	–984.4	–986.9	–915.9	–907.8	–778.5

Note: Receipts include governmental, interfund, and proprietary, and exclude intrafund receipts (which are offset against intrafund payments so that cash income and cash outgo are not overstated).

plus of income over outgo adds to the trust fund's balance, which is available for future expenditures. The balances are generally required by law to be invested in Federal securities issued by the Department of the Treasury.[4] The National Railroad Retirement Investment Trust is a rare example of a Government trust fund authorized to invest balances in equity markets.

A trust fund normally consists of one or more receipt accounts (to record income) and an expenditure account (to record outgo). However, a few trust funds, such as the Veterans Special Life Insurance fund, are established by law as trust revolving funds. Such a fund is similar to a revolving fund in the Federal funds group in that it may consist of a single account to record both income and outgo. Trust revolving funds are used to conduct a cycle of business-type operations; offsetting collections are credited to the funds (which are also expenditure accounts) and the funds' outlays are displayed net of the offsetting collections.

Income and Outgo by Fund Group

Table 24–1 shows income, outgo, and the surplus or deficit by fund group and in the aggregate (netted to avoid double-counting) from which the total unified budget receipts, outlays, and surplus or deficit are derived. Income consists mostly of governmental receipts (derived from governmental activity, primarily income, payroll, and excise taxes). Income also includes offsetting receipts, which include proprietary receipts (derived from business-like transactions with the public), interfund collections (derived from payments from a fund in one fund group to a fund in the other fund group), and gifts. Outgo consists of payments made to the public or to a fund in the other fund group.

Two types of transactions are treated specially in the table. First, income and outgo for each fund group exclude all transactions that occur between funds within the same fund group.[5] These intrafund transactions constitute outgo and income for the individual funds that make and collect the payments, but they are offsetting within the fund group as a whole. The totals for each fund group measure only the group's transactions with the public and the other fund group. Second, outgo is calculated net of the collections from Federal sources that are credited to expenditure accounts (which, as noted above, are referred to as offsetting collections); the spending that is financed by those collections is included in outgo and the collections from Federal sources are subsequently subtracted from outgo.[6] Although it would be conceptually correct to

add interfund offsetting collections from Federal sources to income for a particular fund, this cannot be done at the present time because the budget data do not provide this type of detail. As a result, both interfund and intrafund offsetting collections from Federal sources are offset against outgo in Table 24–1 and are not shown separately.

The vast majority of the interfund transactions in the table are payments by the Federal funds to the trust funds. These payments include interest payments from the general fund to the trust funds for interest earned on trust fund balances invested in interest-bearing Treasury securities. The payments also include payments by Federal agencies to Federal employee benefits trust funds and Social Security trust funds on behalf of current employees and general fund transfers to employee retirement trust funds to amortize the unfunded liabilities of these funds. In addition, the payments include general fund transfers to the Supplementary Medical Insurance trust fund for the cost of Medicare Parts B (outpatient and physician benefits) and D (prescription drug benefits) that is not covered by premiums or other income from the public.

In addition to investing their balances with the Treasury, some funds in the Federal funds group and most trust funds are authorized to borrow from the general fund of the Treasury.[7] Similar to the treatment of funds invested with the Treasury, borrowed funds are not recorded as receipts of the fund or included in the income of the fund. Rather, the borrowed funds finance outlays by the fund in excess of available receipts. Subsequently, any excess fund receipts are transferred from the fund to the general fund in repayment of the borrowing. The repayment is not recorded as an outlay of the fund or included in fund outgo. This treatment is consistent with the broad principle that borrowing and debt redemption are not budgetary transactions but rather a means of financing deficits or disposing of surpluses.[8]

Some income in both Federal funds and trust funds consists of offsetting receipts.[9] Offsetting receipts are not considered governmental receipts (such as taxes), but they are instead recorded on the outlay side of the budget. Expenditures resulting from offsetting receipts are recorded as gross outlays and the collections of offsetting receipts are then subtracted from gross outlays to derive net outlays. Net outlays reflect the government's net transactions with the public.

---

[4] Securities held by trust funds (and by other Government accounts), debt held by the public, and gross Federal debt are discussed in Chapter 4 of this volume, "Federal Borrowing and Debt."

[5] For example, the railroad retirement trust funds pay the equivalent of Social Security benefits to railroad retirees in addition to the regular railroad pension. These benefits are financed by a payment from the Federal Old-Age and Survivors Insurance trust fund to the railroad retirement trust funds. The payment and collection are not included in Table 24–1 so that the total trust fund income and outgo shown in the table reflect transactions with the public and with Federal funds.

[6] Collections from non-Federal sources are shown as income and spending that is financed by those collections is shown as outgo. For example, postage stamp fees are deposited as offsetting collections in

the Postal Service Fund. As a result, the Fund's income reported in Table 24–1 includes postage stamp fees and the Fund's outgo is gross disbursements, including disbursements financed by those fees.

[7] For example, the Unemployment trust fund is authorized to borrow from the general fund for unemployment benefits; the Bonneville Power Administration Fund, a revolving fund in the Department of Energy, is authorized to borrow from the general fund; and the Black Lung Disability Trust Fund, a trust fund in the Department of Labor, is authorized to receive appropriations of repayable advances from the general fund, which constitute a form of borrowing.

[8] Borrowing and debt repayment are discussed in Chapter 4 of this volume, "Federal Borrowing and Debt," and Chapter 8 of this volume, "Budget Concepts."

[9] Interest on borrowed funds is an example of an intragovernmental offsetting receipt and Medicare Part B's premiums are an example of offsetting receipts from the public.

Table 24-2. COMPARISON OF TOTAL FEDERAL FUND AND TRUST FUND RECEIPTS TO UNIFIED BUDGET RECEIPTS, FISCAL YEAR 2017

(In billions of dollars)

Gross Federal fund and Trust fund cash income:	
Federal funds	2,785.6
Trust funds	2,175.2
Total, gross Federal fund and Trust fund cash income	4,960.8
Deduct: intrabudgetary offsetting collections (from funds within same fund group):	
Federal funds	−286.3
Trust funds	−50.8
Subtotal, intrabudgetary offsetting collections	−337.1
Deduct: intrafund receipts (from funds within same fund group):	
Federal funds	−32.7
Trust funds	−6.6
Subtotal, intrafund receipts	−39.3
Federal fund and Trust fund cash income net of intrabudgetary offsetting collections and intrafund receipts:	
Federal funds	2,466.6
Trust funds	2,117.9
Total, Federal fund and Trust fund cash income net of intrafund receipts	4,584.5
Deduct: offsetting collections from the public:	
Federal funds	−235.7
Trust funds	−21.4
Subtotal, offsetting collections from the public	−257.2
Deduct other offsetting receipts:	
Federal fund receipts from Trust funds	−1.1
Trust fund receipts from Federal funds:	
Interest in receipt accounts	−147.1
General fund payments to Medicare Parts B and D	−306.5
Employing agencies' payments for pensions, Social Security, and Medicare	−77.8
General fund payments for unfunded liabilities of Federal employees' retirement funds	−122.4
Transfer of taxation of Social Security and RRB benefits to OASDI, HI, and RRB	−62.3
Other receipts from Federal funds	−4.6
Subtotal, Trust fund receipts from Federal funds	−720.8
Proprietary receipts:	
Federal funds	−127.5
Trust funds	−148.0
Subtotal, proprietary receipts	−275.5
Offsetting governmental receipts:	
Federal funds	−13.7
Trust funds	−*
Subtotal, offsetting governmental receipts	−13.7
Subtotal, other offsetting receipts	−1,011.1
Unified budget receipts:	
Federal funds	2,088.6
Trust funds	1,227.6
Total, unified budget receipts	3,316.2
Memoradum:	
Gross receipts:[1]	
Federal funds	2,263.6
Trust funds	2,103.0
Total, gross receipts	4,366.6

* $50 million or less.
[1] Gross income excluding offsetting collections.

As shown in Table 24–1, 37 percent of all governmental receipts were deposited in trust funds in 2017 and the remaining 63 percent of governmental receipts were deposited in Federal funds, which, as noted above, include the general fund. As noted above, most outlays between the trust fund and Federal fund groups (interfund outlays) flow from Federal funds to trust funds, rather than from trust funds to Federal funds. As a result, while trust funds account for 27 percent of total 2017 outlays, they account for 33 percent of 2017 outlays net of interfund transactions.

Because the income for Federal funds and trust funds recorded in Table 24–1 includes offsetting receipts and offsetting collections from the public, offsetting receipts and offsetting collections from the public must be deducted from the two fund groups' combined gross income in order to reconcile to total governmental receipts in the unified budget. Similarly, because the outgo for Federal funds and trust funds in Table 24–1 consists of outlays gross of offsetting receipts and offsetting collections from the public, the amount of the offsetting receipts and offsetting collections from the public must be deducted from the sum of the Federal funds' and the trust funds' gross outgo in order to reconcile to total (net) unified budget outlays. Table 24–2 reconciles, for fiscal year 2017, the gross total of all trust fund and Federal fund receipts with the receipt total of the unified budget.

Income, Outgo, and Balances of Trust Funds

Table 24–3 shows, for the trust funds group as a whole, the funds' balance at the start of each year, income and outgo during the year, and the end-of-year balance. Income and outgo are divided between transactions with the public and transactions with Federal funds. Receipts from Federal funds are divided between interest and other interfund receipts.

The definitions of income and outgo in this table differ from those in Table 24–1 in one important way. Trust fund collections that are offset against outgo (offsetting collections from Federal sources) within expenditure accounts instead of being deposited in separate receipt accounts are classified as income in this table, but not in Table 24–1. This classification is consistent with the definitions of income and outgo for trust funds used elsewhere in the budget. It has the effect of increasing both income and outgo by the amount of the offsetting collections from Federal sources. The difference was approximately $51 billion in 2017. Table 24–3, therefore, provides a more complete summary of trust fund income and outgo.

The trust funds group ran a surplus of $154 billion in 2017, and is expected to continue to run surpluses over the next several years. The resulting growth in trust fund balances continues a trend that has persisted over the past several decades.

The size of the trust fund balances is largely the consequence of the way some trust funds are financed. Some of the larger trust funds (primarily Social Security and the Federal retirement funds) are fully or partially advance funded, with collections on behalf of individual par-

Table 24–3.   INCOME, OUTGO, AND BALANCES OF TRUST FUNDS GROUP
(In billions of dollars)

	2017 Actual	Estimate					
		2018	2019	2020	2021	2022	2023
Balance, start of year	4,879.3	5,033.8	5,177.6	5,280.8	5,361.0	5,436.7	5,462.4
Adjustments to balances	0.8	....	....	....	....	....	....
Total balance, start of year	4,880.1	5,033.8	5,177.6	5,280.8	5,361.0	5,436.7	5,462.4
Income:							
Governmental receipts	1,227.6	1,238.6	1,305.4	1,358.0	1,433.4	1,495.1	1,570.0
Offsetting governmental	*	5.0	3.7	1.7	*	*	*
Proprietary	166.0	189.4	200.1	207.7	222.5	233.9	245.9
From Federal funds:							
Interest	150.9	145.5	145.2	147.9	151.2	154.4	156.6
Other	624.0	638.7	668.3	692.7	732.6	774.8	823.1
Total income during the year	2,168.6	2,217.2	2,322.7	2,408.0	2,539.7	2,658.3	2,795.6
Outgo (–)	–2,015.0	–2,073.5	–2,219.4	–2,327.8	–2,464.0	–2,632.6	–2,746.4
Change in fund balance:							
Surplus or deficit(–):							
Excluding interest	2.7	–1.8	–41.9	–67.7	–75.4	–128.8	–107.4
Interest	150.9	145.5	145.2	147.9	151.2	154.4	156.6
Subtotal, surplus or deficit (–)	153.6	143.7	103.3	80.2	75.7	25.7	49.2
Borrowing, transfers, lapses, & other adjustments	*	0.2	–0.1	....	....	....	....
Total change in fund balance	153.6	143.9	103.2	80.2	75.7	25.7	49.2
Balance, end of year	5,033.8	5,177.6	5,280.8	5,361.0	5,436.7	5,462.4	5,511.6

* $50 million or less.

Note: In contrast to Table 24–1, income also includes income that is offset within expenditure accounts as offsetting collections from Federal sources, instead of being deposited in receipt accounts.

ticipants received by the funds years earlier than when the associated benefits are paid. For example, under the Federal military and civilian retirement programs, Federal agencies and employees together are required to pay the retirement trust funds an amount equal to accruing retirement benefits. Since many years pass between the time when benefits are accrued and when they are paid, the trust funds accumulate substantial balances over time. [10]

Due to advance funding and economic growth (both real and nominal), trust fund balances increased from $205 billion in 1982 to $5.0 trillion in 2017. Based on the estimates in the 2019 Budget, which include the effect of the Budget's proposals, the balances are estimated to increase by approximately 9 percent by the year 2023, rising to $5.5 trillion. Almost all of these balances are invested in Treasury securities and earn interest.

From the perspective of the trust fund, these balances are assets that represent the value, in today's dollars, of past taxes, fees, and other income from the public and

from other Government accounts that the trust fund has received in excess of past spending. Trust fund assets held in Treasury securities are legal claims on the Treasury, similar to Treasury securities issued to the public. Like all other fund assets, these are available to the fund for future benefit payments and other expenditures. From the perspective of the Government as a whole, however, the trust fund balances do not represent net additions to the Government's balance sheet. The trust fund balances are assets of the agencies responsible for administering the trust fund programs and liabilities of the Department of the Treasury. These assets and liabilities cancel each other out in the Government-wide balance sheet. The effects of Treasury debt held by trust funds and other Government accounts are discussed further in Chapter 4 of this volume, "Federal Borrowing and Debt."

Although total trust fund balances are growing, the balances of some major individual funds are declining. Social Security and Medicare face particular challenges due to the decline in the ratio of active workers paying payroll taxes relative to retired workers receiving Social Security and Medicare benefits. Within the 2017-2023 window presented in Table 24–3, the Social Security and Medicare Hospital Insurance (HI) trust funds will begin to run deficits and their balances will consequently begin to fall. In the longer run, absent changes in the laws governing these programs, the funds will become unable to meet their obligations in full. For further discussion of the longer-term outlook of Social Security and Medicare,

---

[10] Until the 1980s, most trust funds operated on a pay-as-you-go basis as distinct from a pre-funded basis. Taxes and fees were set at levels sufficient to finance current program expenditures and administrative expenses, and to maintain balances generally equal to one year's worth of expenditures (to provide for unexpected events). As a result, trust fund balances tended to grow at about the same rate as the funds' annual expenditures. In the 1980s, pay-as-you-go financing was replaced by full or partial advance funding for some of the larger trust funds. The Social Security Amendments of 1983 (P.L. 98-21) raised payroll taxes above the levels necessary to finance then-current expenditures. Legislation enacted in the mid-1980s established the requirement for full accrual basis funding of Federal military and civilian retirement benefits.

and the Federal budget as a whole, see Chapter 3 of this volume, "Long-Term Budget Outlook."

Table 24–4 shows estimates of income, outgo, surplus or deficit, and balances for 2017 through 2023 for the major trust funds. With the exception of transactions between trust funds, the data for the individual trust funds are conceptually the same as the data in Table 24–3 for the trust funds group. As explained previously, transactions between trust funds are shown as outgo of the fund that makes the payment and as income of the fund that collects it in the data for an individual trust fund, but the collections are offset against outgo in the data for the trust fund group as a whole.

As noted above, trust funds are funded by a combination of payments from the public and payments from Federal funds, including payments directly from the general fund and payments from agency appropriations. Similarly, the fund outgo amounts in Table 24–4 represent both outflows to the public—such as for the provision of benefit payments or the purchase of goods or services—and outflows to other Government accounts—such as for reimbursement for services provided by other agencies or payment of interest on borrowing from Treasury.

Because trust funds and Federal special and revolving funds conduct transactions both with the public and with other Government accounts, the surplus or deficit of an individual fund may differ from the fund's impact on the surplus or deficit of the Federal Government. Transactions with the public affect both the surplus or deficit of an individual fund and the Federal Government surplus or deficit. Transactions with other government accounts affect the surplus or deficit of the particular fund. However, because that same transaction is offset in another government account, there is no net impact on the total Federal Government surplus or deficit.

A brief description of the major trust funds is given below; additional information for these and other trust funds can be found in the Status of Funds tables in the *Budget Appendix*.

- Social Security Trust Funds: The Social Security trust funds consist of the Old Age and Survivors Insurance (OASI) trust fund and the Disability Insurance (DI) trust fund. The trust funds are funded by payroll taxes from employers and employees, interest earnings on trust fund balances, Federal agency payments as employers, and a portion of the income taxes paid on Social Security benefits.

- Medicare Trust Funds: Like the Social Security trust funds, the Medicare Hospital Insurance trust fund is funded by payroll taxes from employers and employees, Federal agency payments as employers, and a portion of the income taxes paid on Social Security benefits. The HI trust fund also receives

transfers from the general fund of the Treasury for certain HI benefits and premiums from certain voluntary participants. The other Medicare trust fund, Supplementary Medical Insurance (SMI), finances Part B (outpatient and physician benefits) and Part D (prescription drug benefits). SMI receives premium payments from covered individuals, transfers from States toward Part D benefits, excise taxes on manufacturers and importers of brand-name prescription drugs, and transfers from the general fund of the Treasury for the portion of Part B and Part D costs not covered by premiums or transfers from States. In addition, like other trust funds, these two trust funds receive interest earnings on their trust fund balances.

- Highway Trust Fund: The fund finances Federal highway and transit infrastructure projects, as well as highway and vehicle safety activities. The Highway Trust Fund is financed by Federal motor fuel taxes and associated fees, and, in recent years, by general fund transfers, as those taxes and fees have been inadequate to support current levels of investment.

- Unemployment Trust Fund: The Unemployment Trust Fund is funded by Federal and State taxes on employers, payments from Federal agencies, taxes on certain employees, and interest earnings on trust fund balances. Unemployment insurance is administered largely by the States, following Federal guidelines. The Unemployment Trust Fund is composed of individual accounts for each State and several Federal accounts, including accounts related to the separate unemployment insurance program for railroad employees.

- Civilian and military retirement trust funds: The Civil Service Retirement and Disability Fund is funded by employee and agency payments, general fund transfers for the unfunded portion of retirement costs, and interest earnings on trust fund balances. The Military Retirement Fund likewise is funded by payments from the Department of Defense, general fund transfers for unfunded retirement costs, and interest earnings on trust fund balances.

Table 24–5 shows income, outgo, and balances of two Federal funds that are designated as special funds. These funds are similar to trust funds in that they are financed by dedicated receipts, the excess of income over outgo is invested in Treasury securities, the interest earnings add to fund balances, and the balances remain available to cover future expenditures. The table is illustrative of the Federal funds group, which includes many revolving funds and special funds.

Table 24–4.   INCOME, OUTGO, AND BALANCE OF MAJOR TRUST FUNDS
(In billions of dollars)

	2017 Actual	Estimate					
		2018	2019	2020	2021	2022	2023
Airport and Airway Trust Fund							
Balance, start of year	14.8	15.1	15.0	16.6	19.0	22.3	20.9
Adjustments to balances	....	....	....	....	....	....	....
Total balance, start of year	14.8	15.1	15.0	16.6	19.0	22.3	20.9
Income:							
Governmental receipts	15.1	15.7	16.5	17.3	18.1	3.4	3.5
Offsetting governmental	....	....	....	....	....	....	....
Proprietary	0.1	0.1	0.1	0.1	0.1	0.1	0.1
Intrabudgetary:							
Intrafund	....	....	....	....	....	....	....
Interest	0.3	0.3	0.3	0.4	0.5	0.6	0.6
Other intrabudgetary	0.1	0.1	0.1	0.1	0.1	0.1	0.1
Total income during the year	15.5	16.2	17.0	17.8	18.7	4.1	4.2
Outgo (–)	−15.2	−16.3	−15.4	−15.4	−15.4	−5.5	−4.3
Change in fund balance:							
Surplus or deficit(–):							
Excluding interest	*	−0.4	1.2	2.0	2.7	−2.0	−0.7
Interest	0.3	0.3	0.3	0.4	0.5	0.6	0.6
Subtotal, surplus or deficit (–)	0.3	−0.1	1.6	2.4	3.3	−1.4	−*
Borrowing, transfers, lapses, & other adjustments	*	....	....	....	....	....	....
Total change in fund balance	0.3	−0.1	1.6	2.4	3.3	−1.4	−*
Balance, end of year	15.1	15.0	16.6	19.0	22.3	20.9	20.9
Civil Service Retirement and Disability Fund							
Balance, start of year	887.2	905.1	923.7	939.7	945.6	950.8	953.6
Adjustments to balances	....	....	....	....	....	....	....
Total balance, start of year	887.2	905.1	923.7	939.7	945.6	950.8	953.6
Income:							
Governmental receipts	4.1	4.7	4.9	7.5	10.2	12.4	14.5
Offsetting governmental	....	....	....	....	....	....	....
Proprietary	....	....	....	....	....	....	....
Intrabudgetary:							
Intrafund	....	....	....	....	....	....	....
Interest	26.4	25.9	24.6	24.7	24.8	25.0	25.5
Other intrabudgetary	71.2	72.8	72.8	62.0	60.7	58.0	56.4
Total income during the year	101.7	103.4	102.4	94.3	95.7	95.4	96.3
Outgo (–)	−83.8	−84.8	−86.3	−88.4	−90.5	−92.6	−94.9
Change in fund balance:							
Surplus or deficit(–):							
Excluding interest	−8.5	−7.4	−8.6	−18.9	−19.6	−22.2	−24.0
Interest	26.4	25.9	24.6	24.7	24.8	25.0	25.5
Subtotal, surplus or deficit (–)	17.9	18.6	16.1	5.8	5.2	2.8	1.4
Borrowing, transfers, lapses, & other adjustments	....	....	....	....	....	....	....
Total change in fund balance	17.9	18.6	16.1	5.8	5.2	2.8	1.4
Balance, end of year	905.1	923.7	939.7	945.6	950.8	953.6	955.0
Employees and Retired Employees Health Benefits Funds							
Balance, start of year	23.7	26.0	26.0	26.1	26.2	26.6	27.3
Adjustments to balances	*	....	....	....	....	....	....
Total balance, start of year	23.7	26.0	26.0	26.1	26.2	26.6	27.3
Income:							
Governmental receipts	....	....	....	....	....	....	....

Table 24–4. INCOME, OUTGO, AND BALANCE OF MAJOR TRUST FUNDS—Continued

(In billions of dollars)

	2017 Actual	Estimate					
		2018	2019	2020	2021	2022	2023
Offsetting governmental	....	....	....	....	....	....	....
Proprietary	15.7	16.7	17.7	18.7	20.0	21.3	22.5
Intrabudgetary:							
Intrafund	....	....	....	....	....	....	....
Interest	0.2	0.2	0.3	0.4	0.5	0.6	0.8
Other intrabudgetary	37.0	38.4	40.3	42.8	44.3	46.6	49.3
Total income during the year	52.9	55.3	58.3	61.9	64.9	68.5	72.6
Outgo (–)	–50.6	–55.2	–58.3	–61.8	–64.5	–67.8	–71.8
Change in fund balance:							
Surplus or deficit(–):							
Excluding interest	2.1	–0.1	–0.3	–0.3	–0.1	0.1	0.1
Interest	0.2	0.2	0.3	0.4	0.5	0.6	0.8
Subtotal, surplus or deficit (–)	2.3	0.1	*	0.1	0.4	0.7	0.8
Borrowing, transfers, lapses, & other adjustments	....	....	....	....	....	....	....
Total change in fund balance	2.3	0.1	*	0.1	0.4	0.7	0.8
Balance, end of year	26.0	26.0	26.1	26.2	26.6	27.3	28.2
Foreign Military Sales Trust Fund							
Balance, start of year	29.6	33.1	43.1	35.1	35.3	35.7	34.8
Adjustments to balances	....	....	....	....	....	....	....
Total balance, start of year	29.6	33.1	43.1	35.1	35.3	35.7	34.8
Income:							
Governmental receipts	....	....	....	....	....	....	....
Offsetting governmental	....	....	....	....	....	....	....
Proprietary	31.9	42.0	44.0	43.0	45.6	44.9	42.4
Intrabudgetary:							
Intrafund	....	....	....	....	....	....	....
Interest	....	....	....	....	....	....	....
Other intrabudgetary	....	....	....	....	....	....	....
Total income during the year	31.9	42.0	44.0	43.0	45.6	44.9	42.4
Outgo (–)	–28.3	–32.0	–52.1	–42.7	–45.2	–45.8	–42.4
Change in fund balance:							
Surplus or deficit(–):							
Excluding interest	3.6	10.0	–8.1	0.3	0.4	–0.9	*
Interest	....	....	....	....	....	....	....
Subtotal, surplus or deficit (–)	3.6	10.0	–8.1	0.3	0.4	–0.9	*
Borrowing, transfers, lapses, & other adjustments	....	....	....	....	....	....	....
Total change in fund balance	3.6	10.0	–8.1	0.3	0.4	–0.9	*
Balance, end of year	33.1	43.1	35.1	35.3	35.7	34.8	34.8
Highway Trust Fund							
Balance, start of year	69.2	56.3	43.6	29.9	15.5	1.0	....
Adjustments to balances	....	....	....	....	....	....	....
Total balance, start of year	69.2	56.3	43.6	29.9	15.5	1.0	....
Income:							
Governmental receipts	41.0	41.8	42.6	43.2	43.6	43.8	43.9
Offsetting governmental	*	*	*	*	*	*	*
Proprietary	0.1	....	....	....	....	....	....
Intrabudgetary:							
Intrafund	0.1	0.1	....	....	....	....	....
Interest	0.4	0.4	0.2	0.1	....	....	....
Other intrabudgetary	0.3	0.5	0.4	0.4	0.4	0.4	0.4
Total income during the year	41.9	42.8	43.1	43.7	44.0	44.2	44.3

Table 24–4. INCOME, OUTGO, AND BALANCE OF MAJOR TRUST FUNDS—Continued

(In billions of dollars)

	2017 Actual	Estimate					
		2018	2019	2020	2021	2022	2023
Outgo (–)	–54.8	–55.5	–56.8	–58.0	–58.5	–45.2	–44.3
Change in fund balance:							
Surplus or deficit(–):							
Excluding interest	–13.3	–13.0	–13.8	–14.4	–14.5	–1.0	....
Interest	0.4	0.4	0.2	0.1	....	....	....
Subtotal, surplus or.deficit (–)	–12.9	–12.7	–13.7	–14.4	–14.5	–1.0	....
Borrowing, transfers, lapses, & other adjustments	–*	....	–0.1	....	....	....	....
Total change in fund balance	–12.9	–12.7	–13.7	–14.4	–14.5	–1.0	....
Balance, end of year	56.3	43.6	29.9	15.5	1.0	....	....
Medicare: Hospital Insurance (HI) Trust Fund							
Balance, start of year	192.5	197.5	201.3	210.1	224.2	238.4	236.2
Adjustments to balances	....	....	....	....	....	....	....
Total balance, start of year	192.5	197.5	201.3	210.1	224.2	238.4	236.2
Income:							
Governmental receipts	256.4	259.7	275.9	287.8	305.1	322.8	340.3
Offsetting governmental	....	....	....	....	....	....	....
Proprietary	9.7	10.4	10.5	10.7	11.0	11.3	11.7
Intrabudgetary:							
Intrafund	....	....	....	....	....	....	....
Interest	7.5	7.2	7.2	7.3	7.7	7.9	7.9
Other intrabudgetary	30.8	29.8	31.2	34.2	37.3	40.5	43.8
Total income during the year	304.4	307.2	324.8	340.0	361.0	382.5	403.6
Outgo (–)	–299.4	–303.4	–316.1	–325.9	–346.8	–384.7	–401.1
Change in fund balance:							
Surplus or deficit(–):							
Excluding interest	–2.5	–3.4	1.6	6.8	6.5	–10.1	–5.4
Interest	7.5	7.2	7.2	7.3	7.7	7.9	7.9
Subtotal, surplus or deficit (–)	5.0	3.8	8.8	14.1	14.2	–2.2	2.5
Borrowing, transfers, lapses, & other adjustments	*	–*	....	....	....	....	....
Total change in fund balance	5.0	3.8	8.8	14.1	14.2	–2.2	2.5
Balance, end of year	197.5	201.3	210.1	224.2	238.4	236.2	238.7
Medicare: Supplementary Insurance (SMI) Trust Fund							
Balance, start of year	62.8	68.0	96.8	105.3	106.1	107.7	83.3
Adjustments to balances	....	....	....	....	....	....	....
Total balance, start of year	62.8	68.0	96.8	105.3	106.1	107.7	83.3
Income:							
Governmental receipts	4.1	6.0	2.8	2.8	2.8	2.8	2.8
Offsetting governmental	....	....	....	....	....	....	....
Proprietary	101.5	113.4	121.0	128.4	138.9	149.3	162.0
Intrabudgetary:							
Intrafund	....	....	....	....	....	....	....
Interest	2.3	1.3	1.2	1.5	2.2	4.1	5.0
Other intrabudgetary	306.5	317.0	335.2	358.2	386.3	417.1	452.8
Total income during the year	414.6	437.6	460.2	490.9	530.2	573.3	622.6
Outgo (–)	–409.3	–408.8	–451.7	–490.1	–528.6	–597.6	–621.3
Change in fund balance:							
Surplus or deficit(–):							
Excluding interest	2.9	27.5	7.3	–0.7	–0.6	–28.4	–3.7
Interest	2.3	1.3	1.2	1.5	2.2	4.1	5.0
Subtotal, surplus or deficit (–)	5.2	28.8	8.5	0.8	1.6	–24.3	1.3

Table 24–4. INCOME, OUTGO, AND BALANCE OF MAJOR TRUST FUNDS—Continued
(In billions of dollars)

	2017 Actual	Estimate					
		2018	2019	2020	2021	2022	2023
Borrowing, transfers, lapses, & other adjustments	....	–*	....	....	....	....	....
Total change in fund balance	5.2	28.8	8.5	0.8	1.6	–24.3	1.3
Balance, end of year	68.0	96.8	105.3	106.1	107.7	83.3	84.6
Military Retirement Fund							
Balance, start of year	584.5	654.3	731.0	811.6	896.0	985.3	1,074.5
Adjustments to balances	....	....	....	....	....	....	....
Total balance, start of year	584.5	654.3	731.0	811.6	896.0	985.3	1,074.5
Income:							
Governmental receipts	....	....	....	....		....	....
Offsetting governmental	....	....	....	....	....	....	....
Proprietary	....	....	....	....	....	....	....
Intrabudgetary:							
Intrafund	....	....	....	....	....	....	....
Interest	21.4	22.4	25.5	28.9	32.0	35.5	37.4
Other intrabudgetary	106.2	108.4	115.5	117.5	121.1	124.6	128.1
Total income during the year	127.6	130.8	141.0	146.4	153.1	160.1	165.6
Outgo (–)	–57.7	–54.1	–60.4	–62.1	–63.8	–70.9	–67.7
Change in fund balance:							
Surplus or deficit(–):							
Excluding interest	48.5	54.3	55.1	55.5	57.2	53.8	60.4
Interest	21.4	22.4	25.5	28.9	32.0	35.5	37.4
Subtotal, surplus or deficit (–)	69.9	76.7	80.6	84.4	89.3	89.3	97.9
Borrowing, transfers, lapses, & other adjustments	....	....	....	....	....	....	....
Total change in fund balance	69.9	76.7	80.6	84.4	89.3	89.3	97.9
Balance, end of year	654.3	731.0	811.6	896.0	985.3	1,074.5	1,172.4
Railroad Retirement Trust Funds							
Balance, start of year	22.0	24.0	22.9	21.8	20.7	19.6	18.7
Adjustments to balances	0.9	....	....	....	....	....	....
Total balance, start of year	22.9	24.0	22.9	21.8	20.7	19.6	18.7
Income:							
Governmental receipts	5.3	5.6	5.7	5.9	6.1	6.3	6.6
Offsetting governmental	....	....	....	....	....	....	....
Proprietary	*	....	....	....	....	....	....
Intrabudgetary:							
Intrafund	4.5	4.9	5.0	5.1	5.0	5.2	5.2
Interest	3.3	1.3	0.7	0.8	0.8	0.8	0.8
Other intrabudgetary	0.9	0.8	0.8	0.9	0.9	0.9	0.9
Total income during the year	14.0	12.6	12.2	12.6	12.8	13.2	13.5
Outgo (–)	–12.9	–13.7	–13.4	–13.7	–13.9	–14.1	–14.3
Change in fund balance:							
Surplus or deficit(–):							
Excluding interest	–2.1	–2.4	–1.9	–1.9	–1.9	–1.7	–1.6
Interest	3.3	1.3	0.7	0.8	0.8	0.8	0.8
Subtotal, surplus or deficit (–)	1.2	–1.1	–1.2	–1.1	–1.1	–0.9	–0.8
Borrowing, transfers, lapses, & other adjustments	*	....	....	....	....	....	....
Total change in fund balance	1.2	–1.1	–1.2	–1.1	–1.1	–0.9	–0.8
Balance, end of year	24.0	22.9	21.8	20.7	19.6	18.7	17.9
Social Security: Disability Insurance (DI) Trust Fund							
Balance, start of year	45.7	69.4	91.7	89.6	77.8	68.9	62.0
Adjustments to balances	....	....	....	....	....	....	....
Total balance, start of year	45.7	69.4	91.7	89.6	77.8	68.9	62.0

Table 24-4. INCOME, OUTGO, AND BALANCE OF MAJOR TRUST FUNDS—Continued
(In billions of dollars)

	2017 Actual	Estimate					
		2018	2019	2020	2021	2022	2023
Income:							
Governmental receipts	162.6	163.0	142.4	136.7	144.4	152.3	160.0
Offsetting governmental	....	....	....	....	....	....	....
Proprietary	0.1	0.1	0.1	0.1	0.1	0.1	0.1
Intrabudgetary:							
Intrafund	....	....	....	....	....	....	....
Interest	1.6	2.2	2.8	2.7	2.3	1.8	1.5
Other intrabudgetary	5.3	5.2	4.6	4.6	4.9	5.2	5.4
Total income during the year	169.6	170.5	149.9	144.0	151.6	159.3	167.0
Outgo (–)	–145.9	–148.3	–152.0	–155.8	–160.5	–166.3	–172.7
Change in fund balance:							
Surplus or deficit(–):							
Excluding interest	22.1	20.0	–4.9	–14.4	–11.2	–8.8	–7.2
Interest	1.6	2.2	2.8	2.7	2.3	1.8	1.5
Subtotal, surplus or deficit (–)	23.7	22.2	–2.1	–11.8	–8.9	–7.0	–5.7
Borrowing, transfers, lapses, & other adjustments	....	0.1	*	....	....	....	....
Total change in fund balance	23.7	22.2	–2.1	–11.8	–8.9	–7.0	–5.7
Balance, end of year	69.4	91.7	89.6	77.8	68.9	62.0	56.3
Social Security: Old Age and Survivors Insurance (OASI) Trust Fund							
Balance, start of year	2,796.6	2,820.1	2,795.6	2,788.5	2,768.6	2,736.6	2,688.7
Adjustments to balances	....	....	....	....	....	....	....
Total balance, start of year	2,796.6	2,820.1	2,795.6	2,788.5	2,768.6	2,736.6	2,688.7
Income:							
Governmental receipts	688.0	689.3	762.7	804.7	850.1	896.6	942.5
Offsetting governmental	....	....	....	....	....	....	....
Proprietary	*	*	*	*	*	*	*
Intrabudgetary:							
Intrafund	....	....	....	....	....	....	....
Interest	84.9	81.5	79.0	76.9	75.2	72.2	70.3
Other intrabudgetary	49.6	48.9	51.3	56.2	60.6	65.3	69.9
Total income during the year	822.5	819.7	893.0	937.8	985.9	1,034.1	1,082.7
Outgo (–)	–799.0	–844.3	–900.1	–957.7	–1,017.9	–1,081.9	–1,149.4
Change in fund balance:							
Surplus or deficit(–):							
Excluding interest	–61.4	–106.1	–86.1	–96.9	–107.2	–120.1	–137.1
Interest	84.9	81.5	79.0	76.9	75.2	72.2	70.3
Subtotal, surplus or deficit (–)	23.5	–24.5	–7.1	–19.9	–32.0	–47.9	–66.7
Borrowing, transfers, lapses, & other adjustments	–*	0.1	*	....	....	....	....
Total change in fund balance	23.5	–24.5	–7.1	–19.9	–32.0	–47.9	–66.7
Balance, end of year	2,820.1	2,795.6	2,788.5	2,768.6	2,736.6	2,688.7	2,621.9
Unemployment Trust Fund							
Balance, start of year	45.7	58.5	75.2	90.1	104.9	119.7	134.6
Adjustments to balances	–*	....	....	....	....	....	....
Total balance, start of year	45.7	58.5	75.2	90.1	104.9	119.7	134.6
Income:							
Governmental receipts	45.8	48.1	46.5	46.6	47.7	49.3	50.7
Offsetting governmental	....	....	....	....	....	....	....
Proprietary	*	*	*	*	*	*	*
Intrabudgetary:							
Intrafund	....	....	....	....	....	....	....

Table 24-4. INCOME, OUTGO, AND BALANCE OF MAJOR TRUST FUNDS—Continued
(In billions of dollars)

	2017 Actual	Estimate					
		2018	2019	2020	2021	2022	2023
Interest	1.3	1.5	1.8	2.2	2.8	3.4	4.1
Other intrabudgetary	0.5	0.5	0.6	0.6	0.8	0.7	0.7
Total income during the year	47.6	50.1	48.9	49.4	51.3	53.5	55.4
Outgo (–)	–34.8	–33.4	–34.0	–34.5	–36.5	–38.6	–40.8
Change in fund balance:							
Surplus or deficit(–):							
Excluding interest	11.6	15.2	13.1	12.7	12.0	11.4	10.6
Interest	1.3	1.5	1.8	2.2	2.8	3.4	4.1
Subtotal, surplus or deficit (–)	12.8	16.7	14.9	14.9	14.8	14.8	14.6
Borrowing, transfers, lapses, & other adjustments	–*	....	....	....	....	....	....
Total change in fund balance	12.8	16.7	14.9	14.9	14.8	14.8	14.6
Balance, end of year	58.5	75.2	90.1	104.9	119.7	134.6	149.2
Veterans Life Insurance Funds							
Balance, start of year	6.0	5.2	4.5	3.8	3.3	2.8	2.3
Adjustments to balances	....	....	....	....	....	....	....
Total balance, start of year	6.0	5.2	4.5	3.8	3.3	2.8	2.3
Income:							
Governmental receipts	....	....	....	....	....	....	....
Offsetting governmental	....	....	....	....	....	....	....
Proprietary	0.2	0.1	0.1	0.1	0.1	0.1	0.1
Intrabudgetary:							
Intrafund	....	....	....	....	....	....	....
Interest	0.2	0.2	0.2	0.1	0.1	0.1	0.1
Other intrabudgetary	....	....	....	....	....	....	....
Total income during the year	0.4	0.3	0.3	0.2	0.2	0.2	0.1
Outgo (–)	–1.1	–1.1	–0.9	–0.8	–0.7	–0.6	–0.5
Change in fund balance:							
Surplus or deficit(–):							
Excluding interest	–1.0	–0.9	–0.8	–0.7	–0.6	–0.5	–0.4
Interest	0.2	0.2	0.2	0.1	0.1	0.1	0.1
Subtotal, surplus or deficit (–)	–0.7	–0.7	–0.6	–0.6	–0.5	–0.4	–0.4
Borrowing, transfers, lapses, & other adjustments	....	....	....	....	....	....	....
Total change in fund balance	–0.7	–0.7	–0.6	–0.6	–0.5	–0.4	–0.4
Balance, end of year	5.2	4.5	3.8	3.3	2.8	2.3	2.0
All Other Trust Funds							
Balance, start of year	99.1	101.0	107.0	112.7	117.8	121.4	125.4
Adjustments to balances	–0.1	....	....	....	....	....	....
Total balance, start of year	99.1	101.0	107.0	112.7	117.8	121.4	125.4
Income:							
Governmental receipts	5.1	4.8	5.2	5.5	5.3	5.5	5.2
Offsetting governmental	*	5.0	3.7	1.7	*	*	*
Proprietary	6.7	6.5	6.6	6.7	6.8	6.9	7.0
Intrabudgetary:							
Intrafund	0.1	0.1	0.2	*	*	*	*
Interest	1.2	1.1	1.4	1.9	2.1	2.4	2.7
Other intrabudgetary	15.6	16.3	15.6	15.4	15.4	15.4	15.5
Total income during the year	28.9	33.8	32.7	31.1	29.7	30.2	30.5
Outgo (–)	–27.0	–27.8	–26.9	–25.9	–26.1	–26.2	–26.2
Change in fund balance:							
Surplus or deficit(–):							

Table 24–4. INCOME, OUTGO, AND BALANCE OF MAJOR TRUST FUNDS—Continued

(In billions of dollars)

	2017 Actual	Estimate					
		2018	2019	2020	2021	2022	2023
Excluding interest	0.7	4.9	4.3	3.2	1.4	1.7	1.6
Interest	1.2	1.1	1.4	1.9	2.1	2.4	2.7
Subtotal, surplus or deficit (–)	1.9	6.0	5.8	5.1	3.5	4.0	4.3
Borrowing, transfers, lapses, & other adjustments	*	0.1	–0.1	....	....	....	....
Total change in fund balance	1.9	6.0	5.6	5.1	3.5	4.0	4.3
Balance, end of year	101.0	107.0	112.7	117.8	121.4	125.4	129.7

* $50 million or less.

Table 24–5.   INCOME, OUTGO, AND BALANCE OF SELECTED SPECIAL FUNDS
(In billions of dollars)

	2017 Actual	Estimate					
		2018	2019	2020	2021	2022	2023
Abandoned Mine Reclamation Fund							
Balance, start of year	2.9	2.8	2.8	2.7	2.6	2.6	2.4
Adjustments to balances	–*	....	....	....	....	....	....
Total balance, start of year	2.9	2.8	2.8	2.7	2.6	2.6	2.4
Income:							
Governmental receipts	0.2	0.2	0.2	0.2	0.2	....	....
Offsetting governmental	....	....	....	....	....	....	....
Proprietary	....	....	....	....	....	....	....
Intrabudgetary:							
Intrafund	....	....	....	....	....	....	....
Interest	*	*	0.1	0.1	0.1	0.1	0.1
Other intrabudgetary	....	....	....	....	....	....	....
Total income during the year	0.2	0.2	0.2	0.3	0.3	0.1	0.1
Outgo (–)	–0.2	–0.3	–0.3	–0.4	–0.3	–0.3	–0.3
Change in fund balance:							
Surplus or deficit(–):							
Excluding interest	–0.1	–0.1	–0.1	–0.2	–0.1	–0.3	–0.3
Interest	*	*	0.1	0.1	0.1	0.1	0.1
Subtotal, surplus or deficit (–)	–*	–0.1	–0.1	–0.1	–0.1	–0.2	–0.2
Borrowing, transfers, lapses, & other adjustments	....	....	....	....	....	....	....
Total change in fund balance	–*	–0.1	–0.1	–0.1	–0.1	–0.2	–0.2
Balance, end of year	2.8	2.8	2.7	2.6	2.6	2.4	2.2
Department of Defense Medicare-Eligible Retiree Health Care Fund							
Balance, start of year	212.0	224.4	237.9	249.9	263.6	278.2	293.3
Adjustments to balances	....	....	....	....	....	....	....
Total balance, start of year	212.0	224.4	237.9	249.9	263.6	278.2	293.3
Income:							
Governmental receipts	....	....	....	....	....	....	....
Offsetting governmental	....	....	....	....	....	....	....
Proprietary	....	....	....	....	....	....	....
Intrabudgetary:							
Intrafund	12.8	15.0	13.6	14.3	14.9	15.7	16.4
Interest	9.4	9.6	9.5	11.0	11.8	12.0	12.6
Other intrabudgetary	....	....	....	....	....	....	....
Total income during the year	22.3	24.5	23.0	25.3	26.7	27.7	29.0
Outgo (–)	–9.9	–11.0	–11.1	–11.5	–12.1	–12.6	–13.3
Change in fund balance:							
Surplus or deficit(–):							
Excluding interest	2.9	4.0	2.5	2.7	2.8	3.0	3.1
Interest	9.4	9.6	9.5	11.0	11.8	12.0	12.6
Subtotal, surplus or deficit (–)	12.3	13.6	12.0	13.8	14.6	15.0	15.7
Borrowing, transfers, lapses, & other adjustments	....	....	....	....	....	....	....
Total change in fund balance	12.3	13.6	12.0	13.8	14.6	15.0	15.7
Balance, end of year	224.4	237.9	249.9	263.6	278.2	293.3	309.0

* $50 million or less.

25. COMPARISON OF ACTUAL TO ESTIMATED TOTALS

The Budget is required by statute to compare budget year estimates of receipts and outlays with the subsequent actual receipts and outlays for that year. This chapter meets that requirement by comparing the actual receipts, outlays, and deficit for 2017 with the current services estimates shown in the 2017 Budget, published in February 2016.[1] It also presents a more detailed comparison for mandatory and related programs, and reconciles the actual receipts, outlays, and deficit totals shown here with the figures for 2017 previously published by the Department of the Treasury.

Receipts

Actual receipts for 2017 were $3,316 billion, $161 billion less than the $3,477 billion current services estimate in the 2017 Budget, which was published in February 2016. As shown in Table 25–1, this decrease was the net effect of economic conditions that differed from what had been expected and technical factors that resulted in different tax liabilities and collection patterns than had been assumed.

Economic differences. Differences between the economic assumptions upon which the current services estimates

were based and actual economic performance reduced 2017 receipts by a net $5 billion below the February 2016 current services estimate. Corporations reported less profits in 2017 than initially projected, which reduced receipts $17 billion below the February 2016 estimate and accounted for most of the net reduction in receipts attributable to economic differences. This was offset by higher deposits of earnings by the Federal Reserve, which increased 2017 receipts by $18 billion above the February 2016 estimate. Different economic factors than those assumed in February 2016 had a smaller effect on other sources of receipts, decreasing collections by a net $5 billion.

Technical factors. Technical factors decreased receipts by a net $156 billion relative to the February 2016 current services estimate. These factors had the greatest effect on individual income taxes, decreasing collections by $141 billion. Decreases in corporation income taxes of $28 billion and increases in social insurance and retirement receipts of $32 billion accounted for most of the remaining changes in 2017 receipts attributable to technical factors. The models used to prepare the February 2016 estimates of individual and corporation income taxes were based on historical economic data and then-current tax and collections data that were all subsequently revised and account for the net decrease in these two sources of receipts attributable to technical factors. The majority of the difference in the original estimate of individual income taxes relative to actuals relates to lower-than-projected tax year 2016 liability, which was due in part to lower-than-expected taxable income from pass-through businesses and capital gains realizations. In addition, both individual income and corporation income taxes may have decreased due to taxpayers shifting income into the future in anticipation of comprehensive tax reform.

---

[1] The current services concept is discussed in Chapter 23, "Current Services Estimates." For mandatory programs and receipts, the February 2016 current services estimate was based on laws then in place, adjusted for certain expiring provisions. For discretionary programs, the current services estimate was based on the discretionary spending limits enacted in the Budget Control Act of 2011 (BCA). Spending for Overseas Contingency Operations, was estimated based on annualizing the amounts provided in the 2016 appropriations and increasing for inflation. The current services estimates also reflected the effects of discretionary and mandatory sequestration as required by the BCA following failure of the Joint Select Committee on Deficit Reduction to meet its deficit reduction target. For a detailed explanation of the 2017 estimate, see "Current Services Estimates," Chapter 25 in *Analytical Perspectives, Budget of the United States Government, Fiscal Year 2017.*

Table 25–1. COMPARISON OF ACTUAL 2017 RECEIPTS WITH THE INITIAL CURRENT SERVICES ESTIMATES

(In billions of dollars)

	Estimate (February 2016)	Changes			Total Changes	Actual
		Policy	Economic	Technical		
Individual income taxes	1,724	–*	4	–141	–137	1,587
Corporation income taxes	343	*	–17	–28	–46	297
Social insurance and retirement receipts	1,139	–*	–9	32	23	1,162
Excise taxes	86	....	–*	–2	–3	84
Estate and gift taxes	22	....	2	–2	*	23
Customs duties	40	–*	–3	–2	–5	35
Miscellaneous receipts	123	....	18	–11	6	129
Total receipts	3,477	–*	–5	–156	–161	3,316

* $500 million or less

Outlays

Outlays for 2017 were $3,982 billion, $107 billion less than the $4,089 billion current services estimate in the 2016 Budget. Table 25–2 distributes the $107 billion net decrease in outlays among discretionary and mandatory programs and net interest.[2] The table also shows rough estimates according to three reasons for the changes: policy; economic conditions; and technical estimating differences, a residual.

Policy differences. Policy changes are the result of legislative actions that change spending levels, primarily through higher or lower appropriations or changes in authorizing legislation, which may themselves be in response to changed economic conditions. For 2017, policy changes increased outlays by $35 billion relative to the initial current services estimates, which included the impacts of sequestration and discretionary cap reductions as part of the Joint Committee enforcement provisions of the Budget Control Act of 2011 (Public Law 112-25). The combined policy changes from final 2016 and 2017 appropriations, including Overseas Contingency Operations, increased discretionary outlays by $33 billion. Policy changes increased mandatory outlays by a net $1 billion above current law. Debt service costs associated with all policy changes increased outlays by less than $1 billion.

Economic and technical factors. Economic and technical estimating factors resulted in a net decrease in outlays of $142 billion. Technical changes result from changes in such factors as the number of beneficiaries for entitlement

---

[2] Discretionary programs are controlled by annual appropriations, while mandatory programs are generally controlled by authorizing legislation. Mandatory programs are primarily formula benefit or entitlement programs with permanent spending authority that depends on eligibility criteria, benefit levels, and other factors. The current services estimates published in the 2017 Budget re-classified certain surface transportation programs as mandatory. The published estimates for nondefense discretionary outlays and mandatory outlays were $1,215 billion and $2,565 billion, respectively. This proposal was not subsequently enacted, so the applicable costs are shown as discretionary in this chapter for comparability.

programs, crop conditions, or other factors not associated with policy changes or economic conditions. The final enacted 2017 appropriations allowed for lower discretionary outlays than the rates included in the February 2016 estimate. Increases in discretionary outlays due to legislation, as discussed above, were offset by a $52 billion decrease in net outlays resulting from technical changes. Outlays for mandatory programs decreased $43 billion due to economic and technical factors. There was a net decrease in outlays of $58 billion as a result of differences between actual economic conditions versus those forecast in February 2016. Outlays for Social Security were $28 billion lower than anticipated in the 2017 Budget largely due to lower-than-estimated number of beneficiaries and cost-of-living adjustments. Income security program outlays were a combined $16 billion lower, while the remaining changes were in veterans benefits and services, deposit insurance, and other programs. Outlays for net interest were approximately $41 billion lower due to economic and technical factors, primarily lower interest rates than originally assumed.

Deficit

The preceding two sections discussed the differences between the initial current services estimates and the actual Federal government receipts and outlays for 2017. This section combines these effects to show the net deficit impact of these differences.

As shown in Table 25–3, the 2017 current services deficit was initially estimated to be $612 billion. The actual deficit was $665 billion, which was a $53 billion increase from the initial estimate. Receipts were $161 billion lower and outlays were $107 billion less than the initial estimate. The table shows the distribution of the changes according to the categories in the preceding two sections. The net effect of policy changes for receipts and outlays increased the deficit by $35 billion. Economic conditions that differed from the initial assumptions in February

Table 25–2.   COMPARISON OF ACTUAL 2017 OUTLAYS WITH THE INITIAL CURRENT SERVICES ESTIMATES

(In billions of dollars)

	Estimate (February 2015)	Changes			Total Changes	Actual
		Policy	Economic	Technical		
Discretionary:						
Defense	601	14	....	–25	–11	590
Nondefense	618	19	....	–26	–8	610
Subtotal, discretionary	1,219	33	....	–52	–19	1,200
Mandatory:						
Social Security	967	....	–3	–24	–28	939
Other programs	1,594	1	–7	–8	–14	1,580
Subtotal, mandatory	2,561	1	–11	–33	–42	2,519
Allowance for disaster costs [1]	6	....	....	–6	–6	....
Net interest	304	*	–47	6	–41	263
Total outlays	4,089	35	–58	–84	–107	3,982

* $500 million or less

[1] These amounts were included in the 2017 Budget to represent the statistical probability of a major disaster requiring federal assistance for relief and reconstruction. Such assistance might be provided in the form of discretionary, or mandatory outlays or tax relief. These amounts were included as outlays for convenience.

Table 25–3. COMPARISON OF THE ACTUAL 2017 DEFICIT WITH THE INITIAL CURRENT SERVICES ESTIMATE

(In billions of dollars)

	Estimate (February 2016)	Changes			Total Changes	Actual
		Policy	Economic	Technical		
Receipts	3,477	–*	–5	–156	–161	3,316
Outlays	4,089	35	–58	–84	–107	3,982
Deficit	612	35	–53	72	53	665

* $500 million or less
Note: Deficit changes are outlays minus receipts. For these changes, a positive number indicates an increase in the deficit.

2016 decreased the deficit by $53 billion. Technical factors increased the deficit by an estimated $72 billion.

Comparison of the Actual and Estimated Outlays for Mandatory and Related Programs for 2017

This section compares the original 2017 outlay estimates for mandatory and related programs in the current services estimates of the 2017 Budget with the actual outlays. Major examples of these programs include Social Security and Medicare benefits, Medicaid and unemployment compensation payments, and deposit insurance for banks and thrift institutions. This category also includes net interest outlays and undistributed offsetting receipts.

A number of factors may cause differences between the amounts estimated in the Budget and the actual mandatory outlays. For example, legislation may change benefit rates or coverage, the actual number of beneficiaries may differ from the number estimated, or economic conditions (such as inflation or interest rates) may differ from what was assumed in making the original estimates.

Table 25–4 shows the differences between the actual outlays for these programs in 2017 and the current services estimates included in the 2017 Budget.[3] Actual outlays for mandatory spending and net interest in 2017 were $2,781 billion, which was $83 billion less than the current services estimate of $2,865 billion in February 2016.

As Table 25–4 shows, actual outlays for mandatory human resources programs were $2,596 billion, $43 billion less than originally estimated. This decrease was the net effect of legislative action, differences between actual and assumed economic conditions, differences between the anticipated and actual number of beneficiaries, and other technical differences. Most significantly, outlays for Social Security, income security, and veterans benefits and services decreased by $50 billion due to economic, legislative and technical factors. Outlays for these programs were offset by a $40 billion increase in Education, training, employment and social services programs. The outlay changes were primarily driven by upward re-estimates and positive subsidy outlays in some student loan accounts. Mandatory outlays for programs in functions outside human resources were $18 billion less than originally estimated.

Outlays for net interest were $263 billion, or $41 billion less than the original estimate. As shown on Table 25–4, interest payments on Treasury debt securities decreased by $55 billion. Interest earnings of trust funds fell by less than $1 billion, increasing net outlays, while net outlays for other interest increased by $14 billion.

Reconciliation of Differences with Amounts Published by the Treasury for 2017

Table 25-5 provides a reconciliation of the receipts, outlays, and deficit totals for 2017 published by the Department of the Treasury in the September 2017 Monthly Treasury Statement (MTS) and those published in this Budget. The Department of the Treasury made adjustments to the estimates for the Combined Statement of Receipts, Outlays, and Balances, which decreased outlays by $34 million. Additional adjustments for the 2019 Budget increased receipts by $1,288 million and increased outlays by $983 million. Most of these adjustments were for financial transactions that are not reported to the Department of the Treasury but are included in the Budget, including those for the Affordable Housing Program, the Electric Reliability Organization, the Federal Financial Institutions Examination Council Appraisal Subcommittee, the Federal Retirement Thrift Investment Board Program Expenses, the Public Company Accounting Oversight Board, the Securities Investor Protection Corporation, fees and payments related to the Standard Setting Body, and the United Mine Workers of America benefit funds. There was also an adjustment for the National Railroad Retirement Investment Trust (NRRIT), which relates to a conceptual difference in reporting. NRRIT reports to the Department of the Treasury with a one-month lag so that the fiscal year total provided in the Treasury Combined Statement covers September 2016 through August 2017. The Budget has been adjusted to reflect transactions that occurred during the actual fiscal year, which begins October 1. In addition, the Budget also reflects agency adjustments to 2017 outlays reported to Treasury after preparation of the Treasury Combined Statement.

---

[3] See footnote 1 for an explanation of the current services concept.

Table 25–4. COMPARISON OF ACTUAL AND ESTIMATED OUTLAYS FOR MANDATORY AND RELATED PROGRAMS UNDER CURRENT LAW

(In billions of dollars)

	2017		
	Estimate	Actual	Change
Mandatory outlays:			
Human resources programs:			
Education, training, employment, and social services:			
Higher education	5	45	41
Other	7	7	–1
Total, education, training, employment, and social services	12	52	40
Health:			
Medicaid	377	368	–8
Other	119	105	–15
Total, health	496	473	–23
Medicare	602	591	–11
Income security:			
Retirement and disability	150	146	–3
Unemployment compensation	32	30	–2
Food and nutrition assistance	101	93	–8
Other	173	166	–7
Total, income security	456	436	–20
Social security	967	939	–28
Veterans benefits and services:			
Income security for veterans	86	86	–*
Other	20	19	–2
Total, veterans benefits and services	106	105	–2
Total, mandatory human resources programs	2,639	2,596	–43
Other functions:			
Agriculture	21	13	–8
International	–0	–5	–5
Mortgage credit	–23	–17	7
Deposit insurance	–10	–12	–2
Other advancement of commerce	18	13	–5
Other functions	25	20	–5
Total, other functions	30	12	–18
Undistributed offsetting receipts:			
Employer share, employee retirement	–88	–85	3
Rents and royalties on the outer continental shelf	–4	–3	1
Other undistributed offsetting receipts	–15	–2	14
Total, undistributed offsetting receipts	–108	–90	19
Total, mandatory	2,561	2,519	–42
Net interest:			
Interest on Treasury debt securities (gross)	512	457	–55
Interest received by trust funds	–147	–147	*
Other interest	–61	–47	14
Total, net interest	304	263	–41
Total, outlays for mandatory and net interest	2,865	2,781	–83

* $500 million or less

Table 25–5. RECONCILIATION OF FINAL AMOUNTS FOR 2017

(In millions of dollars)

	Receipts	Outlays	Deficit
Totals published by Treasury (September MTS)	3,314,894	3,980,605	665,712
Miscellaneous Treasury adjustments	....	–34	–34
Totals published by Treasury in Combined Statement	3,314,894	3,980,571	665,677
Additional Adjustments to the 2019 Budget			
Affordable Housing Program	392	392	....
Electric Reliability Organization	100	100	....
Federal Financial Institutions Examination Council Appraisal Subcommittee	19	19	....
Federal Retirement Thrift Investment Board Program Expenses	....	–5	–5
Public Company Accounting Oversight Board	276	265	–11
Puerto Rico Oversight Board	31	31	....
Securities Investor Protection Corporation	364	138	–226
Standard Setting Body	28	28	....
United Mine Workers of America benefit funds	81	81	....
National Railroad Retirement Investment Trust	....	–164	–164
Environmental Protection Agency	....	75	75
Other	–3	23	26
Total additional adjustments	1,288	983	–305
Totals in the Budget	3,316,182	3,981,554	665,372
MEMORANDUM:			
Total change since year-end statement	1,288	949	–340